ODD MAN OUT

Richard C. Thornton

ODD
MAN
OUT

Truman, Stalin, Mao, and the Origins of the Korean War

BRASSEY'S   WASHINGTON, D.C.

First paperback edition 2001

Copyright © 2000 Brassey's, Inc.

Published in the United States by Brassey's, Inc.

Map on p. ix from *In Mortal Combat* by John Toland. Copyright © 1991 by John Toland. Reprinted by permission of HarperCollins Publishers, Inc.

LIBRARY OF CONGRESS CATALOGING-IN-PUBLICATION DATA
Thornton, Richard C.
  Odd man out : Truman, Stalin, Mao, and the origins of the Korean War / Richard C. Thornton.—1st ed.
    p.   cm.
  Includes bibliographical references and index.
  ISBN 1-57488-240-6
  ISBN (pbk.) 1-57488-343-7
  1. Korean War, 1950–1953—Causes.   2. World Politics—1945–1955.   I. Title.
  DS918 .A555 2000
  951.904′21—dc21   99-086272

Printed in the United States of America on acid-free paper that meets the American National Standards Institute Z39-48 Standard.

Design and composition by Melissa Ehn at
Wilsted & Taylor Publishing Services

Brassey's, Inc.
22841 Quicksilver Drive
Dulles, Virginia 20166

10 9 8 7 6 5 4 3 2 1

No people in history have preserved their freedom
who thought that by not being strong enough to protect themselves
they might prove inoffensive to their enemies.
 —NATIONAL SECURITY COUNCIL, STRATEGY PAPER NO. 68

CONTENTS

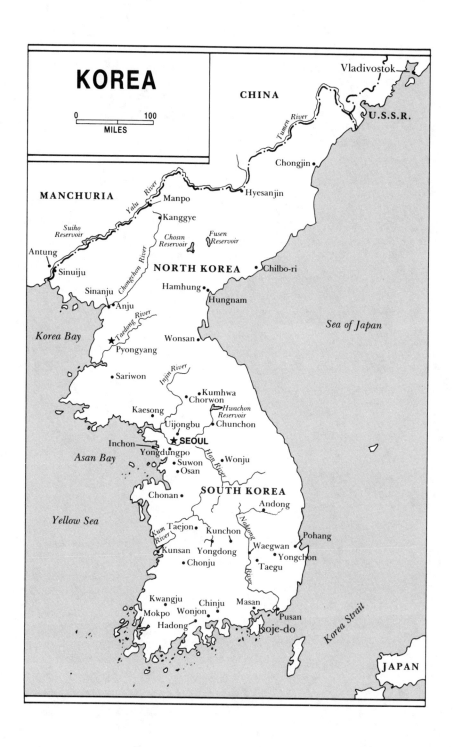

KOREA

0   100
MILES

CHINA

Vladivostok

U.S.S.R.

Tumen River

Chongjin

MANCHURIA

Yalu River

Manpo

Hyesanjin

Kanggye

Suiho
Reservoir

Chosin
Reservoir

Fusen
Reservoir

Antung

Chongchon River

NORTH KOREA

Chilbo-ri

Sinuiju

Sinanju

Hamhung

Anju

Hungnam

Korea Bay

Taedong River

Wonsan

Sea of Japan

Pyongyang

Sariwon

Injin River

Kumhwa

Chorwon

Kaesong

Hwachon
Reservoir

Uijongbu

Chunchon

Inchon

SEOUL

Yongdungpo

Han River

Wonju

Asan Bay

Suwon

Osan

Chonan

SOUTH KOREA

Andong

Yellow Sea

Kum
River

Taejon

Kunchon

Naktong River

Pohang

Kunsan

Yongdong

Waegwan

Yongchon

Chonju

Taegu

Kwangju

Chinju

Masan

Mokpo

Wonjon

Pusan

Hadong

Koje-do

Korea Strait

JAPAN

PREFACE

This book is not another military history of the Korean War. There are many excellent histories, from which I benefited immensely in preparing this study. This is, rather, a political history of the American-Soviet-Chinese interaction that produced the war and determined the shape of global politics from then to now. The Korean War shaped the fate of many nations, particularly the United States, the Soviet Union, the People's Republic of China, Japan, the Republic of China, and North and South Korea. Indeed, the war, as I view it, was the crucible in which was finally catalyzed the entire set of international relationships in Europe and Asia understood as the Cold War.

The Cold War had begun earlier, of course: the date varies by author, but most certainly by the spring of 1947 the structure of Western Europe was already coalescing along East-West lines. But such was not yet the case for Northeast Asia. There, the Chinese civil war was in full swing, raising questions about the future of China and its position in the emerging world order. The same could be said for Korea, Japan, and Formosa. Korea had been divided at the end of the Pacific War and quickly solidified into Soviet- and American-backed regimes, but unification schemes abounded. Japan was preparing for a peace treaty and full independence as the American occupation wound to a close. Finally, there was Formosa, which Chinese Nationalist forces had reclaimed from Japanese rule, and which was fast becoming the island bastion of the defeated followers of Chiang Kai-shek. Yet nothing was certain; everything was in a state of flux.

The status of all four of these states would be determined within the two-year period covered by this book, 1949–1950. China would come under Communist rule and commit to a thirty-year alliance with the Soviet Union. Korea would suffer war, devastation, and, for all intents and purposes, permanent division. Japan would emerge from occupation as an American ally firmly integrated into the Western camp. And Formosa would become an independent, de facto state under Chinese Nationalist rule.

Most important, the United States would emerge from war in Korea rearmed and resurgent, ascending to eventual hegemonic status in global affairs through continuous strife with the Soviet Union, buttressed with alliances in Europe and Asia. During the war in Korea the elements of the containment strategy would be extended to encompass a global structure.

In my view, none of these outcomes was inevitable, except perhaps the last. Even that, the rise of American power, was a matter of timing, which could have occurred much later in history than it did. That the six states covered in this study evolved into the relationships they did was in the first instance a function of the choices of three men: Mao, Stalin, and Truman. I use a literary convention in reference to these three men. The reader will understand that the decision-making process is more complex than a leader simply sitting down to decide on a course of policy. Obviously aides and staffs, options, arguments, and circumstances are all part of the process. To the extent that that process can be captured, I have presented it. Nevertheless, ultimately, the responsibility for choice lies with leaders and it is in this sense that I characterize national choices as those of Mao, Stalin, and Truman.

This study could not have been attempted but for the prior existence of extensive scholarship on the war, and would not have been attempted but for the release of new materials from American, Russian, and Chinese sources. Two projects in particular, combined with the wealth of information contained in the U.S. National Archives, made this study possible. They are the Woodrow Wilson Center's Cold War International History Project, which has for some years now been publishing materials released by Communist and post-Communist governments about their past, and the National Security Archives, located at George Washington University in Washington, D.C., which has persisted in the use of the Freedom of Information Act to pry data from the bowels of U.S. government repositories.

Many people, too numerous to mention, have assisted me in this study, but I must mention those who were particularly helpful. Thanks go to Professor James Millar, Director of the Institute for European, Russian, and Eurasian Studies of George Washington University, for needed research support. Chi-yuan Yung, Paul DuQuenoy, and Catherine C. Nielsen helped acquire and assisted in translation of Chinese and Russian materials. Dr. James Perry, Alan Capps, and Gerson Kuhr facilitated recovery of difficult-to-locate materials in the United States. Alan Capps also compiled the index. Jack Walker, Director of Special Projects of the Tennessee Korean War Association, provided useful technical combat data.

I would like to extend special thanks to Richard M. Valcourt, editor of the International Journal of Intelligence and Counterintelligence, who is also my agent, for invaluable support; to Don McKeon, publisher of Brassey's, for his intellectual fortitude in supporting the pursuit of the difficult truth of the Korean War; and to Nancy Evans, who edited the manuscript with a fine hand. Heartfelt thanks also go to my many students, now colleagues, sprinkled throughout government, who have helped to educate me in its processes. Finally, I wish to extend my deepest gratitude for the encouragement, inspiration, and support of my wife, Joanne, and my sons, Douglas and James.

ODD MAN OUT

INTRODUCTION

The fiftieth anniversary of the outbreak of the Korean War occurs as new data is being made public from Russian, Chinese, American, and, to a lesser extent, North Korean sources. The newly released materials, in combination with what is extant, enable us to peer further into the decision-making processes of Stalin, Mao, and Truman, and offer a reappraisal of their policies. Most important, we are for the first time in a position to construct an interactive analysis of Soviet, Chinese, and American decision-making. The result is an entirely new assessment of the motives, strategies, successes, and failures of the three nations' leaders as they struggled to maneuver their countries into positions of advantage at a critical moment of postwar history and the event that globalized the Cold War.

In short, we may now develop a reasonably comprehensive history that answers the big questions about the conflict. What were the strategic origins of the Korean War? How did the interplay of Soviet, Chinese, and American policies produce it, and why? Up till now, every new release of material has forced a reconsideration of our understanding of this watershed conflict. The volume and quality of data are now such, I am confident, that what is released in the future will only serve to reinforce the interpretations developed in this book.

I offer new interpretations of: the origins of the war, the Sino-Soviet Treaty, the Chinese decision to intervene, overall Soviet and Chinese strategies, and American strategy, including policy toward the Republic of Korea and the reasons for the shifting policy toward Taiwan. Stalin's war—a fact made conclusive by the documents—was designed to serve larger purposes beyond the unification of Korea, which, however, was Kim Il-sung's only interest. Above all, the war marked the decisive step in Stalin's struggle with Mao to pit China against the United States and prevent the Chinese leader from establishing relations with the United States. Yet the conflict also offered the United States the opportunity to put into place a global containment strategy that went far beyond the immediate issue of Korea.

Despite having just entered into a thirty-year alliance, Stalin and Mao were pursuing markedly divergent strategies. Mao wanted to establish rela-

1

tions "with all nations," including the United States, but only after reaching a new relationship with Moscow. (Mao had no intention of isolating his country in subordination to Moscow.) Documents now confirm that Mao negotiated the alliance with Stalin with an eye to gaining Soviet assistance, especially the planes and ships China lacked, to assault Taiwan. The seizure of Taiwan and the defeat of Chiang Kai-shek would, in turn, clear the way to the establishment of relations with the United States. Such were Mao's objectives.

Stalin, on the other hand, perceived Mao's scenario as his own "worst nightmare," as Sergei N. Goncharov, John W. Lewis, and Xue Litai have argued, one that would destroy Soviet security in Northeast Asia. Stalin's response to this problem was to accede to Kim Il-sung's insistence on reunifying Korea, as it served his larger purposes. Kim believed that with the success of the Chinese revolution, Korea was "next in line." For Stalin, however, support for war in Korea was designed to preempt Mao's strategy of conquering Taiwan and establishing relations with the United States. It was Stalin's objective to employ conflict in Korea to maneuver China into confrontation with the United States, and thus subordinate Mao to Soviet strategy.

Documents show that Stalin's decision for war came while Mao was in Moscow in December 1949, when he became convinced that Mao's strategy might succeed. Stalin did not inform Mao of his decision for war in Korea as he negotiated the Sino-Soviet Treaty of Friendship and Alliance, but insisted on treaty terms that would serve Soviet interests in the coming conflict. During the treaty negotiations, Mao became aware of the implications for his own strategy in the coming war in Korea and realized that his only hope lay in seizing Taiwan before war broke out in Korea.

Thus, the essential issue between the Russians and the Chinese through the first six months of 1950 was, who would strike first? Would Mao seize Taiwan first and clear the way for the establishment of diplomatic relations with the United States? Or would Stalin trigger war in Korea first and forestall Mao? The evidence now shows that Stalin's motive in deciding for war in Korea was to isolate China, keeping China weak and dependent upon the Soviet Union, and was not a product of the Soviet leader's later knowledge of the U.S. decision to rearm contained in the mid-April National Security Council strategy paper known as NSC-68. No doubt that knowledge gleaned from his spy network reinforced his decision, but did not produce it.

And what of the United States? Through 1949, Secretary of State Dean Acheson had walked a fine policy line. He wished to establish good relations with Mao as a means to the larger strategic end of keeping the Russians and the Chinese apart, the so-called wedge strategy. His freedom of action was limited by continued strong congressional support (mostly Republican, but also some Democratic) for Chiang Kai-shek. So, while publicly claiming no change in the policy of supporting the Nationalists, Acheson backed away from Chiang and secretly sought to establish working relations with the emerging Communist regime. (Newly released cables by Mao confirm this clandestine U.S. effort.) Only Chiang's complete defeat, squelching domestic support for the Nationalist cause, would enable the United States to move openly to establish diplomatic relations with Mao.

Mao's sudden appearance in Moscow in December 1949, combined with the earlier discovery that the Soviet Union had detonated an atomic device, shocked American leaders, who strove to dissuade Mao from allying with Moscow. Success of the wedge strategy would allay concerns regarding Moscow's newfound atomic power. Truman decided to go public with the decision to abandon Chiang and open the door wider to diplomatic relations with Mao. Thus, in early January 1950, on the 5th and the 12th, Truman and Secretary of State Acheson publicly declared that the United States would no longer provide any military equipment to Chiang, and would present no threat to the People's Republic of China (PRC) in hopes of dissuading Mao from entering into a long-term alliance with the Soviet Union. Their efforts failed. When the Korean War erupted they would be excoriated for giving the green light to Pyongyang for an invasion of the South, but such was not their purpose.

Once certain that Mao would proceed to sign the treaty with Moscow, the United States had little choice but to change strategy, and did so secretly, in part, no doubt, because of probable congressional opposition. Remarkably, on January 31, within forty-eight hours of Stalin's cable to Kim confirming his decision to support war, Truman decided to proceed with the development of the H-bomb and with the formulation of a new geopolitical strategy, which was embodied in NSC-68. The juxtaposition of the two events suggests that U.S. intelligence intercepted Stalin's cable to Kim, but, regardless of whether that happened, the Soviet possession of the A-bomb and the Sino-Soviet alliance were more than sufficient reasons for the United States to change strategy. Knowledge of Stalin's war decision would certainly have added urgency to the decisions.

NSC-68 established the basic rationale for American rearmament and global containment in the face of growing Soviet military power augmented by the Sino-Soviet alliance. But the strategic decision was kept secret until after war broke out in Korea. Through the spring of 1950, American intelligence watched intently as the Soviet Union shipped thousands of tons of weaponry to North Korea and China assembled a massive invasion fleet for Taiwan. The question of who would strike first held implications as significant for the United States as for China and Russia, because the change in American strategy involved a change of policy regarding Taiwan.

Whereas the United States had been willing, if not eager, to abandon

Chiang and Taiwan as part of the price for keeping China independent of the Soviet Union, once the two communist powers allied, that was no longer true. Under NSC-68 the United States now sought to retain Taiwan as part of the containment structure in Northeast Asia, preferably under another leadership than the Kuomintang (KMT), but under the Kuomintang if necessary. Indeed, when it was feared that China might strike Taiwan before war broke out in Korea, Washington sought to remove Chiang and place Taiwan under a U.N. trusteeship as a way of retaining control of the island without prematurely disclosing its new strategy. War in Korea and American involvement solved this problem and offered a plausible rationale to protect Taiwan.

Stalin's strategy of employing Korea as a tar baby to pit China against the United States required that North Korea fail in its attempt to defeat the South. New data regarding the Soviet war plan for Pyongyang, the conduct of the war, the kind of weapons supplied and withheld, and the timing of supply show rather clearly Stalin's intent to prevent the North from winning. Ironically, the closer the North Korean Army came to victory the less chance there was of achieving it. As NKA supply lines grew longer they grew more vulnerable to devastating American air and sea attack. Critically, however, the failure to seize Pusan—which was lightly guarded at the outset—meant that the United States would be able to hold a beachhead.

A lengthy conflict spelled doom for the North. Worse, Stalin did nothing to offset NKA vulnerabilities: he provided no air support, no air defense, no sea support, no modern weapons, and no bridging equipment. Worst of all, Stalin's war plan was fatally flawed. New documents show that the original plan called for the seizure of Seoul with the explicit assumptions that the Republic of Korea (ROK) would promptly fall and the United States would not intervene. Moscow's war planners were experienced World War II general officers. Clearly, while a war planner might have expectations along these lines, to make explicit planning assumptions on these crucial matters was an obvious, deliberate, design flaw. New evidence also demonstrates that the North Korean minister of defense objected to the Soviet plan and was temporarily shelved, returning to his duties only after the offensive had failed.

As soon as the war broke out, cables show, Stalin began pressing Mao to prepare for intervention, yet another indication that the Soviet leader expected Kim to fail. Stalin then, after the initial plan failed and the drive south began, urged Kim to concentrate all his forces against the Pusan perimeter and to ignore defense against the high probability of an American counterstrike in the rear. (Mao had warned Kim against a landing at Inchon, but the Korean leader was well aware of it.) When the Inchon landing occurred, Stalin refused to offer any assistance other than to permit North Korean soldiers to enter Soviet territory for recovery purposes. Instead, he demanded that Mao intervene—even before MacArthur moved north of the 38th parallel.

Documents discussing the Mao-Stalin bargaining over Chinese entry into the war show Mao's initial disinclination to enter—even though Chinese forces were preparing to do so. The sticking point was Stalin's refusal to agree to the joint defense of North Korea through provision of Soviet air support for Chinese forces in Korea. Stalin was willing to extend Soviet air support over Chinese territory, but not to Chinese forces in the field against the United States. Stalin was in the stronger bargaining position. As MacArthur's forces moved toward the Yalu, Mao's options dwindled. Ultimately, Mao's options were reduced to either not entering and permitting the United States to unify Korea under U.N. auspices, or intervening with whatever support he could get from Stalin, in hopes of securing a pro-Chinese buffer regime in North Korea.

Mao decided to intervene. Once he did so, then, and only then, did Stalin deploy a few thousand of the five thousand aircraft the Soviet Union had available in East Asia. Still, however, Soviet air support remained restricted to air defense in the North. No Soviet air-ground support role ever materialized for Chinese armies, as Stalin assiduously avoided conflict with the United States. Furthermore, China was required to purchase all assistance provided by the Soviet Union. Stalin's obvious intent was to prolong the conflict, at the same time deepening China's dependence on Moscow and also keeping the United States in a potentially draining quagmire.

Only when the Korean conflict began was American policy revealed, layer by layer, as one peels an onion. The Korean conflict would be the springboard to American rearmament only if the conflict lasted long enough and produced the desired geopolitical confrontation for congressional appropriations to reach previously programmed levels. The drafters of NSC-68 subsequently divulged what was not included in that document: that they had envisaged successive $50 billion defense budgets to produce the level of rearmament required to satisfy the needs of globalized containment beyond that required for the Korean conflict.

The need to appropriate funds for rearmament partially explains American policy behavior during the Korean conflict. Alternative solutions were available after Inchon and before the Chinese entry that, possibly, could have resulted in a termination of hostilities, but which would not have generated a threat large enough to produce desired appropriations levels. There can be little doubt that a short war in which American forces were victorious would not have resulted in major defense budget appropriations. The need to satisfy the requirements of global strategy explains the president's decisions to authorize MacArthur's relentless push to the Yalu River that precipitated Chinese involvement, although it is not clear whether MacArthur initially understood that limited war in Korea was to be a springboard to larger global objectives.

In a curious sense American and Soviet strategy ran parallel. Stalin precipitated a war in Korea to preclude China's move toward the United States, while Washington secretly prepared to employ a conflict to satisfy larger global containment objectives that no longer included a relationship with China. Stalin started the Korean War, but the United States used it for larger purposes. Thus, in both the Soviet and American strategies, Mao became the Odd Man Out.

PART I
THREE ALTERNATIVE FUTURES

CHAPTER ONE

Truman and the "Wedge" Strategy in 1949

THE EMERGENCE OF the Sino-Soviet alliance occurred against the backdrop of a year-long, cautious, yet persistent effort by the United States to come to terms with the emerging Communist regime in China. This effort influenced the timing and to a significant extent the content of the relationship between the two communist powers. An examination of the U.S. effort is therefore an essential component to any analysis of the origins of the Korean War.

THE ATTEMPT TO KEEP THE CHINESE AND RUSSIANS APART

From the moment American leaders realized that the Chinese Communists were going to win the civil war, they recognized the strategic importance of keeping the Chinese and Russians apart. The primary policy objective of the United States, NSC-34/1, concluded in January 1949, was "to prevent China from becoming an adjunct of Soviet power."[1] A Sino-Soviet alliance would open up the grim prospect of communist domination of the Eurasian landmass and threaten to vitiate the American sacrifice made in World War II. Therefore, from early 1949, the United States sought to come to terms with the emerging Chinese regime under Mao Zedong. The central objective was the establishment of diplomatic relations, which, it was thought, would enable the United States to retain intact its extensive commercial and treaty interests in China, and promote Chinese independence from Russia.

Concomitantly, Washington sought to disengage from its position of long support for the Nationalist government. In January 1949, the United States refused Chiang Kai-shek's request to mediate a peace between the Chinese Communists and the Nationalists. Chiang promptly resigned the presidency to Li Tsung-jen, only to reappear as chairman of an "Extraordinary Committee" on Formosa three months later, his power only thinly disguised. As Nationalist forces retreated into South China, the United States left its entire diplomatic presence in place, including Ambassador J. Leighton Stuart, perhaps the first indicator that Washington anticipated doing business with the new regime.

Ultimately, the Nationalist collapse and defeat would determine the pace of U.S. movement toward recognition of the new regime. American domestic, particularly congressional, support for the Nationalist cause was an accompanying constraint on the administration's policy. Throughout 1949, a determined group of pro-Nationalist supporters doggedly attempted to continue U.S. support, while administration leaders engaged in a very active behind-the-scenes effort to undercut congressional efforts on behalf of the Nationalists. When Communist victory became apparent, the administration became increasingly public in expressing its interests in establishing relations.

On the international level, British-American conversations in January produced a theme that would persist throughout the year, namely, the use of diplomatic recognition as a means of preserving each nation's respective commercial and treaty interests. British officials, however, wondered whether China's "economic weakness . . . might not offer an opportunity to secure reasonable treatment for our interests," while Secretary of State Dean Acheson believed that the new regime's prior demonstration of "respect for treaty obligations" would be the key that opened the door to recognition.[2] The different emphases would increasingly produce different approaches to the timing of extending diplomatic recognition, with Great Britain becoming more inclined toward early, even de facto, recognition, while the United States insisted upon an initiative from the new regime before taking action.

Thus, early in 1949, the strategic objective of the United States was to keep China independent of the Soviet Union; the means to that end was the establishment of diplomatic relations with the new Communist regime. This strategy was based on the assumption that the Chinese Communists were in fact more nationalists than communists and would adopt a "Titoist" orientation between East and West. The assumption was reinforced by the administration's own analysis of China's developmental needs based on the economic devastation of the country. The West alone possessed the necessary resources that could assist China's recovery, and it seemed inconceivable that China's new leaders, even though communists, would isolate themselves from vitally needed resources.

The timing of American policy would be dependent upon two related factors: the uncontestable collapse of Nationalist forces in the field and the evap-oration of American domestic support for the KMT. These were, in a sense, two sides of the same coin. Domestic support for the Nationalist cause re-mained strong as long as Nationalist resistance continued. Early in the year, while there still seemed a chance for Nationalist victory, Senator Pat Mc-Carran (D, Nevada) introduced a bill on February 25 to authorize $1.5 billion in economic and military aid to the Kuomintang. His bill was supported by fifty senators of both parties. The core of the pro-KMT group included Re-publican Senators William Knowland, California, Kenneth Wherry, Ne-braska, and H. Alexander Smith, New Jersey. Henry Luce, publisher of *Time* magazine, influential columnist Stuart Alsop, and the former head of the Flying Tigers, Claire Chennault, provided strong support from the private sector.

Continued congressional support for the Nationalists occasioned the be-ginning of a sustained but behind-the-scenes effort by the secretary of state and his assistants to oppose any further assistance. The State Department's efforts commenced in earnest in March. At this point Nationalist forces were reeling from multiple defeats and retreating into south China. On four occa-sions that month, high State Department officials appeared before the Sen-ate Foreign Relations Committee to testify in closed-door executive session. On March 18, for example, Acheson appeared before the committee to argue that Communist victory was inevitable. In his view, "the disaster is com-plete." Chinese Communist Party (CCP) forces were in command and the KMT had "disintegrated."[3] The United States government, he declared, must be prepared to consider the possibility of relations with a Communist government in China.

W. Walton Butterworth, director of the Office of Far Eastern Affairs, and Philip D. Sprouse, director of the Division of Chinese Affairs, accompanied the secretary to reinforce his views. Butterworth made the point that "we have consuls in Peking and Tientsin who are carrying on in a normal fashion under the Communists. . . . They deal with them about official business pro-vided it is not written on official paper." Butterworth's statement prompted the observation by Senator Claude Pepper (D, Florida) that: "if [the Commu-nists] respect rights, property, institutions, do business, allow our people to function . . . I think we should not appear to just turn our backs upon them."[4]

On March 21, the British Foreign Office issued a statement of general views on the question of diplomatic recognition. "To refuse to accord any sort of recognition to a government which in fact effectively controls a large pro-portion of territory is not only objectionable on legal grounds but leads to grave practical difficulties. It would be open to His Majesty's Government to recognize the Chinese Communist Government as at any rate being a *de facto* government of that part of China which it controls, and . . . at the same time, continue to recognize the Central Government as being the *de jure* government of the whole of China. By so doing His Majesty's Government would be adopting an attitude similar to that which they adopted toward General Franco during the Spanish Civil War." Butterworth passed on "our general agreement with British views on this subject."[5]

On April 25, Chinese Communist troops crossed the Yangtze River and occupied the Nationalist capital at Nanking. Although the Nationalist government had already relocated to China's Southwest, most of the diplomatic corps remained in Nanking with reduced staffs, including the ambassadors of Great Britain and the United States. Indeed, earlier in April, Secretary Acheson had authorized American Ambassador Leighton Stuart to talk to the Communists, but "to avoid any publicity."[6]

At 6:45 on the morning of the 25th a dozen armed Communist soldiers demanded to be admitted into the lightly guarded U.S. embassy compound. On gaining entry, they muscled their way past the Chinese domestic staff and got into the ambassador's residence through the back door. They quickly, and it would seem purposefully, went upstairs to the ambassador's bedroom, rudely awakening him. Although no threats were uttered, the soldiers spoke in "loud and angry tones," brandishing their weapons while "inspecting" the ambassador's personal belongings.[7]

Whether because of the violation of the sanctity of the embassy or for other reasons, Stuart promptly cabled back to Washington his opposition to any early move to recognition. In cables to Acheson four days later, Stuart censured Communist "arrogance," recommended scrutiny of the Communist Party's "intention to maintain basic freedoms and human rights," and urged the creation of a united front among Western nations in establishing preconditions for recognition of the new regime.[8] Stuart was "convinced our tactics should ... be one of reserve, waiting for new regime to make first approach. We can afford to wait." The Communists, Stuart said, although "extremely intelligent," needed to be "educated" out of the "murky haze of [their] own self-indoctrination." He objected to the British notion of de facto recognition because it would 'sacrifice possible long range advantages for immediate and relatively minor ones ... we should not appear anxious to make first move ... "[9]

The intrusion into the American embassy had an almost immediate effect on policy as Secretary of State Acheson announced on May 4 that U.S. policy toward China would remain "unchanged."[10] There would be no consideration of an early establishment of diplomatic relations. Acheson also acted immediately on Stuart's suggestion of building a united front, authorizing embassy staff worldwide to discuss the policy of holding out recognition in return for preservation of the international community's respective interests in China. In adopting this position, however, Washington and London began to diverge on their approaches to the new regime, as British authorities increasingly sought an early opportunity to extend recognition.

Reaffirmation of existing policy but without the resumption of further assistance to the KMT seemed to produce a shift in the Communist position. By early May, Communist control of most of the mainland was evident and the CCP leadership decided to initiate discussions with Ambassador Stuart in Nanking. CCP leader Huang Hua, who had been a student at Yenching University where Stuart had been president, suggested meetings, and Washington responded affirmatively.[11] In a cable on May 13, Acheson provided "guidance" to Stuart, enumerating specific criteria for recognition. The new Chinese government, Acheson stipulated, must exercise effective control over its territory, recognize its international obligations, and have the "general acquiescence" of its people.[12]

In discussions with Ambassador Stuart that day, May 13, Huang Hua "expressed much interest in recognition of Communist China by USA on terms of equality and mutual benefit."[13] Stuart laid out the position that the United States would "await developments in China," but then added that it was "customary to recognize whatever government clearly had support of people of country and was able and willing to perform its international obligations." The respective positions after the May 13 meeting were that China had indicated "much interest in recognition" and the United States conveyed its view that it was "customary to recognize."[14]

The two men met again several weeks later, on June 6. Huang appeared to be "extremely anxious," urging the United States to "break ... off relations with [the] Nationalist Government."[15] Stuart, however, maintained the wait-and-see attitude expressed earlier. At last, Huang extended an invitation for the ambassador to travel to Peiping to meet with the Chinese Communist leadership. Chinese Communist leaders had learned of Stuart's custom of traveling to Peiping to spend his birthday and visit his old university, and sought to combine his annual visit with a meeting with Mao.[16] But Washington procrastinated as events on the battlefield began to unfold rapidly and the recognition question bubbled to the surface.

By late June, Chinese Communist forces had captured Shanghai and were rolling on toward Canton. The remnants of Nationalist forces were retreating to the far Southwest. Under these circumstances, State Department officials recognized that acceptance of Huang's invitation would mean "the *coup de grace*" for the Nationalists, which led to a decision to decline the invitation.[17] Afterward, Stuart concluded that an opportunity had been missed; he believed that Mao and Zhou had "counted on entertaining me and talking to me during this ostensibly private visit to Peiping."[18]

The decision not to authorize Stuart's trip to Peiping was rendered moot because, before it was delivered, Mao Zedong indicated a major shift in the

13

CCP's position. On June 30, Mao issued a statement declaring that China must "lean to one side." We must, he said, "ally ourselves with the Soviet Union, with the People's Democratic Countries, and with the proletariat and the broad masses of the people in all other countries, and form an international united front."[19] Mao's announcement was followed over the course of the next few weeks by the abrupt closure of United States information offices throughout China, but not of its consular offices, which remained unobstructed.

More will be said in the next chapter about the timing and reasoning that lay behind the Chinese leadership's decision to take this step. What was surprising was the manner in which the United States responded. Contrary to what one might have anticipated, given the public announcement of Mao's intention to ally with the Soviet Union and restrict American influence, U.S. officials, instead of ceasing efforts to reach a modus vivendi with the CCP, redoubled those efforts. Acheson and his aides decided that they must accelerate the pace of policy to avoid any further deterioration of relations and move to establish political and commercial ties with Peiping.

The immediate task, it was decided, was to embark upon a public campaign to convince Congress and prepare public opinion for recognition. On July 27, Acheson announced the formation of a policy committee to "review" Far Eastern policy. Headed by Ambassador-at-large Philip Jessup and including the former president of the Rockefeller Foundation, Raymond Fosdick, and the president of Colgate University, Everett Case, the Policy Review Committee was formed primarily for the purpose of establishing a public forum within which a change of policy could be discussed.

In announcing the formation of the committee, Acheson noted that the Nationalist government had been "unable to rally its people and . . . been driven out of extensive and important portions of the country." Battlefield developments confronted American policy with "sharply limited" alternatives.

> We must not base our policy on illusions or wishful thinking. . . . The United States . . . will be prepared to work with the people of China and of every other country in Asia to preserve and to promote their true interests, developed as they choose and not as dictated by any foreign imperialism.[20]

Acheson's statement was the first public signal that the policy, which as recently as May 4 he had said would be "unchanged," would in fact be changed. A few days later, on August 5, the State Department released its "white paper" on China. In his letter of transmittal, Acheson once again declared that it was "abundantly clear that we must face the situation as it exists in fact. We will not help the Chinese or ourselves by basing our policy on wishful thinking." Lamenting China's exploitation by "a party in the interest of a foreign imperialism," the secretary of state declared his belief that ultimately the Chinese people would "throw off the foreign yoke," an objective toward which the United States would work "now and in the future." American policy, he concluded, will continue to be based upon respect for "China's independence and administrative and territorial integrity."[21]

President Truman, commenting on the release of the White Paper, declared:

> the mutual interests of the United States and China require full and frank discussion of the facts. It is only in this way that the people of our country and their representatives in Congress can have the understanding necessary to the sound evolution of a foreign policy in the Far East. . . . The problem of finding ways to give practical expression to that friendship [between the people of the United States and China] will continue to receive, day in and day out, the closest attention of this government.[22]

But the movement of American public opinion toward a way of giving "practical expression" to friendship with China suffered a second, stunning blow only weeks following the issuance of the White Paper.

THE SOVIET ATOMIC BOMB
COMPLICATES AMERICAN CHINA POLICY

The United States Air Force had for months been sending aircraft on long-range patrols along the Alaskan coast "to monitor the Soviet Union's atomic energy program." Prevailing west-to-east winds would carry radioactive dust from the Soviet test sites in Central Asia out to the North Pacific. The planes employed specially treated filter paper which could pick up radioactive dust that had been lifted into the atmosphere as a result of any nuclear tests. The flight of September 3 revealed "an abnormally high count of radioactive particles" on the filters, indicating what U.S. officials had feared, "that sometime the previous week the Soviets had detonated a nuclear device."[23]

To the American leadership neither the "discovery of the Soviet detonation of an atomic device [and] the approaching consolidation of Communist rule on the Chinese mainland" was a surprise. To Paul Nitze, recently appointed director of the State Department's Policy Planning Staff: "The fact that they had occurred almost simultaneously suggested that we were on the verge of a fundamental change in the balance of power." The question was: "How should we react to these developments?"[24]

Truman administration officials immediately began to debate the impli-

15

cations of both developments. Foremost was the nuclear question. Was it advisable to proceed with the development of the next stage of nuclear power based on the fusion process, which offered "a thousandfold" increase in the power generated by the fission process? Opinion in both the scientific and political groups involved was sharply divided and it would be four months before the decision would be made to proceed with the H-bomb. With regard to China policy, on the other hand, the decision was made to proceed rapidly toward the establishment of diplomatic relations with the new Communist regime. More than ever, it was now vital to keep the Russians and Chinese apart.

In truth, Soviet detonation of an atomic weapon greatly complicated Secretary Acheson's China policy. On the one hand, Soviet possession of atomic weapons capability and the imminent establishment of communist rule in China meant that the United States must move to recognition as soon as possible before it was too late to meet the objective of keeping the communist regimes apart. On the other hand, the secretary could not move as long as the Nationalist government continued to mount resistance, however feeble. The continued presence of the Nationalists made an early jump to recognize the CCP unseemly, if not impossible, if only for the domestic furor it would cause, especially among the powerful bloc in Congress that continued to express support for the Nationalist cause.

Acheson's solution had been to attempt to build a united front of Western nations that the United States could employ as leverage to obtain a more cooperative attitude from the Chinese. If he could gain the support of allies, Acheson could buy time by holding out the prospect of recognition and the enticements that that implied to pull the Chinese to the "middle of the road" because of their need for Western assistance in rebuilding war-torn China. The clear assumptions behind this strategy were that the "need" for Western assistance was overriding, that China could in fact be "weaned" from the Soviet Union, and that there was sufficient time to make the Western case. In actuality, Acheson hoped he could hold off recognition long enough for the remnants of the Nationalist regime to fade from the scene and for congressional support for the Nationalists to subside, thus making it possible for the administration to move.

Two weeks later, on September 19, in the midst of heated congressional debate over China policy and in anticipation of the imminent proclamation of the People's Republic (the CCP Political Consultative Conference announced the Party's intention on September 21 but the formal proclamation did not come until October 1), Acheson reentered the fray. In an attempt to strip any moral impediments attached to the issue of recognition, Acheson made a strong bid for extending recognition simply as the way governments "do business" with one another.

We maintain diplomatic relations with other countries primarily because we are all on the same planet and must do business with each other. We do not establish an embassy or legation in a foreign country to show approval of its government. We do so to have a channel through which we conduct essential government relations and to protect legitimate United States interests.[25]

On October 1, the CCP proclaimed the establishment of the People's Republic of China with the capital at Beijing, formerly Peiping. Accompanying the proclamation was the statement that "this government ... is willing to establish diplomatic relations with any and all governments of foreign countries which wish to observe principles of equality, mutual benefit, and mutual respect for territorial sovereignty."[26] A letter was sent out by newly designated foreign minister Zhou Enlai to the international community reiterating Beijing's interest. Declaring the regime's willingness to establish ties with "any and all governments" gave Acheson and his aides some hope **17** that their strategy of keeping China independent of the Soviet Union still stood a chance of succeeding.

The State Department quickly responded to Zhou's letter by bringing up the case of Angus Ward, U.S. consul in Mukden, Manchuria, who, along with his staff, had been seized and held hostage by the Chinese Communists—on Moscow's advice—since November 1948.[27] The State Department had reluctantly closed the Mukden consulate the following May, but the CCP refused to permit Ward and his staff to depart. From the department's point of view, the manner in which the new regime dealt with Ward would indicate whether or not Beijing was willing to observe the norms of international behavior, one of Acheson's key criteria for recognition. Discussion of the issue would also keep communications channels open.

At the same time, October 6–8, the State Department sponsored a "roundtable conference" under the auspices of Ambassador Jessup's Policy Review Committee. Some two dozen influential academic and business leaders attended, the majority of whom advocated the early establishment of diplomatic relations with China. Here the message was unmistakably positive. Raymond Fosdick, chairman of the first day's session, declared: "we have come to the end of an era" in American policy toward the Far East. It is our "hope and expectation," he said, "that with the aid of such groups as this we can get light in the formulation of a new policy."[28] Ambassador Jessup viewed the matter of recognition as the most pressing issue, but the basic position of prior PRC demonstration of willingness to honor treaty obligations remained.

The assumptions underlying Acheson's carefully crafted strategy began to crumble almost immediately, however, and the United States' bargaining position rapidly shifted from demander to supplicant. Not only did the united front idea never get off the ground, but China also proved to be "*un-*

weanable," and time rapidly ran out on Washington's efforts to educate the CCP in its need for the West. Worst of all, Soviet and Chinese relations not only did not become antagonistic—despite Soviet heavy-handedness in Manchuria and Sinkiang—but the two countries also moved toward a formal alliance.

THE CRUMBLING OF AMERICAN STRATEGY

British authorities had since early in the year conveyed their view that prompt rather than delayed interaction offered the best hope for fostering cooperative policy behavior. By this time, India, France, Italy, Canada, Australia, and the Netherlands were becoming increasingly uncomfortable with delay and would have welcomed the opportunity to recognize the new regime. Britain, as head of the Commonwealth, was the key nation and U.S. officials emphasized the need for the Chinese to express their intentions to honor their international obligations before any move to recognize was taken. But it was a losing battle.

On October 10, British officials acknowledged that they had replied to Zhou's letter with the suggestion of establishing "informal relations," even while protesting that this approach did not constitute an offer of de facto recognition.[29] The British action appeared to be in direct response to a possible threat to Hong Kong. The day before, Chinese Communist forces had taken Canton and the CCP's attitude toward the British colony was uncertain. Truman, in conversation with Acheson, "thought that the British had not played very squarely with us on this matter."[30] With Britain vacillating, it seemed that the united front would soon collapse.

The view from the field was more encouraging. On October 7, U.S. Ambassador to Moscow Alan Kirk advised early recognition so as not to replicate the experience with the Soviet Union in 1917, which had resulted in a delay in recognition for sixteen years. On the 11th, the chargé d'affaires in Beijing, O. Edmund Clubb, cabled Acheson to note that there had been surprisingly little anti-American commentary in the press, leading to his conclusion that "there seems good reason [to] believe Communist leaders truly desire American recognition and regularization [of] relations for both political and economic reasons." The chargé d'affaires in Britain chimed in a day later with the view that since Britain had cracked the united front "perhaps we also should take early action . . . so that appearance of UK-US difference of view would be minimized, especially in Communists' eyes."[31]

That morning, October 12, Acheson appeared once again in executive session before the Senate Foreign Relations Committee. In his remarks, he attempted to adhere to his strategy of first obtaining Chinese commitment to uphold its treaty obligations before moving to recognition. He stressed the theme of Russian aggressive domination of China as antithetical to Chinese nationalism, on whose side stood the United States, but he seemed resigned to the prospect that the establishment of diplomatic relations might not come soon.

We have regarded foreign domination of China as hostile to the interests of the United States and hostile to the best interests of the Chinese people.... We hope to take the [public] attitude that the question is Russian Imperialism against Chinese Nationalism, [that]we are on the side of the Chinese people, and we are against this foreign power that is trying to take over in that area.[32]

Ultimately, he said, resignedly, "if the Chinese, after thinking it over, want to be Communist, that is their business." At the very least, he still hoped to be able to do business with the Communist regime. The United States, he said, will not put itself in the position of being the foreign aggressor in China. "If trade can take place at some time, we are not going to put artificial governmental prohibitions in its way."[33]

The secretary explained his three criteria for recognition, then declared: "We could not anticipate that there will be any imminent reason for dealing with this matter, but, on the other hand, I do not want to give you the impression that such an event might not arise." The "real question," he said, "is whether they are going to recognize us rather than whether we are going to recognize them." It would be most desirable, the secretary continued, if the United States could "keep a united front on this and act as much as possible together" with its allies. In a clear reference to Great Britain, Acheson said: "No nation ought to consider that it can get any special advantage by jumping in and recognizing them ahead of somebody else."[34]

Ambassador-at-large Jessup took an optimistic position in his remarks. "We think," he said,

there is a real possibility that in the evolution of the situation of China vis-à-vis the Soviet Union, the attempts which the Soviet will probably make to exercise greater control on the Chinese . . . may bring about that same kind of basic antagonism between the Chinese Communists and the Russians, which would develop a Tito movement.... We think they are going to have increasing difficulty as they take on the main job of running the cities and trying to industrialize and so on.... They are going to see then their dependence is more on the West than the Soviet Union.[35]

The same day, following his testimony, Acheson met with visiting Indian Prime Minister Jawaharlal Nehru. The secretary noted in his memorandum of their conversation that Nehru's "general attitude seemed to be that since recognition was doubtless inevitable, there was little purpose in postponing it by diplomatic maneuvers."[36] At a news conference after their meeting, Acheson revealed publicly for the first time his three "criteria" for recogni-

19

tion of the Chinese Communist government. Acheson said that CCP control of the country, public acquiescence in its rule, and a willingness to honor China's treaty obligations would constitute the basis for recognition by the United States.[37] At the same time, his announcement signaled that the United States would not be stampeded by the actions of others. The ball was in China's court.

The Chinese response came quickly. The CCP reaffirmed a long-held position that all treaties, agreements, and loans made by the Nationalist government were invalid. On October 15, Chinese troops, having taken Canton, began a drive toward Hong Kong, intensifying pressure on London to respond. A week later, the forces of the People's Liberation Army (PLA) began the first of two unsuccessful attempts to take Nationalist-held islands off the coast. The first was Quemoy, an island off the Fukien coast, and the other was Dengbu, an island in the Zhoushan group off Shanghai. In both cases, Nationalist control of the air and sea were decisive in repelling the attacks, but the United States had provided no assistance to the Nationalists.

At the same time, in late October, Chinese authorities announced the formal arrest of Angus Ward and his staff (who had been in their custody for the previous year), and their forthcoming trial. The announcement on Ward sent mixed signals. He was to be tried for assaulting a "Chinese citizen" at the American Consulate, not, as some expected, for espionage, which would have closed off any possibility of improving relations. Since mid-June, the CCP press outlet, Xinhua, had escalated the charges against Ward, alleging that he had been involved in espionage operations in Manchuria.[38]

The Chinese decision on Ward, with its glimmer of a possibility for a diplomatic opening, prompted Acheson to confer with his confidants. In two confidential meetings on October 26 and 27, several decisions were reached. First, it was determined that any further military aid to the KMT was "futile," and would be disadvantageous to American interests. Second, it was felt likely that "great strains" would develop between Moscow and Beijing. "These strains would not only work to our advantage but would contribute to the desired end of permitting China to develop its own life independently rather than as a Russian satellite."

Third, to help strains develop the United States "should acquiesce in trade with China of an innocent character while permitting no strategic items to reach Communist China." The U.S. government "should not consider" financial assistance and should "discourage" private capital investment, although private firms already doing business in China would be permitted to "continue their operations." Nor would the United States "seek to detach Formosa from the Communist-controlled mainland." Finally, Washington's attitude toward recognition should not be "eager," but "realistic."[39]

If not being "eager" reflected expectations that there would be sufficient time for events to unfold, London quickly shattered those expectations. On November 1, the Foreign Office sent a confidential memorandum setting forth a proposal for prompt de jure recognition of the PRC and requested an indication of Washington's views within two weeks. It reflected the success of the CCP's strategy of applying pressure on Hong Kong to prod Britain into recognition. As such, the memo represented the end of Acheson's attempt to maintain a united front on the recognition issue. The British view was that "the disadvantages of nonrecognition were so great as to outweigh any possible advantages to be obtained from [first] securing Chinese Communist assurance of respect for international obligations."[40]

Acheson discussed the issue with British Foreign Secretary Ernest Bevin the following week in Paris, but could not budge him. The best he could obtain was an assurance that Britain would not accord recognition until after the first of the year. Over the following several weeks, the State Department attempted to apply pressure on its allies to delay recognition, but the majority leaned toward the British view. The United States, it seemed, would be isolated on the issue of recognition. On December 16 British Foreign Secretary Bevin sent a note to Acheson indicating that he was "thinking in terms of the 2nd of January 1950" as the recognition date, but later informed the secretary that Britain would extend de jure recognition on January 6, 1950.[41] India planned to recognize the PRC on December 30.

Although the united front had collapsed, the United States maintained its position of insisting that China express its willingness to honor treaty obligations before recognition could be considered. The situation, however, was changing very rapidly. Indeed, by mid-December, Acheson began to change American policy in response to several dramatic developments. First, there can be no doubt that the failure to maintain a united front was a factor. Second, Angus Ward had been tried, found guilty, and then deported on December 7. Third, on December 8, as Communist troops approached the Nationalist government's temporary capital at Chengtu, Nationalist officials fled the mainland to Formosa. It appeared, indeed, that it was only a matter of days before the Nationalists would be eliminated. The main obstacles to recognition were being cleared away.

But the main factor in bringing about a shift in Acheson's view to prompt and early recognition of the PRC was Mao's sudden appearance in Moscow on December 16, which was also the day Acheson received Bevin's memo indicating Britain's intention to extend recognition in early January. Mao's arrival in Moscow raised the grim prospect that the very object of American strategy—to keep the Russians and Chinese apart—was in jeopardy. It was this, above all, that forced Acheson quietly to drop his criteria for recognition.

The first indication of a change came on December 16, when the secretary sent a circular cable to U.S. embassies in Indonesia, Thailand, Pakistan, the

Philippines, India, Burma, Vietnam, and Singapore, requesting embassy opinion of the probable impact of each of three courses of action: 1) if the U.S. joined in early recognition, 2) if the U.S. delayed recognition until a majority of others recognized, or 3) if the U.S. withheld recognition?[42] The clear implication in this internal survey was that the United States was contemplating a change in its policy of delaying recognition. The very act of requesting embassy personnel to engage governments to which they were accredited on the question of a potential change of policy was itself a clear indicator that the existing policy of waiting for China to commit itself to honoring existing treaty obligations would not be maintained.

But time was beginning to run out for Acheson and the United States. Mao had gone to Moscow ostensibly to help celebrate Stalin's seventieth birthday, on December 21. He stayed on afterward and on January 2, 1950, the TASS news agency released an "interview" in which Mao indicated that one of his reasons for extending his stay in the Soviet Union was to resolve several questions related to Soviet-Chinese relations. Replying to the interviewer's question of which problems he was considering, Mao replied: "Among these problems, the problems of first importance are the existing Sino-Soviet Treaty of Friendship and Alliance, the Soviet loan to the PRC, trade and a trade pact."[43]

THE SINO-SOVIET ALLIANCE DEFEATS THE WEDGE

Acheson and the American leadership were stunned. The secretary had assumed that continued Soviet heavy-handedness, especially in Manchuria and Sinkiang, would quickly drive the Chinese into seeking a counterbalance. He had anticipated that the United States would perform that role, assumed there was sufficient time to bring about Chinese appreciation for the benefits relations with the United States could confer, and, even if belatedly, had begun to position the United States to extend recognition. Mao's revelation that a new treaty was about to be negotiated and that the Soviet Union would be extending a loan and developing trade was a most serious blow to Acheson's assumptions.

The United States under President Truman had sought a diplomatic relationship with China as the means of preventing the emergence of any destabilizing groupings of states in Asia. At the worst, an independent China was acceptable, but China allied to the Soviet Union was something very different, and unacceptable, because it altered the global balance of forces. Every effort must be made to dissuade the Chinese from making a long-term alliance commitment to the Soviet Union, although the prospects were not good. Failure would, perforce, require a revamping of American strategy.

Given the reduction in American military power since the end of World

War II, and the Soviet acquisition of atomic weapons, the relative balance of global power was now quite precarious. China's entry into a treaty relationship with the Soviet Union would present a threat to the overall United States global position. With a secure common border, the Soviet Union could concentrate its resources on Europe, while China could focus on Asia, threatening to upset as-yet-unrealized relationships in both areas.

Truman's response would be to mount a last-ditch public campaign, increasing his offer to Mao in an effort to bring about a last-minute change of decision. As an inducement for China to maintain its independence, the United States would present no military threat to China, nor would the United States provide any military assistance to the remnants of the Nationalist regime on Taiwan. Most significantly, American leaders would declare that the defeat of communism in China was no longer a policy goal.

On the contrary, the United States would adopt a most benign posture. No further mention was made of "criteria," or preconditions. The policy of the United States, it would be stressed, was to encourage Asian peoples to pursue their own chosen destinies, offering assistance whenever requested. Ultimately, the United States was interested in regular diplomatic relations with the People's Republic, if the Chinese government and the U.S. Congress concurred. Acheson continued to believe that a falling out between the two communist countries was as inevitable as was the demise of the Nationalist government on Taiwan.

But Mao Zedong and the Chinese leadership confounded American leaders; disdaining the independent future offered by the United States, they proceeded to establish a long-term treaty relationship with the Soviet Union. Mao's choices, in turn, forced the United States to change fundamental (and obviously mistaken) assumptions about the Chinese Communists. These choices and their consequences are the subject matter of this study.

CHAPTER TWO

Mao and Stalin: A Modus Vivendi?

As it became clear, certainly no later than the end of 1948, that the Chinese Communists were going to emerge victorious in the civil war, Mao and the Chinese leadership began to turn their thoughts to how to govern and to the relationships the "new China" would have with other states.[1] Contrary to what actually transpired, it seems indisputable that what Mao did *not* seek was to isolate China from the rest of the world, lodging his country in an indefinite, dependent relationship on the Soviet Union. Rather, Mao sought to establish a state free of the encumbrances of past foreign oppression by imperial powers. He sought to replace the unequal treaties of the past century with new equal treaty relationships with all countries. It is also clear that Mao intended to establish communist rule over China in emulation of the Soviet system. The People's Republic would be a totalitarian dictatorship under the control of the Chinese Communist Party, not a democracy.

The path to the establishment of a new regime was strewn with difficulties, not least of which were the actual circumstances of history. The key to understanding Mao's objectives is a recognition of the contradictory impact of his ideological and organizational ties to the Soviet Union and of his perception of China's national interest. Furthermore, there is no doubt that, as the leader of a large and potentially powerful state, Mao would have to consider China's national interests. The former would have to be addressed before the latter could be realized. In practice, this meant that—first and foremost—China's relationship with the Soviet Union would have to be negotiated, or more accurately, *re*negotiated. Mao consistently made clear that the state-to-state relationship he intended to negotiate with Stalin would be his model for China's relations with all other nations.

Chinese leaders were by no means unified in their objectives. Three distinct groupings can be identified, each with different ideas regarding future relations with the Soviet Union. First, there was Mao, whose views were clearly more nationalistic than *inter*nationalistic, as noted above. Second, there was Liu Shaoqi, whose position was the reverse of Mao's on relations with Moscow. Liu and those who supported him sought a close alliance with the Soviet Union. Third, there was Gao Gang, Manchurian party chief, who sought either to establish Manchuria as a de facto independent state, or, failing that, to annex it to the Soviet Union. Gao's willingness to detach Manchuria from China put him in opposition to both the Mao and Liu groups.

Mao himself was an indivisible part of the Communist Party apparatus. The Chinese Communist Party, of course, was for over a quarter of a century a part of the Soviet Union's international communist movement. Mao Zedong had risen to the top of the Chinese party organization in the course of a series of political struggles with rivals, many of whom were considered Stalin's chosen leaders, which led some outsiders, mostly Americans, to believe that Mao was a potential "Titoist." The fact that Mao had risen within the communist organization on the basis of his own political acumen and not as one of Stalin's men was of mixed benefit. On the one hand, it conferred a strong, independent political base. On the other hand, that very independence raised Stalin's suspicions regarding Mao's "loyalty" to the cause of international communism.

There was also the inescapable logic of the Chinese Communist revolution. New China was emerging as one of the "revolutionary" states, with built-in relationships, if not alliances, to the Soviet camp. Mao had no intention of repudiating his revolutionary heritage and could not do so had he wished. The only alternative open to him was to broaden his appeal to include opening relations with other states, on the grounds of renegotiating unequal treaties and accepting assistance in the reconstruction of a China devastated after so many years of war. To embark upon this course without first firmly establishing his relationship with Stalin, however, would open him up to a charge of "Titoism" and Soviet hostility.

Finally, there was the historical fact of the presence of Soviet armies on Chinese soil, there by virtue of the 1945 treaty between the Soviet Union and the Nationalist government and by their supporting role in the civil war. Mao knew that it would be very difficult to pry the Soviet Union away from positions in Sinkiang, Outer Mongolia, and Manchuria, buffer territories that the Russians had coveted since tsarist times. Any hint of disloyalty, Titoism, or nationalism might well persuade Stalin to claim Soviet "rights" to these areas by virtue of the 1945 treaty. As it was, since 1924 Stalin had incorporated Outer Mongolia as a Soviet satellite state, a status reconfirmed by the 1945 treaty.

Mao's general strategy, then, was to normalize relations with the Soviet Union prior to broadening his position to include relations with other states. Thus, Mao's initial agenda was to demonstrate his bona fides to Stalin and establish China as part of the Soviet camp. The means to this end lay in his determination to renegotiate the 1945 treaty, and ensure China's territorial integrity with regard to Sinkiang and Manchuria. He also hoped to "complete" the Chinese revolution by extending communist control over Tibet and, most of all, Taiwan. None of this was possible without a close, cooperative, even friendly, relationship with Stalin and the Soviet Union. The question was: Could he accomplish this part of his agenda without foreclosing an opening to the West?

26

STALIN ATTEMPTS TO RETAIN WORLD WAR II GAINS IN CHINA

By early 1949 at the latest, Stalin understood that in terms of Soviet strategy as it had evolved in World War II, the imminent victory of the Chinese Communists represented a mixed blessing. On one level it signified the victory of international communism over imperialism and colonialism—the theme of many publications in both countries. But at a deeper level, he knew that the coming victory of the Chinese Communists would most probably result in a degradation of the Soviet position compared to what it would have been had the Yalta Agreement prevailed and the Nationalist government remained in power.

Under the Yalta Agreement worked out with President Franklin D. Roosevelt, the Soviet Union would have secured control of buffer zones around the Soviet periphery, ensuring maximum security against attack. In Asia, this security zone included Outer Mongolia and a strong presence in both Manchuria and Sinkiang—all subsequently legitimized by treaty with the Nationalist government of Chiang Kai-shek and guaranteed for a minimum of thirty years.[2] Thus, under Yalta, the projected postwar outcome was for a China under Nationalist control joined in a coalition with the Chinese Communist Party. In this coalition, the communists would be the junior partner, but in control of Manchuria, a feature that offered further insurance against the use of Manchuria as a springboard for attack against the Soviet Union.

The Yalta Agreement and the Sino-Soviet treaty of 1945 that legitimized them held only through the spring of 1946 when civil war resumed. Three years of conflict brought the Chinese Communists to the verge of victory, and raised clear implications for the Soviet position negotiated with the about-to-be-defeated Nationalist government. The Soviet position was strong by virtue of the facts of international communism, its ideology and organization, the Sino-Soviet treaty, and the dominant presence of Soviet forces in China. Nevertheless, Stalin could anticipate that Mao would insist upon recovering all lands claimed by or belonging to China, proletarian internationalism notwithstanding.

In short, Stalin could not expect to emerge from negotiations with the victorious Chinese Communists with the same position embodied in the 1945 treaty with the Nationalists. Soviet treaty rights on the Changchun Railroad, and to Port Arthur and Dairen on the Liaotung Peninsula, amounted to an intrusive presence no different from that accorded to the "imperialist" powers a century earlier. It was, in fact, the most recent of the "unequal" treaties imposed on China that Mao Zedong was publicly committed to eradicate.

The treaty held broader significance for Chiang Kai-shek, but was controversial even for him. For Chiang the treaty involved a quid pro quo: in return for granting the Soviet Union a long-term presence in Manchuria with use of its ice-free ports, and a Soviet-dominated Mongolia and Sinkiang, the Soviet Union agreed not to support the Chinese Communists. Stalin immediately and quickly violated both the letter and the spirit of the treaty, employing the Soviet presence in Manchuria to facilitate the entry of the Chinese Communists into it and secretly to provide essential support for the Communist war effort against the Nationalists. From this position in Manchuria, the Soviet-arranged transfer of North Korean troops to the Chinese Communists proved to be a critical component in the CCP's victory in the civil war.

On January 8, 1949, when Chiang Kai-shek appealed to the United States, the Soviet Union, Britain, and France to mediate peace in the civil war, Stalin immediately sought to persuade Mao to accept a Soviet mediation, a mediation that if successful would have resulted in a divided China—Stalin's optimum outcome. In all probability, it was Stalin who "inspired" Chiang's request through Soviet Ambassador Nikolai Roshchin, though he accused the United States of doing so. Stalin said in a cable to Mao: "obviously, the government's proposal had been inspired by the Americans."[3] Washington, however, refuting Stalin's claim, declined any mediation role.[4] It was a typical pattern of Stalin's to impute to others what he himself wished to do, and we will see him employ this device on numerous occasions in his dealings with Mao and others.

Mao's reply of January 13 was blunt and to the point, a response remarkable for its assertion of the Chinese Communist Party's interests over Moscow's. In offering a proposed reply for Moscow to Nanking, Mao declared: "It is for the people of China itself to choose the way to achieve peace, unity and

27

democracy. . . . The government of the USSR . . . cannot accept mediation between the two sides." Victory, Mao said, "is already in sight" and "the balance of class forces in China has already changed irreversibly." "We are therefore inclined," Mao said, toward "the unconditional surrender of the Nanking government."[5]

But Stalin would not relent, replying the next day and asserting that "we have to accept it." To refuse, he said, would be to give up "the banner of peace into the hands of the Kuomintang." Then, detailing his proposal of an internal takeover of the coalition government that would result from a mediation, Stalin concluded with the ominous remark: "This is our understanding of the issue and our advice to you. Maybe we were not able to present our advice clearly enough in our previous telegram." Mao immediately responded to Stalin, informing him that the CCP that day had published conditions under which they would be willing to enter peace negotiations.[6] These were Mao's "eight points," which meant Kuomintang surrender. Mao had preempted and defied Stalin.

Throughout these exchanges, Mao pressed Stalin to agree to receive him in Moscow, but Stalin declined. Stalin quite probably would not agree to an early meeting because he did not wish to reveal his hand openly. At the end of January 1949, however, in an attempt to repair the bad feelings that resulted from his blunt pressure on the Chinese to agree to mediation, Stalin offered a substitute for a face-to-face meeting. He sent Anastas Mikoyan to meet with the Chinese leadership *and to try again to stop the offensive*. Mikoyan arrived at the moment when Mao's armies were preparing to cross the Yangtze River, flushed with victory over the Nationalist forces in the decisive Huai-Hai campaign and the seizure of Beijing.

The dispatch of Mikoyan thus came as a last opportunity for Stalin to avert what was for the Soviet Union the worst case: the complete victory of the Chinese Communists—which would call into question the 1945 treaty arrangements and the Soviet "buffer" position in Manchuria, Mongolia, and Sinkiang. Aside from familiarizing himself with the Chinese revolution, Mikoyan's mission was to attempt to persuade the Chinese leadership to stop at the Yangtze River and acquiesce in the creation of two Chinas, the only way Stalin's gains in Manchuria and Sinkiang could be preserved. In other words, since Mao could not be induced to enter into a mediation that would result in the division of China, Stalin sent Mikoyan to try to talk him into stopping at the Yangtze anyway and achieving the same result.

The Russians understandably deny this embarrassing charge, which implies that Stalin put Soviet interests above those of proletarian internationalism, but Mao revealed Soviet advice shortly after Mikoyan's departure. "Some friends abroad," he said, "half believe and half disbelieve in our victory. [They are] persuading us to stop here and make the Yangtze River a

border with Chiang, to create the 'Northern and Southern Dynasties.'"
Zhou Enlai later repeated this charge, and clarified that it had been Stalin
who "demanded that we 'stop the civil war' . . . [and] attempted to create the
'Northern and Southern Dynasties,' namely two Chinas."[7]

For Mao's part, his talks with Mikoyan offered the opportunity to begin
the negotiation process that would culminate when the two communist leaders would eventually meet and establish a new relationship between their
countries. Thus, Mao set out his basic agenda to Mikoyan, covering the entire range of issues regarding the future nature of China's regime, relations
with Moscow, and general foreign policy. Referring to the 1945 treaty, Mao
touched on the Soviet presence in Sinkiang, Mongolia, and Manchuria, observing that "some" Chinese demanded the unconditional return of Mongolia and the Soviet "share" in the Changchun Railroad. Mao's reference to the
Soviet "share" in the railroad was a delicate way of raising the issue of the
Soviet presence and withdrawal from Manchuria. Clearly, he was indicating
that the treaty would have to be renegotiated.

Mao made plain that his intention was to restore the nation's dignity by
eradicating "all traces" of imperialism. This was the principle of "rebuilding
the oven." China would align with the Soviet Union in this struggle—the
principle of "leaning to one side"—but that would not mean perpetuating
an unequal treaty relationship. Finally, Mao described his foreign policy
strategy as "inviting guests after cleaning the house." Mao wanted the Soviet
Union to recognize China first, even before he cleaned the house. Then he
intended to establish relations with all nations "on an equal footing."[8] Mao
would defer action against Hong Kong and Macao because of their economic
value to China and because to seize them would virtually preclude the establishment of diplomatic relations with Britain and Portugal.

In what was a thinly veiled warning to Stalin, Mao also served notice that
he would not tolerate any "evil designs." In a statement that "astonished"
Mikoyan, Mao declared:

> We think that as our liberation war makes more and more victorious progress,
> we will need more and more friends. Here I speak about genuine friends. . . .
> Friends are divided into genuine and false ones. Genuine friends are sympa-
> thetic to us, support and assist us, and demonstrate sincere and honest friend-
> ship. False friends are friendly on the surface. They tell you one thing but do
> another, or even devise some evil designs; they fool the people and afterwards
> take joy in the people's disasters. We should be alert on this point.[9]

Mao's strategy was quite straightforward as he presented it to Mikoyan,
with little room for misunderstanding the policies he intended to follow.
China would align with the Soviet Union against imperialism, but "after
cleaning house" would establish diplomatic relations with all nations. The

relationship with the Soviet Union would have to be based on equality—thus the need to renegotiate the Sino-Soviet treaty of 1945. Implicit was the notion that the 1945 treaty was an unequal treaty and that a renegotiated treaty would serve as the model for relations with other nations. Mao's declaration that the Chinese would be "alert" to the "evil designs" of "false friends" was a clear warning that the old party-to-party relationship in which Stalin attempted to manipulate and dictate to the Chinese was a thing of the past.

At the Second Plenum of the Seventh Party Congress in March, Mao took a similarly tough stance with regard to the West, issuing initial guidelines for the complete eradication of imperialist domination in China. Mao said there was no hurry in seeking diplomatic recognition from other countries. After all, the oven had to be rebuilt and the house cleaned before relations could be established with the imperialists. When they were ready, China would establish relations with "all countries on the principle of equality." In the meantime, China would not recognize the legal status of any foreign diplomatic establishment from the "Nationalist period," would not recognize any of the "treasonable treaties" from that period, would abolish all foreign propaganda agencies, and would assume control over the entire foreign trade and customs system.[10]

Mao had apparently taken a tough stance toward both the Soviet Union and the West as an opening position, which he expected to soften later in negotiations. In fact, the softening toward the West came first. On April 17, a few days before Chinese forces crossed the Yangtze River, Zhou Enlai redefined the Second Plenum "guidelines." Moving from the position that the new Chinese government would not recognize any of the "treasonable treaties" from the Nationalist period, he now said that the government would evaluate all treaties on a case-by-case basis. Some treaties would have to be abrogated, some could stand with revision, and others could be retained intact.

Zhou declared that "no country can any longer interfere in China's domestic affairs." While welcoming aid, he said, China would no longer be dependent. "We should not even depend on the Soviet Union and the new democracies." Nevertheless, China must have an ally and that was the Soviet Union. It was the "fond dream" of the United States to split China and the Soviet Union, but that would not happen. At the same time, he said, "no force can prevent [China] from having two friends or even more." China might not be able to have close relations with the United States, but could conduct trade with it. "Trade could deepen mutual understanding and lead to an exploration of diplomatic ties on the basis of equality."[11]

Zhou's statement, made before a noncommunist audience, was clearly crafted to be encouraging, particularly to the United States, and was a shift

30

from the position taken at the Second Plenum a month earlier. But he also knew that if left unexplained it would alarm Stalin, who was alert and concerned about developments at this critical phase of the Chinese revolution. So Zhou told Stalin's representative to the CCP, Ivan Kovalev, about "feelers" from Washington. He observed that U.S. Ambassador Stuart was "seeking to establish contact." Although the Soviet ambassador, Nikolai Roshchin, had moved south with the Nationalist government, Stuart and the British ambassador, Sir Ralph Stevenson, had remained in Nanjing hoping to talk with Chinese Communist leaders.

Word that China was in discussions with the United States brought a quick response from Stalin. He could not very well object to China's desire to establish diplomatic relations with other states, but at a minimum hoped to delay the process, especially with regard to the United States. In a cable to Mao, he said that "China must not reject establishing official relations with some of the capitalist countries, including the United States," but should do so only if "these states officially abandon military, trade, and political support of Chiang Kai-shek's Nationalist government."[12] Stalin was demanding that Mao adhere to a more rigid criterion than Moscow was. The Soviet Union itself still maintained "official" relations with the Nationalist government.

31

Stalin then elaborated on the reason "this condition is necessary." It was because "the policy of the United States is aimed at splitting China into the south, middle, and north, with three governments." Thus, Stalin argued, "if you want to have a unified China headed by Communists, you ought to establish relations with only those capitalist governments that officially abandon support of the Nanjing and Canton groups." The implication was clear: Be wary of dealing with the Americans who are attempting to split your ranks.

This was an extraordinary argument, but not unlike the one used in response to the Nationalist request for mediation in January. Stalin was imputing to the United States the very policy that Moscow was pursuing, that of dividing China, and securing control of the buffer zones. This was clearly not American policy. The United States had since the end of the nineteenth century pursued a policy of ensuring China's territorial integrity, not division, of supporting China against the depredations of the imperialist powers as they carved up imperial China. Tsarist Russia had been a leading participant in the drive to acquire extraterritorial rights in China and the Soviet government was following in its footsteps. The facade of international communism could not disguise this fact.

Indeed, at this point, April 1949, the United States was busily disengaging from the Nationalist government, as Stalin surely knew. By making the United States the culprit, Stalin was attempting to place obstacles in the path of any possible Sino-American relationship and also slipping around his earlier advice to stop the revolution half way. It was the United States that was attempting to create a divided China, he said, not the Soviet Union. As we shall see, Stalin would repeatedly identify the United States as China's adversary as a way of demonstrating Soviet "friendship."

On April 24, the day before Communist armies crossed the Yangtze River, Mao got word to Stalin through Kovalev that there was a good chance the CCP would be making contact with the United States and Britain. He told Kovalev that "the Americans have reduced the number of security guards at their embassy in Nanjing from 40 to six men" and both the American and British ambassadors had stayed on.[13] Indeed, the next morning after crossing the Yangtze, several PLA men had forced their way into Ambassador Stuart's embassy residence.

What occurred encouraged Mao sufficiently for him to say a few days later, on April 28, that "The U.S. side has entrusted some people to request the establishment of diplomatic relations with our side. The British side is doing its best to do business with us. We may consider the issue of establishing diplomatic relations with the United States (and Britain), provided they cut off relations with the Nationalist regime."[14] Mao made the same statement publicly on April 30, although it was issued in the name of a PLA headquarters "spokesman." The CCP would be "willing to consider the establishment of diplomatic relations with foreign countries ... based on equality, mutual benefit, mutual respect for sovereignty and territorial integrity and, first of all, on no help being given to the KMT reactionaries."[15]

As we have seen in chapter 1, the Stuart–Huang Hua talks that then ensued marked the CCP's "interest" in establishing diplomatic relations with the United States and elicited Washington's view that the establishment of relations was "customary," but in any case not imminent. Both sides had to await further developments before action on the recognition question could be taken, but the talks had clearly established a mutual interest in opening diplomatic relations.

How genuine Mao's interest was at this point is open to debate. Indeed, his exchanges with U.S. representatives in particular may have been purely tactical. The spring of 1949 was the last moment when the Chinese Communist revolution could be reversed, and only if the United States were bent on preventing a Communist victory in China. In this connection, Mao's response to Kim Il-sung's plea to support an attack on the South is illustrative of Mao's broad-ranging thinking.

During his trip to Moscow in March, Kim had proposed an attack on South Korea, but Stalin refused on the grounds that "it was not necessary to attack the south."[16] Stalin agreed only to a North Korean counteroffensive, in response to a first attack by the South. Mao, on the other hand, was supportive and sent back to North Korea two divisions of troops consisting mainly of

Korean soldiers, who had been contributed earlier to assist the Chinese Communists.[17] In taking this action in opposition to Stalin, Mao was apparently attempting to create a North Korean diversion as a way of tying up potential forces that the United States could employ against China.

Washington was in the process of completing the withdrawal of its military forces from South Korea. Although Truman had no intention of intervening in China, Mao may have been concerned that the United States could redeploy these forces to save Chiang Kai-shek's regime. Mao may have hoped that the strengthening of the North Korean Army would persuade Washington to delay withdrawal of troops from South Korea and thus eliminate any possibility they could be employed in China. If so, the issue soon became moot as Washington completed the troop withdrawal from Korea and did not intervene, the Chinese revolution passed the point of reversal by the summer, and Stalin firmly ruled out any North Korean invasion in September. [33]

After this episode, which Stalin could easily have interpreted as a hostile act, Mao was particularly at pains to demonstrate that his first priority was regularizing his relationship with the Soviet Union. To reassure Stalin that the Chinese were not "Titoists," as well as to take a next step in arranging for important negotiations to come, he sent Liu Shaoqi to Moscow, the first meeting between top Chinese and Russian leaders in over a decade.

LIU SHAOQI'S TRIP TO MOSCOW

Liu Shaoqi was the number-two man in the CCP leadership and the most pro-Soviet. Mao, in fact, would send the most pro-Soviet of the Chinese leadership along with Liu, including Gao Gang, Wang Jiaxiang, Deng Liqun, and Ge Baoquan. Kovalev accompanied them along with Shi Zhe, as interpreter. In discussions with him prior to Liu's departure, Mao had given Kovalev advance notice of the issues that Liu would address, so Stalin was well-informed of the Chinese agenda.

To ensure that Stalin was under no misapprehension regarding China's international stance, two days before Liu departed, on June 30, Mao declared in a major address that China would "lean to one side," that is, on the side of the Soviet Union. At the same time, Mao authorized the publication of charges that the American consul in Manchuria, Angus Ward, had been engaged in an espionage operation against China. The espionage case against Ward, who was still under house arrest, was simply made up out of whole cloth. It was undoubtedly designed to reassure Stalin that there was little possibility of an improvement in Sino-American relations, which lenient treatment would imply.[18]

Liu Shaoqi arrived in Moscow on July 10 and remained until August 14.

On the evening of his arrival, just as Mao had done with Mikoyan in January, Liu went over the outstanding issues with Stalin. In a prepared statement, Liu gave the Chinese leadership's view that victory was now inevitable. In the unlikely event that the imperialists attempted to intervene, they could only "delay but not stop" the revolution. Even if the imperialists blockaded the coasts, which they were already doing, and deployed "one or two hundred thousand troops to occupy a few of China's coastal ports," they could only hinder but not change the outcome.[19]

Affirming the relevance of the Chinese revolution to other countries in Asia, Liu asked Stalin if China "could become a member of the Cominform." It was this request that generated Stalin's reply that the locus of world revolution had shifted from Europe to Asia and the Chinese should focus their efforts there. In short, Stalin denied the request. He did not want to create a situation where the Chinese could veto Soviet policy in Europe and so urged them to create a union of Asian Communist parties, which the Soviets would join.[20]

On China's foreign policy, Liu hoped that the Soviet Union would be the first state to recognize new China, but reaffirmed the position that China was prepared to establish relations with imperialist states "if they choose a policy of recognition." However, he said, China would not agree to any relationship that would "tie our hands and feet." Regarding treaties concluded during the Nationalist period, Liu revised the Chinese position yet another notch, saying that they were prepared to "examine them anew and to solve any issues on a case by case basis." The guiding principle would be to "recognize and inherit everything that [was] favorable" and reject that which was not.

This was an obvious reference to Mao's determination to renegotiate the 1945 treaty, which would be examined "anew," and Liu devoted some time to it. Focusing on the Soviet military presence in Manchuria's railroads and ports, he evidently raised the issue of Soviet withdrawal. Liu then offered a concession, in fact the same concession made by Chiang Kai-shek, expressing China's readiness to accept the independence of Mongolia. Liu's concession was clearly structured to elicit a similar concession from Stalin. The Chinese leader then ended his presentation with the proposal for Mao to visit Moscow, and asked Stalin to consider timing and format.

Stalin met with Liu and his group again the next day, July 11, to respond to Liu's proposals. Stalin's first comment was to apologize for being a "hindrance" in the civil war—implicit reference to his demand that the CCP terminate the conflict, but Liu vehemently denied any need for an apology.[21] After several exchanges along these lines, with Stalin lavishing praise on the Chinese for their accomplishment, he then confirmed that Moscow would extend recognition to the new Chinese government as soon as it was established and that Mao Zedong could come to Moscow immediately afterward.[22] But the Soviet leader admonished the Chinese "not [to] worry about getting recognition from the imperialist countries, even less about their attitude toward you."[23]

Since Liu had proffered a Chinese compromise on Mongolia, Stalin reciprocated with one on Sinkiang. In doing so, however, once again the Soviet leader projected his own objectives onto the United States and Britain, who, he claimed, were "promoting ethnic unrest . . . as a pretext for expanding their presence there."[24] He urged a speedup of the PLA's efforts and promised "material help" for the "liberation of China's western regions." Of course, as the Chinese leadership well knew, it had been the Soviet Union, not the United States or Britain, that had backed rebellions in November 1944 in the three northernmost counties of Sinkiang (Tahcheng, Ili, and Ashan) that bordered on the Soviet Union, and had been in control there ever since through their rebel proxies.[25]

Stalin went to great lengths to explain how and why the Soviet Union had signed the 1945 treaty with the Nationalist government, which Mao had severely criticized, and of the necessity for continued Soviet military presence in Manchuria. We dealt with the Nationalist government, he said, because we were committed by the Yalta Agreement and had no choice. As for the presence of Soviet troops in Port Arthur, Stalin went on, they are the "freedom force that is deterring the military forces of America and Chiang Kai-shek." This "freedom force" protects not only the Soviet Union, but also the Chinese revolution.

Offering what he hoped would be seen as an acceptable concession regarding the thirty-year right to remain in Port Arthur and Dairen contained in the 1945 treaty, Stalin declared that as soon as Japan signed a peace treaty and the United States withdrew its troops from that country, the Soviet Union would withdraw from Port Arthur. If the Chinese comrades insisted, however, Soviet troops could be withdrawn "right away." The port of Dairen, on the other hand, was a different matter. It "must be used jointly by China and the Soviet Union. That is the real situation." Liu, no doubt taken aback by Stalin's determination to maintain a Soviet military presence in Manchuria despite Chinese wishes, did not respond.

Instead, Liu raised what was the key issue for the Chinese: Soviet assistance in the liberation of Taiwan. But Stalin wasted no time in rejecting this idea "out of hand," because he said it would risk a confrontation with the United States.[26] "The Russian people would not understand," Stalin said, "if we . . . undertake this." Nevertheless, to mollify Liu, he agreed to turn the matter over to an expanded Politburo group of senior political and military leaders. The second Liu-Stalin meeting thus ended on an unsatisfactory note. Stalin had agreed to relinquish his hold on Sinkiang, but insisted on maintaining a Soviet military presence in Manchuria, and the issue of Soviet assistance in the liberation of Taiwan was left hanging.

During the second meeting, Liu had raised the issue of the nuclear balance and requested a tour of the Soviet Union's nuclear facilities. His trip had coincided with the Soviet detonation of an atomic device, on July 10, an event that Chinese intelligence immediately noted, but which U.S. intelligence would not discover until over a month later. Stalin refused to permit a tour, but arranged for the Chinese to see a documentary of the detonation, which had occurred "somewhere . . . near the Arctic Circle."[27] On the basis of the film, Stalin boasted to Liu that "The Soviet Union is sufficiently strong now not to be afraid of the nuclear blackmail of the United States."

Stalin did not meet again with the Liu group for over two weeks, on July 27. But, judging by what happened when they did meet, the Soviets had had private discussions with individual leaders, as they sought to break down Chinese resistance to the Russian presence in Manchuria. The Soviets evidently persuaded Gao Gang to float a trial balloon at this meeting.[28] Gao proposed that instead of withdrawing, the Soviet Union should station more troops in Port Arthur and deploy warships to Tsingtao on the Shantung Peninsula to counter the American threat. He then went further, proposing to detach Manchuria from China entirely, and incorporate it as the "seventeenth republic of the Soviet Union."

The Soviet Politburo members present "enthusiastically applauded Gao's idea," but Stalin after a few awkward moments dismissed it as "specious and prejudicial," referring to Gao as "Comrade Chang Tso-lin," the Manchurian warlord of the twenties. It was an odd reference because Chang Tso-lin had been responsible for uncovering a Soviet scheme to take over China through the Chinese Communists, and was considered extremely anti-Soviet, hardly analogous to Gao. But if the proposal was designed to probe the depth of the Chinese leaders' determination to recover control of Manchuria, the answer came quickly. Liu Shaoqi and the other members of the Chinese delegation immediately turned on Gao, with Liu calling him a "traitor."

After the meeting, Liu reported the incident to Mao, who ordered Gao's immediate return (he would return to China three days later). Before he left, however, Stalin moved to save his loyal ally. He arranged for Gao as head of the Manchurian trade delegation to sign a trade agreement with Moscow.[29] At a farewell banquet, he goaded the Chinese into toasting their disgraced colleague. On Gao's departure, Stalin told Liu that they had both been "too severe toward Comrade Gao ... without any grounds."[30] When Stalin's words were reported to Mao, he quickly declared that "he had always supported Gao Gang." These exchanges saved Gao for the time being, but there was little doubt now within the Chinese leadership, if there had been earlier, where Gao's loyalties stood. (Mao would purge and execute Gao after Stalin's death on grounds of having "illicit relations with foreign countries," leading an "anti-Party alliance," and attempting to "seize power.")[31]

Also during the meeting on July 27, Stalin reiterated his earlier arguments against support for an assault on Taiwan and Liu withdrew his proposal. Instead, in a step worked out with Mao and the Chinese leadership between meetings, Liu formally requested and Stalin agreed to provide long-term Soviet assistance in the modernization of China's air and naval forces, and of its defense industry.[32] (The head of China's air force, Liu Yalou, immediately flew to Moscow, and in September Zhang Aiping, the head of China's navy, would go to make necessary arrangements regarding naval modernization.) It would seem that while Stalin would not support an immediate attack on Taiwan, he agreed to provide the basis for an eventual assault.[33]

Stalin also agreed to provide extensive advice and assistance on the establishment of the new state structure, political institutions, legal system, and intelligence apparatus. Indeed, ninety-six Soviet specialists would accompany Liu on the return train to China and hundreds more would follow. The Liu-Stalin discussions had covered the full range of future Sino-Soviet relations. Practical, theoretical, strategic, and sensitive issues had been raised and explored. Many had been resolved, but some crucial questions had been left undecided. Nevertheless, the groundwork had been laid for Mao's coming summit meeting with Stalin.

The Liu Shaoqi mission to Moscow had accomplished much, but on the crucial question of Soviet support for the conquest of Taiwan, Stalin had equivocated. While rejecting Liu's proposal for immediate assistance, Stalin had agreed to assist in the future buildup of China's air force and navy, the essential components of any amphibious attack. In effect, Stalin's answer on Taiwan had been yes, but not now. But Mao would not accept a delay and ordered his generals to prepare for an attack by the summer of 1950. As He Di notes, this cable directive "explicitly demonstrat[ed] Mao's impatience and firm determination to initiate the Taiwan campaign at the earliest possible time."[34] An assault on Taiwan, however, would have to be preceded by the capture of key offshore islands: Quemoy just off the Fukien coast and Dengbu in the Zhoushan group off Shanghai.

These islands would become the springboards for an attack on Taiwan, which lay ninety miles off the coast, and Mao ordered the PLA to seize them, even without air and naval superiority. Conversely, Nationalist retention of these islands amounted to the forward defense of Taiwan and would make any attempt to assault Taiwan itself fraught with danger and difficulty.

Mao's decision on Quemoy and Dengbu was based on three probable considerations. First, he believed that Nationalist forces could not withstand one more concerted blow and might even capitulate if the forward island defense positions fell.

Second, Mao correctly assumed that the United States was no longer backing Chiang Kai-shek and would stand aside if Chinese Communist forces attacked. The United States had made no attempt to prevent the PLA from crossing the Yangtze River or seizing Shanghai or Canton (which incidentally was a clear refutation of Stalin's claim that the United States was attempting to divide China). When the White Paper was issued in August, quite inconveniently from Mao's point of view, he authorized a campaign of criticism of U.S. policy, no doubt to reassure the ever-suspicious Stalin of his fealty, but the fact that Washington had disengaged from the Nationalists was nevertheless clear.[35]

38   The third consideration was perhaps most important. Mao wanted to be able to leverage Stalin on the issue of aid to seize Taiwan and complete China's unification. Success in seizing either of the two island positions would strengthen his hand when he met Stalin face to face and would make it difficult for Stalin to deny him the air and naval assault capability without which an attack on Chiang's island fortress was impossible. Thus, while the country celebrated the foundation of the People's Republic, the PLA prepared for the attacks. The results, however, were disastrous.

On October 24, the PLA landed three regiments on Quemoy and encountered fierce resistance. Nationalist forces, controlling both the air and sea, cut off and encircled the invaders and after three days of fierce fighting defeated the assault, capturing or killing some 10,000 men. It was a total defeat, but Mao would not relent. Needing a victory before he met Stalin, he tried again on the night of November 3. Three battalions landed on Dengbu and gained control of almost the entire island by the next morning. Once again, however, Nationalist air and naval superiority turned the tide. Nationalist forces reinforced their positions while preventing the Communists from doing the same, and the PLA was forced to withdraw. The defeats at Jinmen (Quemoy) and Dengbu were among the worst suffered by the PLA during the civil war and undercut Mao's arguments for an early assault on Taiwan.[36]

Mao also realized that he had vastly underestimated the importance of air power in an amphibious assault. Earlier, during Liu Shaoqi's meetings with Stalin, Mao had calculated that the assault on Taiwan would be achieved by reliance upon "internal cooperation," by which he meant Nationalist defections, "and the support of an air force." Indeed, Mao believed that "our plan would succeed if we could meet one of the two conditions, and our hopes would be even greater if both conditions could be satisfied."[37] At this point, Mao believed that if he could purchase an air force of one hundred planes from the Soviet Union and arrange for Moscow to train three or four hundred pilots, that would be sufficient "to seize Taiwan next summer." The defeats at Quemoy and Dengbu brought home forcefully the realization that many more planes would be necessary for the attack. While in Moscow Mao would revise his original estimate upward by a factor greater than ten.

MAO ZEDONG GOES TO MOSCOW

The failure to capture the offshore islands of Quemoy and Dengbu meant that Mao would go to Moscow in a weaker position than he would have held had they been taken. Conversely, Stalin now knew that he held the key card in the coming negotiations with Mao—the air and naval capability without which the PLA could not successfully attack Taiwan. The essential quid pro quo shaping up in the wake of the unsuccessful attempts to take Quemoy and Dengbu was that in the coming meetings between Stalin and Mao, the Chinese leader would be forced to concede a stronger Soviet position in Manchuria in return for Soviet assistance in the assault on Taiwan.

Indeed, Mao could now be almost certain that Stalin would drive a hard bargain and insist on retention of all the concessions gained in the 1945 treaty with the Nationalists in return for provision of assistance for the assault on Taiwan, a bad bargain from Mao's point of view. In early November, after the defeat at Dengbu, the Chinese Politburo convened to discuss the strategy Mao would employ in his meetings with the Soviet leader. Most important was to devise an exit strategy, a way for Mao to walk away from any bad deal that Stalin sought to foist upon him without causing a serious rupture in their relations.

The plan devised by the Politburo was threefold: First, to alleviate the pressure of lofty expectations, they would declare the reason for Mao's trip to be to help celebrate Stalin's birthday, not to negotiate a new treaty. Second, Mao would go without Foreign Minister Zhou Enlai to meet with Stalin and discuss their options. If Stalin attempted to deal high-handedly with the Chinese and refused to renegotiate the treaty, or demanded excessive concessions, then Zhou would stay home. If, on the other hand, he agreed to renegotiate the treaty, then Zhou would be called to Moscow for the negotiations. Thus, if Stalin refused to renegotiate the treaty, Mao, having helped celebrate Stalin's birthday, would return to China with no loss of "face."

Mao departed for Moscow on December 6, stopping along the way in Shenyang, Manchuria. There Mao got off the train for an unplanned tour of the city. He wanted to see for himself whether Gao Gang had complied with an earlier directive to take down Stalin's portraits from every place but Soviet garrison locations and other places were the Soviets were working. Gao had not. Stalin's portraits were hung in profusion, with portraits of Mao much smaller and less in evidence, indicating that Gao's views had not changed. Fuming, Mao reboarded the train and remarked sarcastically that "as he understood it, the Northeast was still part of [China]."[58] Clearly, the situation portended what was to come in Moscow. Stalin's pervasive presence extended into Manchuria and would be very difficult to eradicate. It was also yet another demonstration of Gao Gang's fealty to Stalin rather than to Mao.

Arriving in Moscow at noon on December 16, Mao was met by several Soviet Politburo members, including Molotov and Bulganin, but not Stalin.[59] The arrival ceremony was curtailed because of bitterly cold weather. Although Mao made some remarks from the train, he did not deliver his planned arrival speech, which was published instead. In it, Mao made the point that after the October revolution "the Soviet government, in accordance with the policy of Lenin and Stalin, was the first to abrogate the unequal treaties of the imperialist Russian period."[40] The implication, of course, was that China, having conducted its own revolution, would do the same.

After getting settled in the dacha prepared for him and his entourage in the Moscow suburbs, Mao met Stalin that evening at the Kremlin. With his first words, Mao attempted to put the Soviet leader on the defensive. After exchanging greetings, Stalin said: "We have probably caused you a lot of trouble. Beg your pardon." But Mao responded to this mumbled apology by Stalin with an accusation: "I have been attacked and squeezed within the party in China," meaning by Stalin's men in the CCP. Stalin, refusing to be drawn into any further apology or argument, merely said: "Let bygones be bygones. . . . Who can condemn victors?"[41]

The Soviet leader then changed the subject, asking Mao what he had in mind for his trip. Mao replied elliptically, saying: "for this trip we hope to bring about something that not only looks nice but also tastes delicious."[42] Mao had declined to take the proffered opening to state his wish to renegotiate the 1945 Sino-Soviet treaty, but why? Mao attempted to avoid placing himself in the position of the supplicant asking for favors. Mao wanted Stalin to raise the treaty issue, but even after Mao's interpreter Shi Zhe explained that "looking nice means something with a good form and tasting good means something substantial," the wily Soviet leader would not take the bait.[43]

Mao then tried another indirect approach, asking Stalin whether he should call Zhou Enlai to join them. Stalin understood that to say yes would mean that he was prepared to renegotiate the 1945 treaty, so he replied: "If we cannot make certain what we really want to work out, what is the use to call Zhou to come here?"[44] It was obvious that Mao's ploy to elicit an offer from Stalin to renegotiate the treaty was not going to work, so he switched tack, declaring China's need for a period of peace to stabilize the country and promote recovery. "How long will international peace be preserved?" he asked.[45]

Stalin's reply was most interesting. He said that "we have already had peace for the past four years." As far as China is concerned, he said, "there is no immediate threat," not from Japan, the United States, or Europe. "There is no one to fight with China, not unless Kim Il-sung decides to invade China."[46] Peace, Stalin declared, "will depend on our efforts. If we continue to be friendly, peace can last not only 5–10 years, but 20–25 years and perhaps even longer." Stalin's remarks emphasizing "*our* efforts," and "if *we* continue to be friendly" suggested cooperation between equals and seem to have offered Mao the opening he needed to return to the question of the treaty.

Mao then said: "Since Liu Shaoqi's return to China, [the CCP] has been discussing the treaty of friendship, alliance and mutual assistance between China and the USSR." Stalin's immediate response was to say "this question we can discuss and decide." His obviously considered reply was to offer Mao three options. "We must ascertain whether to declare the continuation of the current 1945 treaty of alliance and friendship between the USSR and China, to announce impending changes in the future, or to make these changes right now." But while offering Mao three possibilities, Stalin employed a curious and insulting argument in support of maintaining the current treaty as it was.

"As you know," Stalin began, the 1945 treaty was concluded "as a result of the Yalta Agreement, which provided for the main points of the treaty (the question of the Kurile Islands, South Sakhalin, Port Arthur, etc.)." In other words, this treaty was concluded "so to speak, with the consent of America and England. Keeping in mind this circumstance, we, within our inner circle, have decided not to modify any of the points of this treaty for now, since a change in even one point could give America and England the legal grounds to raise questions about modifying also the treaty's provisions concerning the Kurile Islands, South Sakhalin, etc."

"This is why," Stalin informed Mao, "we searched to find a way to modify the current treaty . . . while formally maintaining its provisions." In this way, he went on, we could "formally [maintain] the Soviet Union's right to station its troops at Port Arthur while, at the request of the Chinese government, actually withdrawing the . . . forces currently stationed there." We could do the same thing, Stalin said, with the Changchun Railroad. "If, on the other hand, the Chinese comrades are not satisfied with this strategy, they can present their own proposals."[47]

Restating his position that the form of the treaty be maintained but its content changed to reflect the new situation, Stalin said, "the treaty ensures the USSR's right to station its troops in Port Arthur. But the USSR is not ob-

41

ligated to exercise this right and can withdraw its troops upon Chinese request. However, if this is unsuitable, the troops in Port Arthur can remain there for 2, 5, or 10 years, whatever suits China best. Let them [the imperialists] not misunderstand that we want to run away from China. We can stay there for 20 years even."

Mao was clearly taken by surprise by this line of argument, admitting that "in discussing the treaty in China we had not taken into account the American and English positions regarding the Yalta agreement. We must act in a way that is best for the common cause. This question merits further consideration. However, it is already becoming clear that the treaty should not be modified at the present time, nor should one rush to withdraw troops from Port Arthur."

Then Mao asked again: "Should not Zhou Enlai visit Moscow in order to decide the treaty question?" Obviously, Mao now wanted Zhou to come not to renegotiate the treaty that he had just said "should not be modified," but to determine how to respond to Stalin's argument. And Stalin quickly replied: "No, this question you must decide for yourselves." Just as obviously, Stalin didn't want Zhou to add his expertise to Mao's, just when he had Mao nearly convinced by his argument. The reason for Stalin's unhesitating "no" was also clear. It was a bad argument.

Stalin's argument was remarkable for its blatant misrepresentation of the facts regarding Yalta and the 1945 Sino-Soviet treaty. The argument was that the 1945 treaty derived from the Yalta Agreement signed by Roosevelt, Churchill, and Stalin and it was Yalta which provided for the main points of the treaty, "the Kuriles, South Sakhalin, Port Arthur, etc." Therefore, Stalin argued, "a change in even one point could give America and England the legal grounds to raise questions about modifying also the treaty's provisions concerning the Kurile Islands, South Sakhalin, etc." In other words, if changes were made regarding Port Arthur, then America and England could raise questions about the Kuriles and South Sakhalin.

The falsity of this argument was clear enough. The 1945 treaty derived from Yalta, to be sure, but the treaty had nothing to do legally or otherwise with the Soviet position in the Kuriles or South Sakhalin. Neither one is mentioned in the treaty, although both are mentioned in the Yalta Agreement.[48] The treaty, in fact, stood on its own merits. Here was Stalin, who had grossly violated the 1945 treaty to destroy the Kuomintang, saying to Mao that he needed to maintain the treaty because it would invalidate the Yalta Agreement, which was predicated on support for the Kuomintang and which, moreover, had long since been eclipsed by the Cold War. Stalin had muddled together what were separate entities, which he no doubt knew Zhou would recognize. Therefore, the Soviet leader strove to keep him in

China. Did Stalin think he could bulldoze Mao into accepting the Soviet position on the treaty on the grounds that he might not have seen the details of the Yalta Agreement?

Mao Zedong was no doubt confused, but, not wishing to make a hasty decision, now switched subjects entirely and recited a list of China's needs. "We would like to decide on the question of Soviet credit to China." From information reaching the West, Mao sought credit in the amount of $5 billion.[49] Without flinching, Stalin replied: "This can be done." It was also necessary, said Mao, to resolve the question of trade, "especially between the USSR and Sinkiang." Stalin: Let us know what you need. Mao: We need assistance in creating air transportation routes. Stalin: "We are ready to render such assistance." Mao: "We would also like to receive your assistance in creating a naval force." Stalin: We could train cadres at Port Arthur. "You give us people, and we will give you ships. Trained cadre of the Chinese navy could then return to China on these ships."

Mao now ventured tentatively onto the subject that was of the utmost importance, the issue of recovering Taiwan. The Kuomintang, he said, have built a naval and air base on Taiwan. "Our lack of naval forces and aviation makes the occupation of the island by the People's Liberation Army more difficult." Then, without making a direct request for aid, Mao raised the issue indirectly. "With regard to this, some of our generals have been voicing opinions that we should request assistance from the Soviet Union, which could send volunteer pilots or secret military detachments to speed up the conquest of Formosa."[50]

Stalin, however, would not volunteer to provide "secret military detachments to speed up the conquest of Formosa." Cagily, the Soviet leader responded: "Assistance has not been ruled out, though one ought to consider the form of such assistance. What is most important here is not to give the Americans a pretext to intervene. With regard to headquarters staff and instructors we can give them to you anytime. The rest we will have to think about." Then Stalin asked: "Do you have any assault landing units?" To which Mao replied: "We have one former Guomindang assault landing regiment unit which came over to join our side."[51]

Mao's admission that he had only one assault regiment, which was obviously insufficient to mount an attack on Taiwan, confirmed what Stalin's own intelligence must have told him. Mao was totally dependent upon Stalin for any hope of completing the final stage of the revolution—the recovery of Taiwan and the final defeat of Chiang Kai-shek. (The Soviet Union had some twenty-six United States LCI amphibious assault ships, from thirty transferred to Northeast Asia as part of Lend-Lease in 1945.)[52] Since Stalin was not about to give an inch on Taiwan unless and until he had squeezed

43

what he wanted from Mao on the treaty, from this point onward Stalin toyed with the Chinese leader. Thus Stalin's comic suggestion on Taiwan: "One could select a company of landing forces, train them in propaganda, send them over to Formosa, and through them organize an uprising on the isle."[53]

Recognizing Stalin's suggestion for the absurdity it was, Mao immediately switched the subject. "Our troops," he said, "have approached the borders of Burma and Indo-China. As a result, the Americans and the British are alarmed, not knowing whether we will cross the border or whether our troops will halt their movement." But Stalin was not through amusing himself at Mao's expense, saying: "One could create a rumor that you are preparing to cross the border and in this way frighten the imperialists a bit."

Now Mao, no doubt thoroughly roused, attempted to turn the tables and frighten Stalin a bit, raising the prospect he dreaded most. "Several countries," he said, "especially Britain, are actively campaigning to recognize the People's Republic of China. However, we believe that we should not rush to be recognized. We must first bring about order to the country, strengthen our position, and then we can talk to foreign imperialists." But Stalin was not rattled. Instead, he said: "That is a good policy." But, if you "need to put pressure on the British, this can be done by resorting to a conflict between the Guangdong province and Hong Kong. And to resolve this conflict, Mao Zedong could come forward as the mediator."[54]

Now it was Stalin's turn to shift subjects. Mao had carefully conveyed his intention to establish diplomatic relations with the West. There was "no rush," but Mao would act. Stalin did not wish to dwell on this issue. Therefore, and for the rest of their discussion, Stalin asked a series of questions about the situation in China. Were foreign banks operating in China? What about Japanese enterprises? Who controls customs? Do you have inspectors overseeing foreign enterprises? Who owns the mining and petroleum industries? Can rubber-bearing trees be grown in southern China? Was there a meteorological service? Send us a list of your works for translation into Russian. Thus ended, on a most unsatisfactory note, Mao's first meeting with Stalin.

After pondering his conversation with Stalin, Mao sent a cable to Liu Shaoqi and the Chinese leadership on December 18. Mao devoted the bulk of his cable to Stalin's argument for not changing the treaty. "If we . . . abolish the old treaty and sign a new treaty, the status of the Kurile Islands will be changed, and the United States will have an excuse to take away the Kurile Islands."[55] Therefore, Mao said, "on the question of the Soviet Union's thirty-year lease of Lushun [Port Arthur], we should not change it in format; however, in reality, the Soviet Union will withdraw its troops from Lushun and will let Chinese troops occupy it." Stalin, Mao said, agreed to "sign a statement, which will solve the Lushun problem in accordance with the above-mentioned ideas." In regard to this, Mao reported, "Stalin said that it is unnecessary for the Foreign Minister to fly here just for signing a statement."

Continuing, Mao said that he thought it was "necessary for us to maintain the legitimacy of the Yalta agreement," but Chinese public opinion believed that "as the old treaty was signed by the Guomindang, it has lost its standing." Stalin, Mao said, agreed that "the old treaty needs to be revised, and that the revision is necessarily substantial, but it will not come until two years from now." Mao's remark is most interesting. The official Soviet transcript of their conversation mentions nothing about Stalin's agreement to sign a statement on Lushun, or to a substantial revision of the treaty two years hence, although he did mention several time periods, of which two years was one. Did Stalin make these commitments? Had the Soviets altered the transcript? Did Mao make it up to reassure his comrades? In any case, the issue is moot in light of the renegotiation of the treaty that did in fact occur within the month.

Mao closed his cable to Liu by observing that even if the treaty were not renegotiated, Zhou "should come" to be present for the signing of the commercial, loan, and aviation agreements then being prepared. Mao was clearly uncomfortable with Stalin's argument about Yalta and needed advice from his comrades on how to proceed. So he closed with the hope "that the Politburo will discuss how to solve the treaty problem and offer its opinions."

After their meeting, Stalin avoided Mao for five days, no doubt deliberating how to proceed with him, but also softening him up for discussions that were to come. Years later, Mao commented on the deep-freeze tactic Stalin employed following his first meeting, saying that "Stalin refrained from any meetings with me."[56] He had attempted "to phone him" at his apartment, but was told that Stalin was "not home." It was suggested that he "meet with Mikoyan," but this "offended" Mao, so he "decided to undertake nothing further and to wait it out at the dacha."

While waiting, however, Mao decided to begin putting pressure on Stalin in the only way open to him. Mao and his comrades undoubtedly assumed that the Soviets were reading their cables. So Mao decided to communicate with Stalin by this indirect method. Following his reporting cable of December 18, the next day Mao sent another cable to Liu Shaoqi and Zhou Enlai, urging them to respond ("I am awaiting your answer to my [Dec] 18 cable"). In this cable, Mao authorized his government to proceed with the establishment of relations with "a certain capitalist country." The specific issue was the establishment of relations with Burma, but he went on to state that the procedure he had authorized would be followed "toward all capitalist coun-

45

tries."[57] Indeed, "if a certain capitalist country openly announces the desire to establish diplomatic relations with us, our side should . . . request that it dispatch its representative to China for discussions."

Mao's message authorizing the establishment of relations with capitalist countries put pressure on Stalin in a way that the Chinese leader could not have imagined. It triggered Stalin's worst fear—the complete compromise of the Soviet Union's Asian security structure. Stalin knew that India and Great Britain had already decided to extend recognition (they would do so on December 30 and January 6, respectively). Would the United States be far behind? Was it to the United States that Mao referred? Stalin knew that American leaders were formally disengaging from the Nationalists and waiting only for the opportunity to establish relations with Beijing. (Washington's "hands off" policy would be enshrined in NSC-48 on December 30 and be made public by President Truman on January 5.) Stalin certainly had to presume that Mao was fully prepared to establish relations with the United States.

If there was a specific event, a straw that broke the camel's back, as it were, for Stalin's decision for war in Korea, it was Mao's December 19 cable authorizing the establishment of diplomatic relations with the United States— and the realistic prospect of doing so. Up to this point Stalin had been working through the various contingencies to preserve the optimum Soviet position enshrined in the 1945 treaty. Now a larger danger loomed: the establishment of relations between China and the Soviet Union's main enemy—a development that had to be forestalled at all costs. Stalin's choice for the means to accomplish this objective was war in Korea.

STALIN'S DECISION FOR WAR IN KOREA

Stalin had decided on war in Korea but not when the war would begin. The war date would be a function of other factors, including North Korean preparedness, but especially, as we shall see, of Chinese preparedness to attack Taiwan. He immediately sent "a new group of Soviet military advisors . . . in December 1949 to prepare the North Korean Armed Forces for war."[58] At the same time, on December 27, the North Korean leadership sent instructions to their South Korean communist cadre to prepare to go into action when war began.[59] (If this chronology is correct, then we can expect to find additional materials in Soviet archives relating to Moscow's authorization for the North's instructions to southern cadres regarding war mobilization.)

Stalin gave no hint of his momentous decision for war to Mao, whom he continued to let stew in semi-isolation at his dacha for several more days. After four days, however, Mao grew impatient, calling Kovalev to see him. Mao demanded that he meet with Stalin "on about December 23 or 24," for a discussion about the treaty. Mao told Kovalev that he saw two options. He and Stalin could either renegotiate the treaty, negotiate other agreements on a loan, trade, air transport, and so on, and summon Zhou to Moscow "for shaping and signing" them, or simply discuss the same issues "without formalizing them into agreements." In the latter case, "there would be no need for Zhou Enlai to come."[60] Mao did not say what would become of the 1945 treaty in the latter case, but the implied threat was that it could be abrogated just as other treaties concluded in the Nationalist period were. Mao's two options to Kovalev were, in short, an ultimatum.

The next day, December 21, was Stalin's birthday celebration and Mao was accorded the high honor of sitting at Stalin's right hand. We do not know what the two men discussed during the festivities, or if they discussed anything at all. But we do know that Mao was "gloomy and unresponsive" to attempts by others to engage him in conversation.[61] We have only Mao's very brief speech in which he honored Stalin as "a teacher and a friend of the Chinese people," who "developed the revolutionary theory of Marxism-Leninism and . . . made extremely outstanding and extremely broad contributions to the cause of the world Communist movement."[62] From Mao's point of view, Stalin's birthday was anything but a festive occasion.

That Mao was indeed perturbed by Stalin's treatment of him came through clearly in his cable to Liu the next day. Ostensibly discussing preparation of a trade agreement with the Soviet Union, Mao reiterated his view that China would deal with all countries, including the United States. While in Moscow, Mao had been pleased to learn that East Germany, Poland, and Czechoslovakia intended "to do business with us." Reporting this news, he wrote:

> In addition, Britain, Japan, the United States, India, and other states are already doing business with us or will begin to do so pretty soon. For this reason, when preparing the trade agreement with the Soviet Union, you should proceed from a point of view that takes into account the whole situation. The Soviet Union, of course, occupies the first place, but at the same time, it is necessary to get ready to do business with Poland, Czechoslovakia, [East] Germany, Great Britain, Japan, the United States, and other states. We must make a general evaluation of the scope and volume [of potential trade].[63]

Mao undoubtedly hoped that his instruction to "get ready to do business with . . . Britain, Japan, the United States" would place added pressure on Stalin (who he knew was reading these telegrams) to come forth with a generous trade deal in his forthcoming meeting. He closed his cable by saying that "we have arranged with Stalin to have a talk on [Dec.] 23 or 24. After this talk, we will be able to define our guiding principles."

But there apparently was no meeting on either date as Stalin kept Mao dangling until Christmas morning. (On December 29, Mao sent a cable referring to a meeting with Stalin on December 25.)[64] Mao mentions that he discussed Soviet assistance regarding repair of the Xiaofengman hydroelectric station (actually the return of six generators that Soviet forces had stripped and carted off in 1945), but none of the issues Mao had deemed important—the treaty, trade, loan, a civil air agreement—had yet been dealt with, at least insofar as the extant record shows. It seems highly likely that had there been meetings in which these key issues were discussed Mao would have been sending and receiving cables, reporting and receiving advice and comments on proposed text.

In the absence of data to the contrary, we must assume that Stalin kept Mao waiting until his meeting with him on Christmas morning—and then all that was discussed was the relatively minor matter of the repair of a hydroelectric station. Nor does it appear that there were any meetings between Christmas Day and the 29th. In his cable of the 29th, Mao noted that he would be seeing Stalin the next day, but there is no cable from Mao reporting on that meeting, either. In short, it seems, after their first meeting Stalin kept Mao dangling in isolation for over two weeks. Severely irritated by this treatment, Mao "sharply rejected" proposals by Ivan Kovalev and Nikolai Fedorenko to "go on an excursion around the country." Instead, Mao decided "to sleep through it at the dacha."[65]

What should we make of Stalin's tactics? Was he being deliberately insulting to Mao? Undoubtedly, giving Mao the deep freeze was intended to generate anxiety, to soften him up for the coming treaty negotiation. But, most of all, Stalin was preoccupied with the initial planning for the war he intended to precipitate in Korea and did not want to reenter discussions with Mao until he was prepared. Stalin would not be ready to reengage Mao until New Year's Day. On that day, according to Mao's later account, "they handed me a draft of my interview for publication which had been signed by Stalin."[66]

Mao's remark is intriguingly ambiguous. Did it mean that he had given an interview which Stalin then approved for publication? Or did it mean that he had been handed a draft interview which the Soviets had concocted and intended to publish in his name? Putting words in the mouths of others was a common Stalinist practice. In the purported interview, Mao declared that the main problems being considered were the 1945 treaty, a loan, and a trade pact. There was no mention of a civil air agreement, which we know Mao had specifically asked Stalin about and would consistently refer to in his cables. Nor would there be a civil air agreement in the final treaty package, which suggests that Mao's interview was a Stalinist concoction.

Goncharov, Lewis, and Xue say that the Soviets hastily arranged an interview for Mao with a TASS correspondent in order to dispel rumors that Mao was being mistreated in Moscow. But Mao says "they handed me a draft" of his interview. "This document," Mao says, "reported that negotiations are being held in Moscow on concluding a Soviet-Chinese treaty. This already was a significant step forward. Negotiations began right after this."[67] Mao conveys the distinct impression that he was surprised, albeit pleasantly, to learn that negotiations were being held from a document purporting to be an interview he himself gave containing that information.

Whatever the truth of the matter, Stalin sent Molotov and Mikoyan to see Mao that evening. It was the first time these two men had been to see Mao during his visit except for a brief exchange during Stalin's birthday celebration. Mao, who had not the faintest inkling of the reasons behind Stalin's abrupt shift, sought to increase the pressure for an agreement to sign a new treaty. It was like rushing through an open door, however, because Stalin had already decided to renegotiate the treaty. Shifting from the treaty-or-no-treaty ultimatum he had given to Kovalev on December 20, Mao now offered three options.

First, Mao said, they could sign a new treaty, which would confer "enormous advantages." It would "solidify" our relations and enable us to "counter the imperialist states." It would strengthen both China's internal position vis-à-vis the national bourgeoisie and its international position vis-à-vis the imperialist powers. Or, he said, they could issue a joint communiqué stating that they had "reached an identity of views on the important problems." This, of course, said Mao, "would mean we would be delaying the [treaty] problem for several years." Finally, he said, we could simply issue "a statement that sets out the most important points in [our] bilateral relations but would not be a treaty."[68]

Molotov "immediately" picked the first option and said that Zhou Enlai should come. Taken aback by this about-face, and not certain that he had understood correctly, Mao "asked again if we should replace the old treaty with a new one? Comrade Molotov answered: 'Yes.'" They spent the remainder of their meeting determining "a timetable for Zhou's arrival and the signing of the treaty." Mao reported all this in his cable of January 2, excitedly declaring that there had been "an important development." He said that "Stalin has agreed to Comrade Zhou Enlai's arrival here and to the signing of a new Sino-Soviet Treaty of Friendship and Alliance, as well as agreements on credit, trade, civil aviation, and others."

Later that night, after Mao had sent his cable to Beijing, Stalin called him on the telephone, both to express his satisfaction at the decisions made and to clarify the form and content of the new treaty. In discussing the basic structure of the new treaty, Stalin said that there would be "a partial change concerning the problems of Lushun and Dalien [sic]," but the exact language of the changes "still have to be discussed." In what Stalin referred to as the "basic spirit of the new treaty," he specifically noted that the clause recognizing the independence of Outer Mongolia would remain and the clause involving defense against possible aggression by Japan would be enlarged to include Japan's "allies," meaning, of course, the United States.[69] What Stalin declined to tell Mao was how he planned to change the treaty in light of his plans for Korea.

After his telephone chat with Stalin, at 4:00 A.M. Mao sent a second reporting cable home, identifying the basic content of the new treaty, the credit agreement, trade agreement, and civil aviation agreement. Mao emphasized the value of the new treaty. "It will press the capitalist countries to play by rules that will be set by us, it will be favorable for the unconditional recognition of China by various countries, [it will lead to] the cancellation of the old treaties and the conclusion of new ones, and it also will deter the capitalist countries from reckless undertakings."[70]

Mao was euphoric. He had after months of planning and maneuvering finally achieved the centerpiece of his plan to end China's unequal treaty relationships and establish the basis for new equal treaty relationships with all countries based on the about-to-be-renegotiated treaty with the Soviet Union. While he waited for Zhou Enlai to arrive on January 20, he agreed to take a one-day tour of Leningrad and sightsee around Moscow. Stalin, on the other hand, used this time to put into place additional parts of his plan to maneuver China into conflict with the West in Korea.

CHAPTER THREE

Truman Increases His Offer

MAO ZEDONG'S appearance in Moscow galvanized the American leadership into quickly formulating a proposal in hopes of dissuading him from entering into a long-term treaty relationship with the Soviet Union. The success of the wedge strategy depended on it. Acheson took the lead, employing as his vehicle an ongoing study, NSC-48, which was intended to develop a response to the imminent Communist victory in China. Since its inception in July at the insistence of Secretary of Defense Louis Johnson, NSC-48 had already gone through several drafts exploring various political and economic policy combinations. The principal thrust of these policy deliberations was to devise some method of rolling back communist power in Asia.

Now, at the end of December, drawing upon ideas developed earlier in the year in NSC-41 regarding trade with China, Acheson put forth a dramatic proposal for the improvement of overall relations with Beijing, designated NSC-48/1. Acheson's quid pro quo would center on Washington's encouragement of the development of a Chinese economic relationship with Japan and the abandonment of Chiang Kai-shek, which would lead to the PLA's seizure of Formosa. In return, China would decline an alliance with the Soviet Union, maintain its independence, and eventually establish diplomatic relations with the United States. In short, Acheson proposed the creation of a Sino-Japanese counterweight to stabilize the Far East, a grouping that would not only be independent of the Soviet Union, but, except for the defense of Japan, of the United States, too.

Acheson's far-reaching and, it must be said, risky proposal immediately generated objections within the American leadership. Led by Secretary of

Defense Johnson, further discussions produced a revised position, designated NSC-48/2, which, at least for the moment, removed Japan from the quid pro quo and lodged Tokyo firmly within the American defense perimeter in the Pacific. Although Johnson also objected to the abandonment of Formosa, insisting that the United States continue to provide support to Chiang Kai-shek, Acheson, with President Truman's support, was able to defeat Johnson's challenge, and retain Formosa as part of the proposal.

When TASS published Mao's "interview" on January 2, Truman and Acheson hurriedly moved to communicate their proposal to the Chinese leadership. President Truman initiated the process with the announcement on January 5 that the United States would no longer provide any military support for the government of Chiang Kai-shek on Formosa, which should be returned to China. Acheson's news conference the same day explaining the president's statement in actuality made clear the conditions under which the United States would accept a Chinese seizure of the island.

Truman's announcement precipitated an immediate response from both Moscow and Beijing. The Soviet Union commenced a walkout from the U.N., ostensibly in protest of the continued presence of the Nationalist government in China's allotted seat, while Beijing responded with the announcement that the following week the PLA would seize the U.S. embassy grounds and buildings in the Chinese capital. It was thus against the background of increasingly evident Sino-Soviet cooperation and their growing antagonism toward the United States that Secretary of State Acheson conveyed the United States proposal to China.

It was too late, and may never have had a chance of succeeding in the sense that Truman and Acheson had envisaged. Despite informal contacts suggesting the possibility of negotiations, which may only have served to delay Washington's recognition of the actual state of affairs, Mao and the Chinese leadership declined the American offer. They decided instead to pursue an alliance with Moscow, thus marking the failure of the American strategy of attempting to keep the Soviet Union and China apart. The failure of the wedge strategy, in turn, established the need for a new American strategy that would take into account the high probability that the two Communist powers would collaborate against the United States.

A PROPOSAL FOR CHINA

NSC-20/4 of November 24, 1948, had outlined the basic strategy of containment of the Soviet Union. It was based on the assumptions that the Soviet Union did not have an atomic capability or an alliance with China that would open up the prospect of dominating the Eurasian landmass. Under the assumptions of American atomic hegemony and an essentially Euro-centered USSR, therefore, U.S. planners had decreed that the United States could satisfy its security needs with a relatively small $12–13 billion defense budget. As long as these assumptions held, the United States would not need to increase defense outlays and could, instead, allow continued expansion of the domestic economic infrastructure, an advantageous situation. The longer the condition of low defense outlays and an enlarging economy persisted, the better off the United States would be if and when the time came to commit additional resources to defense, for the burden on the economy could be all the more easily borne.

In less than thirteen months, however, the assumptions underlying NSC-20/4 were shattered by the Soviet detonation of an atomic device and Mao's unanticipated trip to Moscow. Mao's appearance in Moscow on December 16, with the connotation that he was there to negotiate an alliance with the Soviet Union, prompted American leaders to reconsider strategy. On the one hand, it was judged that, if Mao decided on an alliance with the Soviet Union, that would open up for Moscow the prospect of dominating the Eurasian landmass, particularly Western Europe, based on its atomic capability and ability to concentrate its resources without concern for its Asian front. Such a shift in the global balance would require a major change in American strategy to counter it. On the other hand, if the United States could persuade the Chinese leadership to maintain an independent position vis-à-vis the Soviet Union, the United States would not be required to make an immediate, fundamental change in strategy.

In late December, therefore, the American leadership formulated its position in two top-secret NSC documents, NSC-48/1 of December 23 and NSC-48/2 of December 30, both titled "the position of the United States with respect to Asia." NSC-48/1 was a report by the executive secretary to the National Security Council, while NSC-48/2 was a report by the National Security Council to the president. The first of these two documents constituted a very generous "offer" to Chinese leaders of a Northeast Asian region conducive to China's growth and development, including U.S. acquiescence in China's seizure of Taiwan, on condition that Beijing maintain its independence of Moscow. The second document constituted a largely unsuccessful attempt by the secretary of defense to reverse, or otherwise hedge, key positions expressed in the first. These two documents are so extraordinary that they deserve comparison.

In NSC-48/1 the United States expressed its willingness to promote a Sino-Japanese counterweight to Soviet (and, to a lesser extent, American) power in Northeast Asia. Portraying the Soviet Union as a threat to all Asia, including China, Washington offered to adopt a "benign" attitude toward both Japan and Korea, and take no action toward Formosa, which, it was believed, "probably will succumb to the Chinese Communists by the end of 1950."[1] NSC-48/1 opened with a statement of United States strategic objectives.

> Our overall objective with respect to Asia must be to assist in the development of truly independent, friendly, stable and self-sustaining states in conformity with the purposes and principles of the United Nations Charter. In order to achieve this, we must concurrently oppose the domination of Asia by any single country or coalition. It is conceivable that in the course of time a threat of domination may come from such nations as Japan, China, or India, or from an Asiatic bloc. But now and for the foreseeable future it is the USSR which threatens to dominate Asia through the complementary instruments of communist conspiracy and diplomatic pressure supported by military strength. For the foreseeable future, therefore, our immediate objective must be to contain and where feasible to reduce the power and influence of the USSR in Asia to such a degree that the Soviet Union is not capable of threatening the security of the United States from that area.[2]

In portraying the Soviet position in Asia, NSC-48/1 argued that the Soviet threat to China was as great as it was to the rest of the region. On the other hand, it suggested that the United States would promote a "middle of the road regime in Japan" that could maintain "normal" relations with the Communist bloc and "resist" complete identification with either Moscow or Washington. In other words, NSC-48/1 held out the prospect that, if China declined to ally with the Soviet Union, the United States would promote a Sino-Japanese relationship that would counterbalance both the Soviet Union and the United States in Northeast Asia. As such it implied a much looser American relationship with Japan than had thus far developed during the occupation.

> The USSR is now an Asiatic power of the first magnitude with expanding influence and interests extending throughout continental Asia and into the Pacific. Since the defeat of Japan, which ended a balance of power that had previously restrained Russian pressures in China and the Pacific, the Soviet Union has been able to consolidate its strategic position until the base of Soviet power in Asia now comprises not only the Soviet Far East, but also China north of the Great Wall, Northern Korea, Sakhalin, and the Kuriles. . . . If Japan, the principal component of a Far Eastern war-making complex, were added to the Stalinist bloc, the Soviet Asian base could become a source of strength capable of shifting the balance of world power to the disadvantage of the United States.
>
> Japan has ceased to be a world power, but retains the capability of becoming once more a significant Asiatic power. Whether its potential is developed and the way in which it is used will strongly influence the future patterns of

politics in Asia. As a result of the occupation, Japan's political structure has been basically altered and notable steps have been taken toward the development of democratic institutions and practices. . . .

A middle of the road regime in Japan retaining the spirit of the reform program, even if not necessarily the letter, would in the long run prove more reliable as an ally of the United States than would an extreme right-wing totalitarian government. Under such a regime the channels would be open for those elements in Japan that have gained most from the occupation to exercise their influence over government policy and to mold public opinion. Such a regime would undoubtedly wish to maintain normal political and economic relations with the Communist bloc and, in the absence of open hostilities, would probably resist complete identification either with the interest of the United States or the Soviet Union.

The basic United States non-military objectives in Japan, therefore, remain the promotion of democratic forces and economic stability before and after the peace settlement. To further this objective the United States must seek to reduce to a minimum occupation or post-occupation interference in the processes of Japanese Government.

In Korea, U.S. objectives were to continue to assist "the efforts of the Korean people to regain that independence promised them at Cairo." Citing NSC-8/2 of March 23, 1949, NSC-48/1 declared that the United States "must continue to give political support and economic, technical, military and other assistance to the Republic of Korea." The objectives of this policy were to strengthen the government of South Korea to the point where it could "successfully contain the threat of expanding Communist influence and control arising out of . . . North Korea" and "serve as a nucleus" for eventual peaceful unification.

As far as China itself was concerned, NSC-48/1 declared forthrightly that the United States "cannot be expected greatly to weaken Chinese communist control of China in the foreseeable future, but may have influence on the relations between the Chinese communists and the USSR." Indeed, it went on, "any attempt on the part of the United States openly to deny Chinese territory such as Formosa to the communists would probably react to the benefit of the communists by rallying all the anti-foreign sentiment in China to their side." Any attempt to "occupy Formosa would inevitably expose the U.S. to charges of 'imperialism' . . . at a time when the U.S. is seeking to expose Soviet imperialist designs."

Citing a CIA estimate of October 19, 1949, and an earlier Joint Chiefs of Staff (JCS) estimate, which was reaffirmed by NSC-37/7 of August 22, and reconfirmed that very day, December 23, NSC-48/1 declared that "denial of Formosa to the Chinese communists [cannot] be achieved by any method short of actual U.S. military occupation," which the administration point-edly declined to undertake, spelling the demise of the Nationalist regime.

> Without major armed intervention, U.S. political, economic, and logistic sup-port of the present Nationalist island regime cannot insure its indefinite sur-vival as a non-communist base. Communist capabilities are such that only ex-tended U.S. military occupation and control of Taiwan can prevent its eventual capture and subjugation by Chinese Communist forces. Failing U.S. military occupation and control, a non-communist regime on Taiwan proba-bly will succumb to the Chinese Communists by the end of 1950.

NSC-48/1 appeared just four days after Mao's cable to Liu of December 19 authorizing the establishment of relations with the United States. The se-quence may have been coincidental, or American intelligence may have bro-ken Chinese codes. In either case, NSC-48/1 is nothing if not an attempt to respond to this decision, to encourage Mao to continue along the path he had seemingly taken (even though, as stated in chapter 2, Mao's purpose in send-ing the cable was primarily to influence Stalin). NSC-48 had been in gesta-tion since July, but NSC-48/1 bears little resemblance to the several drafts, heavily anti-communist in substance, that had percolated in the State-Defense bureaucracy since then, giving added force to the argument that the final document was produced hurriedly and in response to a different stimu-lus.[3] With NSC-48/1, in short, the United States had entered the bidding for China's allegiance.

But before NSC-48/1 could be communicated to the Chinese leader-ship, an explosive reaction came from within the Department of Defense. Secretary of Defense Louis Johnson immediately and strongly objected to NSC-48/1, forcing its reconsideration, despite having been overruled by the president. Johnson had fought for a policy of support for the Nationalist gov-ernment and had lost. Just before the meeting that produced NSC-48/1, on December 22, Johnson learned that "I had lost my fight on Formosa." He was told that President Truman "wasn't going to argue with [him] about the mil-itary considerations but that on political grounds he would decide with the State Department."[4]

But NSC-48/1 had gone too far for Johnson, who continued to object. Tru-man, however, would not be deflected. To ensure that Johnson could not in-terfere personally he gave the secretary "clearance to go on and take 4 or 5 days in Florida following . . . Christmas Day at home." Then, while the secre-tary was in Florida, the president convened the second NSC meeting on De-cember 29 to work out a final draft. Johnson was informed of the meeting, but declined to return from Florida to attend because, as he put it, "the mat-ter was already decided [and] there was no point in my being there."[5]

Thus, on December 30, President Truman approved NSC-48/2, which set forth in some detail the position that the United States planned to take in Northeast Asia, taking into account some but not all of the secretary of defense's objections. The result was to dilute the offer contained in NSC-48/1, particularly the proposal regarding Japan's relations with China, but not on Formosa. NSC-48/2 was in essence a partial retreat from the proposal contained in NSC-48/1.[6]

The secretary of defense had objected to the proposed bargain of relinquishing control of Taiwan in return for China's independence from Moscow and to the notion of a Sino-Japanese counterbalance, with its negative implications for the American position in the Pacific. He argued, instead, for the need to strengthen the overall American position to include Japan, Taiwan, and South Korea as integral parts of the American defense position in Northeast Asia. NSC-48/2 would not go that far, but key portions of the document directly reflected the dispute between Johnson and Acheson, particularly regarding policy toward Formosa, including language supporting both positions.

First and foremost, NSC-48/2 deferred the issue of Japan's future orientation to "a later date . . . after the decision regarding a peace treaty has been made." Where NSC-48/1 proposed a Japan that would "probably resist complete identification with either the interest of the United States or the Soviet Union," NSC-48/2 depicted Japan as an integral part of the American defense perimeter in the Western Pacific. NSC-48/2 stated simply that "the question of a peace settlement with Japan . . . will be presented for the consideration of the National Security Council at a later date and policies with respect to Japan will be re-evaluated after the decision regarding a peace treaty has been made." In short, Japan was taken off the table.

In NSC-48/2 the basic objectives of the United States were superficially similar to those stated in NSC-48/1, that is, the development of the "nations and peoples of Asia on a stable and self-sustaining basis." But there the similarities ended. Where NSC-48/1 sought to "direct" the potential power of Asian countries into "constructive channels," NSC-48/2 placed emphasis on the "development of sufficient military power in selected non-communist nations . . . to prevent further encroachment by communism." Where NSC-48/1 sought "to contain and where feasible to reduce the power and influence of the USSR," NSC-48/2, harking back to earlier drafts of NSC-48, argued for the "gradual reduction and eventual elimination of the preponderant power and influence of the USSR." Both documents agreed on the need for the "prevention of power relationships in Asia which would enable any other nation or alliance to threaten the security of the United States," but NSC-48/2 was a tougher and much less compromising statement of

American objectives and offered no hint of cooperation with "communist" states, instead emphasizing the rollback of communist influence.[7]

While NSC-48/1 made no mention of a defense perimeter in Northeast Asia, or of security arrangements, NSC-48/2 placed the U.S. position at the forefront, arguing that the United States must strengthen its position along the line from Japan, the Ryukyus (Okinawa), and the Philippines, and develop "some form of collective security arrangements," both multilateral and bilateral. While NSC-48/1 did not elaborate on possible threats from Communist aggression, NSC-48/2 pledged to "scrutinize closely the development of threats from Communist aggression, direct or indirect, and be prepared to help within our means to meet such threats by providing political, economic, and military assistance." The United States would also encourage "economic recovery and development in non-Communist Asia" through a liberal trade policy, private investment, and aid programs.

On Korea, NSC-48/2, consistent with NSC-48/1, argued for continued political, economic, technical, and military support for the Republic of Korea through effective implementation of existing programs. But on policy toward the Republic of China on Taiwan, both Johnson's and Acheson's positions were represented. Johnson's position called for the United States to "continue to recognize the Nationalist Government of China until the situation is further clarified." Furthermore, "the United States should avoid recognizing the Chinese Communist regime until it is clearly in the United States interest to do so."

Acheson, however, would not allow this statement to stand unamended, and inserted the following sentence, which rendered Johnson's position moot: "In the event that recognition of the Chinese Communists is anticipated, appropriate steps should be taken to make it clear that recognition should not be construed as approval of the Chinese Communist regime, or abatement of our hostility to Soviet efforts to exercise control in China." Furthermore, the United States would not provide military support for "any non-Communist elements in China." The fate of Taiwan in the event of recognition of Beijing was left unstated, but was self-evident.

As in NSC-48/1, it was agreed to "exploit . . . any rifts between the Chinese Communists and the USSR." But NSC-48/2 argued that it was crucial to prevent the USSR, its East European satellites, and North Korea from obtaining strategic materials "through China." The United States should also prevent China from acquiring such materials, designated as "1A items." On the other hand, the United States "should permit exports to China of 1B items within quantitative limits of normal civilian use . . . and should place no obstacle in the way of trade with China in non-strategic commodities. The United States should seek the support and concurrence of its principal

European allies in these policies. [But] the United States should not extend governmental economic assistance to the Chinese Communists or encourage private investment."

The position of the Joint Chiefs of Staff was also included, which could permit support of Chiang Kai-shek on the grounds of denying the island of Formosa to the Communists. Referring to the policy position approved earlier in NSC-37/2 and NSC-37/5, NSC-48/2 declared that the United States should continue the policy set forth therein of "attempting to deny Formosa and the Pescadores to the Chinese Communists." But Acheson also amended this language to reflect the decision to cut off further military support to the Nationalists. It stated that the policy of denial should be solely "through diplomatic and economic means within the limitations imposed by the fact that successful achievement of this objective will primarily depend on prompt initiatives and faithful implementation of essential measures of self-help by the non-Communist administration of the islands."

Acheson then added a second passage further eviscerating the first. "Since the United States may not be able to achieve its objectives through political and economic means, and in view of the opinion of the Joint Chiefs of Staff . . . that, while Formosa is strategically important to the United States, 'the strategic importance of Formosa does not justify overt military action' . . . the United States should make every effort to strengthen . . . the Philippines, Ryukyus, and Japan." This passage made it clear that the United States would not respond militarily to a Chinese attempt to conquer Taiwan and kept intact the essential trade-off of Taiwan for Chinese independence of Moscow made in NSC-48/1.

Finally, Acheson inserted the following language to preserve the position crafted in NSC-48/1: "Nothing in this paper shall be construed as amending approved NSC papers unless a specific statement to that effect has been made on each point." In other words, NSC-48/2 did not supersede NSC-48/1, whose positions remained in force. To give the president added flexibility, $75 million was set aside for the provision of assistance "to the general area of China," which left a loophole for the secretary to discreetly funnel assistance to Chiang, or to Mao, depending on Mao's response.

What emerges from a comparison of NSC-48/1 and NSC-48/2 is an indication of the magnitude of the policy battle that erupted in the last week of December 1949 over whether to make an offer to Beijing, and what the terms of that offer should include. The chief protagonists were clearly the secretary of state and the secretary of defense, with the former emerging victorious. The formulation of American policy had occurred hastily but was completed in the nick of time, for within forty-eight hours of the president's approval of NSC-48/2, events in Moscow forced Washington to reveal its hand.

59

WASHINGTON BEGINS TO SHOW ITS CARDS

The publication of Mao's "interview" with a TASS correspondent on January 2, 1950, injected a sense of great urgency into the White House, for Mao was quoted as saying that he was considering, as "problems of first importance," a new treaty, a Soviet loan, and a trade pact.[8] It was imperative that the United States convey the position developed in NSC-48 to Chinese leaders if there was to be any hope of deflecting Mao from locking China into a long-term treaty relationship with the Soviet Union. Indeed, as we now know, it was already too late, for that very evening Stalin had informed Mao that he had changed his mind and would negotiate a new treaty (see p. 49).

Not privy to this decision, the administration had clearly been taken off guard: first by Mao's secret trip to Moscow and then by the Chinese leader's apparently sudden decision to strike an alliance. The administration decided that its only hope was to conduct an immediate, public campaign to dissuade China from entering into an alliance with Moscow by revealing its just-formulated offer in NSC-48. Over the next few weeks, in the context of a public campaign stressing that the Soviet Union was a predator state already in direct occupation of vast areas of Chinese territory, U.S. officials sought to set forth the American proposal.

The first step was the president's statement of January 5, announcing that the United States was prepared to accept the Communist conquest of Formosa. Privately, at the same time, the administration sought discussions with Chinese representatives in Hong Kong to explain the implications and consequences of the president's decision.[9] Before going public, however, the administration had to provide to Chiang's congressional supporters its rationale for publicly abandoning Taiwan. Thus, Acheson met with senators William Knowland and Alexander Smith in the morning just before the president issued his statement. It was a hard sell.

Acheson opened the conversation with the two senators, observing that the Chinese Communists had won and that Britain, the Commonwealth nations, and many others would be recognizing the new government "before the passage of any considerable period of time." He pointed out that Manchuria and Outer Mongolia "were firmly under Russian control, achieved as a result of a long-time design," while Inner Mongolia and Sinkiang were under a "less severe measure of control." However, he said, "as far as the rest of China was concerned Russian control as such had in no way been consolidated." And he expected the Russians to encounter "increasing difficulties by way of their program of subjugation."[10]

As regards Formosa, while previewing the arguments he and the president would make publicly later that day, the secretary pointed out that ultimately the United States had to make a choice between two alternatives:

"either that we will fight, if need be, for the retention of the island under our aegis, or in the absence of such a position we must be prepared to accept what now appears to be the real possibility of its collapse." Acheson "did not believe it was in the interest of the American people to hazard a war over Formosa; and secondly, that the mere statement of our intention to so hold the island would be completely defeative of the general line we had been taking." We would be open to the charge that we were following the "same . . . imperialistic design that Russia is following today."

Senator Smith disagreed, saying that he had consulted with Ambassador Stuart and the Far Eastern commanders, General Douglas MacArthur and Admiral Arthur Radford. All believed that "under no circumstances should we permit Formosa to fall into Communist hands." Acheson responded with the view that "there were always differences of opinion among military personnel as to the strategic importance of practically any place . . . in the world and therefore it was necessary in such matters to accept the considered judgment of the Joint Chiefs of Staff." Their view, he said, was that only by directly occupying Formosa ourselves could we keep it out of Communist hands, a policy which we declined to undertake for the reasons stated above.

Acheson averred that the Nationalists had the wherewithal to defend themselves if they had the will to do so, but both Smith and Knowland vigorously disputed the secretary's views. Knowland said that Nationalist morale was high, but their resources limited, and "if we would give a proper measure of both military and economic aid the situation could be saved." Otherwise, he believed the United States was pursing a "fatal" policy of "grave danger to the American people." Smith decried the fact that "no opportunity was afforded for any consultation on this matter, as disclosed by the fact the President was in the act of issuing a policy statement on Formosa without either him or Senator Knowland having been consulted before the policy was given to the public."

Indeed, at that moment the president was issuing a statement of policy toward Formosa, in the process divulging one of the decisions contained in NSC-48. The president declared that the United States had traditionally, since the Open Door policy at the turn of the century, "called for international respect for the territorial integrity of China." This principle, said the president, recently reaffirmed in the U.N. General Assembly resolution of December 8, calls on all states to refrain from either "seeking to acquire spheres of influence or to create foreign controlled regimes within the territory of China," or from "seeking to obtain special rights or privileges within the territory of China."

He observed that the "specific application of the foregoing principles is seen in the present situation with respect to Formosa." In the Cairo Declaration of December 1, 1943, he said, the president of the United States, the prime minister of Great Britain, and the president of China had stated that the "territories Japan had stolen from China, such as Formosa, should be returned to the Republic of China." Similarly, he went on, the United States was a signatory of the Potsdam Agreement, which declared that the terms of the Cairo Declaration should be carried out. Furthermore, Japan accepted the provisions of the Potsdam Agreement at the time of its surrender and the United States duly surrendered Formosa to Generalissimo Chiang Kai-shek. Since that time "the United States and the other Allied Powers have accepted the exercise of Chinese authority over the Island." Then, he said:

> The United States has no predatory designs on Formosa or on any other Chinese territory. The United States has no desire to obtain special rights or privileges or to establish military bases on Formosa at this time. Nor does it have any intention of utilizing its armed forces to interfere in the present situation. The United States Government will not pursue a course which will lead to involvement in the civil conflict in China.
>
> Similarly, the United States Government will not provide military aid or advice to Chinese forces on Formosa. In the view of the United States Government, the resources on Formosa are adequate to enable them to obtain the items which they might consider necessary for the defense of the Island. The United States Government proposes to continue under existing legislative authority the present [Economic Cooperation Agency] program of economic assistance.[11]

President Truman had not mentioned the Soviet Union in his statement; that would be left for the secretary of state. But he had referred to the U.N. resolution decrying efforts on the part of foreign powers to obtain special rights or privileges or to create foreign controlled regimes in China as being antithetical to respect for China's territorial integrity. This, of course, was precisely what Stalin was in the process of doing, although he had not yet broached the subject to Mao of legitimizing Soviet actions in what would be termed the "additional agreement." Indeed, the fact that the Soviets were attempting to create a sphere of influence in Manchuria, Sinkiang, and Outer Mongolia was not yet widespread public knowledge.

Secretary of State Acheson held a brief press conference later in the day to provide "background" to "clarify" the president's statements, but what he said was in the end more puzzling than clarifying. The secretary stressed three points. First, the president's decision had nothing to do with the "great deal of amateur military strategy indulged in in regard to this matter of Formosa," an implicit reference to the argument that Formosa was important to the U.S. security position in the Far East. On the contrary, he said, it had to do with "the fundamental integrity of the United States and with maintaining in the world the belief that when the United States takes a position it sticks

62

to that position and does not change it by reason of transitory expediency or advantage."[12]

Second, he stressed that "our position in regard to China should never be subject to the slightest doubt or the slightest question." It is and has been since the Cairo Conference of 1943 that "Formosa should go back to China." Some say, he went on, that "the situation is changed." As "the forces now in control of the mainland . . . are not friendly to us . . . well, we have to wait for a treaty" with Japan to determine the disposition of the former Japanese-controlled island. But we say no. "We did not wait for a treaty on Korea. We did not wait for a treaty on the Kuriles. We did not wait for a treaty on the islands over which we have trusteeship." So, said the secretary, "whatever may be the legal situation, the United States of America . . . is not going to quibble on any lawyers' words. . . . That is where we stand."

Then Acheson came to his third and last point, which had to do with explaining a curious sentence in the president's statement: "The United States has no desire to obtain special rights or privileges or to establish military bases on Formosa at this time." Reporters wanted to know what was meant by the phrase "at this time." Acheson declared that "that phrase does not qualify or modify or weaken the fundamental policies stated in this declaration by the President in any respect." But then the secretary proceeded to take a position that in fact not only served to "qualify or modify or weaken," but actually reverse the position he and the president had been at pains to establish. He said that the phrase "at this time" was simply "a recognition of the fact that, in the unlikely and unhappy event that our forces might be attacked in the Far East, the United States must be completely free to take whatever action in whatever area is necessary for its own security."

The secretary thus contradicted his president and himself. Far from taking a position and sticking to it and not changing that position for reasons of expediency or transitory advantage and despite the oft-repeated view that "Formosa should go back to China," the secretary acknowledged that if "our forces might be attacked . . . the United States must be completely free to take whatever action . . . is necessary," by which he meant to *prevent* Formosa from being returned to China! In blunt terms, Acheson was saying that the American commitment to return Formosa to China would be invalidated by a Chinese attack on American forces. In the end, Acheson's denial that the president's declaration had anything to do with "amateur military strategy" was precisely the grounds on which he justified in advance a repudiation of the U.S. pledge.

Truman's use of the phrase "at this time" was not a slip of the tongue and Acheson was obviously prepared to "explain" it. This was part of the campaign to dissuade Mao from entering into an alliance with Stalin by offering both carrot and stick at the same time. The formulation was straightforward: China could regain Formosa if it cooperated with the United States, but not if Mao allied with Stalin and collaborated in a conflict against the United States or its allies in Northeast Asia. Such a collaboration would invalidate any American promise on Formosa. On the other hand, clearly, if Mao remained independent of Moscow the United States would keep its word.

Before Mao could react, however, Stalin responded immediately with a scheme designed not only to show Sino-Soviet solidarity, but also to drive a wedge between Beijing and the West. Protesting the continued occupation of Beijing's U.N. seat by Taipei, the Soviet Union declared that it would boycott the U.N. until the slight was rectified. A Soviet resolution on the question of seating Beijing was defeated in the Security Council, leaving Moscow (and Beijing) isolated. Observers thought that Moscow had deliberately courted defeat in order to isolate China from the West.[13] The general consensus was that had Beijing taken no actions to inflame sentiment against itself, the proposal to admit China to the U.N. "would certainly be accepted within a few weeks."[14]

The representative of the Republic of China was president of the Security Council for the month of January, but since the presidency rotated monthly among the permanent members, this would be an obstacle to China's admission only until the end of the month. Seven Security Council votes were required for admission and five of the eleven members of the council had already recognized the Beijing government (India, Norway, U.S.S.R., Yugoslavia, and the U.K.), with France and Egypt planning to do so within a few weeks, at most. There was, in short, every reason to wait, but the walkout of Jacob Malik, Moscow's chief delegate, "inevitably hardened" opposition to what was interpreted as Soviet blackmail. Even so, France remained predisposed to recognize Beijing until the PRC recognized Ho Chi-minh's regime in Indochina on January 19; France "recoiled more definitely" when the Soviet Union followed suit at the end of the month.[15]

More ominously, for Truman's and Acheson's proposal, a response also came from Beijing, and one evidently not coordinated with Mao beforehand (see below, pp. 73–74). On January 6, General Nie Rongzhen issued a proclamation requisitioning the military barracks in the U.S. embassy compound in Beijing. Claiming "military exigencies," and on the grounds of the abolition of "unequal treaties," Nie said, "this type of real property right naturally should be recovered."[16] Action would be taken within seven days, he said. The announcement was a stunning and potentially fatal blow to Washington's efforts to reach agreement with Beijing. It appeared as if it would be Truman who would be odd man out.

A DESPERATE ATTEMPT TO STRIKE A DEAL

The Truman administration kept Nie Rongzhen's announcement of the imminent seizure of U.S. consular offices secret for nine days, while making a last-gasp attempt to reach some accommodation with Beijing. On January 10, Secretary Acheson appeared in closed session before the Senate Foreign Relations Committee, where he attempted to make the case for the establishment of diplomatic relations with China as simply the way states do business with one another. He argued that it was a common "misconception" that "our relations with a country must either be hostile or intimate." In fact, he declared, they are "neither . . . they are simply regular." The secretary observed that unfortunately diplomatic recognition had "become a symbol, which it never should have become."

> We have gotten into more trouble . . . by linking recognition with approval or disapproval. It is an instrument as powerful as a popgun in trying to disapprove of somebody. It hurts the fellow who does not recognize much more than the person who is recognized. It is of absolutely no use in trying to affect the internal operations of a government. . . . You may hate their guts, but [diplomatic representation] is what [recognition] was in the past and that is what I think it should be in the future.

"The fact is clear," he said, "the Communists have complete control of the mainland of China," though they are faced with considerable problems. Primary among these was the Russian effort to gain control over China's northern provinces of Manchuria, Inner Mongolia, and Sinkiang. The secretary averred that the Chinese "have always been particularly against those foreigners who want to seize their territory" and it is the Russians against whom "should be, and I think will be, directed the hostility of the Chinese people." On the explicit question of recognition, the secretary declared that "we see no reason to take hasty action." No step will be taken, he said, "until it has been thoroughly threshed out with the committees of the House and the Senate." But, he added, "I will meet with the committee [to discuss recognition] as often as and whenever they wish."[17]

The *New York Times* account of Acheson's appearance did not disclose the secretary's remarks regarding the issue of recognition, although committee chairman Senator Tom Connally said afterward that in his view "recognition of Communist China would not be accomplished 'in a hurry.'" Connally said that there had been a general discussion of East and Southeast Asia and that there had been disagreement over policy toward Formosa. Acheson had identified "the line Japan-Okinawa-Philippines [as] our line of defense [which] lay east of Formosa." Asked whether any of Acheson's antagonists had been "sold" by his presentation, Connally replied: "I haven't tried to sell them. You can't sell a stubborn fellow who doesn't want anything."[18]

On January 12, Acheson went public with his views at the National Press Club. His speech, combined with the president's statement of the week before on Formosa and his own remarks of two days before to the Senate Foreign Relations Committee, contained the essential elements of the American proposal developed during the last week of December and formulated in NSC-48/1 and 2. As such, the secretary addressed his speech not to an American audience, but to Mao Zedong. Indeed, Acheson went to some lengths to insure that the American people did not know precisely and immediately what he said. In an unprecedented procedure for what was billed as a "major address," the secretary claimed to speak "ad lib," using only a few notes, which of course was not true. But claiming to speak off-the-cuff enabled him to avoid providing a published text to the many assembled members of the press corps.

Perhaps as a result, the next day's *New York Times* failed to report, *misreported,* and omitted key parts of what the secretary actually said. As neither the secretary nor the Department of State made any effort to clarify, correct, or otherwise object, however, one must assume that they were satisfied with the article as it appeared. Nor, as was customary, did the *Times* print a copy of the secretary's speech. The *Department of State Bulletin* carried the presumed "text" of the secretary's speech only on January 23, by which time Acheson had received the answer he was seeking from the Chinese.[19] It is most enlightening to compare the secretary's speech—as later carried in the *Bulletin*—with what the *New York Times* and also the *Washington Post* reported about it.

Continuing a theme he had employed in public and in private for the past year, Acheson stressed the relations between the "peoples" as opposed to the "governments" of the United States and Asia to assert a long-term coincidence of interests. He noted the developing pattern among the "peoples" of Asia in their revulsion against misery, poverty, and foreign domination, "whether that foreign domination takes the form of colonialism, or whether it takes the form of imperialism." The "symbol" of this revulsion became nationalism and he associated the American people with Asian nationalism. "The truth is," the secretary declared, "no nation and no people are wise enough and disinterested enough very long to assume the responsibility for another people or to control another people's opportunities."

Acheson then suggested that "much of the bewilderment which has seized the minds of many of us about recent developments in China comes from a failure to understand this basic revolutionary force which is loose in Asia." The reasons for the fall of the Nationalist government were "preoccupying many people." Among the many reasons which have been adduced, "nobody, I think, says that the Nationalist Government fell because it was confronted by overwhelming military force which it could not resist. Certainly, no one in his right mind suggests that."[20]

> What has happened in my judgment is that the almost inexhaustible patience of the Chinese people in their misery ended. They did not bother to overthrow this government. There was really nothing to overthrow. They simply ignored it ... [and] withdrew their support. ... When that support was withdrawn, the whole military establishment disintegrated. Added to the grossest incompetence ever experienced by any military command was this total lack of support both in the armies and in the country, and so the whole matter just simply disintegrated.
>
> The Communists did not create this condition. They did not create this revolutionary spirit. They did not create a great force which moved out from under Chiang Kai-shek. But they were shrewd and cunning to mount it, to ride this thing into victory and into power.

Now, the secretary asked, what is the attitude of our own people to Asia, the fundamental attitude out of which our policy has grown? The American people, he asserted, were interested in the peoples of Asia, "not ... as pawns or as subjects for exploitation but just as people." Moreover, "our interests have been parallel to the interests of the people of Asia" for a hundred years. The profound belief of the American people has been that "the control of China by a foreign power was contrary to American interests," a view which has been held "since the time of the Open Door policy."

Addressing the "factor" of communism, Acheson said: "I hear almost every day someone say that the real interest of the United States is to stop the spread of communism. Nothing seems to me to put the cart before the horse more completely than that. Of course, we are interested in stopping the spread of communism. But we are interested for a far deeper reason than any conflict between the Soviet Union and the United States." Oddly, the reason he then gave was precisely because of the conflict between Washington and Moscow.

Aside from making the point that "Communism is a doctrine that we don't happen to like," the secretary saw Communism as "the most subtle instrument of Soviet foreign policy that has ever been devised ... the spearhead of Russian imperialism which would, if it could, take from these people what they have won, what we want them to keep and develop, which is their own national independence." "Our real interest," on the other hand, "is in [the Chinese] people as people. It is because Communism is hostile to that interest that we want to stop it." Of course, it followed that if communism was the instrument of Soviet foreign policy, then American interest in stopping it was precisely because of the conflict between Washington and Moscow.

Acheson continued: We put forth "the most affirmative truth that we

67

hold, which is in the dignity and right of every nation, of every people, and of every individual to develop in their own way, making their own mistakes, reaching their own triumphs but acting under their own responsibility. That is what we are pressing for in the Far East and that is what we must affirm and not get mixed up with purely negative and inconsequential statements."

Now what of the Soviet Union's attitude toward Asia, he asked? In particular, what is the Soviet attitude "towards those parts of Asia which are contiguous to the Soviet Union, and with great particularity . . . to north China?" The attitude and interest of the Russian in these areas, he said, long antedates communism, but the Communist regime has added new methods, new skills, and new concepts to the thrust of Russian imperialism. "Armed with these new powers, what is happening in China is that the Soviet Union is detaching the northern provinces of China from China and is attaching them to the Soviet Union."

> This process is complete in Outer Mongolia. It is nearly complete in Manchuria, and I am sure that in Inner Mongolia and in Sinkiang there are very happy reports coming from Soviet agents to Moscow. This is what is going on. It is the detachment of these . . . areas from China and their attachment to the Soviet Union. . . . This fact that the Soviet Union is taking the four northern provinces of China is the single most significant, most important fact, in the relations of any foreign power with Asia.

What this means for us is that nothing we do or say "must be allowed to obscure the reality of this fact." Indeed, the only thing that could obscure it, the secretary said, in his only veiled reference to the dispute over Taiwan, would be "the folly of ill-conceived adventures on our part." He warned: "We must not undertake to deflect from the Russians to ourselves the righteous anger, and the wrath, and the hatred of the Chinese people which must develop. . . . We must take the position we have always taken—that anyone who violates the integrity of China is the enemy of China and is acting contrary to our own interest."

The secretary then shifted to the question of United States military security in the Pacific. The defeat and disarmament of Japan, he said, "placed upon the United States the necessity of assuming the military defense of Japan so long as that is required." Then, in implicit reference to the dispute over policy toward Japan that occurred during the formulation of NSC-48, he said: "I can assure you that there is no intention of any sort of abandoning or weakening the defense of Japan and that whatever arrangements are to be made either through permanent settlement or otherwise, that defense must and shall be maintained."

Switching abruptly to the subject of the United States defense perimeter in the Pacific, the secretary declared that "the defensive perimeter runs along the Aleutians to Japan and then goes to the Ryukyus." Then it runs "from the Rykyus to the Philippine Islands." As far as "the military security of other areas in the Pacific is concerned, it must be clear that no person can guarantee these areas against military attack. But it must also be clear that such a guarantee is hardly sensible or necessary." However, "should such an attack occur . . . the initial reliance must be on the people attacked to resist it and then upon the commitments of the entire civilized world under the Charter of the United Nations which has so far not proved a weak reed to lean on by any people who are determined to protect their independence against outside aggression."

Seeing in these "other areas" more serious problems of "subversion and penetration" the secretary went on to discuss "in more detail some of these areas." He pointed to the "great difference between our responsibility and our opportunities in the northern part of the Pacific area compared to the southern part of the Pacific area. In the north, we have direct responsibility in Japan and we have direct opportunity to act. The same thing to a lesser degree is true in Korea. [In the northern part of the Pacific] we had direct responsibility, and there we did act, and there we have greater opportunity to be effective than we have in the more southerly part." In the southern part of the Pacific, "we are one of many nations who can do no more than help. Direct responsibility lies with the peoples concerned."

The secretary was at pains to point out that "American assistance can be effective when it is the missing component in a situation, which might otherwise be solved. But the United States cannot furnish all the components to solve the question." Having said that, Acheson moved to discuss "some of the problems," aside from military security, in Japan, Korea, and the Philippines. In Japan, he said, "General MacArthur has been very successful [in] . . . hammering out . . . a political system which is based on nonmilitaristic institutions." However, he said, "in the economic field we have not been so successful. That is in large part due to the inherent difficulty of the problem."

The problem arose with the necessity of Japan being able to resume its role as a trading nation, "to buy raw materials and sell goods." The former connections of Japan with the mainland and with some of the islands had been disrupted. That has produced difficulties. The willingness of other countries to receive Japanese goods has very much contracted since the war, Acheson said. These matters must be "solved along lines which permit the Japanese greater freedom—complete freedom if possible—to buy what they need in the world and to sell what they have to offer on the mainland of Asia, in Southeast Asia, and in other parts of the world." It was a "tough" problem on which "the occupation authorities, the Japanese government, ourselves, and others are working. There can be no magic solution to it."

In Korea, "we have taken great steps which have ended our military occupation, and in cooperation with the United Nations, have established an independent and sovereign country recognized by nearly all the rest of the world. We have given that nation great help . . . we are asking the Congress to continue that help. . . . The idea that we should scrap all of that, that we should stop half way through the achievement of the establishment of this country, seems to me to be the most utter defeatism and utter madness in our interests in Asia." So much for the notion that Acheson was abandoning South Korea to its fate.

Turning to the Philippines, Acheson declared that "we acted with vigor and speed to set up an independent sovereign nation." We have given several billions of dollars to Manila since the war. "Much of that money has not been used as wisely as we wish it had been used, but here again, we come up against the matter of responsibility. It is the Philippine Government which is responsible. It is the Philippine Government which must make its own mistakes. What we can do is advise and urge. . . . We cannot direct, we should not direct, we have not the slightest desire to direct."

Elsewhere, in Southeast Asia, in Indochina, Burma, Indonesia, Malaya, Pakistan, and India, the situation is difficult, but we "help where we are wanted." Other nations as well as ourselves "have all had experiences which can be useful to those governments . . . if they want it. It cannot be useful if they don't want it." The secretary concluded by saying that "there is a new day which has dawned in Asia." The old relationships of paternalism and exploitation between East and West are gone and the new relationships must be based on mutual respect and helpfulness. "We are their friends. Others are their friends. We and those others are willing to help, but we can help only where we are wanted."

The secretary had, in the context of accusing the Soviet Union of detaching and seizing control of vast portions of North China and Outer Mongolia, offered the Chinese leadership a rationale for declining to enter into a long-term treaty relationship with Moscow—the Soviet exploitation of Chinese territory. He and the president had also offered an alternative—a rewarding political-economic relationship with the United States and Japan as well as the capture of Taiwan as a bonus. His speech was in its essence the proposal crafted in NSC-48/1. What was reported in the next day's *New York Times*, however, was remarkably different, and included additional elements of the secretary's "proposal."

THE *NEW YORK TIMES* AND ACHESON'S SPEECH

The *New York Times* report, written by Walter Waggoner, but no doubt edited, was nothing less than extraordinary in the extent to which he departed from what Secretary Acheson had said.[21] Waggoner accurately emphasized the Soviet detachment of China's northern areas and Acheson's warning against "ill-conceived follies" that could distract the Chinese from the Soviet Union and divert their anger to the United States. Waggoner emphasized Acheson's view that Chiang Kai-shek had been responsible for his own downfall, causing his armies and popular support to "just melt away." But the similarity between Waggoner's report and Acheson's speech ended at this point.

Acheson had not mentioned Formosa by name in his speech, while Waggoner devoted several paragraphs of his report to "the role that Formosa might play in American security," implying that the secretary had addressed that issue. Moreover, Waggoner had inserted Formosa into the section of Acheson's speech in which he discussed the differences in the "responsibilities and opportunities" for the United States in the northern and southern parts of the Pacific. The secretary specifically referred to Japan, Korea, and the Philippines as countries where the United States had played a formative postwar political, military, and economic role, but not Formosa. Not even by implication could Formosa be included in this section of the speech, for the United States had played no such role there, and Truman had just announced the virtual abandonment of the island a week before.

The secretary had responded to a question about Formosa but said nothing about the island in his speech. On the other hand, Acheson had singled out South Korea twice in his speech for special mention to emphasize that both the United States and the United Nations had helped establish Korea as a "sovereign nation," that the United States intended to continue to support Korea—legislation to that effect was pending—and that it would be the "most utter defeatism and utter madness" to "stop half way [and] scrap all that." Waggoner, however, had not mentioned Acheson's remarks about Korea at all in his report.

Furthermore, Waggoner left out Japan completely from Acheson's description of the "defense perimeter," saying that it ran "from the Ryukyu Islands (Okinawa) and the Aleutians off Alaska down to the Philippines." Was this an attempt to convey to Mao that the United States would step back from Japan if Mao stepped back from the Soviet Union, which was the proposal contained in NSC-48/1? Of course, what the secretary had said was that the "defensive perimeter runs along the Aleutians to Japan and then goes to the Ryukyus. . . . [then it] runs from the Ryukyus to the Philippine Islands." Later, Waggoner mentioned the defense of Japan, but in Acheson's mildest formulation, saying that the United States had "no intention of abandoning or weakening the defenses of Japan." While the secretary had said this, he had prefaced it with the firm assertion that the United States would maintain "the military defense of Japan so long as that is required."

But Waggoner omitted entirely the secretary's proposal for the resolution

71

of Japan's economic difficulties through the development of ties to the mainland, the essence of the proposal crafted in NSC-48/1. Acheson had stated
clearly the "need" to resolve Japan's problems "along lines which permit the
Japanese greater freedom—complete freedom if possible—to buy what
they need in the world and to sell what they have to offer on the mainland of
Asia." It was a "tough" problem, he had said, on which "the occupation authorities, the Japanese government, ourselves, and others are working. There
can be no magic solution to it." Waggoner had omitted this as well as
Acheson's reference to MacArthur's "very successful [efforts in] hammering
out . . . a political system which is based on nonmilitaristic institutions."

Waggoner duly noted Acheson's view that in "other areas of the Pacific"
there could be no "guarantee" against military attack, and that it must also
be clear that such a guarantee "is hardly sensible or necessary within the
realm of practical relationship." Of course, should an attack occur, "initial reliance" must be on the people attacked, and then upon the "commitments of
the entire civilized world under the Charter of the United Nations." And he
correctly reported Acheson's position that in the southern part of Asia the
United States was only "one of many nations who can do no more than help."

Waggoner's account of Acheson's speech badly distorted what the secretary had said. He had excluded Korea as a policy matter, included Formosa to
imply that it was part of America's defense perimeter, and left Japan out of it,
referring only to Washington's "intention" not to abandon or weaken Japan.
Finally, he had omitted Acheson's discussion of the need to resolve Japan's
"economic problems." Acheson had said something quite different. He had,
on the contrary, expressed his firm determination to defend Japan, included
it in the United States defense perimeter, declared support, with the U.N., for
South Korea, and made no mention of Formosa. It was no wonder, based on
what Waggoner had reported, that after the Korean War broke out, Acheson
would be accused of having given the "green light" for the attack on South
Korea. But that was not what the secretary had said.

The *Washington Post*, on the other hand, got it right. *Post* reporter Ferdinand Kuhn gave an accurate rendition of the secretary's speech that covered
all the issues, including the secretary's references to Korea, Japan, the Philippines, the defense perimeter, the Soviet detachment of China's northern
areas, his explanation for Chiang's fall, and the rest. And Kuhn faithfully
made no mention of Formosa, even in summarizing the secretary's responses
during the question-and-answer period.

Kuhn, however, like Waggoner, also missed what was perhaps the most
important part of the secretary's speech: the implied offer to promote a Sino-
Japanese economic relationship. Kuhn, at least, in an inside box adjoining his
article, included Acheson's specific remarks on Japan in a country-by-coun-
try survey.[22] Comparing the two accounts, it would seem that Waggoner's

piece was in effect a trial balloon designed to elicit a response from Mao. If questioned, the deviation from Acheson's actual words could always be explained away as a misunderstanding because there had been no formal text.

The secretary had also arranged to disclose in the *New York Times* that the United States had never regarded Chiang Kai-shek as anything more than a "temporary expedient." In an effort to demonstrate American bona fides, the State Department released a "newly discovered" report by former Vice President Henry Wallace on his visit to China in 1944. The gist of the report was to convey the notion that the United States had for several years considered Chiang Kai-shek as little more than a temporary expedient. "Chiang, at best is a short-term investment," Wallace said. "It is not believed that he has the intelligence or political strength to run post-war China. The leaders of post-war China will be brought forward by evolution or revolution, and it now seems more likely the latter."[23]

On a more substantive note, however, Acheson was also attempting to arrange through the American consulate in Shanghai for Mao to send his representative to Hong Kong for "negotiations" with roving ambassador Phillip Jessup. Unfortunately for the secretary, the effort came to nothing and may, on the Chinese side, have had more to do with attempting to generate leverage on Stalin than with opening the door to relations with the United States. Mao described Acheson's ploy in a discussion with Soviet foreign minister Molotov on January 17. As Molotov recounted it:

> Mao Zedong said that during the past few days the Americans have mobilized the activities of their [diplomatic, intelligence and information] networks and are testing the ground for negotiations with the People's Government of China. Thus, a few days ago, the head of the American telegraph agency in Paris addressed Mao Zedong with a question of how he would react to the famous American expert on far eastern affairs Jessup's trip to Beijing for negotiations. Almost simultaneously, information was received from Shanghai stating that steps are being taken by the American consulate in Shanghai, through representatives of the Chinese national bourgeoisie, to obtain agreement from the People's Government of China to send their representative to Hong Kong for negotiations with Jessup. However, we are paying no attention to this American ground testing, said Mao Zedong.[24]

Indeed, three days before, the Chinese had requisitioned the Marine barracks in Beijing. The State Department had immediately protested that the barracks had "long since" been converted for use as consular offices and residences, and that the United States had acquired the right to the land on which the buildings were constructed in 1901, rights which were reaffirmed in the Sino-American Treaty of 1943 when the United States agreed to relinquish extraterritoriality. All protest was futile. At 9:50 on the morning of January 14, the Beijing police, accompanied by four civilian officials, "invaded" the premises and seized control.[25] The frantic efforts of the Department to avert the seizure of the compound had failed, and with them, seemingly, any prospects for reaching an accommodation with Beijing.

The next morning's *New York Times* emblazoned headline read: "U.S. Recalls Aides In China As Peiping Seizes Offices; Foes Demand Acheson Quit."[26] W. Walton Butterworth, in announcing the Department's recall of 135 embassy personnel from China, explained that the State Department had held up public announcement "in the hope that higher Communist authorities would appreciate the gravity of the contemplated step and would find a way to overrule the action without 'losing face' " and "until it was certain the seizure had taken place and that there would be no official reconsideration." It was now clear that Beijing's action would stand. Indeed, Chinese authorities also seized the property of the French and Dutch in Beijing, making their position unmistakable.[27]

Butterworth described Beijing's act as a "completely unprecedented" treaty violation more akin to "tribal law than international law." Other administration officials said that the "Peiping incident . . . has pushed even further into the future the nebulous possibility of United States recognition of the Chinese Communist Government." In a companion piece under the same headline, William S. White, assessing the reaction on Capitol Hill, quoted senators as saying that "the Communists . . . had now rather clearly demonstrated that they did not want recognition."

THE PROSPECT OF NEGOTIATIONS EVAPORATES

Throughout, there had been no direct communication with Mao, who was still in Moscow. In the slim hope that there was still a chance of working something out if only direct contact could be established, the American side was reduced to grasping at straws. Earlier in January, a noncommunist friend of Hsieh Hsin-tung, the nephew of General Chen Yi [Chen I], contacted a member of the U.S. consulate in Shanghai. The individual, one Chou Minghsun—possibly the national bourgeois referred to by Mao above—represented himself as a spokesman for General Chen Yi, commander of PLA forces in Shanghai and East China, and overall commander of the operation to take Taiwan. Upon Acheson's authorization, Consul General Walter McConaughy and other consular officers met with Chou several times during the course of January.

To establish his bona fides with the Americans, Chou disclosed details of Mao's negotiations in Moscow, which proved to be largely accurate. Incidentally, this information may have been at least part of the basis for Acheson's assertion of Moscow's "complete domination of peripheral China." Chou also said Mao sought planes from Stalin for the invasion of Taiwan, "$5 billion" in aid, and machinery and other capital equipment, but was being asked to make "far-reaching Chinese concessions" to the Soviets regarding control of key ports, and to "minority groups," through which Moscow could exert influence. Chou's information about the secret negotiations in Moscow, however, was designed to establish his credibility for another tale.

Chou purported to have reliable information regarding the possibility of an imminent split in Communist leadership ranks between pro-Moscow and "China-first" leaders centered on General Chen Yi. Chen Yi's position was "not too secure," he declared, having been reprimanded by the top leadership as being "too moderate." He was, therefore, "fed-up" with the Moscow-dominated regime and looking for alternatives. "Chen would not be averse to discussing matter with ConGen [Consulate General] officer through intermediary." He foresaw a "split in CCP developing some time following Mao's return from Moscow," in the spring.

Should such a split occur, the "China-first" elements would depend upon Chen's (and Liu Po-cheng's) military forces. Chen believed that he could "hold East China (Shantung to Fukien) against combined other Communist armies for six months before requiring outside aid."[28] Chen reportedly wanted to know "whether there might be any disposition on part of American Government (a) to provide assistance to Chen in event of open intra-Communist conflict; and (b) to withdraw recognition of Nationalists in Taiwan." The logic of Chou's information proceeded step-by-step until the inquiry about Taiwan, which bore little obvious relationship to the previous inquiry and all that preceded it, raising suspicions.

In evaluating Chou's statements, McConaughy and his colleagues in Shanghai believed that "Chou's approach is genuine," and that he had the "backing of Chen Yi, which he claimed to have." They also felt, however, that "such 'belief' that Chou's approach is probably genuine is not enough, and that some infallible proof that Chou is Chen's authorized spokesman should be required." McConaughy also concluded that "even when authenticity of Chen's approach is established, ConGen should . . . divest itself as quickly as possible of all connection with the matter and be in a position to advise Chou that further contact with American side should be transferred to Hong Kong."

Acheson agreed. Replying a few days later, he instructed McConaughy to "authenticate" Chou's role as Chen Yi's interlocutor. He also agreed that "position of ConGen and other Amer Govt personnel wld be seriously jeopardized by involvement in any negots, commitments or any but most circumspect contact with informant." Therefore, the "locale of further contact shld be shifted to Hong Kong without delay." Finally, the secretary said that "in view extreme delicacy this matter it is at this stage being handled only by high officers in this Dept. and you shld mark later msgs 'Eyes only for Secretary.' "[29]

Further contacts with Chou made increasingly clear that the so-called initiative by Chen Yi was in fact an attempt to induce a formal American break with the Nationalist government on Taiwan and was not an attempt to seek American support in an intra-communist struggle. Chou's now transparent argument went as follows. According to Chou, Chen was part of a "New China Movement" that had "already opened office in Hong Kong and is opening another in Manila." The "movement looks to possible action some time following Mao's return." However, "such action now stymied by Taiwan factor, Generalissimo's continued possession of Taiwan, supported by US recognition of Nationalist regime. . . . Until this threat is removed once for all, Communists must hang together and anti-Moscow faction could not think of forcing Moscow control issue to showdown fight. First immediate objective of all Communists, anti as well as pro-Moscow, is to take Taiwan and end with finality all possibility of political comeback by Generalissimo."[30]

At this point, certainly, if not sooner, consulate officers became skeptical about "Chen's approach." McConaughy wondered "how serious is his intention of combating Moscow domination and whether he is primarily interested in that or in getting US withdrawal of recognition of Nationalist Government with view to thereby hastening Nationalist collapse and his bloodless occupation of Taiwan. Our guess is that both factors probably involved."[31] The reaction within the State Department, however, was more skeptical.

The State Department Policy Planning Staff, after careful evaluation of the "initiative," concluded that "the feelers allegedly put out by General Chen Yi . . . and our response to them have come to naught, at least for the time being. The unsavory middle man, Chou, may have fabricated out of whole cloth his reports. . . . On the other hand, Chou's story to us may have had considerable foundation in fact at the time he approached us but in the meantime Chen Yi has for any of a number of reasons become much more cautious." In any case, "we may conclude . . . Chen Yi's alleged overtures . . . appear to have vanished into thin air."[32]

And with them vanished any hopes Acheson may have harbored that Mao would decline to enter into an alliance with Stalin. The so-called "overture" was in reality a Chinese attempt to persuade Washington to formally divest itself of any relationship with the Nationalist government prior to a Chinese assault on the island. Acheson, on the other hand, had hoped that in entertaining this overture he could establish contact with the leadership and communicate his own proposal to Mao. But that had "come to naught."

How realistic was Acheson's "offer" to Mao? Did the secretary really expect Mao to get up from the negotiating table, spurn Stalin, return to China, and deal with the United States? Acheson seems to have formulated his proposal as one would formulate a business deal in the expectation that Mao would choose the better offer. Did he not realize that whatever Mao's thinking, he was locked into a relationship with the Soviets by virtue of his own history, his role in the Communist Party, and his subscription to communist ideology? Mao was simply not free to choose the best offer. Indeed, Mao was neither consulted nor informed beforehand about the crucial decision to seize the Marine barracks, his first reference to the issue coming in a cable sent to Beijing the day before it was to be carried out.[33] Mao had agreed to the fait accompli, but the episode indicated rather clearly that there existed forces within the Chinese Communist Party that were independent of the Chairman's will.

If Acheson was in fact sincere, the episode speaks volumes of the State Department's self-delusion about the nature of the Chinese Communist Party. President Truman, on the other hand, held no such illusions. While Mao and Stalin moved to conclude their negotiations for a treaty, Truman was authorizing the Policy Planning Staff to formulate a new strategy for the United States. We will turn first to the negotiation of a new Sino-Soviet treaty, however, before we focus on the American reaction to the failure of the wedge strategy.

77

PART II
MAO'S CHOICE
AND ITS CONSEQUENCES

CHAPTER FOUR

Mao Wants It Both Ways, But First the Treaty

STALIN HAD ALREADY sent military advisers to Pyongyang in late December to begin preparations for the invasion (see p. 46), without prior coordination or discussion with Mao, still languishing in isolation in Moscow. He had undoubtedly learned, through his secret agent network in the United States, of the Truman administration's December 30 decision (NSC-48/2) to adopt a hands-off policy toward Taiwan.[1] Was the idea of Mao's interview announcing that he and Stalin were about to negotiate a new treaty designed to prod Truman into revealing U.S. policy, or to preempt it?

In any case, Truman's announcement on January 5 that the United States would no longer support the Nationalist government on Taiwan, and the next day's declaration that Great Britain intended to recognize the People's Republic, confirmed Stalin's suspicion that there was "an emerging tacit understanding between Beijing and Washington on the 'liberation' of Taiwan in exchange for the normalization of Sino-American relations," a development that would be his "worst nightmare come true."[2] Stalin was prepared to respond immediately and between early January and the beginning of treaty negotiations he repeatedly sought to maneuver Mao into anti-Western positions.

STALIN SETS THE STAGE

As the object of war in Korea was to maneuver China into conflict with the West, one of Stalin's first steps had to be to facilitate the unity of the West under American leadership. This pointed directly at the United Nations, where any breach of the peace would be addressed. If a Soviet representative sat on the Security Council, it would be impossible for the U.N. to unify in support of South Korea in the wake of an attack by the North. With a single vote Moscow could veto any unified reaction. So Stalin contrived to withdraw the Soviet representative and employed the issue of the Nationalist government's occupation of China's seat on the Security Council as a pretext.

At one o'clock in the morning of January 7, only a few hours after London's announcement, Stalin sent Foreign Minister Andrey Vyshinsky to Mao's quarters with a proposal. After affirming Soviet readiness to sell aircraft fuel to China (which perhaps implied a willingness to sell the aircraft it would power), and agreeing to restore the Xiaofengman hydroelectric station to working order, Vyshinsky came to his main purpose. He proposed that Beijing send a letter to the United Nations "denying the legitimacy" of the Nationalist government's occupation of China's seat on the Security Council. Vyshinsky said that "if China publishes such a statement, the Soviet Union is ready to take action." Specifically, he went on to say that if the Nationalist delegate "remains in the Security Council as a representative of China ... then the Soviet Union will refuse to participate in the Security Council meetings."[3]

Mao immediately took the bait, agreeing without a second's hesitation. He said that he would send a cable to Beijing that very day and the statement would be published the next day, or the day after at the latest. Beijing's formal notification cable in fact reached the U.N. headquarters at Lake Success, New York, on January 8, and Soviet representatives immediately began walking out of all U.N. agencies and departments to which they had been accredited. Jacob Malik, Moscow's chief delegate, completed the total walkout on January 13, coincidentally the day after but not because of Secretary of State Acheson's speech about U.S. policy in Asia.

Of course, the Soviet ploy failed. The Nationalist representative retained his seat and Beijing remained isolated, but Stalin achieved his underlying objective.[4] The absence of a Soviet representative at the U.N. would enable the United States, without hindrance, to mobilize that body under American leadership in the wake of a North Korean attack on the South. It would not only leave China permanently dependent upon Moscow, but it would also make a formal United States declaration of war extremely unlikely. Gaining passage of a resolution condemning aggression would be far simpler than gaining each member state's agreement to join in a formal declaration of war—assuming that Washington would seek one. The legal intricacies and responsibilities involved in such an action were beyond realization.

Unknowingly, Mao had fallen completely into Stalin's trap, but he could be forgiven for not being able to see through Stalin's ploy. The possibility of

82

war in Korea had not yet entered fully into his thinking, as it would shortly. Furthermore, the Soviet leader had not yet removed the trigger that would deactivate the Sino-Soviet treaty and Moscow's responsibilities under it to come to Beijing's assistance as soon as China became "involved in hostilities." That step would not come until treaty negotiations began (see below, pp. 97–98), but, in retrospect, the U.N. ploy opening the way for Beijing's isolation indicates conclusively that Stalin's decision for war in Korea had already been taken.

Of course, Stalin could have returned his representative to the U.N. at any time—even the day following the outbreak of the conflict—to thwart Washington, but chose not to do so until August 1, when the Soviet representative was slated to assume the chairmanship of the Security Council. In other words, it would be over a month after war had broken out and the United States had successfully completed all arrangements to commit the U.N. to its side in the conflict before the Soviets returned to the U.N. Stalin would do nothing to interfere with the American effort, which served his purpose of further isolating China. Incidentally, in late May, Stalin also recalled General Kuzma Derevyanko, his representative to the Far Eastern Commission in Tokyo, which conveniently removed a potential stumbling block to the U.S. use of Japan as a forward staging area during the Korean War.[5] It also alerted MacArthur to coming trouble.

Regarding Japan, war in Korea would logically call for an attempt to disrupt American response capability, at least initially, behind the lines. In this connection, Stalin brought to Mao's attention an article in the January 6 issue of the Cominform *Bulletin* criticizing the head of the Japanese Communist Party, Nosaka Sanzo. Consistent with earlier Soviet policy toward Japan, since the end of World War II Nosaka had followed a policy of the peaceful path to power. The article now severely criticized that policy and exhorted the JCP to adopt a policy of violent resistance against the United States' use of Japanese soil for defense purposes.[6]

Earlier, Mao had refused to enter into discussion of Japanese matters, but now, under pressure from Stalin, he assented. There can be little doubt that Mao understood the implications of the policy change toward Japan. It made sense only in the context of a conflict in Korea and the American use of Japan as a forward base. A conflict in Korea, it seems, would now increasingly inform Mao's dealings with Stalin. Nosaka, having spent the war years in Yenan, was an ally of Mao's. Thus, Mao's admonition to change policy added to Stalin's would be very persuasive. When Mao arranged for *Renmin Ribao* to run an editorial echoing the Soviet line, Beijing issued no criticism, and simply expressed the lukewarm "hope that the Japanese Communist Party will take appropriate steps to correct Nosaka's mistakes."[7] The Japanese

83

Communist Party Politburo followed Mao's lead, explaining that they could not adopt a "more active revolutionary policy" because of MacArthur's tight control.[8]

In actuality, the early and public Soviet demand for the Japanese Communist Party to resort to violent resistance against the United States simply gave MacArthur advance notice of the JCP's planned actions and allowed him to take preventive steps. The Japanese Communist Party's efforts to disrupt American operations in Japan during the war were largely ineffectual. U.S. officials, puzzling over the JCP's unresponsiveness to the Soviets, believed that the Chinese had "interceded with Moscow on behalf of the JCP," allowing the Japanese Communists "to confess that their theory was wrong, but which did not require them to alter fundamental policies."[9]

Stalin also sought to turn Secretary Acheson's bombshell speech of January 12 to advantage. There can be little doubt that Acheson's exclusion of Formosa got Mao's attention; it was an open invitation to seize the island, with the clear indication that Washington would not interfere. But Acheson's speech contained much more than a declaration of what was or was not included in the United States' defense perimeter in the Western Pacific, and what else he said was incendiary to Stalin and created a dilemma for Mao.

Acheson had charged that Moscow was slicing off vast portions of northern China "and attaching them to the Soviet Union." The process, Acheson said, "is complete in Outer Mongolia. It is nearly complete in Manchuria, and . . . in Inner Mongolia and in Sinkiang." Acheson described "the fact that the Soviet Union is taking over four northern regions of China [as] the most important and the most significant fact, in the relation of any foreign power with Asia."[10] Whatever Acheson's motive was in making this charge, which was stunningly close to the truth, as we shall see, he had created a dilemma for Mao Zedong.

What should Mao do? To respond publicly to the charge of Soviet annexation of Chinese territory would raise questions about possible concessions Mao might make that would undercut him politically, but to remain silent would raise Stalin's ire on the eve of the all-important treaty negotiations. Mao's response was to ignore Acheson's speech altogether, hoping to avoid the dilemma. (His cables to Beijing between January 12 and 17, when the situation changed, contain no mention of Acheson's speech.)[11]

But Stalin could not allow the secretary's remarks to go unanswered because they exposed him for the national-imperialist that he was, rather than the so-called international communist he professed himself to be. So the Soviet leader decided to take the bull by the horns and attempt to employ the issue to serve his own ends. After five days of silence on the Acheson speech, on January 17, Stalin sent Molotov and Vyshinsky to see Mao and demand a response. Molotov called Acheson's remarks "a clear slander against the Soviet

Union" and said that Moscow would react with a declaration from the foreign ministry. "However," he went on, "we would prefer for the Chinese government to be the first to make a statement on this matter, and afterwards . . . the USSR Ministry of Foreign Affairs would make an appropriate statement."[12]

Unable to avoid the issue, and this time seeing a trap coming, Mao agreed to a response, but attempted to downplay it by issuing a reply through the Chinese news agency instead of the foreign ministry. But Molotov would not allow it. In reply to Mao's inquiry if "it would not be better for Xinhua to make this kind of declaration," Molotov retorted that since the matter concerned a speech by the U.S. Secretary of State "the declaration should not be made by a telegraph agency, but rather by the Ministry of Foreign Affairs of the People's Republic of China."[13]

Momentarily outmaneuvered, Mao initially agreed to prepare a reply to be issued through the foreign ministry, and then attempted a maneuver of his own to avoid it. He said that since Zhou Enlai was in transit to Moscow, he would authorize the deputy secretary of Foreign Affairs to issue the declaration, instead. Molotov hastily arranged for Mao to converse with Zhou by telephone during a stopover in Sverdlovsk, giving him the opportunity to arrange for a direct reply through the Foreign Ministry. Despite Molotov's pressure, however, Mao would prevail on this issue. The reply to Acheson's charges would be issued through the New China News Agency under the name of its chief, Hu Qiaomu, and not through the Foreign Ministry, or Zhou Enlai, or even his deputy.[14]

At this point, hoping to put an end to this line of talk and seeing an opening to put some pressure on Stalin to sweeten the upcoming treaty negotiations, Mao asked whether Molotov thought Acheson's declaration was "a kind of smokescreen" for an American attempt "to occupy the island of Formosa?" Molotov, following Mao's lead, agreed, replying that since U.S. China policy had gone bankrupt, it was "impossible to disagree that they are using the dissemination of slander as a kind of smokescreen . . . to carry out their plans of occupation." Moreover, he said, finally getting around to a reason for a Chinese response, Acheson's "fabrications . . . are an insult to China."[15]

Mao then moved to deflate the Soviet leader by revealing to him that Washington was at that moment exploring a venue to make contact in order to discuss recognition! "During the past few days," he said, "the Americans have mobilized . . . their networks and are testing the ground for negotiations with the People's Republic of China." We are being asked by the American consulate in Shanghai, Mao said, to send a representative to Hong Kong for "negotiations" with the "famous American expert on Far Eastern affairs," roving ambassador Philip Jessup. (Ambassador Jessup was at that time in the middle of a fourteen-nation fact-finding tour that spanned December 14,

1949, to March 15, 1950.) "However," Mao quickly added, "we are paying no attention to this American ground testing."

Indeed, as you know, he continued, a few days ago we appropriated the U.S. compound in Beijing and are "forcing the American consular representatives out of China." We are in no hurry, said Mao. "We need to win time . . . to put the country in order, which is why we are trying to postpone the hour of recognition by the USA. The later the Americans receive legal rights in China, the better it is." Mao's revelation no doubt alarmed Molotov, who may or may not have been as fully informed about events in China as was Stalin. Mao was openly declaring to Molotov that he fully intended to normalize relations with the United States, but not just now. Stalin, of course, knew from Mao's cable of a month earlier, December 19, that the Chinese leader had already authorized prompt movement toward normalization should the United States express its interest, as it was now doing.

It was with some urgency, therefore, that Stalin pressed forward with his plan to push China into conflict with the West. He urged Mao to seize Hong Kong, on the grounds that there were "a lot of imperialist agents in this city," and to recognize Ho Chi-minh's breakaway regime in North Vietnam.[16] Mao firmly disagreed with the Soviet dictator's advice to seize Hong Kong. It was transparently obvious that a Chinese assault on the British Crown Colony would scotch any possibility of establishing diplomatic relations with London, which were just getting under way. Such an act would, of course, carry even larger negative implications for China's prospective relations with London's Commonwealth allies.

Recognition of Ho Chi-minh's regime was a different story. Mao saw here not only an opportunity to further the anti-imperialist cause, but to box in and hopefully remove those Nationalist troops who had eluded his armies and were still carrying out cross-border raids from bases in Vietnam and Laos. Thus, on January 17, he approved the establishment of diplomatic relations with the Democratic Republic of Vietnam.[17] Stalin, however, would not take concurrent action, but only followed suit two weeks later in February, citing implications for the Soviet Union's relations with France for the delay. Mao had avoided the Hong Kong trap, and had independently taken an anti-French stand in Indochina. But Stalin had yet one more card up his sleeve: it was to implicate Mao in the coming Korean conflict.

THE KOREAN FACTOR ENTERS

On January 8, Stalin instructed Ambassador Terentii Shtykov to prod Kim Il-sung into requesting that China return those remaining Korean troops sent earlier to fight with Chinese Communist forces in the Chinese civil war.[18] Troop transfers had begun the previous year when the PLA's 166th Division was returned to North Korea to be reorganized into the NKA's Sixth Division and the PLA's 164th Division returned to become the NKA's Fifth Division. Shtykov replied three days later, reporting that Kim was preparing to send a special emissary to make the request.[19] The timing of the request was important to Stalin. He was carefully orchestrating the arrival of a Korean request for troop transfers while Mao was still in Moscow so that he would find it impossible to refuse.

At any rate, carefully following Stalin's orders, even if not fully understanding them, Kim prepared the ground for his request. On January 17, he held a luncheon for his newly designated ambassador to China, Yi Chu-yon (in Chinese Li Zhou-yuan).[20] In addition to second-in-command Pak Hon-yong, Premier Kim Tu-bong, and Deputy Minister of Foreign Affairs Pak Chong-jo, the guest list included Chinese trade representative Wang Shizhen, Soviet ambassador Shtykov, and two Soviet advisers, Aleksei Ignatiev and Ivan Pelishenko. Premier Kim regaled his guests with an account of his trip to Moscow to celebrate Stalin's birthday and underscored the repeated wishes he had received for the prompt unification of Korea.

Kim Il-sung and the Chinese Wang Shizhen "enthusiastically" discussed the CCP victory in China and the situation in Korea, with Kim repeatedly declaring that "Mao Zedong [was] his friend and will always help Korea." After the luncheon was over, and the Chinese guests had departed, Kim continued excitedly to discuss the prospects for Korean unification with the Soviet advisers. His view was that now that "China is completing its liberation, the liberation of the Korean people in the south of the country is next in line." Kim said that Stalin would only permit a counterattack if the South struck first, "but since Rhee Syngmann [*sic*] is still not instigating an attack, it means that the liberation of the people of the southern part of the country and the unification of the country are being drawn out."

Kim declared to Shtykov that "he needs again to visit Comrade Stalin and receive an order and permission for offensive action by the People's Army for the purpose of the liberation of the people of Southern Korea." He said that "he himself cannot begin an attack, because he is a communist, a disciplined person and for him the order of Comrade Stalin is law." Kim proposed a meeting with Stalin followed by one with Mao, who he "underscored . . . promised to render him assistance after the conclusion of the war in China." And, he went on, if it was "impossible to meet with Comrade Stalin, then he wants to meet with Mao Zedong, since Mao after his visit to Moscow will have orders on all questions." Responding, Ambassador Shtykov allowed that it would be "possible that Comrade Stalin will receive him."

Two days later, on January 19, Kim Il-sung sent his emissary General Kim Kwang-hyop to Beijing with the request to transfer forthwith all remaining North Korean troops who had fought in the Chinese civil war.[21] Acting Chief of Staff Nie Rongzhen received Kim's request and immediately forwarded it to Mao, who quickly approved it. Mao could not very well refuse Kim Il-sung's request for the return of his own troops, with Stalin looking on. Final troop transfers began in February. In all, some 23,000 troops from the PLA's 156th Division were returned and reorganized into the NKA Seventh Division.[22] When completed, in May, this transfer essentially concluded the repatriation process begun the previous year. The three battle-hardened, combat-experienced units, comprising between 50,000 and 70,000 troops, would be the main attack force for the invasion of the South.

Mao and Zhou, who had just arrived in Moscow for the treaty negotiations, were acutely aware of the implications of the troop transfers, which began while they were still in Moscow. They knew that troop movements would be (and were) monitored by American intelligence, which would conclude (erroneously) that Mao was cooperating with Stalin in preparing for conflict in Korea. Mao's decision to arrange for the troops to return with old Japanese and American weapons, but without any ammunition, could not alter this impression.[23]

Most ominous of all, Kim Il-sung's request, coming on the eve of their negotiations for a new Sino-Soviet treaty, raised to the forefront the fundamental question of "Who first?" Would a North Korean attempt to unify the peninsula preempt Mao's determination to complete the Chinese revolution with the seizure of Taiwan? Was Stalin attempting to gain leverage on them in the coming treaty negotiations? What was he up to?

It would thus have been perfectly natural for even the most unsuspecting leader, which of course Mao was not, to have inquired of Stalin about his intentions in North Korea and there can be little doubt that a discussion occurred at this point. Of several versions of their conversation, there is only one firsthand account, that of Mao's interpreter Shi Zhe. As was Stalin's practice, he attributed the idea for an invasion solely to the "young and brave" Kim. Then, without divulging his own view, he asked Mao for his, particularly regarding the possibility of an American intervention. According to Shi Zhe, Mao replied after some reflection that "the Americans might not come in because this is Korea's internal affair, but the Korean comrades need to take America's intervention into account."[24]

However one examines this exchange, there is little ground for interpreting it as a "green light for Kim's plans to attack the South."[25] Several years later, in a conversation with Soviet Ambassador Pavel Yudin, Mao disclosed what had transpired. Aside from pointing out Stalin's "serious miscalculation" regarding American intervention in the Korean War, Mao said: "When I was in Moscow, there was no talk about conquering South Korea, but rather on strengthening North Korea significantly. But afterwards, Kim Il-sung was in Moscow when a certain agreement was reached about which nobody deemed it necessary to consult with me beforehand."[26] Mao, in short, claimed that he had not been consulted "beforehand" on the decision for war in Korea.

Mao's conversation with Stalin about Korea was not a "green light" for war. It was rather the opposite, marking the beginning of Mao's determined efforts to delay the outbreak of war in Korea until after his forces had seized Taiwan. If, as Shi Zhe recounts, Mao concluded from his exchange with Stalin that "Kim Il-sung would attack the South no matter what happened," then the issue that would lie just beneath the surface for the remainder of the negotiation with Stalin was, "Who first?"

Stalin, of course, now acted to gain leverage on Mao's own war preparations by reversing himself on the issue of air and naval support for the attack on Taiwan.[27] Having refused to provide such assistance for six months, he abruptly changed his mind and agreed to provide support for the attack. He could do no less, for Mao must have demanded that Stalin provide the materiel support for a Chinese assault on Taiwan just as he was providing the support for Korean unification. Moreover, Stalin realized that to refuse would spur Mao to attack Taiwan as soon as possible.

Although it appeared on the surface that Stalin's promise to provide the needed air and naval support for the assault on Taiwan placed the prospect of success within Mao's grasp, in reality it put the Soviet leader into position to thwart Mao's drive. We can be certain that Stalin had no intention of making his "worst nightmare come true." Agreeing to support an assault on Taiwan may have momentarily eased Mao's growing sense of anxiety about Korea, but it gave Stalin a measure of control over the operation to take Taiwan. His promise of support was his best insurance against any precipitate Chinese action.

Even more important, being in control of the weapons supply for both the Korean and Taiwan assaults enabled Stalin to exert decisive leverage on which would occur first. And which one occurred first was crucial to the successful outcome of his strategy to maneuver China into conflict with the West and into dependence upon Moscow. The issue was fundamental and straightforward and the stakes were of the highest magnitude.

A Chinese conquest of Taiwan before the outbreak of war in Korea would indeed open the door to the establishment of diplomatic relations between Beijing and Washington. This would be Mao's preferred sequence and Stalin's "worst nightmare." A war in Korea under those circumstances would make it highly unlikely that China could be maneuvered into conflict against the United States. Indeed, they could conceivably cooperate to settle it. On the other hand, in what was obviously Stalin's preferred sequence and Mao's worst nightmare, the outbreak of war in Korea before China seized Taiwan would prevent Chinese action against the island, forestall establishment of diplomatic relations between Beijing and Washington, and leave Beijing isolated and in a position to be maneuvered into conflict on the peninsula.[28]

THE TREATY NEGOTIATIONS BEGIN

On January 22, 1950, when Mao Zedong and Zhou Enlai sat down with Joseph Stalin to negotiate a new treaty, Mao realized that he was in a race against time.[29] The possibility of war breaking out in Korea before he could seize Taiwan must have preoccupied him, and for good reason. The answer to the question of "Who first?" would determine the success or failure of his strategy of dealing with both East and West. Moreover, with the future of China very much at stake, there was precious little that he could do about it.

Mao knew that he was completely at the mercy of Stalin for the planes, if not also the ships, he needed to ensure a successful assault on Taiwan and he knew that Stalin did not share his strategic objectives. Professions of international solidarity only papered over fundamental differences. Mao had placed orders for the purchase of over twelve hundred aircraft and arranged for the training of the pilots to fly them.[30] This was the decisive component of his attack plans, but he could not be certain when or even if Stalin would deliver. Mao's only hope was to get the best deal that he could—on the treaty, on the planes and ships—and proceed with his plans. There was only an outside chance that he could take Taiwan first and he must prepare for it—with or, most probably, without Stalin's help.

A second question, crucially related to "Who first?," would actually drive the treaty negotiations. It was: if Korea first, "What then?" If war in Korea broke out first, frustrating Mao's attempt to take Taiwan, Mao must avoid being drawn into it, if it went badly for the North. Mao must be prepared to act and have the freedom to act if the opportunity presented itself on Taiwan, yet not be forced by the treaty to go to war over Korea. It was absolutely crucial, as he told his interpreter Shi Zhe, that the treaty "must not bind my hands."[31] Yet the worst case could occur and, if it did, the immediate pressure would be on China rather than the Soviet Union to come to Pyongyang's aid because of China's long border with North Korea. In the worst case, in other words, Mao wanted treaty language that would require at the very least massive Soviet support, if not direct military involvement, if China was forced into war with the United States.

Stalin, on the other hand, controlled the timing of the outbreak of conflict in Korea. The particular moment the war broke out was inconsequential to him, just so long as it came before Mao made his bid for Taiwan. Stalin knew that Mao would attempt to attack Taiwan, if he could, before the onset of the monsoon season in July. The summer monsoon meant turbulent waters in the Taiwan Strait, making amphibious operations extremely difficult for even the most seaworthy craft. This explains, by the way, why the conflict in Korea broke out in late June, just before what was the rainy season there, which was decidedly not the optimum time for a tank-led assault. If conditions in Korea had been the determining criterion, beginning an assault well before or just after the rainy season would have been better for a rapid war of maneuver—and would have given Kim a genuine chance to defeat the South. The attack during the rainy season—with swollen rivers and soggy roads—hindered the NKA's mobility.

In other words, Stalin's first concern was to ensure that war broke out in Korea before Mao attacked Taiwan. In this ironic sense Mao's preparations for an assault on Taiwan would determine the timing of the outbreak of war in Korea. Second, Stalin would also ensure that the North Korean assault would fail—a subject treated in depth in chapter 9. The failure of the North Korean attack would create the basic condition for maneuvering China into conflict with a U.S.-led United Nations, leaving China dependent upon the Soviet Union and crystallizing the basic architecture of the postwar period, Stalin's main objective.

For Stalin a less desirable, less likely, but acceptable outcome was a successful North Korean attack against the South from which the United States, despite many signals to the contrary, abstained. In that case, a pro-Soviet Korea would emerge on China's flank—an outcome that would settle a century-long struggle among China, Japan, and Russia for control of the peninsula. It would also signal another communist victory over an American ally. Stalin's main objective, however, was not to settle this historic struggle, but to employ a conflict on the peninsula to produce a structural outcome that had far greater, indeed global, significance. From Stalin's point of view, war in Korea seemed to be a win-win proposition no matter what the United States did.

Thus, in the treaty negotiations with Mao, Stalin strove on the one hand to obtain the loosest possible construction on the treaty so as to minimize any legal commitments to come to China's assistance in the event of war. The treaty must not enable Mao to drag the Soviet Union into war. On the other hand, Stalin sought to structure the treaty to create a long-term antagonism between China and the United States. Superb negotiator that he was, Stalin gave Mao the impression that he had been won over to Mao's view. In fact, however, both leaders had reversed positions. The crucial issues of "Who first?" and especially "What then?" brought about a reversal of objectives regarding the new treaty compared to the positions taken by both Mao and Stalin up to and on December 16.

When their discussion opened, now it was Stalin who insisted on scrap-ping the 1945 treaty entirely because it had become an "anachronism" and Mao who wanted to keep substantial portions of it intact in the interests of "friendship and cooperation."[32] Stalin opened the conversation after an exchange of greetings with the remark that there were "two groups of questions which must be discussed: the first group of questions concerns the existing agreements between the USSR and China; the second group . . . concerns the current events in Manchuria, Xinjiang, etc."[33]

Regarding the first group of existing agreements, Stalin said: "We believe that these agreements need to be changed, though earlier we had thought that they could be left intact." In response to Stalin's request to hear his "opinion," Mao replied cautiously: "So far we have not worked out a concrete draft of the treaty, only a few outlines." We believe, Mao continued, "we should strengthen our existing friendship using the help of treaties and agreements. This would resonate well both in China and in the international arena." Two points, he thought, were "cardinal" compared to the previous treaty. First, the new situation establishes the conditions for "real friendship and cooperation," not the empty words of the 1945 treaty with the KMT. And second, since Japan's defeat, "now attention must turn to preventing [renewed] Japanese aggression."

Mao wanted "a paragraph on consultation regarding international concerns," which would "strengthen our position, since among the Chinese national bourgeoisie there are objections to the policy of rapprochement with the Soviet Union on questions of international concern." Stalin immediately agreed, observing that "the inclusion of such a paragraph goes without saying." The two leaders then agreed to remand the drafting of the treaty to Vyshinsky and Zhou and, at Stalin's suggestion, moved on to discuss the agreement on Manchuria—the Changchun Railroad, Port Arthur, and Dairen, which had also been part of the 1945 treaty.

At this point, Mao presented the first of several reversals from his previous position, observing that "perhaps we should accept as the guiding principle the idea of making practical changes . . . while legally continuing them in their present state." Surprised, Stalin asked: Do you mean that "you agree to declare the legal continuation of the current agreement while, in effect, allowing appropriate changes to take place?" Well then, said Stalin, reversing himself as well from what had been his position of December 16: "we believe that the agreement concerning Port Arthur is not equitable."

Mao quickly countered, referring to Stalin's adamant stand in December to maintain the existing status of the agreement on Port Arthur in terms of Yalta, "but changing this agreement goes against the decisions of the Yalta Conference." Stalin: "True, it does—and to hell with it! Once we have taken up the position that the treaties must be changed, we must go all the way."

Mao: "This question worries us only because it may have undesirable consequences for the USSR." Stalin noted that changing the treaty terms "entails certain inconveniences, and we will have to struggle against the Americans. But we are already reconciled to that."

Stalin, recovering, offered Mao two options on Port Arthur, either of which was acceptable. Either declare that the current agreement will remain in force until a peace treaty is signed with Japan, "after which the Russian troops would be withdrawn from Port Arthur," or declare that the current agreement "shall remain in place, while in effect withdrawing troops from Port Arthur." Mao quickly chose the first option, clarifying it and making an additional proposal. He noted that when a peace treaty is signed with Japan the agreement "shall become invalid and the Soviet soldiers will leave." But, said Mao, "we would like for Port Arthur to be a place for military collaboration, where we could train our military naval forces."

Declining to respond to Mao's offer for "military collaboration" at Port Arthur, Stalin quickly shifted to the issue of Dairen, saying: "We have no intention of securing any Soviet rights in Dalny." Mao was incredulous. "Will Dalny remain a free port?" Stalin: "Since we are giving up our rights there, China must decide on its own the question of Dalny." Stalin had come full circle. He had gone from insisting that Soviet forces would remain in Port Arthur and that Dairen "must be used jointly" (the position he had taken with Liu Shaoqi the previous June), to declining to maintain a presence in Port Arthur at all, or even to collaborate with China, and abdicating any "rights" in Dairen.

Mao, too, had reversed position, from attempting to regain complete control to insisting on a Soviet presence. Thus, he now declared, "we believe that Port Arthur could serve as a base for our military collaboration, while Dalny could serve as a base for Sino-Soviet economic collaboration. In Dalny there is a whole array of enterprises that we are in no position to exploit without Soviet assistance. We should develop a closer economic collaboration there." It is obvious, in retrospect, that Mao now wanted a Soviet presence in Manchuria to facilitate involvement should the worst case of a crisis in Korea occur.

But Stalin wasn't interested. Instead, he moved on to a discussion of the Changchun Railroad, saying: "Tell us, as an honest communist, what doubts do you have here?" Once again, Mao switched from his earlier position (which he had stated to Mikoyan the previous March) of complete recovery of the Soviet "share" in the railroad to the view that the Soviets must stay, but without control. "The principal point is that the new treaty should note that joint exploitation and administration will continue in the future." But Mao wished to "take the lead role" in administering the railroad, abolishing the 1945 system of a management board of directors, in which the Russians participated, and replacing it with a commission staffed entirely with Chinese cadres.

Mao's proposal produced a spate of objections from the Russian delegation. Molotov interjected at this point to insist on "equal participation," and Stalin proposed that management positions "be alternated." When Zhou proposed that China increase its investment ratio from 50 to 51 percent, Molotov argued that "this would go against the existing provision for parity," and Stalin said that "we might as well have equal participation," since we have similar agreements with the Czechs and the Bulgarians. Mao refused to give in. Agreeing to give the issue "more thought," he said, "the question needs to be further examined, keeping in mind the interests of both sides." No doubt, Mao and Zhou wished to ponder why Stalin was so determined to maintain a strong position on the railroad, but wanted nothing whatever to do with the ports.

Moving to a discussion of a Soviet credit (only $300 million, not the $5 billion that had been rumored), Mao approved of the repayment rate of 1 percent interest, but wanted to know whether "the shipment of military arms [could be] considered a part of the monetary loan?" Stalin said: "This you can decide yourself." So Mao determined that "part of the military shipments will have to be billed towards the loan, while the other part will have to be paid with Chinese goods." Could the delivery period be shortened, Mao asked? Stalin replied that it depended on how quickly the Chinese side presented the necessary requisition lists. "The sooner a list is presented, the better for the matter at hand."

Turning to the trade agreement, Stalin, perhaps to set Mao up for what else he had in mind from these areas, wanted to know whether the Soviets would "be signing separate agreements with Xinjiang, Manchuria and other provinces, or a single agreement with the central government?" Mao immediately replied that "we would like to have a single, central agreement. But in time Xinjiang may have a separate agreement." To Stalin's query: "What about Manchuria?" Zhou snapped: "A separate agreement with Manchuria can be ruled out."

With this the substantive portion of the conversation about Stalin's "first group" of issues ended. The two sides agreed to delegate the questions of economic cooperation and the reconstruction and development of the Manchurian economy to their negotiators. Mao thanked Stalin for the use of a Soviet air transport regiment and hoped he would "allow it to stay a little longer," to help transport provisions to the PLA Second Field Army currently preparing for an attack on Tibet. Stalin approved of Mao's plans. "The Tibetans need to be subdued," he said.

94

STALIN'S "SECOND GROUP" OF ISSUES

At this point in their meeting, for which there are only the recollections of the interpreters Shi Zhe and Mikhail Kapitsa, Stalin moved to discussion of his "second group" of issues regarding current events in "Manchuria, Xinjiang, etc."[34] Stalin, understanding that he had Mao at his mercy regarding the provision of weapons for Taiwan, decided to push hard for everything he could get and made an extraordinary demand. He proposed that "citizens of third countries not be allowed to come to live in the Chinese Northeast and Xinjiang." Stalin's proposal was all the more extraordinary for the fact that just the day before he and Mao had issued a statement repudiating Secretary Acheson's charge of January 12 that the Soviet Union was detaching Manchuria and Xinjiang from China.

It is evident from what little public reportage is available on what is termed the "Additional Agreement" that this proposal was received unhappily by Mao and Zhou. They resented what was gross intrusion into China's internal affairs, and what Mao later termed Stalin's attempt to create "spheres of influence,"[35] and a Soviet attempt to establish "colonies" in China.[36] But the proposal itself was puzzling. Zhou immediately pointed out to Stalin that "many people of Korean nationality live in the Northeast . . . should we consider them to be citizens of a third country? This is all the more true of the Mongolians who came from foreign countries." Stalin hastily and lamely explained that his intent was not to exclude these peoples, but only people "from the United States, Japan, Britain and other imperialist countries."

As originally presented, Stalin's proposal would have applied solely to China, which precipitated an outburst of indignation from Mao and Zhou. In a heated argument, Mao declared himself to be "highly dissatisfied," demanding reciprocity, while Zhou declared that "he would rather resign than accede to [Soviet] demands as presented."[37] To gain their concurrence, Stalin agreed to apply the exclusionary provisions of the Additional Agreement to the Soviet Far East, as well. Of course, Stalin's "concession" meant nothing because the Soviet Union prohibited "imperialists" from living and doing business in sensitive areas anyway. In the end, Stalin got his way.

Following this discussion, the Chinese and Soviet sides each drafted agreements. This, too, is a process about which we know little, except for what Mao revealed in cables to Beijing and in later commentary. According to him, for example, the Chinese side completed a draft of the treaty on January 24, an agreement on the Changchun Railroad, Port Arthur, and Dairen on the 25th, and a barter agreement on the 28th.[38] The Chinese side also drafted a civil aviation accord, an agreement on the loan and its repayment schedule, and a statement reaffirming the independence of Outer Mongolia and the establishment of diplomatic relations with Ulan Bator.

The Soviet side drafted its own agreements at the same time. These included the Additional Agreement, four agreements establishing "joint stock" companies (on scientific-technical cooperation, mineral exploitation in Sinkiang, and two agreements to construct rail lines connecting China and the Soviet Union, one through Sinkiang and the other through Outer Mongolia) giving the Soviet Union preferential terms, an agreement on espionage cooperation, and one on extraterritoriality—exempting Soviet citizens and troops from Chinese law.[39]

By the end of January the drafting process had been completed and the two sides got down to the task of negotiating the final agreements. The negotiation was in fact a series of horse-trading sessions lasting until just hours before the treaty and related agreements were signed and published, on February 14, as both sides maneuvered for advantage until the last moment.[40] Only a brief glimpse of the extent of trading is possible in the absence of a full record of the negotiations, but enough exists to offer a broad outline of the negotiation.

Stalin's main objectives when the two sides sat down to negotiate their drafts of the treaty were to explicitly identify the United States as the main enemy and raise the threshold for Soviet commitments to support China should Beijing become engaged in a future conflict. Mao and Zhou, on the other hand, sought to strengthen the automaticity of Soviet commitments and retain a substantial Soviet military presence in Manchuria, while avoiding explicit mention of the United States as the main enemy.

On the title of the treaty, just as in the 1945 treaty with the KMT, the Soviet draft read "treaty of friendship and alliance," but Zhou sought to strengthen it by adding "and mutual assistance," a phrase that Stalin accepted.[41] Stalin, seeking to drive a wedge between China and the United States, attempted to inject the United States directly into the treaty by name with reference to "American and Japanese imperialists" (which he succeeded in doing in the Additional Agreement), but Zhou insisted on the formulation "Japan or any state allied with her," which, even though everyone knew the term "any state" referred to the United States, did not directly identify it.

In the sentence dealing with consultation, Stalin inserted the word "common" before the word "interests," restricting its application. Consultations would occur only regarding those "international problems affecting the common interests" of the parties, requiring prior discussion of what constituted a "common" interest. At Zhou's insistence, clauses were inserted declaring each party's adherence to the "principles of equality, mutual benefit, and mutual respect for the national sovereignty and territorial integrity and

96

noninterference in the internal affairs of the other." He also insisted on including the phrase "[rendering assistance] by all means at its disposal" if attacked, which implied a commitment of the Soviet Union's nuclear power.

All this was peripheral to the central change that Stalin succeeded in
making in the treaty, which was to change the term that would automati-
cally trigger Soviet involvement on China's behalf in the event of conflict. In
the 1945 treaty, Stalin's intent was to legitimize and facilitate Soviet military
intervention in China. Thus, the language of article III read:

> in the event of one of the High Contracting Parties becoming involved in hos-
> tilities with Japan in consequence of an attack by the latter against the said
> Contracting Party, the other High Contracting Party shall at once give to the
> Contracting Party so involved in hostilities all the military and other support
> and assistance with the means in its power.[42]

97

This formulation justified Soviet intervention on the slightest pretext and
could obviously be turned to Mao's advantage. Since Stalin was now planning to trigger a conflict in Korea and maneuver China into it, while staying
out himself, this commitment had to be expunged. When China became involved in a conflict on the Korean peninsula, there must be no grounds on
which Mao could demand Soviet involvement. Thus, the language of the
1945 treaty that facilitated Soviet involvement had to be changed to make
such involvement extremely difficult, if not impossible. In the event, the language of the new treaty, shifted to article I, read:

> in the event of one of the Contracting Parties being attacked by Japan or any
> state allied with her and thus being involved in *a state of war*, the other Con-
> tracting Party shall immediately render military and other assistance by all
> means at its disposal.[43]

Stalin substituted the term "a state of war" for "hostilities." Legally, a
state of war required a formal declaration of war which, as we shall see, Stalin had reason to believe would be very unlikely. (As it actually turned out, at
Stalin's suggestion, China's participation in the conflict was in terms of "volunteers," while the United States fought a "police action" under the U.N.
banner, virtually precluding a declaration of war by either party against the
other.) In other words, China, according to the new formulation, would have
to be in a formally declared state of war before the treaty's support provisions
could be invoked. In the 1945 treaty, on the other hand, simply being involved in "hostilities" of any magnitude was sufficient to trigger Soviet
involvement.

But, while Stalin succeeded in changing the term "hostilities" to "state of
war" in the treaty, in the agreement on Manchuria the Chinese succeeded
in retaining the original term "hostilities," and more. In article II of the

Agreement Between the People's Republic of China and the Union of Soviet Socialist Republics on the Chinese Changchun Railroad, Port Arthur, and Dairen, February 14, 1950, the treaty language was restated according to Mao's wishes.

> In the event of either of the contracting Parties becoming the victim of aggression on the part of Japan or any state that may collaborate with Japan, and as a result thereof becoming involved in *hostilities*, China and the Soviet Union may, on the proposal of the government of the PRC and with the agreement of the government of the USSR, jointly use the naval base at Port Arthur for the purpose of conducting joint military operations against the aggressor.[44]

Furthermore, regarding Port Arthur, Soviet troops would be withdrawn and installations transferred to the PRC "on the conclusion of a peace treaty with Japan, but not later than the end of 1952." Thus, Mao would regain full control of the port "not later than the end of 1952," but he sought to cover himself in the short term, arranging for joint military operations with the Russians in case China became "involved in hostilities."

Regarding the port of Dairen, it was agreed to form a joint commission to arrange for the transfer of the property to be "fully carried out in the course of 1950." Then, "on conclusion of a peace treaty with Japan," the "question of Dairen harbor [would] be further considered." In other words, China would regain control of Dairen immediately, but would be willing to give consideration to how the Soviet Union could use the port in the future after conclusion of a peace treaty with Japan.

Like Port Arthur, the Changchun Railroad would revert to the PRC "after the conclusion of a peace treaty with Japan, but not later than the end of 1952." Pending the transfer, however, "the existing Sino-Soviet joint administration . . . shall remain unchanged." In other words, for the following two years or less, the 1945 treaty terms would govern usage of the railroad. Mao had backed away from his proposal of January 22 for Chinese control and 51 percent ownership. These terms included the Soviet right to transport troops, military goods in sealed cars, and other goods for through transit, free of customs and inspection. Although the 1945 treaty restricted the transportation of troops only to "time of war against Japan," this restriction was amended to permit the Soviet Union to transport troops during the period pending transfer.[45] In fact, the Manchurian railroad system would become the main supply corridor for the transport of Soviet weapons and equipment during the Korean War, but not prior to it.

Stalin and Mao had each compromised on key points, but Stalin appeared to have gotten the better of the horse-trading. Particularly on the crucial issue of what would trigger Soviet involvement in the coming conflict, Stalin had made it most difficult for Mao to demand Soviet participation. The

United States would have to declare war on China before the Soviet Union would be under any obligation. Even though Mao and Zhou had managed to retain the term "hostilities" in the agreement on the Changchun Railroad, Port Arthur, and Dairen, the treaty language would govern in case of any conflict.

Although Stalin had failed to gain the explicit identification of the United States as China's main enemy in the treaty, he had managed to do so in the Additional Agreement, which declared that the treaty "had crushed the aggressive plans of the American and Japanese imperialists." Mao had managed to avoid the insertion of the United States in the treaty itself, employing the term "Japan or any state allied with her" instead. But the Additional Agreement was scheduled to be published along with the treaty and other agreements on February 14, thus, it seemed that Stalin would achieve his objective of driving an explicit wedge between Washington and Beijing.

As late as February 10, Mao cabled Liu to say that "both sides are to publish the treaty and the agreements on the same day."[46] The agreements scheduled to be published were the treaty, the agreement on the Changchun Railroad, Port Arthur, and Dairen, the agreement on the Soviet loan, the agreement on Civil Aviation, and the Additional Agreement. Both sides had agreed to keep secret the agreements on extraterritoriality, espionage cooperation, and the joint stock companies.

But Mao had one more trick up his sleeve. The signing ceremony was scheduled for the evening of the 14th followed by a great dinner celebration. At five o'clock in the morning of the 14th, however, Mao sent instructions to the Politburo deleting all mention of the Additional Agreement, and the Civil Aviation Agreement, and all references to Chinese commitment to repay the Soviet Union for the loan with "strategic raw materials."[47] Mao had decided to keep secret the Additional Agreement, which explicitly mentioned the United States as China's enemy and, equally importantly, contained his acquiescence in Stalin's demand that "China not allow citizens of third countries to settle or to carry out any industrial, financial, trade, or other related activities in Manchuria and Xinjiang."[48]

Outmaneuvered, and with no choice but to accede to Mao's wishes, Stalin was furious, and he vented his anger during the dinner following the signing ceremony. The Soviet leader devoted the majority of his banquet speech to indirectly putting Mao on notice, warning him against perfidy by vilifying Tito and Yugoslav treachery. The point was plain. Don't break ranks as Tito did and attempt to deal with the United States.

In reality, the treaty was the result of a year-long contest of move and countermove by Stalin and Mao, each attempting to promote the interests of his state as he saw them. Each sought to employ the relationship with the other as part of his respective foreign policy. Mao was moving on a course

99

that would be anathema to Stalin, who sought to head him off. Least of all was there any friendship between the two leaders. Still, for all of the back-stage maneuvering, the publication of the Sino-Soviet Treaty of Friendship, Alliance, and Mutual Assistance signaled a major event in international affairs. To the outside world, at least, China and the Soviet Union had committed to a thirty-year alliance against the West by forging a powerful "communist bloc." It was only to be expected that the two powers would put their strategic partnership to some use.

CHAPTER FIVE

Stalin Versus Mao, Korea or Taiwan: The Race to Strike First

STALIN PLOTS PREEMPTIVE WAR

From the turn of the year Stalin and Mao were actively engaged in preparations for coming conflict. Even as they were negotiating the treaty of friendship and alliance, Stalin and Mao were clandestinely assembling the military forces each hoped to employ preemptively against the other's objectives. Stalin was building up the North Korean Army for an invasion of the South, while Mao was marshaling his forces for an assault on Taiwan.

While negotiating the treaty at the end of January, Stalin, behind Mao's back, secretly arranged for Kim Il-sung to come to Moscow to work out joint preparations for the war. In a message of January 30, to Ambassador Shtykov, Stalin declared that he was "ready to grant approval" for war in Korea, although, he said, "an operation on such a large scale demands preparation. It is necessary to organize the operation in such a way as to minimize risk."[1]

Shtykov acted immediately and, in his reply cable of January 31, reported to Stalin that he had conveyed "your orders." Shtykov observed that "Kim Il-sung received my report with great satisfaction. Your agreement to receive him and your readiness to assist him in this matter made an especially strong impression." Kim was elated. Hardly able to contain himself, and "apparently wishing once more to reassure himself, [he] asked me if this means that it is possible to meet with Comrade Stalin on this question. I answered that from this communication it follows that Comrade Stalin is ready to receive you."[2]

Kim immediately began to think through the preparatory tasks. On the top of his list was the enlargement of his army. North Korea had seven divisions and Kim wanted to add three more for the coming assault. On February 4, Kim met with Shtykov again. Exploring ways to enlarge his army, he wanted to know if they could obtain a loan to finance "three additional infantry divisions?" He also wanted to know whether for the same purpose he could "use in 1950 the credit the Soviet government had allocated for 1951?"[3]

Kim also reported that they had decided to convene a session of the Supreme People's Assembly to discuss the 1950 budget, the national economic plan, and the criminal code. He added, in what was probably coded language referring to military matters, that he wished to send "a group of textile workers to the Soviet Union in order to prepare them to work on the Soviet equipment that is arriving." This was probably a reference to the training of tank drivers to drive the tanks Moscow was delivering. Stalin received Shtykov's telegram on February 7, and approved Kim's requests on the same day.

102

In subsequent discussion about payment terms, the Soviets prevailed upon Kim to defray the cost of the weapons by sending 9 tons of gold, 40 tons of silver, and 15,000 tons of monazite concentrate (for use in the Soviet nuclear program), a total value of 133,050,500 rubles.[4] Kim also decided to use 70 million rubles from the 1951 Soviet credit allocation for "arms, ammunition and military-technical equipment for the Korean People's Army."[5] Stalin replied to Kim on March 18, informing him that "the Soviet government has decided . . . to satisfy fully this request of yours" for "arms, ammunition and technical-equipment."[6]

Two days later, Stalin decided to bring Kim to Moscow. When Shtykov delivered this message, Kim requested that Pak Hon-yong accompany him. Reporting to Stalin, Shtykov noted that "they want to make the trip to Moscow and the meeting with Comrade Stalin unofficially, in the manner as in 1945."[7] In other words, they wished to make another secret trip. Stalin agreed, for it was his aim to keep Mao in the dark for as long as possible. Kim and Pak, accompanied by Ambassador Shtykov and interpreter Mun Il, left Pyongyang aboard a Soviet aircraft on March 30.[8] They remained in Moscow for almost four weeks, until April 25.

In Moscow, while making arrangements for the North Korean attack, Kim exhibited some ambivalence, which Stalin sought to dispel. Kim wondered how the people of South Korea would react to the invasion, observing that "he did not know how the people would respond to decisive measures in that direction." Stalin sought to reassure him with a tale from Greek mythology about Pan, god of goatherds and flocks. "The people are like a flock of sheep," Stalin said. "They would follow the leading ram wherever he might go." (Had Kim known his Greek mythology he would not have been reassured by Stalin's example. Pan was also the god of misadventures, one of which involved the amorous pursuit of the nymph Syrinx. Just as he was about to catch her at the river's edge, she was transformed into a tuft of reeds in his arms, leaving Pan empty-handed. The unification of Korea would prove equally elusive.)

But on this occasion Pak Hon-yong supported Stalin, saying that there was a "200,000-strong detachment of communists in South Korea . . . ready to rebel at the first signal from the North." In his view, "the population of the South was waiting for land reform and other democratic transformation such as those already conducted in the North."[9]

For all of his encouragement, however, Stalin made it quite plain that in the event things went wrong "the Korean friends should not expect great assistance and support from the Soviet Union, because it had more important challenges to meet than the Korean problem. . . . The situation in the West was very difficult and was occupying much of his time."[10] He told Kim that "if the United States participated in the war, the Soviet Union had no intention of fighting against the United States."[11] Then Stalin nudged Kim toward Mao, according to his plan. "The Korean friends," he said, "should consult more with Mao Zedong because he had a good understanding of Oriental matters."[12] Indeed, Stalin stated flatly: "If you should get kicked in the teeth [meaning if the United States entered the war and defeated the invasion], I shall not lift a finger. You have to ask Mao for all the help."[13]

The danger of American intervention was obvious and had been a part of every discussion about the war, but Kim, with Stalin's encouragement, had decided that it was a risk worth taking. The United States had severely pared its military power to the bone and had little in the way of actual military forces. Of a total of ten divisions, only one and a half were combat ready; of the four divisions deployed to Japan, none were combat ready, and all were under strength. The mighty nation that had fought a global conflict a brief five years before was no more, or so it seemed.

Even if the United States did intervene, Kim believed that his forces—qualitatively superior to both South Korean and American forces combined at this moment—would gain victory before the United States could mobilize to prevent it. Besides, did he not have the backing of the newly united communist world, which now also had the atomic bomb? Kim thus understood that while Stalin would equip his forces and plan the invasion, the war would be an all-Korean endeavor from which Moscow would stand back, in much the same way that the Soviets had aided China during the civil war. As the United States had not intervened in China, when the stakes were greater and it was strong, why should Washington intervene in Korea, when the stakes were so much smaller and it was much weaker?

Kim was determined. This was, after all, his opportunity of a lifetime to fulfill the dream of unifying his nation, an opportunity that might not ever come again. For the same reason, Kim would do no more than "consult" with

Mao. The Korean leader would not allow Mao to exercise any veto over his plans (nor, for that matter, would Stalin), disdainfully and repeatedly observing to his colleagues that "Mao Zedong is Mao Zedong and Kim Il-sung is Kim Il-sung": Mao was master in China, but Kim was master in North Korea.[14]

Stalin had wished to maintain the tightest secrecy, to keep not only South Korea and the United States ignorant of the war preparations, at least for the moment preserving the element of surprise, but also Mao Zedong, lest the Chinese leader move first. Keeping war preparations secret was most difficult and Mao seems to have deduced Stalin's plot. As reported in an April 10 cable from Ignatiev to Vyshinsky, just as Kim and Pak were preparing to depart for Moscow, the North Korean ambassador to China, Yi Chu-yon (Li Zhou-yuan), met with Mao and Zhou to discuss "the question of a meeting between Kim Il-sung and Mao Zedong."[15] Recall that Kim had proposed a meeting with Stalin or one with Mao in his January discussion with Shtykov. Yi's meeting with Mao was thus consistent with Kim's plans, if not Stalin's.

Mao agreed to meet with Kim Il-sung, but attempted to elicit from Ambassador Yi information regarding Kim's plans for war. In a remarkably transparent formulation, Mao proposed that "if there is a concrete plan for the unification of Korea, then the meeting should be organized secretly, but if there is not yet such a plan . . . then the meeting with Kim Il-sung can be conducted officially."[16] Yi said that he would convey this proposal to Kim, who was then "undergoing medical treatment." Medical treatment was the cover story to explain why Kim, who was in Moscow, was not available in Pyongyang to give a prompt answer, as Mao and Zhou deduced.

In another attempt to pry information from the North Korean ambassador, Mao declared that "if a third world war begins, Korea will not escape participation in it, therefore the Korean People's Democratic Republic should prepare its armed forces." Once again Yi was noncommittal and unable to give an answer, which raised Mao's suspicions. He was after all acutely sensitive to any indicators of war in Korea that could spoil his own plans. If Kim was meeting secretly with Stalin and keeping Mao in the dark, it could only be to prepare for war in Korea before Mao could attack Taiwan. There could be no other reason for a secret meeting that excluded Mao.

In late February, Stalin had sent another team of experienced and highly ranked advisers led by a Lieutenant General Vasiliev (a pseudonym) to Pyongyang to oversee war preparations.[17] Also, from the spring, the Soviet Union accelerated the shipment of military equipment to North Korea. "Deliveries of tanks, artillery, small arms, ammunition, medical supplies and oil from the USSR were stepped up."[18] At the same time, Stalin began to slow down deliveries to China for the Taiwan attack. However good or bad Mao's intelligence of Soviet deliveries to North Korea was, he was extremely sensitive to the implications of the slowdown of Soviet deliveries to China.

Did the slowdown in deliveries to China mean that Stalin was arranging for Korea first, Mao wondered? To test this hypothesis, in late April Zhou sent a cable to Soviet Defense Minister Nikolai Bulganin "requesting a speed-up in the delivery of such naval requisitions as ships, airplanes, and coastal artillery."[19] The reply, which is unavailable, undoubtedly alarmed Mao, because he immediately began to accelerate his own preparations.

Meanwhile, Stalin knew about the exchange between Mao and Yi, by virtue of Ignatiev's April 10 reporting cable to Vyshinsky, but declined to tell Kim, even though he was then in Moscow making preparations for the coming war. To tell Kim would only raise the question of why Mao was being kept in the dark, particularly after Stalin had urged him to consult and seek assistance from Mao. This would undoubtedly raise questions in Kim's own mind about his role in the whole affair. So Stalin remained silent, permitting Kim to assume that, in some way or other, Mao would support his war of liberation. But a week after Kim returned to Pyongyang, with war preparations well under way, Stalin casually informed Mao through Ambassador Roshchin that "Korean comrades visited us recently. I'll inform you shortly about the results of our conversations."[20]

Ironically, Stalin's decision not to inform Kim of his ambassador's meeting with Mao encouraged the Korean leader to attempt to deceive the Soviet dictator on the eve of his own meeting with Mao. Kim did not read the report of his ambassador's meeting with Mao and Zhou until after he returned from Moscow.[21] Nor, evidently, did he realize that Stalin had already received a report of this meeting from Ignatiev while he and Shtykov were in Moscow. This is the only explanation for Kim's attempt to mislead Stalin about Mao's views. When informing Shtykov about the meeting, Kim completely misrepresented what Mao had said to reinforce his own view of the coming conflict. A comparison of Ignatiev's April 10 and Shtykov's May 12 cables reveals Kim's ploy.

According to Ignatiev, Ambassador Yi had reported that Mao said: "If a third world war begins, Korea will not escape participation in it, therefore the Korean People's Democratic Republic should prepare its armed forces." In this report, although there is no direct mention of the United States, American military involvement on the Korean peninsula is clearly implied in the idea of a third world war from which Korea could not escape participation. According to Kim, on the other hand, what Mao said was that peaceful unification "is not possible, solely military means are required to unify Korea. As regards the Americans, there is no need to be afraid of them. The Americans will not enter a third world war for such a small territory." Thus,

Kim portrayed Mao as being completely supportive of the coming conflict and dismissive of the prospect of American involvement, when the opposite was the case.

Kim's intention was evidently to reinforce Stalin's decision for war by emphasizing Mao's support, which Stalin had directed him to obtain. Kim obviously assumed that to have revealed Mao's reservations would have placed Stalin's war decision in jeopardy. In fact, however, Stalin had successfully duped Kim. There is nothing in Kim's behavior to suggest that he suspected that Stalin was using him in a larger game, plotting behind Mao's back, or that there was any antagonism between Stalin and Mao. Kim seems to have assumed that Stalin had discussed the issue with Chinese leaders "at the same time or after the meetings with the Korean leaders."[22] Thus, Kim Il-sung was oblivious to the role he was to play in Stalin's race with Mao to strike first.

KIM IL-SUNG AND MAO ZEDONG

When Kim and Pak Hon-yong departed for Beijing on May 13, they fully expected to enlist Mao's support. Their trip would be completely secret, as only Politburo member Kim Chaek was told of their plans. Kim's intention was to "inform" Mao about the decision for war, the "results of the discussions on this question in Moscow," but not the start date because that had not yet been finally determined. Kim wanted to conclude a trade agreement with China "in the nearest future, but . . . sign an agreement on friendship after the unification of the country." He also wanted to establish "closer communications" between their two parties, and discuss questions of mutual interest.[23]

Kim had initially intended to ask Mao to supply the "ammunition for the Japanese and American arms which the divisions that arrived from China have," but, after discussions with his army chief of staff, decided against it. There was more than enough ammunition. He decided that "he doesn't have more requests for Mao about assistance, since all his requests were satisfied in Moscow and the necessary and sufficient assistance was given him there." In discussing his trip with Shtykov just before departure, Kim reported that "with regard to the question of the preparation of the operation he had given all necessary orders to the chief of the general staff, who already has begun to implement them, that his wish is to begin the operation in June, but he is still not convinced that they will manage it in this period."[24]

Kim and Pak arrived by plane on the evening of May 13 and promptly sat down to a late evening meeting with Mao Zedong and Zhou to convey "the directives of comrade Filippov [Stalin]." It was Stalin's view, they said, that "the present situation has changed from the situation in the past and that North Korea can move toward actions." However, Stalin also instructed that "this question should be discussed with China and personally with comrade Mao Zedong."[25] When Mao heard what Kim had to say he was stunned and outraged, although he disguised his reaction to the Koreans. For Mao, this was the first concrete indication that Stalin had decided on Korea first!

Immediately after their meeting, at 11:30 P.M., Mao sent Zhou to see Soviet Ambassador Roshchin to demand an immediate explanation from Stalin himself. Referring to Stalin's cable of May 3 promising to disclose the results of his conversations with Kim, Zhou insisted emphatically that "Mao Zedong would like to have [the] personal clarifications of comrade Filippov on this question." Stalin replied promptly, sending a cable at 4:10 the next morning, reinforcing the position expressed by Kim and Pak. "Filippov and his friends," he said, "expressed the opinion, that, in light of the changed international situation, they agree with the proposal of the Koreans to move toward reunification."[26]

What had Stalin meant by reference to "the changed international situation?" Was it to the implications inherent in the recent Soviet acquisition of the atomic bomb? Would Soviet possession of atomic weapons enable Stalin to deter the United States from supporting South Korea once the invasion began? Or was Stalin referring to the secret American decision of April 15 to rearm contained in NSC-68, of which he probably had knowledge from his extensive intelligence network? Did the Soviet leader seek to unify Korea before American rearmament was accomplished? Or was Stalin attempting to egg Mao on, secure in the knowledge that he would win the race to strike first? Did Stalin now want Mao to know of the coming attack and attempt to beat Kim Il-sung to the punch? If he did, would it not appear that the communists were mounting a coordinated attack against the West, even though that was not the case?

In typical Stalinesque style, the Soviet leader had imputed the "proposal" for war to the Koreans, to which he "and his friends" had agreed. Even though Stalin added the "qualification" that the question of war "should be decided finally by the Chinese and Korean comrades together, and in case of disagreement by the Chinese comrades the decision on the question should be postponed until a new discussion," Mao knew better. Whoever "proposed" the war, all knew that Stalin "disposed" on the matter, which, for Mao, meant that Stalin would very likely win the race to strike first, no matter what objections he raised.

And Mao did object, putting forth "various arguments" in hopes of persuading Kim to reconsider. As Marshal Peng Dehuai recalled, he vehemently disagreed with Kim's proposed action, "but he had no way of opposing or stopping it."[27] Mao raised the dire possibility of American intervention, "but Kim did not take it seriously."[28] The Korean leader insisted that "he would achieve victory within a month, and that the United States could not deploy its forces before then."[29] Nor was any Chinese assistance needed, he said. "Soviet assistance in hand or in the pipeline was all that would be needed." The NKA would "solve the Korean problem" on its own. After Kim's visit, Sino-Korean relations, as might be expected, became very tense in the weeks leading up to the outbreak of war.

Several points should be made regarding Kim Il-sung's trip to Beijing to meet Mao. It was not an attempt to secure Mao's support, but to present him with a fait accompli. Nor was Stalin's support for war in Korea in any way contingent upon Mao's agreement, which was not forthcoming. The Soviet Union had begun to escalate deliveries of war materiel to North Korea before the trip and deliveries continued to be made afterward. In this month before the outbreak of the war, Soviet equipment deliveries were made primarily by sea from Vladivostok to North Korean ports, not by land across Manchu-

ria, as would be the case once war broke out. As the North Korean head of logistics General Chung Sang-chin put it, this was done "for the specific purpose of denying the Chinese any hard intelligence about the North's preparations."

> . . . even before Mao gave his "approval" of Kim's intentions, the Soviet leader began to act. . . . "After [Kim's] April meeting with Stalin, Moscow . . . began to send additional weapons. As soon as Kim Il-sung returned home, the weapons began to arrive in huge numbers at the port of Chongjin. The quantities were obviously bigger than before. This was a final stage in the preparations for war. On arrival, the weapons were immediately distributed among the troops deployed along the 38th parallel."[30]

Once the conflict erupted, prisoner interrogations confirmed the prewar Soviet use of Chongjin as a major supply depot. As Roy Appleman notes:

> One captured North Korean supply officer stated that in May 1950, when he went to Chongjin to get supplies for the N. K. 5th Division, Soviet merchant ships were unloading weapons and ammunition, and that trucks crowded the harbor waterfront area. Korean-speaking crew members told him the ships had come from Vladivostok.[31]

Moreover, the size and extent of the delivery surge just prior to the invasion can be estimated with a fairly high degree of reliability. The Central Intelligence Agency issued a study of the *Current Capabilities of the Northern Korean Regime* on June 19, 1950, one week prior to the outbreak of the war. The study, however, was based on data available to the agency only as of May 15. Comparing the CIA's estimate of NKA strength with what is known of weapons inventories on June 25 gives a reasonably close estimate of the surge in Soviet weapons deliveries over the final month before the outbreak of the conflict. Indeed, the CIA estimate omits any mention of Soviet weapons deliveries even while describing North Korea as "a firmly controlled Soviet Sat-ellite that exercises no independent initiative and depends entirely on the support of the USSR for existence."

The CIA estimated the strength of the NKA at 66,000 men, augmented by a paramilitary Border Constabulary of 20,500 men. Both forces were be-ing "expanded with ex-Manchurian levies." Although the report grossly underestimated the size of the forces transferred from China at 16,000, it noted that "an additional sixty to seventy thousand Koreans who have seen service with the Chinese Communists . . . are believed to be available in Manchuria if needed." The CIA evaluated the total size of the North Korean armed force to be "at least three infantry divisions and an independent bri-gade."[32] (At that moment it was already a seven-division force that would grow to ten by the end of June.)

The report identified "an armored unit, estimated to possess 65 Soviet T-34 tanks" (there were sixty-five tanks to a Soviet brigade), and an unde-termined number of 76mm self-propelled guns and 122mm howitzers. (The normal complement of these weapons per division was twelve 122mm and twenty-eight 76mm guns, which, for a three-division-plus force would amount to around 150 guns.) The air force consisted of 1,500 men, 150 pilots, forty-five Yak-9 and IL-10 fighters, three twin-engine bombers, two trans-port aircraft, thirty-five training planes, and anti-aircraft units in the border regions. Finally, the North Korean navy of 5,100 men was mainly "a coast guard force," whose "shore installations and ships are of little conse-quence."[33]

Despite the fact that the CIA believed that North Korea's forces possessed a superiority over the South in "armor, heavy artillery, and aircraft," and that "as presently constituted . . . have a capability for attaining limited ob-jectives in short-term military operations . . . including the capture of Seoul," there was no expression of alarm or warning of imminent attack. That was because the forces of north and south were seen to be "nearly equal in terms of combat effectives, training, and leadership." Indeed, the report concluded that it was "not certain that the northern regime . . . would be able to gain effective control over all of southern Korea" without the active participation of Soviet and Chinese military units, which was believed to be unlikely.[34]

But North Korea began the war with a much larger force than contained in the CIA estimate. Citing Soviet data, Goncharov, Lewis, and Xue report that when hostilities commenced on June 25 the North had ten infantry di-visions, 258 tanks, 1,600 artillery and mortar weapons, and 178 planes.[35] We have already discussed Stalin's decision to authorize the enlargement of the NKA by three divisions. Except for the number of tanks, this estimate is con-sistent with U.S. military estimates. A South Korean estimate gave the North

183 tanks on June 25, a number nearly more than three times as large as that estimated by the CIA in mid-May, although Moscow would supply more once the war began.[36]

Thus, in the month and a half before the war began, it would be fair to conclude that the Soviet Union doubled the number of North Korean planes, tripled its infantry divisions, more than doubled and possibly even quadrupled the number of tanks, and massively increased the NKA's artillery and mortar capability. What had been essentially a "defensive-type army," in Appleman's characterization, and, as late as mid-May had caused no undue alarm in the CIA, had suddenly been transformed into a massive strike force of overwhelming superiority by the end of June.

Following Kim's return from Moscow, Stalin's trusted team of military advisers, headed by Generals Vasiliev, Postnikov, and Marchenko, began to draft the war plan.[37] In early May, they discarded the North Korean invasion plan because, they said, it was "a defensive one," and set about to "draft one themselves."[38] After drafting the new plan they passed it on to Kang Kon, chief of the NKA general staff. General Kang, in turn, ordered the chief of the Operations Bureau, General Yu Song-chol, to translate it from the Russian, in which it was titled the "Preemptive Strike Operational Plan."

Yu quickly translated it and a small select group of Korean leaders discussed it among themselves. According to Yu: "Everyone who participated in this project was a Soviet-born Korean. The Yenan faction individuals who had entered various military positions were excluded from this effort because . . . we had to maintain security," that is, keep Mao ignorant of their plans.[39] The small group that discussed the Soviet-drawn invasion plan included: Kim Il-sung himself; the Minister of Defense, Choe Yong-gon; NKA Chief of Staff Kang Kon; Deputy Chief Kim Chaek; and Politburo member Ho Ka-yi. Also involved were key operational commanders: Chief of Armor Command, Major General Kim Pong-yul; Chief of Artillery Command, Major General Chong Hak-chun; the Chief of the Engineering Bureau, Senior Colonel Pak Il-nam; and the Chief of Operations, General Yu. All took an "oath of secrecy."

It is evident that Stalin was now in a hurry. Soviet advisers drew up the invasion plan in a mere "three or four days." Moreover, according to Yu, "they did not consult with anybody. They did everything themselves. They did not study the terrain and did not know it. . . . Because of that, they made a lot of mistakes."[40] The reason for Stalin's haste, as will be shown below, was that Mao was rapidly preparing for the assault on Taiwan, despite Stalin's refusal to provide the equipment Mao needed. The effect of the hasty invasion planning, however, was to cause immediate dissension at the very pinnacle of the North Korean leadership.

The North Korean regime was composed of three main factions: the dominant Manchurian (pro-Soviet) faction, led by Kim Il-sung, Choe Yong-gon, and Kim Chaek; the Yenan (pro-Chinese) faction, led by Kim Tu-bong, Pak Il-yu, and Mu Chong; and the domestic faction, led by Pak Hon-yong. The Soviet and domestic factions were ascendant over the Yenan faction as reflected in the Kim Il-sung–Pak Hon-yong coalition. Their supporters staffed the majority of high-level positions, while the Yenan men occupied second-level command positions. The Yenan men were, however, as Yu Song-chol noted above, completely excluded from the decision to go to war.

The principal opponent of the war was none other than Minister of Defense Choe Yong-gon. Choe was one of the senior members of the Korean Communist movement, and from the pro-Soviet Manchurian faction. Choe would in fact hold the defense post in the Pyongyang regime from the time of its founding until his death in 1976. His name appears on all important documents issued by the Ministry of Defense during these years—except for the crucial months between late April and August 1950, when orders relating to the war were issued by Vice Minister of Defense Mu Chong, of the pro-Chinese group.[41] Choe would resume an active role only after the North Korean offensive had failed, in late August.

Choe disagreed with the decision to go to war and for that reason was antipathetic to the Soviet war planning team. He subsequently withdrew from active participation in the planning and conduct of the war through mid-August, and during this period his duties were assumed by others. Choe's inactivity coincided with the arrival of Vasiliev's war planning team. American intelligence believed at the time that Choe "was opposed to the invasion of South Korea and to the new group of Soviet military advisers" for reasons evidently associated with the war plan.[42] The Soviet plan called for an assault across the 38th parallel and the seizure of Seoul, but offered little detail beyond. Furthermore the plan discounted the likelihood of American intervention. Head of the Operations Bureau Yu Song-chol also believed that Choe "opposed an all-out war, pointing to the possibility that the United States would intervene."[43] More will be said about the Soviet-designed war plan and its implications in chapter 9.

Choe's opposition to the war led Vasiliev to bypass him during the weeks leading up to the war and prompted Kim Il-sung to reorganize the high command around him once the war broke out. Kim did name Choe as one of the seven-man military council set up on June 26, although he was not active on it at the outset of the conflict. Kim Il-sung named himself Supreme Commander on July 1, effectively assuming Choe's role, and named Kim Chaek Battlefield Commander and Kang Kon Chief of Staff. Choe thus had no operational role during the early months of the offensive, a fact supported by the absence of combat orders issued by him. The chain of military command thus passed from Kim Il-sung to Kim Chaek and Kang Kon, bypassing Choe.

Kim Il-sung was not hesitant in purging those with whom he had disagreements. The list is long.[44] But Choe was not purged, as might have been expected on an issue of this magnitude, although Kim appears to have been preparing to remove his defense minister. Just after naming himself Supreme Commander, Kim Il-sung transferred "all of Choe's executive staff within the defense ministry . . . to the newly created Front Headquarters." Choe, in effect, became "a minister without any subordinates" and ripe for removal.[45] But Stalin saved him, instructing Kim Il-sung that "the Minister of National Defense will remain in his post. He will manage the formation of new units and the organization of anti-[amphibious?] landing defense, and also supply troops with everything needed."[46]

The reasons for Stalin's actions are obscure, but to purge the Minister of Defense at the very outset of the war would clearly have a negative impact throughout. Choe, Kim Chaek, and Kim Il-sung were the original troika of the pro-Soviet Manchurian faction. To remove Choe would reveal disagreement at the highest levels of the leadership over the war, clearly weaken the army command, and undermine Kim's own power base. Furthermore, once the fortunes of war turned, Choe's military experience would be put to good use in attempting to organize a defense against advancing U.N. forces. He would take command of the Defensive Headquarters in mid-August.

According to Yu Song-chol, "we formulated an operational plan at the end of about one month's work." Yu himself "completed the final composite of the plan" in early June, presumably at which time the date for the invasion was established.[47] Yu thought that the reason for choosing June 25 was "because that was when the South Korean National Defense Forces would be at their weakest, with soldiers on pass and guard duty being lax."[48] He also said that the date "was proposed by the [Soviet] advisers. It was Sunday, and they may have used the experience of war with Germany, when Hitler attacked Russia on . . . a Sunday."[49] Pearl Harbor, too, was attacked on a Sunday.

According to Shtykov, in a top-secret report on the military situation the day after the war began, the concentration of NKA units near the 38th parallel "began on June 12 and was concluded on June 23." Shtykov noted that "the planning of the operation at the divisional level and the reconnaissance of the area was carried out with the participation of Soviet advisers." He also thought it probable that "the intelligence service of the enemy . . . detected the troop redeployment, but we managed to keep the plan and the time of the beginning of troop operations secret."[50]

Troop deployments were carried out under the guise of troop training exercises combined with a propaganda campaign proposing the peaceful unification of the peninsula. As Yu notes, "we had put a particular amount of effort into concealing this large-scale troop movement as training. To do this, we passed bogus mobility training plans not via encoded communications, as is normally done, but rather through plain-text wire communications." To make the deception convincing, "even training evaluation reports were passed in plain-text via wire. We even rewarded some units for training well, while punishing other units for being lax in their training discipline. Of course, the South had monitored such exchanges of messages."[51]

When North Korea began military operations at 4:40 A.M. on June 25, Stalin had not only triggered a major war, he had beaten Mao Zedong in the race to strike first. But having beaten Mao to the punch did not mean that the Chinese leader would conform meekly to Stalin's preemptive move. Mao would attempt to keep open the prospect for an assault on Taiwan even after the Korean War began. Only the gradual revelation of the new American strategy, North Korea's collapse, and the Chinese decision to enter into the Korean conflict would finally close off any hopes Mao may have had for the seizure of Taiwan, the defeat of Chiang Kai-shek, the completion of the Chinese revolution, and the opening to the United States.

113

MAO: BETWEEN THE DEVIL AND THE DEEP BLUE STRAIT

Like Stalin in his decision for war in Korea, even as Mao was negotiating the Sino-Soviet treaty he was giving the go-ahead for action against Taiwan. Mao was attempting to mount a preemptive assault against Taiwan before war could come in Korea, although he appears to have let Stalin believe that the attack would be contingent upon receipt of weaponry, especially aircraft, from the Soviet Union. There was a credible basis for Mao's attempted deception. The Chinese Communist defeats at Jinmen and Dengbu had clearly demonstrated the decisive value of air power and the folly of attempting an amphibious assault without it.

But Mao could not permit Stalin to control the initiative. He fully understood the strategic significance of "Who first?" and would not wait for Stalin to keep his promise of supplying the aircraft, assault ships, and coastal artillery that Mao had ordered. He would attack Taiwan with what he had on hand, assuming that Chiang's forces could not mount a successful defense without American aid. Mao continued to assume that Washington would not support Chiang, an assumption reinforced by the absence of any subsequent indications that Truman had changed policy.

Mao had designated General Su Yu to command the assault on Taiwan. Su's analysis led him to conclude that the assault was feasible and that the United States would not protect Chiang Kai-shek. General Su had delivered his "Report on the Problem of Liberating Taiwan and Establishing Military Forces," on January 27.[52] Mao was convinced and on February 4, while still in Moscow, he ordered the formation of paratroop units for the assault. They would be transported in the several cargo planes the Communists had captured from the Nationalists. Then, on February 10, a few days before he signed the Sino-Soviet treaty, Mao authorized Su Yu to "deploy four divisions in naval operation maneuvers."[53]

Administering final defeat to the Nationalists, however, would not be an easy task. Having retreated to Taiwan, ninety miles off the China coast, Chiang had constructed an island fortress buttressed by several hundred thousand troops, over four hundred planes, and seventy ships.[54] Hoping beyond hope that the United States would change policy and support the Nationalist government once again, Chiang had deployed forces on close-in islands from Shanghai to Canton in an attempt to deflect any attack on Taiwan, control movement along the China coast, launch raids on the mainland, and act as intelligence-gathering centers. Thus far, he had successfully beaten back all attempts to take these positions.

114

On Hainan Island, under General Hsueh Yueh, there were five corps, two divisions, and several air and naval units, some forty thousand troops in all. During the month of March, Hsueh Yueh's men had repulsed several small-scale attempts by forces under the command of Lin Biao to take the island.[55] Chiang had also deployed forces to the islands of Lintin and Mansan off Canton, Tungshan off Fukien, Jinmen off Amoy, Matsu off Foochow, Dazhen off Jejiang, and Zhoushan off Shanghai. Most heavily fortified were Jinmen and Zhoushan, where Chiang had deployed seventy thousand and one hundred thousand troops, respectively.

Not only were Chiang's ground forces in control of key points off the China coast, but his air force and navy were also largely intact and had dealt telling blows in repelling the PLA's attacks on Jinmen and Dengbu in late 1949, as we have seen. Nationalist ships were carrying out attacks on Communist coastal shipping and controlled the sea approaches to Shanghai; Chiang's planes were carrying out periodic bombing raids against China's coastal cities, especially Shanghai, Nanking, and Xuzhou, using island airstrips as forward bases. Indeed, Nationalist air attacks had become sufficiently worrisome to generate a response from Moscow.

From mid-February to early March, amid proclamations of undying unity following the signing of the Sino-Soviet treaty, the Soviet Union deployed several air regiments of MIG-15s and anti-aircraft batteries to Shanghai, Nanking, and Xuzhou to provide air defense against the Nationalist bombing campaign. Stalin, no doubt, relished the prospect of tantalizing Mao with the deployment of some of the world's most modern jet aircraft to China, just what Mao needed most for his assault against Taiwan. But Stalin kept these weapons just out of his reach. The entire air defense operation was controlled by the Soviets, including some 1,500 Russian pilots, crews, and ground technicians.[56] The MIGs, in their first appearance in Northeast Asia in April, downed five Nationalist planes, but Mao was denied the employment of these aircraft for his own purposes.[57]

After returning to Beijing, on March 11 Mao authorized former Nationalist General Chang Chih-chung to offer a negotiated surrender, the so-called "peaceful liberation" of Taiwan, while at the same time conducting a major propaganda campaign touting the inevitable and imminent assault on the island. The end of March, recall, saw Mao's and Zhou's meeting with North Korean Ambassador Yi Chu-yon and the likely deduction that Stalin and Kim were meeting secretly in Moscow. Their clandestine meeting could only have meant one thing: war was imminent in Korea. But could Mao strike first? More important, if he struck, could he succeed in the face of Nationalist air and naval superiority?

Mao quickly authorized plans for another attempt to seize Jinmen and Dengbu as well as for stepped-up operations against Hainan Island off China's southern coast—as a prelude to the assault against Taiwan. Mao and the Chinese leadership must have been driven to a frenzy following the unsatisfactory reply to Zhou's cable in late April to Soviet Defense Minister Nikolai Bulganin that requested an acceleration of the delivery of naval requisitions that Stalin had promised.[58] The slowdown clearly signified that Stalin had no intention of assisting Mao to conquer Taiwan.

Judging by the virtually nationwide effort to commandeer urgently needed financial resources, Mao was in a panic. He intensified the propaganda campaign proclaiming the "liberation of Taiwan" and instructed Party organizations in East China "to provide all necessary assistance in preparations for the Third Field Army to cross the Taiwan Strait." One form of "assistance" was a massive effort to bleed local business and banking interests through "impossible tax and bond demands," which were crippling the economy. As the outgoing U.S. consul in Shanghai observed: "Bond collecting methods creating near state terror, with collectors ... taking line that all must contribute in order to raise funds for conquest of Taiwan."[59] Mao was clearly less concerned about reconstructing the economy than he was with taking Taiwan.

The need to squeeze all available resources, it seems, reached into the PLA itself. On April 21, Mao issued orders for the large-scale demobilization of the People's Liberation Army—a demobilization that, as it turned out, did not occur. As Communist forces had largely completed ground actions in gaining control of mainland China, their very large army of 5.4 million men was clearly unnecessary and a growing drain on state coffers. Demobilization could shift resources from military operations to reconstruction as well as obtain needed resources for other investment. The basic concept of cutting 1.4 million men from the PLA was to improve the quality of the force, and shift resources, as Nie Rongzhen put it, "to construct our air force and navy," for the obvious tasks at hand—the seizure of the offshore islands, first and foremost, then Taiwan.[60]

On the night of April 16, Lin Biao's Fortieth and Forty-second Armies aboard four hundred sampans and motorized junks crossed the shallow, fifteen-mile strait separating Hainan Island from the mainland to launch a large-scale invasion, without air or naval support, but in coordination with guerrilla forces in the island interior. Although suffering extensive losses, by one estimate amounting to around 10,000 men, by the morning of the 19th, Communist forces had lodged in force on the north coast.[61] Nationalist forces, after what was termed "dispirited resistance," withdrew from Hainan's capital city of Huichow to the southern tip of the island where they were evacuated to Formosa. The PLA conquest of Hainan had taken less than a week, but it had been misleadingly easy.

116

Just as the battle was beginning, Chiang Kai-shek had decided to alter his strategy from a widely dispersed defense of the close-in islands to a concentrated defense of Taiwan and Jinmen. The reason for his change in policy lay not in the quality or morale of his troops, nor in the strength of the PLA, but in a decision in Washington. Military attachés in Hong Kong and Taipei thought that Nationalist military forces had "repeatedly shown the will to fight" and that the Chinese navy and air force were "doing their most effective work since the end of World War II with morale and reliability the highest in years." However, they pointed out that "present stocks of ship and aircraft ammunition and maintenance parts will be exhausted within a few months at the present rate of military activity."[62]

Chiang had reassumed the presidency on March 1, believing that the Sino-Soviet treaty signified the failure of Washington's attempts to come to terms with Beijing. He hoped that the Truman administration would revert to its earlier policy of support for the Nationalist government as part of a broader effort to contain China and the Soviet Union in the Western Pacific. Chiang also knew there were those within the U.S. administration who supported such a change in policy, if only to deny Taiwan to the Communist Chinese on military grounds. Secretary of Defense Louis Johnson, Supreme Commander Allied Powers, Japan, General Douglas MacArthur, and Commander in Chief of the Pacific Fleet, Admiral Arthur Radford, had taken this position, among others.

To test the waters, or perhaps to force the issue, on March 7 Chiang forwarded to the Department of State an application for export licenses to purchase twenty-four Sherman tanks and twenty-five F-80 jet aircraft. The Nationalist government proposed to pay for the jets from its own funds and pay for the tanks from what remained of the $125 million allocated for military assistance under section 404 (b) of the China Aid Act of 1948.[63]

On April 14, citing President Truman's January 5 policy pronouncement that "the United States Government will not provide military aid or advice to Chinese forces on Formosa," Secretary of State Acheson ruled against the application. Acheson enjoined Secretary of Defense Johnson to "discontinue procurement for the Chinese Government or the transfer of military materiel from U.S. Government stocks to the Chinese Government." Furthermore, he added, "the President's statement would also appear to require that no assistance or advice be given to the Chinese Government in their purchase of any other military materiel," although Washington would "allow for Chinese Government purchases of military materiel in the American commercial market with its own funds."[64]

In short, the U.S. position of January 5, formally disengaging from the Nationalist government, remained unchanged. Reaffirmation of that policy, it would seem, was the catalyst for Chiang's decision to pull his forces back from all forward island positions, except for Jinmen and Matsu, which lay directly in the path of any invasion attempt. Chiang needed to prepare for the imminent assault on Taiwan. Thus, when the PLA attacked Hainan Island on April 16, Nationalist forces did not put up much of a fight and instead withdrew to Formosa. Then, two weeks later, when Communist forces mobilized for another assault on Dengbu in the Zhoushan islands, Chiang evacuated his entire one-hundred-thousand-man force between May 10 and 16. The PLA took the Zhoushan islands without firing a shot and turned to prepare for an attack on Taiwan itself.[65]

The crucial decision had come from Washington. When Acheson denied the aid request, Chiang Kai-shek knew that the Communist-Nationalist struggle had come down to a battle of financial and military attrition. It served no purpose to allow the Communists to defeat his forces piecemeal on isolated outposts, so he concentrated his forces. No matter how difficult the problem of an amphibious landing on Taiwan was, and no matter how determined the defenders were, the simple fact was that without U.S. support the Nationalists could only hold out for so long against a foe determined to seize the island, for at some point the defenders would run out of weapons, ammunition, and money. (Nor did Chiang know that the modern jet planes defending Chinese cities against his propeller-driven bombers would not be used in an assault against Taiwan.)

The chargé d'affaires in Taipei, Robert Strong, interpreted the pullbacks to mean that the "fate of Taiwan [was] sealed" and that "Communist resources can now be concentrated against Taiwan solely (whether Jinmen is evacuated or not)." Earlier, the CIA had estimated that the Communist assault would come later "during the period June–December."[66] But with the evacuation of the Zhoushans, Strong now believed it would come much sooner, "between June 15 and [the] end [of] July."[67]

117

Indeed, over the course of the next month, Mao marshaled his forces for the assault. Based in part on their experience gained from the Hainan invasion, Mao's generals had assembled a flotilla of 4,000 motorized wooden junks, in some cases lashing several together to promote seaworthiness, to ferry his invasion force across the Taiwan Strait. The junks, slow but virtually unsinkable, were fitted with 40mm guns for anti-air and anti-ship defense.[68]

Mao was exerting all efforts to get his force ready for an immediate attack. He was moving his forces to the coast in preparation for embarkation to Taiwan, just as Stalin was shipping mountains of munitions to North Korea for their attack. Secretary of Defense Johnson, who had traveled to Tokyo for a week's visit (June 17–23) to discuss the situation with MacArthur, noted in testimony before Congress that between the time he and General Omar Bradley "went to the Far East and our return, 12 or 14 days, the troops opposite Formosa had been increased from less than 40,000 to about 156,000."[69]

As noted above, North Korean forces had begun to concentrate along the 38th parallel on June 12. Two days later, in a cable to Su Yu and Third Army commanders, Mao exhorted them to "pay attention to the problem of seizing Taiwan immediately."[70] Mao's exhortation to seize Taiwan immediately just as North Korean forces began to concentrate along the parallel suggests that Mao had better intelligence regarding decision-making in Pyongyang than is evident from the record. And Secretary Johnson's admission that U.S. intelligence was carefully watching the Chinese buildup along the China coast indicates a much better appreciation for the impending attack than has hitherto been admitted.

American intelligence expected Mao to attack between mid-June and the end of July, but Stalin's proxy in Pyongyang beat him to the punch by starting the war on June 25. Prior to the Korean attack, however, American leaders were in a quandary, not knowing who would win the race to strike first. Their quandary arose out of the fact that the United States had changed its strategy and was no longer willing to permit the Communist Chinese to seize Taiwan. NSC-68 meant a retention of Taiwan in the American sphere. The earlier quid pro quo of exchanging Taiwan for Chinese independence from Moscow had been discarded. Thus, as Mao and Stalin raced to strike first at their respective targets, the quandary for the United States was, how to keep Taiwan out of Mao's hands if he won the race?

CHAPTER SIX

Truman's Dilemma and the Decision to Change Strategy

AMERICAN LEADERS watched intently as the Soviet–North Korean buildup accelerated along the 38th parallel and the Chinese marshaled their forces for a cross-strait assault on Taiwan. The pace of events over the previous six months had greatly accelerated and would be the determining factor governing the timing and content of policy. They, too, pondered the implications of "Who first?" for, in its own way, the question posed as much of a dilemma for Truman as it did for Mao and Stalin. Anticipating the coming conflict, or conflicts, the United States had secretly changed strategy after China had entered into an alliance with the Soviet Union. In NSC-68 of April 15, 1950, the Truman administration had decided to rebuild U.S. military power, including its nuclear component, and to extend European containment to Asia around the entire periphery of the new communist alliance area.

STRATEGY AND CONSEQUENCES

The U.S. decision had profound implications for Taiwan and Mao's attempt to administer a final defeat to the Nationalist government. Since NSC-41, February 28, 1949, the United States under Secretary of State Dean Acheson had attempted to develop a diplomatic relationship with the emerging Communist regime in China in an effort to wean Beijing into an independent stance vis-à-vis the Soviet Union, the wedge strategy. Washington's final effort to build a relationship with Beijing had occurred in early January 1950, with the attempt to communicate the offer contained in NSC-48. That offer had included the public announcement of Washington's decision to wash its hands of the Nationalist government and acquiesce in the Chinese seizure of Taiwan, as a prelude to the establishment of relations.

When Mao and the Chinese leadership declined the American offer, instead deciding to pursue an alliance with Moscow, the United States had no choice but to change strategy, for the Sino-Soviet alliance marked the failure of the strategy of attempting to keep the Soviet Union and China apart. A new strategy would have to take into account the high probability that the two communist powers would collaborate against the United States. Indeed, the new strategy, NSC-68, anticipated a crisis in the near term and called for the affirmative mobilization of the noncommunist world against the communist bloc.

The change in strategy dictated that Taiwan must now be held, however distasteful American leaders found Chiang Kai-shek. Aside from the political significance of the Kuomintang as a noncommunist ally of the United States, the island of Formosa stood at the mid-point of the U.S. defense perimeter in the Western Pacific. The entire China coast lay within easy reach from the island, with no point farther than 1,100 miles away. In addition, the island stood astride the main sea lanes connecting Japan with Southeast Asian markets and Middle East fuel supplies.

Thus the control of Taiwan by a hostile power would severely weaken the U.S. position in the Western Pacific. U.S. bases in the Philippines, Okinawa, and Japan would be within easy reach of a hostile power in control of the island. Retention of access to the island would enable the United States to build a formidable and sustainable security structure in the region, closing the ring of containment in the Pacific. Taiwan logistically was the cork in the bottle, the strategic linchpin; therefore, the United States would retain the island, if need be, with Chiang Kai-shek in control of it.

In retrospect, high-level political and personnel changes implicitly signaled the change in policy. At the end of March, Acheson removed Walton Butterworth, who personified the accommodation with China strategy, as director of the Office of Far Eastern Affairs, and replaced him with Dean Rusk, who expressed a more tolerant attitude toward the Nationalist government on Taiwan. Shortly thereafter, in early April, following a public pledge by President Truman and Republican Senator Arthur Vandenberg to pursue a bipartisan foreign policy, Acheson named the tough-minded John Foster Dulles as a "top adviser" to the State Department and six weeks later placed him in charge of negotiating the Japanese peace treaty. At the same time, department officials formerly sympathetic to the Chinese Communists expressed "revised" opinions.[1]

Under the new strategy, another place where the United States must hold its ground was in Korea, an obvious focal point where Chinese, Soviet, and

American interests converged. Indeed, it was the only place on earth where such a convergence existed. This fact was well understood by American leaders, if not by the general public. There, a line had already been drawn and had to be held. The Republic of South Korea was, after all, the creation of the United States and the United Nations. Its defeat at the hands of the Soviet-built armies of North Korea would amount to a major defeat in the rapidly evolving Cold War struggle between East and West. But more than Cold War prestige was involved.

The defeat of an American client and ally would reverberate throughout the United States' global alliance structure and raise questions regarding the steadfastness of the United States, not least in Tokyo, without question the most important of Washington's Asian allies, and still without a fixed treaty tie to the United States. Furthermore, Washington's linkage of the Republic of Korea with the United Nations would also undermine the utility of that organization if Seoul should fall to northern invaders. Yet, compared to its behavior toward other areas, Washington was curiously ambivalent in its policies toward the Republic of Korea in the months preceding the outbreak of war, even as American leaders saw the war clouds forming. The subject of Washington's policy toward South Korea will be treated in depth in the next chapter.

As American leaders watched the military buildups along the 38th parallel and on the China coast across from Taiwan, however, the implications of Mao striking first were most alarming. Under its new but still secret strategy, the United States would not permit Taiwan to fall to Communist conquest and, if the Nationalist regime were about to fall, would come to its aid, an outcome that ipso facto would rescue Chiang Kai-shek. This, of course, would also raise the prospect not only of a war with China, but also, because of the Sino-Soviet treaty, of a potential war with the Soviet Union, or global war. Before the outbreak of the Korean War resolved this dilemma, therefore, U.S. leaders explored ways of quietly providing additional military and political assistance to Taiwan, removing Chiang Kai-shek, and placing the island under U.N. trusteeship. But providing military assistance would also strengthen Chiang, making his removal ever more difficult.

When war broke out in Korea first, the United States was absolved of the necessity of making an unpalatable choice. Instead, Washington would connect what up to then had been separate issues. Within two days of the outbreak of war in Korea, President Truman revealed that not only would the United States enter the war in Korea as the leader of a U.N. defense force, but also that Washington would not permit a Chinese conquest of Formosa. In short, American entry into the Korean War permitted the United States to prevent a Chinese attack on Taiwan in the context of securing the Korean flank. This chapter will trace the change in American strategy, and some of the political, military, and intelligence preparations prior to the outbreak of the Korean War, including Washington's response to the growing dilemma over Taiwan.

THE QUESTION OF FOREKNOWLEDGE

The Chinese decision to enter into a long-term alliance with the Soviet Union was grounds enough to recast American strategy, but it may have been advance warning of probable conflict in Korea that gave urgency to the decision to begin the process of change. President Truman's twofold decision on January 31 to begin a high-priority feasibility study regarding production of thermonuclear weapons (which was in reality a decision to proceed with their production and development) and to initiate formulation of a new geopolitical strategy, came less than forty-eight hours after Stalin had sent a telegram to Kim Il-sung granting his approval for war in Korea (see chapter 5, p. 101). Once again, as in the instance of Mao's December 19 telegram to Liu, which U.S. intelligence may also have intercepted (chapter 2, pp. 45–46), an important American decision followed hard upon a decision communicated by the other side.[2]

The juxtaposition of decisions suggests that American intelligence had broken Soviet codes, providing advance warning of coming events. In fact, in the spring of 1948, the Army Security Agency, precursor of the National Security Agency, in cooperation with the FBI, had achieved a major breakthrough in its effort to break Soviet codes.[3] Special agent Robert Lamphere's memoir, describing the breakthrough, focuses only on the domestic, counter-intelligence side of the story, but the extensive cooperation that he recounts between the FBI and ASA strongly suggests an at-least-as-large and probably larger effort on the foreign intelligence side. Indeed, as he notes,

> I can now tell enough of the story so that anyone reading this account will comprehend the magnitude of the breakthrough that the deciphered KGB messages provided.... In the best possible scenario, the enemy would never know of our penetration; we would learn in advance his every move, though, and we would achieve the ultimate counter-intelligence goal, complete control of the enemy's moves against us.[4]

To restate, the Sino-Soviet alliance was itself necessary and sufficient grounds to persuade American leaders to change strategy. The thesis presented here does not hinge on the issue of codebreaking. It is entirely possible, even though I believe unlikely, that no codes were broken and that American and Soviet decision chains were parallel but separate. It is beyond question, however, that the United States was expending a great effort on intercepting and decrypting Soviet communications—and, no doubt, Chinese and North Korean communications, too, and that a significant measure of success had been achieved. Knowledge of Stalin's decision to authorize conflict in Korea would account for the timing of the study that became renowned as the strategic directive that would govern U.S. policy for over two decades.

From early January, even before Truman's decision to formulate a new strategy, the administration moved to tighten control over and access to intelligence information, particularly with regard to the very broad category defined as "communications intelligence." On January 6, 1950, the National Security Council issued Intelligence Directive No. 11, designed to protect "sources and methods" of intelligence collection. The same day, the NSC also issued Intelligence Directive No. 12, which instructed all departments of the government to "take steps to prevent the unauthorized disclosure . . . of any information concerning intelligence or intelligence activities."[5]

In early March, as the drafting of NSC-68 was under way, the NSC established the "communications intelligence board," which was authorized to control access to all intelligence "produced by the study of foreign communications." The board's mandate was "to effect the authoritative coordination of the Communication Intelligence activities of the Government." In a self-serving tautology, communications intelligence was defined as "all intelligence based in whole or in part on communications intelligence." To leave no room for obfuscation, communications intelligence activities were seen to comprise:

> all processes involved in the collection, for intelligence purposes, of foreign communications, the production of information from such communications, the dissemination of that information and the control of the protection of that information and the security of its sources.[6]

One of the most curious aspects of the period leading up to the outbreak of the Korean War was the nearly total press blackout and disregard by American leaders of numerous specific, tactical, battlefield intercepts warning of a North Korean attack, and the comparatively voluminous secret *and public* warnings of a Chinese Communist assault on Taiwan.

New York Times press accounts and diplomatic cable traffic from Washington's Pacific outposts monitored the Chinese force buildup for the cross-strait assault from the beginning of the year. For example, in early January, Walter McConaughy, the consul general at Shanghai, noted the "dramatic crescendo of publicity and preparations demonstrating [the] new regime's irrevocable determination to 'liberate' Taiwan [which] has been a major feature of this political scene [in] recent months."[7] McConaughy emphasized the relative enormity of the effort.

While Department doubtless has fuller information, Consulate General's information at least sufficient to indicate clearly that effort and expenditure have gone and will go into Chinese Communists 'Operation Taiwan' . . . on scale which for Communists must be relatively as great as invasion [of] North Africa was for Western Allies. Fleets are being built and assembled, oil stocked, armies trained, soldiers taught to swim, etc. Large proportions of nation's budget and army specifically allocated to project.

Writing from Taipei, *New York Times* reporter Burton Crane detailed expectations for an invasion before August. Citing "informed persons," Crane noted the belief that the Chinese Communists would attack Formosa "before August, provided they manage to capture Hainan and provided they are not smashed too badly in doing so." The Communists, he said, were "thoroughly committed" to the conquest of the Nationalists' island bastion. "Intelligence reports" indicated that they were "throwing every resource into preparations for the invasion, apparently without regard for the fact that they may be wrecking their fishing industry and otherwise complicating their already difficult economic position."[8]

Crane doubtlessly received his information from Robert Strong, the chargé d'affaires in Taipei, who was saying the same thing in his reporting cables to Washington. At the end of April, following the Communist conquest of Hainan Island, Strong was highly pessimistic. In his view, if the next target, the Zhoushan islands off Shanghai, were taken, "the Communists . . . can expect eventual success on Taiwan." Indeed, it was his belief that the "loss of Chusans [Zhoushan] within next month will probably seal doom of Taiwan within nine months thereafter or even sooner, depending on capabilities of Communists."[9] In less than three weeks, by mid-May, after the Nationalists unexpectedly withdrew from the Zhoushan islands without a fight, Strong advanced his estimated timetable for the conquest of Taiwan to between one and three months.

In opinion of attaches and myself fate of Taiwan sealed, Communist attack can occur between June 15 and end July. Although probably mid-June too early a date we are not in position [to] prove it, nor is it worthwhile arguing whether [it] will occur in one month, two months or three months.[10]

Strong recommended and the Department of State concurred in advising all American citizens on Taiwan to leave. "Milit[ary] developments along the China coast made it appear possible that hostilities might spread to points hitherto peaceful, with the result that normal transportation facilities from Taiwan might be disrupted." American citizens were "strongly advised," therefore, to consider "the desirability of leaving Formosa while normal transportation facilities remained available."[11] The State Department, attempting to ensure that "no publicity be given to the issuance of the above notice," instructed Strong to contact the three-hundred-odd Americans on the island by "registered mail." Unfortunately, but perhaps inevitably, Strong's advisory immediately leaked to the press.[12] Indeed, the *New York Times* piece was more alarmist than the official advisory, saying that Americans were being urged to "leave as soon as possible," fearing an invasion "within the next three months."

As noted in the previous chapter, Secretary of Defense Johnson, in subsequent testimony before Congress, divulged the estimated number of troops involved in the Chinese buildup for the invasion of Taiwan, information that he expected "the censor may strike ... out," but did not.[13] At that time, a week prior to the outbreak of the Korean War, Johnson disclosed a buildup from approximately "40,000 to about 156,000." Press reports at that time confirmed "heavy Communist troop movements ... toward the Southeast coast" where "large numbers of invasion craft were massed" and noted Nationalist expectations of an attack "early in July."[14]

A few weeks after war had begun in Korea, Johnson estimated in a cable to the secretary of state that "the Chinese Communists have the capability now of lifting 200,000 armed troops from the mainland to Formosa.... The numbers of craft available to the Communists [are] estimated to be as many as 4,000."[15] The evidence thus confirms not only a close monitoring and evaluation of the Chinese buildup for the assault on Taiwan, but also that American leaders believed that an invasion was imminent.

The evidence regarding foreknowledge of the North Korean attack, on the other hand, is equally persuasive, but virtually nothing reached the press. As discussed above (chapter 5, pp. 108–110), the classified June 19 CIA estimate, *Current Capabilities of the Northern Korean Regime*, was based on data received as of May 15. As of that date, the CIA observed that "trained and equipped units of the Communist 'People's Army' are being deployed southward in the area of the 38th Parallel.... Tanks and heavy artillery have also been moved close to the Parallel in recent months." The very existence of the estimate indicated a continuous monitoring of North Korean "capabilities" and troop movements. Furthermore, it is obvious that if American intelligence was able to detect the deployment of North Korean army units, tanks, and heavy artillery "to the Parallel" in the months *before* May 15, it is highly unlikely that it did not observe the far greater surge of equipment deliveries and troop movements that occurred *after* May 15, when the bulk of Soviet arms deliveries occurred and the North Korean army coiled to strike.

In mid-April, the U.S. Air Force Office of Special Investigations (OSI) reported that Moscow had "definitely ordered an attack on South Korea." In early May, U.S. Army intelligence noted that the "movement of North Korean forces steadily southward toward the 38th parallel . . . could indicate preparation for offensive action." On May 23, Army intelligence warned that "the outbreak of hostilities may occur at any time in Korea." On June 19, the same date as the CIA's estimate cited above, MacArthur's Far East Command forwarded an intelligence report offering "strong evidence of an imminent enemy offensive." As General Matthew Ridgway, who replaced MacArthur, observed about this last report:

> Only six days before the NKPA crossed the border in force a Central Intelligence field agency reported "extensive troop movements" north of the 38th parallel, together with "evacuation of all residents from the northern side of the parallel to a depth of two kilometers"; suspension of civilian freight service from Wonsan to Chorwon and reservation of this line for transporting military supplies only; movements of armed units to border areas; and "movements of large shipments of ordnance and ammunition to border areas." How anyone could have read this report and not anticipated an attack is hard to fathom.[16]

"Stay-behind" agents, Koreans dispatched months and, in some cases, years earlier to North Korea to work under cover and report on the specific possibility of war against the South, were crucial sources for the intelligence estimates. According to General John Singlaub, the CIA station in Seoul from mid-1949 had been receiving "a good flow of intelligence from these agents. It was not likely they'd all simply dried up before the invasion. If they had, *that* would have been a clear warning in itself." These stay-behind agents had in fact "sent specific reports of North Korean preparations" detailing repairs to railroad lines, "reinforcement of roads . . . to carry heavy equipment and armor," and the prohibition of civilian traffic along arteries "linking major military centers with the border."[17]

Publicly, in contrast to the rather voluminous reports of the coming Chinese attack on Taiwan, there was a virtual blackout in the press on North Korean preparations. The *New York Times* carried only one news report, the May 10 press conference by the Republic of Korea's Minister of Defense, Sinh Sung-mo, in which he warned that a North Korean invasion was "imminent."[18] This report made barely a ripple against the background of the uproar created by Tom Connally, chairman of the Senate Foreign Relations Committee. In an interview in *U.S. News & World Report*, Connally declared that the United States was "seriously considering abandoning Korea" since South Korea was not part of the U.S. defense strategy. (More will be said about the Connally interview in the next chapter.)

Although a crisis atmosphere was evident, secret information was available only to the highest-ranked members of the administration. The rank and file of the highly compartmentalized government bureaucracy, including the intelligence bureaucracy, was not fully informed of the entire range of specific information indicating imminent conflict. For example, as historian Joseph C. Goulden notes, "from March 1 through the outbreak of war there was no mention of Korea in the CIA's daily summaries."[19]

It was in the context of a growing crisis atmosphere, however, that the administration moved to change strategy and to strengthen and consolidate the American position worldwide, preparing the groundwork for the extension of containment around the periphery of the Sino-Soviet bloc.

THE UNITED STATES CHANGES STRATEGY

When Truman made the twin decisions of January 31, he also had before him a Joint Chiefs of Staff study entitled "Need of Defense Measures Against Increasing Threat of Atomic Attack Against the Continental United States." In it, the Chiefs, describing a national emergency, concluded that the Soviet Union would have a stockpile of 10 to 20 atomic bombs within six months and between 70 and 135 within three years. In his covering letter to the president, Lieutenant General Alfred M. Gruenther declared:

> Friday, 23 September 1949, when the President announced that we had evidence of an atomic explosion in the USSR, is to us as historic a date as Pearl Harbor or Hiroshima, for it has posed us with the possibility that the atomic bomb, which ended World War II, and which we now believe is produced by the Soviet, might in the future be used against us in a new type of a Pearl Harbor attack of infinitely greater magnitude than that of 1941.[20]

The urgency of the situation was such that the president spent only a few moments considering the recommendations of his advisers. The White House released a statement that afternoon announcing the president's decision to continue nuclear weapons development, but kept secret his decision regarding the reappraisal of American foreign policy he had also just authorized. Indeed, the study that would emerge, NSC-68, would remain officially classified for twenty-five years, although it seems that much of its contents shortly became known to Stalin through his agent network in the United States government.[21]

NSC-68 was a "fundamental reassessment" of the requirements of American national security. Formally a joint State-Defense effort, in actuality the main task of drafting the report was done by Paul Nitze, director of the State Department Policy Planning Staff, and his colleagues in that office.[22] Secretary Johnson, believing the study was "a conspiracy . . . to subvert his attempts to hold down the military budget," refused to participate in the drafting, but, in the end, appended his approval. The policy review committee drafted the report in two months, circulated it for comments at the end of March, and delivered it to the president on April 11.

In form, NSC-68 was a broad comparison of American and Soviet "capabilities and intentions," to make the case that the relative balance of power was shifting toward the Soviet Union and that the United States must take immediate corrective action. It described a "Kremlin challenge" to the United States and its allies in Eurasia and called for an immediate program of general rearmament and strengthening of positions expected to come under attack and pressure. While the scope of the analysis was global, Asia was singled out as an area where the communist model has "found a particularly receptive audience" and where the greatest overall weaknesses of the free world lay.

Although reaffirming the validity of the strategy of containment elaborated in NSC-20/4 (see pp. 52–53), NSC-68 extended its applicability to the entire Eurasian landmass. The main difference between the 1948 study and NSC-68 was that the threat was greater and "more immediate than had previously been estimated." The heightened threat arose because of two unanticipated developments that had occurred in the meantime—the consummation of the Sino-Soviet alliance and Moscow's detonation of the atomic bomb. Thus, the United States

> now faces the contingency that within the next four or five years the Soviet Union will possess the military capability of delivering a surprise atomic attack of such weight that the United States must have substantially increased general air, ground, and sea strength, atomic capabilities, and air and civilian defenses to deter war and to provide reasonable assurance, in the event of war, that it could survive the initial blow and go on to the eventual attainment of its objectives. In turn this contingency requires the intensification of our efforts in the fields of intelligence and research and development.[23]

The authors of NSC-68 justified the call for rearmament on the grounds that military strength was the "ultimate guarantee of our national security." Without military superiority "in being and readily mobilizable, a policy of containment . . . is no more than a policy of bluff." And bluff from a position of relative weakness was a prescription for disaster. In the face of a presumed Soviet attempt to dominate the Eurasian landmass the United States must be prepared "to fight if necessary to defend our way of life."

Although acknowledging that the United States' total economic strength was four times as great as that of the Soviet Union, the authors argued that the Soviet Union was devoting proportionately more to investment in military hardware than the United States. Moreover, the authors declared that the Soviet Union had committed much of its resources to production and already possessed "armed forces far in excess of those necessary to defend its national territory."

This excessive strength, coupled now with an atomic capability, provides the Soviet Union with great coercive power for use in time of peace in furtherance of its objectives and serves as a deterrent to the victims of its aggression from taking any action in opposition to its tactics which would risk war.

To make their point, the authors cited Joint Chiefs of Staff estimates that imputed to the Soviet Union what appeared to be an exaggerated military capability. The JCS estimate claimed that "should a major war occur in 1950," that is, in the next several months, the Soviet Union and its satellites were in a sufficiently advanced state of military readiness immediately to:

1. overrun Western Europe
2. launch air attacks against the British Isles
3. launch air and sea attacks against lines of communication in the Atlantic and Pacific
4. attack selected targets with atomic weapons

Moreover, "after the Soviet Union completed its initial campaigns and consolidated its positions in the Western European area," it could "simultaneously" conduct "full-scale" air and "limited" sea operations against the British Isles, invade the Iberian and Scandinavian peninsulas, and carry out "further operations in the Near and Middle East." The authors of NSC-68 also exaggerated the JCS estimate of Soviet atomic capability, expecting the Soviet Union to possess 10–20 atomic bombs by mid-1950 and 200 by mid-1954. (The JCS had estimated a Soviet atomic stockpile of 135 by 1953.) They referred to "some evidence" that Moscow was also developing thermonuclear weapons.

Several conclusions flowed directly from the analysis. The Soviet Union, devoting "a far greater proportion" of its resources to military production than were the free nations, was "widening the gap between its preparedness for war and the unpreparedness of the free world for war." In addition, "the Communist success in China, taken with the political, economic situation in the rest of South and Southeast Asia, provides a springboard for a further incursion in this troubled area." Furthermore, the Soviet Union held "positions in Europe which . . . could be used to do great damage to the Western European economy" and, despite the Titoist defection, the Soviet Union had "accelerated its efforts to integrate satellite economies with its own."

On the free world side of the ledger, by comparison, the outlook was grim. Western Europe, and especially West Germany, needed further economic integration to promote an environment "conducive to political stability." The United Kingdom must also be strengthened "if it is to be a focus of resistance to Communist expansion in South and Southeast Asia." Throughout Asia the stability of current moderate governments was "doubtful." There were indications of "disillusion" arising from "excessively optimistic expectations" regarding American aid programs. Finally, there were some grounds for predicting that the United States and other free nations would soon "experience a decline in economic activity of serious proportions."

This was a bleak outlook indeed. Though Soviet power was indeed great, in truth the estimate of Soviet military power and by implication the economic capability that undergirded it was inflated. If the Soviet Union had the sustained capability imputed to it in 1950 the Cold War would have been settled then and there in favor of Moscow. But facts in the Soviet era were always difficult to come by because of the closed Communist system. Thoughtful readers no doubt understood the rhetorical nature of the argument that urged and justified American rearmament by exaggerating Soviet capabilities. A lesser threat would not serve the desired purpose of justifying the construction of a "superior" American military capability, which was "cardinal."

Even though the Soviet world's overall "capabilities are inferior to those of our allies and to our own . . . they are mobilized close to the maximum possible extent." The point was that although American forces were potent, the United States had failed to maintain relative position. "In the face of obviously mounting Soviet military strength ours has declined relatively." When current American military strength was "related to the world situation and balanced against the likely exigencies of such a situation, it [was] clear that our military strength [was] becoming dangerously inadequate." Indeed, "the integrity and vitality of our system is in greater jeopardy than ever before in our history. . . . The Kremlin's possession of atomic weapons puts new power behind its designs, and increases the jeopardy to our system." Rapid rearmament was imperative. "No people in history have preserved their freedom who thought that by not being strong enough to protect themselves they might prove inoffensive to their enemies."

As a result, the Kremlin was "growing bolder" and facing us with "difficult decisions." As the existing trend favored the Soviet Union, a continuation of the status quo would lead to clear Soviet superiority. A retreat to isolation would lead to the same outcome. Preemptive war, on the other hand, was unacceptable to the American people, which left rapid rearmament as the only realistic alternative. The United States was faced with the stark choice of either responding to the Soviet challenge and rearming to achieve dominance, or acquiescing to the emergence of a dominant Soviet Union, with its attendant dire consequences for the global balance of power and the American position in it.

The ultimate objective was not to administer military defeat to the Soviet Union, but to "foster a fundamental change in the nature of the Soviet system." In what was a prescient statement of the future strategic outcome, the authors described the ultimate purpose of the United States as being "to negotiate a settlement with the Soviet Union (or a successor state or states) on which the world can place reliance as an enforceable instrument of peace." In this necessarily protracted struggle "we can expect no lasting abatement of the crisis unless and until a change occurs in the nature of the Soviet system."

> The United States cannot therefore engage in war except as a reaction to aggression of so clear and compelling a nature as to bring the overwhelming majority of our people to accept the use of military force. In the event war comes, our use of force must be to compel the acceptance of our objectives and must be congruent to the range of tasks which we may encounter.

The resort to force, although "the last resort of a free society," may become necessary. "But if war comes," the authors asked, "what is the role of force?" As if expecting that NSC-68 would become known to the Kremlin's leaders, the authors quoted the Federalist Papers (no. 28) to illustrate the historical character of American leadership. The United States would seek no war of annihilation should it be forced to fight. "The means to be employed must be proportional to the extent of the mischief." The mischief may be a global war or it may be a Soviet campaign for limited objectives. "In either case we should take no avoidable initiative which would cause it to become a war of annihilation, and if we have the force to defeat a Soviet drive for limited objectives it may well be to our interests not to let it become a global war." In other words, the United States would not transform a small war, should it come, into a global conflict, but keep it limited.

To defeat the Kremlin's challenge we must not only "make ourselves strong," but also "lead in building a successfully functioning political and economic system in the free world." Toward this end, "a comprehensive and decisive program to win the peace and frustrate the Kremlin design should be so designed that it can be sustained for as long as necessary to achieve our national objectives." The long-term program should thus aim to develop an adequate political-economic and security framework for the free world. This would require substantial increases in foreign military and economic assistance programs. The United States would also need to intensify covert operations and improve and intensify intelligence activities. This last, as we have seen, was already being done.

The American house must also be put into better order to be able to afford the cost of the new strategy and build confidence in American strength and resolution. Toward this end, the authors recommended that the United States embark upon a "dynamic expansion of the economy," which would permit the necessary buildup "without a decrease in the national standard of living," although some tax increases might be necessary. Contributing to this end would be improvement in the balance of payments position and the reduction of federal expenditures other than those for defense and foreign assistance. The authors closed their study with exhortation.

> The whole success of the proposed program hangs ultimately on recognition by this Government, the American people, and all free peoples, that the cold war is in fact a real war in which the survival of the free world is at stake.

Yet, paradoxically, the call to arms was not to be made public. Secrecy was essential. "It is recognized, of course, that any announcement of the recommended course of action could be exploited by the Soviet Union in its peace campaign and would have adverse psychological effects in certain parts of the free world." Therefore, the decision to rearm would be kept secret. How a major rearmament program, at home and abroad, could be kept secret and simultaneously gain the support of the American people was left unexplained.

Nor was the cost of the recommended program divulged, although most of those involved in the study privately assumed expenditures in the $40 to $50 billion per year range for four or five years. When the sixty-page study was delivered to the president on April 11, he was informed of the cost estimate, but reserved final judgment on the levels of funding to be requested of Congress "until the agencies and departments had submitted their implementing requests and . . . budget advisers had had a chance to go over them in close detail."[24] Truman promptly established an ad hoc committee of the NSC, which included officials from the Treasury Department, the Council of Economic Advisers, the Bureau of the Budget, and the Economic Cooperation Agency (ECA), to provide cost estimates for implementation of the report's recommendations. Those cost estimates were under way but not completed by the time the Korean War erupted.[25]

The thrust of NSC-68 was clear. The balance of power was shifting toward the Soviet Union because of the acquisition of atomic weapons power and the alliance with China. As a result Moscow was growing bolder. The United States must rearm to be able to meet a threat at any point around the periphery. In the interim, the likelihood of conflict was high and "since the United States cannot . . . engage in war except as a reaction to aggression" the nation must be prepared to respond when war came. Explicit was the principle that the adversary would be permitted to strike the first blow.

WASHINGTON GIRDS FOR CONFRONTATION

Although President Truman had not formally approved NSC-68 in April 1950 (it would become official American policy in September), even before

132

the cost estimates of the study's policies had been completed the administration acted immediately on the basis of its recommendations to build a "successfully functioning political and economic system for the free world," and took certain preparatory military steps. From the spring onward, Washington acted to raise the threshold for war by strengthening its allies and warning its adversaries. Melvyn P. Leffler describes the scope and breadth of the administration's activities as a "diplomatic offensive":

> The diplomatic offensive that was contemplated in the spring of 1950 was of enormous scope. Around the Eurasian land mass, U.S. officials hoped to regain the initiative by strengthening NATO, co-opting the power of West Germany . . . deploying additional troops to Europe, expanding military assistance to the Near East and Southeast Asia, inaugurating new programs of economic aid in the underdeveloped world, launching covert operations in the general area of China, negotiating a Japanese peace treaty, neutralizing Taiwan, and forming a Pacific alliance.[26]

The general problem only addressed by implication in NSC-68 was that the nations in the margin between the American and Soviet spheres would, as a result of the perceived shift in the American-Soviet military balance, attempt to move to the middle and adopt a neutral position between the two blocs. This was particularly true of West Germany and Japan, the anchors of the U.S. forward position in Eurasia, as well as countries in between like Greece, Turkey, Iran, Burma, Thailand, Indochina, Malaya, Indonesia, the Philippines, and South Korea; the administration sought to strengthen ties to these nations by its various programs. The United States allocated $1.3 billion in Mutual Defense Assistance Programs (MDAP) for fiscal year 1950 and another $1.2 billion for fiscal year 1951.[27]

Against the backdrop of increasing strife throughout Asia and potential serious conflict over Taiwan, South Korea, Indochina, the Philippines, and elsewhere, U.S. officials mused publicly about "where the main move will come." State Department "experts" believed that "an important driving force in present Russian policy is a tremendous sense of triumph born out of the victory in China. By this line of reasoning Russia is now primarily interested in keeping the influence of world communism rolling forward."[28] In response, Secretary Acheson actively sought to strengthen the U.S. political and economic positions around the globe to be ready for the expected challenge.

But first Acheson issued a clear warning to the "Communists" who were using "China as a base for probing for other weak spots which they can move into and exploit." In an address to the Commonwealth Club of San Francisco on March 15, the secretary expressed sympathy for the Chinese people that "their present unhappy status within the orbit of the Soviet Union is not the result of any choice on their own part, but has been forced upon them," and declared that "we do not intend to engage in any aggressive adventures against them." But they should understand, he warned, that "whatever happens within their own country, they can only bring grave trouble on themselves and their friends, both in Asia and beyond, if they are led by their new rulers into aggressive or subversive adventures beyond their borders."[29]

The Chinese and North Korean buildups were the most advanced, but not the only danger points. Moscow was also building an East German army and strengthening its own positions elsewhere in Eastern Europe, and there were increasing signs of strife in Indochina and Tibet, as China concentrated forces along these borders. The possibility that conflict in Korea, Taiwan, or Indochina would be opening shots to tie down American forces in East Asia while Moscow struck at Western Europe was a subject of discussion between the United States and its allies that spilled into the public arena.

During meetings in London and Paris in May, Acheson divulged plans for coordinated allied action to secure all fronts. The secretary spoke to British and French officials of the United States' intent to deploy five additional divisions to Europe to ensure stability.[30] At the same time, he publicly called upon Moscow to disband the East German army it was building on the grounds that the Yalta and Potsdam agreements, as well as other allied wartime agreements, required the "complete disarmament and demilitarization of Germany."[31] The Soviet arming of East Germany naturally raised the question of arming West Germany, about which the French, in particular, were not enthusiastic.

The United States, assured Acheson, would not only join the European powers to block the communist advance in the West, but would also provide assistance to maintain their positions in the East. In the East, the United States had primary responsibility for Northeast Asia, while Britain and France had primary responsibility for Southeast Asia. In the event of conflict Acheson "hoped for a successful holding action in Southeast Asia, while the Western Alliance seized the offensive in Western Europe."[32] Britain's Foreign Secretary Ernest Bevin quickly went public with that connection, warning against the Soviet inspiration of multiple crises.

> If you look at a map of the world you will see what extreme trouble it would cause to have a big civil war in Indo-China and one in Europe. It could be a very nasty thing for the rest of the world. Hence, other countries are watching with very great interest what is developing.[33]

American analysts saw similar possibilities. Hanson Baldwin, the military affairs writer, saw the East German and Chinese "salients" as the ones to watch.[34] He viewed with deep foreboding an East German army of "30,000 to 40,000 strong . . . armed with tanks and artillery," while the Soviet "sending of jet fighters . . . to China [had] an immediate twofold significance." Soviet jets to China "foretells the doom of Formosa" and "may mean, in time, that Southeast Asia will become a kind of Oriental Greece—riven by civil war between Communist and anti-Communist forces each helped by outside aid." Baldwin reinforced Secretary Acheson's warning that "the free world must hang together or it would hang separately."

THE PROBLEM OF JAPAN

In Asia, the key problem was Japan, whose role had been altered as a result of the change in American strategy. Under NSC-48/1, recall, the United States was prepared to countenance the establishment of a neutral, "middle of the road regime in Japan" free to "maintain normal political and economic relations with the Communist bloc," and one that "would probably resist complete identification either with the interest of the United States or the Soviet Union."[35] Sino-Japanese cooperation would be mutually beneficial economically and politically, and serve the larger American interest of precluding a Sino-Soviet alliance and stabilizing Northeast Asia along earlier, prewar lines.

In view of Mao's decision to enter into an alliance with Moscow, of course, that proposal had been discarded in favor of binding Japan closely to the United States as part of the global containment envisaged in NSC-68 and thereby denying Japan's considerable resources to the Sino-Soviet bloc. It would be too risky to permit Japan to shift to the middle as a neutral state. The shift in U.S. policy regarding Japan went counter to the initial hopes of Japan's leaders for the conclusion of a peace "treaty with all" of the victorious powers that would enable Japan to assume a neutral position.[36] Since the fall of 1949, the Japanese Communist Party had mounted a campaign for such a peace treaty, denouncing a separate peace and demanding that the Soviet Union and China be included.[37]

The problems posed by the U.S. shift were many, but chief among them was how to gain Japanese acceptance of the new U.S. position without informing Japan's leaders of the change in U.S. strategy. MacArthur, the American shogun, had pronounced in March 1947 in favor of an early peace treaty that would establish Japan as an independent, neutral nation. The question was: How to reorient Japan politically to exclude the communist bloc, build a close Japanese-American relationship, yet provide Japan with the economic opportunity to grow and prosper independently and not as a long-term dependent on the United States? The issue of the peace treaty required decision. Could a peace treaty be signed without the Soviet Union and China, and, if so, when should the United States sign it?

The American leadership decided to proceed unilaterally on the question

135

of a peace treaty as soon as it was clear that Mao would ally with Stalin, as part of the general decision to change strategy. On January 24, Dean Rusk belatedly filed a memorandum of a conversation that had ostensibly taken place during an NSC meeting on December 29 reporting President Truman's view that the United States could proceed to sign a peace treaty with Japan whether the Soviet Union participated or not. Truman's view was that at the Potsdam conference the United States with Great Britain and China had "drawn up and proposed" surrender terms to Japan, which Japan accepted. "The Soviet Union did not participate in this action since it was not then at war with Japan."[38]

After declaring war on Japan, the Soviet Union had "concurred in the surrender terms already offered." It was therefore the president's view that the peace settlement with Japan must in the first instance "be a matter which is satisfactory to the United States and the United Kingdom." He "had no doubt that the United States and the United Kingdom could negotiate a peace treaty with Japan whether the USSR participated or not." Thus, the argument was that since the Soviet Union had not been a party to the original formulation of surrender terms to Japan, but had only adhered subsequently, so also in the signing of the peace treaty the United States could proceed unilaterally, offering the Soviet Union the opportunity to sign the treaty later.

The entire episode of the Rusk memorandum of January 24 recording a presidential decision of twenty-six days earlier suggests an attempt to obfuscate a decision date. The circumstances surrounding Rusk's memorandum suggest a later decision time. It is highly improbable that the State Department would delay recording a presidential opinion or decision by several weeks, especially one of such importance. Indeed, one would have expected the memo to have been crafted that same day of the decision, immediately following the meeting. Moreover, it finessed the role of China, which had joined the United States and Great Britain in proposing surrender terms to Japan.

Indeed, the reason why it was highly unlikely that Truman had made the decision to proceed unilaterally on December 29 was precisely because of China. December 29 was the day before the meeting regarding NSC-48/2, which dealt with the offer to Mao for a settlement in Northeast Asia designed to keep the Russians and the Chinese apart. The American offer had not yet been made and Mao had not yet revealed to American leaders his decision to ally with the Soviet Union. As long as the issue was still open there was, therefore, no need to proceed unilaterally.

Had Mao decided to accept the U.S. offer, the United States would have proceeded with the early peace treaty according to its original terms, no doubt including Beijing in place of Taipei, and with or without Moscow.

Mao's signature on a Japanese peace treaty would have been a major step in the Sino-Japanese relationship that the United States offered to build in NSC-48. Once Mao declined the U.S. offer, however, it became necessary to change the terms of the peace treaty procedure, excluding both the Soviet Union and China. Once rejected, the Truman administration was at pains to obscure the fact that an offer had ever been made. Thus, the pre-dating of the Rusk memorandum.

It is plain that since the United States did not make the offer until early January and Mao did not reject it until the middle of the month, Truman's decision must have come at that time and not on December 29, before the offer had been made. Thus, it would seem that Rusk's memorandum, though referring to a meeting that took place on December 29, actually represented a decision made some time later in January. The December 29 date was selected to seal over the period of the offer to Mao and imply that it had never been made.

137

Having decided to proceed unilaterally on the treaty, the next decision was to delay it, because it would take time to reshape Japanese opinion. Washington would not proceed until Japanese opinion could be changed, reducing if not eliminating Japanese opposition to a continued American military presence in Japan. It had to be clear to the Japanese people that their preferred status, neutrality, was not a viable option. (The United States was, in any case, building a major military base complex on the island of Okinawa in the Ryukyu Islands, which it would retain for the indefinite future.)

The means of delay employed was a variation on the good-cop, bad-cop routine, in this case an actual dispute between the Joint Chiefs and the State Department, of which Japanese leaders were made aware. The Joint Chiefs (bad cop) claimed that a peace treaty was "premature" and insisted on the transparently impossible condition that any peace treaty be both acceptable to the Soviet Union and provide for American bases (from which the United States could attack Moscow in the event of war). It went without saying that the Soviets would not accept these terms, but it bought Washington the time it needed.

The State Department (good cop), on the other hand, after much internal deliberation, developed an elaborate scheme involving a peace treaty without the Soviet Union or China, and a separate security agreement with Japan to provide for American bases. An early idea for lodging Japan securely in the Western camp was to form a Pacific Treaty Organization along the lines of NATO, which would include the United States, Japan, Canada, Australia, New Zealand, and the Philippines. But this conception was discarded in favor of separate pacts between the United States and countries of the Pacific when it was learned of their aversion to entering into a pact with Japan.

The basic document, which would ultimately comprise the Japanese peace treaty and the security agreement regarding bases, was completed in draft form by early March 1950, but would not be signed until a year and a half later.[39] The United States wanted wholehearted Japanese support, not merely acquiescence, for its scheme and sought through delay and suasion to bring about a change in Japanese views. It would not be easy. When, in late January, Premier Shigeru Yoshida had floated a trial balloon, hinting that Japan might have to "rely on Western democracies for protection even after a peace treaty," he had been severely criticized by opposition leaders for suggesting that Japan would permit an American military presence in Japan after the signing of a peace treaty.[40]

The unprecedented visit to Japan by the entire Joint Chiefs of Staff in early February, however, began to shift opinion. An *Asahi* newspaper poll revealed what was termed a "complete switch" on the bases question. "Japanese were deeply impressed by the arrival here for the first time of top United States military authorities and their apparent interest in the base question." The Liberal Democratic Party was now "willing to grant bases inside Japan . . . in exchange for an American-Japanese military agreement." The opposition Democratic Party believed that "bases should be granted in Japan if this does not mean the loss of Japanese neutrality." The right-wing Socialist Party thought that "bases should be granted . . . in the Ryukyus . . . but not in the homeland." The parties on the left, however, the Left-wing Socialist Party and the Japanese Communist Party, continued to resist the notion of bases entirely, and demanded a peace treaty that included the Soviet Union and Communist China. Their views would not change, but they were in a minority. Majority opinion in Japan had begun to shift in favor of granting base rights.[41]

By early May, the shift was in full swing. The Japanese government had agreed to a "treaty with many," rather than its original position of a "treaty with all," excluding the Soviet Union and China, and also agreed to offer bases for a post-treaty American military presence.[42] The trip to Washington of Hayato Ikeda, Japan's finance minister, tipped the scales in favor of the U.S. position. Ikeda was the first Japanese cabinet-level officer to travel to the United States since the war. In a conversation on May 2 with Joseph Dodge, former financial adviser to MacArthur, who had crafted the plan to balance the Japanese budget and erase inflation, Ikeda revealed that "the Government desires the earliest possible treaty. As such a treaty probably would require the maintenance of U.S. forces to secure the treaty terms and for other purposes, if the U.S. Government hesitates to make these conditions, the Japanese Government will try to find a way to offer them."[43]

One week after the Ikeda-Dodge meeting, Premier Yoshida revealed the shift in leadership opinion to the Japanese people, declaring that a "separate" de facto peace already existed with the United States, and Japan sought to "transfer these relationships to a legal basis as soon as possible." Since there were those countries that did not want to conclude a peace treaty with Japan, he said, "it is therefore most difficult for Japan to have an over-all treaty which will include these countries."[44] Japan, he said, would conclude a treaty with many, rather than a treaty with all. Yoshida's public stand indicated his willingness to "go to the Japanese electorate on this basis in the June elections." While there would remain serious issues to negotiate regarding the peace treaty and bases agreement, the fundamental decision to proceed on the basis of an alliance with the United States had been made before the outbreak of the Korean War.

General MacArthur's views also had to be taken into account. As noted above, three years earlier the supreme commander had taken the position that the occupation had run its course and an early and generous peace settlement would ensure a friendly, and neutral, Japan. There was no need for American bases. His position had helped shape the original Japanese expectations of emerging from the occupation as an independent, neutral nation. Accordingly MacArthur now revised his views to take account of the changed circumstances. In an interview with *New York Times* reporter C. L. Sulzberger at the end of May, MacArthur declared:

> I wish to see a demilitarized Japan. But, naturally, that thought deals with the prospect of a world at peace. It is an ultimate aim. Neither side would profit by the arming of Japan. We don't care to use her as an armed ally but we don't want to see Russia or Communist China use her against us. Japanese neutrality would be a benefit to everyone including not only Japan but also the United States, Russia and China. But we cannot see the country left open to a coup de main by Communist China or Russia.
>
> My views concerning a neutralized and totally disarmed Japan do not necessarily apply to the immediate situation involving the period of a peace treaty and right afterward. I am talking of long-range terms. Japan may have to be protected during the interim. Possibly bases might have to be maintained with Japanese consent in order to protect her and to prevent her from being used against us.[45]

Three weeks later, two days before war erupted and undoubtedly reflecting his own intelligence reports regarding its imminence, MacArthur's views evolved further. Now, he saw the need not only for bases, but also for the use of "the entire area of Japan . . . as a potential base for defensive maneuver."[46] He justified this change on the grounds that "pre-determined" bases had "become outmoded by the accelerated speed and power of modern war." MacArthur's concern was "to insure complete freedom of strategic planning and tactical disposition to meet any change in the requirements for successful defense." To allay Japanese concerns, he gave assurances that there would be no change in the disposition of the security forces "except in time of hostilities or imminently threatened hostilities."

Thus, before the outbreak of war in Korea, the United States had effected a fundamental reorientation of position regarding the role Japan would play in Washington's global containment strategy. The peace treaty would be put off until the war had occurred, leaving the United States unhindered use of Japan as a forward base for support of military operations in Korea.

The reorientation of Japan also involved a change in its traditional economic zone, to provide Japan with a substitute for the loss of the China market. This process had, in fact, commenced immediately after China refused the U.S. offer. This process had begun in mid-February, just as the drafting of NSC-68 had gotten under way, with a meeting in Bangkok, chaired by Ambassador Jessup, of American diplomats from State, Defense, ECA, and the Supreme Command Allied Powers (SCAP) in Japan. The purpose of the gathering was specifically to explore ways of reorienting Japanese economic activity from Chinese to Southeast Asian markets, as well as to convey the new policy line to those expected to carry it out. Survey missions from the departments of State, Defense, and Agriculture were sent to develop estimates of the nature and amount of assistance the United States might provide to facilitate the political-economic integration of Southeast Asia with Japan.[47]

There was the usual internal bureaucratic wrangling as each agency sought to carve out for itself as large a piece of the aid turf as possible, but Washington had established the basic policy to be followed. More serious objections came from London, where concern arose that the policy of directing Japan's economic activity into Southeast Asia would undermine the position of Britain's Commonwealth partners there. Britain would engage in a prolonged but ultimately unsuccessful attempt to reorient Japanese economic activity toward mainland China and away from Southeast Asia until the Korean War broke out and ended that possibility.

The decision to reorient Japan into Southeast Asia also led to a temporary but major change in strategy toward France and French colonial policy in Indochina. Long-term American strategy had been to work for the dismantling of the colonial system and the promotion of new independent states, a strategy that had up to this point included opposition to the French colonial empire in Indochina. But the United States decision to develop Southeast Asia into an economic market for Japan forced a temporary change in long-term strategy. Citing the dangers of a communist victory following Chinese and Soviet recognition of Ho Chi-minh, the United States reversed policy toward the French in Indochina from attempting to get them out to encouraging them to remain.

Reversing the earlier American position, from early February Acheson began to praise French policy in Indochina and pledged American support for French efforts. As part of this support, President Truman announced the diplomatic recognition of the Vietnamese regime under Bao Dai on February 7.[48] By the end of the month, the administration had produced a formal policy paper on Indochina, NSC-64, which now declared Indochina a "priority area" and cleared the way for the extension of military assistance. On May 1, the president authorized the initial disbursement of $18 million for support of the French in Indochina in a program of aid that would ultimately total more than $2 billion over the next four years.[49] In testimony before the Senate Foreign Relations Committee on the same day, Acheson emphasized that the United States would do whatever was necessary "to keep the French in there."[50]

THE PROBLEM OF TAIWAN

The problem of reversing policy toward Taiwan was complicated by the return of Chiang Kai-shek. In future, the United States wished to effect a rapprochement with Beijing and therefore felt the eventual need to dispense with Chiang. American leaders assumed that support for Chiang as a claimant to power in China precluded any rapprochement with the mainland. Were the United States to reverse and support Chiang on Taiwan, then the die would be cast toward the mainland, or so it then appeared. (They could not foresee the time, or circumstance, when Chinese leaders would be not only willing but also eager for rapprochement with the United States without first regaining control over Taiwan, as would be the case two decades later.) Once Mao declined the U.S. offer and American leaders decided to retain Taiwan as part of the U.S. defense perimeter, the issue of Chiang arose anew. The problem was how to retain Taiwan, but dispense with Chiang.

The prospect of a Chinese Communist attack on Taiwan before war broke out in Korea prompted U.S. leaders to concoct several schemes by which the United States could openly retain Formosa as part of the de facto defense perimeter in the Western Pacific, without also being forced to accept Chiang Kai-shek in the bargain. In early May, there seemed to be some prospect for accomplishing this objective. Chiang had become quite rattled by the Soviet deployment of MIG jets to China, assuming, as noted earlier, that they would form part of the Communist invasion force, which he could not hope to counter with his World War II–era, propeller-driven aircraft. Chiang had intimated then that "he might consider a SCAP defense of Taiwan if his sovereignty were not impaired."[51] He had, in fact, sent a letter to Truman offering to step aside in return for U.S. support (see chapter 8, p. 203).

On the assumption that Chiang was open to pressure, in mid-May John Foster Dulles worked out the rationalization for defending Taiwan against attack. Dulles, recall, had just been named to negotiate the peace treaty with Japan and, in a May 18 memorandum, he now put forth an argument linking Taiwan and Japan. The defense of Taiwan was essential for the defense of Japan, he said. The Japanese were concerned that the United States was showing no inclination to resist communist pressure on mainland Asia following the Chinese Communist conquest, and questioned whether Washington would "stand firm" with respect to Japan.[52]

Echoing the analysis in NSC-68, Dulles argued that the Japanese believed that the Chinese victory on the mainland signified a "shift in the balance of power in favor of Soviet Russia and to the disfavor of the United States." They were eagerly awaiting some sign that would indicate whether the United States intended to stand fast or retreat. Dulles believed it was imperative that Washington "quickly take a dramatic and strong stand that shows our confidence and resolution." Formosa was the place where a "stand must be taken."

With little risk of war with the Soviet Union, he said, the United States could "neutralize" Formosa and impress the eyes of the world with American determination to oppose communism outside Europe and the Western Hemisphere. (MacArthur, having read Dulles's memorandum, wrote his own on June 14, reinforcing Dulles's plea to prevent the communist conquest. "There can be no doubt," he said, "but that the eventual fate of Formosa rests with the US." In MacArthur's view, "the domination of Formosa by an unfriendly power would be a disaster of utmost importance to the US, and I am convinced that time is of the essence.")[53]

On the basis of Dulles's memorandum, Dean Rusk immediately began working secretly with a few high-ranking officials to prepare the groundwork for a change in policy toward Taiwan. In a meeting with Secretary Johnson's special assistant, General John Burns, on May 25, Rusk alerted the Defense Department to be prepared to act when policy changed, as expected. At issue was the broadening of existing restrictions on sales of equipment to the Nationalist government contained in Secretary Acheson's letters to Johnson of March 7 and April 14. Rusk promised to "facilitate the granting of export licenses" to permit shipments when that occurred and Burns promised to "expedite the supply of that equipment which can be provided."[54]

Burns also promised that the Defense Department would review the situation in Formosa and indicate "at an early date" the desirability of recommending a change of policy. Both agreed that the "augmentation and intensification of the covert effort [was also] desirable" and Rusk took responsibility for gaining "presidential release of such 303 funds as might be required for authorized projects." The 303 funds were a reference to section 303 of the Mutual Defense Assistance (MDA) Act of October 6, 1949, which

142

provided for $75 million in emergency funds designated for the "general area of China."

Rusk then retitled Dulles's memorandum of May 18 and sent it on to the secretary of state with additional comments of his own. He admitted that "the determination to withhold Formosa from the Communists would involve complications with the Nationalist Government and with their elements on Formosa. . . . However, these aspects are of a secondary order. It is within our power to solve the political complications if we have the resolute will." Rusk concluded with the observation that "it will not leave a good taste if we allow our political problems to be solved by the extermination of our war allies."[55]

The chief political problem Rusk referred to was, of course, the continuation in power of Chiang Kai-shek, which a U.S. decision to defend Formosa would ensure. On May 31, Rusk met with a handful of selected top officials— **143** Paul Nitze, Philip Jessup, Livingston Merchant, Jonathan Howe, and Philip Sprouse—to work out a plan to spook Chiang into voluntarily relinquishing power. These six men, plus Dulles and Secretary Acheson, "constitute the only ones who are aware of this move on Rusk's part," reported Howe.[56] Rusk's initial idea was to neutralize Formosa through a quid pro quo with Beijing. In return for Beijing's agreement to a U.S. trusteeship for Formosa, the United States would recognize the PRC, and support its seating in the U.N. As discussion unfolded, however, the quid pro quo with Beijing was discarded as unlikely given the invasion buildup and the focus centered on the immediate problem of forcing out Chiang and making a unilateral effort to neutralize Formosa through a trusteeship.

The plan decided upon was to approach Chiang with the view that "the fall of Formosa in the present circumstances was inevitable," an outcome the United States "would do nothing" to prevent. "The only course open" to him was "to request UN trusteeship" for the island. If Chiang did this, the United States "would be prepared to back such a move . . . and would ready the fleet to prevent any armed attack on Formosa." In that event, the United States was prepared to locate a place where Chiang could retreat in exile. Negotiation of a trusteeship would probably be "extremely difficult and prolonged," however, and would "probably have to include Russia," but "it would give the US a chance to prevent the fall of Formosa under circumstances sponsored by the UN."

The pressure to get Chiang to step aside continued, according to one scholar, beyond the outbreak of war in Korea and included plans to support a coup to topple the Nationalist leader and a search for a successor.[57] Nationalist leaders Sun Li-jen and Hu Shih were sounded out, among others, but all declined. In truth, time ran out on the U.S. effort to find a successor to Chiang before the invasion. As preparations of Mao's invasion force neared completion, measures to strengthen the island took priority over schemes to remove Chiang. Acheson began a gradual relaxation of the arms cutoff that Truman had announced on January 5 and the secretary himself had reaffirmed on April 14. On June 1, one day after receiving Rusk's memo regarding the defense of Formosa, Acheson sent a letter to Secretary Johnson, making clear that:

> It was not the Department's view . . . that a deadline should be established for the submission of requisitions by the Chinese Government under the $125 million grants, with the Departments of the Army, Navy, and Air Force refusing to honor new Chinese Government requests. It is the opinion of the Department of State that assistance by the Departments of the Army, Navy, and Air Force under section 404(b) of Public Law 472 should be continued until all funds allocated to those Departments from the $125 million grants have been exhausted, including not only orders under procurement or delivery as of April 14 but also any subsequent requisitions which the Chinese may submit while these funds remain available.[58]

Acheson had opened the door ever so slightly for the continuation of American assistance to the Nationalist government. Jet planes and tanks continued to be prohibited, but everything else could be supplied until all remaining granted funds were "exhausted." Yet, while declining to provide planes, Washington was considering plans to provide for air defense by reviving the "flying tigers" concept of World War II, permitting the creation of a volunteer flying force.[59] This would keep the planes out of Chiang's hands, while serving the purpose of defending the island. Commitment of the Seventh Fleet would ensure the defeat of any invasion attempt.

Five days later, on June 5, President Truman signed a bill passed by Congress authorizing $94 million in aid to Formosa and non-Communist China.[60] Public sentiment favoring support to the Nationalists was also growing. The easing of the cutoff, passage of aid, and growing popular support, of course, all served to put the United States into position to protect Taiwan from attack, if attack of the island came first, but it also had the effect of reinforcing Chiang's determination to remain in power.

By mid-May, the Truman administration had become actively committed to blunting any possible Communist offensive against Taiwan and to moving forward on a peace treaty with Japan. In addition, the administration had acted to strengthen "control of that portion of Asia between East Pakistan and India to the west and the China Sea to the east." In what was termed the "Eastern 'Truman Doctrine,'" the administration had taken measures to strengthen Burma, Thailand, and Indochina. Twenty-three million dollars had already been allocated to the French Union "and the three Indochinese states of Viet Nam, Laos and Cambodia." Washington had pledged substantial economic aid to Burma and Thailand, with $10 million in military aid pledged to Bangkok and an as yet undetermined amount to Rangoon. It was believed that "when a firm line is drawn and the Soviet bloc is warned it would risk a conflict if its forces advanced beyond it, the situation would be clarified."[61]

Completing the containment ring, the administration allocated military assistance of $27,640,000 from its $1.3 billion Mutual Defense Assistance Program for Iran, the Philippines, and South Korea.[62] Ten million was allocated to Iran, $10.2 million to South Korea, and the remainder, roughly $7.5 million, to the Philippines. Thirteen countries, in all, were included in the U.S. effort to strengthen containment of the communist threat. But therein lay a tale. While South Korea was allocated $10.2 million on paper, and while the president declared that "Korea is under the constant menace of the Communist-dominated regime in North Korea, whose purpose is to destroy the new republic," the United States declined to maintain, let alone strengthen, the defenses of the ROK during the months prior to the outbreak of the war.[63]

CHAPTER SEVEN

Korea and Containment

ONCE THE DECISION to change to a strategy of containment had been made, as we have seen, Washington altered global policies accordingly. Washington's policy was to strengthen *all* possible areas of conflict—regardless of local conditions—except for South Korea. Despite the fact that the governing policy paper for the Republic of Korea, NSC-8/2 (of March 1949), declared that the loss of the peninsula "would enhance the political and strategic position of the USSR with respect to both China and Japan and adversely affect the position of the United States . . . throughout the Far East," Washington blithely proceeded to ignore the growing imbalance of forces on the peninsula because the Republic of Korea was to be the tethered goat employed as bait in a much larger game with global ramifications.[1]

Washington changed policy toward South Korea in the opposite direction from its policies elsewhere. Not only did the Truman administration ignore its own policy of maintaining a military balance between North and South, it also demanded that the Rhee government further reduce its already strained defense capabilities in the name of fighting inflation. Secretary Acheson himself demanded that President Rhee raise taxes and cut defense spending to combat inflation, and threatened to cut U.S. support unless he did so. At the same time, U.S. officials trumpeted Seoul's military capability to defend the country, in the face of growing evidence to the contrary.

Inflation in South Korea was real enough, but the remedies Washington suggested to combat it only weakened the state. Inflation was the inevitable consequence of the division of the peninsula and its resources, combined with the North's continuing campaign to subvert the South. Virtually all of

Korea's industrial capacity and raw materials were in the North. Further-more, according to a Central Intelligence Agency estimate, "the withholding of northern Korea power, fertilizer, coal, iron, and steel from the southern Republic has been offset only in part by large-scale US economic aid."[2] In other words, cutting aid further would not improve the inflation outlook, only worsen it.

Then there was the impact of North Korea's subversion campaign. "Communist-trained guerrilla operations in Southern Korea ... [have] forced the Republic to expend large sums of money in 'suppression cam-paigns,' and thus have contributed materially to the dangerous inflationary situation in South Korea." Communist operations, the estimate concluded, have "forced" the Republic "to make serious political and economic sacrifices in order to counter the ever-present Communist threat. At the same time, the cost to the Communists has been relatively slight, and their ability to continue the campaign far exceeds the Republic's capability to continue effective resistance without US aid."

SOUTH KOREA IN U.S. STRATEGY

The Truman administration's policy toward South Korea in 1950 resembled nothing so much as tethering a goat to trap a tiger, a tiger that American leaders knew was preparing to spring. In truth, there was only one course that would accomplish Washington's larger objectives. If the issue were confined to the Korean peninsula, Washington could match the buildup oc-curring in the North by strengthening the ROK, as originally intended by NSC-8/2. This course would either discourage an assault, or, if one occurred anyway, quickly contain it. A brief conflict, quickly contained, would not, however, serve the larger strategy of global containment, which now re-quired a sustained national commitment to build up American military power to contend with the multiple threats expected to emanate from the Sino-Soviet bloc.

The second response—the response decided upon—would be to ignore the North Korean buildup, acclaim South Korean defense capability, but de-cline any compensatory buildup in the South. In fact, Washington would wait until the Communists struck the first blow and then come to the de-fense of the Republic of Korea. In that case, during what would be a lengthy conflict because of the initial advantages gained by the aggressor, the United States would mobilize the "free world" in justifiable defense against the communist menace, giving firm structure to the Cold War. A long conflict against Communist aggression would be ample justification to fund the al-ready planned rearmament called for in NSC-68.

As the following pages will demonstrate in detail, the United States pro-

147

ceeded to treat the Rhee government in a manner designed to leave South Korea vulnerable to invasion. American leaders knew war was brewing on the peninsula—if not because United States cryptographic and signals specialists had broken Communist codes and tracked military unit movements, then through unambiguous tactical indicators provided by the truly massive Soviet arms supply in the spring, which dramatically changed the relative balance of forces between North and South. Yet American leaders took no steps to strengthen the Republic of Korea against attack. Despite the rapidly escalating military capabilities of the North, which were evident in intelligence dispatches, in 1950, before the war began, Washington had supplied a grand total of military assistance to the ROK of $108 in signal wire!

Not only did American leaders deliberately decline to rectify the changing military balance on the peninsula, but they also took steps to weaken South Korea's armed forces and convey public disinterest in South Korea's fate, even in the event of an outright invasion by the North. This posture contravened Washington's stated policy contained in NSC-8/2 of March 23, 1949, which called for the United States to build and maintain military and police forces in South Korea capable of providing for internal security and defending against armed provocations from the North.[3]

Explicit in this commitment was the requirement for constant monitoring of the North Korean threat to ensure a continuing South Korean capability to accomplish the objectives set. Thus, if North Korea became stronger, the United States would be bound to increase support for the South to maintain the desired equilibrium. At the time NSC-8/2 was formulated in the spring of 1949, the North Korean Army was a four-division infantry force supplemented by a small armored regiment of light tanks. This was a purely defensive force, incapable of mounting an invasion of the South.

In mid-1949, Pyongyang's army was actually smaller than its paramilitary Border Constabulary force (46,000 to 56,000), but pursuant to a military assistance pact signed with the Soviet Union on March 17, U.S. Army intelligence expected the North Korean Army shortly to surpass the Border Constabulary in strength and grow from a four- to a six-division infantry, and from a single armored regiment to "three mechanized 'units.'"[4] U.S. intelligence also anticipated that the Soviet Union would provide the North with a 150-plane air force of World War II vintage fighters, bombers, and reconnaissance aircraft, once "North Korea has sufficient air force trained personnel." Thus, according to this estimate, the mid-1949 North Korean force total of 102,350 men was expected to grow to at least 132,000 once the two divisions and the three armored units were added.

On the basis of this anticipated growth in the size of the North Korean armed forces, the United States determined the size of the force it believed would be adequate to provide for South Korea's defense following the planned withdrawal of American forces in June of that year. The nature of the threat—based on North Korea's estimated capability—was determined to be internal subversion through infiltration of spies, guerrillas, and saboteurs, and armed incidents along the 38th parallel, but not an outright invasion.

American leaders thus decided to provide arms, equipment, supplies, and training for a 65,000-man army, a 35,000-man police force, and a 4,000-man coast guard, for a total force of 104,000 men. On the assumption that a three- or four-to-one advantage was required for a successful invasion, this force was thought to be adequate to defend the Republic of Korea. In fact, however, the United States only provided a full complement of arms for an infantry force of 50,000 men. When conditions began to change rapidly in 1950, Washington held rigidly to commitments established in NSC-8/2, and refused all requests to provide additional arms, or upgrade South Korea's defensive capability.

As early as mid-1949 it was clear that the NKA was a qualitatively superior force to the South Korean Army, a deficiency that the Truman administration declined to redress. Although North Korea possessed a growing air force, the United States provided neither an air force nor an anti-aircraft capability to the ROK. Although the North possessed a growing tank corps, Washington provided neither tanks nor anti-tank mines, the most effective (and most obvious) weapon to employ against tanks in Korea's narrow valley roads. Although the North possessed a large, long-range artillery capability, no comparable long-range artillery was provided to the ROK Army. There were serious ammunition shortages in all categories of arms and the armed forces possessed only a ten-day supply of reserve munitions. In addition, although the North was increasingly attempting to insert guerrilla forces by sea into the South, Washington provided no coastal patrol boats.

The public rationale for declining to provide South Korea with heavy weapons, especially planes, tanks, and long-range artillery, was fear that the Rhee government would attack the North in an attempt to unify the country, a threat that the president frequently uttered in his bombastic public speeches. This was a possibility to be taken seriously, and Washington did. But, of course, anti-tank guns, anti-tank mines, anti-aircraft guns, and coastal patrol craft could not provide the basis for an invasion of the North. They could only be employed in defense. Yet they were pointedly not provided, which leaves the conclusion that the United States did not wish to deter an attack. Indeed, from its actions and inaction in 1950, Washington invited one.

TETHERING THE SOUTH KOREAN GOAT

Roving ambassador Philip Jessup, as part of his regional tour of East Asia, visited South Korea from January 11 to January 14. Jessup's visit included a one-day trip to the demilitarized zone (DMZ) in the Uijongbu area, which straddled the main, traditional invasion route to Seoul. Jessup's trip report, along with Ambassador John Muccio's report on his visit, constitute in microcosm a snapshot of the respective status of the forces of North and South Korea. Their observations, in turn, establish a baseline of sorts from which to measure the rapid divergence of capabilities that then evolved, as well as of Washington's refusal to maintain an equilibrium.

In reporting on the condition of South Korean forces, Jessup observed that they were adequately trained and equipped for counter-guerrilla operations, but were successful "only by devoting to the campaigns overwhelming superiority ... [and] tying up considerable numbers of troops in this work." He approved of efforts by General Lynne Roberts, chief of the Korean Military Advisory Group (KMAG) to organize "national police units which will operate as constabulary and relieve the demands on the regular army."[5] It was reportedly Roberts's view that the "Korean Army had the capability of containing the North Korean forces in being. However, he pointed to the need for additional U.S. aid for the Korean security forces, especially the air forces and the coast guard."[6]

Ambassador Jessup was impressed with the "smartness of the Korean troops in drill," but observed that they had "only six" anti-tank guns, and no anti-tank mines. South Korean officers in the field "stressed the need for more anti-tank guns since the North has a good many light tanks." The exchange regarding the need for anti-tank guns to contend with North Korean light tanks is of interest on two counts. Curiously, it would be the last such reference in the public record to, let alone request for, anti-tank weapons of any kind before war erupted. Second, the reference to "light tanks" indicated that South Korean intelligence, and perhaps the Korean Military Advisory Group (KMAG) as well, were at this time unaware of the fact that the North Korean Army's main armored vehicle was, or would soon become, the T-34 medium tank, a decidedly different level of threat, against which the South would have no defense. More will be said about the "tank problem" below (see p. 170).

Ambassador Jessup also noted that "northern artillery is heavier than theirs and outranges them by at least a thousand yards." Additionally, General Roberts stressed the absolute need for anti-aircraft weapons, saying: "Five or ten bombers could come over and be absolutely unopposed and probably disrupt South Korea by the panic which would result from a raid on Seoul." Jessup observed that the ROK had "anti-personnel land mines ...

and their combat engineers are well trained in demolition of bridges, etc., in case of an enemy attack." He also believed that the morale of the troops was high, but the "defensive positions laid out near the 38th Parallel ... arranged in collaboration with KMAG ... are considered by our people to be quite useless."[7]

In discussions with Korean officers and KMAG personnel, Jessup learned that they had experienced considerable success recently in cutting down infiltration across the parallel, which, however, was "driving the communists to intensify their efforts to smuggle in men and arms by sea." Unfortunately, he observed, "the Korean lack of coast guard patrol craft makes it very difficult to control this." Jessup also felt that his interlocutors "all make out a good case for the need for at least a few aircraft and antiaircraft guns." General Roberts said that he would like to have "a few light tanks, [but] these were low on his priority list." Roberts himself made no request for anti-tank guns or anti-tank mines, indicating that he viewed the tank threat as negligible.

Thus, during his brief stay in Korea, Jessup clearly recognized the military advantages that the North already held over the South and the shortcomings in the southern defense posture. Jessup was openly critical of KMAG competence in laying out defensive positions along the 38th parallel, but was impressed with troop morale and training in demolition work. Over the next six months, the gap between the advantages of the North and the shortcomings of the South would grow rapidly and Ambassador Muccio and General Roberts would try, increasingly frantically, to remedy the South's deficiencies, to no avail. All requests for additional, critically needed defensive equipment were denied, or simply given the classic bureaucratic Ping-Pong treatment and passed from one office to another with no resolution.

Whatever good feelings were generated by the visit of one of the State Department's highest ranking officers dissipated completely a few days after he departed. On January 19, a week after Acheson's Press Club speech, the House of Representatives voted down a $60-million economic aid bill for South Korea. Although the vote was very close (originally believed to have been by two votes, but later discovered to have been by the margin of a single vote), the defeat of the bill was regarded as a slap at Truman's Far East policy and indifference toward the Republic of Korea. It was the first rejection by either body of Congress of an administration foreign policy measure since 1939 and it created a storm in Congress for three weeks over American foreign policy before the aid bill was passed in an amended form.[8] Ironically, the storm broke just as the Truman administration was changing strategy and, in retrospect, raises questions about the relationship of the House action to it.

During the debate before the vote, congressional opinion on South Korea was sharply divided. Southern Democrats joined Republicans to mount a challenge to the administration over Asia policy in general. There was particular objection to Truman's January 5 announcement to terminate military assistance to the Nationalist government on Taiwan and to Acheson's speech on the 12th. Congressional opponents decided to exert pressure on the Truman administration to change policy by voting against appropriations bills. The Korean aid bill was the first target.

Ohio Republican John Vorys declared that passage of the aid bill would be " 'money down a rathole' because Communist forces in North Korea might overrun United States–controlled South Korea at any time." The North Korean army, he said, "could move . . . on Russia's orders." Democratic supporters of the administration countered with the view that there was little reason for Russian aggression against South Korea. One member, Adolph Sabath of Illinois, declared that he was "authoritatively informed" that "there is no such danger." Administration officials, reassuring Democratic supporters "on background" that there was no war danger, were careful to say that there was no danger from overt "Russian aggression."

President Truman and Secretary of State Acheson immediately responded. Acheson sent a letter to the president expressing "concern and dismay" about the impact of the vote on American foreign policy, should it be allowed to stand. Truman quickly sought to retrieve the Korean aid legislation by issuing a statement urging congressional leaders to take "immediate action" to ensure that "important foreign-policy interests of this country are properly safeguarded."[9] The president's ally in congress, Tom Connally, chairman of the Senate Foreign Relations Committee, told reporters that, if the House failed to reintroduce a Korean aid bill, then the Senate would either introduce a Korean aid bill of its own or "provide funds by a simple amendment of existing ECA legislation."

Connally said it was important "that we go ahead and extend aid to Korea. We have a very fine program there, and it is being well administered." It's important, he said, because "Korea is a democratic country, a kind of testing ground for keeping other countries in Asia out of the Communist system." The Senate Foreign Relations chairman did not regard the House vote on Korea "as any indication of what Congress would do on other foreign aid measures." In his view, the House action was "caused partly by the strong feelings of some Republicans over Formosa," but, he said, "they'll get over their dissatisfaction."

In fact, the administration's response to what appeared on one level to be a brouhaha with pro-Kuomintang supporters, Republicans and Southern Democrats, was on another level and in retrospect the first public indication that the United States was changing strategy. Coming in the wake of the Chinese seizure of U.S. consular offices in Beijing four days earlier (see chapter 3, p. 74), which marked the failure of the wedge strategy, the administration "reluctantly" agreed to include short-term assistance to the Nationalists on Formosa in the newly redesignated Korean Aid Bill, a decision that transformed the original bill into a "far different measure." One Republican lawmaker, Donald L. Jackson of California, declared that "it resembles the original Korean-aid bill ... about as much as Forever Amber resembles Mother Goose."[10]

The revised bill was reported out of committee by a vote of 17 to 1 and sailed through the House on February 9, by a 240 to 134 majority. It contained two principal measures: first, the $60 million in the original Korean aid bill and, second, economic assistance for the Nationalist government on Taiwan, in the form of an extension of the period in which existing appropriations could be spent from February 15 to June 30, 1950, the end of the fiscal year. There was roughly $103 million still available from the previous fiscal year's appropriation, although it was estimated that not more than $10.5 million could be spent in territory remaining under Nationalist control.[11]

In response to a series of pointed questions raised by Republicans on the House Foreign Affairs Committee, the president reaffirmed his earlier decision to bar any further military aid to Taiwan. Republicans wanted to know whether the secretary of Defense, the Joint Chiefs, and General MacArthur were asked their views before President Truman cut off military aid to the Nationalists? In response, the administration arranged for Secretary Johnson and JCS Chairman Omar Bradley to issue a statement of support. In it, they "accepted" the president's policy decision on Formosa and said that MacArthur's view was the same, except that he "attaches more urgency to the situation."[12]

Their considered view was that Formosa held strategic significance only if it "fell to an enemy." By enemy, they meant "not necessarily the Chinese Communists, as such, but any force ... with hostile designs on the United States," a thinly veiled reference to the Soviet Union. Nevertheless, MacArthur and the Joint Chiefs agreed that while "Formosa in hostile hands would be a menace to our lifelines," this did not justify sending forces in advance to occupy the island. Finally, Secretary Johnson sought to clear the air about rumors of a division between the Pentagon and State Department, saying: "Rumors about a fight between himself and Acheson were unfounded."

Several questions from House members related to the mainland-Taiwan issue. The administration's responses to two of them, however, were "permanently classified as secret." The questions were: "Has any recent survey of defense resources of Formosa been made by any agency of this Government?" and "Have the Chinese Communist forces obtained, and are they obtaining, amphibious assault equipment from the Soviet Union or elsewhere?"[13] As we now know, the answer to the first question was no. No government "agency"

153

had conducted a survey of Formosa, but several private groups composed of retired military and intelligence officers and others had made assessments.[14] As to the second, we also now know that Stalin had declined to provide Mao with amphibious assault equipment, which, however, had not deterred the Chinese from invasion preparations.

The administration's response was sufficiently satisfactory, even though not everyone was satisfied, to permit passage of the Far East Economic Assistance Act, the now redesignated Korean Aid Bill. Even though aid to Korea was restored by passage of the FEEA Act, which now linked Korea and Taiwan, the furor created by the original defeat of the bill reinforced the erroneous impression conveyed by Acheson in his January 12 speech that the United States was not overly concerned about the fate of the Republic of Korea.

The three weeks between the bill's defeat and resurrection spanned the period when the United States changed strategy, and served to divert attention away from that crucial decision. Also at this time, in early February, Senator Joseph McCarthy began to publicize claims of communists in the government, particularly in the State Department, which precipitated Senate hearings and further muddled public perceptions. During this same period, on January 31, Truman secretly authorized the formulation of a new strategy, NSC-68 (see chapter 6, p. 122). That strategy would, of course, incorporate Taiwan and South Korea into the U.S. defense perimeter in the Western Pacific, but that step would not be taken publicly until after war erupted on the Korean peninsula.

MUCCIO'S AND ROBERTS'S PLEAS FOR ASSISTANCE IGNORED

Just after the news broke regarding congressional disapproval of the Korean economic aid bill, administration officials arrived in Seoul to obtain the Rhee government's signature on the congressional military appropriation for the ROK passed in October 1949. The Mutual Defense Assistance Program allocated a combined $27.64 million for Iran, the Philippines, and the Republic of Korea, without publicly divulging the share for each. In fact, the administration had determined that Korea's share would be $10.23 million for fiscal year 1950, which ended June 30, 1950. The Rhee government signed the military assistance agreement on January 25, although there was great dissatisfaction over the amount in Seoul, particularly within the U.S. embassy and the Korean Military Advisory Group.

Muccio and Roberts immediately attempted to obtain an increased allotment on the grounds that $10.23 million "was far from adequate to meet the minimum all-around needs of the Korean Security Forces in the light of the situation existing in this part of the world."[15] The ambassador recommended that the basic allotment be supplemented by $9.8 million with funds provided under section 303 of the Mutual Defense Assistance Act "to bring the total funds available for military assistance to Korea, in the fiscal year '50 to a minimum of $20 million." He pointed out that "the strengthening of the defenses of the Republic of Korea would obviously contribute to the accomplishment in the general area of China of the policies and purposes set forth in the MDA Act."

Muccio enclosed Roberts's recommendations for additional fiscal year 1950 military assistance, "scaled down to fall within the approximate dollar limitations of $9,800,000."[16] Roberts's concern was to "strengthen the existing Security Forces without providing means for an increase in numerical strength." The original intent under NSC-8/2, he noted, was for a U.S. total supported ground force of 65,000 men, but Washington had provided equipment sufficient for only a 50,000-man force. The 15,000 additional men were armed "with individual arms only." Roberts's request sought to close the gap in this commitment with "crew served weapons, additional artillery with supporting Ordnance and Signal equipment, and a limited quantity of Engineer items." The ground force portion of his supplemental recommendation came to $4.57 million.

Roberts also strongly recommended provision of forty F-51 fighter aircraft to counter the high performance Yak-3 fighters that the Russians had transferred to North Korea.[17] North Korean air strength had already been confirmed at thirty, with more expected. "The South Korean Security Forces are totally without means of combating this type aircraft." The Korean government had purchased with its own funds ten AT-6 trainer aircraft from Canada and was seeking American assistance in refitting them, but, even if armed, these planes would be no match for the Yak-3s. Roberts also recommended provision of "minimum essential equipment" to ensure adequate training and maintenance for the planes. The total estimated cost for the air force portion was $3.91 million.

Lastly, Roberts recommended the provision of ordnance and signal equipment to outfit three U.S. Navy–type coastal patrol boats as well as related shore signal installations. The Korean government had purchased one patrol boat in the United States with its own funds, which the United States had outfitted, and now expressed its intention of purchasing three additional coastal patrol boats, which Roberts proposed the United States should similarly outfit with armament, ammunition, and communications gear. The estimated cost of this assistance was $1.31 million.

The secretary of state, replying to Muccio nine days later, completely ignored the pleas for supplemental military assistance, and instead focused on ways to solve the inflation problem in South Korea. His principal recommendation for bringing inflationary forces under control was for the Seoul ad-

155

ministration to reduce defense spending, which was seen to be "one of [the] big destabilizing factors."[18] Since military spending was determined to be the inflation stimulus, Acheson instructed, "we should be prepared [to] indicate how such expenditures can be controlled and reconciled with stabilization objectives."

There was a sort of backwards legitimacy here. The Rhee government, having noted the growing capability of the North, had decided on its own to increase its infantry force from the 65,000 authorized by the United States to 100,000 and, against the advice of KMAG, had established a Korean Air Force, even though it had only a handful of planes and pilots. In addition, as Jessup had urged, the government was attempting to expand its police force to take over counter-guerrilla tasks from the army and was seeking to enlarge its coast guard to improve defense against infiltration by sea. Acheson sought to place limits on this expansion of forces.

Acheson wanted to know how the ROK apportioned its defense expenditures and what the "minimum fixed expenditures [were] for a basic security force of 100 thousand men, a police force of 50 thousand, and existing naval forces given the present military situation." Acheson's concern was to establish "a benchmark from which to evaluate [the] desirability of additional expenditures for combat aircraft, heavy weapons, patrol craft, etc., in terms of their internal budgetary costs." He wanted to know the "anticipated budgetary effects" of the embassy's recommendation to increase military assistance funds to $20 million.

The secretary suggested that it would be "useful" to include a representative from KMAG as well as from the government's Ministry of Defense on the "joint stabilization committee" to control defense expenditures in the name of combating inflation. In other words, through his request to obtain information on defense expenditures, Acheson was attempting to exert pressure on the Korean government to reduce defense spending. His request was for information on which to base an evaluation, an evaluation that had been made months before, and which explicitly called into question the recommendations from Muccio and Roberts, not to mention from Ambassador Jessup, regarding the ROK's defense needs. Of course, responding to the secretary's requests would take time, delaying the delivery of military assistance. Acheson was stalling.

Chargé d'Affaires Everett Drumright, reporting some success, replied to Acheson a week later: "After prolonged discussion between KMAG and officials [of the] Ministry National Defense, chief of staff Korean Army agreed to limit allocation for fourth quarter Korean fiscal year ending 31 March to 4.37 billion won for national defense."[19] At an exchange rate of roughly 900 won to the dollar, this meant defense expenditures for the fourth quarter, January to March, were $4.8 million. The Korean defense chief agreed to limit expenditures by "eliminating all expenditures for Youth Corps, Reserve Corps, and other irregular forces . . . deferring maintenance and repair of buildings and by reducing food ration allowance for units." Still, Drumright added, despite "strongest representations," the Korean leadership "does not recognize grave consequences [of] continued deficit spending." Rhee himself wanted the joint stabilization committee to "correct [the] impression that there was a financial crisis in Korea."

Drumright calculated that the defense authorization for 100,000 army troops, 7,500 navy and 2,500 air force personnel "can be supported . . . on total appropriation for Ministry of National Defense of 27 billion won in contrast to 36 billion won included in budget for fiscal year 1950–51 submitted to National Assembly without mission concurrence." In other words, Drumright believed that a 25 percent smaller defense budget (from $40 million to $30 million) would still be sufficient to support the authorized force level. This, he said, "assumes minimum present value of won and military situation as it now exists and flow of military aid continuing in future years as at present." In Drumright's view, the "limitations" of Korea's heavy industry made it essential that "this flow continue." To clarify, the chargé d'affaires believed that defense cuts could be sustained *if* the exchange rate remained stable, *if* there was no increase in the North Korean threat, and *if* U.S. military assistance continued.

The secretary responded four days later, continuing to ignore the defense requests. Instead, he pressed anti-inflation measures and sought to dampen spirits following congressional passage of the Far East Economic Assistance Act, which included $60 million in economic aid for South Korea. Acheson wanted to drive home to the Rhee government that it should not now throw caution to the wind on the assumption that the United States would continue to provide support. "Pres Rhee should be most candidly informed that passage on 9 Feb of Bill authorizing $60 million for Second period FY 1950 is not occasion for relaxation of AMIK [American Military in Korea]-ROK efforts to curb inflation."[20] The House action "did not constitute any commitment beyond 30 June." The secretary declared that the House had expressed "serious reservations . . . concerning ability and willingness ROK to utilize ECA program effectively and to promote democratic processes in south Korea." He warned that "halfway anti-inflationary measures by ROK could possibly result in ROK receiving no more than $30 million."

On March 15, the day that the final terms of the Mutual Defense Assistance agreement were signed, nine top State Department and ECA personnel concerned with Korea met under the chairmanship of Walton Butterworth to discuss the political and economic situation. Not a word was devoted to a discussion of the military threat, or to requests for more defense support. Instead, the entire discussion focused on cutting off military support as a

157

means of obtaining greater compliance from the Korean government to cut spending.

Complaints were raised about the tendency "on the part of President Rhee toward a personal authoritarian type of government backed by police support." Not only was President Rhee exhibiting "police state tendencies," he had "failed completely to appreciate the nature and the gravity of the inflationary threat in Korea and . . . had continued to by-pass the provisions of the Constitution with respect to the financing of the Government."[21]

Some believed that "Rhee might be more compliant with our wishes if he were made to feel a little more uncertain about continuing U.S. support." There was some suggestion of employing the threat of terminating all aid as an "ultimatum," before it was acknowledged that "Rhee's strongest weapon is his knowledge that the U.S. could not let the Republic of Korea fall without incurring the gravest political repercussions." Then the point was made that "if the present trend continued very long, the time might come when the lesser of two evils would be to cut [South Korea] loose and run the risk of incurring such consequences."

The question was raised "of whether any useful purpose would be served by using the threat of stoppage of military assistance as a weapon with the Korean Government." Rhee, it was pointed out, as an old revolutionary, "had a more ready understanding of bullets than of capital investments," and the threat of a military cutoff "might get more directly at the heart of the obstacles to stabilization interposed by the defense and police officials." Butterworth suggested at this point that "a State-ECA working group be set up . . . to formulate recommendations." This engendered some objections. It was felt that no new group was necessary since

> all the technical and administrative problems had been thoroughly explored by the Economic Stabilization Committee and that the crucial remaining and unsolved problem was the basically political problem of the ability and willingness of the present Korean Government to enforce the measures which had been recommended.

But Butterworth disagreed, declaring, in closing the session, that the problem of inflation was compounded by several factors; he mentioned "political, economic, and administrative." Butterworth had made no mention of military spending as a factor, yet the "working group" he authorized was to "concentrate on all the steps that could be taken to get the Korean Government to deal in a responsible fashion with this problem." That is, this working group was empowered to recommend the extreme measure of cutting off military aid to gain the Korean government's agreement to reduce defense expenditures as a means of combating inflation.

While administration officials in Washington were contemplating a military aid cutoff, in Seoul the North Korean invasion threat loomed larger. On March 6, Ambassador Muccio had received a letter from President Rhee requesting that obsolescent F-51 fighter planes being phased out in Japan be sent to Korea, to counter the growing North Korean air threat. South Korea's intelligence sources now indicated the Soviet Union had delivered to the North "between 70 and 100 fighters and bombers," which was more than triple the number they were believed to have had in January. Rhee pointed out that "there would obviously be a disastrous effect on South Korean civilian morale as well as on the military situation north of Seoul if enemy planes could bomb and strafe without any fear of retaliation."[22]

On March 16, Muccio sent a cable to Acheson forwarding Rhee's request and enclosing Roberts's supporting memorandum. The KMAG chief declared forthrightly that it was "obvious that immediate measures must be taken to provide Korea with effective air means of countering the growing air threat from the North. This has consistently been the attitude of KMAG." Roberts pointedly noted that "it is understood that this matter has been under discussion in the Department of Defense since last October," that is, for six months, and suggested that for information on the problem "together with a proposed solution," reference should be made to the "numerous proposals" that KMAG had made not only for aircraft, but for air advisers and training of pilots.

Roberts was careful not to pass policy judgment. "I am not in a position to comment on the availability or proposed use of obsolescent aircraft now in Japan." But, he said, "it is known that F-84's and F-86's are now being sent to Japan to replace some or all of the F-51's now in FEAF [Far East Air Force]. I feel that aircraft rendered excess by this substitution will . . . be used to supply MDAP countries. . . . I doubt that they will be 'discarded' or 'junked' as President Rhee presumes." In summing up, Roberts wanted the embassy to forward President Rhee's letter "with a strong statement as to the urgent necessity for a well equipped Korean Air Force."

Muccio agreed. Referring to earlier dispatches recommending the provision of aircraft in his cover letter, he said: "If it is a fact that air equipment in Japan is being rendered obsolescent and declared surplus, it is earnestly hoped that such of this equipment as will meet the requirements of the Republic of Korea will be allocated to this country." But Muccio's and Roberts's urgent pleas fell on deaf ears in Washington. Secretary Acheson was not interested in strengthening the Rhee government.

The secretary of state replied a week later, once again ignoring Muccio's cable, Roberts's memo, and Rhee's request. Now Acheson raised the stakes, referring not only to the "critical . . . problems created by apparent inability or unwillingness ROK recognize and deal effectively with inflation threat," but also to the Rhee government's "increasing anti-democratic tendencies."

159

The secretary asked the ambassador to return to Washington for a "brief consultation," and, upon departing, to "issue brief statement . . . to effect your recall for consultation due your Govt's concern over inflationary situation."[23]

The ambassador delayed a response for almost a week, largely because of the eruption of another issue. The Economic Cooperation Agency had taken action following the discussion of measures to compel greater cooperation from Seoul. One possibility, recall, was the threat to terminate aid. The administrator of the ECA, Paul C. Hoffman, now, on March 27, made that threat in a harsh reply to an earlier letter by President Rhee downplaying the severity of the inflation problem. Hoffman flatly disagreed with the president, bluntly declaring that "the appraisal of the present economic situation in the Republic of Korea which your letter sets forth is invalid and that the optimism which the letter seems to reflect is unwarranted." Government spending continued to exceed its revenues, he said. "Unless tax revenues are sharply increased and expenditures are drastically reduced, prices will continue to rise, probably at an accelerating rate."[24]

Berating the president, Hoffman said that he could "hardly believe that the true nature of the situation is not known to you. I am, therefore, impelled to raise with you the question of whether your Government has a real intention to deal with the problem of inflation." The ECA chief closed with the blunt threat of cutting aid. "Unless I am convinced that a forthright, immediate effort will be made to control inflation . . . I must consider the advisability of requesting a lesser sum from the Appropriations Committee than the $60,000,000 authorized. . . . Similarly, I must further review the request of $100,000,000 which the ECA is making for Korea aid during fiscal year 1951."

Muccio had been sent a copy of this letter, but there can be no doubt that President Rhee immediately complained to him about this personally demeaning and undiplomatic exchange. No doubt Muccio was concerned about adding fuel to the flames, which affected his response to Acheson's cable. In his reply on March 29, Muccio agreed that a brief consultation would be most useful but thought issuing a statement indicating a "lack of cooperation" on the part of the ROK "would in my opinion not serve [a] helpful purpose," and might boomerang. It was his view that "while there are many disturbing developments in situation here, there are equally a number of favorable developments." Muccio felt that the projected late May elections "may mark an important turn in developments," and wished to return to Korea to be on hand when they were held.

The ambassador's reasons for objecting to issuing a statement on lack of cooperation from the government had to do with the "progress" he said had occurred over the previous two months.[25] Specifically, the food program was now in operation, the National Assembly had passed a measure to implement land reform, agreement had been reached on the pricing of subsidies to government enterprises, and a balanced budget for fiscal year 1950/51 was now before the National Assembly. Muccio admitted that, except for the current year's food plan, results were still in the "paper stage," but he insisted that "progress is being made and we have all pushed Korean counterparts as strongly as possible, and almost to breaking point at times."

Acheson replied two days later, explaining that the suggested statement did not envisage a reference to a "lack of cooperation" (diplomatic jargon for severe censure), but "merely to our 'concern over inflationary situation.'" The secretary was "still inclined" to have Muccio issue such a statement, but was willing to leave it to his discretion. In any case, he said, the State Department would be conveying its attitude when the Korean ambassador called on the Department prior to his departure on a goodwill mission to Australia and New Zealand. At that time, the ambassador "will be handed aide memoire setting forth Dept's views on inflationary situation."[26]

Muccio replied to Acheson on April 1, to report yet another new and disturbing development. President Rhee had threatened to postpone scheduled general elections from the end of May until sometime in November unless the National Assembly passed the government's budget proposals then before it. Muccio thought that postponement of the elections "would become more serious than economic problems discussed in proposed aide memoire," and intended to urge President Rhee "most strongly" against postponement. Muccio wanted the secretary to include the electoral problem in the aide memoire being prepared for Ambassador John Chang.[27]

When Ambassador Chang called at the State Department on April 3, Dean Rusk, newly promoted to Assistant Secretary of State for Far Eastern Affairs, handed him the aide memoire and proceeded to summarize it orally, focusing on the twin topics of combating inflation and the postponement of elections. Rusk emphasized that "whatever the reasons might be, the postponement of the long-scheduled May elections would certainly be widely interpreted as an arbitrary action and one inconsistent with the democratic principles in accordance with which the Republic of Korea had been brought into being." On inflation, Rusk declared that it was the Department's "firmly-held belief that the success of the Republic of Korea in maintaining itself as a free nation was at the present juncture dependent in large measure upon its ability to deal effectively with the mounting inflation."[28] Indeed, Rusk subtly inserted the threat that "continued inflation . . . would serve to destroy the basis for further American aid."

Chang agreed with Rusk's admonitions and promised to convey the Department's views to President Rhee, but the Korean ambassador had come with his own agenda. Most important, he wished to "express the hope of the Korean Government that the American defense line in the Far East could be extended to include South Korea." Rusk quickly replied that "this was not a subject which he was in a position to discuss," but he cautioned the ambassador "against putting too much faith in what he read in the newspapers." Rusk pointed out that the "so-called 'defense line' to which the Ambassador had referred was in actuality merely an enumeration of those sectors in the western Pacific in which the United States had firm military commitments."

Ambassador Chang impressed upon Rusk "the importance which the Korean Government and people attached to their apparent exclusion from the defense plans of the United States," but Rusk replied that the "inference that the United States had decided to abandon the Republic of Korea to its enemies was scarcely warranted in the light of the substantial material aid and political support which we had furnished and were furnishing." Then Niles Bond, the country desk officer, declared: "It had been the carefully considered judgment of this Government that the most efficacious means of defending against Communist expansion was to bring about the creation in South Korea of a strong, self-reliant, Korean government, and that it was to that end that our policy in Korea continued to be directed." With that, Ambassador Chang changed the subject to his forthcoming trip, and then departed.

On April 13, Secretary Acheson finally cabled Muccio to "acknowledge receipt" of the now five-week-old request for aircraft and the nearly three-month-old request for patrol boats. The secretary said that "the Department submitted the requests of the Republic of Korea for air and Coast Guard assistance to the Department of Defense for consideration" and was enclosing their "tentative" views. They were devastating. The DOD memorandum flatly declared that "based on the existing authority and intent of NSC 8/2, there appears to be no military necessity for an increase in the Fiscal Year 1950 MDA Program for Korea at this time."[29]

Specifically, a separate Korean Air Force "would be beyond the concept of NSC 8/2, which authorizes an Army of 65,000 men with air detachments," that is, light aircraft for liaison and courier service, but no combat aircraft. Regarding the ground forces, the fiscal year 1950 program provided "adequate support" to "maintain internal security and protect the Republic of Korea from border incidents." Finally, regarding the coast guard, NSC 8/2 established a 4,000-man unit. "Vessels are on hand for this number of men and the present program provides maintenance spare parts for these vessels."

Despite what was by now a rapidly shifting military balance based on the influx of Soviet fighter aircraft to North Korea, the increased rate of infiltration into South Korea by sea, and the growing preponderance of heavy weapons in the hands of Pyongyang's forces, the Department of Defense determined that "there appears to be no military necessity for an increase" in the

1949 program! In closing, perhaps in an attempt to soften the blow, Acheson promised that the "whole question of aid to the Republic of Korea will be reviewed with Ambassador Muccio upon his arrival in Washington within the next few days."

In fact, however, Acheson sidestepped the issue. While Muccio was en route to Washington, the State Department sent the final, approved MDAP for fiscal year 1950 to Seoul. It was for $10.23 million. Incredibly, not only would there be no supplemental assistance, but also, according to the enclosed delivery schedule, the meager assistance previously determined upon would not begin to arrive until fiscal year 1951. Chargé d'Affaires Drumright could not contain his dismay, as he cabled his response to Acheson. It is worth quoting at length.[30]

Most significant aspect of approved program is scheduled deliveries by which only $108 of military aid will arrive in FY1950, two-thirds of total dollar value will be shipped in FY1951 and remaining third in FY1952. Impact of this very serious, delay in deliveries is greater than at first appears in that all vehicle and weapons spare parts and all powder and primers for arsenal program are scheduled for delivery in FY 1952. Owing to quick wearing out of weapons and vehicles (a factor of limited equipment used by large number of troops) and due to critical need of supporting Korean arsenal program, it is essential these 2 categories of MDAP arrive Korea soonest. Material wearing out so fast and currently so seriously in need of spare parts that unless prompt shipment of parts can be assured KMAG considers real danger exists. Major items for which needed will be beyond repair by FY1952. As you know in attempt to stabilize economy, Republic of Korea has cut defense budget substantially. One of first items to be cut was arsenal program (from about 4 billion won to 1.2 billion) which results in increased early need for US assistance in form of powder and primers. Early delivery consonant with US desire that Korea balance budget. Year and half delay contemplated in deliveries these categories should not be accepted except as matter of utmost necessity.

Korea now faced with a condition of materially lessened US military supplies with new flow not coming in significant amounts for 9 months versus enemy force north of parallel which periodic reports put at constantly increasing materiel potential. . . . General Roberts and I request that you do everything in your power to speed dates of delivery of MDAP materials, especially of critical items such as vehicle and weapons spare parts, powder and primers.

Not only did Secretary of State Acheson not reply to this cry of alarm, but the official record contains only a solitary communication from the secretary to Seoul from this date until after the outbreak of the war. This, on June 13, was a brief seven-line message asking for clarification of an earlier embassy comment, which bore no relevance to defense needs. In other words, from April 20 until the outbreak of the war, a span of over two months that covered the period of the massive Soviet buildup in North Korea, Secretary

Acheson said nothing in response to the Seoul embassy's repeated requests to bolster the Republic of Korea's defenses. Of course, the secretary's silence should not be taken to mean there was indifference.

WASHINGTON GIVES MUCCIO THE RUNAROUND

Meanwhile, Ambassador Muccio had arrived in Washington to plead in person for provision of needed armament for Seoul's forces. His pleas went unheeded as he was shunted like a Ping-Pong ball from the State Department to the Defense Department and to the White House. At a large, top-secret, inter-departmental meeting on April 27 at the State Department, Ambassador Muccio made the case for Korea.[31] In discussion with twenty-nine of the department's top officials, Muccio declared that President Rhee had "accepted" and acted on "every recommendation of the Joint Commission on Economic Stabilization." Rhee had moved to balance the budget, raise taxes, cut defense, and regulate foreign exchange. In the long run, Muccio believed, these measures "presaged an improvement in the economic situation." Their immediate effect, however, was to weaken the regime.

For a government only twenty-one months old, following forty years of Japanese control and three years of U.S. military government, the Republic of Korea was doing remarkably well. They were privatizing industries that had previously belonged to the Japanese and were also strengthening the agricultural sector, in which 80 percent of the Korean people worked. Indeed, the peasantry "constitute a strong element of stability." South Korea was in fact on the verge of initiating a grand socioeconomic experiment combining land reform and industrial privatization to jump-start economic development—a scheme not attempted since the Meiji Restoration in Japan nearly a century earlier.

On June 1, the government would initiate a plan whereby it would take over all land holdings in excess of 7.35 acres and convey land ownership to over one million tenants.[32] In recompense, landlords would receive government bonds, with which they would purchase some five thousand government-owned industrial plants previously built by Japan. The ingenious scheme transferred landownership to the tiller, and in theory would transform landlords into industrialists, in exactly the same way the Japanese did in the mid–nineteenth century to trigger the growth of Japan into an economic superpower.

The key question, Muccio said, was whether the Koreans could "handle their own affairs." In this regard, he believed it was heartening to see the National Assembly display a "growing sense of responsibility" and the president not only commit to free elections, but also to request United Nations observance of them. Muccio was enthusiastic about the coming elections. Two thousand candidates had filed for two hundred positions. Many independent candidates were running for office, which, Muccio felt, "indicates that the National Assembly is considered an important body."

"Also heartening," Muccio said, was the "effective training of the Army," which has been "successful in controlling the constant flow of saboteurs and special agents from North Korea." Nevertheless, he said, the Koreans "need help in the economic and military fields." It was Muccio's considered judgment that the Korean people "have the will and ability to defend themselves [and] the U.S. should provide the 'missing component', which will enable them to hold on to the area." (Acheson in his January 12 speech had referred to U.S. assistance as providing the missing component to a country needing but a modicum of assistance to succeed.) In closing, Ambassador Muccio declared that "Korea is a symbol of U.S. interest in Asia . . . and it is important to help the Korean people keep their freedom and independence."

As convincing as Ambassador Muccio's report on the Republic of Korea's progress, potential, and need for continued American assistance may have been, his views ran contrary to policy. Publicly, support for South Korea was totally undercut a few days later by the appearance of the widely read weekly magazine *U.S. News & World Report*. The magazine contained an interview with Senate Foreign Relations Chairman Tom Connally on the subject of "World Policy and Bipartisanship." Two key questions were about Korea and his answers exploded on Washington like bombshells, casting a pall over Korea's future that stretched all the way to Seoul.

Connally was asked whether "the suggestion that we abandon south Korea is going to be seriously considered?" Connally said:

> I am afraid it is going to be seriously considered because I'm afraid it's going to happen, whether we want it to or not. I'm for Korea. We're trying to help her—we're appropriating money now to help her. But South Korea is cut right across by this line—north of it are the Communists, with access to the mainland—and Russia is over there on the mainland. So that whenever she takes a notion she can just overrun Korea just like she probably will overrun Formosa when she gets ready to do it. I hope not, of course.

Secondly, he was asked: "But isn't Korea an essential part of the defense strategy?" He answered:

> No. Of course, any position like that is of some strategic importance. But I don't think it is very greatly important. It has been testified before us that Japan, Okinawa and the Philippines make the chain of defense which is absolutely necessary. And, of course, any additional territory along in that area would be that much more, but it's not absolutely essential.[33]

Connally's response was a stunning one-hundred-eighty-degree turn from his views on Korea stated as recently as late January in the context of passing economic aid for South Korea (see p. 152). Then, he had declared that "Korea is a democratic country, a kind of testing ground for keeping other countries in Asia out of the Communist system." Now, three months later, he had reversed his position from keeping South Korea out of Communist hands to abandoning it to Communist domination. South Korea, he said, was not "greatly important" strategically and not part of the American defense strategy. Moreover, coming from a close partner of the president, his words conveyed a most ominous message.

Connally's remarks appeared in the May 5 issue of *U.S. News & World Report*, which appeared on newsstands on May 2. In what seems to have been a coordinated step, Secretary Acheson held a news conference the next day, where he was asked to comment on Senator Connally's views on Korea. Quoting from a memorandum prepared for him by Dean Rusk, Secretary Acheson recounted the brief history of Soviet obstruction to Korean unification and "how under the United Nations Commission the United States had gone forward with the other nations in establishing Southern Korea; that the United States had been and was now giving them very substantial economic help, military assistance and advice."[34] The secretary "doubted very much whether Senator Connally took a different view from that which the Secretary had just stated." But Acheson did not contradict Senator Connally.

Connally's flat statements about the abandonment of South Korea and its exclusion from America's Asian defense perimeter were met with shock and outrage in Seoul. Fortunately, as Drumright reported, Secretary Acheson's reassuring remarks at his press conference the next day were "received with acclaim and largely vitiated [the] damage resulting from Connally statement."[35] Ambassador Muccio had paid a visit to President Truman on May 4, and afterward "was quoted as saying that there could be no doubt of the eagerness of the United States to maintain Korean independence." Muccio also noted provision of military and economic assistance, and "expressed optimism about the Korean Government's ability to control inflation." President Rhee had also calmed things down by declaring that Acheson's statement had "clarified" Connally's remarks.

But the damage had not been entirely "vitiated." Privately, Rhee continued to seethe. In a conversation with Chargé d'Affaires Drumright a few days later, the president was "deeply bitter" about Senator Connally's remarks, regarding them as "an open invitation to the Communists to come down and take over South Korea. He wondered how any man, in his right senses, not to mention Senator Connally, the Chairman of the Senate Foreign Relations Committee, could make such an irrational statement." It was clear from the "sarcastic" tenor of Rhee's remarks that he believed Connally's statement had "done much harm and that it could not be easily disassociated from United States policy in view of Senator Connally's close relation to the

State Department."[36] Rhee was also extremely "bitter" about what he termed "the failure" to respond to his request to provide air support. Drumright concluded his report by saying:

> It seems clear that the President's faith in the determination of the United States to assist Korea in the event of North Korean aggression has been shaken to an appreciable extent by Senator Connally's remarks, by failure of the United States thus far to take any discernible action to meet Korea's request for air support, and by what appears to be the failure of the United States thus far to supply Korea with military supplies and equipment under the terms of the MDA program. The foregoing factors, coupled with persistent "talk" that Korea lies outside the United States' Far Eastern strategic defense zone, [are] having a decidedly unsettling effect on Korean officials and the public.[37]

In Washington, meanwhile, Ambassador Muccio continued his struggle to gain support for supplemental assistance, seemingly oblivious to the fact that the issue had already been foreclosed against him. In a meeting with armed services directors of military assistance in the Pentagon on May 10, Muccio pointed out the "gaps" in military assistance "thus far committed to South Korea." It was imperative, he said, to plug these gaps "so that our stake in South Korea could be more adequately protected." Muccio pointed out the "lack of any defense against possible attack by air, and a similar lack of sufficient coastal patrol facilities, in both of which respects the Koreans themselves, from their own funds, had been endeavoring to provide a remedy."[38]

The military chiefs had the same two answers for every request Ambassador Muccio made. Existing policy represented by NSC-8/2 prohibited additional assistance to South Korea and, should provision of additional military assistance be desired, there would have to be a political decision from the Department of State. General Lyman Lemnitzer, director of the Office of Military Assistance, began the game by immediately throwing the ball to State, pointing out that the "question of military assistance to the Republic of Korea at the present time was essentially a political one, in as much as South Korea was not regarded as of any particular value to the overall American strategic position in the Far East." It followed for him that "military aid . . . was therefore a matter of concern principally to the Department of State which should take the initiative."

William Galbraith, of the State Department, took the same line. He pointed out that NSC-8/2 made "no provision for an air force" and for an air force to be provided "a revision of that directive . . . would have to be made." Muccio responded by attempting to skirt the directive, replying that "a fully effective air force was not essential but that South Korea should have a few combat planes at least for morale purposes." General Idwal H. Edwards, Acting Deputy Chief of Staff, Operations, U.S. Air Force, "stated, and several times reiterated," the mantra that a revision of NSC-8/2 "would be necessary to cover combat aircraft." Edwards did admit that "language might be stretched to include a limited number of transport aircraft, such as C-47s, for logistic support of ground forces"—but no combat planes.

Ambassador Muccio then said that he had been placed in a "difficult position" when President Rhee learned "surplus aircraft, including F-51's, were being 'junked' by FEAF (Far East Air Force) in Japan." The Koreans found it "difficult to understand" why the United States was junking planes despite their "desperate need for a few such planes." Lemnitzer's immediate response was to say that "if F-51s were . . . transferred to Korea from Japan, the Air Force would have to be reimbursed for their handling and transportation even though they might be surplus."

Realizing that the Korean government might well offer to pay for the handling and transportation costs to obtain the planes, just as they had paid out of their own funds to obtain patrol boats and trainer planes, Lemnitzer then dropped that line of argument. So he reverted to the original formula and "went on to add that . . . the Department of State would have to take the policy initiative." Defense would, of course, "support such a program if the NSC directive were to be appropriately amended." But "since the question was a political one . . . he did not feel that Defense should sponsor such a policy revision."

At this point, Niles Bond, country desk officer for Korean Affairs, spoke up, observing that the combat aircraft portion of the KMAG request for a supplemental $9.8 million "comprised only a part of the Mission's recommendations for additional military aid to Korea for FY 1950." Indeed, he said, "well over half of the recommended program . . . fell well within the terms of NSC 8/2 as presently written." The ground force items were "designed to bring the total U.S.-supported ground forces in Korea to the level of 65,000 called for by the terms of NSC 8/2 . . . [and] together with the coast guard portion of the proposed additional aid, accounted for almost 5.9 out of a total of 9.8 million dollars."

Recall that the ground force portion of Roberts's supplementary request was for $4.57 million, the coast guard portion was for $1.31 million, and the air force portion was for $3.91 million. Bond urged that "prompt action be taken" on the almost 60 percent of the supplementary request that "did not involve the question of the transfer of combat aircraft." Bond's argument was straightforward. Except for the combat aircraft issue, Roberts and Muccio were pleading for fulfillment of commitments stipulated in NSC-8/2.

But Ambassador Muccio, supported by Bond, would not relent on the combat aircraft issue, even though they were now reduced to pleading for a handful of planes. First, Muccio "raised the question of the training of Korean ground crew personnel by FEAF in Japan, for which a precedent had already been established in the training of Korean Army officers in FECOM [Far East Command]." General Edwards thought that the Air Force "would go along with such a proposal insofar as it could, and suggested that the matter might be arranged locally with FEAF."

Muccio then asked whether technical personnel could be sent from FEAF to Korea "for a short period to train Korean personnel." Here Edwards demurred, saying that "it would be difficult to find such personnel who might be available at the present time" in view of worldwide demands. In this regard, Bond asked "whether State's request for the temporary assignment of FEAF personnel to assist the Koreans with their newly-acquired AT-6's had ever received Air Force consideration." Edwards said he did not know but would look into it. (It turned out that "no action was taken on this matter prior to the outbreak of hostilities in Korea.")

Muccio now made his last attempt at obtaining for the Korean government a few combat aircraft and help for the Coast Guard. He referred to the U.S. Air Force's recent request that the Korean government turn over a North Korean Stormovik fighter plane recently flown in by a defector. Muccio said that perhaps Washington could "compensate the Koreans with one or more F-51 aircraft" in return for turning over the Russian fighter. He also asked whether the proposal to send additional advisers for the Korean Coast Guard "had been given consideration." General Lemnitzer replied that "he did not know what had been done," but that he would check on it. (In the event, nothing came of this either.)

Bond followed with the argument he had raised earlier, asking whether it was proper for the State Department, "pending ... revision of NSC 8/2 to permit the transfer of combat aircraft, to request the immediate allocation of funds to cover the other portions of the requested additional aid to Korea." It seemed, at the last, that General Lemnitzer had been won over, saying that he "perceived no objection to that procedure and that such a request would be sympathetically received." In fact, however, he was simply preparing to pass the ball once again. Lemnitzer suggested that the necessary funds could "be more expeditiously obtained from surplus Title II funds than from funds available under Section 303, but that the final decision on this point would have to be left up to the FMACC [Foreign Military Assistance Coordinating Committee]."

The acting director of the Mutual Defense Assistance Program, John Ohly, replied to Dean Rusk at the State Department later that very day. Ohly, referring to "the meeting held this morning at the request of Ambassador Muccio with Major General Lemnitzer, Lieutenant General Edwards and other Defense officers," gave the same answer. Any decision to approve fighter aircraft for Korea would entail "revision of NSC 8/2" and require establishment of reliable sources for "obtaining funds to cover the costs of providing and maintaining such a force."[39]

Assuming that NSC-8/2 were revised, Ohly said, there were several additional questions that would have to be answered. Were funds available to provide training, maintenance, and operational facilities? "From General Edwards' comments during this morning's meeting this appeared doubtful." Ohly also doubted that funds could be found to pay the costs of keeping such aircraft operational. Even if funds were located for fiscal year 1950, no funds had been requested for fiscal year 1951. Finally, according to General Edwards, "the supply of spare parts for the F-51s rapidly will become difficult, thus posing another serious problem."

Thus, Ohly's version of the runaround was that even if NSC-8/2 were revised *and* planes authorized *and* the funds to pay for them were found for fiscal year 1950, that is, the next month and a half, future funding and the spare parts to keep the planes operational beyond that were probably not going to be available. In short, it was not worth the effort. Then, capping his argument, and passing the ball back to State, Ohly said, "it will be recalled that Defense has maintained, and still maintains that there is no military justification for military assistance to Korea." If additional military assistance is approved, "the justification will have to be wholly on political grounds."

Ohly's only agreement was that "the furnishing of additional Army and Coast Guard equipment can . . . be justified on other than strictly military grounds. The real question concerns the provision of fighter aircraft to ROK." With the ball back in its court, State's response was to stall. On the question of providing fighter aircraft, on May 19, over a week later, the Department "requested further information from the Embassy in Seoul" and on the question of whether the rest of the supplementary request could be fulfilled exclusive of combat aircraft, Rusk passed the ball back to Ohly. In a memo on May 19, he suggested "that the matter be referred to the FMACC for approval." (In the event, "no action was taken by the FMACC prior to the outbreak of hostilities.")

THE TANK THREAT EMERGES

As this chapter has demonstrated, between January and May 1950, Muccio and Roberts valiantly sought to fill the "gaps" in the American defense commitment to South Korea. Yet, of all the ROK's security shortcomings, defense against a tank threat was not perceived to be one of them. There is no evidence in the record to indicate that either KMAG or ROK Army intelligence had identified a large and threatening North Korean tank presence during this period. According to Appleman, "the North Koreans had never used tanks in any of the numerous border incidents, although they had possessed them since late 1949."[40] Appleman assumes, but provides no support for the assertion, that the type of tanks "possessed . . . since late 1949" were T-34s. During Ambassador Jessup's tour of the 38th parallel in January, recall, ROK officers mentioned only "light tanks," not medium tanks, which would have indicated the presence of the T-34.

Furthermore, throughout the first half of 1950, the record contains not a single request for anti-tank weapons—anti-tank guns, rocket launchers, or anti-tank mines—indicating, however incredibly, that a prepared defense against a major tank-led thrust across the parallel was not part of contingency planning. Instead, as we have seen, Muccio and Roberts focused specifically upon requests for F-51 fighter aircraft and coast guard patrol boats. Of course, the F-51 was a potent anti-tank weapon in good flying weather, but the stated rationale in all requests for combat aircraft was to counter the growing North Korean air threat.

KMAG chief Roberts was himself a World War II tank commander and was presumably attuned to the requirements for defending against a tank-led assault. The total apparent disregard of the tank threat led one exasperated historian, Clay Blair, to find Roberts's "apparent indifference to the NKPA armored forces . . . simply inexplicable."[41] The answer, however, is straightforward. There were no references to a serious tank threat, or requests for anti-tank weapons, because the tank threat had yet to emerge.

Indeed, had a serious tank threat been identified, the obvious countermove would have been the emplacement of anti-tank mine fields all along the invasion routes—a handful of narrow roads running along the valley floors. The United States had delivered no anti-tank mines to Seoul before the war, although large stocks were maintained in Japan.[42] The United States had provided 140 57mm anti-tank guns and a few hundred 2.36″ rocket launchers, the World War II "bazooka."[43] Little ammunition was included, however, and what was available frequently misfired, or did not detonate at all. The 2.36″ rocket launcher was touted as a "wonder weapon" against tanks in World War II and saw service in both the European and Pacific theaters, but never lived up to its reputation. While it was most useful against bunkers, pillboxes, armored personnel carriers, jeeps, and trucks, and even light tanks, it could not "kill" the German tiger tank and, of course, was completely ineffective against the more heavily armored T-34. The 57mm anti-tank gun was similarly ineffective, and had been abandoned by the United States Army.

The ineffectiveness of the 2.36″ rocket launcher had been well known for years, indeed, since it was first introduced in World War II. In 1944, development of a new and improved model began and by August 1948 the 3.5″ rocket launcher had completed development and entered production. The new model, formally designated T80E2, could penetrate up to 12 inches of armor plate, more than enough to penetrate the 4-inch armor on the T-34 tank. By 1950, before the outbreak of the Korean War, the 3.5″ rocket launcher was being supplied to the U.S. National Guard, but not yet to U.S. troops in Japan or to the ROK Army.[44]

In view of the fact that the North Korean invasion was led by, and based upon, an initial minimum of 150 T-34 medium tanks (U.S. sources estimated that the North lost 767 T-34s and 1,327 total tanks in the entire war),[45] it is curious that there was no reference by either American or South Korean officials to "medium" tanks until very late in the day. That reference first came from South Korean intelligence, on May 10, only six weeks before the outbreak of war. How is it that the existence of so large a number of medium tanks escaped detection? The answer must be that the North Koreans either had not acquired the T-34 until spring, or, having begun to receive them earlier, had kept them hidden until the spring, which was when Soviet equipment deliveries surged.[46] Still, as late as June 15, KMAG intelligence reports included no references to a large North Korean tank presence, or to tank exercises.[47]

The first public reference to the T-34 medium tank came on May 10, when South Korea's Acting Prime Minister and Minister of Defense Sinh Sung Mo (Shin Sung-mo) "hurriedly" called a press conference with foreign correspondents to release an intelligence estimate. He said that the "arrival of two divisions of Chinese Communist troops in Northern Korea since last August has raised the fully-armed effective fighting force there to 183,100."[48] This was a misstatement on two counts. What he obviously referred to were Korean returnees from China, not Chinese Communist troops, and his numbers breakdown did not add up to his total. But Sinh's purpose was to convey to the United States, through the foreign press (the Korean press corps was excluded from his press conference), Seoul's "carefully calculated estimate" that a North Korean invasion was "imminent."[49]

The defense minister provided a detailed breakdown of North Korean forces. He identified six army divisions and three border constabulary brigades for a total of 118,000 men. To this he added 37,000 "mixed troops, including women," a tank brigade of 10,000 men, a navy of 15,000, and an air force of 2,500. This came to a total force of 182,500 (600 fewer than his initial figure). His most alarming revelations were the identification of 173 tanks and 195 planes. There were, he said, "155 medium tanks and 18 small tanks." The aircraft estimate was almost double the highest estimate for North Korean planes given on March 6. Finally, he said, there were 609 artillery pieces (76mm and 122mm), 1,162 mortars (82mm and 120mm), 32 patrol boats, and numerous small weapons.

South Korean intelligence had, if anything, underestimated the North Korean order of battle. As we now know, the North Korean Army had eight full- and two understrength divisions by this time, and was raising three more. Yet, in commenting on this report, Drumright thought that "Korean figures [were] exaggerated." He averred that the report was designed to elicit additional military aid from the United States, but his attempted rebuttal was not only weak and unconvincing, it was also puzzling.[50] Just three weeks before, on April 20, he had sent a cable to Acheson expressing alarm about the refusal of Washington to send vitally needed military assistance and demanding prompt delivery precisely because of a growing Northern military threat (see p. 163). Now, in what appeared to be a complete turnaround, he pooh-poohed the North Korean threat and sharply discounted the minister's estimate.

Furthermore, in his attempt to demonstrate the defense minister's exaggeration, Drumright's rejoinder was vague where it should have been concrete and failed to address the specific allegations made by the South Korean defense minister. Basing his comments on "our current estimate of North Korean strength," he asserted that North Korea's "total armed forces [were] 103,000," not 183,100.[51] He offered no specific breakdown of the NKA force structure the way Sinh had, did not state the number of divisions the North had, and simply lumped together the " 'People's Army,' Korean volunteer army returnees from Manchuria, border constabulary, air division, armored formation and navy." In addition to this, he identified a 25,000-man "provincial police" unit.

Drumright said that the "only armored formation in North Korea is of brigade size and composed of estimated 65 tanks, heaviest of which is Soviet model T-34," a curiously ambiguous statement. Minister Sinh had identified 155 T-34 medium tanks, which implied a force larger than two brigades. Drumright's, and indeed the CIA's, estimate of the number of tanks seemed to have been taken from the Soviet order of battle handbook rather than from direct observation. The handbook called for 65 T-34s to a brigade, and North Korea had a brigade; ergo, Pyongyang must have only 65 T-34s.

Furthermore, Drumright was no more precise regarding the number of T-34s than he was in the number of troops in units, saying only that there were an "estimated 65 tanks, heaviest of which is Soviet model T-34," implying that only a few were T-34s. Oddly, the CIA estimate from which he took his number, and the only declassified U.S. source to identify T-34 tanks in North Korea before the war began, stated that North Korean heavy weaponry included "an armored unit, estimated to possess 65 Soviet T-34 tanks." The CIA estimate, however, while crediting Pyongyang with 65 T-34s, declined to identify this armored "unit" as a "brigade."

173

Drumright said there were only 296 artillery pieces, not 609, and 780 mortars, not 1,162. He ignored the North Korean navy, but declared that the U.S. estimate of the air force was 75 planes, not 195, and included 35 fighters, 35 trainers, 3 bombers, and 2 transports. This estimate, too, was straight from the CIA and, again, he failed to identify plane types other than "fighters," "bombers," "transports," and "trainers." He did include information from the North Korean pilot who defected in late April, which, he said, raised those estimates to 200 aircraft, although he did not give full credence to this information. The pilot claimed, accurately as it turned out, that the North had 100 Yak fighters, 70 IL-10 attack bombers, 22 trainers, 8 reconnaissance planes, and 2 liaison aircraft, for a total of 202 aircraft.

Drumright's estimate of the total North Korean force of 103,000 was almost exactly the estimate of military intelligence a year earlier (see pp. 148–49). But that mid-1949 estimate had anticipated the growth of the NKA from a four- to a six-division infantry force and from a one- to a three-"unit" mechanized force, which implied a force structure of at least 132,000 with the addition of two infantry divisions and two armored units. (It was unclear what was meant by the term "unit," but if "unit" is roughly equated to "brigade," three units would be close to the number of T-34s identified by ROK intelligence.) Thus, Drumright's lowball numbers, implying that the North Korean armed forces had not grown at all from the four-division force of a year ago, were hardly credible, especially in view of the chargé d'affaires' own reference to "periodic reports" of North Korea's "constantly increasing materiel potential" (see p. 163).

The chargé d'affaires' evident purpose, as he was no doubt instructed to do, was to play down the danger of invasion. Thus, he dismissed the defense minister's statement as being expressly issued for "foreign consumption." In a real sense, this was true, because the Korean press had been excluded from the conference with foreign correspondents and was later given a much less detailed report of North Korean military strength. It was only the United States, after all, that could help. Thus, the ROK had sought to convince with specific figures. Drumright acknowledged that to have given specific figures to the local press "would alarm ROK populace," which explains their exclusion. The chargé d'affaires also noted that President Rhee "during recent conversations . . . including one today . . . has spoken emphatically of need for further military aid."

Indeed, two days later, President Rhee held a press conference in which he referred to the defense minister's press conference. Stating that "North Korea is concentrating [troops] near the 38th parallel," he complained that "we can do nothing. We will solve this matter through the UN and the United States." Rhee disparaged those "American friends" who expressed the "useless worry" that if the United States gave weapons to us "South Korea would invade North Korea." It was the other way around. He thought that May and June would be the "dangerous months" and severely castigated the United States for having

> one foot in South Korea and one foot outside so that in case of an unfavorable situation it could pull out of our country. I daresay that if the United States wants to aid our country it should not be only lip-service. General Roberts and Ambassador Muccio have worked to obtain more arms for Korea, but people in the United States are dreaming.[52]

Washington declined to respond to Seoul's pleas. It would appear that the United States was battening down the hatches with regard to inflammatory news from South Korea. The *New York Times* buried the defense minister's press conference on page 14, reporting only briefly (in thirty-three words) Sinh Sung-mo's warning of imminent invasion, and did not carry Rhee's press conference at all.[53] No mention was made of the sudden emergence of the T-34 tank threat. The administration strove to keep the lid on news of the increasingly explosive situation in Korea and continued to stall on the question of aid to Seoul.[54]

A few weeks later, "in late May," an informant from North Korea provided an almost identical report on the North Korean buildup to Far East Command intelligence. He included "an extraordinarily detailed report on the formation of a new North Korean People's Army (NKPA) tank brigade, with an estimated 180 medium and light tanks, 10,000 officers and men, and such support equipment as antitank guns, field guns, and motorcycles." But MacArthur's intelligence chief, Major General Charles Willoughby, took the same line that Drumright had taken, declaring the "personnel and armor totals," in particular, "excessive." In his view "the NKPA would not form so large a tank unit."[55]

Nor was any warning sent to Seoul. On May 19, nine days after the meetings with Muccio, Acting Secretary of State Webb sent a cable to Seoul replying to the ambassador's request for F-51 combat planes. It was the same delaying tactic as before. Before any consideration could be given to the request, Webb wanted to know "how [the ROK] intended to provide maintenance and other ground facilities necessary to keep such planes operational?" How would these be paid for? How would the government meet the "continuing expense of support of such aircraft . . . for FY 1951 and thereafter," including internal financing? How would they "provide adequately trained Korean air and ground personnel, especially mechanics?" Finally Webb said that

> although Dept appreciates Mission not advocating estab modern air force for ROK, it nevertheless true that support even small force obsolescent fighters

wld require considerable outlay in specialized equipment and trained personnel, none of which Dept understands to be presently available in Korea, as well as considerable continuing financial burden if such force is to be kept operational.[56]

An exasperated Muccio, having returned to Seoul, responded to Webb's cable four days later. Hoping to clear away the "confusion" that may have existed from the "various recommendations sent [to the] Department," Muccio declared firmly that "this message concurred in by KMAG and ECA and should be regarded as definitive and authoritative recommended program for support ROK Air Force."[57] Muccio recommended forty F-51 fighters, ten T-6 trainers, and three C-47 transports, with spare parts and maintenance equipment, and seventeen air advisers, including flight instructors and mechanics, "assuming NSC 8/2 is revised to provide support for air force."

176   Ground facilities, such as airfields and buildings, "are now in existence," although these required a "limited amount" of rehabilitation. The cost of the program would be offset through additional taxes or other revenues. South Korea already had sixty pilots "qualified for transition training to fighter aircraft" and a mechanic school was already in operation training ground personnel. "Main reliance for pilot and mechanic training, however, must be on air advisory personnel recommended above," although "a limited number of Korean air technicians and mechanics [could] be authorized for training with FEAF [in Japan]."

Muccio's assumption that NSC-8/2 would be revised was either terribly optimistic or a sarcastic commentary on the runaround he had been given over the past half year. The journal editor of *Foreign Relations of the United States* (*FRUS*) noted in a footnote to this cable that "between the time of the receipt of this telegram and the outbreak of hostilities, no effort was made to revise NSC 8/2." "No effort" meant, of course, that the secretary of state had decided against it. No action had been taken to provide South Korea with any combat aircraft, or, for that matter, anything else, except, as noted above, $108 in signal wire.

On May 29, Chargé d'Affaires Drumright sent a telegram to the secretary of state regarding the logistical situation of the Korean Army. Although his cover letter placed a positive interpretation on the existing condition of the ROK Army, the report itself, issued by General Roberts, starkly laid bare the truth. The situation was so bad, he said, that "Korea is threatened with the same disaster that befell China." Roberts then proceeded to describe a Korean Army "dangerously reduced in fire power, mobility and logistical support." Roberts was ending his tour as KMAG chief and would depart in mid-June before the outbreak of war. His evident purpose was to leave behind for his successor an accurate report of the Korean Army's logistical situation, but it was also to exonerate himself from responsibility for the sorry state of affairs.[58]

Roberts briefly recapitulated the original U.S. commitment, which was "to supply the Korean Army with an initial issue of equipment and a six months supply of spare parts for a strength of 50,000. Later an additional 15,000 individual weapons were supplied." The subsequent South Korean decision to increase the Army's strength to 100,000, he said, resulted in "a serious deficiency in major items of equipment." It was a simple case of too many men using too little equipment, and wearing it out at an unprecedented rate.

> The six months supply of parts is exhausted, and it is estimated that 10 to 15% of the weapons and 30 to 35% of the vehicles are unserviceable. It is tentatively planned by Dept. of Army that the spare parts approved for issue to Korea under 1950 MDAP will not arrive until some time in FY 52. The Korean economy lacks the resources to supply these parts from its own production or from foreign exchange.

The secretary of state declined to reply to this dramatic description of an army in an advanced state of disintegration and incapable of defending its nation, as he had to all requests to provide additional military assistance to South Korea since April 20. Of course, had he acknowledged the need for military assistance, he would have been duty-bound to provide it. Since it was the purpose of the United States to leave South Korea vulnerable to the first blow, however, Acheson was deaf to all entreaties from Seoul.

DISCOVERY AND RESPONSE

The secretary's silence stemmed from the discovery of the massive Soviet supply effort to North Korea, which had begun in April and included over 150 T-34 tanks. The supply effort had begun while Kim Il-sung was in Moscow making final arrangements for the coming conflict—March 30–April 25 (see chapter 5, pp. 103–104). The supply line ran by freighter from Vladivostok along the coast to Chongjin, Najin, and Wonsan. Najin and Chongjin were close to the Soviet border, while Wonsan, south of Chongjin, was about ten hours' sailing time from Vladivostok. The ships used by the Soviets were U.S. lend-lease Victory and Liberty ships, of which they had some two hundred in Northeast Asia, and had refused to return.

Chongjin was the largest port in North Korea and second only to Pusan in the South. It had a discharge capacity of over 19,000 tons per day, 17 berths alongside, unlimited anchorage space, 11 acres of open storage, and 200,000 square feet of covered storage.[59] The Soviets had decided upon the sea route specifically to prevent Chinese discovery (see chapter 5, p. 108), but the supply effort could not be hidden from U.S. intelligence, particularly naval intelligence. The U.S. Navy, for example, had maintained a submarine watch on Vladivostok since 1946, precisely to monitor ship movements.[60] No doubt aerial reconnaissance and stay-behind agents on the docks confirmed the worst.

Discovery of the massive Soviet supply effort confirmed to American leaders that war was certain and imminent; the appearance of the T-34 meant it would be unlike anything that had been anticipated—a blitzkrieg-like attack to topple the ROK before the United States could intervene to prevent it. Or so it was meant to appear. The North Korean Army was superior to the ROK Army without the T-34, but heretofore had lacked the mobility to execute a rapid conquest. The T-34 provided the mobility for a quick victory and presented American leaders with a strategic dilemma.

178 On the one hand, if Washington continued to do nothing for the South, the NKA might mount a blitzkrieg attack, win quickly, and present the United States with a fait accompli. On the other hand, if Washington sent in weapons that could counter the T-34, such as the 3.5″ rocket launcher, ground attack aircraft, such as the F-51, or anti-tank mines, the ROK Army might contain the attack at the 38th parallel. Blunting an invasion at the parallel, however, would not produce the needed stimulus to effect the general rearmament planned in NSC-68. So Washington provided no anti-tank weapons, but began to prepare against the worst case.

The appearance of the T-34s in May had suddenly transformed Korea into a high stakes gamble. The United States had secretly changed strategy and awaited a conflict in Korea to provide the rationale and stimulus for planned rearmament. A lengthy conflict would clearly provide that rationale, and Washington awaited the attack. The appearance of the T-34, however, raised a crucial question: Could the United States prevent South Korea from falling victim to a lightning assault before Washington could respond? In that case, the planned rearmament program might never get off the ground and the political repercussions—"Who lost Korea?" on top of "Who lost China?"—would be fatal.

Thus, in late April, as soon as the Soviet supply effort had been identified, the Pentagon began to assemble the elements of what would be necessary to defeat the worst case threat—a T-34–led lightning assault. In North Carolina, the U.S. Army and Air Force jointly carried out Operation Swarmer, a 60,000-man, 600-plane exercise designed to insert by airlift and air drop a multi-division armed force, specifically to stop a tank-led assault.[61] Under the command of Lieutenant General John R. Hodge, former commander of the U.S. Army in Korea, over two hundred transport aircraft "operating 'round-the-clock' in all weather had air-dropped or landed 20,196 combat troops and 11,689 tons of equipment" in a four-day span. Ultimately, 44,000 troops from the Eleventh and Eighty-second Airborne Divisions and 46,000 tons of supplies were airlifted during the exercise.[62]

Air Force Chief of Operations Lauris Norstad declared that "the air drop of heavy equipment including anti-tank guns (aggressor forces had medium tanks) had been outstandingly successful and that the C-119 Fairchild Packet, the latest version of the 'Flying Boxcar,' has passed its initial 'combat' test with flying colors." This meant, Norstad said, that a "mass airlift" could be employed "anywhere in the world." Furthermore, with the development of proper equipment "an Alaska-mounted trans–Bering Sea operation would be 'entirely feasible.' "

In other press accounts, the exercise was said to demonstrate "the practicality of an entirely airflown attack or counterattack. Conceivably the method might be employed in some circumstances rather than establishing amphibious beachheads."[63] The exercise was also said to have demonstrated the "strengthening [of] one of the admittedly weak areas of military teamwork—tactical air support of ground troops." Operation Swarmer, it was disclosed, "was also a limited experiment of close air support techniques." Air Force ground controllers parachuted in with Army troops and "called in jet air power at decisive times to help the ground troops overcome opposition."[64]

In retrospect, it seems clear that the United States was preparing for the anticipated North Korean use of the T-34 as an assault spearhead, in response to the belated discovery of deliveries of the weapon. In any case, Operation Swarmer practiced a number of new military techniques that would be crucial to the early weeks of the Korean conflict. The exercise suggested a lightning-like assault on South Korea in a blitzkrieg tank strike. If North Korea threatened to seize Pusan before a beachhead could be secured, the United States would presumably be able to insert a sufficiently large force, with combat air support, to defend a perimeter within which a beachhead could be established. Moreover, the reference to an Alaska-mounted trans–Bering Sea deployment was a thinly disguised description of an operation mounted from Japan to Korea.

Hanson Baldwin, military analyst for the *New York Times*, wrote about the preparedness of the United States strategic reserve. The 28,000-strong Second Infantry Division posted at Fort Lewis, Washington, he said, was "ready for instant action" in case of crisis.[65] (The Second Infantry would in fact debark at Pusan on August 1, 1950, along with the First Marine Division, in the nick of time to help in defense of the Pusan perimeter.) General Walton H. Walker, commander of Eighth Army stationed in Japan, was also enthusiastic about the combat readiness of his forces. In an address to his troops, he said that "the present state of combat training was 'entirely satisfactory,' with considerable progress in the last year."[66] (Walker spoke of the adequacy of "training," not of weapons or of troop levels, which were well below autho-

179

rized strength. Even so, as we now know, the level of combat training still left a great deal to be desired.)

At the same time, the USAF announced that the Military Air Transport Service (MATS) was "being revamped to transform the organization into a strategic airlift force that could be expanded swiftly in wartime mobilization."[67] Operating nearly three hundred aircraft, mostly DC-4 transports, the aim was to double the number of air crews available for service in time of need. "Many of the training flights for new crews will be over overseas routes to keep personnel continually familiar with foreign areas." The new program was expected to provide a "substantial increase in airlift available to the Defense Department."

The Navy was also taking subtle preparatory steps. The Seventh Fleet, depleted though it was, had conducted combined exercises with British naval forces in March and when war broke out cooperation was effected quickly and smoothly. As Rear Admiral R. W. Andrewes, head of Task Group 96.8 later put it, "it all seemed familiar, joining up in Formation . . . as it was just what we had done so often during the exercises in March with very similar forces. We didn't feel out of things."[68]

In late May, the Seventh Fleet's thirty-three ships gathered at Apra Harbor in Guam. Under the command of Vice Admiral Arthur D. Struble, task forces built around the carriers *Boxer* and *Valley Forge* were to establish a "new rotation system that keeps one first-line carrier showing the flag in Southeast Asia" at all times.[69] Guam was the same distance from Manila as it was from Tokyo, some 1,350 miles, and within fast cruising distance of Korea. Immediately thereafter, the Seventh Fleet's Amphibious Group One, comprising "the most seasoned group of amphibious experts in the Pacific Fleet," began conducting amphibious training exercises in Japanese waters and its troop training unit "was engaged in indoctrinating the U.S. Eighth Army in Japan."[70]

By early June, the Marine Corps was also engaged in intense preparations for amphibious operations. Traveling to the marine base at Quantico, Virginia, President Truman personally observed the Marines "new 'invasion by helicopter' technique—hailed as the amphibious warfare method of tomorrow—bazookas, jet fighters and intricately coordinated close air support of ground troops."[71] It would seem that all branches of the U.S. military services were moving to a higher state of readiness.

Perhaps most intriguing of all was the prewar contingency plan determining United States military strategy in a war on the Korean peninsula. War Plan SL-17 assumed an invasion by the North, "a retreat to and defense of the Pusan perimeter, buildup and breakout *and an amphibious landing at Inchon to cut enemy supply lines.*" The plan also called for two subsequent, additional landings on the east and west coasts pursuant to destroying the

North Korean Army and occupying the entire country. This plan "was approved, printed and distributed to the General Staff and the technical services early in the week of 19 June, 1950." It was an obvious plan for peninsular warfare, and had been drafted by September 1949.[72]

The situation in Northeast Asia is, perhaps, best described by Robert Futrell.

> Since [September] 1949, when Russia had detonated its first atomic burst, everyone in FEAF had realized that the Cold War might, at any moment, break into the flames of World War III. Such a new world holocaust would begin with air attacks against Far Eastern air bases, launched from Communist airfields in Asia. Everyone was tautly ready.[73]

Finally, in what was a remarkable coincidence if the invasion was truly unexpected, the day before the North Korean attack, the U.S. Army alerted "all combat units of the Army ... for tests that will determine how quickly they could start moving toward ports of embarkation in an emergency."[74] The tests were to begin in July. It was to be a nationwide command-post exercise to prepare the orders for the actual movement of troops in case of crisis.

While American military preparations were under way, American leaders betrayed no sense of alarm. Secretary Acheson, in mid-June, for example, publicly declared that the United States would not act preemptively against the Soviet Union, and implied that the United States would accept the first blow in any conflict. In a foreign policy speech before the Civic Federation of Dallas, Texas, focusing on the defense of Western Europe, from whence he had just returned, Secretary Acheson declared that the "United States could not insure its own peace and security through isolation, appeasement, or 'preventive war.'" Instead, he said, "this country must strengthen the free world militarily to prevent aggression while cooperating with all friendly nations 'in advancing our common welfare.'"[75] The Republic of Korea obviously did not fit within the Secretary's definition of the free world.

Acheson declined to attribute all the world's problems to the Soviets. "It is good to remind ourselves that we would still have enough problems left to keep us well occupied, even if the Soviet Union were to be, as we hope it will some day become, our good neighbor." Some day was a long way off; for the moment, the Soviets were the problem. Acheson ruled out isolationism as unworkable and expensive, and "appeasement of Soviet ambitions as a policy that would only encourage Soviet aggression." There was, he said, "a third course of action which might be considered in earlier times and by another type of government and people than ours." That course, sometimes called by the euphemistic phrase of "preventive war," is "that we should drop some atomic bombs on the Soviet Union." But, he said, "all responsible men must agree that such a course is unthinkable for us. It would violate every moral

181

principle of our people. Such a war would necessarily be incredibly destructive. It would not solve problems, it would multiply them."

Acheson advocated yet a fourth course, the "continuance of present policy—the strengthening of the North Atlantic pact, the adoption of measures to unite Europe more closely militarily and economically, and continued American military and economic cooperation." Turning his back on plans for peace talks with the Soviets, Acheson declared that "there is a prior condition which we must fulfill in order to have successful and meaningful negotiations with the Soviet Union. That condition is for the Soviet leaders to be convinced that they cannot profit from a policy of expansionism—that their own self-interest as well as that of the rest of the world would be advanced by a settlement of some, at least, of our outstanding differences." In other words, as far as Acheson was concerned, the United States would issue no warnings to Moscow, but simply wait until Soviet leaders realized that expansionism would not work. The United States and South Korea would accept the first blow.

PART III
KOREA: A WAR OF SURPRISES

CHAPTER EIGHT

The First Week:
June 25–June 30

STRATEGY ALWAYS governs policy: the Korean War was no exception to this rule. The great, brutal irony of the war was that the Soviet Union and the United States each independently employed the Korean battlefield to achieve the identical structural outcome—Chinese isolation, dependence upon the Soviet Union, and antagonism toward the United States. For both countries these were predetermined objectives, which conflict in Korea was ultimately designed to serve, although only in retrospect do the two states' common aims become apparent. It is not at all clear that the principals engaged in the conduct of policy perceived the similarity of objectives at the time—although a few on the U.S. side came close to such an understanding of Stalin's motives.

Of course, the reasons for Soviet and American parallel policy behavior were entirely different. From the early days of the war Moscow sought to maneuver Beijing into conflict with the United States to foreclose any possibility of Sino-American rapprochement—Moscow's worst nightmare. Washington, however, was intent upon the same end to make manifest the threat implicit in the Sino-Soviet alliance, which would permit execution of the rearmament program already called for in NSC-68. Both would succeed. That Stalin's primary and fundamental purpose in Korea was directed against Mao, and that Mao's planned invasion of Taiwan was directed against Stalin, were essentially immaterial to U.S. leaders, who were pursuing a larger goal of their own. The crucial question is whether Stalin realized that in triggering war in Korea he was playing into the hands of the United States.

185

For American leaders, the fact of the formal Sino-Soviet alliance had already been decisive, forcing a shift to containment and the rearmament program necessary to support the new global strategy. The Communist threat was real to American leaders, and war would demonstrate that threat to the public. It was the people, after all, through their representatives in Congress, who would authorize the funding for rearmament. The war that resulted in Korea would enable the United States to implement a pre-planned rearmament program which would keep the United States well ahead of the Soviet Union in the emerging global struggle.

Whatever the reasons for the dual Communist war preparations through the spring, which were apparent, the central question was what to do about them. American leaders saw war coming, as we have seen, and sought to take advantage of it when it came. The U.S. response to the dual war threat was to prevent a Chinese Communist attack on Taiwan, which would be effectively incorporated into the U.S. defense perimeter (even though disaffection with Chiang Kai-shek would linger), while taking no action to prevent an attack on South Korea, or to contain it immediately when it erupted. Indeed, for a conflict in Korea to serve the larger purpose of stimulating general rearmament, a lengthy conflict was necessary. Therefore, as we will see in this chapter, President Truman would not move immediately to contain the North Korean invasion, but instead would commit fully to the defense of South Korea only when the NKA breached the Han River and attempted to overrun the country.

For Stalin, however, the outbreak of the Korean War preempted Mao's planned attack on Taiwan. Since Stalin's main objective in preempting was to prevent Mao from eliminating Chiang Kai-shek and opening the door to relations with the United States, Stalin's next step was to maneuver China into conflict with the United States. This *required*, ipso facto, that the North Korean invasion fail. A close examination of the Soviet-devised invasion plan and its execution, and weapons and their employment, in this and the next chapter, reveals Stalin's intent. But it was the Soviet leader's direct and immediate orchestration of pressure on Mao to intervene in Korea that removes all doubt about his ultimate purpose. In fact, Stalin began urging Mao to prepare to intervene in Korea from July 5, the tenth day of the war and the first day North Korean forces encountered, and swept effortlessly through, American troops.

INITIAL ASSAULT: THE FIRST SURPRISE

When the war began on June 25, it soon became apparent that the NKA attack was not proceeding according to expectations. American leaders were not surprised by the North Korean invasion, but they were initially taken aback by Pyongyang's war plan. Instead of mounting the expected, tank-led, blitzkrieg attack, driving for Pusan to prevent U.S. entry by sealing off access, Pyongyang's forces moved forcefully but deliberately against Seoul, delayed their drive south for over a week, and provided the United States with the opportunity to enter.

Nor did Pyongyang execute other moves of which it was capable to deny, or even delay, American access to Pusan, such as mining the harbors or launching an air- or seaborne assault on the port. Even haphazard minelaying in the harbor area would have complicated shipping; and Pyongyang had some two dozen transport aircraft with which to attempt an airborne assault against the undefended port. Only one ship with six hundred troops was unsuccessfully sent down the east coast of the peninsula on an apparent mission to take the vital port.

Given the initial, overwhelming superiority of the NKA against the ROK Army, Stalin's generals, who devised the North Korean war plan, had to meet but one condition to ensure victory. That condition was to isolate the ROK from external support. Whatever they may have believed the odds were for or against American entry, it was only prudent to guard against the worst case. Only American entry could prevent the defeat of the South. If the United States stayed out, was deterred from entering, or was even delayed in entering by a few weeks, NKA victory would be certain. If the United States entered quickly, on the other hand, the odds changed dramatically. Victory was still possible if the assault were swift, but defeat was certain if the war were prolonged.

The point is indisputable. The strategic key to North Korean victory was control of a single objective, which would ensure that the ROK remained isolated and also prevent U.S. entry. That objective was the capture or denial of the port of Pusan, the only port in all of South Korea with sufficient capacity to accommodate a relatively high supply level, whether to reinforce the ROK Army or to support an American ground combat presence. Moreover, as Field notes, at this point Pusan was "almost wholly defenseless."[1] The failure to seize Pusan or to deny it to the United States was, without doubt, the single most decisive act of omission of the war, for it enabled the United States to come to the assistance of the Republic of Korea. It would be but the first of many surprises on both sides.

THE FIRST BLAIR HOUSE MEETING

Truman and Acheson, too, proceeded with due deliberation when conflict erupted. By the time that Truman returned from his home in Independence, Missouri, where he had gone to spend a weekend, Secretary of State Acheson and his colleagues at the State Department, Secretary of Defense Johnson and his military brass, and MacArthur in Tokyo had already taken several decisions, with the president's approval. State prepared a resolution to place before the United Nations to legitimize American action and to unite that body in opposition to the aggression. Defense alerted MacArthur to prepare U.S. troops for immediate combat and to send ammunition from Japan to the ROK. And Ambassador Muccio was authorized to execute a prearranged plan for the evacuation of American and other foreign nationals from Seoul.

Truman and his secretary of state had decided not to convene a meeting of the National Security Council, but instead to call an ad hoc meeting restricted to selected Defense and State Department officials. Thus, Secretary Acheson and four of his top aides—James Webb, Dean Rusk, John Hickerson, and Philip Jessup—were invited. Also invited were Secretary of Defense Johnson and the service secretaries, Francis Matthews (Navy), Frank Pace (Army), and Thomas Finletter (Air Force); the Joint Chiefs of Staff; the Chairman, General Omar Bradley; and the chiefs, General Joe L. Collins (Army), General Hoyt Vandenberg (Air Force), and Admiral Forrest Sherman (Navy). These fourteen men assembled at Blair House on the evening of June 25.

By deciding to call an ad hoc meeting instead of the National Security Council, the president was able to exclude certain persons who would otherwise be participants. Excluded from the meeting were Vice President Alben Barkley and the Chairman of the National Security Resources Board, Stuart Symington, who were by law designated members of the NSC. Also excluded were two others who normally attended NSC meetings: the Secretary of the Treasury and the Director of the Central Intelligence Agency. The exclusion of the latter, Admiral Roscoe Hillenkoetter, in particular seemed odd. One would have thought that his presence and the intelligence that he possessed would have demanded his attendance. But perhaps the opposite was the case, as we will see below.[2]

What is termed the first Blair House meeting convened that Sunday evening at 7:45 P.M., barely two hours after the United Nations had adopted the U.S.-sponsored resolution on the attack. The vote was 9 to 0, with Yugoslavia abstaining. The resolution identified the North Korean attack as a "breach of the peace." It called for a cease-fire and withdrawal to the 38th parallel, and requested "all members to render every assistance to the United Nations . . . and to refrain from giving assistance to the North Korean authorities."[3] Passage of the U.N. resolution enabled the United States to stake out the political high ground, without hindrance from Moscow, whose representative did not attend.

The resolution did not call for provision of assistance to the Republic of Korea, nor the application of military sanctions against North Korea, or even request that the Security Council determine that aggression had been committed. The blandness of the resolution led some "informed observers" to believe that "the United States would not do anything really effective to cope with the disaster in Korea."[4] According to Acheson, however, the original draft did include the phrase "an unprovoked act of aggression," but several council members felt that such a conclusion was not yet warranted. They were only prepared to say that a "breach of the peace" had occurred and that phrase was substituted.[5] But U.S. officials were already formulating a tougher, follow-on resolution in the expectation that the North Koreans would disregard the call for a cease fire and continue their attack.

If the U.S.-sponsored resolution had been puzzlingly mild, Moscow's reaction was totally inexplicable. Moscow made no attempt to veto the U.S. resolution, even though its representative, Jacob Malik, was nearby and could easily have done so. A Soviet veto obviously would have complicated if not prevented the United States from making a timely response and/or rallying U.N. members to support the American position. Indeed, a Soviet veto would have paralyzed the U.N. Security Council by precipitating a raucous debate, forcing the United States to gain passage of a similar resolution in the General Assembly, delaying a unified response by at least two weeks, and forcing the United States to act unilaterally on the battlefield. Moscow obviously did not wish to prevent the United States from rallying the U.N. to its cause. The result, as high U.N. officials observed, was not only that the U.N. was unified under American initiative, but that the seating of the Chinese Communists was now "out of the question."[6]

189

There was never any doubt in the president's mind, or the secretary of state's, that the United States would come fully to the assistance of the Republic of Korea. Here was the crisis they had been waiting for these many months. In Truman's view, "if this was allowed to go unchallenged it would mean a third world war, just as similar incidents had brought on the second world war. It was also clear to me that the foundations and the principles of the United Nations were at stake unless this unprovoked attack on Korea could be stopped."[7] Acheson also believed that "we could not accept the conquest of this important area by a Soviet puppet."[8]

In fact, "shortly before the president arrived in Washington," the Joint Chiefs had been authorized to notify MacArthur via teletype conference, often referred to as telecons, to prepare to execute several military measures that Truman would formally decide at the first Blair House meeting a few hours later. In addition, most significantly, they "alerted him to be ready to send U.S. ground and naval forces to stabilize the combat situation and, if feasible, to restore the 38th Parallel as a boundary."[9] In other words, before he had held a single meeting about the crisis and a week before he would decide to commit ground troops to Korea, President Truman had alerted MacArthur to prepare to take immediate action in the event that the NKA undertook, as originally expected, a rapid drive directly for Pusan.

Diary entries of President Truman's daughter support the interpretation that Truman was prepared to order immediate military intervention. According to her entry of June 25, "everybody is extremely tense. Northern or Communist Korea is marching in on Southern Korea and we are going to fight." For June 26, she entered: "Last night Dad said we would resist the aggression of Northern Korea. Tonight he sent the 7th Fleet to guard Formosa and he is going to send planes and troops."[10] The president's decision to send troops, however, was not one that he shared with his top aides or the Congress, and the president would delay commitment of troops until it was clear precisely what the NKA strategy was.

The men who convened at Blair House with the president that Sunday evening were not united on the extent or the manner in which the United States should become involved in Korea. The president and the secretary of state would be the prime movers carefully molding internal unity in crafting the response to Pyongyang's attack because, within the president's selected decision-making group, there were serious doubts within the military regarding a full commitment to the defense of Korea. It was, after all, an article of faith among them that in a general war with the Soviet Union, Korea would be a bad place for combat. All believed that the war was a Soviet initiative and could escalate into global conflict. They were not yet attuned to the notion of limited, or proxy, war. And they were not the only ones.

In the Congress, Republicans, especially, expressed a "moral obligation" to assist South Korea to defend itself, but lawmakers perceived no obligation to deploy combat troops to Korea. Indeed, their view was that the United States should provide all aid short of war, but that "the incident should not be used as a provocation for war."[11] Such public congressional division made prompt decision-making impossible and was undoubtedly the principal reason the president did not consult Congress before making his decisions regarding U.S. policy in the conflict.

Finally, there was MacArthur in Japan, who initially assumed that early reports indicated North and South Korea were engaged in another of the many border skirmishes that had characterized their relationship over the past year. Indeed, when Special Assistant John Foster Dulles, then in East Asia, conferred with MacArthur the day of the North Korean attack, MacArthur at first believed that it was not an "all-out" attack, that Moscow was "not necessarily" behind it, and that the ROK "would gain victory."[12]

Once MacArthur realized that an invasion was indeed under way, he sought to contain the North Korean attack as far forward as possible, at the

Han River, as called for by South Korean contingency plans (but not War Plan SL-17). Thus, MacArthur's intelligence chief, Major General Charles Willoughby, interpreting early reports in terms of these plans, noted the "orderliness of withdrawing South Korean units."[13] But Truman and Acheson wanted no defense at the Han River; they would delay a response to all proposals for forward defense until it was absolutely clear that Pyongyang's forces had breached the Han River and had begun their southward drive, and forward defense was no longer feasible. Containing the NKA attack at the 38th parallel was inconsistent with strategic dictates requiring a lengthy conflict.

At Blair House, in preliminary conversation over drinks in the living room before dinner, the president and his aides attempted to grapple with the key issues raised by the invasion. Why now? Was the invasion part of a larger Soviet and Chinese plan? Was an invasion of Taiwan, or perhaps Iran, or Yugoslavia imminent? Was Moscow now willing to risk war with the United States? The absence of CIA chief Hillenkoetter, who most certainly could have shed light on these deliberations, is puzzling. In any case, they concluded that Moscow was not ready for war with the United States, but was moving its North Korean pawn in a limited challenge. They were nevertheless alert to the possibility that other pawns might be moved, which would indicate that Korea was a diversion and that a wider war was in the offing.

Secretary Johnson, who, along with Bradley, had just returned from a meeting with MacArthur in Tokyo, wanted the group to hear a memorandum of MacArthur's on the strategic importance of Formosa, which Johnson felt "entered into our security more than Korea."[14] Secretary Acheson immediately recognized Johnson's ploy "as an opening gun in a diversionary argument that Johnson wished to start with me."[15] This "diversionary argument" reflected a fundamental difference between Truman-Acheson and Johnson. Johnson wanted no U.S. commitment to Korea, but wished to employ the opportunity presented by the conflict to incorporate Formosa into the U.S. Western Pacific defense. Nevertheless, the president acceded to Johnson's request and General Bradley proceeded to read aloud the entire memorandum.

Dated June 14, MacArthur's position was that "Formosa should not be allowed to fall into the hands of a potential hostile power or of a regime which would grant military utilization of Formosa to a power potentially hostile to the United States."[16] The island was an "unsinkable aircraft carrier and submarine tender," which, in hostile hands, could "checkmate counteroffensive operations by United States Forces based on Okinawa and the Philippines." It was not that the United States should employ Formosa itself, MacArthur said, but that it must not allow any other adversary to employ it against U.S. positions in Northeast Asia.

Secretary Johnson's action was curious. MacArthur's view was already public knowledge, the result of a congressional query in January (see chapter 7, p. 153). Moreover, he evidently did not know or realize that MacArthur's view had already been secretly adopted as part of the earlier change in strategy embodied in NSC-68. As noted above, Johnson had limited his role in the formulation of NSC-68 and evidently had not thought through its implications for Formosa. Unless the secretary wanted a greater, or, perhaps a different kind of commitment than had already been decided upon, he was, in effect, riding a horse through an open barn door.

Most important in the present context, however, was a phrase MacArthur used that all present fixed upon to conceptualize the policy which the president favored. The Far Eastern commander said, regarding Formosa, that "the time must come in the foreseeable future when *a line must be drawn* beyond which Communist expansion will be stopped." This phrase, later articulated by General Bradley, would describe in a nutshell the private and public rationale for coming to the defense of the Republic of Korea. They all agreed that it was time to draw the line, but not on how or where it should be drawn. Recognizing the potential for immobilizing disagreement among his aides, Undersecretary James Webb drew the president aside as they were repairing to the dining room, and said: "Let's not do it too fast," to which Truman replied: "Don't worry, I won't."[17]

The president then announced that further discussion would be deferred until after dinner when they could speak privately. As Secretary Johnson recalled, dinner was taken up with discussion of general "world conditions." Then, "during dessert . . . the Secretary of State again brought up the Korean question; and . . . I interrupted to say that before we got into that too deeply I wanted to discuss Formosa further." At that point, Johnson recalled, "the only really violent discussion Secretary Acheson and myself ever had took place." Johnson felt that U.S. security was "more affected by Formosa than Korea," and insisted on discussing it, but he was overruled by the president, who said that "we would take up Formosa later."

As their deliberations began, the president directed Secretary Acheson to take the lead and he related the most recent intelligence on the battlefield. As the invasion had only been under way for approximately thirty-three hours, initial details were sketchy. Daylight saving time was in effect in both the United States and Korea, with Seoul fourteen hours ahead of Washington.[18] At this early stage, it was too soon to determine whether Pyongyang was attempting the expected blitzkrieg-like strike against the South.[19] It was clear, however, that the NKA had attacked in force: they employed an estimated (severely underestimated as it turned out) seventy T-34 tanks as the

192

spearhead of their advance, crossed the border at eleven points, but moved along four major axes, and attempted amphibious landings at several points.

The attacks, from west to east, were in the Ongjin peninsula; through the Uijongbu corridor, the traditional invasion route leading to Seoul; in central Korea; and along the east coast. In addition, several landings had been made by sea along the east coast south of the 38th parallel. All landings had been successfully accomplished, except for one. In what naval historian James Field described as "the most important surface engagement of the war," PC 701, South Korea's only modern patrol boat, had encountered and sunk a 1,000-ton armed steamer with six hundred troops aboard heading for Pusan.[20] The South Korean information office declared the ship involved to be a Soviet vessel.[21]

It is not clear from the record whether Acheson also discussed a cable from Ambassador Muccio, which had arrived some eight hours earlier, reporting on his meeting with President Rhee and the acting and former prime ministers, although some of President Truman's remarks in the discussion that followed hint that he may have been informed. Muccio said that, against his protestations, an "incoherent" Rhee, "under great strain," had decided to "move government to Taejon tonight." Rhee, like his troops in the field, was terrified by the seemingly unstoppable T-34 tanks. Muccio had

193

> endeavored to persuade President to keep government in Seoul pointing out that armament and troops were available and should be thrown into fight to stop tanks with bazookas, anti-tank guns, and land mines. Prime Minister said that 57 millimeter anti-tank guns had failed to penetrate North Korean tanks armor whereupon I stressed the land mines.[22]

Muccio followed these remarks with the parenthetical observation, "(Prime Minister's allegation seems doubtful; Korean roads and bridges would not support extremely heavy tanks)," which indicated that he had been uninformed about the late-emerging T-34 tank threat and the critical deficiencies of the South Korean Army's defense capabilities against that threat. The facts were that the 57mm anti-tank gun and the 2.36" bazooka were virtually useless against the T-34, and there were no anti-tank land mines then in South Korea.[23]

At any rate, following his battlefield report, Acheson proposed that Mac-Arthur quickly supply arms and other equipment to ROK forces, that air power provide protection for the evacuation of Seoul, and that the Seventh Fleet proceed to Formosa to neutralize the island. Acheson advised, however, that the United States "not tie up with the Generalissimo," and suggested that the "future status of Formosa might be determined by the UN." (The president interposed: "or by the Japanese Peace Treaty.") Acheson also suggested that "our aid to Indochina should be stepped up."[24] Finally, referring to the just-adopted U.N. resolution, he suggested that "consideration should be given to what further assistance we might render to Korea in pursuance of this or a supplementary Security Council resolution."

In accordance with the admonition not to "do it too fast," Truman attempted to put the conferees at ease, saying that he was there with an "open mind," and that "for the present he was not planning to make any crucial decisions."[25] He then "asked each person in turn to state his agreement or disagreement and any views he might have in addition."[26] In the discussion that then ensued, Bradley and the other chiefs spoke first, followed by Secretaries Pace, Matthews, Finletter, and Johnson. As they spoke, the president asked specific questions about force levels and deployments.[27] The overall tenor of the discussion was one of tension and reluctance to commit U.S. power.

194

On the crucial question of how best to meet the North Korean challenge to South Korea, at this meeting none of those present advocated deployment of combat troops. The chiefs, in particular, displayed several degrees of aversion. JCS Chairman Bradley, although declaring that the Soviet Union was "not yet ready for war," and "the Korean situation offered as good an occasion for action in drawing the line as anywhere else," then went on to say paradoxically that he "questioned the advisability of putting in ground units particularly if large numbers were involved."[28] General of the Army Collins was silent on the issue of combat troops and largely confined his remarks to actions then under way. He reported the earlier telecon with MacArthur and noted that materiel from Japan would reach the Koreans "within the ten-day period for which they already have supplies." Finally, Collins's only recommendation was to urge "that authority be given MacArthur to send a survey group to Korea."[29]

Admiral Sherman was the most bellicose, saying that "the Russians do not want war now but if they do they will have it. The present situation in Korea offers a valuable opportunity for us to act." He thought that the Navy should "stop the use of the sea as a means of attack on South Korea" and agreed that, on Formosa, "we must apply our military guarantees against military action both ways." In response to the president's question about the disposition of naval forces, Sherman said that it would take two days to bring the fleet up from the Philippines and "the movement should be ordered now." He also wanted to move more ships, including at least one carrier, from the mainland to Pearl Harbor.[30] The president agreed.

Air Force General Vandenberg was perhaps most cautious of all the military chiefs. "He would not base our action on the assumption that the Russians would not fight." Moreover, "we could knock out the North Korean tanks with our air if only the North Korean air force is involved. However, Russian jets might come into action and they would be operating from much closer bases." At this point, the president asked if the Air Force could knock out Russian bases in the Far East? Vandenberg thought that "this might take some time," but allowed that "it could be done if we used A-bombs." Thus, whatever their assumptions, none of the military chiefs was, as Acheson acknowledges, "in favor of using ground forces under conditions then existing."[31]

Now it was the service secretaries' turn to speak. Secretary of the Army Pace "expressed doubts about the advisability of putting ground forces into Korea." But he "stressed the need for speed and for encouraging General MacArthur to take action" in support of South Korea. Secretary of the Navy Matthews "also stressed the need for prompt action," which, he thought, "would get popular approval." Air Force Secretary Finletter was more cautious, saying that "we should go as far as necessary in protecting our evacuation. . . . [But] he expressed some doubt on the additional items which had been suggested by the Secretary of State." He felt that "our forces in the Far East were sufficient if the Russians do not come in." Finally, he advised that "only the necessary decisions be made that night."

Then it was Secretary of Defense Johnson's turn to speak. He agreed with Acheson's proposed instructions to MacArthur, but cautioned against giving him "too much discretion." There should "not be a real delegation of Presidential authority to General MacArthur." Referring to the defense of Formosa, he mentioned "three islands south of Okinawa in the Ryukyus which could be made ready in a few days as air bases." (These were Nishiomote, Ishigaki, and Miyako islands in the Sakishima archipelago.) These islands were "under our jurisdiction" and, in his view, "the Formosan situation could be handled from them."

On the question of combat troops, the secretary of defense was unequivocal. He declared in no uncertain terms that "he was opposed to committing ground troops in Korea." What followed Johnson's statement is unclear from the record. Jessup's memorandum simply notes that "Mr. Webb, Jr. Jessup, Mr. Rusk and Mr. Hickerson made brief comments in amplification of Mr. Acheson's statements."[32] Truman omits the exchange entirely from his memoirs.[33]

Bringing the discussion to a close, Truman announced his decisions. Based on Acheson's proposals but consistent with Webb's recommendation not to "do it too fast," Truman concentrated on the situation in Korea and excluded any action regarding Taiwan. Accordingly, the president authorized MacArthur to send the suggested supplies to the Koreans and also to dispatch a survey group, although the president was "not yet ready" to name MacArthur Commander in Chief in Korea. That would be done later. Indicated elements of the fleet were to be sent to Japan, but not yet to Formosa, which was to be left out of the equation for the moment.

The Air Force was to "continue to give cover for evacuation destroying tanks if necessary," but they were also to "prepare plans to wipe out all Soviet air bases in the Far East," should the Soviet Union enter the conflict. As General Vandenberg had declared during their discussion that the only way to accomplish this task was through the use of atomic weapons, the president was evidently quietly laying the groundwork for at least the threat to use atomic weapons against the Soviet Union.

The president then asked, perhaps in reference to Muccio's earlier cable on the subject, "whether more bazookas and possibly recoilless rifles could be sent." (Bradley said we had few recoilless rifles available and were short on ammunition, but was silent about the bazookas.) The president then wanted "careful calculation . . . made of the next probable place in which Soviet action might take place." Nevertheless, he said, "our action at this moment would be confined to the United Nations and to Korea" (not Formosa). The president "stressed that we are working entirely for the United Nations. . . . We would wait [to take] further action until the UN order is flouted."

As the meeting adjourned at 11:00 P.M., both Truman and Acheson say in their memoirs, the secretary showed the president a message Dulles had sent to him from Tokyo some twelve-and-a-half hours earlier. In it, he suggested that "US forces should be used" if South Korean forces were unable to "contain and repulse" the attack.[34] Acheson had this message in his pocket during the Blair House meeting and, had he produced it, he possibly could have influenced the discussion toward an early decision on the use of ground troops. An early commitment of combat troops would be desired, however, only if the NKA was making a dash for Pusan. As the fog surrounding the initial NKA attack had not yet dissipated, Truman and Acheson decided to await the clarification of Pyongyang's and Moscow's objectives, as well as the coalescence of opinion within their own leadership in favor of sending troops to combat, before proposing a larger commitment.

The next morning, June 26, amid a growing uproar in Washington over charges that the administration had been caught "flat-footed" by the attack, Secretaries Acheson and Johnson made a previously scheduled appearance before the Senate Appropriations Committee. The State Department had been solely responsible for South Korea—not Defense, and not MacArthur, whose responsibility had formally ended with the withdrawal of American occupation troops a year earlier. Under questioning from the committee, Secretary Acheson replied that President Truman had enjoined them not to discuss the Korean situation publicly. Committee member Styles Bridges (R, New Hampshire) thereupon requested that the hearings be closed in order to permit discussion.

Although Acheson insisted for the record that the committee "would have to talk to Rear Admiral Roscoe Hillenkoetter, Director of Central Intelligence,"[35] for information regarding intelligence warning indicators, he obviously discussed the issue for, by noon, unnamed committee members had "leaked the news that the North Korean attack represented a shocking 'failure' of American intelligence."[36] Outraged by what they were told, committee chairman Kenneth McKellar (D, Tennessee) demanded that the CIA director appear before the committee that very afternoon.[37]

Acheson, the source of the "intelligence failure" charge, now attempted an uncharacteristically clumsy ploy in an attempt to preclude Hillenkoetter's appearance before the committee. As Chairman McKellar was arranging for the CIA director to appear, Acheson "telephoned after his testimony to tell Hillenkoetter he had 'done his best' to defend the intelligence community in the face of savage attacks by the outraged senators."[38] Acheson also made an appointment for the director to brief the president that afternoon at the same time that he was scheduled to appear before the committee.

Learning of Acheson's action, Hillenkoetter smelled a rat. He knew that there had not been an intelligence failure and if he were detained by his briefing of the president and unable to make an appearance before the committee, the false charge of intelligence failure would spread, with predictable consequences for himself, not to mention the intelligence community. The CIA director thus instructed his legislative counsel, Walter Pforzheimer, to "assemble all the agents' reports from North Korea and the latest Intelligence Estimates, which had already been sent to key policy makers." If he was "delayed very long with the President, Pforzheimer was to continue on to testify on the Hill."

Hillenkoetter's meeting with the president was, however, "cordial, brief, and straightforward." The director showed the president the documentary evidence negating the "intelligence failure" charge and Truman made only a perfunctory attempt to dissuade the director from proceeding to the Hill, asking: "Do you really want to go up there?" When Hillenkoetter replied that "I believe we have a good story to tell," the president agreed and told him to "go ahead." In the meantime, the committee deferred the meeting time by an hour to accommodate Hillenkoetter's briefing of the president.

When Hillenkoetter and Pforzheimer arrived at the committee room "they discovered the reason Acheson had tried to stall them at the White House. During his testimony that morning, the Secretary of State had tried to shift the blame for the Korean debacle onto the CIA."[39] An angry but composed Hillenkoetter "read from the Estimates and agents' reports, which clearly cited specific evidence of the North Koreans' invasion plans." Going into detail, Hillenkoetter "read a number of information bulletins his agency had distributed to the Government personnel entitled to receive them, each one giving information about continuing troop and tank concentrations near the border." The bulletins "went back for two or three months," specifically, since April.[40]

In response to Chairman McKellar's demand to know why the information had not been disseminated to key officials, Hillenkoetter declared: "every Estimate was circulated to the key cabinet officials." At this, McKellar became highly agitated, expressing considerable skepticism. "That very morning," he said, "Secretary Acheson had sworn he had received no such warning." Standing his ground, Hillenkoetter "promised to deliver signed receipts, proving these cabinet officers had received the Estimates, including the critical June 20 document containing the specific warnings."[41]

Hillenkoetter had been convincing. When the closed hearing ended, Republican committee members expressed their satisfaction. Senator Bridges declared that the CIA "was doing a good job, although he had not thought so before today's hearing." And Senator Knowland, who had earlier declared that the invasion had caught the administration flat-footed, said: "I am satisfied that the C.I.A. is and was performing its function." Democratic committee members Richard Russell (Georgia), John McClellan (Arkansas), and Joseph O'Mahoney (Wyoming) "concurred in the opinions of their Republican colleagues."[42]

Not so Chairman McKellar, who demanded that Pforzheimer return the following day with the signed receipts, "showing the Estimates had been received by Acheson and other cabinet members." When Pforzheimer produced the signed receipts the next day, McKellar "took one look at them and threw them on the committee room table," declaring "these are forgeries!" But Pforzheimer refused to be intimidated, patiently assisting as McKellar "examined each signature, comparing the handwriting with other authenticated documents." After meticulous examination, McKellar was "forced to acknowledge the validity of the receipts. But he never shared this information with the press."[43]

That afternoon, after somewhat desultory debate in both houses of Congress, the Senate Republican Policy Committee caucused. Afterward, Senator Joseph McCarthy of Wisconsin publicly denounced Secretary Acheson, while Senator William Jenner of Indiana charged that "the Korean debacle . . . reminds us that the same sell-out-to-Stalin statesmen, who turned Russia loose, are still in the saddle." A committee spokesman announced that in their view "the United States should give maximum aid to the Republic of Korea in the form of weapons and other military supplies but should not let the fighting drag it into a war." The consensus was that the United States was under a "moral obligation" to help the Koreans help themselves, but was under "no obligation" to go to war.[44]

Meanwhile, it was becoming apparent that the NKA was not making a dash for Pusan as expected, but was driving on Seoul. U.S. leaders had anticipated the former and—if War Plan SL-17 of June 19, Operation Swarmer, the preparations of the Second Division, Marine exercises at Quantico, the amphibious instruction being given to the Eighth Army, and the instructions issued to MacArthur just the day before meant anything—were preparing to respond with the classic peninsular defense: fall back, overextend the aggressor's forces, and counterattack behind his lines. When the NKA seized Seoul and hesitated at the Han River, however, U.S. leaders in Washington decided to temporize and wait until the NKA made its move for Pusan. The decisive act would be the North Korean crossing of the Han River, which would clearly indicate a plan to subdue the entire country. Then, and only then, would Truman commit combat troops.

Thus, from the outbreak of the war until the end of the first week, the Truman leadership made no U.S. effort to stem the attack beyond air strikes designed to ensure the safe evacuation of foreign nationals from Seoul. Indeed, early press coverage suggested that the United States would not send troops to come to the aid of South Korea.[45] The administration's immediate efforts were concentrated on building a political coalition in the United Nations to isolate the aggressor, providing military supplies to the ROK, and deploying naval forces to prevent any Chinese attack on Formosa. Only on June 30, when it was clear that the NKA had begun to cross the Han River and attack southward, did the Truman administration decide to commit ground troops to battle.

199

A continuing stream of reports from Ambassador Muccio traced the evolving situation. While the president and his aides were conferring at Blair House, Muccio had sent a generally upbeat cable describing the "gallant comeback" by ROK forces, who "seem to have stabilized [the] situation."[46] There was, he said, "some evidence that North Korean armor and artillery are withdrawing all along the line." Korean forces had given an "extremely good account of themselves, and I am confident that they will not be found wanting in the tests to come." But, he urged, "it is obviously essential that we give them not only adequate but sustained aid. Already General MacArthur has been most helpful in this respect."

In three cables received the morning of the 26th (the evening of the 26th in Korea), Muccio reported that overnight the situation had changed dramatically for the worse. In two cables received ten minutes apart at daybreak, Muccio reported the departure of the bulk of the evacuees, 682 people, who had crowded aboard the commandeered commercial freighter *Reinholt*, but the ambassador now realized that "North Korean advances have created dangerous situation with possibilities of rapid deterioration." Three hours later, at 9:31 A.M., State received yet another cable from Muccio, this time expressing great alarm. Referring to the remaining 300 evacuees still in Seoul, he said: "the situation is disintegrating so rapidly that we may not all be able to get out."[47]

Secretary Acheson, perusing these cables, did not promptly pass on the growing concern to congressional leaders. In telephone calls between 10:15 and 10:50 A.M. to Senate Foreign Relations Chairman Tom Connally, second ranking minority member of the committee Alexander Wiley, and Chairman of the House Foreign Affairs Committee John Kee, Acheson said that "the situation seemed to be in hand." It was only when Wiley called the secretary back nearly three hours later, no doubt reflecting his own sources reporting a different view, that Acheson conceded that "things were now not going so well in Korea."[48]

A few hours later, at 4 P.M., the president, accompanied by Secretary Acheson, received the South Korean ambassador, John Chang. The ambassador came bearing President Rhee's plea for planes, tanks, and heavy artillery to enable their forces to stand up to the invaders. "Nothing had as yet arrived," he said. Truman replied that he had already issued orders to MacArthur to "supply all items of ammunition and equipment which, in MacArthur's opinion, the Korean army was trained to use," that is, small arms, but not heavy equipment. The president pointed out that "the battle had been going on for only forty-eight hours and that other men and other countries had defended their liberties under much more discouraging situations through to ultimate victory."[49]

The president reiterated that "help was on the way," and that it was vital that the Koreans "develop the steadfast leadership which would carry them through this crisis." As their meeting was ending, the president and Acheson enjoined the ambassador to say to the awaiting newsmen only that "he had presented a petition asking for help and that the President had assured him that he had issued the necessary orders to give necessary supplies at the earliest possible moment in order to support the resolution of the UN and the efforts of the Koreans to defend themselves." This "was agreed."[50] In other words, there would be no mention of direct American involvement. When the ambassador emerged from his meeting with the president, "reporters, noting Chang's long face . . . were strengthened in their impression that the United States was treading hesitantly."[51]

THE SECOND BLAIR HOUSE MEETING

Cables from Muccio continued to arrive describing the deteriorating situation. At shortly after 5 P.M. he reported the enemy's "numerical superiority vicinity Seoul," and proposed to "stick it out here . . . until bitter end."[52] (He was immediately disabused of this notion and instructed to withdraw.) But it was the ambassador's cable nearly two hours later that persuaded Acheson that it was time for the president and his chief advisers to meet again. At a few minutes before 7:00, Muccio cabled to say that the acting prime minister had told him that the "fight will be all over by this afternoon" and inquired of the possibility of the "President and Cabinet moving to Japan as 'government in exile.' "[53]

The question of Rhee fleeing to Japan to establish a government in exile galvanized Acheson into action. If Rhee fled Korea the game would be lost. Therefore, within half an hour, at 7:29 P.M., Acheson called the president to say that "the Korean news was now so bad that another meeting was advisable." The president, referring to the group that had met the night before, immediately instructed the secretary to "have them here at nine p.m."[54] Oddly, when they met, despite the secretary's urgent report that the "Korean news was now so bad," the bulk of the group's discussion—as recorded by Ambassador Jessup—was mainly about Formosa, allies, Congress, and the United Nations. Only a few minutes of the forty-minute meeting were devoted to Korea.

As the meeting began, General Bradley read from what was purportedly MacArthur's "latest message." It read:

> ... Piecemeal entry into action vicinity Seoul by South Korean Third and Fifth Divisions has not succeeded in stopping the penetration recognized as the enemy main effort for the past 2 days with intent to seize the capital city of Seoul. Tanks entering suburbs of Seoul. Govt transferred to south and communications with part of KMAG opened at Taegu. Ambassador and Chief KMAG remaining in the city. FEC [Far East Command] mil survey group has been recalled under this rapidly deteriorating situation.
>
> South Korean units unable to resist determined Northern offensive. Contributory factor exclusive enemy possession of tanks and fighter planes. South Korean casualties as an index to fighting have not shown adequate resistance capabilities or the will to fight and our estimate is that a complete collapse is imminent.[55]

This message fragment, printed only in Truman's memoirs and attributed to MacArthur, contains so many errors of fact, as of the time it was purportedly sent, as to suggest that it is a fabrication. Indeed, not even the usual "fog of war" confusion accounts for these errors, which exhibit a pattern. It would appear to be part of a sustained effort to obscure fundamental differences between Truman and MacArthur over how to proceed. Truman and Acheson wished to delay commitment of troops until North Korea began its drive for Pusan, while MacArthur, not privy to this plan, sought to defend South Korea at the best, most obvious place at that moment, which was the Han River. Truman's so-called message from MacArthur suggested MacArthur's agreement that a defense of the Han was impossible.

Of these errors, first, it was not the ROK Third and Fifth Divisions that

201

had been moved north "into action vicinity Seoul" to contain the NKA drive on Uijongbu, but the First and Seventh Divisions. Second, NKA tanks would not enter the "suburbs of Seoul" until the next morning, Tuesday, at 5:30 Washington time (7:30 P.M. Korea time), and Seoul would not fall until Wednesday. Third, MacArthur had not recalled the survey team; Major General John Church was on his way and would arrive early the next morning Washington time. Fourth, the KMAG chief was not remaining in Seoul, but leaving it, with the departing ROK Army headquarters.

As to how "adequate" South Korean resistance was, ROK soldiers fought determinedly, especially against those NKA units not supported by tanks, and were suffering large casualties, although it was also true that their withdrawals were not orderly and some units disintegrated in combat because of poor leadership. The situation was certainly grave, but it would be an exaggeration to say at this point that "the South Korean units [were] unable to resist" and that "complete collapse is imminent."[56]

Furthermore, the decisions taken at the second Blair House meeting bear only marginal relevance to the thrust of this purported message from MacArthur describing imminent collapse, which would seem to call for immediate response. And finally, Jessup's official memorandum of the meeting does not mention a message from MacArthur, although in a footnote the *FRUS* volume editor notes Truman's citation of it in his memoirs. In short, the only source for this message is Truman.

As discussion began, General Vandenberg reported that the first Yak plane had been shot down and the president remarked that "he hoped that it was not the last."[57] Then Vandenberg "read the text of the orders" sent to FEAF calling for "aggressive action" against any North Korean interference with the evacuation mission. He indicated, however, that pilots "had been avoiding combat where the direct carrying-out of their mission was not involved." Acheson immediately suggested that an "all out order" be issued to Air and Navy forces waiving any restrictions on their mission to "offer fullest possible support to the South Korean forces, attacking tanks, guns, columns, etc., of the North Korean forces in order to give a chance to the South Koreans to reform." The president approved.

There followed an exchange among Secretary Pace, Vandenberg, and Acheson over the area of air operations, and it was decided that there would be "action only south of the 38th Parallel." The president agreed, saying "no action should be taken north of the 38th parallel . . . not yet." Secretary Pace added that "care should be used to avoid hitting friendly forces." Acheson, ever mindful of the political dimension of the conflict, said that it might be useful for the orders to FEAF to stress that U.S. actions were "to support South Korean forces in conformity with the resolution of the Security Council."

202

Acheson then took command of the discussion. He said that he wished orders issued "to the Seventh Fleet to prevent an attack on Formosa." The president agreed. Continuing, the secretary said that "at the same time the National Government of China [on Formosa] should be told to desist from operations against the mainland and that the Seventh Fleet should be ordered to see that those operations would cease." Acheson also wished to increase U.S. forces in and accelerate aid to the Philippines "in order that we might have a firm base there." The president agreed. Acheson then proposed that the United States send a military mission and step up aid to Indochina. Summing up, the secretary said that "if orders were issued tonight" on all these matters, "it would be desirable for the President to make a statement tomorrow." At this, he handed to the president a rough draft of "the type of statement which might be issued." Truman said "he would work on the statement tonight."[58]

The president then startled his listeners with the remark that "he wished consideration given to taking Formosa back as part of Japan and putting it under MacArthur's Command." Acheson quickly acted to shelve this idea, saying that "he had considered this move but felt that it should be reserved for later." It required further study, he said, and nothing should be done at this time. Truman then unloosed a second shocker. He said that "he had a letter from the Generalissimo . . . to the effect that the Generalissimo might step out of the situation if that would help." The president explained that "this was a private letter and [was why] he had kept it secret," but "we might want to proceed along those lines in order to get Chinese forces helping us." He thought that "the Generalissimo might step out if MacArthur were put in."

Again, Acheson responded negatively. "The Generalissimo was unpredictable," he said, "and . . . it was possible that he might resist and 'throw the ball game.'" It would be well "to do this later." The president then said "alright." He had just "thought that it was the next step." Secretary Johnson piped up to say that Acheson's proposals "pleased him very much." And Acheson added, with finality, that "he thought it undesirable that we should get mixed up in the question of the Chinese administration of the Island." Truman agreed and, reversing his position completely, declared that "we were not going to give the Chinese 'a nickel' for any purpose whatever."

Did Truman truly want to get the Chinese Nationalists in on the U.S. side? To do so would end for the foreseeable future any possibility of opening relations with Beijing, and would clearly draw the line of containment in the Pacific around the Sino-Soviet alliance. Or was it a charade? Truman had a visceral, public dislike for Chiang Kai-shek, most recently displayed only a moment before. Was this exchange a subtle device cooked up between Truman and Acheson designed to shift opinion within the military toward agreement to employ U.S. combat troops? Whatever the purpose, none of the military chiefs volunteered an opinion one way or another—except for Johnson's brief remark—and the subject was abruptly dropped. (But Truman would raise the issue of employing Nationalist troops again on Friday when he finally decided to commit U.S. combat troops.)

Admiral Sherman next raised the subject of Seventh Fleet Command, saying that since the previous day's orders for the fleet to proceed to Japan had "placed" the fleet under MacArthur, today's orders diverting the fleet from Japan to Formosa would not alter command arrangements and "would be issued from the Joint Chiefs of Staff to General MacArthur." It was agreed. MacArthur would control the Seventh Fleet's activities around Formosa just as he was around Korea.

Secretary Acheson observed that the U.N. Security Council would meet the next afternoon and that the Department had proposed a further resolution for adoption. John Hickerson then read the draft, including its key phrase "recommending that UN members render such assistance as was needed to the Republic of Korea to repel the attack." Truman interjected to state that "that was right. . . . We wanted everyone in on this, including Hong Kong." Bradley said that he had spoken with British Air Marshal Lord Tedder, chairman of the British Joint Services Mission in Washington, who supported our "firm position," and who had extended a full report of British forces in the area.

Dean Rusk then raised the possibility of a Russian veto, saying "in that case we would still take the position that we could act in support of the [U.N.] Charter." Truman said "that was right," but "he rather wished they would return," observing that "we needed to lay a base for our actions on Formosa." Truman's meaning was unclear, but presumably he was suggesting a Soviet return to the Security Council and objection to its resolutions would enable the United States to "lay a base" for extending U.N. responsibility for Formosa, or, at the very least, to revisit existing arrangements on the disposition of the island, but the president did not clarify his statement. At this point, only U.S. actions in Korea were covered by U.N. mandate; all other U.S. actions were unilateral.

Moving to the question of where the Communists' next move would be, Rusk reported that Soviet expert George Kennan thought it might be Formosa, while Johnson thought it might be Iran. General Collins and Secretary Pace said that they had asked for "full reports from all over the world in regard to any developments, particularly of Soviet preparations." Acheson said that he would talk with the British and the French about possible Soviet actions. The secretary then asked Admiral Sherman about using the air bases on the Sakishimas, suggesting that "it would be better to put any necessary supporting air forces on these islands than to try to put them on Formosa itself." Acheson then suggested that the president bring in "Senator Connally and other members of the Senate and House and tell them what had been decided." Truman replied that he had already scheduled a meeting with them for the next morning and he wanted Acheson and Johnson to attend.

It was only at this point in the meeting that the discussion turned to the deteriorating situation on the battlefield. General Collins said that "the military situation in Korea was bad. It was impossible to say how much our air can do. The Korean Chief of Staff has no fight left in him." Acheson said that "it was important for us to do something even if the effort were not successful." Johnson reinforced this notion, declaring that "even if we lose Korea this action would save the situation," presumably a reference to the larger strategy embodied in NSC-68.

These quite defeatist statements seemed to have alarmed the president, who then began what can only be described as a soliloquy for the record. His purpose seemed to be to lay the groundwork for the argument that unless the military chiefs agreed to commit troops, they would be blamed if Korea were lost. Truman declared that "he had done everything he could for five years to prevent this kind of situation. Now the situation is here and we must do what we can to meet it." He was "wondering about the mobilization of the National Guard and asked General Bradley if that was necessary now." Continuing, the president said, "if it was, he must go to Congress and ask for funds." He was not attempting to exert any pressure and was "merely putting the subject on the table for discussion." Then, he repeated that "we must do everything we can for the Korean situation—'for the United Nations.'"

General Bradley responded cautiously, saying that "if we commit our ground forces in Korea we cannot at the same time carry out our other commitments without mobilization." Then, he "wondered if it was better to wait now on the question of mobilization of the National Guard. He thought it would be preferable to wait a few days." The president said that "he wished the Joint Chiefs to think about this and to let him know in a few days time," then added: "I don't want to go to war." Truman seemed to be taking both sides of the question. On the one hand he wanted "to do everything we can for the Korean situation" and on the other hand he was saying, "I don't want to go to war." In other words, he would defer to military judgment.

General Collins spoke up to say that "if we were going to commit ground forces in Korea we must mobilize." Acheson quickly suggested that "we should hold mobilization in reserve" and Johnson said that he "hoped these steps already authorized will settle the Korean question." Truman continued: "the next question would be the mobilization of the Fleet Reserve"; Admiral Sherman responded approvingly with the remark that "there must be a degree of balance." Truman noted that there was "some pretty good air" in the Air National Guard, but thought that the Air National Guard "should be like the Naval Reserve." General Vandenberg was "very glad to hear the President say this."

Admiral Sherman asked whether MacArthur could anchor the fleet in Formosan ports and Truman asked Acheson what he thought. Acheson said that "they should go ahead and do it." Sherman replied that "this would be the best procedure." General Collins then remarked, apparently apropos of the overall situation, "if we had had standing orders we could have stopped this. We must consider this problem for the future." Truman agreed. Finally, as the meeting drew to a close, Johnson said that "if there was danger of a Russian veto in the Security Council the President's statement should be put out before the Security Council meets tomorrow." Acheson agreed and the meeting ended.

Secretary Pace and Undersecretary Webb immediately went to the Pentagon to communicate the president's decisions to MacArthur via telecon, around 10:30 P.M. (12:30 P.M. Tuesday, June 27, in Tokyo, which was fourteen hours ahead). When told that Air Force and Navy aircraft were now permitted unrestricted action against North Korean targets anywhere below the 38th parallel, MacArthur "requested permission to make an immediate announcement to the Republic of Korea that American military assistance was on the way," including the dispatch of ground troops.[59]

Webb, speaking on behalf of the president, said that "no announcement could be made until the Chief Executive had discussed his decisions with members of the Congress" the next day. Premature revelation would jeopardize Congressional support. But MacArthur insisted. "If he were to accomplish his mission, there could be no delay in the employment of any measure that could nourish the will to fight of the ROK Army. The South Koreans had to be told at once that the Americans were coming to help them."[60]

The exchange between Webb and MacArthur revealed once again the difference between the president and the general over the proper strategy to employ. MacArthur's evident purpose was to strengthen the ROK Army's "will to fight" where it stood, that is, to mount a defense at the Han River, one of three major water barriers between Seoul and Pusan. (The other two were the Kum River midway between Seoul and Pusan and the Naktong River near Pusan.) Although Webb's objection was couched in terms of the president's prior need to consult Congress, in fact, Truman wished for no defense at the Han at all, and most certainly did not wish to divulge at this early date that the United States would commit U.S. combat troops to the fighting. Indeed, Truman sought to convey the very opposite impression in the Tuesday morning editions of the press and to congressional leaders with whom he would confer that morning.[61]

After arguing for several minutes, Webb proposed an ingenious compromise that MacArthur accepted. "While the impending American military involvement was to be announced in Korean, nothing was to be said in English." Thus, from 3 A.M. Tuesday, Washington time (5 P.M. Tuesday, Korean time), South Korean radio stations played the following announcement every ten minutes for several hours.

At 4:00 P.M. June 27 an official notification was received from General MacArthur's Headquarters that a combat command post of General MacArthur's Headquarters will be immediately established in Seoul.

From tomorrow morning American Air Force planes will directly participate in the fighting and *American troops will gradually participate in the fighting*.

The national Defense forces will resolutely hold their present positions. All citizens are requested to carry out their tasks calmly and march to crush the Communist bandits.[62]

Over the next several days, this message was also conveyed through KMAG personnel to ROK Army forces. Indeed, KMAG personnel, initially instructed to withdraw from their ROK units, were now ordered to return. They were told that the United States was coming into the fight and that "we do what we had to do to contain the enemy north of the Han until U.S. ground troops could join the struggle." The ROK command "had been told that the Americans hoped we could hold at the Han for at least three days to allow them time to deploy U.S. ground forces from Japan to the front in Korea."[63]

The effect of this so-called compromise between Webb and MacArthur may have bolstered the spirits of President Rhee and the Korean leadership, but it was disastrous for the ROK Army. Its leaders sought to reconstitute their forces and mount a defense at the Han River *in the expectation that United States forces would shortly arrive to reinforce them*. There would be no U.S. reinforcement at the Han River line, and while South Korean forces would make a valiant defensive stand at the river, it would shortly lead to greater losses than would have been the case had they engaged in a mobile delaying action to the south. In short, the effect of the compromise was to encourage ROK forces to persist in an unequal battle at the river and, when the river line was breached, leave a greatly weakened defense capability to combat the enemy afterward.

Meanwhile, the president and his cabinet officials met with a dozen congressional leaders Tuesday morning, June 27, at 11:30 A.M. Before the meeting began, the president knew that Seoul had already fallen to the invaders (midnight Tuesday, June 27 in Seoul was 10 A.M. Tuesday, June 27 in Washington), but he omitted that fact in his remarks. Nor is it recorded that Acheson mentioned the fall of Seoul in his summary of developments. Then, the president read aloud the text of an announcement he would release after the meeting.[64] Reflecting the decisions made the night before, he said that he had "ordered United States air and sea forces to give the Korean Government troops cover and support."

"Communism," he said, "has passed beyond the use of subversion to conquer independent nations and will now use armed invasion and war" in defiance of U.N. orders. "In these circumstances," he said, "the occupation of Formosa by Communist forces would be a direct threat to the security of the Pacific area and to United States forces performing their lawful and necessary functions in that area." Accordingly, the president had "ordered the Seventh Fleet to prevent any attack on Formosa." As a corollary, he was also "calling upon the Chinese Government on Formosa to cease all air and sea operations against the mainland. The Seventh Fleet will see that this is done." The president declared that the "future status of Formosa must await the restoration of security in the Pacific, a peace settlement with Japan, or consideration by the United Nations."

208

The president also noted that he had "directed" accelerated delivery of military assistance to U.S. forces in the Philippines and to French forces in Indochina, along with a military mission. He addressed his closing remarks to the United Nations, whose members, he knew, would "consider carefully the consequences of this latest aggression in Korea in defiance of the Charter of the United Nations." Warning against a return to the "rule of force," he affirmed American intentions to uphold the "rule of law."

During ensuing questioning from congressional leaders regarding the adequacy of the forces deployed to Korea, Secretary Pace "mentioned that no ground troops had been sent in."[65] Then, as discussion of this question continued, according to Secretary Johnson's later testimony, congressional leaders "were told there at that meeting that ground troops were not planned to be used."[66] (Later, in attempting to rebut the charge of misleading the congress following the commitment of combat troops, Assistant Secretary of State Rusk offered the crude distinction that "the statement that there were no plans to commit ground forces should be distinguished from a decision not to commit them.")[67]

Congressman Charles A. Eaton (R, New Jersey) asked whether the "United States was now committed to defend South Korea from invasion." The president replied that "his statement made this clear," but Secretary Acheson quickly added that "we were doing this in support of the UN."[68] Senator Alexander Smith (R, New Jersey) wished to clarify which action was in support of the United Nations and which was unilateral and received confirmation that exclusive of Korea "in regard to Formosa and other areas the action was US action and not UN action." Senator Connally said that "we must be careful in handling the Formosan question not to divert attention from Korea." The president agreed.[69]

The president's meeting with congressional leaders had the desired effect as their reports to their respective bodies in the House and Senate brought general expressions of support and congratulation for the president's firm decision to act. The House and Senate voted overwhelmingly to extend selective service for another year. A few Republicans, however, criticized the president for failing to obtain a "mandate" from Congress, but the administration's view that events were moving too fast to await a mandate momentarily satisfied all but the most steadfast critic.

Simultaneously, the administration sought to prepare the ground for the passage of the second resolution to be voted on in the U.N. Security Council that afternoon. Toward this end, the State Department prevailed upon George Kennan, the outgoing head of the Policy Planning Staff, to brief allied representatives in Washington before the Security Council convened. The choice of Kennan to "explain" the president's decisions was curious because he had not been an insider in the decision-making process, but rather, as he described it, a "floating kidney," that is, a person "outside the chain of command and one step removed from the real decisions."[70]

The aptness of his selection, however, lay not in his proximity to the decision-makers, but in his convictions. It was Kennan's belief, which was well known and which Truman wished to propagate, that the United States should do no more in Korea than repel the attack and drive the North Korean forces back across the parallel. Since this view would resonate well with the allies, whose support was required for passage of the resolution to be presented that afternoon, Kennan was "suddenly and unexpectedly . . . obliged to brief the assembled NATO ambassadors in Washington on what it was we were trying to do in Korea."[71] Moreover, he had been "brought into the briefing without forewarning, unable to confer in advance with the Secretary of State."[72] As Kennan phrased it: "I confidently and innocently assured them that we had no intention of doing more than to restore the status quo ante."[73]

Clearly, Truman and Acheson did not wish to show their hand before the U.N. vote. Indeed, to declare that the United States would commit combat troops at this point and carry the battle into North Korea would be prematurely disastrous. It would arouse opposition in the U.N., making difficult if not impossible successful passage of the resolution calling for aid to South Korea. It would immediately elicit an outcry from Congress, especially from those Republican members determined to prevent a decision to commit combat troops. It would certainly generate concern among the allies, especially Great Britain, who were seeking means to resolve the conflict short of all-out combat. And it would risk deterring Pyongyang from driving south, prompting a decision to adopt a fortress Seoul defense instead.

Thus, for all these reasons, the president and his top aides all declared that the United States had no "plans" to deploy troops. The only caveat to this

209

general position was contained in the Tuesday morning *Washington Post*. In an article explaining that current policy barred sending troops, it said: "This policy may change if the United Nations should call on its members to send armed forces."[74] The forthcoming U.N. vote would thus be crucial, for it would not only establish the basis for international and American support for South Korea, it would also generate the political stimulus and create the legal basis for sending troops.

Until the last moment it seemed that Jacob Malik, the Soviet representative to the U.N., would attend the session, veto the U.S. proposal, and thoroughly disrupt Washington's efforts to build a strong anti-Communist coalition. At a previously planned luncheon at the Stockholm restaurant in Syosset, Long Island, near the United Nations, attended by Secretary-General Trygve Lie, Soviet Ambassador Malik, U.S. Ambassador Earnest Gross, and other delegates, Malik deflected conversation from the obvious question, keeping all in suspense until the lunch had ended and the delegates were leaving for the U.N. Security Council. Secretary-General Lie approached Ambassador Malik, expressing the view that the interests of the Soviet Union required his presence, but, to the relief of Ambassador Gross, Malik replied: "No, I will not go there."[75]

Meeting that afternoon, but not voting until just before midnight to permit delegates to contact home governments for instructions, the U.N. Security Council approved the U.S.-sponsored resolution. The vote was seven to one, with two abstentions and one absence. Britain, France, China, Cuba, Norway, and Ecuador voted with the United States; Yugoslavia voted against; Egypt and India abstained. The key recommendation called for "members of the United Nations [to] furnish such assistance to the Republic of Korea as may be necessary to repel the armed attack and to restore international peace and security in the area."[76]

The failure of the Soviets to veto the American resolution has generally been assumed to have been a blunder, resulting in a mix-up in orders from Moscow. But, as Beverly Smith, an early commentator, put it, the Soviets "had known for months" that the NKA would attack; "they had helped train and equip it—and they knew the issue would certainly come before the UN." Smith suggests that the Kremlin "was not unwilling for the United States and the UN to intervene." Given the power of the NKA, the United States might "be kicked humiliatingly out of Korea," or be "tied down in the Korean morass."[77]

The language of the resolution, "to repel the armed attack and to restore international peace and security in the area," clearly implied a policy of returning to the status quo ante, an objective that was explicitly spelled out by administration spokesmen like Kennan, and emphasized in the press. John Norris of the *Washington Post*, for example, in reporting the second Blair

House meeting's decisions, bylined an article titled: "U.S. Forces' Goal Is to Drive North Koreans Back to Border." A sub-heading blared: "No Advance Into Red Area."

While this decidedly modest objective facilitated passage of the resolution, it was not the administration's true goal and would present problems for Truman and Acheson later when the decision was made to carry the battle north of the 38th parallel. Then, U.S. spokesmen would argue that the only way "to restore international peace and security in the area" was through unification of the Korean peninsula under U.N. auspices, lest a return to the status quo ante simply reestablish the circumstances for a replay of the current conflict. As we shall see, discussion about the question of driving north of the 38th parallel and of ways to get around the language of the resolution began in mid-July, at Truman's request, two months before the Inchon landing would offer that possibility.[78]

211

TRUMAN PREPARES TO COMMIT GROUND FORCES

The Truman administration sought to provide Moscow with an opportunity to disavow its involvement not only in the Korean events, but also in two other areas of tension—Formosa and Yugoslavia. In a very well-informed article appearing in the *New York Times* on the morning of June 28, Hanson Baldwin carefully laid out the intelligence on all three cases, but repeatedly made the point that there was little or no direct Russian involvement in any of them.[79] There can be no doubt that the article was an intelligence leak designed to convey a signal to Moscow, for Washington certainly knew the extent of Russian involvement in the Korean and Yugoslav cases, if not in the Chinese.

In the case of Korea, Baldwin laid out the intelligence indicating that United States leaders had had clear and unequivocal advance warning of war preparations (thereby incidentally vindicating CIA Director Hillenkoetter). Baldwin noted that

> The Central Intelligence Agency (and presumably other intelligence agencies) reported and circulated to the President and to Government departments a marked buildup by the North Korean People's Army along the Thirty-eighth Parallel beginning in the early days of June. This buildup was described in a report of June 9 and substantiated on June 13. Capabilities of an invasion at any time were mentioned.... Commencing in early June, light and medium tanks ... and other heavy equipment were assembled at the front, and troop concentrations became noticeable.

While Baldwin acknowledged the presence of between 3,500 and 4,500 Russian advisers in North Korea, "down to company level," none had been identified with the "attacking forces." The tanks were said to be "probably of Japanese manufacture," and "no tanks of Russian manufacture have yet been definitely identified." Of the 150 planes of the North Korean air force, there were "half of Japanese origin and half Russian." Overall, Baldwin asserted, there was "probably more Japanese than Russian equipment in use." (Of course, Baldwin was not privy to the June 19 CIA estimate that had identified both T-34 tanks and Soviet fighter aircraft in a North Korean armed force almost totally equipped by the Soviet Union, but his informant most assuredly was.)

On Formosa, the Chinese buildup along the coast for the invasion had been completed by June 15 and Beijing "between now and the start of typhoon season in August could launch the invasion attempt." The Chinese had an air force of some 200 planes, including Japanese Zeroes, American C-47 transports, and "some Russian types." Of these, there were 20 jets flown by Russian pilots. "It is significant, however, that at least in air battles against Nationalist planes, the Russian-manned jets have not as yet fired a shot." The Chinese Communists had no navy to speak of and "reports here indicate little evidence that the Russians have remedied this weakness." (This description was largely accurate, except that Russian-piloted MIGs had in fact fired on and downed at least three Nationalist aircraft.)

Baldwin repeated the same pattern of argument with regard to the tension surrounding Yugoslavia. Identifying the multi-division buildups in Bulgaria, Romania, and Hungary, he asserted that there were "no Russian troops" in any of them. (Of course, Baldwin omitted the salient fact that Moscow had created, armed, maintained, and controlled these forces.) There can be no doubt that the United States, through this report and others of this kind, was attempting to offer Moscow an opportunity to pull back from what could be the brink of the abyss leading to global war. The Truman leadership would also attempt to position itself so that events would not drag the nation, willy-nilly, into a larger conflict than it bargained for.

Wednesday morning, June 28, in Washington was Wednesday evening in Korea and, although Seoul had fallen, there were signs that South Korean forces were regrouping at the Han River south of the city. At that time Major General John Church, whom MacArthur had sent to survey the military situation, sent a message to the Far East Commander. Church felt that "a reasonable defense of the Han River line from the south bank could be accomplished." However, "if the 38th Parallel were to be restored . . . American ground forces would have to be used."[80] MacArthur immediately sent Church a reply indicating that he would visit him the next morning. It is unknown whether MacArthur also informed Washington of his plans.

Whether Truman knew of MacArthur's plans to visit Korea or not, that day the president began to prepare the political ground for the commitment of ground troops, but not to the defense of the Han. Up to this point, orders to MacArthur had restricted him to the use of air, naval, and logistical support of ROK forces south of the 38th parallel. On Wednesday, the president and his secretary of state now began to consider the implications of enlarging the battlefield to include the area north of the 38th parallel. An important part of this consideration was the possible effect that U.S. action north of the 38th would have on Moscow and on domestic U.S. opinion.

Secretary of State Acheson had prepared a draft policy statement that addressed "the situation which would arise if Soviet forces appeared and took an active part in the present operations in Korea." Because of its "great urgency," he wrote to Secretary Johnson, he hoped that "we can place it before the President for decision at the National Security Council meeting this afternoon."[81]

The Wednesday NSC meeting, which convened in the Cabinet Room of the White House, was the first meeting of that body since the outbreak of the war. By law, the NSC principals numbered five: the president, vice president, secretary of state, secretary of defense, and chairman of the National Security Resources Board. The president, at his discretion, could invite others to attend. On this occasion, the three service secretaries were invited, as were James Lay, executive secretary of the NSC, and Averell Harriman, hastily summoned from his post in Paris to be named "Special Assistant to the President." Apparently, neither the director of the CIA nor the members of the Joint Chiefs were invited.[82]

Secretary Acheson's draft was discussed in the context of intelligence regarding all possible contingencies involving Soviet moves on the global chessboard, including Formosa and Yugoslavia, but also French Indochina, Iran, and Austria, where "some uneasiness has been felt in Washington."[83] The secretary's three-sentence draft policy statement noted that the decision to commit air and naval forces did not "in itself constitute a decision to engage in a major war with the Soviet Union if Soviet forces intervene in Korea." However, the decision "was taken in the full realization of a risk of war with the Soviet Union." If "substantial" Soviet forces did enter, "United States forces should defend themselves, should take no action on the spot to aggravate the situation, and should report the situation to Washington."[84]

In this way, Acheson reasoned, the United States would retain the initiative in determining whether or not to interpret such Soviet action as the opening shot in World War III, and respond accordingly. In a global conflict with Moscow, the United States would not elect to employ Korea as a major battlefield. It was decided, upon advice from Defense, that this directive should be included as part of the orders sent to MacArthur, but not issued as a separate directive. The statement itself, however, strongly implied that American forces would be going into action north of the 38th parallel into

213

North Korea where Soviet entry could occur. Indeed, target lists in North Korea were discussed, but no decisions taken.[85]

The implications of going north also prompted Acheson to point out that "we could not count on the continuance of the enthusiastic support that our staunch attitude in Korea had evoked in the country and in the world." He noted that "firm leadership would be less popular if it should involve casualties and taxes."[86] But Truman replied that there was now no backing out of Korea "unless a military situation elsewhere demanded such action."[87] Harriman observed that, in Europe, after the president had decided to aid Korea "there had been a general feeling of relief." Vice President Barkley noted, however, that during Senate debate, Senator Wherry had questioned whether any NATO countries would support the United States. Truman then revealed that he had just received a British offer to place its Far Eastern warships at the disposal of MacArthur.

Following the NSC meeting, Secretary Acheson returned to the Department of State where he held a press conference. His clear intention was to preempt domestic opposition by affirming unity of purpose, of leadership, and of the nation. In this way he sought to prepare the people for the president's forthcoming decision to commit the United States to a major conflict in Korea. In his opening statement, the secretary expressed deep gratitude for the almost unanimously favorable response given in support of the United States and the United Nations.

He emphasized that "all action in Korea has been under the aegis of the United Nations." Furthermore, "the entire action of the Government of the United States . . . has been taken under Presidential leadership." Within that leadership, "there has been complete unity among the President's advisers, civil and military." Acheson also asserted "complete unity" regarding congressional "understanding of the problem." Finally, he averred, there was "similar unity among the people of the United States."[88] During the question-and-answer session, the secretary would not discuss the Soviet role in the conflict on the grounds that Moscow had not yet replied to a note sent the day before. But Acheson declared that the "willful absence" of a member of the Security Council did not invalidate its deliberations and he dismissed the Soviet charge that the June 25 resolution was illegal as "totally unfounded."

As Secretary of State Acheson was finishing his press conference at the State Department, General MacArthur in Tokyo was boarding his personal aircraft, *Bataan*, for a trip to Korea and a firsthand look at the battlefield. After his assessment of the military situation, MacArthur would recommend the immediate dispatch of combat troops in order to mount a defense at the Han River. The Far East commander's recommendation, however, clashed directly with the plans of Truman and Acheson to wait for an NKA breakthrough across the Han before committing troops. When the NKA began crossing the Han on June 30, Truman would commit ground troops, and made moot any incipient clash between the President and his theater commander. It nevertheless became politically necessary to conceal this policy difference.

THE ARGUMENT OVER FORWARD DEFENSE

At 6:10 A.M. Thursday (4:10 P.M. Wednesday in Washington), MacArthur departed Haneda Airport in Tokyo for a personal evaluation of the battlefield situation in Korea. Accompanied by his top aides, Chief of Staff Major General Edward Almond, intelligence chief Major General Charles Willoughby, aide Brigadier General Courtney Whitney, FEAF Commander Lieutenant General George Stratemeyer, and four newspaper correspondents, the party, a total of fifteen, including crew, arrived at Suwon airfield, twenty miles south of Seoul, at around 10:30 A.M.[89]

En route, General Stratemeyer discussed with MacArthur the difficulty his airmen were experiencing in gaining air superiority. The proximity of North Korean air bases gave their planes greater time in the air over South Korean air space than American planes based in Japan three hundred miles away. Stratemeyer argued and MacArthur agreed that knocking out the main close-in North Korean bases was the only way to gain control of the air. MacArthur also realized that gaining control of the air would contribute significantly to a defense of the Han River, the main focus of his efforts. Indeed, General Church was then attempting without much success to direct U.S. bombing strikes at North Korean positions along the north bank of the Han, having advised the Korean chief of staff, General Chae Byong-duk, "to defend the Han River line at all costs."[90]

The problem in gaining air superiority, as MacArthur phrased it, was "How can I bomb north of the 38th Parallel without Washington hanging me?"[91] At this point, Truman's orders restricted action to south of the parallel. MacArthur's solution was to justify his decision on a broad interpretation of the June 27 U.N. resolution. Based on the directive to "restore peace in the area," with the emphasis on "area," MacArthur reasoned that striking North Korean airfields was the best means available to him as theater commander to accomplish his mission to defend South Korea; it carried no connotation of invading North Korea. Thus, in flight over the Sea of Japan, MacArthur authorized the following message to be sent to the deputy chief of FEAF: "Stratemeyer to Partridge: Take out North Korean airfield immediately. No publicity. MacArthur approves."[92]

It would require tortured reasoning to argue that MacArthur was gratuitously defying the president here. Both the problem and the solution were

215

straightforward. The best method of gaining air superiority was to knock out the enemy's aircraft while they were still on the ground. His clear intent was to provide maximum support for South Korean defense. He had anticipated the president's authorization to strike north of the 38th parallel by less than twenty-four hours and was technically in violation of the president's directive until the next day when the orders were changed to permit such attacks.

That afternoon at 4:15 P.M., as MacArthur was preparing to leave Korea, the Third Bombardment Group, based at Johnson Air Base outside of Tokyo, "sent 18 B-26s to attack the enemy's main military airfield at Pyongyang."[93] After-action reports estimated that twenty-five enemy aircraft were destroyed on the ground. Pyongyang and Moscow charged that B-29s had bombed Pyongyang itself, a charge which was denied. However, on the morning of the 29th, in an action fully within MacArthur's authority, B-29s did bomb Kimpo airport outside Seoul to prevent its use by North Korean aircraft.[94]

Although MacArthur had spent, at most, only eight hours in Korea, being briefed by General Church and discussing the overall situation with President Rhee, Ambassador Muccio, and the South Korean high command, his most important step was driving directly from Suwon twenty miles to the south bank of the Han River to evaluate the prospects for a river defense. In less than half an hour of direct observation of the forming battle lines, his evaluation went a step beyond that of General Church; a defense of the Han River line was possible, but necessitated an immediate commitment of American ground troops to stop the North Korean Army.

Upon returning to Suwon to board his waiting aircraft, MacArthur offered a lift to reporter Marguerite Higgins, who joined the four other reporters who had come along on the trip. During the return flight to Tokyo, MacArthur discussed with her and the other members of the party his decision to recommend commitment of American combat troops for defense of the Han. She noted that MacArthur felt that Korean soldiers "could be rallied with example and leadership." Therefore, he said, "the moment I reach Tokyo, I shall send President Truman my recommendations for the immediate dispatch of American divisions to Korea. But I have no idea whether he will accept my recommendation."[95]

Sources differ on MacArthur's departure time from Suwon. Appleman, whom the majority of authors cite, says that MacArthur left Suwon "within an hour" of 5:15 when his plane arrived, or, around 6:00, while Schnabel says that his plane "departed about 1600 [4:00]."[96] The difference is of some significance because it alters MacArthur's arrival time in Tokyo by some two hours. The flight time between Suwon and Tokyo was four hours and means that MacArthur arrived back in Tokyo sometime between 8:00 and 10:00

P.M. The Department of State account, agreeing with Appleman, says that "MacArthur had arrived back in Tokyo shortly after 10 P.M."[97] But Russell Brines, one of the reporters aboard the plane, established the actual time of departure. In a dispatch from Tokyo he wrote: "Gen. MacArthur and his party left Suwon at 5:15 p.m., a short time after two other transport planes had been attacked in the air nearby."[98]

Brines's contemporaneous report established MacArthur's arrival in Tokyo at shortly after 9 P.M. The general's arrival time in Tokyo bears on his remark to Higgins that "the moment I reach Tokyo, I shall send Truman my recommendations." In fact, Tokyo Headquarters had begun a teleconference with Washington at 8:48 P.M. (6:48 A.M. Washington time),[99] presumably in response to instructions radioed ahead from the plane. According to Truman's memoirs, "General MacArthur had asked for the conference immediately upon his return from a flying trip to the Korean front line."[100]

General Almond, a member of MacArthur's party, also recalled that "that night we began a series of telecon conferences with our Government . . . in the Pentagon, which enabled General MacArthur to personally, from personal observation, interpret how bad the situation was."[101] Thus, from both the president and General Almond, MacArthur had "asked for the conference immediately upon his return," and "that night," "personally," communicated his recommendations to Washington.

Several accounts confirm that General MacArthur had drafted his evaluation and recommendation to commit ground troops during the return flight to Tokyo.[102] It would seem to follow that immediately upon his return, during one of the "series of telecon conferences" held that night, General MacArthur related his recommendations to commit combat troops. If telecons were recorded in numerical sequence, there were eight teleconferences over a twenty-hour period, beginning with number 3437, which commenced just before 7:00 A.M. Washington time, Thursday, June 29, and ending with number 3444, which began at 3:40 A.M. Friday, June 30.[103] Of these telecons, a complete transcript of only the last is available. In other words, from just before the time MacArthur landed in Tokyo his office was in virtually continuous contact with the Pentagon during the next critical day.

Based on these facts, there is little ground for the argument, held by nearly all historians of the conflict, that upon arriving in Tokyo, MacArthur did not immediately communicate his recommendations via the ongoing series of telecons being held that night, but instead, despite the desperate urgency of the situation and his professed intention, simply decided to go to bed.[104] Furthermore, according to this version, which is based on the Department of State account, MacArthur waited to cable his recommendation, unchanged, to Washington some fifteen hours after he had returned from his

217

trip to Korea. Aside from defying all logic, this argument is contradicted by the president, MacArthur's chief of staff, and the content of MacArthur's message itself.

The mystery of when MacArthur sent his recommendation to Washington lies in the confusion of two different modes of communication, which, when clarified, resolves the problem. But clarifying the communications confusion reveals the dispute between Truman and MacArthur over strategy, which was the reason for the coverup. There can be little doubt that MacArthur communicated his recommendations to Washington immediately upon his return to Tokyo, Thursday evening (Thursday morning in Washington). Moreover, what he communicated was the recommendation for the immediate dispatch of combat troops for the defense of the Han, a recommendation he had drafted during his return flight.

218   MacArthur communicated with Washington that Thursday evening upon his return via telecon, as both the president and Gen. Almond attest, and then sent his full recommendation the next day by cable. It is this later cable that appears in the State Department record as MacArthur's *first* recommendation. Basing the subsequent narrative upon the cable, rather than the telecon, covers up the dispute between Truman and MacArthur over *where* to mount the defense of South Korea. When we revisit the chronology from the time that MacArthur first sent his recommendation to Truman by telecon Thursday evening in Tokyo, this dispute becomes apparent.

MacArthur's telecon recommendation was received in the Pentagon sometime Thursday morning. According to Truman: "MacArthur said he was convinced that only American ground units could stop the North Korean advance. He had asked for permission to commit one regimental combat team at once and to build up to two divisions as rapidly as possible."[105] President Truman did not cite all of MacArthur's recommendation, but, if what the general said in his telecon approximates his later cable, as one must assume it does, then what MacArthur called for was the commitment of combat troops to shore up a defense of the Han River line. The content of MacArthur's cable makes plain that it refers to the situation he observed during his trip to the Han River and not to the changed situation that existed a day later when the NKA had broken through. Thus, MacArthur wrote:

> I have today inspected the South Korean battle area from Suwon north to the Han River. My purpose was to reconnoiter at first hand the conditions as they exist and to determine the most effective way to further support our mission.
>
> The Korean Army and coastal forces are in confusion, have not seriously fought, and lack leadership through their own means. Organized and equipped as a light force for maintenance of interior order they were unprepared for attack by armor and air. Conversely, they are incapable of gaining the initiative over such force as that embodied in the North Korean Army.

The Korean Army had made no preparations for defense in depth, for echelons of supply or for a supply system. No plans had been made, or if made, not executed, for the destruction of supplies or material in event of a retrograde movement. As a result, they have either lost, or abandoned, their supplies and heavier equipment and have absolutely no system of intercommunication. In most cases the individual soldier, in his flight to the south, has retained his rifle or carbine. They are gradually being gathered up in rear areas and given some semblance of organization by an advance group of my officers I have sent over for this purpose. Without artillery, mortars, and anti-tank guns, they can only hope to retard the enemy through the fullest utilization of natural obstacles and under the guidance and example of leadership of high quality.

The civilian populace is tranquil, orderly and prosperous according to their scale of living. They have retained a high degree of national spirit and firm belief in the Americans. The roads leading south from Seoul are crowded with refugees refusing to accept the Communist rule.

219

South Korean military strength is estimated at not more than 25,000 effectives. North Korean military forces are as previously reported, backed by considerable strength in armor and a well trained, well directed and aggressive air force equipped with Russian planes. It is now obvious that this force has been built as an element of Communist military aggression.

I am doing everything possible to establish and maintain a flow of supplies through the air-head at Suwon and the southern port of Pusan. The air-head is most vital but is subject to constant air attack. Since air cover must be maintained over all aircraft transporting supplies, equipment, and personnel, this requirement operates to contain a large portion of my fighter strength. North Korean Air, operating from nearby bases, has been savage in its attacks in the Suwon area.

It is essential that the enemy advance be held or its impetus will threaten the overrunning of all Korea. Every effort is being made to establish a Han River line but the result is highly problematical. The defense of this line and the Suwon-Seoul corridor is essential to the retention of the only air-head in central Korea.

The Korean Army is entirely incapable of counteraction and there is grave danger of a further breakthrough. If the enemy advance continues much further it will seriously threaten the fall of the Republic.

The only assurance for the holding of the present line, and the ability to regain later the lost ground, is through the introduction of US combat forces into the Korean battle area. To continue to utilize the forces of our air and navy without an effective ground element cannot be decisive.

If authorized, it is my intention to immediately move a US regimental combat team to the reinforcement of the vital area discussed and to provide for a possible build-up to a two division strength from the troops in Japan for an early counter-offensive.[106]

Chargé d'Affaires Everett Drumright, in Suwon, had alerted Acheson that MacArthur's recommendations were forthcoming. He had sent a cable from Suwon at 9 P.M. Thursday evening (received 9:50 A.M. Thursday) reporting on MacArthur's trip and informing the secretary that "MacArthur arrived at certain momentous decisions which he will no doubt communicate to Washington."[107] There could be little doubt what these "momentous decisions" were. Nor can there be any doubt that the secretary immediately inquired at Defense, learned of MacArthur's recommendation conveyed via the telecon that morning, and promptly informed Truman.[108]

MacArthur's recommendation for the immediate commitment of a regimental combat team (RCT) to reinforce the South Korean positions along the Han River caused a dilemma for Truman and Acheson. The moment was fast approaching when the president would make a full commitment of ground troops. But it was imperative to wait until the NKA had crossed the Han and had begun a drive for Pusan. On the other hand, the president could not deny the theater commander's request for troops. Yet to accede to his request for immediate commitment of troops would mean to defend at the Han, which Truman did not want to do.

Truman's and Acheson's way out of this dilemma was to put MacArthur off by directing him to secure Pusan, rather than attempt to defend at the Han, and to satisfy his demand for immediate action by authorizing him to strike targets north of the 38th parallel by air. Because this decision did not correspond directly to MacArthur's recommendation, Truman and Acheson decided to conceal the fact that it had been received early Thursday morning. Then, the president arranged to hold a press conference at 4:00 P.M. and to convene an NSC meeting an hour later to formally implement these decisions.

Truman's purpose at his press conference was to establish the essential limits of American involvement, encapsulated in the concept of a "police action," rather than a full-scale war. Before a packed room, when asked whether the nation was at war, Truman emphatically replied: "We are not at war." He "refused to talk about the possibility of sending American ground troops to Korea, and was adamant in not commenting about the possible use of atomic bombs" because, he said, these were "tactical matters." Asked if there had been "any differences in opinion in his Cabinet or advisers about the decision he took to give sea-air aid to South Korea," Truman replied that "there never was or had been." Every decision he had made, he said, was "in favor of peace." Asked to explain what he meant, the president said:

> The Republic of South Korea was set up with United Nations' help and was recognized as the legal government by the members of the U.N. It was unlawfully attacked by a bunch of "bandits," neighbors in North Korea. The U.N. met and passed a resolution to go to the relief of the republic to suppress a bandit raid. The action this country has taken is police action—U.N. police action. That was exactly what it amounted to.[109]

Immediately following his press conference, the president convened an NSC meeting where he authorized new orders for MacArthur. The brief, forty-minute meeting was essentially for the record, for the decision had already been formulated. Furthermore, the sparse record of the proceedings seems only marginally related to MacArthur's new directive.[110] Secretary Johnson presented what amounted to a hastily drawn and specious rationale for a new directive to MacArthur on the grounds that existing orders were "impediments to the effective accomplishment of the military mission." These impediments were: the restriction of air and naval action to below the 38th parallel, limited air time over targets because of distance of bases, poor air-ground liaison, and inadequate South Korean transportation facilities for delivering munitions to the front. In fact, MacArthur's new orders addressed only the first of these concerns.

MacArthur's new directive "consolidates, broadens and supplements existing instructions governing your actions with regard to situation in South Korea and Formosa."[111] What was new was the authorization to "extend your operations into Northern Korea against air bases, depots, tank farms, troop columns and other such purely military targets, if and when, in your judgment, this becomes essential for the performance of your missions." However, he was to take "special care . . . to insure that operations in North Korea stay well clear of the frontiers of Manchuria or the Soviet Union."

Secondly, "army forces will be limited to essential communications and other essential service units, except that you are authorized to employ such army combat and service forces as to insure the retention of a port and air base in the general area Pusan-Chinhae." In other words, where MacArthur had recommended a large-scale commitment of two divisions of ground combat troops to defend the Han River line, Truman had circumvented that request and, instead, ordered MacArthur to employ limited "combat and service forces" to secure control of Pusan, two hundred miles to the south.

Finally, the paragraph that had been worked out the day before regarding his actions should the Soviet Union intervene was inserted. "The decision to commit United States air and naval forces and limited army forces to provide cover and support for South Korean troops does not constitute a decision to engage in war with the Soviet Union." However, the United States government fully realized the "risks" involved. If Soviet forces did "intervene," MacArthur was to "defend," but "take no action to aggravate the situation," and then "report" to Washington.

What should have been included in MacArthur's directive, but was only discussed at this meeting, no doubt for the record, was Truman's insistence that U.S. objectives were limited to the reestablishment of the status quo ante. He wanted it "clearly understood that our operations in Korea were designed to restore peace there and to restore the border." Truman "wanted to

221

take every step necessary to push the North Koreans back behind the 38th parallel. But I wanted to be sure that we would not become so deeply committed in Korea that we could not take care of such other situations as might develop."[112]

Secretary Acheson then brought up the negative Soviet reply to the U.S. note sent two days before asking Moscow to use its influence to bring about North Korean withdrawal. He also discussed Beijing's harsh response to Truman's decision to neutralize Formosa. In his view, the two notes "taken together . . . seemed to indicate that the Soviets would not intervene themselves but might help the Chinese Communists to do so."[113] Truman agreed, saying, "that means . . . that the Soviets are going to let the Chinese and the North Koreans do the fighting for them."[114] The NSC meeting ended at 5:40 P.M.

222

Shortly afterward, Secretary Acheson returned alone to the White House to discuss a communiqué from Chiang Kai-shek. His ambassador had met with a representative of the State Department that afternoon to say that the Nationalist government was "prepared to furnish one army of approximately 33,000 men, composed of three divisions with the best field equipment available to the Chinese. [However,] they lack sufficient shipping to transport the entire body."[115] Truman's "first reaction" was to accept this offer, but Acheson once again talked him out of it. The president then told the secretary to "bring up the matter the next day" with the chiefs.[116]

Following the NSC meeting, Secretary Johnson and the chiefs returned to the Pentagon to send the new directive to MacArthur. JCS 84681 was dispatched at 6:59 P.M. (8:59 A.M. Friday in Tokyo). One can only surmise the general's reaction to his new instructions, which surely must have been a combination of astonishment verging on incredulity. To MacArthur and his close aides, Truman's "new directive" was in fact a flat rejection of the general's recommendation to defend South Korea at its most logical and appropriate place under existing circumstances—the Han River.

Perhaps the president had misunderstood? Perhaps his teleconference communication had not been clear? Time was of the essence. Therefore, MacArthur sent his recommendation again, unamended, this time in cable form to Secretary of State Acheson. MacArthur's C-56942 was sent off at 12:50 P.M. Friday, some three-and-a-half hours after his receipt of JCS 84681. It arrived in Washington at 1:31 A.M. Friday, June 30.[117] As soon as it arrived, the duty officer awakened General Collins, who hurried over to the Pentagon to consider the request. Collins roused Army Secretary Pace "at once," telling him that he would talk to MacArthur by telecon and report back.[118] While arranging for the teleconference, Collins also alerted Dean Rusk at the State Department. Rusk and Niles Bond, the Korean desk officer, went over to the Pentagon to join half a dozen other general officers and Collins. (Rusk would later admit that MacArthur's cable "was not the first time that General Mac-Arthur's report on his reconnaissance was known in Washington.")[119]

The teleconference with MacArthur, no. 3444, began at 3:40 A.M. and lasted well over an hour and a half because of several interruptions to consult higher authorities.[120] From the beginning, however, it is clear that Collins sought to dissuade an insistent MacArthur from any attempt to defend at the Han River and MacArthur only relented when, during their teleconference, reports came in which confirmed that the North Koreans had breached the river barrier, making such a defense impossible.

Collins opened the telecon with the statement that MacArthur's specific proposal to send an RCT to defend at the Han "will require Presidential decision which will take several hours for consideration." Attempting to divert MacArthur away from the Han idea, he said: "Meanwhile, you are authorized in accordance with paragraph 2B JCS 84681 to move one RCT immediately to Pusan Base Area." (In actual fact, JCS 84681, while directing MacArthur to employ limited "combat and service forces" to Pusan, did not specifically authorize movement of an RCT for that purpose.)[121]

223

Without waiting for a reply, Collins went on to say that he knew "the president would wish carefully to consider with his top advisors before authorizing introduction of American combat forces into the battle area," meaning the Han River area; he then suggested that while awaiting a presidential decision, the authorization to deploy an RCT to Pusan would at least "permit initiation of movement." Before this movement was completed, he concluded, "we should be able to obtain definite decision on your proposal." Does this, he asked, "meet your requirement for the present?"[122]

MacArthur's answer was a flat "no." He wanted authorization for his proposal to defend at the Han River immediately and would accept nothing less. "Your authorization, while establishing basic principle that US ground combat troops may be used in Korea does not give sufficient latitude for efficient operation in present situation. It does not satisfy the basic requirements contained in my message C 56942. Time is of the essence and a clear cut decision without delay is imperative."[123]

Collins realized that he had no authority to break this deadlock and so informed MacArthur that he would "proceed immediately through Secretary of Army to request Presidential approval your proposal to move RCT into forward combat area. Will advise you soon as possible, perhaps within half hour." At this, "Collins stepped out of the telecon room, called Pace and explained the situation."[124] Secretary Pace then telephoned the president. It was 4:57 A.M. when the president picked up the telephone. He was already awake and dressed. An hour and seventeen minutes had elapsed since the telecon began.

The president immediately authorized sending a regimental combat team "to the combat area and promised he would give a decision on the additional build-up to two divisions within a few hours."[125] Pace quickly got word to Collins about the change in deployment of the RCT from Pusan to the Han. But, despite the fact that the president promised a decision within a few hours on the two-division buildup, orders to MacArthur would not be sent for almost eight-and-a-half hours, until the North Korean breakthrough across the Han had been confirmed. Nor would an RCT move to the Han. The NKA breakthrough would resolve the dispute between Truman and MacArthur, at which time the president would authorize the general to employ two of the divisions at his disposal, as he requested.

In the telecon room, meanwhile, while awaiting word from the president, Collins, and perhaps others, peppered Tokyo with questions about the current situation. Had FEAF conducted air strikes north of the 38th parallel as authorized in JCS 84,681? Were attacks carried out on North Korean troop concentrations along the north bank of the Han? Although the main Han River bridge had been blown prematurely on the 28th, Washington wished to know whether there were "any bridges remaining over Han River in Seoul area?"[126]

The replies from Tokyo came quickly. FEAF had conducted several strikes on airfields north of the 38th parallel. "Reported results good on field near Pyongyang, but no detailed reports of strikes yet received." B-26s carried out two strikes "along north bank of Han River"; results not reported. There was "little indication of enemy activity west of Seoul," but "three railroad bridges still remain over Han south of Seoul. They are being covered with wooden planking for vehicle use and covered by artillery direct fire."

At this, the questions from Washington began to zero in on the issue of crossing the Han. "Have Reds any facilities for transporting any heavy equipment across Han River?" Tokyo answered: "Yes. Ferry and barge services and planking of RR bridges vicinity Seoul. Bridge repairs by North Koreans reported." Then came the question whose answer resolved the dispute between Truman and MacArthur over where to defend. "Press dispatch just received reports break through across Han east of Seoul. Have you any confirmation?" The answer from Tokyo flashed on the teletype screen. It was a simple: "Yes." Just minutes before, General Church had reported in a message to Tokyo headquarters that the NKA "had ferried tanks and troops across the river southeast of Seoul."[127]

After a few more questions, Collins came back on line. He knew that the NKA breakthrough across the Han meant that Suwon was lost. Suwon was then the only accessible airfield in all of South Korea, aside from Pusan, that was capable of handling large C-54 transport aircraft and the only airfield by which to supply the Han front. Without the use of Suwon there could be no thought of forward deployment. Therefore, without yet giving authorization to employ the RCT, and knowing what the answers to his questions must be, Collins asked: "What is your estimate as to time until RCT can be in action in Suwon area? Do you contemplate moving it by air? Can you move heavy equipment and artillery into that area by air?"

The answer from Tokyo reconfirmed the unfeasibility of MacArthur's plan to defend at the Han. "Not feasible to make such an estimate until full extent of breakthrough at Han River is determinable. In any event movement by air would be impossible in view of lack of security of Suwon airhead." This, of course, clinched it. Both Collins and MacArthur knew that MacArthur's plan had been overtaken by events. Knowing that MacArthur could not rapidly deploy a fully equipped RCT to the Han River without access to the Suwon airfield, Collins said: "Your recommendation to move one RCT to combat area is approved. You will be advised later as to further build up." Then, with a sense of irony that still emanates from the telecon text, Collins ended their communication. "Everyone here delighted your prompt action in personally securing first hand view of situation. Congratulations and best wishes. We all have full confidence in you and your command. Nothing further here."

While the dispute with MacArthur was settled, the president still wished to be certain of the North Korean breakthrough. Therefore, at 7:00 A.M. "Col. Henry Ahalt came in from the Pentagon to brief the President more fully on the telecon talks and the military situation."[128] It is apparent that Ahalt confirmed the North Korean breakthrough. Following the briefing, at 7:30 A.M. Truman called Acheson to discuss the new developments. It was decided to meet with Secretary Johnson and the chiefs to discuss two issues: MacArthur's request for two divisions and Chiang Kai-shek's offer of 33,000 troops. The military would be offered a choice.

At 9:30 A.M., Secretary of Defense Johnson, Deputy Secretary of Defense Steven Early, along with the service chiefs and the joint chiefs, slipped into "a side door of the White House" where they joined the president, Acheson, and Harriman.[129] It was another ad hoc gathering along the lines of the Blair House meetings, and not a formal NSC meeting. Truman refers to it twice simply as a "meeting."[130] Since it was not a formal conclave, neither Vice President Barkley nor Chairman of the National Security Resources Board Stuart Symington, nor John Foster Dulles, who had attended the meeting the day before, were invited. Nor were those who usually attended the formal NSC meetings included, such as James Lay, executive secretary of the NSC, or CIA Director Hillenkoetter.

Truman informed the group that he "had already granted authority for the use of the one regimental combat team and . . . now desired their advice on the additional troops to be employed."[131] Truman then brought up Chiang Kai-shek's offer of 33,000 troops. "Would it not be worth while to accept the

225

Chinese offer?" asked the president. They were ready to go and time was of the essence. We must also consider, he said, "places where trouble might break out," suggesting that the United States should conserve its own forces for use against other possible threats. "What, for instance, would Mao Tse-tung do? What might the Russians do in the Balkans, in Iran, in Germany?"

Secretary Acheson, in an exchange reminiscent of the one during the second Blair House meeting, argued against the president's suggestion. He felt that if Nationalist troops were employed in Korea, the Chinese Communists "might decide to enter that conflict in order to inflict damage on the Generalissimo's troops there and thus reduce his ability to defend himself whenever they might decide to try an invasion of Formosa." The chiefs immediately agreed, pointing out that Chiang's troops "would be as helpless as Syngman Rhee's army against the North Korean tanks." Furthermore, U.S. transportation assets "would be better used" if we employed them for our own troops. As a last order of business, Admiral Sherman suggested, and the president authorized, a full naval blockade of North Korea.

The chiefs and the civilian secretaries were at last on board. The president and the secretary of state had deftly maneuvered them over the course of the week into agreeing to the decision to commit U.S. ground troops to Korea. Truman then decided that Chiang's offer would be "politely declined," and "MacArthur . . . given full authority to use the ground forces under his command."[132] The United States was now fully committed to the defense of South Korea.

Although Truman's account suggests that MacArthur could use all of the forces under his command, that was not yet the case. The actual directive, JCS 84718, sent at 1:22 P.M. that afternoon, removed "restrictions on use of Army Forces imposed by JCS 84681" and granted authority "to you as proposed your C56942 subject only to requirements for safety of Japan in the present situation which is a matter for your judgment."[133] In other words, MacArthur's request for two divisions was granted, but it would be Truman's strategy that would be followed. It had, indeed, been a week of surprises, and there were more to come.

226

CHAPTER NINE

Stalin and Truman: Different Means to the Same End

In triggering war in Korea, Stalin had won the race with Mao over who struck first, but it was only the first step in a two-step plan. For Stalin, initially, the war offered a win-win outcome, although the "wins" were not of equal value. Moreover, they were mutually exclusive. North Korea could win if the United States did not come in, or came in too late. In that case, Stalin would have achieved a substantial victory in "unifying" Korea on Communist terms, strengthening the Soviet position in Northeast Asia, particularly against China and Japan, and weakening the American worldwide position. But that was not Stalin's preferred outcome; his objective was far more ambitious.

A North Korean "win," as significant as it would be, would not solve Stalin's most pressing problem of preventing Sino-American rapprochement, and therefore was of relatively lesser value to him than foreclosing on that dangerous possibility. Starting the war, however, was a necessary prerequisite, which placed Stalin in position to take the second step in his larger plan to ensure against Sino-American rapprochement, his ultimate objective. The means to this end was to prod China into conflict with the United States, an outcome that would keep China isolated and dependent upon the Soviet Union for years to come. Such a "win" would be of infinitely greater value than a North Korean victory over the South.

However, Stalin could not achieve both objectives, at least not simultaneously. For Stalin to preempt Sino-American rapprochement, the North Korean assault would have to fail. The ways in which the Soviets devised and executed the war plan, allocated the NKA's weapons mix, and parceled out logistical support ensured failure.[1] Nor, in a wider sense, did Stalin take any steps to cause Truman to hesitate about committing troops to Korea, such as hindering United States use of Japan as a forward base, or raising tensions in Europe or Iran, to name the more obvious spots.

Despite the fact that the Korean War lasted for three years, the issue of North Korean victory or defeat was determined within the first few weeks. Indeed, U.S. policymakers realized that the NKA assault would fail to conquer the South less than three weeks after the war began. The responsibility for failure was Stalin's, not Kim Il-sung's, whose troops fought tenaciously, but in vain. Yet within Stalin's failure lay the seeds of a greater success—a Sino-American conflict that would crystallize the structure of global politics for the next two decades.

Truman's calculations, on the other hand, were more complicated than Stalin's, but his ultimate objective was identical—to insure against any possibility of Sino-American rapprochement, which had been ruled out by the secretly adopted containment strategy of NSC-68, the reciprocal of the Sino-Soviet Treaty. His means were also the same: once the North Korean assault was thwarted, to prod China into conflict with the United States in Korea. Indeed, Truman had already taken the first step toward that outcome by extending U.S. protection to Taiwan on the second day of the Korean conflict. In short, if Stalin had preempted Mao's attack on Taiwan with the Korean assault, then Truman made certain that Mao could not still attempt an assault on the island by deploying the Seventh Fleet to Formosan waters.

Then, once North Korea's armies had been destroyed, certainly no easy task but a foregone conclusion by the third week of the war, the United States pressed northward toward the Yalu River, ignoring Beijing's warnings and leaving Mao no choice but to commit his forces against the United States and United Nations. Sino-Soviet cooperation, based on their just concluded treaty of alliance, in combat in Korea against the forces of the United States and United Nations, served the strategic requirements of containment, graphically demonstrating the very real global threat of communism and justifying the expenditure of additional resources to counter it.

STALIN'S "PREEMPTIVE STRIKE OPERATIONAL PLAN"

Aside from equipment and armament omissions, inadequate provision of supplies and troops, and crippling limitations on ammunition and tank fuel, the Soviet-designed war plan exhibited numerous strategic and tactical flaws, which doomed the invasion from the start. First and foremost was a jejune conception of the war. It is now apparent that whatever Kim Il-sung believed, Stalin sold him on the idea of a short war, according to which a quick military seizure of Seoul, combined with uprisings in the South, would "liberate" the South Korean capital in a few days and all of Korea within a month. Kim was susceptible to this idea because Stalin's men had been propounding it to him for the past year. This conception could only succeed if the United States declined to come to the assistance of the Republic of Korea, a dubious assumption at best.

Moreover, the planning for the war was done quickly, literally at the last minute, and was not completed by the time the war began, suggesting an external stimulus for Stalin's haste, which, as argued here, was Mao's imminent strike against Taiwan. General Yu Song-chol, former North Korean Operational Bureau Commander, who translated the Russian-designed plan into Korean and helped to formulate a war plan based on it, provided a unique insider's account of that war plan and its hasty formulation. According to Yu, in May, Stalin sent a new advisory team to Pyongyang specifically to create a new war plan under the pseudonymous Lieutenant General Vasiliev, "replacing the military advisers who had been dispatched to North Korea with individuals with extensive combat experience."

> The draft plan for the 6-25 Southern invasion was prepared directly by this Soviet military advisory group. Its title was "Preemptive Strike Operational Plan." After the plan was handed over to Kim Il-sung, he passed it on to Kang Kon, the Chief of the General Staff of the KPA, who in turn passed it on to me. Kang instructed, "translate this into Korean and formulate a plan." That was in early May 1950.[2]

Yu and a handful of selected top military officers, all "Soviet-born Koreans" sworn to secrecy, quickly "formulated an operational plan at the end of about one month's work," completing it by early June even as troops were being moved into position for the assault.[3] During this time, Soviet advisers conducted "reconnaissance of the area" and participated in the "planning of the operation at the divisional level."[4] In order to "maintain security," which was a euphemism for keeping Mao ignorant of the imminent assault, the "Yenan faction individuals who had entered various military positions were excluded from this effort."

According to the Soviet scheme, however, the "invasion plan ended with the occupation of Seoul after four days." The plan was based on the assumption that "once we occupied the South Korean capital, then the entirety of South Korea would come into our hands." Simultaneous uprisings throughout the south were critical to the success of this plan, for military operations would be concentrated on the taking of Seoul. Pak Hon-yong, chief of South Korean Workers Party affairs, had assured Kim that "once we ... occupied Seoul, then the 200,000 South Korean Workers Party members who were in hiding throughout South Korea would rise up and revolt, toppling the South Korean regime."[5]

Thus, according to Yu, the assurance that uprisings would accompany the invasion was "one of the major factors in hardening Kim Il-sung's resolve to invade." Kim Il-sung said later, when purging Pak Hon-yong as a traitor, that contrary to expectations "not even one uprising had occurred" and that "if only a few thousand workers had risen in Pusan, then we certainly could have liberated all the way down to Pusan, and the American scoundrels could not have landed." Yu concluded that "in this manner, our war scenario was flawed from its basic inception."[6] Of course, the "war scenario" was Stalin's. Yu's account, however, does suggest a reason for the otherwise inexplicable failure to seize Pusan and deny it to the United States. Kim had not attempted to seize the key port militarily because he assumed that a locally inspired uprising would secure it for him.

On the first day of the war, command problems were already evident, as was the reason for them. Stalin had withdrawn the Soviet advisers from combat units and, along with them, their communications. Offering his typically specious rationale for withdrawing this critical component from the NKA, Stalin said that it was "too dangerous to keep our advisers there. They might be taken prisoner. We don't want there to be evidence for accusing us of taking part in this business. It's Kim Il-sung's affair."[7] Of course, it was a fact that North Korea, Kim Il-sung, and the North Korean Army were Stalin's own creation. Soviet complicity was therefore a foregone conclusion, with or without the presence of advisers in combat units. But their absence would have a critical effect on the conduct of battle. As Khrushchev conceded, as a result of the withdrawal of Soviet advisers "the North Korean army was in trouble from the very start."

Ambassador Shtykov's report describing the first day of the war, although generally congratulatory, confirmed the debilitating impact of the absence of the advisers. "The command staff of the KPA [NKA] does not have battle experience, after the withdrawal of Soviet military advisers they organized the battle command poorly, they use artillery and tanks in battle badly and lose communications." Indeed, singling out the communications failure, he noted that from the very "beginning of military actions and the forward advance of units and formations, staff communication was lost from top to bottom. The general staff . . . already on the first day did not direct the battle, since it did not have firm communications with a single division."[8]

Nevertheless, despite the lack of command experience and communications with the general staff, the main body of the NKA took Seoul more or less according to plan. At that point, however, Kim began to realize that he had been deceived as the war began to evolve in a manner totally opposite from that which Stalin had led him to expect. There were no uprisings, the South Korean government did not fall, and the United States quickly began to provide air support and logistical assistance. As Yu observed, the leadership was "bewildered" by the fact that the ROK did not collapse. "The Front Line Command received reports that Yi Sung-man [Syngman Rhee] and the South Korean government had moved to Taejon and the resistance by the National Defense Forces continued."[9]

While the troops of the North Korean Army celebrated the capture of Seoul, Kim, Stalin, and their respective aides argued over whether or not to continue the attack. Yu recounts that "orders to urgently continue advancing were passed down."[10] It appeared to him "as though the orders to press southward were discussed and decided upon directly by Chief of the General Staff Kang Kon and Kim Il-sung," but there can be little doubt that Stalin took part in this discussion. Only Stalin could decide questions regarding Soviet provision of supply and armament, which would be crucial to any decision to continue. The extant record, however, contains only Stalin's last message in what was undoubtedly a tense exchange of messages on this issue. Interestingly, the Soviet leader's views suggest that there was considerable reticence within the North Korean high command about pressing southward.

In a cable to Shtykov dated July 1, Stalin demanded to know what Kim had decided to do. What were the plans of the Korean command, he asked? "Does it intend to push on? Or has it decided to stop the advance? In our opinion the attack absolutely must continue and the sooner South Korea is liberated the less chance there is for intervention."[11] He wanted to know "how the Korean leaders regard the attacks on North Korean territory by American planes. Are they frightened or do they continue to hold firm?" To bolster Kim, Stalin promised "to fulfill fully by July 10 the Koreans' requests for delivery of ammunition and other military equipment."

This cable clearly indicated Stalin's views in the argument over whether or not to press the attack and its insistent tone indicated that the North Korean leadership was doubtful about proceeding in the face of the commitment of American combat troops to battle. To obtain Kim's agreement to press the attack, Stalin promised additional equipment for the offensive. In the Soviet leader's opinion, "the sooner South Korea is liberated the less chance there is for intervention," but, of course, Stalin knew when he sent the cable that the "chance" to prevent American "intervention" had already been lost. Yet he demanded that the "attack absolutely must continue."

Shtykov responded to Stalin's queries about the political mood in North Korea the next day, noting that "the political mood of the population is somewhat worsening." Shtykov went on to say that, while the top leadership of the party and army still "believe in full victory," there was "some portion of the leading figures" who were uncertain. Relating information passed to him by Kim Il-sung's secretary, he noted that some leaders were speaking about the difficulties of conducting a war against the Americans with the forces of Korea and in a cautious way have tried to ascertain from Kim Il-sung the position of the Soviet Union on this question.[12]

After several critical days' delay, however, Kim and the North Korean leadership agreed to press the war southward.[13] The Soviet advisory group under Lieutenant General Vasiliev hastily drew up a new war plan and reorganized the NKA field command, installing Yenan faction commanders to lead the attack south.[14] For the initial invasion, Stalin's advisers had crafted a two-corps structure controlled by a Front Line Command for the attack on Seoul. Their original plan had called for the First Corps, commanding the First, Third, Fourth, and Sixth Divisions, supported by the 105th Armored Division, to strike along the main axis (Kaesong, Yonch'on, Uijongbu) to seize Seoul and Inchon. The Third and Fourth Divisions drove for Seoul and its adjacent industrial suburb and transportation hub, Yongdungp'o, while the Sixth moved for Kimpo airfield and the port of Inchon.[15]

232

The Second Corps, commanding the Second, Fifth, Seventh, and Twelfth Divisions, supported by a mechanized tank regiment, was to proceed through the central Korea region and the east coast.[16] Their assignment was to execute a broad envelopment of Seoul from the east. The Second Division drove for Chunchon and the Seventh Division for Hongchon. They were to join at Ichon, take Suwon, and then strike northward to close the pincer at Seoul.[17] The Fifth Division drove south along the east coast road in support of amphibious landings there, then dispersed its forces into the mountains to assume a blocking position. The action of the NKA Fifth, in retrospect, was perhaps the earliest indicator that a blitzkrieg attack to conquer all of Korea was not the objective. Appleman's analysis is to the point:

> one of the enemy's major tactical mistakes of the Korean War was failure to press rapidly south on the east coastal road after crossing the Parallel. . . . [Had the NKA Fifth Division] pressed south with all possible speed and effort the division could have been in P'ohang-dong within two weeks after the war began and thus have turned, on this flank, the entire ROK and American line across the peninsula. Once in P'ohang-dong it would have been in a position to advance directly on Pusan.[18]

In other words, according to Appleman, the NKA could have been in Pohang-dong by July 8, denying use of that critical port to the United States, or at the very least making its employment costly and time-consuming. Even more important, from that point, the NKA Fifth would have been in position to seize Pusan. That the Fifth failed to do so was not because it was a "mistake," as Appleman declares, or because naval bombardment of the coast road by U.S. and British warships blocked their advance, but because the original Soviet plan simply did not call for the military seizure of Pusan.[19]

North Korean tanks did not cross the Han from Seoul in force until July 3, the eighth day of the war. They were delayed by the discussion over whether or not to proceed south, by the need to await supplies, and by the need to repair bombed out and blown bridges. On that day, General Vasiliev and Ambassador Shtykov met with Kim Il-sung and Pak Hon-yong to discuss Soviet proposals for the coming campaign, including the new war plan. But Kim opened the meeting by complaining about the situation at the front. Reflecting his understanding of the need for speed, Kim thought that the "troops [were] moving very slowly, especially in the Central direction [sector].[20]

Kim was referring to the difficulties being experienced by the Second and Seventh Divisions of the Second Corps. The Second Division stalled in heavy fighting at Chunchon, while the Seventh Division's tanks had become bogged down in the mountains, encountering "fierce resistance" at Hongchon.[21] Having recovered from the initial shock of the invasion, ROK forces were giving a good account of themselves, especially against those NKA units operating without tanks, or with light tanks. Privately, the North Korean command was furious with the Russians for sending tanks into this "difficult mountainous terrain." They felt it was "an absurd error which arose because Soviet military advisers . . . were not familiar with Korea's terrain."[22] As a result, not only had the pincer at Seoul never materialized under the original plan, but also the Second Corps was having difficulty proceeding southward under the revised plan.

Kim was particularly concerned with the troop crossing of the Han River, which he said was "disorganized, although there was a minister in place there." Kim was being disingenuous. He could not openly criticize Stalin for his failure to provide any "large-scale river crossing equipment, such as floating bridges," so he pointedly expressed dissatisfaction with his own minister.[23] In fact, throughout the period of the offensive, and obviously hindering it, the Soviets declined to provide river crossing equipment; the NKA would be forced to devise time-consuming ad hoc measures to surmount Korea's numerous river obstacles. Most could be forded without undue difficulty, but the Han and Naktong were formidable barriers.

Kim also realized that the change of plans meant that he would need additional forces both to sustain a southward push and to defend North Korea from an enveloping attack. Therefore, he crafted an argument on which to justify a major expansion of his armed forces. He expressed a natural and obvious concern about the "danger of landings by American troops in the rear at North Korean ports or airborne landings of troops."[24] Then he requested "quick delivery" of sufficient arms to outfit an additional "two divisions, 12 battalions of marines and . . . the formation of security detachments." He also requested "arms and tanks" to equip "reserve regiments and 2 tank brigades."

233

At this point, Kim gave his Soviet interlocutors the opening for which they were waiting. "Since the People's Army is fighting against American troops," he considered it "necessary to strengthen the leadership of the army" and asked "how better to organize troop command" in this unexpected situation? He also wanted advice on "what kind of organizational command structure to choose so that the General Staff is brought closer to the troops." Taking advantage of this opening, General Vasiliev and Ambassador Shtykov proposed a series of staff and organizational changes. First, they suggested that Kim appoint himself "as Supreme Commander of troops." Kim agreed.

The Soviet representatives then proposed that the Front Headquarters and each of the two corps established earlier now be "headed by Military Councils composed of: a commander, a member of the Military Council and a chief of staff." In other words, instead of individual commanders, the Front Headquarters and each corps would be directed by a collective leadership, including a member from the military council that had been established on the second day of the war. That seven-man military council consisted of: Kim Il-sung and Pak Hon-yong, vice ministers Hong Myong-hui, Kim Chaek, and Choe Yong-gon, interior minister Pak Il-yu, and planning board director Chong Chun-t'aek.[25]

Shtykov and Vasiliev next proposed to "preserve the Ministry of National Defense that already exists only in a reduced form." This was a proposal to rehabilitate Defense Minister Choe Yong-gon, who, recall, had earlier objected to Kim's decision to go to war, had been shunted aside and nearly purged, only to be protected by Stalin. Choe was to "remain in his post"; his role would now be "the supply of combat troops with everything needed (foodstuffs, fuel, transport, ammunition) as well as the training of reserves, new troop formation and the organization of anti-aircraft defense for the northern part of the republic."[26]

In response to Kim's next question about who should be placed in charge of the Front Line Command and the two corps, Shtykov and Vasiliev proposed that Kim Chaek become Front Line Commander and Kang Kon Chief of Staff. They further recommended General Kim Ung for command of the First Corps and General Mu Chong for command of the Second Corps.[27] Both corps commanders were, as Yu notes, "from the Yenan faction."[28] In short, for the drive south, Shtykov and Vasiliev had reorganized the NKA high military command, bringing the leadership "closer to the troops," as Kim requested, but also inserting members of the Yenan faction into front line command positions to carry on the battle.

There can be little doubt that the Soviet advisers had acted on Stalin's orders, but, in their zeal, they proposed to make a substantial improvement in the NKA's fighting capabilities by allowing General Vasiliev and his staff "to go to Seoul" and by assigning "two [Soviet] advisers in every army group (adviser for the group commander and adviser for the artillery commander)." Not authorized to make this decision, and not privy to Stalin's plan, Shtykov asked for "permission" to make the changes.[29] Stalin replied to Shtykov two days later, denying permission for Vasiliev to move to Seoul, saying that "we consider it more useful for him to be in Pyongyang."[30] Stalin was silent on the request to assign advisers to combat command, but agreed to "give fully the arms, tanks and other military equipment for 2 divisions, 2 tank brigades and 12 battalions."

At this point, at what was obviously Soviet direction, the Front Line Command "assigned new roles," that is, the objectives of the revised war plan, to the First and Second Corps. The First Corps was now ordered "to go southward along the Kyongbu road" to Pusan, while the Second Corps "was entrusted with the central and east coasts." According to Yu, "beyond that . . . operational plans were left to be decided as the situation developed either at the command posts or at the division level." Remarkably, "the NKA had no established fronts, joint operations between artillery and infantry, or even a basic strategy. Each division simply pushed southward on its own."[31]

As Stalin had not replied explicitly to Shtykov's request for permission to assign Soviet advisers to the army groups, Kim Il-sung repeated the request. In a letter to Stalin of July 8, Kim appealed to the Soviet leader "to allow the use of 25–35 Soviet military advisers in the staff of the front of the Korean Army [the Front Line Command] and the staffs of the 2nd Army Group, since the national military cadres have not yet sufficiently mastered the art of commanding modern troops."[32] The extant record contains no reply from Stalin to Kim's request, but, as no Soviet advisers were ever captured with Korean front line forces, the answer must have been negative.[33]

To recapitulate the policy record to this point, the Korean War bears the heavy stamp of Soviet dictate in every aspect. It was Stalin who, directly and through his representatives, determined the war plans—both the original plan to seize Seoul only, and the follow-on plan to seize Pusan; provided the weapons and supplies; trained the cadre; assigned commanders; and determined strategy and tactics, including the day the war would begin. Kim undoubtedly wanted to unify his country, but it was Stalin who decided whether, when, and how it would be attempted.

The irony was that Stalin had, in fact, furnished the North Koreans with a formidable army, which was superior to that provided by the United States to the Republic of Korea. Under a blitzkrieg scenario, spearheaded by the fast-moving T-34 tank, combined with other measures to hinder American entry at Pusan, such as air strikes, or the mining of harbor approaches, this army might well have gained victory over the South. Stalin knew that only a strategy of rapid conquest could bring victory, yet, as the record clearly indicates, he eschewed that strategy despite providing the wherewithal to pursue it.

PLAN "B": THE DRIVE SOUTH

When, despite the fall of its capital, the South Korean government did not capitulate and the United States came to its support, Stalin's men hastily devised an alternate plan. After a delay of several days, Stalin then urged the NKA to drive toward Pusan. This was after the United States had already committed combat troops to battle and the prospect for quick victory was growing slimmer by the day. At this point, Kim's interests would have been better served by not attempting to conquer the entire country, but by fortifying his control of Seoul instead, but Stalin would have none of it.

236

At Stalin's urging, North Korean forces began to cross the Han River and drive southward, even before a new plan had been finalized, causing further confusion and providing time for the United States to establish a beachhead at Pusan. The new plan, which General Yu described as not "even a basic strategy," was akin to winding up a mechanical toy and pointing it in the general desired direction. Stalin, through his advisers, continued to provide policy advice to Kim, who followed it, though with increasing concern, for that advice ensured failure.

It must be kept in mind that for North Korea to succeed speed was of the essence to prevent an American lodgment. Yet even now, having crossed the Han River and having become committed to a southward drive, the NKA exhibited little inclination to move quickly, a delay that puzzled observers on the scene, but which, as indicated above, was because plans had yet to be finalized, promised supplies to be delivered, and bridge repairs made. A Western newsman filing a report from the front on July 1, for example, noted that with no opposition before them, the "North Korean invaders ... appeared stalled on the plains south of Seoul."[54]

The central question was: Could North Korean forces drive southeastward along the Kyongbu road and reach Pusan before the United States could deploy enough troops to stop them? This question would be resolved within three weeks of the decision to drive south. During this period Stalin made two crucial command decisions that ensured that the NKA would not succeed. Rather than concentrate NKA forces along the main axis of attack —Seoul-Taejon-Kumch'on-Taegu-Pusan—Stalin dispersed North Korean forces, indeed, their best forces, to weaken the main axis of attack and slow the rate of advance to Pusan. These two decisions were: first, to split off the

Sixth Division from the Third and Fourth, and, second, to split off the Fourth from the Third.

First was the decision taken at Ch'onan, some twenty miles south of Osan, to split the NKA Sixth Division off from the main force and send it on a two-week-long trek westward and southward down the west coast. Stalin made this decision when the NKA appeared to be an unstoppable juggernaut and the United States had been able to deploy parts of only six poorly armed and trained battalions of the Twenty-fourth Division to combat against three NKA tank-supported divisions. In skirmishes at Osan, Pyongtaek, Ch'onan, Chonui, and Chochiwon, July 5–12, the NKA hardly slowed, while shouldering American troops away in bloody confusion.

American forces, like the ROKs before them, had nothing yet with which to stop the T-34 tank, or to counter the enveloping tactics of the more numerous NKA infantry, a lack that made a shambles of attempted withdrawal actions, despite growing air support.[35] Reporter Marguerite Higgins, describing the North Korean sweep through Task Force Smith a few miles north of Osan on July 5, said: "Why they did not push their tanks straight through to Pusan then and there is one of the war's mysteries. A hard push would have crumbled our defenses, as everyone from General MacArthur on down now concedes."[36] Indeed, at this point, MacArthur himself began to wonder if a foothold could be held in Korea.

But the NKA immediately slowed its advance rather than accelerated it, a fact that U.S. officials on the scene quickly picked up. Chargé d'Affaires Drumright, for example, describing the "continued fluid situation around Chonan" in a cable to the State Department sent late on July 9, noted that the "military situation has taken turn for better today. Enemy thrusts diminishing in strength and appear halted in most areas." Drumright attributed this "turn for [the] better" to ROK forces "who have won two small scale victories in past two days."[37]

The air historian Robert Futrell believed that "if the Communists had vigorously prosecuted their attack following their capture of Chonan on 8 July, they might well have destroyed the 24th Division, leaving the route to Taejon, Taegu, and Pusan bare of defenders."[38] That they did not, in Futrell's view, was because the NKA was "feeling the effect of the damage wrought upon them by American air attack." There can be little doubt that American air power was inhibiting the NKA advance when weather conditions permitted, but the reason for the slowdown lay not in Korea, but in Moscow.

The reason for the temporary lull in action was that, at this point, Stalin had issued new orders to the NKA Sixth, which split off from the main force and reassembled at Yesan, fifteen miles west of Ch'onan. After resting for four days, on July 13 the Sixth moved fifty miles south, taking the port of

237

Kunsan without a fight. It then marched inland southeast and took Chonju, pausing there until July 20. The Sixth was now, according to Appleman, "poised to make an end run . . . toward Pusan." However, despite the fact that "in all Korea southwest of the Taejon-Taegu-Pusan highway . . . there were only a few hundred survivors of the ROK Seventh Division," that is not what the Sixth did.[39]

Instead of driving toward Pusan, the Sixth dispersed its entire force, sending them deep into the southwest corner of Korea *away* from Pusan, on an apparent mission to secure control of the remaining southern ports to facilitate supply by sea.[40] (U.S. control of the sea made this a dubious tactic for anything but sporadic supply at best.) Arriving at Kwangju, the Sixth sent the Thirteenth Regiment to the extreme southwest coast to Mokp'o, the Fourteenth Regiment to Pesong, and the Fifteenth to Yosu—each port one of the farthest points of land reachable on the southwest Korean peninsula.

Throughout this sojourn, the Sixth encountered minimal resistance and disappeared for a time from the scrutiny of U.S. intelligence, but it had outrun its supply lines. When the division regrouped at Sunch'on on July 25, ninety miles west of Pusan, "its supply was poor and rations were cut in half and on some days there were none."[41] This cannot be described as an end run toward Pusan. If anything, it was a decision to leave the field temporarily and observe the action from the sidelines. Later, the Sixth Division would indeed present a major threat to the Eighth Army's southern flank, but removing this powerful strike force from the battle at the critical moment for over two weeks not only weakened the main axis of attack through the center, but also gave the United States time to deploy forces in strength.[42]

Stalin's second command decision came hard upon the victory of the NKA Third and Fourth Divisions at Taejon, which opened the road to Kumch'on and Taegu, and thence to Pusan. After taking the city on July 20, this force rested for two days and received replacements. Instead of exploiting the breakthrough, however, on July 23 the Fourth was split off from the main axis and sent south to Kumsan along a route inside but parallel to the route that the Sixth had taken two weeks earlier. (By this time, the Sixth had already completed its trek and was moving to reassemble at Sunch'on.) At Kumsan, the Fourth received about one thousand barely trained replacements, but "left behind the tank regiment that had accompanied it ever since they had crossed the 38th parallel together a month earlier."[43]

For the second time, at the crucial moment when the NKA appeared to be poised for a concentrated breakthrough against beaten and inferior American forces, Stalin reduced its strength and slowed its advance. I say that these decisions had to have been made by Stalin and not Kim Il-sung, or the NKA field command. The decisions to divide and weaken the main axis of attack by advancing on a broad front instead of concentrating forces for a break-

238

through were command decisions of the utmost importance that altered the course of the war. Such decisions, in my view, could only have been taken by Stalin.

By the last week of July, Stalin had sent two of the NKA's three best divisions onto circuitous envelopments that removed these units from combat at absolutely decisive moments. By the time these two divisions were returned to combat, the United States had been able to deploy forces in greater numbers, with superior firepower, and to establish a defense perimeter around Pusan, which the NKA was unable to crack.[44] In brief, if the United States needed time to deploy forces to Korea and establish a beachhead, Stalin contrived to give them just enough.

Even more astonishing was the Soviet logistical failure. When North Korean forces reached the Pusan perimeter, they were already perilously low on food, fuel, ammunition, weapons, and even trained men. In some cases, the NKA was forced to leave tanks and artillery behind and continue their assault with light arms. Appleman estimated that the NKA had "probably had no more than . . . forty tanks at the front on 5 August."[45] Nor did Stalin provide the NKA with anti-aircraft weapons, initially not even to protect Pyongyang, despite the fact that American air power was increasingly effective at long-range interdiction and close air support. Indeed, from late July, as the weather cleared, U.S. air attacks forced the NKA to shift virtually all logistics efforts and troop movement to after dark. Stalin refused to replenish lost aircraft, or to provide North Korea with any jet aircraft to contest the American mastery of the skies, or any assistance whatsoever to contest American domination of the seas, although some mines were supplied.

Stalin declined to assist the North Korean invasion on the broader game board as well. For example, the Soviets held several hundred thousand Japanese POWs in Siberia. By infiltrating even some of them into Japan, Stalin could have severely hindered the extremely valuable Japanese support for the United States' war effort and compelled MacArthur to retain forces in Japan for security purposes that he could otherwise send to battle in Korea. In fact, unconcerned about the security of his Japan base, MacArthur virtually denuded Japan of the four infantry divisions stationed there on occupation duty. Nor did Stalin make threatening moves in Europe, Iran, or anywhere else to constrain Truman's commitments to Korea.

Victory or defeat in Korea was, in essence, a question of timing. Even though the NKA Sixth and Fourth Divisions would eventually pose a major threat to the Pusan perimeter, that threat came too late, after the United States had deployed sufficient forces and firepower to defend its lodgment. Had the Sixth and the Fourth Divisions remained with the First Corps in its drive along the main axis of attack to Pusan, there was every possibility that the NKA could have been victorious. That, in fact, was General Walton's conclusion. Speaking about the NKA Sixth Division, he said: "Had the enemy force driven straight and hard for Pusan instead of occupying all of the ports in southwestern Korea, he [Walton] would not have had time to interpose the strength to stop it."[46]

MacArthur gave a similar assessment in different terms. In a teleconference discussion with the Joint Chiefs on July 24, after the defeat at Taejon, the chiefs warned him of the NKA Sixth and Fourth move "around the left end of his line which resembled the start of a double envelopment. General MacArthur admitted that he lacked the strength to prevent it, but saw it as no serious threat." He observed that as long as the NKA outnumbered his forces at a particular point they would always be able to mount enveloping attacks. "Their main effort continued to be in the center of the line, and the basic question was whether they had sufficient strength to force withdrawals there." If his own forces could hold the center, he would have no special worry about the incipient envelopment. On the other hand, he said, "if our center is unable to hold . . . our perimeter will have to be contracted."[47]

Of course, the center did hold, courtesy in part of Stalin himself. And even though the NKA would come close to victory, as Appleman observes:

> Never afterward were conditions as critical for the Eighth Army as in the closing days of July and the first days of August 1950. Never again did the North Koreans come as close to victory as when their victorious 6th and 4th Divisions passed eastward through Chinju and Koch'ang. Costly, bloody battles still remained, but from a . . . strategic point of view, the most critical phase had passed. Heavy . . . reinforcements were then arriving, or [were] on the point of arriving in Korea.[48]

TRUMAN BUILDS A NUTCRACKER

The U.S. contingency plan for responding to an invasion of South Korea (War Plan SL-17) called for a fighting retreat to the southern tip of the peninsula to an established beachhead at Pusan.[49] Then, during the engagement of an overextended attacking force against this beachhead, the plan called for an amphibious envelopment in the enemy's rear at Inchon to sever lines of communications and supply. The contingency plan, perforce, could say little about the speed of the NKA advance, or how rapidly the beachhead could be established, factors that would determine the timing of the amphibious envelopment. The concept was to execute the amphibious strike when the NKA was overextended, locked in the grip of the perimeter defense, and unable to recover and defeat the enveloping attack. In short, the faster the assault toward Pusan, the sooner the amphibious envelopment could be executed.

Logic suggested that once the NKA had crossed the Han River and the

U.S. had committed ground troops to combat, the NKA would employ its T-34 tanks in an all-out drive for Pusan before the beachhead could be consolidated. It was on the basis of such an expected NKA blitzkrieg that MacArthur planned for an early amphibious envelopment at Inchon, code-named "Bluehearts." In fact, he had initiated planning for an amphibious strike based on this assumption before the first encounter had occurred between North Korean and American forces on July 5. His plan was to execute a landing at Inchon on July 22, by which time, he assumed, the NKA would have proceeded too far down the peninsula to be able to recover to defeat the landing at Inchon.[50]

But Stalin confounded MacArthur. The NKA's advance had been far slower than expected (not more rapid, as is commonly believed), forcing him to cancel Bluehearts on July 10.[51] Nor was the slowness of the advance due to U.S. delaying actions. At this point, the U.S. had deployed to combat only six **241** understrength battalions of the Twenty-fourth Division: the Nineteenth, Twenty-first, and Thirty-fourth Regiments, with supporting units (slightly over five thousand men). Their mission was not to stop the enemy advance, which was impossible, but to remain in contact with and delay the much larger enemy force of three divisions, while withdrawing toward Pusan. Their task was to buy time till reinforcements arrived, but the odds were daunting, as was enemy firepower.

By July 10, the NKA had advanced only a few miles beyond Ch'onan, which they had taken two days before, and were a mere sixty miles from Inchon. In view of the fact that from this position the NKA force could easily recover and retreat to defend against an Inchon landing, MacArthur canceled Bluehearts, but continued planning for a future amphibious strike. (Recall that, at this point, Stalin had removed the NKA Sixth Division from the main force and it was assembling at Yesan, west of Ch'onan, and in position to move either south or north, depending on the need.)

Less than two weeks later, however, the situation had changed. The NKA Sixth had moved to the far south and the NKA main force had just crushed the U.S. defenses at Taejon. Therefore, on July 23, MacArthur informed the Joint Chiefs that he intended to mount "major amphibious operations" in mid-September.[52] By September, MacArthur could anticipate that the NKA would be engaged by larger American forces which would have arrived by then, and be unable to extricate their forces to defend against an assault behind their lines. In his cable to Washington MacArthur stated:

> Operation planned mid-September is amphibious landing of a two division corps in rear of enemy lines for purpose of enveloping and destroying enemy forces in conjunction with attack from south by Eighth Army. I am firmly convinced that early and strong effort behind his front will sever his main lines of

communication and enable us to deliver a decisive and crushing blow. The alternative is a frontal attack which can only result in a protracted and expensive campaign.[53]

In the meantime, all concerns were focused on establishing a perimeter beachhead around Pusan. Generals Hoyt Vandenberg and Joe L. Collins, of JCS, had traveled to Tokyo to meet with MacArthur and the newly appointed Eighth Army Commander in Chief Walton Walker, on July 13. They carried with them the latest estimate of the situation in Korea. In discussion with MacArthur and Walker, the chiefs noted that the NKA as then constituted "can continue to advance in the face of the available United Nations forces and is capable of threatening the security of Pusan by 25 July 1950."[54] The problem was seen to be the last week of July. It was vital to delay the NKA advance until heavy reinforcements arrived at the end of the month and the Pusan perimeter was consolidated.

Help was on the way, however. Elements of the Twenty-fifth Division had begun deploying from July 10, and its three regiments (the Twenty-fourth, Twenty-seventh, and Thirty-fifth) would add thirteen thousand more men to the defense by July 15. The First Cavalry Division would also begin arriving on July 18, adding ten thousand more men, although these units were all at less-than-authorized wartime strength and lacked heavy weapons in quantity. Additional massive reinforcements accompanied by heavy armament were scheduled to arrive at the end of the month, but it would be a close call.

Worse, the chiefs identified "70,000 Koreans now included in the Military District troops of the Chinese Communist Army in Manchuria." If released by Beijing, these forces could be deployed to the front "in from five to ten days. . . . Such reinforcements would increase the capability to threaten the security of Pusan by 25 July 1950." This force, as we shall see, would be of intense concern to American leaders, who would go to some lengths to ensure that it not be added to the assault on the perimeter at the end of the month (see chapter 10).

The chiefs also believed that both China and the Soviet Union could reinforce the NKA. They counted 210,000 troops in the Beijing-Tientsin area, which "could be put into combat in Korea from 20 to 30 days from the time a decision is made to commit them." Moscow could also deploy forces from four divisions stationed in China's Liaotung Peninsula and seven more deployed around Vladivostok, although they believed that "nothing in the Korean situation has as yet indicated that the USSR would deliberately decide to employ organized Soviet forces in direct military action precipitating a global war."[55]

The chiefs offered three possible defensive positions for Walker's consid-

242

eration. The first, fanning out in a radius from Pusan with Kumch'on at the apex some 80 miles from Pusan, was 162 miles in length. It was clearly unfeasible to defend this line given the troop numbers then in Korea and on the way and was offered only as a possible delaying point. The second, an "outer Pusan defense line," was about 50 miles from Pusan, had its southern anchor at Chinju, then swept northward to Waegwan, encompassing Taegu, the provisional capital of the Republic of Korea, and then eastward to the east-coast port of Pohang. It was 144 miles in length.[56]

The chiefs also offered an "inner and final Pusan defense line," 35 miles in radius from Pusan. This line, later called the "Davidson Line," was 75 miles in length, connecting Masan in the south, Miryang in the north and Ulsan in the east. The "inner and final" line would relinquish Taegu, but still offer sufficient depth to permit unhindered activity within the beachhead beyond the range of NKA artillery. Indeed, even the "inner and final" defense line would be larger than the Anzio beachhead of World War II. Both the "Outer" and "Inner" defense positions had the advantages of being supportable on both flanks by naval gunfire, interior lines of communications, and terrain generally favoring the defense, that is, offering high ground against the attackers, especially in the southwest sector.

General Walker designed his defensive perimeter on the spot, closely following the "Outer" Pusan defense line as proffered by the chiefs, with minor changes.[57] Based on their discussion, it was Walker's view that "barring unforeseen developments, he could hold a sizable bridgehead in the southern tip of the peninsula."[58] Thus, by the end of the second week of July, when American troops had been in combat for all of nine days against overwhelming odds, General Walker had concluded that he could maintain a foothold in Pusan.

Although MacArthur agreed, he waited for another week to convey this conviction to Washington. On July 19, less than three weeks after the commitment of American ground troops and on only the twenty-fourth day of the war, MacArthur informed President Truman that, despite desperate battles to come, "our hold upon the southern part of Korea represents a secure base." The reason for his optimism, MacArthur explained, was the NKA's actions. When the NKA "crashed the Han line the way seemed entirely open and victory was within his grasp," he said, but

> the enemy's plan and great opportunity depended upon the speed with which he could overrun South Korea once he had breached the Han River line and with overwhelming numbers and superior weapons temporarily shattered South Korean resistance. This chance he has now lost through the extraordinary speed with which the Eighth Army has been deployed from Japan to stem his rush.[59]

MacArthur's conclusion was correct, but for the wrong reasons. Although the Twenty-fifth Division had arrived by July 15, its regiments had been deployed to protect Taegu: the Twenty-fourth regiment to Kumch'on, the Twenty-seventh to Andong, and the Thirty-fifth to Yongchon. The First Cavalry Division had begun to deploy on July 18, the Fifth and Eighth regiments arriving at the east coast port of Pohang on that date, but the Seventh was delayed until July 22. The First Cavalry's regiments were deployed along the Taegu-Naktong corridor.[60] All six regiments had been deployed to blocking and reserve positions east of the main axis of the NKA advance and had not yet engaged in combat by the time MacArthur sent his message to Truman.

Thus, when MacArthur referred to "successive holding actions by the ground forces [that] forced the enemy into continued deployments, costly frontal attacks and confused logistics, which so slowed his advance and blunted his drive," he could only mean the six understrength battalions of the Twenty-fourth Division, which had been in action for two weeks. Moreover, it was difficult to know what he meant by these assertions. The battalions of the Nineteenth, Twenty-first, and Thirty-fourth regiments had hardly "forced" the enemy into "continued deployments," or "costly frontal attacks."

Battle reports showed confusion among U.S. units, cautious NKA deployments, and few frontal attacks.[61] The NKA operational style at all levels was encirclement of the enemy and infiltration behind his lines, not frontal attack. While NKA logistics were confused, that was not due to U.S. ground actions. General Walker calculated that enemy forces "could only sustain offensive operations for a period of three days," before being forced to break off their advance to await resupply.[62] It was, of course, the Soviets who controlled the NKA's logistics, and thereby in great measure controlled the rate of advance.

MacArthur acknowledged that a rapid advance was the NKA's only hope for victory, but claimed that it was the Eighth Army's speed of deployment that was responsible for stemming the NKA's "rush."[63] As we have seen, the facts were otherwise. First, there had been no NKA rush and, second, the bulk of the Eighth Army had yet to enter combat and thus could hardly be responsible for stemming the enemy drive. Finally, the pitifully small numbers of inadequately armed men of the Twenty-fourth Division delayed the NKA advance by no more than a few days, at most, and at great cost.[64]

Kim Il-sung himself acknowledged that it was the deliberate slow pace of his own forces' advance that was his undoing. "The first error we committed was, instead of making a complete siege [meaning blitzkrieg] and annihilating the enemy, we gave them enough time to regroup and increase their strength while retreating."[65] Both Kim and MacArthur agreed that a rapid advance was the key to victory, but differed on the reasons for the slowdown. While MacArthur attributed the slowdown to the speed of Eighth Army deployment, Kim actually indicted Stalin. When he says that "we gave them enough time to regroup," the use of the term "we" was an implicit criticism of Stalin, who controlled Kim's forces.

President Truman had eagerly awaited news that the South Korean beachhead would be secure. On July 19, he sent a message to Congress announcing as a matter of course the new strategy of worldwide containment that until then had been kept under wraps. The president addressed the immediate situation in Korea, its global ramifications, both for the United States and for the free world, and the economic strength that would be required to sustain a defense of freedom against the forces of aggression. He also subtly revealed that the United States would seek the unification of Korea under U.N. auspices once the North had been defeated. In a radio broadcast that same evening, the president quoted from MacArthur's message received that day that U.S. forces had established a "secure base" in the southern part of Korea.[66]

The United States, he said, went to the aid of the Republic of Korea "as a matter of basic moral principle" in support of a nation unjustifiably attacked by an aggressor force. The president acknowledged that it would take time to "slow down the forces of aggression, bring those forces to a halt, and throw them back." But, he declared, hinting at what was to come, "we are determined to support the United Nations in its effort to restore peace and security to Korea, and its effort to assure the people of Korea an opportunity to choose their own form of government free from coercion, as expressed in the General Assembly resolutions of November 14, 1947, and December 12, 1948." Although Truman did not elaborate, these resolutions called for the unification of Korea under U.N. auspices.[67]

The president also said that the outbreak of aggression in Korea "requires us to consider its implications for peace throughout the world." In this regard, he said, he had already directed that support for the Philippines and Indochina be strengthened and ordered the Seventh Fleet to prevent any attack on Formosa as a matter of elementary security. He wanted no doubt to exist about "our intentions regarding Formosa." The United States had no territorial ambitions concerning the island and "the present military neutralization of Formosa is without prejudice to political questions affecting that island. . . . With peace reestablished, even the most complex political questions are susceptible of solution." With these words, the president seemed to be suggesting that, if patient, Beijing might still gain control of Taiwan.

The president went on to say that the outbreak of aggression in the Far East "increases the importance of the common strength of the free nations in other parts of the world," which must now "increase and . . . unify their common strength, in order to deter a potential aggressor." Increasing the strength of the free world, he said, requires efforts in three different categories. "In the first place, to meet the situation in Korea, we shall need to send additional men, equipment, and supplies to General MacArthur's command as rapidly as possible. In the second place, the world situation requires that we increase substantially the size and materiel support of our Armed Forces, over and above the increases which are needed in Korea. In the third place, we must assist the free nations associated with us in common defense to augment their military strength."

Toward this end, he said, he would be transmitting to the Congress "specific requests for appropriations in the amount of approximately 10 billion dollars" and urged the prompt enactment of the authorization bill for the Mutual Defense Assistance Program for 1951 that was already before the House of Representatives. He said that "we must recognize that it will be necessary for a number of years to support continuing defense expenditures, including assistance to other nations, at a higher level than we had previously planned."

The president, concerned about possible strains that could be placed on the nation by the defense buildup, went to some lengths to illustrate the "tremendous productive power" of the economy. Total GNP was nearly $270 billion, 5 percent higher than a year earlier, and over $100 billion higher than in 1939. The U.S. was producing more steel than during the peak year of 1944. Electrical power generation had risen to 317 billion kilowatt hours, compared to 228 billion kilowatt hours in 1944. Food production was "practically as high as it was during the war years, when we were sending far more food abroad than we are now." Furthermore, he believed, "the potential productive power of our economy is even greater" and everything would be done to increase production.

The president had laid down the gauntlet. The United States would not only stay the course in Korea, but there was every expectation that America would defeat the aggressor and move to unify the country. Beyond Korea, the United States would increase its military strength and the strength of its allies to confront Moscow and its minions. In short, in the few weeks that had passed since the outbreak of the war, the Truman administration was already actively preparing the ground for national rearmament and global containment, as called for in NSC-68.

CHAPTER TEN

Mao Attempts to Avoid Entrapment

THE OUTBREAK of the war quickly compromised Mao Zedong's grand strategy and Stalin and Truman soon forced him to abandon it. It is important to review precisely what Mao was attempting to accomplish to understand how the war compromised his plans and how Stalin's "preemptive strike operational plan" and Truman's decision to commit ground troops forced their abandonment. Recall, Mao intended to establish relations with both the Soviet camp and the West, in that order. In that way, Mao would satisfy his profound obligation to the communist camp and also keep the channels open to Western wealth and technology, which China desperately required for economic recovery and development. Mao hoped that China could thus occupy a straddling position in the rapidly evolving bipolar world, with ties to both, even while establishing a communist society. In short, Mao sought to pursue a twentieth-century Middle Kingdom strategy.

Although this may seem to have been a quixotic idea, in retrospect it was simply too advanced for its time. Mao lacked the power to pursue such a strategy against the more powerful international forces then ranged against him. Ironically, Mao's later adversary and successor, Deng Xiaoping, would quite successfully pursue this same strategy some thirty years later. But in the early years of the Cold War, as Washington and Moscow demanded allegiance to their respective camps, few would successfully maintain a stand on the middle ground unless they were irrelevant to the East-West global power struggle, or could actually serve the interests of both powers as "neutral," such as Austria, Yugoslavia, or India. Mao's mistake was to assume that he

247

could ally with the Russians and still have access to American wealth and technology at a time when neither power would permit a straddle.

MAO'S FUNDAMENTAL MISCALCULATION

Mao simply and severely underestimated both the lengths to which Stalin would go to prevent Sino-American rapprochement and the depth of American concern regarding a Sino-Soviet alliance. Thus, Mao proceeded through the first half of 1950 as if he could occupy this middle stance, which, moreover, appeared to be feasible and actually unfolding according to his plans. He had signed the treaty with Stalin and Truman had withdrawn American support for Chiang Kai-shek, giving Mao the green light to assault the island. Thus, Mao and the Chinese leadership were clearly focused on mounting the strike against Taiwan before war erupted in Korea.

Mao was, however, completely uninvolved in Kim Il-sung's war plans, notwithstanding his agreement to return those Korean troops who had fought in China's civil war in the spring, and so was not privy to his timetable for assault. Furthermore, Mao was totally unaware of the secret change in American strategy. Mao had not calculated the impact of his commitment to a thirty-year treaty with the Soviet Union on the United States and was unaware of Truman's decision to craft the new strategy of containment, whose main component was a reversal of policy toward China.

Under the new, but still secret, strategy of containment, Washington no longer sought to keep China and the Soviet Union apart, but now would ensure that they remained bound together, which meant—above all—preventing Mao from taking the middle position. This fundamental change would also directly impact policy toward Taiwan, which would be reversed. Earlier, Truman had been willing to sacrifice Taiwan and the strategic position it represented in return for Beijing's independence of Moscow. Now, he would preserve Taiwan's independence and, in fact if not in name, include the island bastion into the U.S. Western Pacific sector of containment.

When the war erupted and Truman extended U.S. protection to Taiwan on the second day, Mao was hit with a double-barreled shock. Not only had Stalin beaten him to the punch by beginning the Korean War before he could strike Taiwan, but also Truman had administered what seemed to be a fatal blow to Mao's strategy by reversing his publicly held position and reentering the final phase of China's civil war on Chiang's side. By the single stroke of ordering the deployment of the Seventh Fleet to Formosan waters Truman had frustrated Mao's plans to finish the revolution and compromised his grand strategy—all without firing a shot.

Mao would go to considerable lengths to avoid entry into the war, as his negotiations with Stalin and proposals to Truman suggest. While preparing for the worst case, as all leaders must, Mao repeatedly sought for the most obvious of reasons to extricate himself from the trap he saw forming. War between China and the United States would be a disaster for China, threatening the possible collapse of the Communist regime. Communist rule had by no means been consolidated. Even a Sino-American conflict on the Korean battlefield that did not extend to a full-scale war between the two countries would mean China's indefinite isolation from the West and its resources.

But as the Korean conflict wore on and North Korean prospects for victory dimmed, Mao's focus shifted and the future structure of the Korean peninsula came to dominate his thoughts. The course of the conflict soon forced Mao to set aside the objective of attaining the middle position between East and West and concentrate on dealing with the immediate problem of achieving an advantageous outcome in Korea. Mao could not accomplish both goals simultaneously. By intervening, Mao would successfully reestablish the North Korean buffer zone, but at a very high cost.

Chinese entry crystallized the structure of the global political balance for the next two decades in a manner wholly disadvantageous to China. Mao would succeed in establishing a pro-Chinese, North Korean buffer state, but little else and not for very long. Far from assuming the middle position between East and West, Mao's main foreign policy objective, China would find itself isolated from the West, politically subordinate to Moscow within the communist camp, and economically dependent upon the Soviet Union for developmental assistance—technology, skilled manpower, trade, loans, and virtually everything else.

EARLY WARTIME DISCUSSIONS WITH STALIN

Mao moved early to prepare for any military contingency in Korea, but delayed a decision on entry into the conflict until all hope of a negotiated settlement had evaporated. Soon after the war began and Truman committed U.S. combat forces, Mao and Stalin commenced a running discussion over how to respond. Stalin insisted that China prepare to intervene in the conflict, while Mao sought to involve Moscow through provision of combat air support. Three points should be made about this lengthy discussion. First, it was nothing less than remarkable that Stalin should have raised the issue of Chinese involvement in the Korean conflict at this early stage in the war when the NKA appeared to be invincible. Second, Mao clearly wished to avoid entanglement. And third, Kim Il-sung wanted no Chinese assistance and assiduously sought to keep Mao out of any involvement in the war, until the NKA's fortunes turned and left him no alternative.

As far as the Korean peninsula was concerned, Mao had a clear view of

Chinese interests and would doggedly pursue them. Here, one must distinguish between national interest and the rationale employed to justify action in its name. Throughout, Mao justified Chinese intervention in terms of defending Chinese security (particularly the potential military threat to Manchuria) and assisting in the defense of his North Korean neighbor, but there were unstated reasons that more accurately explain Chinese actions.

The fact was that Mao took the opportunity of the Korean War to alter the most important factor relating to China's security in the northeast—the internal political dynamics of the North Korean regime. The ultimate, unspoken purpose of Chinese intervention in the war was to change Kim Il-sung's regime from pro-Soviet to pro-Chinese. Moreover, the timing of Mao's actions was not a function of negotiations with Stalin over the provision of materiel, but according to his own timetable derived from a combination of his objectives and the events on the battlefield. Clearly, Mao sought to obtain a maximum contribution from Stalin, including direct Soviet participation, but that did not fundamentally determine Mao's actions. In fact, Mao initially committed Chinese troops to battle without Soviet military assistance.

There were six different possible outcomes to the Korean War, three if Korea were unified, and three if the country reverted to a divided state. Regarding the former: Kim Il-sung's invasion could succeed without Chinese support and establish a unified, pro-Soviet Korea. Alternatively, the United States could defeat the invasion and succeed in establishing a unified, pro-American Korea. And, least likely, China could intervene and succeed in establishing a unified, pro-Chinese Korea. Of the three remaining possibilities, in a reversion to the status quo ante, there could be in the north a pro-Soviet regime, a pro-Chinese regime, or a form of Sino-Soviet coalition ranged against a pro-American South Korea.

Of these six possible outcomes, ideological and propaganda positions aside, only two would genuinely serve China's long-term interest of a secure area free of threat. Chinese interests would best be served by a divided Korea that was either a pro-Chinese buffer state, or a coalition. A unified pro-Chinese Korea was a very unlikely outcome because China could not hope to accomplish this objective unilaterally and Stalin would not support it. Besides, it was undesirable. A unified Korea under *any* regime would in all probability be as destabilizing a factor in Northeast Asia in the future as it had been in the past, as the object of big power competition. Therefore, for all concerned, it was the least likely outcome.

Only through direct intervention could Mao pursue his objectives in Korea, the only means through which Chinese influence could be inserted decisively to alter what up to this point was a thoroughly pro-Soviet North Korea. Thus, while the Korean War would present Mao with a major crisis, involving war against the United States, it also offered him an unprecedented opportunity to change the political dynamics of North Korea. Only if he took advantage of the proffered opportunity could Mao ensure that China would have sufficient leverage in Pyongyang to prevent war on the peninsula in the future.

Thus, like Stalin, but for a different reason, Mao did not wish the NKA to win, which would lead to the least desirable outcome—a unified, pro-Soviet Korea on China's border. But neither did he wish the North to be completely defeated, which would lead to the equally undesirable outcome of a unified, pro-American Korea, and a proximate, long-term threat to China's security. Rather, Mao sought a North Korean buffer state in a divided peninsula, in which his influence—not Stalin's—would be substantial, if not dominant. Ironically, but for entirely different reasons, then, Stalin, Mao, and obviously Truman all sought the identical outcome to the North Korean invasion— **251** that the NKA should fail.

It followed that Mao would do nothing to contribute to a pro-Soviet victory, or to a completely pro-Soviet regime in a divided Korea. Nor would Mao accept a unified, pro-American Korea without a struggle. From the outset, through the venue of the U.N., Mao would explore a trade-off with the United States. The quid pro quo involved Chinese assistance in arranging for a return to the status quo ante bellum in Korea, in return for U.S. support for Beijing's seat in the U.N. and non-support for Taiwan, an outcome that would allow Mao eventually to realize his grand Middle Kingdom strategy.

But prospects for this trade-off quickly evaporated. In truth, not only was Mao's price too high for Truman, but it also contradicted American strategy. Therefore, as Truman pressed forward with plans to unify Korea and evinced little interest in either a Korean settlement or an agreement with China, Mao began preparations in earnest to contend with the probability of conflict with the United States. He would prepare his forces and wait for the optimum moment to intervene. That moment would be after the defeat of the NKA, but before complete American control of the North—thence to pursue his objective of ensuring a pro-Chinese, North Korean buffer regime.

Chinese action, or rather inaction, between the outbreak of the invasion and mid-October illustrates the thesis that Mao waited for the NKA to lose. There were four times when the commitment of Chinese forces would have either ensured a North Korean victory or prevented total defeat. Mao could have ensured North Korean victory with a commitment of forces in late July or early August. At that point, he had just deployed a quarter of a million troops to the Sino-Korean border; the NKA had just begun its assault on the Pusan perimeter; and large U.S. reinforcements had yet to arrive. Chinese leaders recognized that this was a potentially decisive moment, and some urged action, but Mao declined. American leaders, too, believed that Chinese entry could have been decisive at that vulnerable time and, as we shall see, sought to counter that possibility.

Alternatively, in September, Mao could have prevented NKA defeat with commitment of forces either shortly before Inchon or soon afterward. North Korean vulnerability to an amphibious envelopment increased as NKA forces drove deeper into the south and concentrated forces against the Pusan perimeter. A limited, even if unannounced, deployment of Chinese forces in early September to the Seoul-Inchon area—the crucial communications nexus for the country—would have forced a change of Washington's plans away from Inchon and prevented the disastrous reversal of fortune that the amphibious attack produced.

A Chinese deployment immediately after Inchon to contest the U.S. drive to recover Seoul would certainly have provided for the escape of the NKA as it attempted to withdraw from the American envelopment and enabled a stronger defense of the north. Finally, in early October, Mao could have committed Chinese forces to the defense of Pyongyang following the U.S. decision to cross the 38th parallel, ensuring the survival of the regime. Mao did, in defiance of Stalin's demands, none of these things, because all four would have tended to reinforce a pro-Soviet North Korea.

In this regard, Stalin's secret plotting with Kim Il-sung actually worked to Mao's advantage. The fact that neither Stalin nor Kim permitted any Chinese involvement in or even knowledge of prewar preparations served Mao's purposes. Also, the fact that Kim declined to seek Chinese support as long as the NKA was victorious on the battlefield made it easy for Mao to stand aloof from the conflict and pick his moment to intervene afterward. When the war began, therefore, Mao declined to provide any support for the NKA.

Indeed, there was not even a Chinese ambassador in Pyongyang until August 13, although Beijing formally opened an embassy there on July 10. Even Stalin's sarcastic prodding would not hurry Mao. On July 8, Stalin had sent a message urging that he send a representative "soon . . . if, of course, Mao Zedong considers it necessary to have communications with Korea."[1] Although Mao opened an embassy within two days of Stalin's telegram, he would wait five weeks before sending his ambassador. Instead, Mao remained alert to the rapidly vanishing possibility that he could still avoid involvement in Korea through an agreement with Washington, and assault Taiwan.

By early July, Mao and his colleagues had begun to realize what Stalin and Truman had wrought. Stalin had created a crisis on China's border by triggering preemptive war in Korea and Truman had acted quickly to foreclose Mao's grand strategy by extending protection to Chiang Kai-shek. Worse, the United States had committed its power to the Korean battlefield and, in the likely event that Kim would fail to seize a quick victory, China could be faced with a truly major crisis should the United States defeat Kim's forces and drive north in an attempt to unify the peninsula.

Mao had known war was coming in Korea, but not when, and was initially unaware of its full implications for China. The Beijing press kept all news of the conflict out of its pages for the first two days (although other Chinese papers covered the event).[2] President Truman's announcement that the United States would neutralize the Formosa Strait, however, brought an immediate response. Clearly stunned, Mao, in a speech to a meeting of the Central People's Government Council the next day, lashed out at Truman for breaking his word. "On January 5, Truman said in an announcement that the United States would not intervene in Taiwan. Now his conduct proves that what he said was false."[3]

In his rage, Mao followed that charge with another, which, however, bore little relationship to reality. "Moreover," he said, Truman "shredded all international agreements related to the American commitment not to intervene in China's internal affairs." The fact was that the only international agreements the United States had entered into over China, as opposed to unilateral statements, like Truman's pronouncement of January 5, were the Cairo agreement of 1943 and the Potsdam Agreement of 1945 (agreements that Mao had denounced). In these the United States promised to "restore" Formosa to the Republic of China. It would confound reality to twist the "purpose" of the Cairo Declaration, for example, into a "commitment not to intervene in China's internal affairs." The Potsdam declaration simply reiterated that "the terms of the Cairo Declaration shall be carried out."

That same day, Zhou Enlai issued an even stronger statement, bordering on paranoia. Going beyond Mao's accusation of intervention in China's internal affairs, Zhou charged that Truman's decision to protect Taiwan was "armed aggression against the territory of China in total violation of the UN charter." Furthermore, he claimed war in Korea was merely a "pretext for the United States to invade Taiwan, Korea, Viet Nam, and the Philippines." Zhou pledged that China would "liberate" Taiwan no matter what the American imperialists did.[4] Both Mao's and Zhou's outbursts shrilly reflected China's complete impotence to contest Truman's action. But Mao's inability to counter U.S. action over Taiwan quickly paled before his growing realization of the magnitude of the problems he began to face as Kim's forces stalled at the Pusan perimeter.

Stalin's revised invasion plan, which sent virtually the entire NKA southward, leaving rear areas vulnerable to amphibious encirclement, immediately raised alarms in Beijing, as the Soviet leader no doubt expected it would. In a conversation with Soviet Ambassador Roshchin on July 2, Zhou Enlai leveled a thinly veiled criticism at Stalin by complaining that Kim Il-sung had ignored Mao's prewar warnings about American intervention. Now that the worst had occurred, Zhou wanted to pass on additional advice from Mao "to create a strong defense line in the area of Inchon because American troops could land there." Mao feared that Kim was leaving himself vulnerable to "landing operations by Americans in other parts of the Korean peninsula as well."[5]

Strategically, the probable American response to the invasion—an amphibious strike in the rear—was obvious to all. Chinese analysts needed only to have read *Time* magazine to be informed of U.S. plans. In its weekly "strategy" section on the war, *Time*'s editors described the "three-phase war" to their readers. First, establish the Pusan beachhead; second, build up strength for a counterblow; and third, break out from the beachhead "supported by Allied amphibious attacks behind the North Korean lines on either coast."[6] No doubt Chinese analysts had other sources of intelligence information that lent credence to this plan.

The only surprise could be tactical, regarding the precise time and place for the American counterblow. Only a handful of places were suitable for large-scale landing operations and the time could be narrowed as intelligence monitored preparations for the assault. That all on the Communist side expected an amphibious counterthrust, however, was beyond doubt. As noted in the previous chapter, Kim was already raising this concern to Stalin and MacArthur was in fact planning for precisely such an early strike at Inchon, which, however, he postponed.

It is not clear from Roshchin's cable, of which only a fragment is currently available, whether it was the Chinese or the Russians who proposed Chinese military involvement in support of Kim, but Zhou "confirmed" that in the event of a near-term American landing behind North Korean lines, "Chinese troops, disguised as Korean, would engage the opponent." Zhou said that for this purpose China had already deployed near Shenyang (Mukden), Manchuria, 120,000 men in three Chinese armies comprising nine divisions and he inquired whether "it would be possible to cover these troops with the Soviet air force?"[7]

Zhou's conversation with Roshchin established the basic theme of a running dialogue between Mao and Stalin, which began at this time and continued for the next three months, that ultimately would lead to Chinese intervention in the conflict. The basic question the Chinese side pressed to resolve was: If Mao were to send troops, would Stalin provide combat air cover for them? In short, would it be a joint effort? At this early stage, unwilling to provide overt Chinese assistance, Mao offered only emergency covert support in case Kim's forces were encircled. Covert support could easily be denied and/ or withdrawn. In return, however, he wanted an overt Soviet commitment in the form of air cover, which, once committed, could not easily be withdrawn, and, moreover, could lead directly to conflict with the United States.

Stalin replied affirmatively to Mao three days later, saying that "we consider it correct to concentrate immediately 9 Chinese divisions on the Chinese-Korean border for volunteer actions in North Korea in case the enemy crosses the 38th parallel. We will try to provide air cover for these units."[8] Stalin wanted to pit China directly against the United States and so suggested that rather than commit forces covertly "disguised as Korean," Mao should deploy them openly as "volunteers." That, of course, would mean that Chinese forces, whatever their formal designation, would engage American forces, even though the latter were configured as a United Nations force, in Korea—Stalin's objective. Moreover, to encourage Mao, he declared that he would "try" to provide air cover for these units, but without making an irrevocable commitment.

255

Each was attempting to involve the other more directly in conflict with the United States while minimizing entanglement for himself. Mao wanted to conceal his role—in the form of "disguised" troops—and thus avoid a direct Sino-American clash and possible retaliation against China, but sought to have Soviet planes directly involved over Korean airspace. The term "air cover" here clearly meant combat air support for ground operations in Korea, not air defense of the Chinese homeland. When Stalin said, "we will try to provide air cover for these units," he was referring to those "units" that would move into combat in Korea against the United States. The question was: What did Stalin mean by the word "provide"?

The exchange with Stalin in the second week of the war, with its clear expectation that the NKA invasion would fail even before the first engagement with American combat troops, was the factor that undoubtedly produced Beijing's shift of interpretation on the war the very next day. The July 6 front-page editorial of the *People's Daily* (*Renmin Ribao*) changed the interpretation of three days before that "complete victory is not far off." Now, in view of the fact that Washington was unlikely to "concede defeat," Beijing believed that North Korean victory would "come not so fast."[9] The realization that any hope for a quick victory had vanished led Mao to begin immediately to prepare the way for possible Chinese involvement in Korea.

But, while Mao began to reposition his forces for any Korean eventuality, he did so, initially at least, in a manner that would still allow him to strike at Taiwan if the opportunity arose. Although Truman had declared his intention to neutralize the Formosa Strait and protect Taiwan from invasion, as of the first week of July the United States had deployed no forces to the Formosa area. The only "show of muscle" thus far had been the overflight of jets over the Formosa Strait and the city of Taipei as the carrier *Valley Forge* steamed north from the Philippines to Korean waters. Air reconnaissance patrols would begin in the second week of July, but all available ships were being directed to Korean waters for gunnery duty. Consequently, the first "Formosan patrol" was submarines, the Catfish on July 18, followed the next day by the Pickerel.[10]

On July 7, the same day that General MacArthur was named U.N. Commander, Mao and the Central Committee "decided to establish a Northeast Border Defense Army [NBDA] in order to strengthen border defense forces in Northeast China and to prepare to enter the Korean War in case of necessity."[11] In a series of subsequent meetings between July 7 and 13, the Chinese high command worked out requirements of organization, structure, and logistics. Four additional armies of infantry were deployed into Manchuria— the Thirty-eighth, Thirty-ninth, Fortieth, and Forty-second—along with the First, Second, and Eighth Artillery Divisions, three newly established air force regiments, and other units.

Units of these armies were at that time widely dispersed across China, some as far south as Kwangtung and Kwangsi, China's southernmost provinces. Movement orders were issued on July 13, instructing troop units to arrive at designated points in the Northeast by August 5, when they were to undergo further training. The Thirty-eighth, Thirty-ninth, and Fortieth Armies became the Thirteenth Army Corps under the command of Deng Hua, while the Forty-second Army remained independent under the command of Lin Biao. By the end of July, Mao would more than double the number of troops along the Sino-Korean border from 120,000 to 260,000.[12]

The six armies that Mao had marshaled for the invasion of Taiwan, the Twenty-fourth, Twenty-fifth, Twenty-eighth, Twenty-ninth, Thirty-first, and Thirty-second armies, remained in place for the time being, but the high command of this force was reassigned to the NBDA. Thus, Su Yu was named commander of the NBDA, with Xiao Jingguang and Xiao Hua as vice commander and political commissar, respectively. (Xiao Jingguang was also commander of the PLA navy.) These command changes would never be implemented and the Taiwan invasion force would remain in place along the China coast, biding its time in a make-work project "suppressing local bandits and stabilizing the rear area," until August 11. At that time the plan to invade Taiwan was formally postponed and this force, too, was shortly deployed to Manchuria, where its armies became the nuclei of the Ninth and Nineteenth Army Corps.[13]

On the day Mao issued the movement orders for the NBDA, Stalin sent him a cable inquiring "whether you have decided to deploy nine Chinese divisions on the border with Korea" as Zhou Enlai had indicated in his discussion with Roshchin eleven days earlier? This message, which clearly indicated that Mao had not coordinated his decision with Stalin, also revealed how the crafty Soviet leader began to lay the groundwork for circumventing his promise of providing Soviet air cover for Chinese troops in combat. He said: "If you have made such a decision, then we are ready to send you a division of jet fighter planes—124 pieces for covering these troops." Moreover, he said, "we intend to train Chinese pilots in two to three months with the help of our pilots and then to transfer all equipment to your pilots. We intend to do the same thing with the aviation divisions in Shanghai."[14]

In other words, Stalin had now clarified the meaning of his earlier promise to "provide" air cover for Chinese troops in Korea. There would be no joint defense of North Korea. He was, instead, proposing to train Chinese pilots and transfer jet fighters to China—those he had sent earlier to Shanghai and   **257** an additional division, so that Mao could employ them as Chinese aircraft for covering his troops. If this proposal were to transpire, Stalin would have "provided" air cover while evading direct Soviet involvement, and strengthened prospects for a direct Sino-American war. As it turned out, however, Chinese pilots were not ready to fly the jets when Mao made the decision to send in combat troops in October, so he reopened the issue of Soviet air combat support, much to Stalin's discomfiture.

INITIAL SINO-AMERICAN INTERACTION

The end of July was the first of the four crucial periods discussed above when a Chinese deployment of forces could have tipped the balance in favor of the NKA. Of course, American leaders could not have known that it was not Mao's strategy to assist the North Koreans to victory, but they had to guard against this worst-case possibility. In any case, American leaders assumed that the Russians and Chinese were cooperating. American leaders had carefully monitored the Chinese deployment and sought to forestall early Chinese entry by creating a diversionary threat to Beijing's flank. That flank was Taiwan.

The crucial question facing American leaders from the end of July onward was whether or not the Chinese would commit their just-deployed forces in Manchuria to support the NKA. The press treatment of this extremely delicate issue was phrased in terms of whether North Korea itself had additional reserves to commit to battle, but the question was actually addressed to Beijing. Thus, according to Hanson Baldwin in the August 2 edition of the *New York Times*, MacArthur believed that the NKA "had mustered their maximum strength—perhaps 200,000 men—in an effort to push us into the sea before sufficient reinforcements could arrive." Other "observers," however, "were not so sure that the Communists had yet utilized all their available strength." Indeed:

> the great question mark of the North Korean reserves, believed by Washington to be concentrated somewhere in the north near the Manchurian-Korean frontier, still made accurate assessment of the outcome of the current campaign impossible.[15]

The phrase "reserves . . . concentrated somewhere in the north near the Manchurian-Korean frontier" was a thinly veiled reference to the massing of Chinese forces in Manchuria, in addition to the 70,000 Koreans the JCS had identified earlier as being present there. In either case, it was a matter of what the Chinese would do with them. The JCS estimate calculated that, once committed, these forces could be in action at the perimeter in "five to ten days."[16] Given the precarious situation then existing around Pusan, it was vital to dissuade Beijing from committing troops to action. American strategy ultimately was to prod Beijing into intervention in Korea, but later from a position of strength, not at this early stage, which would only court disaster.

At this most critical point in the battle, when General Walker had pulled his "entire force . . . back behind the Naktong River," and had issued his "stand or die" order to hold the Pusan perimeter at all costs against the existing level of NKA attacking strength, it was vital to forestall Chinese involvement, which could tip the balance before reinforcements arrived and the beachhead was secured. The situation was so dire that MacArthur had decided to send the First Marine Brigade and the Second Infantry Division, then en route, to reinforce the perimeter, instead of holding them out for his amphibious envelopment as originally planned.[17]

Therefore, at the end of July, the U.S. leadership prepared a subtle countermove, born of the desperation of the moment. Its surface aspect came in the form of a trip by MacArthur to Taipei to confer with Chiang Kai-shek, and the deployment of nuclear-capable B-29s to Northeast Asia. Buried in the two events, as we shall see, was the message that if China intervened in Korea at this point, the United States was prepared to employ Chinese Nationalist forces in attacks against the mainland, and, if necessary, conduct nuclear strikes on the mainland. There can be little doubt that only the most critical situation would have prompted Truman to "unleash" Chiang or consider nuclear attacks. Once the moment of danger passed and the Pusan perimeter was consolidated, it should be noted, Truman re-imposed constraints on the Nationalists and quietly returned the B-29s to the United States, but the process was messy and became enmeshed in domestic politics.

Although MacArthur had conveyed to General Collins in mid-July his

intention to visit Formosa as soon as the Korean situation had become sufficiently stabilized, it was a message from the Joint Chiefs on July 28 that precipitated the general's trip. The message itself was the product of a presidential decision taken at a National Security Council meeting of the day before.
Truman says that at this meeting he only "approved three specific proposals": to extend immediate military assistance to the Nationalist government,
to authorize MacArthur's headquarters to conduct a military survey of what
was needed, and a plan "to carry out reconnaissance flights along the China
coast to determine the imminence of attacks against Formosa."[18]

But the president had approved at least two more proposals, one of which
the chiefs informed MacArthur about the next day. The chiefs said that in
view of the Chinese Communist buildup along the coast the Nationalists
should be "permitted to break up hostile concentrations through military action, even if it meant attacks on the mainland."[19]

When informed, MacArthur, realizing its significance for operations in
Korea, immediately gave full concurrence to the chiefs' proposal and informed them that he would visit Formosa two days hence "to survey the situation."[20] Although the chiefs suggested that MacArthur could send a senior
officer in advance of his own visit, the general decided to make the trip himself, a decision in which the chiefs concurred. In view of the president's decision to extend prompt military aid to the Nationalists, it was only natural
that the senior officer in command, MacArthur himself, go immediately to
Taiwan to convey the news of this major policy decision to Chiang and, no
doubt, to explain its precise parameters.

Chiang Kai-shek had reluctantly acquiesced in President Truman's June
27 decision prohibiting attacks against the mainland. On July 14, however,
he had requested permission to break up naval assault concentrations along
the coast, fearing that the Communists were preparing to launch an attack
on the island of Quemoy.[21] The chiefs responded three days later, denying
this request and declaring that the islands were not included in the area de-
lineated by the president's directive and that any "offensive action directed
against the mainland from these islands may not be supported in combat by
military forces based on Formosa or the Pescadores," although the United
States "should not prevent the Nationalists from defending these islands."[22]
Rebuked, Chiang had devised a defensive strategy that, according to Nationalist Foreign Minister George Yeh, "was to let Communists land and wipe
them out on beaches rather than destroying invasion forces at sea before
reaching Formosa."[23]

Both the chiefs' position and Chiang's had been taken before intelligence
indicated that Mao had begun to deploy substantial forces into Manchuria in
mid-July. By the end of July, in a rapid action, Mao had assembled over a
quarter of a million troops in Manchuria along the Korean border. Mao may

259

have been surreptitiously sending individual Chinese soldiers into Korea even at this early date to surrender to U.N. forces, quietly signaling his concern and raising an implicit threat of intervention. One such POW, according to Marguerite Higgins, who reported on him, had in his possession "Chinese army manuals, complete with pictures of Mao Tse-tung, the Chinese dictator, and Chu Teh, the head of the Chinese armies."[24]

The Chinese buildup in Manchuria, with its terrible implications of probable defeat for United States forces in Korea, prompted the president to agree to a change in Taiwan's role, although the stated rationale for temporarily changing policy was the invasion threat along the coast to Taiwan. Thus, on July 29, Secretary Johnson sent a message to Acheson recommending that

> the pertinent part of the President's statement of 27 June [see p. 208] be so clarified as to permit the Nationalist Government to employ its military forces in defensive measures to prevent Communist amphibious concentrations directed against Formosa or the Pescadores. Such measures should include attacks on such concentrations and mining of those mainland water areas from which such an assault could be staged.[25]

On July 30, two days after MacArthur's trip was announced, Chiang Kai-shek, undoubtedly in coordination with MacArthur, sent his forces into action. Nationalist planes carried out a highly publicized air strike against shipping concentrated along the coast across from the island of Quemoy, "sinking and damaging more than 150 Communist ships." According to Chargé d'Affaires Robert Strong, who inquired into the matter, while the general was in Taipei "other bombing and strafing missions on mainland [occurred] which have been kept secret."[26]

To make clear to the leaders in Beijing that the Nationalists were in fact responding to American wishes, both MacArthur and Chiang issued communiqués after MacArthur's departure hailing the arrangement of "effective coordination." In his communiqué, MacArthur graciously acknowledged Chiang's offer to send troops to Korea, but declined because it "might so seriously jeopardize the defense of Formosa that it would be inadvisable." On the other hand, MacArthur declared: "Arrangements have been completed for effective coordination between the American forces under my command and those of the Chinese Government the better to meet any attack which a hostile force might be foolish enough to attempt. Such an attack would . . . stand little chance of success."[27]

Chiang Kai-shek, in turn, extolled MacArthur's "deep understanding" of the Communist menace, declaring that

> an agreement was reached between General MacArthur and myself on all the problems discussed in the series of conferences held in the past two days. The

foundation for a joint defense of Formosa and for Sino-American military co-operation has thus been laid. It is our conviction that our struggle against Communist aggression will certainly result in final victory.[28]

Chiang said that "now that we can again work closely together with our old comrade in arms, General MacArthur, I am sure not only will our determination in the struggle for this common cause be strengthened but the peoples of all Asia will be aroused to fight communist aggression."[29] MacArthur reciprocated with assurances promising "effective military coordination between the Chinese and American forces."

An irate Robert Strong had been given the cold shoulder during MacArthur's visit and he along with the military attachés had not been included in the discussions between the general and Chiang Kai-shek. He was obviously not privy to the plan to utilize the Nationalists to apply pressure to Beijing's flank, a fact that colored his reporting. Strong wrote to Acheson that he thought the attacks were a "deliberate test case" to see how far Chiang Kai-shek could go in defiance of the United States.[30] The chargé d'affaires did note, however, that MacArthur had arranged to "put three squadrons of USAF jet fighters into Taiwan by end of week," that several transport aircraft had already flown in from Okinawa and the Philippines, and that two more cargo planes were due to arrive from Tokyo the next day. All this, of course, indicated an American initiative rather than an instance of Nationalist defiance.[31]

In Washington, Secretary Acheson took exception to this decision, about which he was apparently not consulted in advance. He agreed with Nationalist mining operations, but objected to air attacks against the mainland on the grounds that they might bring about the very outcome the U.S. sought to avoid. In his view "if we or the Chinese Nationalists should now precipitate hostilities between Formosa and the mainland, the probability of Chinese Communist overt intervention with armed forces in Korea ... would be greatly *increased*." Furthermore, Acheson placed high value on the universally held view of North Korea as the "aggressor" and believed that "we should take considerable military risks rather than place ourselves in the role of an aggressor by launching an attack on our own initiative, unless there are overwhelming considerations of national security involved."[32]

Acheson's argument convinced the president. At a meeting with him on August 3, Truman decided to reverse policy and send a personal emissary, Averell Harriman, to MacArthur to explain. No doubt the timely arrival of large-scale reinforcements in Korea made the decision easier. On July 31, the Fifth RCT from Hawaii and lead elements of the Second Infantry Division from Seattle arrived at Pusan and on August 2 the First Provisional Marine Brigade landed, with its organic air support. All came equipped with armor

261

and heavy weapons. Indeed, by the second half of July, the port of Pusan was bursting with activity, handling over two hundred ships a week bringing cargo and personnel to Korea, and an air lift was in full swing.[33] The battlefield balance of forces had begun to change.

The next day, August 4, Secretary Johnson sent a message to MacArthur formalizing the policy reversal and reiterating the president's original policy. The gist of it read: "you are to stop attacks from Formosa upon the mainland. No one other than the President as Commander-in-Chief has the authority to order or authorize preventive action against concentrations on the mainland. . . . The most vital national interest requires that no action of ours precipitate general war or give excuse to others to do so. This message has the approval of the President and Secretary of State."[34] The deployment of the three fighter squadrons into Taiwan was also canceled.

MacArthur replied immediately saying that "the president's decision of June 27 is fully understood here and this headquarters has been and is operating meticulously in accordance therewith." He "thoroughly" understood the limitations of his authority and reassured the secretary that he would not "in any way" exceed them. The general closed with the "hope neither the President nor you has been misled by false or speculative reports from whatever source, official or non-official."[35] MacArthur's comment was in reference to speculation already appearing in the press that he had exceeded his authority with the trip to Taiwan.

The president's emissary, Harriman, arrived the next day for two days of intensive conversations. Harriman drove home the point that MacArthur "must not permit Chiang to be the catalyst for a war with the Chinese Communists."[36] MacArthur wanted, at least, to keep alive the potential threat of Nationalist attacks on the mainland as a deterrent. Harriman attempted to explain why Chiang "was a liability, and the great danger of a split in the unity of the United Nations on the Chinese Communist–Formosa policies." Although Harriman did not believe that he and MacArthur "came to a full agreement on the way . . . things should be handled on Formosa and with the Generalissimo . . . he accepted the president's position and will act accordingly, but without full conviction."[37]

Publicly, the president sought to end the incipient controversy by declaring that he had been "reassured" and that he and the general "saw eye to eye on Formosa policy." Privately, Truman also sent MacArthur reassurance through his "personal representative," Major Frank E. Lowe, whom he had had assigned to MacArthur's headquarters. Lowe was Truman's "back channel" directly to MacArthur and through him sensitive communications could pass. Truman instructed Lowe to "say to General MacArthur I have never had anything but the utmost confidence in his ability to do the Far Eastern job and I think I've shown that by action, as well as by words."[38]

262

But that was not the end of it. In retrospect, it seems, the president was being disingenuous, for while expressing his confidence in the general, the administration was at the same time adding fuel to the controversy by putting out the word to the press that MacArthur had been responsible for the flap over Formosa and Chiang. It would seem that Truman had decided to employ a controversy to obscure key policy decisions and, perhaps, begin the process of establishing the grounds for future political action against MacArthur, who was widely perceived to be a Republican presidential candidate.

Quite aside from the issue of MacArthur's visit and with no reference to him, Truman had in fact decided to change policy and arm the Nationalist government in accordance with the strategy of containment. The idea of authorizing Nationalist attacks on the mainland had also come from the JCS, not MacArthur, and related to the threat of Chinese entry into Korea. But Truman, having had second thoughts regarding the attacks, now moved to obscure the events by allowing blame to be placed on an all-too-independent MacArthur.

For example, in the United Nations the "complaint" was heard that MacArthur's visit to Taiwan was "taken without specific instructions at the time from Washington" and was a "triumph of mistiming," coinciding as it did with the return of Soviet envoy Jacob Malik to the Security Council. Moreover, "responsible officials still insist" that those in charge of Far Eastern policy in the State Department "did not know about the MacArthur visit to Formosa until they had read about it in the newspapers." Despite a statement from MacArthur suggesting that the criticism was being spread for "divisive purposes" and one from Harriman saying that the general's trip had been "planned in advance," officials at the U.N. and in Britain and France "were told that General MacArthur had chosen this particular time for his visit to Formosa on his own initiative."[39]

The flap over MacArthur also revealed something of Truman's decision-making procedure. The president sometimes dealt separately with his top advisers, particularly State and Defense, producing decisions based on discussions with one, of which the other was not informed, and could only object to after the fact. This had evidently been the case regarding the authorization of Nationalist strikes against the mainland. Truman had agreed with the JCS proposal, only to be persuaded against it after the fact by Acheson. MacArthur became the convenient scapegoat that all sides could castigate.

Aside from its domestic aspects, there was an even more important reason to promote the notion of presidential disagreement with MacArthur. The president hoped to use the budding MacArthur controversy to obscure what were his two most important decisions of the war thus far. These were his decision to convey subtly a nuclear threat to Beijing, should Mao decide to intervene in Korea at this vulnerable time, and to authorize the long-planned and awaited amphibious strike behind North Korean lines.

On July 29, the Joint Chiefs proposed to supplement the three B-29 bombing groups already in the Far East with two more for a thirty-day period to augment FEAF's capability for strategic bombing "deep in North Korea."[40] To this group they then "added ten nuclear-configured B-29s to the task force about to cross the Pacific."[41] In mid-August, these aircraft, although unarmed and carrying only non-nuclear components, would fly to Guam, while the two bomber groups would fly on to Japan. The impression, deliberately false, of course, was that these planes, set apart from the FEAF B-29 Bomber Command in Japan, were carrying atomic weapons.

In authorizing this deployment, the president also ensured that the Chinese learned of it. Secretary of State Acheson instructed Ambassador Loy Henderson in Delhi to commit a "calculated indiscretion," revealing the deployment in his discussions with the Minister of External Affairs, Girja Bajpai.[42] They knew that Bajpai would convey Henderson's views to India's ambassador to China, K. M. Panikkar, who would pass the information on to Zhou Enlai. Indeed, Washington regularly employed the "Panikkar channel" as an informal means of communicating to Beijing. It worked both ways. Panikkar would report his discussions with Zhou to Bajpai, who would in turn pass these views on to Henderson.

Acheson also arranged to leak news of the B-29 deployment to the press. In a front-page article in the *New York Times* on August 1 appeared the revelation that additional B-29s were being sent (but not the nuclear-configured ones). The reinforcement was "the second since the Communist attack on South Korea" and was one that would "bolster United States fighting power in Korea in a matter of days."[43] (The B-29, the heavy bomber of World War II, had been redesignated as a medium bomber; the B-36 now held the heavy bomber title.) The administration even made use of misfortune. On August 3, one of the planes crashed in California, killing the commander of the strike force. Instead of attempting to hush the matter up behind a veil of secrecy, it was exploited. The crash was compared to an atomic blast, but press photos of the crash showed no nuclear components aboard the aircraft.[44] The very fact of comparing the crash blast to an atomic detonation was suggestive enough.

Truman's second major decision was to authorize the long-awaited amphibious strike behind North Korean lines. Indeed, the landing was one of the major topics of conversation between Harriman and MacArthur. In their meeting of August 8, attended by Generals Lauris Norstad, Edward Almond, and Matthew Ridgway, MacArthur argued with "dramatic eloquence," according to Ridgway, that the time had come for an amphibious campaign "by about 25 September." Such a stroke behind enemy lines offered a "reasonable chance of decisive success," that is, the destruction of the North Korean Army.[45]

MacArthur argued that time worked against the United States. The longer the delay the more likely the chance of direct military intervention by the Chinese Communists, the Soviets, or both. The general believed that the sooner he struck the better and, if his forces were augmented by two infantry divisions and an airborne RCT, decisive success was "reasonably attainable by early winter." The alternative, he declared, was "the certainty of a more difficult and costly operation later, of an incalculable loss of military prestige world-wide and consequently of political advantage, and the probability of greater non-battle casualties during a Korean winter, than of battle losses in the operation as planned."

Immediately upon his return to Washington, on August 9, Harriman reported to Truman. The President wasted no time in requesting the Secretary of Defense and the Joint Chiefs of Staff "to give immediate consideration to General MacArthur's proposals for a military offensive." Later that same morning Harriman conferred with Johnson, the service secretaries, and the Joint Chiefs and "within twenty-four hours approval had been given to the plan discussed for an offensive in Korea."[46] The amphibious counterthrust was on, although the exact time and place had yet to be determined.

MAO DECIDES AGAINST EARLY INVOLVEMENT

Meanwhile, in Beijing, Chinese leaders had indeed recognized the vulnerability of the American position in early August, but Mao, acting consistently with the view that he would not assist Kim and Stalin, decided to put off a decision regarding intervention until a later date. Mao had convened a Politburo meeting on August 4 to discuss the current situation and China's options. Several issues were on the agenda, including a cable from Manchurian party chief Gao Gang, the implications of MacArthur's visit to Taiwan, and the B-29 deployment. Although the public response to MacArthur's visit was a "mild" editorial comment the next day, which declared that the visit represented no threat to China, it was apparent that Chinese leaders took the implied threat very seriously.[47]

The Politburo had discussed the full ramifications of Chinese entry into combat against American forces, including responses to the possible U.S. use of atomic weapons. Plainly, Chinese intelligence had learned of the planned, nuclear-configured, B-29 deployment to Guam and had begun to consider the possibilities. Nevertheless, Zhou Enlai argued in favor of early intervention, declaring "in order to win the war, China's strength must be added to the struggle." In his view, "if China's strength were added, the whole international situation could be changed," suggesting that an early commitment of Chinese forces could bring victory.[48]

Mao, however, took a different position. While making clear his agreement on the need to intervene, and accepting Stalin's suggestion of employing "volunteers," he put off a decision on when to send troops until later. Said Mao:

> If the U.S. imperialists won the war, they would become more arrogant and would threaten us. We should not fail to assist the Koreans. We must lend them our hands in the form of sending our military volunteers there. The timing could be further decided, but we have to prepare for this.[49]

The Politburo also discussed a cable from Gao Gang that the troops dispatched on July 13 had all arrived in Manchuria. Following the Politburo conference, Mao instructed Gao Gang to prepare the NBDA "for battle by the first 10 days of September" on the grounds that it "seems unlikely that operational tasks will be assigned to these troops in August." In other words, there would be no early entry. Gao was instructed to "convene a meeting of the cadres at the corps and division levels in the second 10 days of the month [of August] and there instruct them on the purpose and significance of the operation and its general direction."[50]

Gao Gang duly convened a high-level cadre conference on August 13 and 14, to discuss requirements for intervention. At this conference, the issue of U.S. use of atomic weapons was discussed further and it was decided that China should not be deterred by the bomb. It was generally agreed that China should adopt a strategy of forward defense and to meet the Americans in Korea, rather than attempt to defend at the Chinese border. But it was also recognized that "it would be very difficult for the army to complete its preparations" by the end of August as required by the August 5 directive.[51] After receiving the report of this conference, Mao agreed that "the deadline . . . can be extended up to the end of September."[52] Thus, it would not be until some time in October that Mao would be prepared to send substantial numbers of "volunteers" into Korea, and then only after he had had an opportunity to discuss the issue fully with Stalin and probe the prospects of a settlement with Truman.

MAO PROBES UNSUCCESSFULLY FOR A DIPLOMATIC SETTLEMENT

Until August 17 the United States had offered only veiled, public hints about its war aims and Mao had been content to explore settlement possibilities through third parties, mainly Britain, India, and the Soviet Union. All that changed with Ambassador Warren Austin's statement before the U.N. Security Council on that date. Austin's declaration that the United States sought a "free, unified, and independent" Korea, not merely a return to the status quo ante bellum, immediately prompted Beijing to attempt to move on its own toward a settlement through the U.N. Both Moscow and Washington, however, in different ways quashed Beijing's bid, leaving Mao no alternative but to prepare for intervention. It is to a survey of the diplomatic context that we now turn.

Ambassador Austin's statement that the United States would seek the unification of Korea under U.N. auspices had preempted frenetic diplomatic maneuvering by Britain and India, as well as internal argument within the Departments of State and Defense, over the question of American war aims. Washington's careful silence regarding war aims in Korea and unilateral policy toward Taiwan had created growing concern in U.N. circles. There was also sentiment within the Department of State, expressed by George Kennan and others, for a return to the status quo ante bellum as a war aim, on the grounds that going beyond the 38th parallel "might" force a Soviet or Chinese reaction, thus enlarging the conflict.[53] (These internal deliberations within the administration will be explored in detail in the next chapter.)

London and Delhi also argued for this policy, but for additional reasons. For London the complicating factor was Washington's policy toward Taiwan. British leaders were concerned that a war aim of Korean unification would lead to Chinese involvement and compromise British policy toward Beijing. Britain, associated with the United States in Korea, would find itself drawn willy-nilly into an anti-Chinese position, raising concerns regarding the security of Hong Kong, trade with China, and completion of recognition negotiations. British leaders therefore sought to forestall this unpleasant prospect by arguing for a return to the status quo ante bellum. They also favored Chinese entry into the United Nations.

London's concern to avoid impairment of its close and beneficial relationship to Washington, however, led British leaders circumspectly to encourage India to explore possible solutions to the conflict along these lines, a task that Nehru was more than happy to undertake for his own reasons.[54] The People's Republic had been forthright in expressing its intention to carry the revolution to semi-autonomous Tibet, a development Nehru sought to forestall by being instrumental in effecting China's entry into the United Nations. Presumably, Beijing could be more effectively constrained from invading Tibet as a member of the U.N. Security Council than as an outsider.

Thus, in early July, India informally put forth a two-part proposal designed to serve multiple ends. China would be admitted into the U.N., which would permit the return of the Soviet Union. For this to occur, however, there would have to be prior agreement by both powers to a cease-fire and withdrawal of North Korean forces from the South, followed by nationwide elections under U.N. supervision.[55] Beijing agreed to both parts of this formula, but Moscow refused to agree to any prior conditions.[56]

These responses immediately prompted George Kennan to note the existence of "a serious difference of policy between the Soviet and Chinese Communist Governments," which possibly offered a way out of the growing Korean morass. At the very least, he said, we could put the Soviets in "an embarrassing position" were we to "favor and achieve the admission of the Chinese Communists to the UN and the Security Council under some understanding which involved Chinese Communist support for a settlement of the Korean affair along the lines the Indians had suggested." He was, however, "shouted down on this."[57]

As an aside, it is not at all clear that Kennan had seen or been aware of the new strategy embodied in NSC-68. He certainly had not been involved in its formulation. Acheson had sent him on a tour of Latin America during February and March when drafts of the new strategy were being circulated in the department. It was a journey Kennan found "anything but pleasant." Whether involved or not, however, it is clear that Kennan was diametrically opposed to the strategy whose original concept had been his own.[58]

Stalin, of course, as we have seen so many times in this history, sought to have it both ways, cabling Zhou Enlai that "we agree with the opinion of the Chinese comrades regarding the mediation of India on the question of the entry of People's China into the membership of the UN," but he refused to take any serious steps to bring the conflict to an end.[59] In truth, to have done so would have been contradictory to his own strategy of prodding China into conflict with the United States.

Rebuffed, Nehru watered down his formula to make it more palatable to Stalin. In letters to Washington and Moscow on July 13, he changed his proposal from requiring prior Soviet and Chinese agreement on cease-fire, withdrawal, and elections, as a prerequisite to Chinese admission, to merely granting Beijing admission outright accompanied by agreement of the two communist powers to "informally explore" means to bring the war to an end and arrive at a permanent solution to the Korean problem. In other words, Stalin's rejection had persuaded Nehru to turn his proposal inside out. Stalin, of course, was more than happy to agree to this "formula," for it committed him to nothing.

Cleverly, Stalin published Nehru's letter and his own response before Acheson had a chance to reply, ensuring that there would be no agreement along these lines, even while placing himself on record as seeking both an end to the conflict and the admission of Beijing into the U.N. And Acheson did refuse Nehru's proposal on the grounds that it would mean that the United States would be forced to "pay a substantial price for termination of

Soviet aggression in Korea," which was, moreover, a bad bargain. Nehru's proposal would simply amount to Chinese entry into the U.N. in exchange for nothing more than a return to square one in Korea, with no real guarantee of a long-term peaceful outcome.[60] Outmaneuvered, Washington had been placed in the position of seeming to reject an early termination of hostilities, which heightened concerns in London and Delhi.

The wrangling in the United Nations provided an opening for Moscow to sow further confusion. On August 1, despite all earlier proclamations that the Soviet Union would boycott the U.N. until Beijing had been admitted and Taiwan expelled, Stalin returned his representative Jacob Malik to the U.N. to assume the position of Security Council president, a position that rotated monthly among the members of the council. From that position, through the month of August, he carried on what can best be described as a procedural guerrilla warfare campaign designed to confuse the issues and immobilize the Security Council in its deliberations.

Malik refused to accept or acknowledge any Soviet responsibility for Pyongyang's actions, declaring the conflict a "civil war," which evaded the issue of who attacked whom. He also refused to recognize the validity of all resolutions passed since the Soviet walkout in January, especially the Security Council resolutions of June 25 and 27, which committed the U.N. to oppose North Korean aggression in Korea. Instead, elaborating on the Indian proposal, on August 4 he put forward a so-called settlement formula that denied the relevance of all previous Security Council action. He proposed a cease-fire and return to the status quo ante bellum followed by a U.N. invitation to China and North and South Korea to discuss the conflict. American and British representatives, responding with their own guerrilla tactics, contested on procedural grounds, arguing that the issue before the council was North Korean aggression, which must receive priority.[61]

In the heat of these diplomatic exchanges, President Truman decided to make public American objectives in Korea. The announcement came in Ambassador Austin's statement before the Security Council on August 17, and followed efforts to canvass and formulate views of U.N. members, especially those of the U.N. Committee on Korea (UNCOK). The views of UNCOK, in particular, were solidly in favor of unification, recommending that "the commander of the UN security force . . . assume full responsibility for the administration of North Korea." Within twelve months of the cessation of hostilities, "free and democratic" elections would be organized and held under U.N. auspices.[62]

For Mao, the revelation of Washington's war aim clearly indicated that the United States had ruled out stopping at the 38th parallel and returning to the status quo ante bellum. Austin's speech revealed that the United States was bent on the defeat and destruction of Kim Il-sung's regime and the es-

tablishment of a unified, pro-American Korea, an outcome wholly unacceptable to China. Moreover, Austin's announcement, combined with the growing stalemate around Pusan, signaled that Washington's counterblow was
imminent.

MAO'S TRIAL BALLOONS

Up to this point, China had taken no position on the outcome of the war,
other than generally supporting Kim Il-sung. Austin's declaration meant
that it was time to engage the United States on the issue, particularly as Chinese forces were not yet prepared to undertake large-scale military action. At
best, engagement could lead to a mutually satisfactory, peaceful settlement.
At worst, it could provide more time to prepare. Therefore, on August 20, in
a cable from Zhou Enlai to the U.N., Beijing moved to indicate its "concern"
regarding the "solution of the Korean question." Zhou declared that the conflict "must and can be settled peacefully." Seconding Malik's proposal of
August 4, Zhou demanded that Beijing be represented "when the Korean
question is discussed in the Security Council," but did not demand that Beijing be seated as a permanent member in place of Taipei. In the meantime,
Zhou urged, the Security Council must terminate U.S. bombing "in North
Korea."[63]

If Mao and the Chinese leadership hoped or expected Washington to respond to this offer to settle the Korean conflict peacefully, or even to haggle
over terms, they would be disappointed. Washington ignored the telegram
entirely. Of course, it would have been inconsistent with the new strategy of
containment to have probed for differences between the two communist
powers. Nor was Washington interested in terminating hostilities before its
now proclaimed war aims were fulfilled.

Instead, it was Moscow that responded, and in a manner that only served
to confuse the meaning of the Chinese overture. Two days after Zhou's cable
reached the U.N., Soviet delegate Malik rose before the Security Council to
declare that "any continuation of the Korean War will lead inevitably to a
widening of the conflict with consequences, the responsibility for which will
lie with the United States." The proximity of Malik's sharp attack on the
United States with Zhou's cabled demands tended to suggest that the two
states had coordinated their response, when that was probably not the case,
but Washington had no intention of finding out. Austin and Sir Gladwyn
Jebb, British representative to the U.N., immediately charged Malik with
"Hitler like tactics," focusing on Malik and ignoring Zhou's telegram.[64]

Zhou was not deterred, however. He next attempted to float a trial balloon
over Taiwan, both publicly and through the well-used back channel of In-

dia's ambassador to Beijing, K. M. Panikkar. As noted above, Panikkar's role as messenger between Washington and Beijing had been well established. (It was only later, when Panikkar conveyed Zhou's warnings against the movement of U.S. troops to the Yalu, that Acheson would discredit the Indian ambassador as being untrustworthy and his message, therefore, unreliable, a classic case of "shooting the messenger.") On August 24, following a discussion with Zhou, Panikkar cabled his chief Girja Bajpai:

> It might be possible to persuade Peking not to press issue Formosa if assurances could be obtained from US on one of following alternatives: (a) after Korean situation was eased, US would withdraw protection Kuomintang remnants in Formosa or (b) if UN would accept Peking as sole representative China or (c) if UK, India and other powers which had recognized Peking could give assurances that they would use their influence to see that US did not aim … at keeping Kuomintang remnants in Formosa permanently under US protection.[65]

271

Bajpai provided Henderson with excerpts of Panikkar's reporting cable for transmission to Acheson. The Indian ambassador felt that there was "no reason to think that China has any immediate intention to attack Taiwan. Apart from all other considerations she feels that her very substantial gains may themselves be jeopardized if a world war now intervenes and confuses issue. Also she realizes that while she has great powers of resistance, she cannot carry on a war against America. Chinese leaders are therefore determined to avoid a war unless they are forced into it by a direct threat to their authority on the mainland."[66]

Publicly, on August 24, Zhou sent another cable to the U.N., protesting U.S. policy toward Taiwan as "an open encroachment of the territory of the People's Republic of China." Zhou declared that Beijing was "determined to liberate from the tentacles of the United States aggressors Taiwan and all other territories belonging to China." He was placing before the U.N. Security Council the case of Formosa and urged that body to "condemn the United States Government for its criminal act in the armed invasion of the territory of China and to take immediate measures to bring about the complete withdrawal of all the United States armed invading forces from Taiwan."[67]

In the span of five days, Zhou had sent two cables to the U.N., the first to register China's interest in a peaceful settlement in Korea and the second to place before that body its claims on Taiwan. Obscured by Malik's obstreperous attack of August 22, Beijing was clearly indicating its willingness to work through the U.N. to settle both issues. As we now know, Mao had in fact already called off the invasion of Taiwan, while pressing forward with preparations for a possible confrontation in Korea. Was Mao making one last attempt to keep the door open for achieving his grand strategy? Were the two cables an implicit suggestion for a trade-off, that if Washington were willing to withdraw support from Taiwan, Beijing would not intervene in Korea? Or had Mao already closed the door to negotiations and was he simply attempting to buy additional time to complete preparations for an intervention?

President Truman, continuing to ignore China's expression of interest in a peaceful settlement of the war in Korea, responded promptly regarding Taiwan by restating his original position. Zhou's démarche actually offered Truman the opportunity he had been waiting for to place the issue of Formosa under U.N. protection. The decision to deploy the Seventh Fleet on June 27 had been unilateral; referring Formosa to the U.N. would multilateralize it. The next day Ambassador Austin sent a letter to U.N. Secretary-General Trygve Lie reiterating President Truman's policy decision of June 27 and its further elaboration on July 19, in which the president sought to remove any doubt about American "intentions regarding Formosa."

In an effort to refute the allegations made by Zhou Enlai, the president declared that "the United States has not encroached on the territory of China, nor has the United States taken aggressive action against China." The action taken by the United States on June 27, the president said, "was an impartial neutralizing action addressed both to the forces on Formosa and to those on the mainland." It was designed to keep the peace and was "therefore, in full accord with the spirit of the Charter of the United Nations." The president stressed that the United States had "no designs on Formosa."[68]

Then the president set forth the legal grounds for U.S. action toward Formosa. "The actual status of the island," he said, "is that it is territory taken from Japan by the victory of the Allied Forces in the Pacific. Like other such territories, its legal status cannot be fixed until there is international action to determine its future. The Chinese Government was asked by the Allies to take the surrender of the Japanese forces on the island. That is the reason the Chinese are there now." Stressing the record of U.S. friendship for "the Chinese people," the president declared that the United States "would welcome United Nations consideration of the case of Formosa. We would approve a full United Nations investigation here or on the spot. We believe that United Nations consideration would contribute to a peaceful, rather than a forceable solution of that problem."

But not yet. While holding out the carrot of possible U.N. disposition of the issue of Formosa, agreeing to place the case before the Security Council, the president went on to say that the United Nations should not take up the case until after the Korean War had ended. "We do not believe," he said, "that the Security Council need be or will be diverted from its consideration of the aggression against the Republic of Korea. There was a breach of the

272

peace in Korea.... If the Security Council wishes to study the question of Formosa we shall support and assist that study. Meanwhile, the President of the Security Council should discharge the duties of his office and get on with the item on the agenda, which is the Complaint of Aggression Against the Republic of Korea." Once peace was reestablished, he said, "even the most complex political questions [would be] susceptible of solution."

At this point, Truman went to some lengths to avoid Chinese political as well as military involvement in Korea. His plans for an amphibious landing behind North Korean lines, the decisive counterstroke of the war, were rapidly maturing. Now that North Korean forces were concentrated around the Pusan perimeter, MacArthur intended to strike at the earliest possible moment. Thus, even a mere discussion of Chinese proposals about a Korean settlement might have the unwanted consequence of delaying military action, and missing the opportunity to crush the North Korean armed forces. It is to the issue of Truman's continuing efforts to deter Chinese involvement in Korea until the decisive counterstroke, and then to compel Chinese involvement after it, that we now turn.

PART IV
EMERGENCE OF
A NEW WORLD ORDER

CHAPTER ELEVEN

Truman: From Deterrence to Compulsion

THE CRITICAL MOMENT of the war arrived at the end of August as MacArthur was moving with great speed and intensity to execute the decisive enveloping stroke that would destroy the NKA. As we have seen, this was also the moment that Mao, also realizing that the decisive moment had arrived, had attempted to insert China politically into the Korean issue, and Stalin had moved to close off any peaceful settlement. Washington had ignored Beijing's sally because it was imperative that the United States not be deflected from executing the decisive blow, but Washington could not ignore its allies, who were also intensely concerned about the prospect of global war.

All concerned anticipated and no doubt planned for a decisive U.S. counterstroke, which was expected in the near future. The end of August thus saw extensive activity along three lines of development, as the decisive moment approached. Stalin prodded Kim into an all-out drive to overrun Pusan, while attempting to block any Chinese opening to Washington. Truman strove to deter Mao from committing troops, while reaching an understanding with Britain and France regarding future actions. And Mao intensified his war preparations, while subtly exploring his options through Delhi's representatives.

Truman's concern to deter Beijing from entering the Korean conflict continued only until the successful strike at Inchon, which destroyed the NKA and opened up the possibility of unifying the peninsula under U.N. auspices. From that point, in late September, Truman would shift policy from deterrence to compulsion—from attempting to keep the Chinese out of the war to forcing them into it. Combating the Sino-Soviet menace was the strategy

277

called for in NSC-68 and Truman would act consistently with its precepts, disdaining any opportunity to divide Moscow and Beijing. Ironically, Stalin paralleled this strategy by pressing Mao into conflict with the United States as the means of subordinating China to the Soviet Union, the object of his own strategy. Mao, ultimately, would intervene, but only on his own terms— after the NKA had been destroyed and United States' forces were moving to unify the country.

Washington's war-fighting strategy was divided into two broad phases, the defensive and the offensive. In the defensive phase, until the defeat of the NKA, the objective was to prevent intervention by third parties, which in the first instance meant Moscow, whose entry would transform the Korean war into a world war, and in the second Beijing, whose early commitment of troops could spell defeat for the United States. Then, based on the strategic concept set forth in War Plan SL-17, MacArthur was to withdraw to the Pusan beachhead, overextend the invading force, and strike behind enemy lines, severing vital logistics and communications sinews to defeat the NKA. At that point, once the NKA was destroyed, the war would move from the defensive to the offensive phase.

U.S. policy toward the Soviet Union remained constant in both phases. From early in the conflict the Truman administration had decided that Soviet intervention would signify the outbreak of global war. This position was subsequently codified in NSC-76 of July 27.[1] In the event of overt Soviet intervention, the United States would curtail its involvement, perhaps withdrawing entirely from the Korean peninsula, which could not be a decisive battlefield in a global war against the Soviet Union, and activate its contingency plans for World War III. No doubt the administration made sure that Moscow learned of this fundamental decision through leaks to spies or in other ways, for it was the epitome of a high-risk, zero-sum deterrence strategy, and it was vital that Stalin understand Truman's intention to limit the conflict to avoid miscalculating American resolve.

Should China intervene, on the other hand, particularly in the second phase, Washington would respond much differently. According to NSC-73/4 (finally adopted on August 24, four days after Mao's initiative, but under consideration since July 1), the United States would continue to pursue its objectives in Korea as long as there was a "reasonable chance" of success. In other words, Truman had made a command decision to engage in limited war with China in Korea long before that was an immediate prospect. Indeed, the Truman administration constructed the options for China, which were also zero-sum: either acquiesce in complete Korean unification by American military power, under "UN auspices," or intervene to prevent it.

The meaning of "reasonable chance" in NSC-73 was left vague, giving the president considerable latitude to continue military action even after

Chinese forces had entered. Although still determined to prevent any escalation to a major war, according to the directive, Washington would be prepared "to take appropriate air and naval action outside Korea against Communist China."[2] This particular formulation, we shall see, would become the nub of the disagreement between Truman and MacArthur when China did intervene, for despite this provision Truman had no intention of expanding the war with China outside the Korean peninsula.

These different considerations regarding possible Soviet or Chinese entry into the Korean conflict meant, in effect, that while Soviet intervention in Korea would signal a new, global war, Chinese intervention would mean continuation of the existing one. The threat of Soviet intervention was, therefore, of less concern for military operations in Korea than was the threat of Chinese intervention. In the defensive phase, Chinese intervention could defeat U.S. plans, and Truman, sensitive to this possibility, strove to deter Beijing from involvement. But in the offensive phase, once the NKA was defeated, Truman would dismiss not only the rising crescendo of threats from China, but also the actual presence of Chinese troops in Korea, to press forward with his objectives, until Chinese and American forces were fully engaged.

MAO, STALIN, MACARTHUR, AND INCHON

Quite ironically, on August 23, the same day that MacArthur in Tokyo was delivering his spellbinding oration to assembled officers involved in the decision-making and planning for the amphibious counterstroke behind NKA lines at Inchon, Mao Zedong in Beijing had come to the identical conclusion as to the target for the counteroffensive. This was the second of the four moments of the war when Mao declined to authorize, and Stalin declined to press for, Chinese intervention that could have tipped the balance decisively in favor of North Korea. At the very least, such intervention would have forced the United States to alter its plans for a counterattack at Inchon. Of course, this was a moment that American leaders also recognized and which partly animated discussions about Inchon.

Although MacArthur had informed the Joint Chiefs that he intended to deliver a decisive amphibious counterstroke at the end of September, in the interests of security the U.N. commander had been noticeably reticent about discussing his specific plans with them. By mid-August, growing constraints on force availability for the landing, Navy objections to the site of Inchon, and concern that the landing could become a debacle prompted the chiefs to dispatch two of their number to Tokyo to "review" MacArthur's plans. More than a review, the visit of Army Chief of Staff General J. Lawton Collins and Navy Chief of Staff Admiral Forrest Sherman, from August 21 to 24, was an unsuccessful attempt to dissuade MacArthur from executing the amphibious attack at Inchon.

The crucial briefing occurred on the afternoon of August 23. Navy planners under Admiral James Doyle, commander of the proposed amphibious assault, led off the discussion. Lieutenant Commander Arlie G. Capps, gunnery officer of Admiral James Doyle's staff, declared: "We drew up a list of every natural and geographic handicap—and Inchon had 'em all." Doyle's men proceeded to express serious concern with the difficult and narrow sea approaches to Inchon restricting ship maneuverability, the great tidal variations in excess of thirty feet limiting landing operations to only a few hours at high tide, the extensive, impassable mud flats at low tide, and the twelve-foot-high sea walls the Marines would have to scale to gain entry to the port city. In closing, Admiral Doyle offered the unenthusiastic assessment that

"the best I can say is that Inchon is not impossible."[3]

General Collins, chief critic of the Inchon plan, then expressed his concerns. He was worried about the tides for another reason—they determined the only time for a landing and thus opened up the possibility of a trap. The seasonal tidal action saw low tides between May and August followed by rough tidal water between October and April. Only in September, the transition season, and in particular on September 15, would the tidal action favor a large-scale landing with gentle flowing waters and sufficiently high, thirty-foot tides to permit landing by LSTs (landing ship-tank) against the sea walls protecting the city. Collins's critique was trenchant. Raising the specter of an ambush, he said:

> Of course, an alert enemy, familiar with these local conditions, could read the same charts and arrive at the same optimal dates for a flanking amphibious attack. He thus could be prepared to bomb or shell the approaching troop convoys moving through the restricted channels.[4]

Collins was also concerned that General Walker would be unable to link up with the Inchon landing force in time to prevent a debacle. He observed that "in many instances, throughout military history the division of forces beyond supporting distances has led to disastrous defeats."[5] To ensure mutual reinforcement, Collins proposed an envelopment closer to Pusan, at Kunsan, where there would be no tidal constraints. Surveys had been taken there, and it was found that the beaches were satisfactory at all times. In the course of discussion, other landing sites were offered, at Posun-Myong thirty miles south of Seoul, and even at Chinnampo, Pyongyang's port.

MacArthur's chief planner, General Edwin "Pinkey" Wright, voiced still another concern. The original forces tabbed for the landing, the Fifth Marines RCT and the Second Infantry Division, had been diverted for employment in defense of the Pusan perimeter. Although the Marines were scheduled to be withdrawn, Wright did not believe that the proposed substitute force for the Second Division, the heavily cannibalized Seventh Division, would be ready in time. In his view, "any plan based on use of the 7th Division would be 'visionary and impracticable.' "[6] He proposed that the landing be postponed until the next satisfactory tide, on October 11. By that time sufficient replacements would have arrived to fill out the division's ranks.

MacArthur, who had sat quietly throughout the discussion, which had lasted more than an hour, rose to respond. In what has been universally acclaimed as a masterful and eloquent exposition of his plan, but which unfortunately was not recorded for posterity, MacArthur effectively rebutted all perceived difficulties and dismissed proposed alternatives in explaining why only Inchon could be the target, how he would respond if it were a trap, how only September 15 could be the date for the landing, and how the Seventh Division would be ready.

Admitting the difficulties presented by an amphibious landing at Inchon, MacArthur, turning Admiral Doyle's assessment inside out, declared that they were indeed *not* "insuperable." He believed that the Navy had never let him down before and would not let him down now. Perhaps, he said, "he had more confidence in the Navy than the Navy had in itself."[7] MacArthur believed that the North Koreans would regard an Inchon landing as impossible, which meant that he would have an element of surprise in his favor. This same factor would militate against the possibility that his forces would be sailing into a trap. Acknowledging the possibility of a trap, however, he said:

> If my estimate is inaccurate and should I run into a defense with which I cannot cope, I will be there personally and will immediately withdraw our forces before they are committed to a bloody setback. The only loss then will be to my professional reputation. But Inchon will not fail. Inchon will succeed. And it will save 100,000 lives.[8]

Addressing the issue of dividing and thus fatally weakening his forces, MacArthur declared that "the bulk of the enemy" was committed to the Pusan perimeter. There were thus insufficient reserves to contend with a flank attack at Inchon. Moreover, the main force was too distant to recover and defend against the landing and naval air support and ship bombardment would effectively seal off Inchon from attempted reinforcement. This point led directly to discussion of proposed alternative landing sites. Delivering a lesson in military strategy, MacArthur forcefully clarified the theory of envelopment. "The amphibious landing is the most powerful tool we have. To employ it properly, we must strike hard and deeply into enemy territory."[9]

It was, he said, "the deep envelopment, based on surprise, which severs the enemy's supply lines [that] is and always has been the most decisive maneuver of war. A short envelopment, which fails to envelop and leaves the en-

281

emy's supply system intact, merely divides your own forces and can lead to heavy loss and even jeopardy."[10] That was why Kunsan, Posun-Myong, or Chinnampo would not do. Responding to Collins's suggestion, he said that an envelopment at Kunsan would be too shallow, would not sever the NKA supply lines, and was close enough to the perimeter to allow the enemy to recover. Posun-Myong was too far from Seoul, the main objective, and Chinnampo was too far north. Both of the latter would offer a tempting opportunity for Chinese intervention.

On timing, MacArthur insisted that the strike must occur as soon as possible. If they did not act at the first available opportunity, he feared that the Russians and the Chinese would send supplies to strengthen the NKA and turn the conflict into a war of attrition. If that occurred, U.N. cohesion would suffer and confidence in the United States would wane. "If there were one vital spot in the enemy's line of communications, the Seoul-Inchon area was that spot."[11] That was the place to strike. According to the tide tables, the earliest time for a landing there was September 15. That was the moment to strike. Even a delay of one month until the next high tide on October 11 would be too late. Winter would be setting in and there would be insufficient time for the "pursuit and breakout" phase of the operation. By that time, too, the North Koreans might have taken countermeasures, such as the laying of extensive mine fields. Thus far, there had been only sporadic indications of mine-laying efforts.

Finally, on the question of the Seventh Division's readiness, MacArthur had for some weeks been diverting a portion of all arriving replacements to the division to ensure that it would be at full strength for Inchon. Still, at this point, the division was well under strength. In desperation, MacArthur decided to impress able-bodied South Korean civilians to fill out the division's ranks. Over the next several weeks, some 8,637 Korean civilians would be sent to Japan for incorporation into the division. They would be paired with American servicemen in what MacArthur loftily termed a buddy system. By early September, when the Seventh Division embarked for Inchon, it would have a full, if not thoroughly trained, complement of 24,845 troops.[12]

MacArthur's impressive exposition had been persuasive. Of the two members of the Joint Chiefs attending, Admiral Sherman had been convinced that Inchon was the proper target even before the briefing, but Collins still had lingering reservations.[13] He insisted that the Kunsan alternative be open for selection if things went wrong and, in fact, that option would be included in the final JCS cable of approval to MacArthur.[14] MacArthur, however, never wavered from his focus on Inchon-Seoul, the "vital spot" in the North Korean logistical system.

Strikingly, Mao had also recognized the vulnerability of the NKA at Inchon, but declined to take any action in support of Kim Il-sung. For Mao, late

August was the second moment of the war when he had the opportunity to assist Kim—if not to victory, then to avoid disastrous defeat—and he demurred. Chinese intelligence had, of course, been following the evolution of the war. It was already clear that the NKA would fail to drive U.N. forces into the sea at Pusan, although Pyongyang was preparing for what would be a final attempt. Ambassador Austin's declaration of August 17 made plain that the United States would not accept a return to the status quo ante bellum, but would seek the unification of Korea under U.N. auspices. Intelligence indicators, moreover, suggested that MacArthur was soon planning to execute an amphibious counterstroke somewhere along the coast with the intention of encircling and destroying the NKA.

For Mao the crucial questions were: When and where would the attack come and should China do anything to counter it? Chinese analysts noted the concentration of large numbers of ships and landing craft in Japan, and the assignment of the First Marine and Seventh Army Divisions to a newly formed organization, the X Corps. These forces, they observed, were not being employed to reinforce the Eighth Army's position around Pusan, nor were they being deployed for the defense of Japan. Instead, they were undergoing "crash combat training," an indication, they believed, that the war soon "might escalate with landing operations."[15]

Chinese intelligence identified five places suitable for a landing. These were Inchon, Chinnampo, and Kunsan on the west coast and Hungnam and Wonsan on the east. Of these "all agreed on one point: there was a great possibility for an Inchon landing by the enemy." Inchon was "the most favorable point." A landing there would "cut off north-south strategic communication between Pyongyang and the offensive forces in the Naktong River area, and interrupt logistical supplies to the Korean People's Army." A landing at Inchon would permit adoption of "a strategy of surrounding and attacking the Korean People's Army from north and south."[16]

Lei Ying-fu, Zhou Enlai's military secretary, reported these findings to the premier on the evening of August 23. Zhou promptly called Mao, who wanted an immediate detailed briefing, which was arranged for that very evening. During the course of the briefing, Mao acknowledged that the war would be "protracted, complicated and tough," but, he believed, it would be limited. In his view, "America was not yet ready" for a third world war. In response to Lei's conclusion that "the enemy would most likely land at Inchon," Mao asked about the "geographic and hydrographic conditions of those possible landing points in Korea."

If Mao had in fact homed in on Inchon as the target for an American amphibious landing, then his perceptive inquiry regarding "geographic and hydrographic conditions" there would lead quickly to the answer of the key question of when an attack could occur. Checking the tide tables, as General

283

Collins had surmised an alert enemy would do, Mao would have learned that the only time for large-scale, amphibious landings was during the high tides of September 15 and October 11. This information, combined with intelligence of the "intense activity" of American preparations in Japan, as ships, men, and supplies concentrated at Kobe, Sasebo, and Yokohama, would clearly suggest the earlier date.[17] At the close of the meeting, Mao "emphasized again that a possible American army landing at Inchon was indeed a very important strategic issue to which we needed to pay close attention."[18]

The crucial question now was: Should China take any action? Over the next several days the Chinese leadership debated the issue. One point was clear: the war would soon enter a new and dangerous phase for North Korea, and China must accelerate preparations to be ready for any eventuality. Thus, on August 27, Mao instructed Peng Dehuai to triple the force in Manchuria from the four corps already deployed, to twelve, a total of thirty-six divisions, some 700,000 troops. This involved the movement of two additional corps, the Ninth and the Nineteenth Army Corps. No decision on the use of this force would be made until the end of September, presumably when preparations would have been substantially completed.[19]

The Chinese leadership was divided over the necessity of entering the conflict. Some, represented by corps commanders Xie Fang, Deng Hua, and Hong Xuezhi, urged early action to assist North Korea as soon as American forces crossed the 38th parallel, and perhaps before, "to maintain the initiative on the battlefield." Their recommendation was based on the assumption that American forces would execute an amphibious landing, placing the NKA in a "very difficult situation." They believed that China should take preemptive action, but only in conjunction with Soviet support.

Their recommendation was not, therefore, unconditional. It was based on prior negotiation with the Soviet Union of an agreement to fully equip Chinese forces with all necessary weapons, including artillery, anti-aircraft, tank, and anti-tank weapons. Moreover, the provision of Soviet air support to cover Chinese troops in battle was seen as crucial. With such Soviet support, they were prepared to recommend commitment of the entire force, the Thirteenth, Ninth, and Nineteenth Army Corps, but advised the delay in commitment of Chinese armies without Soviet air support.[20] They were, in short, willing to contribute men, if Moscow contributed materiel, in a joint defense of North Korea.

Other leaders opposed Chinese involvement under any conditions. Lin Biao, and no doubt others as well, opposed involvement on the grounds that China was too weak and America too strong. Lin refused (on medical grounds) Mao's offer to command the planned Chinese volunteer force in Korea. He suggested that the NKA fight alone and, in the event of defeat, Kim Il-sung revert to a defensive strategy of conducting guerrilla warfare in the mountains. Mao himself was publicly defiant in his speeches, arguing that the United States was weaker than it appeared, but he, too, declined to press for an early commitment.[21]

In short, a familiar range of opinion evolved. Some argued in favor of early involvement in a policy of forward defense beyond China's border, while others wished to wait, and defend only when the enemy reached the border, or actually attacked the country. The issue of Soviet support was central to the discussion. The upshot of this pre-Inchon discussion within the Chinese leadership was that Mao allowed the moment for early intervention to pass. It was true, as Chen Jian notes, that there had as yet been no request from Kim Il-sung for military assistance, although some contacts had occurred at this time, during which Mao passed on a warning about Inchon, but the absence of a request did not shape the discussions in Beijing.[22]

The most unusual development, however, was the absence of pressure from Stalin, which contrasted sharply with the weeks immediately after the outbreak of the war. Between the outbreak of the war and mid-July, as we have seen, Stalin had prodded Mao several times to deploy troops to the Yalu, but between mid-July and Inchon there is in the extant record no evidence of any attempt by Stalin to press Mao to commit troops to Korea. Aside from two cables regarding the timetable for the training of Chinese pilots and notification of the dispatch of air defense personnel to China, the record is bare.[23] It is as if Stalin, having prodded Mao to deploy troops to the Yalu, was then content to wait for the right moment to apply pressure on him to intervene.

In other words, there is no record of Stalin pressing Mao to intervene during the first two moments of U.S. vulnerability that we have noted, in late July and late August, when Chinese intervention could have been decisive. In the sense of the dog that doesn't bark in a famous Sherlock Holmes mystery, the failure of Stalin to press Mao to commit troops in late July and late August provides added confirmation of the thesis that he was not interested in victory for North Korea. Had Stalin sought a North Korean victory, the record would be filled with entreaties to Mao to commit troops in both periods. Only after Inchon, when American forces had destroyed the NKA, did Stalin begin to generate great pressure on Mao to commit troops. Stalin was active, however, on another front, in attempts to prevent any Sino-American dialogue, as we shall see below.

The notion that Stalin was awaiting the North Korean debacle also comes through in his cable to Kim Il-sung, a cable marked by its complete disregard of the growing peril facing the NKA. In a message of August 28, on the eve of the NKA's final, major assault on the perimeter, Stalin hailed Kim's "brilliant success." He had "no doubt that in the soonest time the interventionists will be driven out of Korea with ignominy." He comforted Kim not to be "embarrassed by the fact that he does not have solid successes in the war against the interventionists, that the successes are sometimes interrupted by delays in the advance or even by some local set-backs. In such a war continuous successes do not occur."

Stalin compared the Korean conflict with the Allied intervention in Russia of 1919 and World War II, noting that "the Russians also did not have continuous successes during the civil war and even more during the war with Germany." He said that Kim's "greatest success . . . is that Korea has now become the most popular country in the world," whose example other enslaved peoples will imitate. Stalin also gave small comfort with the notion that "Korea is not alone now, that it has allies, who are rendering and will render it aid." The position of the Russians "during the Anglo-French-American intervention in 1919 was several times worse than the position of the Korean comrades at the present time."

Closing with a bit of impractical tactical advice, Stalin advised Kim "not to scatter the air force, but to concentrate it on the front." Employ the air force to deliver "decisive blows" against enemy troops, he advised, and use fighter planes to "defend the troops of the People's Army from the blows of the enemy planes as much as possible." In a revealing final comment, Stalin offered to "throw in" additional assault aircraft for the Korean Air Force, if necessary. Stalin's advice was nothing less than extraordinary, especially when one considers that at this point in the war, the Korean Air Force consisted of all of nineteen planes, the remnants of the force with which the NKA had begun the war!

What Kim needed most was more equipment, not "comforting" comparisons showing that the North Koreans were better off now than the Russians had been at other times past. In light of the NKA's desperate, pressing need for additional weapons, Kim's reply to Stalin must be understood as being nothing less than facetious. Replying three days later, he said: "we bring to you, our dear teacher, gratitude for the warm sympathy and advice. In the decisive period of the struggle of the Korean people we have received great *moral* support from you."[24]

Soviet and Chinese policy during the period from late August through mid-September can best be characterized as two onlookers watching while a cobra prepares to strike its victim. Stalin stood silent during these weeks leading up to Inchon, while Mao, realizing where and probably when the American landing would occur, also decided to stand back and await the outcome. Truman, however, was not privy to these calculations; understanding full well that Chinese intervention would force a change in the choice of landing place, or defeat the landing, he marshaled all the forces at his command in an effort to deter Chinese intervention before Inchon.

U.S. DETERRENCE PRIOR TO INCHON

The planned strike at Inchon was crucial, for unless it succeeded and the NKA were crushed quickly the United States would be faced with a long war of attrition leading to a stalemate, which would serve no strategic purpose. Because Inchon was so crucial and because only Beijing could thwart American plans, Truman was willing to offer Mao the carrot of a favorable future resolution on Taiwan, including placing the issue before the Security Council. But Truman's attempt to deter Mao from committing troops to Korea at this critical juncture produced unexpected reactions, both inside and outside of the administration. Internally, the Taiwan carrot brought a public but indirect objection from Secretary of Defense Johnson, a public but inadvertent objection from General MacArthur, and a most unusual response from Stalin.

Johnson's objection first surfaced through Secretary of the Navy Francis T. Matthews. In remarks inserted into a previously planned speech at the Boston Naval Shipyard on August 25, Matthews urged preventive war "to compel cooperation for peace." The United States, he declared, "should be willing to pay any price for a world at peace." In his view, "we have no choice other than to build our military power to the strength which will make it impossible for any enemy to overcome us." Indeed, our generation must become "aggressors for peace."[25] Both the White House and the State Department immediately "disowned" the speech, saying that Matthews's remarks had not been not cleared by them, but neither Matthews nor Johnson, who was believed to have instigated the idea, was disciplined, at least not immediately.[26]

MacArthur's objection to relinquishing Formosa immediately followed in the form of a message to the Chicago convention of the Veterans of Foreign Wars. The message, which was a close paraphrase of his June 14 cable to the JCS describing the strategic value of the island, explicitly denounced "those who advocate appeasement and defeatism in the Pacific." Formosa in the hands of a hostile power, he said, would "breach and neutralize our western Pacific defense system." MacArthur warned against any step that would "turn over the fruits of our Pacific victory to a potential enemy."[27]

MacArthur's letter had to be dealt with immediately because it was about to become public and contradict the president's proffered carrot to Beijing. In fact, MacArthur had sent the letter to the Department of the Army ten days earlier. At that time, of course, there was nothing "objectionable in it." Between the time he sent in his letter and its imminent publication, at the end of August, Truman had decided to placate Beijing. Since the letter had already been released to the press and was beyond recall, President Truman decided the most effective means of reemphasizing both his authority and his new (and temporary) policy position—the carrot to Beijing—was to demonstrate his control over his field commander and order the general to issue a formal statement "withdrawing" his message. This, the general did without public, but with considerable private, objection.

But the process of determining what was to be done brought to a climax the continuing rift between Secretary of State Acheson and Secretary of Defense Johnson, which, in a two-week-long struggle, resulted in the Defense Secretary's removal from office on September 12.[28] Johnson refused to order MacArthur to withdraw his statement, even after being instructed to do so. Truman ended up dictating the withdrawal letter personally to Johnson, and directing him to send it.

The defense secretary's insubordination, his opposition to limiting the war (as suggested in Matthews's remarks), combined with his behind-the-scenes efforts to orchestrate Secretary Acheson's ouster, was enough for the president to demand his resignation, and MacArthur's letter offered the opportunity. When the president informed him he would have to resign, however, Johnson procrastinated. When the president issued a point-blank demand, Johnson handed him an unsigned resignation letter, then wept when the president ordered him to sign it.[29] (The president immediately replaced Johnson with former Secretary of State and World War II JCS Chairman George C. Marshall.)

The fact was, however, that Truman and MacArthur did not disagree over policy toward Formosa, only over the president's current means of attempting to deter Beijing through its use as a carrot. Truman had no intention of allowing Taiwan to slip into Beijing's grasp, but was not broadcasting that fact, particularly at this delicate moment. Indeed, on September 8, concerned lest the president and secretary of state actually do what they proposed to do, the Joint Chiefs sent a memorandum to the secretary of defense emphatically reaffirming MacArthur's view and formally disagreeing with the proposal for a U.N. "solution" for Taiwan. In closing they said:

> The strategic consequences of a communist-dominated Formosa would be so seriously detrimental to United States security that, in the opinion of the Joint Chiefs of Staff, the United States should not permit the disposition of Formosa to be recommended in the first instance or decided by any commission or agency of the United Nations in which the United States has no voice.[30]

Hard upon the internal perturbations produced by Truman's offer of a "deterrence carrot" to Beijing, there came Zhou Enlai's complaint to the U.N. on August 28 that "United States planes bombed and strafed Chinese territory damaging buildings and vehicles and injuring and killing civilians."[31]

The planes involved were identified as F-51 fighters. The provocative attacks came at an inopportune time and threatened to undermine, if not contradict, Truman's attempt to deter China through the conciliatory proposal regarding Formosa. The questions were: What had actually happened and who was responsible?

Air Force Chief of Staff Vandenberg immediately investigated Zhou's charge, querying Lieutenant General Stratemeyer, Commander, Far East Air Force. Zhou had charged that three cities had been attacked: Linkiang, Tsian, and Talitzu, all located along the upper reaches of the Yalu River in the central sector of the Chinese–North Korean border. Vandenberg's investigation established that "no United States aircraft have at any time attacked the three cities mentioned." Pilots are issued flight plans with "specific instructions . . . concerning specific targets to be attacked," he said, and "General Stratemeyer has reported no attacks in violation of his instructions." In addition, "strike reports and strike photos indicate that no target instructions have been violated."[32]

But if the United States did not carry out the air strikes, who did, and why? Could MacArthur, given his antipathy to Communist China, have surreptitiously authorized the attacks and covered up incriminating evidence? In view of his preparations for the Inchon landing, which was only a little more than two weeks away, it was obviously not his doing. Provoking Chinese entry before Inchon would at the very least force a change of landing location, and perhaps more. The very last thing MacArthur would favor at the approaching critical moment of the Inchon landing was to precipitate the one event that could possibly deny him victory—the entry of Chinese forces.

If it was contradictory for the United States to incite the Chinese leadership with air attacks at the same moment that Truman was attempting to deter Mao from sending troops into Korea with the Taiwan carrot, then who would have had an interest in provoking a Sino-American clash over Korea at this critical moment? The definitive answer was, of course, elusive, but the circumstantial evidence pointed directly to Stalin and his North Korean allies. Aside from Stalin's obvious motive of provoking a clash as a small step toward his larger objective of bringing about a major Sino-American conflict, a little-noted event in Pearl Harbor some two weeks earlier suggested that he also possessed the means to carry out such a provocation.

Crew members of a U.S. Navy patrol plane reported at a news conference on August 12 that "their plane was attacked July 23 over the Formosa Strait by two American-built F-51 fighters 'with Communist markings.' " They observed that "the attacking planes carried the Red Star and blue circle markings of the North Korean Air Force."[33] The intriguing possibility suggested by this report was that Stalin had ordered the attacks on Chinese towns, using F-51s in Soviet possession, probably World War II lend-lease aircraft painted with U.S. markings, to destroy any possibility of a dialogue between Mao and Truman.

To keep the deterrence theme alive, the Truman administration decided to attempt to turn the incident to advantage, but in a way that made clear to Chinese leaders (and no one else) that the United States had not been responsible for the attacks. After initially denying U.S. responsibility, on September 1, Ambassador Austin declared before a surprised Security Council that there was "a possibility" that an American F-51 fighter "might have mistakenly violated the territory of Communist China on August 27, by strafing an airstrip at Antung [present-day Dandong]." Austin urged the Security Council "to send out a United Nations Commission to investigate the incident without delay." He promised that if there was evidence of a U.S. attack, then the United States would pay "damages" and take "appropriate disciplinary action" against those responsible.[34]

The flimsy basis for Austin's declaration of possible U.S. responsibility was an item in Vandenberg's investigation report, which had included the fact that on August 24 (not the 27th) a reconnaissance aircraft had "reported receiving anti-aircraft fire from gun positions across the Yalu River in the Antung (Manchuria) area."[35] This aircraft, however, was unarmed, carrying neither bombs nor bullets, and therefore could not have bombed or strafed anything, but that part of Vandenberg's report had not been revealed.

Austin's admission was an attempt to turn the tables on Stalin and kill two birds with one stone. On the one hand, the conciliatory gesture was designed to defuse Chinese hostility by admitting possible U.S. responsibility (even though Antung and the cities in Zhou's complaint were over 150 miles apart, which, of course, the Chinese understood); on the other hand, the proposal to send a commission to investigate was an obvious ploy to insert a U.N. presence at the major troop-crossing point from China to Korea. Antung lay on the Chinese side of the Yalu River bridges whose Korean terminus was Sinuiju.

The United States proposed placement of an "on the spot" investigation of the Chinese "complaint" on the Security Council agenda, which was passed 8 to 3, with the U.S. in favor. But before the vote Soviet representative Malik sought to muddle the issue by introducing a resolution "condemning the United States for the bombings," a pure propaganda ploy designed to upset the U.S. proposal. Indeed, in the debate preceding the vote, Malik devoted most of his long speech to an attack on the "monarcho-fascist government of Greece" for its persecution of Greek "democrats." In the end, although Malik's diversionary ploy failed and the proposal was passed, the Soviets' purpose was fulfilled. Beijing complained of additional attacks (probably also Soviet inspired), and no commission was sent.[36]

Not to be diverted, on August 30, Acheson said bluntly in a press conference that "the United States was trying to discourage the Chinese Communists from entering the Korean war by making it plain in every possible way that this Government felt no hostility toward the Chinese and had no aggressive intentions in the Far East."[37] President Truman followed Acheson's statement the next day, reemphasizing his carrot regarding Formosa.

> The Formosan situation as set out in my various messages is one for settlement—in the Japanese peace treaty with the allies who fought in the Japanese war and with those occupation forces—by those nations that have occupying forces in Japan now. Of course, it will not be necessary to keep the 7th Fleet in the Formosa Strait if the Korean thing is settled. That is a flank protection on our part for the United Nations forces.[38]

On September 1, Acheson and Truman continued efforts, privately and publicly, to dissuade Mao from taking any action that would defeat the coming landing at Inchon. (By this time, it was apparent that the NKA had begun an all-out drive to take Pusan, making it doubly vital that Mao not commit Chinese forces to the battle.) Privately, Acheson sent Ambassador Henderson a lengthy statement of his views for transmission through the Panikkar channel to Beijing. The United States was an old friend of the Chinese people, Acheson said, and was "not irrevocably committed" to support for or opposition to any particular group in China. Acheson urged China "not to engage in aggression against its neighbors."

It was not the United States that was the "real obstacle" to Beijing's U.N. seat, he said, but rather the majority of the world's free nations which held "misgivings" about China's bona fides. On Formosa, U.S. military measures were taken purely to "localize" the conflict to Korea. These measures were "without prejudice" to the peaceful settlement of the issue, as evidenced by the readiness of the United States to have the "question of Formosa considered by UN." Then, Acheson got to his main point, which was a subtle threat to retaliate against China directly if Beijing intervened in the war. Chinese leaders, he said, "need not fear US military action against China unless it lends itself to indirect or direct aggression against neighboring countries."[39] In that case, the United States would have to reconsider its position.

Truman continued Washington's deterrence barrage with a major radio and television address that same evening of September 1. The president was more forceful in his public address than Acheson had been in his private message, setting forth the U.S. position. After a lengthy discussion of the course of the fighting in Korea, in which the president asserted that the North Korean assault would be "crushed," he declared that the United States was rebuilding its military power to support free nations threatened by com-

291

munist tyranny. Truman noted that "Hitler and the Japanese generals mis-calculated badly, ten years ago," and he warned: "let would-be aggressors make no such mistake today."

Truman declared unequivocally that the United States would keep its pledges to seek peace and security through the U.N. "We believe," he said, "the Koreans have a right to be free, independent and united—as they want to be." He said that "we do not want the fighting in Korea to expand into a general war. It will not spread unless Communist imperialism draws other armies and governments into the fight of the aggressors against the United Nations." Then, the president said: "we hope in particular that the People of China will not be misled or forced into fighting against the United Nations and against the American people, who have always been and still are their friends."

292   In his view, "the Communist imperialists are the only ones who can gain if China moves into this fight." The president repeated the view that "we do not want Formosa or any part of Asia for ourselves. We believe that the future of Formosa . . . should be settled peacefully . . . by international action, and not by the decision of the United States or any other state alone. The mission of the Seventh Fleet is to keep Formosa out of the conflict. Our purpose is peace, not conquest." The president referred to earlier references of preventive war with the statement that "we do not believe in aggressive or preventive war. Such war," he said, "is the weapon of dictators, not of free democratic countries like the United States." Closing, he declared: "we want peace and we shall achieve it."[40]

The same day's edition of the *New York Times* carried an authoritative article by Hanson Baldwin titled "War of Prevention," in which he pulled together the themes of the previous several days. He noted that along with reports about the fresh massing of enemy divisions on the Korean front, there were also "threatening Chinese Communist troop movements in Manchuria toward the Korean frontier." Baldwin evaluated these troop movements "at the moment as of more political and diplomatic importance than military significance," particularly when combined with "the careful ground-work of complaints and proclamations about Korea that Peiping has been issuing."

In a remarkably astute analysis, based upon his Pentagon sources, Baldwin said that "the Chinese Communists are making troop dispositions that will enable them to intervene militarily in Korea if they wish" and went on to observe that Chinese military intervention in Korea "may well occur, however, particularly when and if most of the available North Korean manpower has been committed and when and if United States offensive operations threaten a North Korean defeat. Such intervention is, therefore, a contingency that must be planned for and, if it occurs, met." (Unbeknownst to

Baldwin, this was precisely Mao's calculation, but it also suggests that the newspaperman's Pentagon sources had anticipated Mao's plan.)

Baldwin then made explicit what had until now only been alluded to, namely, connecting the theory of preventive war to events in Korea. "Some suggestions—unfortunately from responsible quarters," he observed, "advocate preventive war against the Soviet Union as a means of meeting Chinese Communist military intervention in Korea, or as a counter to the start by Soviet satellites of other 'hot wars' elsewhere in the world." But Baldwin deplored the theory of preventive war "as a course of political bankruptcy and moral frustration that would be militarily ineffective and which would lose for the United States the very values we are trying to defend."[41] The United States, in other words, would not expand the war against the Soviet Union and, as before, would accept the first blow in a Chinese intervention.

293

THE DEBATE OVER WAR AIMS

While the press was consumed with covering the course of daily events on the battlefield, conveying the impression of impending American defeat, the atmosphere inside the administration was of an entirely different order. From the beginning the discussion centered not on an American defeat, but on the course of action to follow when the North Koreans were defeated, which was seen to be only a matter of time. The battle that raged within the administration over its war aims through July and August until Inchon was fierce, and was affected critically by input from British and French leaders.

The spectrum of opinion ranged from the extreme left, which argued that the United States should terminate its involvement in Northeast Asia entirely, beginning with Korea, as soon as possible in order to avoid world war with the Soviet Union, to the extreme right, which argued that the United States should employ military force to unify Korea regardless of possible consequences of enlarging the war.[42] And there were gradations in between. Generally speaking, for there were obviously individuals who disagreed with the prevailing opinion in their respective departments, within the Department of State the Policy Planning Staff was on the left, while the Bureau of Northeast Asian Affairs was on the right. The CIA was on the left, while the Department of Defense was on the right. The British and French were on the left, while Rhee was on the right.

From the outset, whether posed explicitly or implicitly, the question was: How far should the United States go in employing the opportunity of war to fulfill the U.N.-declared objective of building a unified, free, and democratic Korea? Those on the left, in the administration and in the United Nations, stressed the limiting factors, particularly as they might lead to World War

III, while those on the right stressed the opportunities presented by the defeat of a Soviet satellite, the prospect of driving a wedge between the communist powers, and of rolling back the communist tide. Truman and Acheson would employ elements of both views in moving toward their own goals.

Those on the left within the administration were inspired and animated by outgoing Soviet expert George F. Kennan, former head of the State Department Policy Planning Staff.[43] Kennan, his policy position rejected, would leave the Department at the end of August. Before leaving, however, he would detail comprehensively the strategic views that had lain at the basis of his and his supporters policy proposals during this period.[44] An analysis of Kennan's views helps illuminate the strategic issues that lay just beneath the surface of the policy debate.

294

Kennan was unalterably opposed to both the strategy and policy the Truman administration was pursuing. To press forward in Korea, he believed, would only lead to war with the Soviet Union, which must be avoided at all costs. (As it turned out, it would be Moscow's determined *refusal* to come to the direct assistance of North Korea, or even to threaten to do so, which ultimately discredited his thesis.) In any case, Kennan argued that "we should . . . terminate our involvement [in Korea] . . . as rapidly as possible and on the best terms we can get." While he believed that Truman had been "correct" to go to the defense of the ROK, the United States should not seek to unify Korea.

> It is not essential to us to see an anti-Soviet Korean regime extended to *all* of Korea for all time; we could even eventually tolerate for a certain period of time a Korea nominally independent but actually amenable to Soviet influence, provided this state of affairs were to be brought about gradually and not too conspicuously, and were accompanied by a stable and secure situation in Japan.

Kennan believed that it was "beyond our capabilities to keep Korea permanently out of the Soviet orbit. . . . [Moreover] a period of Russian domination, while undesirable, is preferable to continued U.S. involvement in that unhappy area." He also favored Chinese admission to the U.N., a U.N. plebiscite on Formosa, and "permanent supervision" by the U.N. over whatever regime emerged on the island. And Kennan rejected current policy toward Japan. "We cannot, in the long run, continue successfully to keep Japan resistant to Soviet pressures by using our own strength as the main instrument in this effort. . . . Precisely because we have forces there, we will not be able to establish a healthy diplomatic relationship with the Japanese."

Kennan's "solution" to the problems of Northeast Asia lay in reaching an accommodation with Moscow as a prelude to a retreat from the region. "Our best bet," he believed, was "to establish real diplomatic contact with the Russians . . . aiming at the achievement of something like the following state of affairs: we would consent to the neutralization and demilitarization of Japan . . . whereas the Russians would agree to a termination of the Korean War involving withdrawal of the North Korean forces and of our forces and a period of effective United Nations control over Korea for at least a year or two."[45]

Kennan's overriding objective was to avoid any risk of war with Moscow and he was willing to surrender much of the U.S. position in Asia, earned through World War II, to avoid that prospect. Thus, stripped to its essence, Kennan's position was akin to the proverbial giving up a bird in the hand for two in the bush. He urged the United States to relinquish its dominant position in Japan in return for U.N. control of a presumably unified Korea. The U.N. would also manage a presumably independent Formosan government and the United States would not stand in the way of Beijing's entry into the U.N., acquiescing in the displacement of the Nationalist government.

The central assumptions underlying this prescription were that the United States was too weak to obtain its objectives in the region, that China would agree to relinquish Formosa to permanent supervision by the U.N., and that the Soviet Union, though ready for war, would be more than amenable to reaching an accommodation with the United States to achieve the Japan-Korea trade-off. Among the contradictions in Kennan's views was the argument that Moscow would inevitably dominate Korea, yet would be willing to relinquish it if the United States stepped away from Japan. There was a faint resemblance in this position to the proposal Acheson had attempted to make to Mao in early January, except that Acheson had tied U.S. willingness to back away from Japan to Mao's break with Moscow.

This weltanschauung underlay the policy proposals of what I shall call the "State-CIA left." The facts that this worldview was totally divorced from current reality and completely antithetical to Truman's and Acheson's newly devised containment strategy, which was based on strength not weakness, did not dissuade Kennan's supporters from pressing policy recommendations based on this view. Indeed, before American forces had entered combat on July 5, a memorandum from the Policy Planning Staff was already recommending that MacArthur should be instructed to announce that his forces would not conduct "close pursuit" if the NKA "offer to withdraw" behind the 38th parallel and that he should further undertake to prevent his troops and those of the Republic of Korea from "crossing into North Korean territory in force."[46]

President Syngman Rhee posed the issue of the 38th parallel squarely in a speech on July 13 when he declared that the parallel was not a formal dividing line and his forces would not stop at that line in repelling the invaders. Rhee's unambiguous position, no doubt based on General Walker's

295

expressed conviction of the day before that Pusan could be held, was to favor complete unification. Truman, when asked about it at a news conference the same day, immediately dodged the issue, saying: "I will make that decision when it becomes necessary to do it." But the president instructed the National Security Council on July 17 to determine what policy should be toward the parallel.[47]

Rhee sent a letter to Truman on July 19, formally stating his position. By invading, Pyongyang had "ended any possible claim to the maintenance of the 38th Parallel as a political or military dividing line." We consider, he said, that "this is the time to unify Korea, and for anything less than unification to come out of these great sacrifices of Koreans and their powerful allies would be unthinkable." Rhee closed with the warning against any deals. "Any future agreement or understanding made regarding Korea by other states or groups of states without the consent and approval of the Government of the Republic of Korea," he said, would not be binding.[48] Truman waited three weeks to reply to Rhee, and then, avoiding any commitment to unification by force, simply restated the formal position of the United States to support the unity and independence of Korea.[49]

In the meantime, opposition to the proposal to halt at the 38th parallel immediately arose within the administration. First, John Foster Dulles, Republican appointee named to negotiate the Japanese peace treaty, expressed a nuanced view short of complete unification and designed to avoid a larger war. In a memorandum dated July 14, Dulles agreed that the parallel was "not a political line." Moreover, "the United Nations, has, from the beginning, insisted that equity and justice require a united Korea." North Korea must be punished for its aggression. "There must be a penalty to such wrongdoing unless we want to encourage its repetition." He believed "it would be folly to allow the North Korean army to retire in good order with its armor and equipment and re-form behind the 38th Parallel from whence it could attack again. . . . The North Korean Army should be destroyed, if we have the power to destroy it, even if this requires pursuit beyond the 38th Parallel. That is the only way to remove the menace."

Dulles advised that there be no public declaration of intention "at this time." "Perhaps expediency would make it wise to stop at the 38th Parallel. But I believe strongly that we should not now tie our hands by a public statement precluding the possibility of our forces, if victorious, being used to forge a new Korea which would include at least most of the area north of the 38th Parallel." In his view, the "new Korea" would not necessarily include North Hamgyong Province, adjacent to Vladivostok, or North P'yongan Province, which borders the Yalu River. Dulles's position, then, was substantial unification with a buffer zone between China and the Soviet Union. But he wanted no public statements at this time. We should, he said, "preserve our freedom to act in the way that seems best at the time when a decision is practically needed."[50]

Of course, Dulles's position was the obvious one to implement if the objective were substantial unification without undue provocation of either the Soviet Union or China. Later, this would be developed as the intermediate position between the minimum of stopping at the 38th parallel and the maximum of driving all the way to the Yalu River. Dulles's position sought to avoid a larger war and did not preclude future efforts to achieve complete unification at a later date, but it was not Truman's position.

The next day, July 15, John Allison, director of the Office of Northeast Asian Affairs, supported and went beyond Dulles in expressing his "most emphatic disagreement" with the recommendation to declare U.S. intent to stop at the 38th parallel, but also "with the reasoning back of them." Not only would it be "utterly unrealistic to expect to return to the *status quo ante bellum*," it would cause the people of South Korea "to lose all confidence and faith in the moral position of the United States." Referring to the U.N. resolution of June 27, he said, a "perpetuation of the division of that country at the 38th Parallel will make it impossible 'to restore international peace and security in the area.'"

297

Finally, he said, "determination that the aggressors should not go unpunished" would serve notice to the aggressor, "who is the same as the covert aggressor in Korea, that he cannot embark upon acts of aggression with the assurance that he takes only a limited risk—that of being driven back only to the line from which the attack commenced." At the very least, he said, "we should destroy the North Korean Army." We should then "insist upon the full implementation in North Korea of the procedures laid down by the General Assembly resolutions," that is, the unification of Korea. No statement should be made, Allison concluded, "which commits the government not to proceed beyond the 38th Parallel or implies that we will agree to any settlement which merely restores the *status quo ante bellum*."[51]

Neither Dulles nor Allison spoke to the issue of Soviet or Chinese intervention, but both agreed that the 38th parallel was of no political or military significance in determining policy, which accorded with U.N. resolutions, and urged the destruction of the NKA. Both were sensitive to the effect on the ROK of any declaration implying a restoration of the status quo ante bellum. Therefore, they recommended that no public statement be made regarding U.S. war aims, but urged that policy be determined forthwith. Both clearly sought, if the opportunity arose, to unify the country in the course of defeating the North Korean Army, even if they disagreed on precisely how much unification would occur.

The Policy Planning Staff responded to the Dulles-Allison position with two draft memoranda of July 22 and 25, the second an elaboration of the first. They raised the red flag of war with the Soviet Union should the United States go north of the 38th parallel. The PPS draft bowed to the sentiments of the South Korean people, "having been the victim of armed attack," and of public and congressional opinion, which "might be dissatisfied with any conclusion falling short of what it would consider a 'final' settlement of the problem." In the U.N., however, the drafters saw allies who would oppose the "multilateral use of force . . . to bring about the complete independence and unity of Korea."

They believed that "carrying the military struggle into a new phase by a land offensive beyond the 38th Parallel" would raise the clear danger of war with the Soviet Union. Because of the "strategic importance to Russia of the Korean peninsula," they argued, "it is unlikely that the Kremlin at present would accept the establishment in North Korea of a regime which it could not dominate and control." When it becomes apparent that the North Korean aggression "cannot succeed," the Kremlin will reach a decision "which would mean in substance that U.N. military action north of the 38th Parallel would result in conflict with the U.S.S.R. or Communist China."

The clearly stated assumptions in this analysis were that Stalin would not accept the total defeat of Kim Il-sung, and that his assistance would in all likelihood involve the commitment of Soviet troops. The analysis also assumed that Stalin could command the commitment of Chinese troops. (Indeed, there was no analysis of Chinese interests independent of Moscow's.) Finally, the analysis assumed that Stalin would risk global war for the preservation of North Korea, that he considered the outcome of a Korea unified by the United States under the U.N. worse than the precipitation of a global war to save Kim Il-sung. Curiously, the drafters argued the very obverse of this thesis for the United States. "The advantages of an effort involving the use of military forces to attain the complete independence and unity of Korea . . . must be weighed against the disadvantages of such a course," the most serious of which was, of course, the risk of global war.

The PPS draft concluded that while it was U.S. policy "to help bring about" the unification of Korea, "the Korean problem must be dealt with in the wider framework of the conflict between the communist and non-communist countries." The U.S. must "maintain a realistic balance between our military strength on the one hand and commitments and risks on the other hand." Moreover, "the need for additional information . . . makes it impossible to take decisions now regarding our future course." Therefore, "decisions regarding our course of action when the U.N. forces approach the 38th Parallel should be deferred until military and political developments provide the additional information necessary" to make them.[52]

The immediate consequence of the argument that the Soviet Union would risk global war to prevent North Korean defeat was NSC-76, the presi-

298

dential decision of July 27 determining what the United States would do in that event. The president decided that should the Soviet Union commit troops to the Korean conflict the United States would immediately execute plans for global war with the Soviet Union. This determination would permeate all subsequent analyses of U.S. policy toward Korea, and neutralized the PPS argument.[53]

DEFENSE PRESSES FOR UNIFICATION

On July 31 and August 7 the Defense Department produced its position. Noting that the U.N. resolution of June 27 did not "specifically limit" military operations "to the area south of the 38th Parallel," the memo concluded that North Korean forces "can be engaged and defeated wherever found." Indeed, the unified command "should seek to occupy Korea and to defeat North Korean armed forces wherever located north or south of the 38th Parallel." The principal deterrent to military operations north of the 38th parallel "would be entry of major Chinese Communist or Soviet forces in action in order to oppose further advances by the ground forces of the unified command."

299

The Defense Department draft memorandum disputed the assumption of the Policy Planning Staff that the Soviet Union would "risk general war to prevent a full-fledged, rapid, and determined UN effort to unite Korea." But should either Russia or China "enter overtly into the hostilities in Korea, the courses of action in NSC-73/1 and NSC-76 would apply." In other words, if China entered, according to NSC-73, the United States would continue to fight for its objectives in Korea, as long as it was feasible, but if the Soviet Union entered, according to NSC-76, it would mean the beginning of world war, requiring a curtailment of military operations in Korea.

The Defense memo then laid out the procedure that the administration would ultimately follow once the tide of battle turned in its favor. At the appropriate times, the president should first "proclaim that our peace aim is a united, free, and independent Korea, as envisaged by the UN." Second, "the U.S. should seek to translate this aim into UN objectives." In the meantime, the United States should energetically act to "forestall any Soviet effort to mediate the conflict on any terms short of the unification of all Korea on a free and representative basis under UN auspices."[54]

In war aims, Defense saw three options: a minimum effort seeking only to force the North Korean Army to withdraw north of the 38th parallel; an intermediate objective involving the occupation of North Korea, including its capital of Pyongyang, between the 39th and 40th parallels, setting an unoccupied, demilitarized zone along the Chinese and Soviet frontiers, much as Dulles had proposed; and a maximum effort including the pacification and occupation of all Korea by the unified command. The U.N. would then arrange to hold elections and establish a government for the entire country. Defense preferred the maximum objective.

The Defense Department position paper was persuasive. John Allison, chief of the State Department's Office of Northeast Asian Affairs, accepted much of it in his own analysis of August 12. In attempting to bridge the gap between the PPS argument that the Soviet Union would enter the Korean conflict and the Defense argument that it would not, Allison concluded that

> it is possible that, notwithstanding its considerable military strength located in the Far East, the Soviet Union is not yet ready to risk a general war to prevent a determined and rapid effort by the U.N. to create a unified Korea. This possibility might be increased if the U.N. should adopt by a large majority a program recommended by UNCOK and if some means can be devised of assuring the Soviet Union that a U.N. settlement would not be only a U.S. settlement and that it would not be directed against legitimate Soviet interests.[55]

The thrust of Allison's analysis was that the United States should do everything possible to shape its objectives in terms of U.N. objectives, but to seek a unified Korea. He noted that since November 1947, the U.N. had passed "by overwhelming majorities" three resolutions looking for the establishment of a "free, independent and unified Korea." A U.N. Commission on Korea had since then been charged with the task of "seeking Korea's unification by pacific settlement," although he acknowledged that the U.N. had "never formally considered nor explicitly approved the unification of Korea through military means."

He urged the United States to "continue its efforts . . . to repel the aggressors and restore the integrity of the Republic of Korea, taking such military action north and south of the 38th Parallel as is necessary." He urged that "after the successful repulsion of the aggression in Korea and the unification of the country . . . Korea be demilitarized . . . the United Nations . . . to recommend the methods by which this could be done." He foresaw that a "United Nations military force" would be retained in Korea "during the natural period of readjustment" after the conflict had ended.

Sensing that his side was losing the policy argument, Kennan employed an incident that occurred at this time to raise higher the threat of war with the Soviet Union. On the morning of August 12, the State Department learned that American B-29s had bombed the east coast port city of Najin (sometimes also referred to as Rashin, or Rajin), located seventeen miles from the Soviet border. Deputy Undersecretary of State Freeman Matthews expressed the department's deep concern to Air Force General Lauris Norstad, reminding him of the president's directive that all bombing missions north of the 38th parallel were to stay "well clear" of the Manchurian and Soviet borders. Matthews emphasized the "sensitivity of Soviet authorities to any military activity in the neighborhood of their territory and the dangers involved, particularly in view of their presumed state of tenseness and irritation."[56]

Two days later, Kennan took up this issue in a memorandum to Acheson, based on a *New York Times* story of that morning. The story declared that Najin was being used as a Soviet submarine base and that it was no longer being used to ship supplies to the NKA. Kennan believed that the Soviets would interpret the bombings as "United States intent to damage their strategic interests under cover of the Korean war." Given the fact, he said, that the bombing occurred during heavy cloud cover and by radar guidance, and in view of "the speed at which these planes operate . . . it is obvious how easily they could not only have overflown the Soviet frontier but actually have inflicted damage on the Soviet side of it."

He said that stories coming out of MacArthur's headquarters were "making it entirely plain that the relationship of Rashin to the hostilities in South Korea was only a pretext for our bombing and that the real reason for it was the desire to injure the Soviet strategic position in the Far East." The "pathologically sensitive" Soviets were bound to see this as a provocation. Indeed, said Kennan, "it is entirely possible that a Soviet military re-entry into North Korea might occur at any time; or the Soviet Government might take other local measures, such as putting strategic bombing planes nominally at North Korean disposal, and beginning operations with them against our forces and our bases in Japan."[57]

Kennan's alarmist interpretation prompted Undersecretary Webb to raise the bombing issue in a cabinet meeting with the president on August 18. Webb declared that London had also protested against bombing targets in North Korea, because of its concern that indiscriminate bombing might inflame public opinion against the U.N. General Bradley said that the British concern was due to a misunderstanding which had since been cleared up. Besides, he said, bombing decisions were left to the discretion of the commander in the field. The president stated that while he understood the "point" being raised by State, he wanted "to go after any targets which were being used to furnish supplies to the North Korean troops fighting the UN forces."[58]

The issue of the Najin bombing dragged on for three more days, until Secretary of Defense Johnson replied definitively to yet another Kennan memorandum denying that any supplies were flowing to the battlefield from Najin. Johnson reemphasized that not only had the president decided the issue, "the bombing of Najin was directed by the Joint Chiefs of Staff in accordance with their military responsibilities for the conduct of war operations." The mission was "definitely within the terms of the directive" authorizing air operations into North Korea and Najin's location was "well clear" of the border. The primary target at Najin, Johnson concluded, was a petroleum storage plant that was "obviously a military asset to the operations of North Korean forces and, therefore, important to our own forces as a military target."[59] Perhaps coincidentally, the day of Johnson's memorandum was also the day Kennan submitted his departing critique of American policy to Acheson.

In the meantime, the Central Intelligence Agency had weighed in with its own analysis, presenting the worst of worst cases. It was the agency's view that even if the United States succeeded in complete unification of Korea, it would ultimately fail because the Soviet Union was strong enough to prevent a lasting solution. It was felt "doubtful whether the US could secure the support of its allies" for a conquest of the north. "Consequently, US action would provide the USSR with a strong wedge for attempting to separate the US from its Western European allies."

The Chinese "might well take up defensive positions north of the 38th parallel," a development that the Soviet Union "might welcome," giving Moscow additional leverage. The CIA made the same assumption as all other agencies at this time, namely, that Moscow controlled Beijing. No analysis of Chinese interests independent of Moscow was presented. The CIA analysis argued that "the USSR might use Chinese Communist troops at any stage in the fighting, but their participation would be especially useful at the 38th parallel where UN members could legally discontinue their support of the US policy."

Raising the specter of global war, the analysis went on to say that the Soviet Union "might become involved, either directly or indirectly, in hostilities with Soviet forces." The Soviets could deploy their forces on the 38th parallel and "oblige the US to initiate hostilities against Soviet forces under conditions which would alienate most of Asia from the US-UN cause." And, if general war ensued, the Soviet Union could "conquer most of Europe and the Near East before the impact of US industrial mobilization could be felt upon the defensive capability of those areas."

But even if Moscow did not choose war, "it is probable that the Kremlin would be prepared by one method or another to prevent UN occupation of North Korea." The Soviets could "provide sufficient ground, air, or naval assistance to interdict UN communications, halt the ground advance, and neutralize UN air and naval superiority." They could "inaugurate new limited aggressions elsewhere" and "strain further UN military capabilities."

If none of this transpired, the CIA analysis continued, even the conquest of North Korea "would not provide assurance of peace throughout the country or of true unification." The Soviets would "almost certainly" withdraw the remnants of North Korean forces into Manchuria or the U.S.S.R. and "from these areas . . . continue to threaten aggression and infiltration and thus produce such instability as to require the continuing presence of large numbers of US or UN forces."

As far as the Republic of Korea was concerned, the outlook was equally bleak. Syngman Rhee was "unpopular among many—if not a majority—of non-Communist Koreans." To establish his regime over all of Korea "would be difficult, if not impossible." Even if this could be done the regime would be unstable. If, on the other hand, "a new government should be formed consequent to a UN-supervised free election, there is no assurance that the Communists would not win either control of or a powerful voice in such a government."

Finally, if a U.N. trusteeship were formed "instability would nevertheless continue," as even the non-Communist Koreans would rebel against the denial of independence. "Korea once more would become the catspaw of international politics, and its ultimate status would be dependent upon the comparative strength and ambitions of the countries whose representatives supervised the trust administration." One could not have conceived of a more hostile, negative, and depressing analysis. The logical conclusion, never stated, was that the United States was making the worst of all possible errors in supporting the Korean cause and should extricate itself from this multiple dilemma at the first opportunity.[60]

Three days later, Policy Planning Staff offered up precisely such a prospect, devised to meet "only one particular contingency: an indication from the Soviet side, before the tide of battle has turned, that Moscow and/or Peiping are prepared to negotiate a settlement involving the withdrawal of the North Koreans to the 38th parallel." Completely unrealistic, it was based on the assumption that the Communists would surrender North Korea without a struggle, and permit the U.N. to hold free elections. In sending this memorandum to Assistant Secretary Dean Rusk, John Emmerson appended a note suggesting that the proposal be sent to Beijing via the Indian channel. "Having this reach Peiping's ears would irritate the Russians, promote the cleavage, and might possibly intrigue the Chinese Communists," he thought. Rusk didn't think so, and delayed a response for almost three weeks, before turning the suggestion down on the grounds that it was inappropriate and overcomplicated.[61]

On the same day the CIA memorandum appeared, John Allison distributed a revised version of his August 12 draft paper. His analysis incorporated points from earlier Policy Planning Staff proposals, but retained the essential thrust of his earlier paper calling for Korean unification. Allison acknowledged that Moscow "would probably take extreme measures" to prevent the establishment of a regime in North Korea that it could not dominate or control, but he did not believe that the Soviet Union would take any action "likely to bring on general war." Allison agreed that "when the tide of battle begins to turn," Stalin might commit Soviet or Chinese Communist troops "at least occupying Korea north of the 38th parallel," or offer to settle.

Surveying public opinion, Allison believed that "there is growing sentiment in the United States favoring a 'final' settlement of the Korean problem as opposed to any settlement which smacks of compromise or a 'deal,'" although he acknowledged that should "a peace offer be made" on the basis of a return to the status quo ante bellum, "there would doubtless be strong efforts made by large sections of the public and the Congress to stop the fighting and return to a peace basis." Allison noted that UNCOK would soon be making recommendations "to bring about the unification of Korea under UN auspices," to which the United States should pay heed.

Although the United States had interests and obligations to the Korean people, "we have a moral obligation as well to support previous General Assembly recommendations on Korea," because "the problem of Korea is primarily a United Nations problem and its final solution must be one which is carried out under the authority of the United Nations." In his view "the independence and unification of Korea conform with Korean aspirations, United States objectives, and the expressed objectives of the United Nations."[62]

THE ALLIES ALTER THE POLICY EQUATION

Two days later, on August 23, in preparation for a scheduled meeting with British and French representatives, the secretary of state placed a hold on the ongoing argument and moved to establish a unified position. First, in a memorandum to the NSC, he recommended that "decisions regarding the course of action when the United Nations forces approach the 38th parallel should be deferred until military and political developments provide the additional information necessary to enable us" to base our decisions on events occurring in Korea "and in other parts of the world," to consult with our allies, and to keep our "capabilities and commitments in a safe balance."[63]

While recommending that the president defer a decision, on August 25, State proceeded to forge a unified position within the department. It was, in essence, the position that had been advocated by Allison and the Defense Department. Washington would enter discussions with the allies with a very firm stand, which it no doubt expected would weaken in the discussions. There was "agreement" that MacArthur had authority to "make operational amphibious landings behind the North Korean lines, [even] north of the 38th parallel," as long as U.N. forces kept "well clear of the Russian frontier." On the east coast, U.N. forces "might occupy the neck reaching into the mountain area up to the 39th parallel" just south of Wonsan.

What if the Chinese or the Soviets entered? It was agreed that "if Chinese

Communist forces have entered the fighting," NSC-73 would govern: "we continue our operations as if we were still fighting North Koreans." On the other hand, "if major Soviet units are engaged," then, according to NSC-76, "the US should minimize its commitments and execute war plans," that is, prepare for global war. What if Soviet troops entered unannounced? "In the absence of an announcement by Russia of its intentions of moving into North Korea we would bomb Russian troops as if they were North Korean troops." If they announced an intention to reoccupy North Korea, then we should take the case to the Security Council, because "we could not make a war issue with Russia out of their announced intention to re-occupy North Korea."

Should U.N. forces stop at the 38th parallel? It was agreed that "in the absence of Chinese Communist or Soviet participation we should not stop"; indeed, it was recognized that "it might be desirable for South Korean troops to pursue North Korean troops beyond the 38th parallel." What about the ultimate solution of the Korean problem? It was agreed that "questions of ultimate solution should not be decided until the military situation has cleared up." It was, however, agreed that the United States would "favor neutralization," but not demilitarization of a unified Korea. Finally, it was agreed that "while leaving open the question of our war aims we should announce what we wish ultimately to accomplish."[64]

State conveyed this position in a draft memorandum to the NSC on August 30, elaborating on several points, emphasizing that "the political objective of the United States in Korea is to carry out the UN mandate of establishing under the auspices of the United Nations a unified and independent Korea without provoking a general war with the Soviet Union." Therefore, "the objective should be to obtain the maximum strategic and political benefits from operations north of 38 with a minimum of provocation to the Soviet Union and Communist China." Since it was "unlikely that the North Korean forces can be entirely disarmed and dissolved south of 38 . . . a halt at this point would not make political or military sense unless the risk that it would provoke a major clash with the Soviet Union or Communist China were so great as to override all other considerations."

The closer U.N. forces moved to the Siberian-Manchurian borders, the greater the risk of provoking a clash. Therefore, U.N. forces "should . . . refrain from any ground activity, either combat or occupational, in areas close to the international borders of Korea." The U.N. commander should be informed, the memorandum continued, "that the foregoing is the sole restriction on his freedom to carry out operations north of 38 degrees." Nevertheless, the U.N. commander "should also be authorized to conduct continuous roll-back operations against North Korean forces well into the northern part of the peninsula if such operations are necessary to the dissolution of the North Korean armed resistance."[65]

The State memorandum seemed to end the argument within the administration, erasing the PPS position that had sought to limit U.N. military action solely to defeating North Korean aggression south of the 38th parallel, and establishing a clear conception of policy objectives looking toward Korean unification. The memorandum emphasized the desirability of both the military defeat of North Korea and the political unification of the country. However, this clearly stated set of objectives lasted for less than a week. In conversations at the end of the month between representatives of the Department of State and their counterparts in the British and French embassies, the thrust of the argument moved the administration's position away from the firm Allison–Defense Department position and closer to the PPS-CIA position. The result was a contradictory, stitched-together compromise that would emerge as NSC-81 on September 1.

The State Department sent forward a memorandum the next day that reflected the discussion with the allies. The Soviet threat was paramount. The new position focused concern on possible Soviet responses to a move north of the 38th parallel, and narrowly limited the contingencies under which unification could be pursued. The memorandum so hedged its proposals that several were patently illogical and some were contradictory, as is usually the case with documents of multiple, and multi-national, authorship reflecting divergent interests. Ironically, one contradictory passage forecast Stalin's actual strategy.[66]

The memorandum maintained the view that Moscow would not passively accept the loss of Korea if "it believes that it can take action which would prevent this and which would not involve a substantial risk of general war." Moscow "may decide that it can risk reoccupying Northern Korea before United Nations' forces have reached the 38th parallel," or reach an agreement with Pyongyang pledging the defense of North Korea, or "initiate some move toward a negotiated settlement while hostilities are still in progress south of the 38th parallel," or some combination of these.

Having described the Soviet commitment of forces as not involving the risk of war, however, the memorandum then illogically recommended that "in view of the importance of avoiding general war, *we* should be prepared to negotiate a settlement." Of course, it went on, we should refuse terms that would leave the aggressor with an advantage, would invite renewed aggression, or undermine the U.N. The memorandum did not elaborate on how it would be possible to negotiate victory after surrendering to what patently would be blackmail, nor was the command decision of NSC-76 referred to as the response to Soviet entry into the conflict, indicating that the allies were not privy to that decision.

The memorandum then argued in contradictory fashion that Moscow would and would not use Chinese Communist forces to occupy North Korea "because the Soviet Union probably regards Korea as being in its own direct sphere of interest." The conferees did not believe Communist forces would be committed "in the southern part of the peninsula, for it is believed that neither the Soviet Union nor the Chinese Communists are ready to engage in general war at this time for this objective." It was possible, they said, hitting on Stalin's actual strategy, that Moscow might attempt "to persuade the Chinese Communists to enter the Korean campaign with the purpose of avoiding the defeat of the North Korean forces and also of fomenting war between the United States and the Chinese Communists should we react strongly."

The conferees were prepared to support ground operations north of the 38th parallel only in the "unlikely contingency . . . that the Soviet Union had decided to follow a hands-off policy, even at the expense of the loss of control of Northern Korea." Even so, military operations that go beyond the Security Council resolution "to compel the withdrawal of the North Korean forces behind the 38th parallel" to accomplish the "political objective of unifying Korea under the Republic of Korea are not clearly authorized by existing Security Council resolutions." Such authorization would be a necessary "prerequisite to their initiation." The memorandum emphasized the

> importance of securing support of the majority of U.N. members for any action that might be taken north of the 38th parallel and the advantage of establishing a record that will clearly show that every reasonable effort has been made to avoid carrying the military struggle into a new phase by a land offensive beyond the 38th parallel.

The memorandum concluded with the view that "final decisions can not be made at this time . . . since the course of action which will best advance the national interest of the United States must be determined in light of the action or inaction of the Soviet Union and the Chinese Communists and in consultation and agreement with friendly members of the United Nations." The result of the discussion with the allies was a compromise guidance directive, NSC-81, whose foremost purpose was to maintain a semblance of unity. Allied unity, however, came at the cost of renewed internal dissent, this time from the Joint Chiefs and MacArthur, just before Inchon.

NSC-81, THE JOINT CHIEFS, AND MACARTHUR

NSC-81, circulated for discussion on September 1, was a complete retreat from the decisions arrived at on August 25 by the senior State Department staff. It completely reflected the reluctance of the British and French allies to carry operations north of the 38th parallel and in actuality represented a position very close to the "State-CIA left." Although the sharp retreat from the

307

Allison–Defense Department position immediately caused a furor within the administration, it is clear that the purpose of the shift was to secure the support of Britain and France and through them the majority of the nations in the U.N. as the critical phase of the war approached, and was not a change of Truman's position. In short, it was a tactical maneuver.

Truman went as far as he had to go to keep his allies on board, but he had not changed his own position. Indeed, between the time that NSC-81 was circulated for discussion and the time Truman formally approved it as NSC-81/1 on September 11, several subtle but critical changes were made in the directive, which gave him sufficient "wiggle room" to do what he wished when the time came. The changes also gave the president greater control over MacArthur, not less, as some have suggested.

The revision of NSC-81 was prompted by a memorandum from the Joint Chiefs to the Secretary of Defense on September 7. The chiefs thought the basic approach of the paper was "unrealistic," because it envisaged "the stabilization of a front on the 38th parallel." No doubt anticipating the dramatic results of the forthcoming Inchon envelopment, the chiefs declared that they agreed in discussions with MacArthur that "the initial objective to be attained is the destruction of North Korean forces." They believed that "after the strength of the North Korean forces has been broken, which it is anticipated will occur south of 38th degrees North, that subsequently operations must take place both north and south of the 38th parallel."[67]

The chiefs' conception of what subsequent operations would be, however, was markedly different from anything that had been said to date, namely, that with the strength of the NKA broken, the war would be over, except for mopping-up operations. These operations "will probably be of a guerrilla character," and "should be conducted by South Korean forces." They added that "General MacArthur has plans for increasing the strength of the South Korean forces so that they should be adequate at the time to cope with this situation." Indeed, the chiefs and MacArthur "agree that the occupation of Korea by U.N. forces subsequent to the cessation of actual hostilities should be limited to the principal cities south of the 38th parallel." The chiefs recommended that "NSC-81 be redrafted to reflect the foregoing principles."

Of course, while the chiefs' memo did point out the limiting factors that permeated the first draft of NSC-81, and attempted to shift the focus from the 38th parallel to the destruction of the NKA as the main objective, theirs and MacArthur's notion of an abrupt end to the war, the surrender of the North, and mop-up operations by ROK forces in the North, was hopelessly Pollyanna-ish. Nor, it is plain, did they contemplate a major drive by large forces north to the Yalu River. Nevertheless, their memo did open the way for a revision of the directive, which emerged on September 9.

Surprisingly, despite the chiefs' and MacArthur's view that the war would end quickly, in the final draft the threat of Soviet or Chinese intervention was strengthened slightly from "does not appear likely" and "seems unlikely" in NSC-81, to "it is possible" and it is "also a possibility" in NSC-81/1. Paragraph five declared that it would "not be in our national interest . . . to take action in Korea which would involve a substantial risk of general war." Furthermore, allied interests would receive strong consideration. "It would not be in our national interest to take action in Korea which did not have the support of the great majority of the United Nations, even if, in our judgment, such action did not involve a substantial risk of general war."

For the rest, however, the wording of NSC-81/1 was altered to remove all independent initiative from MacArthur and lodge it directly in the hands of the president, or from him through the chiefs, and to open loopholes for the president to control the action. Thus, in paragraph fifteen, it was acknowledged that "United Nations forces have a legal basis for conducting operations north of the 38th parallel to compel the withdrawal of the North Korean forces behind this line or to defeat these forces. It would be expected that the UN commander would receive authorization to conduct military operations . . . north of the 38th parallel."

Such operations could take place, however, only if "there has been no entry into North Korea by major Soviet or Chinese Communist forces, no announcement of intended entry, nor a threat to counter our operations militarily." Since military operations in North Korea "involve a risk of major war with the Soviet Union and would directly involve the interests of other friendly governments, the UN Commander should, prior to putting any such plan into execution, obtain the approval of the President."[68]

NSC-81 stipulated that "UN operations should not be permitted to extend into areas close to the Manchurian and USSR borders of Korea." In NSC-81/1 the wording was changed to read "UN operations should not be permitted to extend across the Manchurian or USSR borders of Korea." The change was a significant shift toward Truman's as yet undisclosed goal of driving to the Yalu. The initial formulation refusing to permit operations in "areas close to" the border could be interpreted to mean that U.N. forces must stop well short of the border. The revised formulation allowed operations up to the border, but not to "extend across" it.

While NSC-81 stated unequivocally that only ROK forces "be used in the north-eastern province bordering the Soviet Union or in the area along the Manchurian border," NSC-81/1 weakened that position to state that "it should be the policy not to include any non-Korean units in any UN ground forces which may be used in the north-eastern province bordering the Soviet Union or in the area along the Manchurian border." Policy, of course, could be changed.

In paragraph sixteen, NSC-81 stipulated that "UN forces should be developed and plans should be perfected with a view to the possible occupation of North Korea. However, the execution of such plans should take place only with the explicit approval of the President, and would be dependent upon prior consultation with and the approval of the UN members." In NSC-81/1, this was changed to give the Joint Chiefs, that is, the president, the authority to direct MacArthur. Thus, "the Joint Chiefs of Staff should be authorized to direct the Commander of the UN forces in Korea to make plans for the possible occupation of North Korea. However, the execution of such plans should take place only with the explicit approval of the President . . . and would be dependent upon prior consultation with and the approval of members of the UN." Clearly, it would be Truman himself who held the power to authorize MacArthur to proceed.

Paragraph twenty-three further restricted MacArthur. In discussing operations in the North under the specific circumstance of the "collapse" of North Korean forces, but with the refusal of Pyongyang to accept surrender terms, NSC-81 had said that as long as there was "no evidence of a substantial risk of a clash with Soviet or Chinese Communist forces," the U.N. commander "should request new instructions before continuing operations north of the 38th parallel." That was changed in NSC-81/1 to read that the U.N. commander could continue operations north of the 38th parallel "only if so directed," once again shifting the initiative from MacArthur to the president.

The main purpose of NSC-81/1, as in its earlier drafts, was to construct a series of hedges constraining the conduct of military operations north of the 38th parallel. These contingencies included what MacArthur should do in light of "open or covert" entry of major Soviet units north or south of the 38th parallel, "open or covert" entry of major Chinese Communist units south of the 38th parallel, entry of "small" Soviet or Chinese units "covertly" south of the 38th parallel, and the "announced" intention by either Moscow or Beijing to occupy North Korea.

Without specifically saying so in the directive, MacArthur's responses to each contingency would be governed by NSC-76 and NSC-73, respectively. NSC-73 was in fact a command decision to engage in limited war with China in Korea. If the Soviets entered anywhere, then we would "proceed on the assumption that global war is probably imminent." If the Chinese entered south of the 38th parallel, on the other hand, MacArthur was to continue operations "as long as action by UN military forces offer[s] a reasonable chance of successful resistance." If "small" Soviet or Chinese units entered "covertly" south of the 38th, "the UN Commander should continue the action." Only in the case of an announced intention by either communist power to occupy North Korea would MacArthur stop operations while the administration took the issue to the Security Council.

The discussion did not anticipate the kind of turnaround that shortly occurred at Inchon. The several references to "open or covert" entry of Soviet or Chinese forces south of the 38th parallel implied a breakout from Pusan and an advance up the peninsula, which would provide the opportunity for a Communist intervention south of the 38th parallel. Clearly, the successful envelopment at Inchon eliminated or severely reduced the possibility of such action, rendering much of the contingency planning of NSC-81/1 irrelevant.

But there was yet another oddity about NSC-81/1. Despite a lengthy dissection of various contingencies and proposed responses by the U.N. commander, the most obvious contingency was not included. This was the covert entry of Chinese forces into North Korea. It was obvious that Chinese entry south of the 38th parallel would not be possible without first entering into North Korea. Covert Chinese entry into North Korea, if discovered, would, of course, constitute a major indicator of Chinese intent to intervene.   **311**

This glaring omission would be rectified in early October after MacArthur's forces crossed into North Korea, but it is impossible to believe that the omission went unnoticed earlier. Indeed, the reason for the omission in NSC-81/1 may well have been not to provide advance warning of the kind of response Washington would make. As the product of discussion with the allies, it must be assumed that the contents of NSC-81/1 would shortly end up in the hands of the adversaries. Perhaps it was felt that to have included the issue of possible responses to Chinese covert entry into North Korea would precipitate such action before Inchon when Washington was not prepared for it.

NSC-81/1 was manifestly not a license to go north of the 38th parallel. Rather, it was a series of hedges constructed by the allies against doing so. But Truman had inserted sufficient qualifications to enable him to authorize military operations in North Korea should circumstances permit. Nevertheless, the deal with the allies would drive later intelligence. According to NSC-81/1, MacArthur would not be authorized to proceed north of the 38th parallel if there was evidence of the entry in some form of Russian or Chinese forces. Thus, after Inchon, when operations in the north were decided upon, intelligence would be forced to deny the presence of enemy forces. Such denials would assume ludicrous proportions in early November when American intelligence would be forced to minimize the size of Chinese forces, then engaged in major battles with American forces.

STALIN, KIM IL-SUNG, AND INCHON

On September 1, Kim Il-sung sent virtually his entire army into action in a suicidal assault on the Pusan perimeter. Hugely outgunned and outmanned, Kim marshaled thirteen infantry divisions, one armored division, and two armored brigades for an all-out assault at five points around the perimeter—at either end of the perimeter and at three points in between—converging on Taegu, the gateway to Pusan. Despite mounting intense pressure at each point and manufacturing breakthroughs or near-breakthroughs at all of them, the NKA did not have sufficient forces in reserve to exploit any success.

American forces fought with exceptional skill and tenacity, ingeniously employing mobility and firepower to plug gaps in lines when NKA forces punched holes in the perimeter. The result was that by a few days before the Inchon landing, the NKA offensive had been spent, with little chance of renewal. Indeed, on September 13, General Walker was publicly telling his troops that "he noted signs of weakening of the North Koreans along the entire front [and] . . . added that the time was rapidly approaching when the United Nations forces would take the offensive."[69]

312   The question arises of why Stalin authorized an all-out invasion against the perimeter, knowing as he did that an amphibious counterattack was imminent? There can be little doubt that it was Stalin who made this decision. In addition to providing the weaponry for it, he would not have left this decision, the crucial decision of the war for North Korea, to Kim Il-sung alone. Nor can there be any doubt that Stalin knew a counteroffensive was imminent. As established by this chapter, the Communist side (as well as everyone else) anticipated a near-term amphibious attack, and perhaps had even identified the actual date and place, yet took no defensive precautions.

The general view, as expressed by Clay Blair, is that "the best NKPA defense to an amphibious envelopment in its rear—indeed, the *only* feasible defense—was to make one last do-or-die attempt to crack the Pusan Perimeter and overrun Eighth Army. A decisive NKPA victory in the perimeter would almost certainly force a cancellation of the amphibious invasion."[70] To this might be added the point that even if a landing occurred during the assault, once victorious, North Korean forces could wheel and defeat the landing. Yet Blair undercut his own argument by correctly pointing out the North Korean "blunder" in their organization of the attack. Focusing on the southwest sector, but in an analysis that applies all across the front, he notes:

> rather than mass . . . divisions on a single line of advance for a power punch-through, they spread them out along a long front for a simultaneous frontal attack. . . . By this arrangement the NKPA denied itself power in depth to exploit a breakthrough.[71]

A closer look at the problem belies the notion that the best and only defense was "one last do-or-die attempt to crack the Pusan Perimeter." The fact was that the NKA had virtually no chance of overrunning Pusan. Indeed, that opportunity had long passed. The American position had simply become too strong, with overwhelming superiority in tanks, artillery, mortars, and men, not to mention continued superiority in the air and on the sea. Although the NKA had marshaled what was initially estimated to be some 98,000 men for the attack, almost one-third of them were untrained conscripts who were in many cases unarmed. (It was later learned that the assault was mounted with closer to 70,000 men, and some 21,000 effectives.) The NKA supply system was simply no longer capable of sustaining its army in combat.[72]

At this point, U.N. forces in the Korean theater totaled just under 250,000 men: 83,000 American ground forces in four-plus divisions and support units; 91,000 men in nine ROK divisions; and some 70,000 in air and naval forces. Within the perimeter the United States had amassed around six hundred tanks against less than one hundred for the NKA and held major advantages in artillery and mortars, all zeroed in for concentrated fire at potential breakthrough points.[73] The United States had the further advantage of fortified defensive positions and interior lines of communication and supply, which permitted rapid movement within the perimeter to meet crises. This is not to argue that the defense would not involve extreme difficulty, but that a successful assault against this position was extremely unlikely.

From Pyongyang's strategic perspective, even the best possible outcome of a somehow successful assault that pushed U.N. forces into the sea would still fail if the Americans landed successfully behind NKA lines and cut off their source of supply. In this scenario, the NKA would have driven the United States off the peninsula only to see themselves trapped there instead, cut off by the successful landing at Inchon. This would not even be a Pyrrhic victory; it would be a total defeat. MacArthur made this point in a response to a JCS request for reconsideration of the timing of the Inchon attack. The chiefs were concerned that the NKA offensive might succeed. One week before the landing, the general declared:

> There is no slightest possibility ... of our force being ejected from the Pusan beachhead. The envelopment from the north will instantly relieve the pressure on the south perimeter and, indeed, is the only way that this can be accomplished.... The success of the enveloping movement from the north [moreover] does not depend upon the rapid juncture of the X Corps and the Eighth Army. The seizure of the heart of the enemy distributing system in the Seoul area will completely dislocate the logistical supply of his forces now operating in South Korea and therefore will ultimately result in their disintegration. This, indeed, is the primary purpose of the movement.[74]

If a suicidal charge of a proverbial Light Brigade was not the best offense, what was? From the beginning, Kim's strategy (but manifestly not Stalin's) hinged on a quick victory. As we have seen, all hopes for a quick victory had evaporated quite early in the war, by the end of the third week. Frantically, Kim had redoubled his drive to overrun the Pusan perimeter through the

313

first two weeks of August, but had failed because the United States was now ensconced in growing strength behind the Naktong. No amount of encouragement from Stalin would change the balance of forces on the ground. Nor had Stalin provided a sufficient level of weapons supply to change it. A September 15 CIA estimate of North Korean military supplies for the offensive observed that "intelligence reports do not indicate a preinvasion stockpile of a magnitude required to support current operations."[75] The NKA September offensive against the perimeter was thus sustained more by North Korean fanaticism than by Soviet weaponry.

For Kim, then, with all but the dimmest possibility of victory extinguished, his only option was not to risk everything on a single throw of the dice, but to gird for a war of attrition in the twin hopes that his allies would sustain him and that the United States would weary of a long struggle and sue for peace. Furthermore, with the prospect of amphibious encirclement imminent, Kim's strategy should have been to take steps to defeat or at least contain the landing, wherever it occurred, prevent the closing of the pincers, and, ultimately, prepare to withdraw to defensive positions in North Korea, from which to wage a long war. But, of course, Kim did not determine North Korea's policy, Stalin did.

From a strict North Korean perspective, assuming Kim was in charge, two principal steps were mandatory. First, Kim had to shift from offensive to defensive warfare. In this regard, it was necessary to build fortified positions around the perimeter to delay an Eighth Army breakout, and to prepare for a phased withdrawal once the landing occurred. (In fact, there is some evidence of this. The Eighth Army experienced considerable difficulty in initial attempts to break out of the perimeter once Inchon had begun.) This would, at the very least, slow the closing of the pincers and provide an escape route for his forces.

Second, it would have been necessary to assemble a mobile reserve of several divisions so positioned as to be able to rush to the landing point. In truth, with only five possible landing sites, preparatory defenses could have been constructed to hinder a landing. As we have seen, of these five, Chinnampo, Inchon, and Kunsan on the west coast, and Hungnam and Wonsan on the east coast, only an attack at Inchon held the possibility of severing logistical and communications lines to the southern forces. Thus, as Mao noted, Inchon should be watched most carefully for any signs of coming attack and, of course, defenses should be constructed there first.

It is the supreme irony that Stalin himself—no doubt to exculpate himself from blame—urged the creation of something like a mobile reserve to contend with the Inchon envelopment—except that he did so *after* Inchon, not before it! On September 18, Stalin urged Kim to withdraw four divisions from the perimeter to contain the drive from Inchon to Seoul.[76] Of course, had Kim withdrawn four divisions *before* Inchon and positioned them as a mobile reserve, he would have stood a fighting chance of either defeating the landing or containing the drive to Seoul. Either outcome would have preserved an escape route for his forces. The actual outcome was disaster for the North Korean Army.

With the Inchon landing on September 15, the stage was set for the final act in the Korean drama, of maneuvering China and the United States into conflict in Korea. It is to an examination of the consequences of Stalin's and Truman's policies for Mao Zedong that we now turn.

CHAPTER TWELVE

Mao and the Decision to Enter the Korean War

INCHON, AND THE events surrounding it, crystallized the main lines of what had been developing since the outbreak of the war. For Truman, the defeat of the NKA opened up a win-win situation. He would either unify Korea, dealing a major setback to Communist aggression, or prod Mao into a military commitment to save Kim Il-sung. Indeed, the attempt to accomplish the one was the path to the other. In the latter, more probable, and strategically desirable case, the engagement of American and Chinese forces in battle under their respective U.N. and volunteer cloaks would, without leading to another world war, define the structure of global politics for the indefinite future, fully in accordance with the strategic conception of NSC-68. Truman, however, would get more than he bargained for.

For Stalin, North Korean defeat also opened the final act in the long-planned drama of maneuvering China into conflict with the United States—his object in the first place. Chinese entry would finally defeat Mao's strategy of attempting to play both sides of the fence, preclude any near-term possibility of diplomatic relations with the United States and subordinate China to Soviet strategic design. China would find itself isolated from the West and dependent upon the Soviet Union for future assistance. Moreover, the Sino-Soviet alliance would make secure the Soviet Union's Asian security zone. Conflict in Korea would at the same time shift the U.S. focus away from the great prize of Europe, or so Stalin believed. Stalin would get far less than he wished for.

For Mao, North Korean defeat and the American determination to unify Korea brought a historic decision to intervene in the conflict, but not until after a complex negotiation with Stalin. Stalin exerted tremendous pressure on Mao to commit forces against the Americans, while Mao strove to gain the Soviet leader's agreement on the joint defense of North Korea through the provision of combat air support for Chinese ground troops. When Stalin refused, Mao, acting consistently with his objective of shifting the political dynamics of the North Korean regime from pro-Soviet to pro-Chinese, waited until the United States had destroyed most of the NKA before entering. In intervening, Mao satisfied his minimum objective of creating a more pro-Chinese North Korea as a buffer state, but his decision consigned China to a terrible future of isolation and backwardness for decades.

TRUMAN UNWRAPS HIS PACKAGE OF COMPULSION

The two-week period immediately after Inchon was the third of the four instances when Chinese intervention could have been very effective against vulnerable American forces. (The Eighth Army drive across the 38th parallel to Pyongyang would have been the fourth.) Beijing's intervention at this time would have been equally as effective as intervention in the earlier two instances. Indeed, it probably would have been more effective because American forces were divided and the Inchon force was only two divisions strong. In the first two instances, as we have seen, American leaders sought to deter Mao from entering. But now American policy had changed.

With Inchon, the turning point of the war, Truman reversed position from deterring Beijing's entry to compelling it. Truman's shift was precisely intended to prod Beijing into a commitment to North Korea, thereby demonstrating the community of interests of the Communist bloc against the West. In conjunction with the Inchon landing, he unveiled a broad array of initiatives that clearly signaled American plans. These were the determination to isolate Beijing, reorganize U.N. procedure to permit action in the face of Soviet veto, show Sino-Soviet cooperation in Korea, retain Formosa within the U.S. sphere, propose to rearm Japan and West Germany, integrate the Western alliance, strengthen the Republic of China within the U.N., and gain passage of a U.N. resolution to send forces into North Korea.

On the day of the Inchon landing, the United States announced that it was now ready to proceed with a peace treaty with Japan. The United States, a *New York Times* account said, "will propose a Japanese peace treaty placing no restrictions on rearmament, allowing the maximum of economic and commercial freedom and encouraging the admission of the former enemy into the United Nations and the community of anti-Communist allies."[1] Moreover, "responsible officials" also revealed that Washington would provide for Japan's security by stationing U.S. military forces in the country through a long-term arrangement.

Aside from establishing the anchor of the American security position in Asia and harnessing Japan securely to the Western alliance, the decision to proceed unilaterally with the treaty was a blow to Mao because it denied Beijing any legal voice in the disposition of Formosa. Although the United States had proposed a U.N. commission to consider how the purpose of the Cairo pledge to return Formosa to China could be carried out, Beijing was not in a position to influence those considerations. In the meantime, the Japanese Peace Treaty would legally supersede the pledges made at Cairo and Potsdam.

Press accounts about the treaty decision were subtly misleading. Although publicly placing "no restrictions" on Japan's rearmament, the United States had no intention of rearming Japan. Nor was there any thought of permitting Japan "maximum economic and commercial freedom," which implied that Japan's extensive prewar economic relationship with the China mainland would be resumed. The United States would strictly limit all "land, sea, or air forces" the Japanese government would be permitted to establish,[2] but the impression created was for the imminent revival of Japan as a military power.

The Big Three foreign ministers (of the United States, Great Britain, and France) were meeting in New York City when Inchon occurred. Acheson made a big show of proposing West German rearmament during the meetings, "even though the State Department knew the views of the British and French before the conference convened."[3] Not only were they opposed to actual rearmament, but they also rejected a disguised rearmament through an expansion of the German police force.[4] Nevertheless, five days after the landing, the Big Three agreed to end the state of hostilities, reinforce the internal police, endow the Bonn government with diplomatic privileges, and ease economic curbs.[5] The steps taken toward the integration of West Germany at the same time as the announcement of the decision to proceed on a Japanese Peace Treaty clearly indicated a decision to strengthen the Western alliance against the Communist world.

Successive blows then rained down on China in the United Nations, extinguishing Mao's hopes for admission. In a report sent to the Security Council on September 18, the day before the Assembly was to vote on the seating of the People's Republic of China, MacArthur accused the Russian and Chinese Communists of continuing to provide materiel and manpower to the North Korean war effort.[6] U.N. Ambassador Warren Austin made a great spectacle of demonstrating MacArthur's charges by pulling out a Russian-made submachine gun from under the Council table and passing it around to the Council delegates as evidence. Few doubted that Moscow had and was continuing to support North Korea, despite Malik's denials.

The surprise allegation was that China was cooperating with Moscow in supplying men. Ostensibly covering the period of August 16–31, 1950, the report said that the Chinese had sent some forty to sixty thousand Koreans who had fought in the Chinese civil war back to North Korea, thus providing military assistance that MacArthur described as "substantial, if not decisive." In fact, the evidence of Chinese manpower support was less than substantial and was not recent. A close reading of the report revealed that the Chinese had, indeed, sent back ethnic Koreans to become part of the NKA, but had done this in 1949 and early 1950, months before the outbreak of hostilities. There was no evidence of current and continuing support, but the damage had been done.

Nor was the timing of MacArthur's report accidental. Five weeks earlier, during Harriman's trip to Tokyo, the presidential envoy was instructed to inform MacArthur on "the importance of getting evidence on the participation of the Chinese Communists in supporting the North Korean attack and present operations." Harriman said that "there will be considerable support for seating the Chinese Communists at the next meeting of the Assembly" and he explained that "if we could obtain real evidence of direct support for the North Koreans, this might be the reason by which we could prevent the seating of the Communists on the moral issue involved."[7] The fact was that Beijing had provided very little assistance to the NKA forces and MacArthur was forced to manufacture some.

The plan to marshal enough votes to deny Beijing admission to the U.N. showed clearly that earlier U.S. proposals for commissions on bombing in Manchuria and the Formosa issue were but tactical ploys to keep Mao's hopes for admission alive and deter him from taking actions that would defeat vulnerable American forces on the battlefield. Now the U.S. position had changed. When the General Assembly met on September 19 to consider the Indian resolution to admit the PRC, Acheson urged them to "vote it down." The U.N. Assembly duly complied, voting 33–16 to deny Beijing admission.[8]

To add insult to injury, the next day during the election of seven vice presidents and six chairmen for the U.N. basic committees, "Nationalist China drew more support than had been predicted in obtaining a vice presidency, even to the extent of winning votes from delegates whose countries have recognized the Communist regime of Peiping."[9] Of the full U.N. membership of fifty-nine nations, the Nationalist government received forty-five votes. The Nationalist government's position was thus strengthened within the U.N.

With China effectively barred from U.N. membership, Secretary Acheson moved to neutralize the Soviet Union within that body. On the same day, the secretary delivered a major speech proposing that the General Assembly be empowered to take action on "a breach of the peace or an act of aggression" if the Security Council were prevented from doing so.[10] Acheson proposed that the Assembly "establish a 'security patrol' or 'peace patrol' to make an immediate investigation in any area where an international conflict was threatened." He wanted each member to "set aside specially trained United Nations units" to be in constant readiness for prompt service. All of this was directed explicitly at the Soviet Union, "the main obstacle to peace," which has "lengthened the shadow which war casts over us."

The final piece of Truman's new policy dealt directly with Korea. There was little doubt that the U.N. resolution of June 27 calling upon its members to furnish "such assistance . . . as may be necessary to repel the armed attack and to restore international peace and security in the area" permitted the conduct of tactical military operations in and around the 38th parallel. But additional authorization would be necessary if there were to be an attempt to unify Korea. During the Big Three meetings, Acheson had persuaded British Foreign Secretary Bevin, who now needed little persuasion, to compose a resolution authorizing such an objective. On September 23 the British Foreign Office had produced the first draft of a resolution and had begun to circulate it to selected members.[11]

The key points of the first draft were that "all necessary steps be taken to promote conditions of stability and security throughout the whole of Korea" and "when such conditions have been created, new elections be held throughout the whole of Korea with a view to the establishment of a unified, independent and democratic government of all Korea." After discussion with U.S. officials, these two points were, in fact, strengthened. In the final resolution, the first point was strengthened to read "all appropriate steps be taken to *insure* conditions of peace and stability" and the second to read "elections be held *and other constituent acts* be taken." Firmly based on U.N. resolutions of 1947, 1948, and 1949 calling for the unification of Korea, the British resolution was a clear statement anticipating the defeat of the North Korean regime and the establishment of a unified Korea under U.N. auspices.

By September 23, then, Mao and the Chinese leadership realized that the die had been cast. Truman had promoted a global structure of relationships that clearly excluded Beijing and firmly lumped together China and the Soviet Union. Furthermore, whatever slim hopes may have existed for an end to the war on the basis of a return to the status quo ante bellum were now dashed with the British proposed resolution to proceed toward unification. The grim prospect for Mao was that at the very least the United States would soon be sending its forces, already on the verge of recapturing Seoul, into North Korea, perhaps to the Yalu River, in an effort to eradicate Kim Il-sung's regime.

Mao responded immediately, in fact, the next day. In a formal note to the United Nations dated September 24, Foreign Minister Zhou Enlai declared that "the peace-loving peoples all over the world definitely will not stand in the face of this with folded arms." In an attempt to intimidate U.N. members, Zhou said that "if a majority of United Nations members continued to support United States action in Korea and China 'they shall not escape a share in the responsibility for lighting up war flames in the East.' " Finally, Zhou charged again that U.S. planes had violated Chinese air space and demanded that China be invited to "take part in discussions of the charges against the United States."[12]

The next day a spokesman from the Ministry of Foreign Affairs succinctly recapitulated Truman's new policy package, indicating that Beijing's leaders understood it precisely.

> We Chinese people are against the American imperialists because they are against us. They have openly become the arch enemy of the People's Republic of China by supporting the people's enemy, the Chiang Kai-shek clique, by sending a huge fleet to prevent the liberation of the Chinese territory of Taiwan, by repeated air intrusions and strafing and bombing of the Chinese people, by refusing new China a seat in the U.N., through intrigues with their satellite nations, by rearing up again a fascist power in Japan, and by rearming Japan for the purpose of expanding aggressive war. Is it not just for us to support our friend and neighbor against our enemy? The American warmongers are mistaken in thinking that their accusations and threats will intimidate the people of China.[13]

The kind of pressure generated by Truman was indirect and Mao's response prompt and direct. The kind of pressure simultaneously generated by Stalin, on the other hand, was direct and Mao's response delayed and indirect. Nevertheless, these combined pressures would constitute a closing political vise on Mao and the Chinese leadership, leaving but a single avenue by which to proceed—the commitment of troops to Korea. The only questions were where and when and under what circumstances the commitment would be made. In this way Mao's options were at once created and circumscribed.

STALIN INTENSIFIES THE PRESSURE FOR COMMITMENT

Stalin's strategy entered the end game with the assault on Inchon, and as soon as American troops landed, he began to pressure Mao to send troops, subtly at first, then with increasing heavy-handedness. The day after the landing, he sent a cable asking Mao how many troops he had deployed in Manchuria between Shenyang (Mukden) and Antung and whether he could send them to assist Kim.[14] Mao was in no hurry to send troops and Zhou Enlai procrastinated two days before replying. In his reply, he asked Stalin for an evaluation of the military situation, offered a litany of excuses as to why Bei-

321

jing could do nothing, and avoided any discussion of his troop request.[15] Alerted by Stalin's request, however, Zhou moved quickly to prepare the ground for a negative response.

Zhou said that Kim had not kept the Chinese ambassador, Ni Zhiliang, informed and thus Beijing had no knowledge of the Inchon landing except that carried in the Western press and over Pyongyang radio. Zhou complained that they had "very poor contacts" with the North Korean government and were "absolutely in the dark" about Kim's operational plans. Moreover, Kim had "persistently ignored Mao's advice and predictions." In response to Soviet Ambassador Roshchin's query about what Kim should do, Zhou said that if Kim had 100,000 men in reserve in the Pyongyang-Seoul area he could defeat the Inchon attack. If not, he must withdraw his "main forces" from Pusan for that purpose.[16]

322   Meanwhile, Stalin seemed to be acting on these very lines. On September 18, he sent Kim a cable ordering him to withdraw four divisions from the Naktong front toward Seoul. But later that day, perhaps after receiving Zhou's cable, he also sent a special envoy, General Matvey V. Zakharov, deputy chief of the General Staff of the Soviet Army, to Pyongyang with orders "to pull out *all* his divisions from the Naktong River front and redeploy them to defend Seoul in the northeast and east."[17] In fact, North Korean forces began to withdraw from the perimeter the next day. Stalin also issued orders for the establishment of the air defense of Pyongyang, a paper exercise, as it turned out, since no Soviet air defense of the North Korean capital materialized, but it momentarily raised Kim's hopes that Moscow would defend his regime.

Responding to Zhou's cable on September 20, Stalin criticized the NKA's "underdeveloped command and control system and weak cadres." However, he went on, had it fought only against Syngman Rhee's troops, "it would have cleaned up Korea from the reactionary forces a long time ago." Attempting to lay the basis for better relations between Beijing and Pyongyang, Stalin stressed that poor communications were "abnormal," but excusable because the regime "was young and ill-experienced." Kim, Stalin explained, failed to provide Mao with military intelligence "because of difficulties in his own . . . command, rather than his reluctance to share this kind of information [with Mao]." He himself, Stalin went on, had received some "odd and belated reports about the front line situation."

In closing, Stalin professed to agree with Zhou that the only hope of halting the unfolding U.N. offensive around Seoul was through "a pullout of main forces from the southeastern front and creation of formidable lines of defense east and north of Seoul."[18] In other words, there were no large North Korean reserves left. Although Stalin had professed his agreement with Zhou regarding the withdrawal of forces from Pusan to defend Seoul, Zhou had not advised that Kim pull out all of the forces from Pusan, only that he withdraw his "main forces." Stalin, however, had secretly ordered the withdrawal of the entire force, with predictable and disastrous consequences.

Kim Il-sung was, of course, the pivotal figure in the intensifying exchanges between Stalin and Mao. If he could be persuaded to request assistance from the Chinese, it would be difficult for Mao to refuse, despite the fact that Kim had been adamantly opposed to any Chinese role to date. Thus, both sides sought to persuade Kim to embrace their view—Stalin wanting Kim to ask Mao for help and Mao wanting Kim to continue the war, but to turn to the defensive and rely on his own resources.

The first skirmish for Kim's mind went to Mao. Before replying to Stalin, Zhou Enlai had instructed Ambassador Ni Zhiliang to elicit from Kim the opinion that his forces would continue to fight on, shifting to "protracted war on the basis of self-reliance."[19] When Zhou replied to Stalin on September 21, he informed him of Ni's conversation with Kim. While expressing satisfaction that the Soviet assessment of the military situation after Inchon "matched the Chinese one," he passed on to the Soviet leader Kim's reported view that "the Korean people were ready to fight a protracted war." Of course, if Kim held to that view, there would be no need to dispatch Chinese troops.[20] But the struggle for Kim's mind had just begun.

Stalin had entrusted General Zakharov, as part of his special mission to Pyongyang, with the task of persuading Kim to request immediate help from the Chinese.[21] In his first report to Stalin on September 26, following his arrival in Pyongyang, Zakharov described the "severe" disintegration of the NKA and the efforts he was making to organize a fighting withdrawal of the southern units to a defensive line spanning Seoul, Yoju, and Ch'ungju. He noted that the delivery of ammunition and fuel had been "virtually halted," and sought to restart it. In an effort to strengthen overall command and control, Zakharov recommended, and Kim agreed, that Kim take over the post of Defense Minister. Finally, observing that the NKA had a "dire shortage of [truck] drivers" to move supplies, he closed with the question: "It may be expedient to propose to Kim Il-sung that he ask the Chinese friends to dispatch not less than 1,500 drivers to Korea, may it not?"[22]

Thus, Stalin hoped to entangle Mao in the defense of North Korea step by step, by prodding Kim to ask for minimal assistance at the start. He was, of course, confident in his ability to persuade Kim, particularly as the NKA was disintegrating before the onslaught of American forces moving north. At this point, September 23, U.S. forces from Inchon stood poised for the assault on Seoul and Eighth Army units were moving northward from Pusan to effect a junction with X Corps. Although NKA forces had managed to throw together close to forty thousand poorly armed and loosely organized troops for the defense of Seoul, including the deployment of some fifty tanks and the placement of extensive minefields on the roads between Inchon and Seoul, there were not enough forces available for defense, making the outcome a foregone conclusion. American battlefield successes worked to Stalin's advantage by inexorably increasing the pressure on Mao.

In any case, after receiving General Zakharov's report, Stalin immediately convened an emergency Politburo meeting on September 27, the first of several, as Mansourov notes, "to minimize Soviet exposure on the peninsula," but actually to establish an official cover-up of his own policy. At this meeting, Stalin blamed everyone but himself for the looming disaster. The North Korean high command and field commanders had made a "series of grave mistakes." Soviet military advisers, "who are even more to blame," displayed "strategic illiteracy and incompetence" and had failed to carry out Stain's orders "scrupulously and in a timely fashion."[23]

In Stalin's view, Soviet advisers, failing to grasp the significance and implications of Inchon, procrastinated in withdrawing four divisions from the south for the defense of Seoul as he had ordered, "despite the fact that at the moment of adopting this decision such a possibility existed." Consequently, "they lost seven days which brought about an enormous tactical advantage in the vicinity of Seoul to the U.S. troops." Stalin claimed that "had they pulled out these divisions on time, this could have changed the military situation around Seoul considerably."

What Stalin declined to note, however, was that he himself had instructed Zakharov to withdraw not four divisions, but *all* of the forces in the south. Moreover, he had made this decision only after and not before Inchon, when it would have made a difference. At this point, the withdrawal of the entire force only threw the NKA into chaos and facilitated the Eighth Army's breakout from the perimeter and its drive north against blindly retreating NKA troops. To have had *any* hope of defeating the Inchon landing the southern front had to have been held, while some forces were sent to contain the lodgment, as Zhou suggested. But, of course, Stalin had not intended for the NKA to succeed either in the initial invasion or in the later defense, which would only have contradicted his strategy. Thus the reason for the cover-up.

Stalin complained that the single division that had been redeployed for the defense of Seoul "was thrown into combat in a disorganized manner and in odd units, which made it easier for the enemy to decimate and annihilate it." Criticizing Zakharov directly, his telegram read: "you should have deployed this division for combat at the line northeast and east of Seoul," instead of to the southeast on the Seoul-Yoju-Ch'ungju line. "As a result of this," Stalin maintained, "the KPA [NKA] troops, in essence, are beyond control; they are engaged in combat blindly and cannot arrange the coordination between the various armed services in battle." Disaster complete, the Politburo then arrived at the obvious conclusion that "after the fall of Seoul the KPA's main goal should be to withdraw all its troops to North Korea and defend its own homeland by all means."

It would appear that Stalin's telegram of September 27 to General Zakharov and Shtykov was not divulged to Kim Il-sung. Nevertheless, acting on Zakharov's recommendation to assume command of the Defense Ministry, Kim convened a Politburo meeting the next day. The atmosphere was grim and the North Korean leadership in a state of panic. They had lost contact with both the First and Second Front Line Commands, and there was no news from Seoul, as American forces advanced. Kim decided to organize a defense along the 38th parallel and form fifteen new infantry divisions, from six that were then being created in the north, and nine that were among the remnants of those divisions fleeing from the south. As discussion continued, however, Kim realized that this plan was a fantasy. Once Seoul fell

325

> nothing would stop the UN forces from crossing the 38th parallel; that if they did cross the parallel, the remaining KPA units would not be able to render any serious resistance, and, consequently, the war would be over in a very short period of time, with the North Korean state being eliminated by the aggressive American imperialists.[24]

Their only hope, Kim and his cohorts concluded, was to send an urgent plea to Moscow and Beijing for immediate and direct military assistance. Then and there, in a meeting lasting past midnight, they discussed, composed, and approved two letters addressed to Stalin and Mao "begging them to intervene directly and without delay to save the North Korean regime."

Discussing the Politburo decisions with Shtykov later that day, Kim ritualistically reaffirmed his determination to unify the country by his own means, but then repeated the argument made in the Politburo to the effect that if the enemy crossed the 38th parallel "they would be unable to form new troops and they would have no means to render any serious resistance to the enemy." Shtykov urged Kim to "set up defenses along the 38th parallel," as Stalin had instructed, but sensed utter "confusion and hopelessness" in Kim's eyes. Shtykov, the man who previously had had all the answers, now had none.[25]

Kim turned to the matter of the letter to Stalin, seeking advice. Shtykov, however, had been forewarned and "dodged" the issue, saying he "could give no advice on this matter." After the North Korean Politburo meeting of the day before, one of Zakharov's group had had a chance encounter with Pak Hon-yong, who told him that the Politburo had agreed to send a letter to Stalin requesting Soviet air support. He also learned that they had already dispatched a letter to Mao containing "a hint about aid." (As noted above, Kim had asked for more than a "hint" of aid from Mao and wanted far more than merely air support from Stalin.)

Shtykov immediately sent Stalin a cable alerting him to the imminent arrival of a letter requesting direct Soviet intervention. Kim's and Pak Hon-yong's letter to Stalin was dated September 29, but evidently did not reach Stalin until the first of October, for reasons to be explained below. It reiterated the arguments discussed above, noting in particular the devastating effectiveness of the U.S. air force to "inflict great losses to our manpower and destroy our armaments."[26] These were, the letter said, "very unfavorable conditions for us," and should they remain so, "then the American aggression ultimately will be successful."

Insisting that the Korean people were "determined to overcome the difficulties facing us," and promising to fight to "the last drop of blood," Kim and Pak said that "first of all, we need to have an appropriate air force," even though we have no "well-trained pilots." We were also "arming the entire people so as to be prepared to fight a protracted war." Notwithstanding our determination, "if the enemy does not give us time to implement the measures which we plan, and, making use of our extremely grave situation, steps up its offensive operations into North Korea, then we will not be able to stop the enemy troops solely with our own forces."

> Therefore, dear Iosif Vissarionovich, we cannot help asking You to provide us with special assistance. In other words, at the moment when the enemy troops cross over the 38th parallel we will badly need direct military assistance from the Soviet Union. If for any reason this is impossible, please assist us by forming international volunteer units in China and other countries of people's democracy for rendering military assistance to our struggle.[27]

Upon receipt of Shtykov's cable alerting him to Kim's forthcoming request for direct Soviet intervention, Stalin made several quick decisions. Hastily convening a Politburo meeting, he dashed off a reply to Zakharov, approving the suggestion that Kim become Supreme Commander in Chief by assuming the duties of the defense minister. (Defense Minister Choe Yong-gon, desperately attempting to mount a defense of Seoul, had not been heard from for days.) Second, he approved the formation of six divisions and the withdrawal of "manpower reserves," a euphemism for those troops fleeing from the south. Third, he promised to supply the necessary "armaments, ammunition, and other materials" over a two-week period beginning October 5. Finally, he agreed with Zakharov's suggestion that "Kim ask the Chinese friends to dispatch [truck] drivers to Korea," but not say that the idea came from Moscow.[28]

Then, without waiting for Kim's letter to arrive, indeed to avoid receiving it, Stalin left Moscow and flew to his dacha on the Black Sea. Kim's letter would be forwarded to him there. Why leave Moscow at what was from his point of view the crucial moment of the war? Stalin clearly did not want to reply to Kim before dealing with Mao. A prompt reply would only be crushingly negative; moving to his dacha gave him time and something of an excuse to delay. In fact, he would not reply to Kim for over a week, until October 8, and even then his reply would be devastating for Kim, because his initial discussions with Mao would be unsuccessful.

Arriving at his dacha, Stalin prepared to confront what was perhaps the most serious crisis since the German attack on Moscow in World War II. It was a crisis, it bears restating, that was entirely of his own making. His departure from Moscow at this time, unusual given the fact that all the resources for managing a crisis existed there, can best be explained by Stalin's intention to minimize the number of individuals involved in the difficult negotiations to come. But this was the moment Stalin had been planning for these many months, the moment when he hoped to nudge Mao into battle against the United States. As Stalin prepared for his dramatic negotiation with Mao, Truman was making an equally portentous decision to send MacArthur into North Korea.

MACARTHUR'S "WONSAN GAMBIT"

All summer long, U.S. and allied officials had discussed the advisability of crossing the 38th parallel and had reached the decision to do so under certain conditions. Truman, of course, had already made the command decision to engage Chinese troops in battle in NSC-73. After the brilliantly successful strike at Inchon it would have been politically impossible to stop short of an effort to unify Korea. Foreign opinion, with India's prominent exception, anticipated U.N. operations in North Korea to end the war and Great Britain had sponsored the U.N. resolution that would authorize these operations. President Syngman Rhee, naturally enough, was urging U.N. forces as well as his own troops on to the Yalu River. In Washington, Republicans and Democrats were calculating the impact of a Korean victory for upcoming mid-term elections.

Yet, following the Inchon landing and the drive on Seoul, no instructions were sent to MacArthur for operations beyond the 38th parallel. It was not until Seoul was about to fall, on September 27, that a directive was sent to MacArthur. All accounts explain the reason for the almost two-week delay as the result of the transition from Secretary of Defense Johnson to George C. Marshall, but this was an obvious administration "spin." President Truman had forced Johnson to resign on September 12, but the decision to replace him and the arrangements for Marshall to succeed him had been completed some days earlier.[29]

The decision to send U.N. forces into North Korea was transcendent and would not have gotten lost in the shuffle as Marshall familiarized himself with his new job. Indeed, that decision as well as the decision to take Wonsan by amphibious assault were, according to James Schnabel, "among the most significant of the Korean War."[30] Besides, the decision to proceed north of the 38th parallel had already been made. The delay in sending MacArthur his action directive had to do with the issue of how the enemy would respond to the dramatic reversal effected by Inchon.

All calculations about Inchon had focused on cutting off and trapping the North Korean forces concentrated around Pusan. It was assumed that North Korea had no large reserve forces concealed somewhere in the North and that the Chinese would not intervene with the large force known to be assembled in Manchuria. As long as these assumptions were correct, MacArthur's amphibious assault would succeed. When Inchon occurred, the first assumption had been proven correct: the NKA had few reserves to send to contain the landing and mount a defense of Seoul, although the troops that were there fought doggedly. But the second assumption had yet to be tested.

As MacArthur's forces conducted mopping-up operations around Seoul and proceeded unhindered toward the 38th parallel, the question was: Would the Chinese now intervene to bar access to North Korea?[31] This was, recall, the third instance when Chinese forces could intervene, perhaps most decisively, as MacArthur's forces were divided and the Inchon force was vulnerable to a large-scale Chinese attack, particularly if the NKA force in Pusan prevented an Eighth Army breakout and linkup. If Beijing intervened, of course, Truman would have achieved his ultimate objective of engaging China in conflict without provoking them into it. And so Truman waited.

When Beijing did not intervene immediately after Inchon, American planners, certainly MacArthur, began to gird for the possibility that Mao would attempt to prevent the complete destruction of the Pyongyang regime as U.N. forces drove into North Korea, which would be Mao's fourth and final opportunity to do so. It seemed inconceivable that Mao would make no effort to save Kim. The plan to counter a possible Chinese intervention as U.N. forces crossed the 38th parallel was the impetus behind what I call the "Wonsan gambit."

The issue was far larger than the destruction of the North Korean Army itself. Had the objective simply been the stated one of trapping and destroying the fleeing North Korean armies, then the scheme generally concurred in by MacArthur's planners, as well as by General Walker, would have been implemented without delay.[32] These proposed plans followed standard Army doctrine, actually universal military doctrine, which called for the rapid pursuit of a retreating and disorganized enemy. Prompt action would also most likely overtake North Korean efforts to mount a defense at the 38th parallel, if not also of Pyongyang.[33]

Operational plans grew logically out of the force dispositions of late September following the recapture of Seoul. The X Corps' First Marine and Seventh Army Divisions were deployed north and south of Seoul, poised to advance, while Eighth Army forces were still arriving from the south. Eighth Army units had not, by the way, pursued the retreating NKA with the objective of capturing or destroying them. Instead, eschewing the "palms in" method of short envelopments approved by Army doctrine, they drove rapidly north, led by armor, in an "attack to unlimited objectives." They thus bypassed enemy troops in a race to link up with X Corps at Seoul.[34]

It was generally assumed that following the successful Inchon attack the X Corps, specially created for the amphibious operation, would be joined to Walker's Eighth Army, and its commander, General Almond, would return to his position on MacArthur's staff in Tokyo. Under a single, powerful command, then, the First Marines and the Seventh Division would set out toward Pyongyang "almost immediately" to capitalize on the enemy's confusion, seize his capital, and establish one of several lines of control across the peninsula to close the door on the fleeing NKA. Seizure of Pyongyang and its port of Chinnampo would support further operations eastward toward Wonsan.

The best lateral road net in Korea, despite extensive bomb damage, was the triangle of Seoul-Pyongyang-Wonsan-Seoul. Part of Eighth Army, I Corps, composed of the U.S. First Cavalry and Twenty-fourth Divisions, along with the ROK First Division and the British Twenty-seventh Brigade, would establish a second line, driving from Seoul overland along the northeast leg of this triangle to Wonsan. I Corps would link up with the ROK Third and Capital Divisions moving up the east coast road toward Wonsan. Gaining control of the port of Wonsan would enable the support of additional operations westward back toward Pyongyang.

After taking Wonsan, elements of I Corps would drive westward to link up with the Marines and the Seventh Division moving east and seal off all remaining escape routes for the NKA. Once completed, these forces would advance another fifty miles north to the "narrow neck" of the Korean peninsula, the Chongju-Yongwan-Hamhung line, which would provide for two additional ports—Sinanju at the mouth of the Ch'ongch'on River on the west coast and Hungnam on the east coast. The four forward ports of Chinnampo, Sinanju, Wonsan, and Hungnam would permit sustained operations in North Korea, if needed, to eradicate all remaining North Korean resistance.

These plans made perfect sense if, but only if, there were no Chinese intervention. Were the Chinese to intervene either while the Marines and Seventh Division were driving on Pyongyang and/or while I Corps was moving to Wonsan, U.S. forces would be at a severe disadvantage, without forward supply and with little possibility of rapid reinforcement. Without forward supply, and restricted to the limited logistical capabilities of Inchon and distant Pusan, even adequate defense, let alone timely large-scale offensive operations, would be very problematical. When presented to MacArthur, he immediately rejected these plans, but without explaining his reasons.

Instead of going with the obvious plans outlined above, MacArthur offered what his aides thought was an "astonishing" alternative. He would not merge X Corps and Eighth Army, but keep the commands separate, controlling Almond's force from Tokyo. Furthermore, he would not attack promptly, but would delay the advance across the parallel, at least until given U.N. authorization, but by at least two weeks, or more. Perhaps the most astounding portion of MacArthur's plan was the decision to remove X Corps from the field of battle around Seoul entirely, leaving the escape route north open to the fleeing NKA.

He would, instead, send already weary Eighth Army units through X Corps lines north to assault Pyongyang and send X Corps by sea for an amphibious assault on Wonsan. Eighth Army was not to commence its drive north until October 15, while the Wonsan landing was scheduled for October 20. In this operation, the First Marines would outload at Inchon, tying up the port for weeks and denying its use to the Eighth Army, while the Seventh Division would move overland all the way to Pusan, completely clogging northbound supplies for the Eighth Army, there to embark on ships for a Wonsan landing behind the marines. Blair rightly described this as "a logistical nightmare."[35]

It is no wonder that some military historians view MacArthur's plan as "one of the more glaring blunders of American military history."[36] If the object truly was to trap and destroy the remnants of the retreating NKA, speed was of the essence. Even if it worked to perfection, MacArthur's plan would not accomplish that objective because it took too long to develop. Obviously, withdrawing the main force that could close the gate against the NKA and delaying the start of operations by two or three weeks would allow what remained of the enemy to escape. But, of course, MacArthur as well as the president, who not only promptly authorized, but also "warmly endorsed" this plan, understood that more was at issue than trapping and destroying the North Korean armies.[37]

MacArthur's plans were not only in conformity with the operational guidance sent to him at this time, but also anticipated the possibility of

330

Chinese intervention. The directive of September 27 authorized airborne, ground, and amphibious operations north of the 38th parallel to effect "the destruction of the North Korean armed forces." This authorization was contingent upon the proviso that "there has been no entry into North Korea by major Soviet or Chinese Communist forces, no announcement of intended entry, nor a threat to counter our operations militarily in North Korea."[38] To ensure against the possibility of inadvertent clashes with Chinese or Russian border units, not only were operations to be restricted to North Korea itself, "no non-Korean Ground Forces" were to be employed "in the northeast provinces bordering the Soviet Union or in the area along the Manchurian border."

As in NSC-81/1, the alliance compromise document from which this military directive was derived, the decisions of NSC-76 and NSC-73 governed, even though they were not identified explicitly. Should the Soviets intervene with major units, it would signal the beginning of World War III and MacArthur should assume the defense and refer the matter to Washington. Should the Chinese intervene with major units, "you should continue the action as long as action by your forces offers a reasonable chance of successful resistance." Finally, "in the event of an attempt to employ small Soviet or Chinese Communist units covertly south of the 38th parallel, you should continue the action."

MacArthur's military directive retained the same ambiguity of purpose found in NSC-81/1, in that the directive was almost entirely focused on operational contingencies that could occur *south* of the 38th parallel, contingencies that had already been overtaken by events. The gist of MacArthur's orders was that as long as the Soviets or Chinese did not openly deploy "major" units into Korea, he was authorized to continue military operations. The president would evaluate the accumulating announcements and threats from Beijing, but it was left to MacArthur to determine what constituted "major" units in the field against his forces. In short, he was provided with both an incentive and an opportunity to downgrade the size of the forces he would encounter.

As the military directive of September 27 was explicitly based on NSC-81/1, there can be little doubt that MacArthur would have compared the two documents and immediately noticed discrepancies and omissions. Most strikingly, what had been omitted from his military directive, but contained in NSC-81/1, was what else the administration was ostensibly prepared to do should the Chinese Communists intervene. NSC-81/1 stated that if the Chinese Communists intervened "the U.N. Commander should continue such action and be authorized to take appropriate air and naval action outside Korea against Communist China." This latter "action," that is, against China *outside* Korea, "should be continued pending a review of U.S. military commitments in the light of conditions then existing to determine further U.S. courses of action."

In unambiguous language, MacArthur was being told to take aggressive action into North Korea. Should his military operations provoke Chinese intervention, then the administration was prepared to "take appropriate air and naval action outside Korea against Communist China." Strikingly, MacArthur himself could initiate such action, "pending a review." Immediately upon receipt of the military directive, MacArthur briefed his commanders on his Wonsan plan, sending an outline description of it to the Joint Chiefs for approval, as required.

Presidential approval was forthcoming within twenty-four hours, accompanied by a personal message from Secretary of Defense Marshall urging MacArthur to "feel unhampered tactically and strategically to proceed north of the 38th parallel." The administration, he said, did not wish to be "confronted" in the U.N. by the necessity of a vote on the issue. The reference to feeling "unhampered ... strategically" could only have been a veiled assurance regarding Truman's commitment to back MacArthur if Beijing intervened. MacArthur promptly cabled back his understanding that "unless the enemy capitulates ... I regard all of Korea open for our military operations."[39]

MacArthur's "Wonsan gambit" was an attempt to lure Mao into a trap and was specifically designed to accomplish two ends. First, it would permit enough NKA stragglers to escape to justify military operations in North Korea to destroy them. Second, it would prepare to counter the possibility of Chinese intervention when his forces moved into North Korea. Removing the X Corps from its positions around Seoul without question opened the door for the fleeing North Koreans and initially reduced the risk to Beijing of intervention. Sending X Corps by sea to Wonsan gave MacArthur a potent weapon to counter any Chinese attack on the units of the Eighth Army moving northward toward Pyongyang. Delaying the start of operations provided time for both things to happen.[40]

MacArthur issued the operations order for his plans on October 2, even as the ROK Third and Capital Divisions were speeding across the 38th parallel toward Wonsan along the east coast road. That same day Mao, replying to Stalin's insistent entreaties that he send Chinese troops into battle, informed the Soviet leader that he would not do so, at least not yet. Unbeknownst to Mao, MacArthur had prepared an elaborate countermove for a Chinese intervention that would not occur, at least not when or where he and Truman expected it. Mao, as we shall see below, had his own agenda.

Nevertheless, that China would intervene was becoming increasingly obvious. In private messages and official announcements, Beijing was issuing warnings against any entry into North Korea. The Chinese Chief of Staff, Nie Rongzhen, had sent a message to the United States through the Panikkar channel on September 25, declaring that "the Chinese did not intend to sit back with folded hands and let the Americans come up to their border."[41] Panikkar, who up to this moment had not believed that China would intervene, changed his mind. He now felt that "Chinese intervention in Korea had become much more probable."[42] This was a message neither American nor British officials wished to hear, and henceforth they conveniently disparaged Panikkar's opinion.

Publicly, on September 30, before the Chinese People's Political Consultative Conference, Zhou Enlai removed all doubt about Beijing's intentions, announcing that "the Chinese people absolutely will not tolerate foreign aggression, nor will they supinely tolerate seeing their neighbors being savagely invaded by the imperialists."[43] American intelligence had also learned that Zhou had told another conference that "if the Koreans were pushed back to the Manchurian frontier China's policy would be to fight outside her borders and not wait for the enemy to come inside."[44]

As Alan Whiting concluded, by October 2 the Chinese government had "clearly defined the casus belli as the entry of U.S. forces into North Korea, and its own response as military intervention on behalf of the DPRK [Democratic People's Republic of Korea]."[45] Indeed, Beijing was complying with Washington's own criteria, announcing its intention to intervene and threatening to counter U.N. operations militarily. The United States and China were clearly on a collision course.

MAO ATTEMPTS TO "NEGOTIATE" CHINESE ENTRY

During the first two weeks of October, Mao, in a complex negotiation with Stalin, reached the decision to intervene in the Korean War. The Mao-Stalin exchanges revealed a sharp conflict of interests on matters that would affect the global position of their respective states, not to mention the fate of, and their relations with, North Korea, for decades to come. Extremely sensitive and complex, as are all high-stakes negotiations involving issues of grand strategy, both sides pulled no punches, engaging in protracted hard bargaining to the extent of reneging on earlier commitments.[46]

Shortly after arriving at his Black Sea dacha, Stalin received the forwarded message from Kim and Pak. He may also have learned of Zhou Enlai's statement of September 30. In any case, he immediately drafted a cable to Mao, and transmitted it at 3:00 in the morning on October 1. Stalin omitted any mention of having received Kim's and Pak's letter, but undoubtedly realizing that Mao must have received his from them by now, Stalin assumed

333

a studied, casual attitude. Feigning unconcern, he started by saying that he was "far away from Moscow on vacation and somewhat detached from events." Of course, except for the fact that he was not in Moscow, the truth was precisely the opposite. He was neither "on vacation" nor "detached."[47]

Sticking to the cover story crafted four days before, he blamed the North Korean high command for failing to follow Kim's orders. He said that although he had warned Kim that Inchon had "great significance" the day after it happened, and "admonished them to withdraw at least four divisions from the south immediately, to set up a frontline to the north and east of Seoul, and later to gradually pull out most of the troops fighting in the South northward, thereby providing for the defense of the 38th parallel," they had paid him no heed. (As discussed above, Stalin had ordered a wholesale pullout, not a graduated one.)

As a result, he said, the situation is getting "desperate": "Our Korean friends have no troops capable of resistance in the vicinity of Seoul. Hence, one needs to consider the way toward the 38th parallel wide open." The fact was, as Stalin must have known, by October 1 Seoul had already fallen, North Korean troops were fleeing across the parallel, U.S. forces were already at the parallel, and some ROK forces were already across it. The way to Pyongyang was now wide open. Was this description of the current situation part of Stalin's charade to convince Mao that, being on vacation and somewhat detached, he was uninformed? Or did Stalin hope that Mao, realizing the situation was worse than Stalin portrayed it, would be prompted into immediate action?

Continuing in a casual mode, Stalin did not demand that Mao openly intervene, but suggested that he could give Kim time to organize his forces by providing a screen of Chinese "volunteers" at the 38th parallel. He said, deferentially: "I think that if in the current situation you consider it possible to send troops to assist the Koreans, then you should move at least five–six divisions toward the 38th parallel at once so as to give our Korean comrades an opportunity to organize combat reserves north of the 38th parallel under the cover of your troops. The Chinese divisions could be considered as volunteers, with Chinese in command at the head, of course."

Mao received Stalin's message on October 1, 1950, the first anniversary of the Chinese People's Republic. As the people celebrated throughout the country, Mao was faced with a deep crisis. He now had Kim's and Pak's request in hand as well as Stalin's telegram, which he apparently kept to himself. He had also received Ambassador Ni Zhiliang's message conveying an oral request for assistance from Kim. Late on the evening of October 1 and carrying over into the 2nd, Mao met with several key members of the Politburo—Zhou Enlai, Zhu De, and Liu Shaoqi—to discuss the Korean situation. They were joined later in the day by Chief of Staff Nie Rongzhen and Manchurian party chief Gao Gang, whom Mao called to attend.[48]

At this meeting, given the rapid deterioration of the Korean situation, Mao was concerned with "how fast" China could act. He sent a message to NBDA commander Deng Hua querying whether his forces could "begin operations immediately?" They also discussed the choice of an overall commander for the proposed volunteer force and, in light of Lin Biao's continued objection to intervention, settled on Peng Dehuai. Finally, they decided to send troops into Korea on October 15. At the end of the meeting, "Mao mentioned that he was going to send Stalin a telegram in his own name, informing the Soviets of the main decisions of the meeting." All agreed and Mao sent a telegram that evening, October 2.[49]

Mao's telegram, however, did not in the least reflect these decisions. Instead, he initiated a two-week-long campaign to bring the Soviet Union into the war for the joint defense of North Korea, a commitment that would raise the risk of a Soviet-U.S. world war. Indeed, maneuvering Stalin into war with the United States seems to have been Mao's underlying objective during the negotiations, the modern-day equivalent of the ancient Chinese strategy of sitting on the mountain to watch the two tigers fight. The exchange of messages made it immediately apparent that both leaders were engaging in a high stakes game of "chicken," each wagering that the other would blink first before American forces gained control of all of Korea.

Thus, as the negotiation unfolded, Mao attempted to predicate his commitment of troops to Korea on Stalin's provision of combat air support. Stalin, for his part, while willing to provide weapons for Chinese troops and air defense for Manchuria, would not budge on combat air support in Korea. Stalin won this "game" because, as U.N. forces advanced to the Yalu, he was willing to allow the United States to gain complete control of Korea, and believed that Mao was not. Time ran out for Mao when U.N. forces advanced to the Yalu and Stalin still held out. It was Mao who flinched and intervened to ensure his minimum objective—the existence of a divided Korea, a buffer zone under strong Chinese influence.

Mao wanted Stalin to provide combat air support for Chinese ground forces in Korea, which was tantamount to Soviet entry into the conflict and the prospect of world war with the United States. Mao certainly understood the import of his request. Recall, in chapter 10 (p. 255), Stalin had promised air support for Chinese troops, then attempted to finesse his promise by transferring jet aircraft to China and training Chinese pilots to fly them. Although jets had at this point been transferred, the pilots had not yet been trained. Thus, Mao's opening and Stalin's dilemma. When Mao replied to Stalin's message of October 1, he said:

We originally planned to move several volunteer divisions to North Korea to render assistance to the Korean comrades when the enemy advanced north of the 38th parallel. However, having thought this over thoroughly, we now consider that such actions may entail extremely serious consequences.[50]

In the first place, Mao explained, his commanders had "no confidence" that they could succeed by sending a few poorly equipped divisions into battle against American troops. In the second place, he went on, "an open conflict between the USA and China" could drag the Soviet Union into it, leading to a world war. He said that "many comrades . . . judge that it is necessary to show caution here." Of course, Mao continued, "not to send out troops to render assistance is very bad for the Korean comrades, who are presently in such difficulty, and we ourselves feel this keenly." There was no alternative, he believed, except for the Koreans to suffer defeat "temporarily," while shifting to guerrilla warfare.

But, he reiterated, "if we advance several divisions and the enemy forces us to retreat; and this moreover provokes an open conflict between the USA and China, then our entire plan for peaceful construction will be completely ruined." In his view, "it is better to show patience now, [and] refrain from advancing troops." We should, instead, "actively prepare our forces, which will be more advantageous at the time of war with the enemy." In any case, he said, we will convene a meeting of the Central Committee, "at which will be present the main comrades of the various bureaus."

Mao concluded by saying that this was a "preliminary telegram," and that "a final decision has not been taken on this question." We want "to consult with you. If you agree, then we are ready immediately to send by plane Comrades Zhou Enlai and Lin Biao to your vacation place to talk over this matter with you."

The subtext contained in these two messages requires little elucidation. Based on Kim's "desperate" situation, Stalin had asked Mao to deploy a small force of five to six divisions to the 38th parallel to provide cover for the North Koreans to reorganize their own forces. He did not offer to provide equipment or any other kind of support. In other words, Stalin's opening proposal was for Mao to deploy a weak and overextended force to the 38th parallel where supply would be difficult against powerful U.N. forces fighting close to their supply bases. This was a prescription for disaster, particularly as MacArthur was readying a devastating blow with X Corps through Wonsan. But Mao would not fall for the trap.

In his reply, Mao did not say that he would not commit his forces. What he did say was that he would not commit them now because they were "extremely poorly equipped" and not able to contend with American troops (the enemy can force us to retreat). He implied that a Sino-U.S. conflict would bring into play the Sino-Soviet treaty, which he mistakenly thought obligated Stalin to assist China. (No doubt, if he did not already know it, he would soon be apprised of the fact that only a specific declaration of war by the U.S. against China obligated Stalin. Stalin incurred no obligation in a conflict between the U.N. forces and Chinese "volunteers.")

The implication was that, once Stalin agreed to provide weapons and other support, particularly air support, then Mao would be willing to commit troops. The fact was that Mao would commit troops with or without Soviet weapons or air support, but Stalin could not be certain of that. Mao's main consideration was that his forces fight from a position of advantage, which meant close to their support bases in Manchuria, and not at the 38th parallel, a distance of over 150 miles. This, of course, also meant that Mao would wait to commit his troops until U.N. forces approached the Yalu and ipso facto that North Korean forces would be almost totally destroyed in the meantime.

337

Did Mao believe he could outwait Stalin? Did he hope that the imminent collapse of Kim's regime, with the resulting loss of Soviet influence, would prompt Stalin to risk global war? If he did, it was a miscalculation. The chances were, however, that Mao understood that his delay tactic was a long-shot gamble that would in all likelihood not succeed. He was playing a weak hand. Mao's plan from the beginning was to wait until the NKA was nearly demolished before entering, so that the outcome of China's intervention would be a pro-Chinese Korea. Delay was his only hope of avoiding the crushing burden of unilateral involvement in Korea—even with Soviet weapons.

Upon receipt of Mao's cable, Stalin immediately decided on another turn of the screw to increase the pressure on Mao to commit troops. On the one hand, he authorized a cease-fire proposal in the U.N., which he knew would not be accepted because it would leave North Korea better off than it had been before the conflict began. For Truman, this would have been like snatching defeat from the jaws of victory. (The proposal was essentially Stalin's old World War II ploy of supporting a cease-fire and withdrawal of all foreign troops followed by national elections observed by neighboring states, envisioning a coalition government outcome). The General Assembly voted it down, 47 to 5.

At the same time, Stalin sent a message to General Zakharov instructing him to pull out all remaining troops in the south to North Korea immediately.

In the current situation, without delay, you must give instructions to the soldiers and officers who are still fighting in the south to retreat by any means, in groups or person by person, to the north. There is no continuous frontline. . . .

They must leave heavy weapons behind and try to get to the north by all means, by using the cover of night and the areas unoccupied by the enemy yet.[51]

Mao, on the other hand, having bought some time from Stalin, sought to gain some from the Americans. Zhou Enlai called Ambassador Panikkar out of his bed shortly after midnight on October 3 for an urgent conversation. Declaring that "no country's need for peace was greater than that of China," he said, "there were occasions when peace could only be defended by determination to resist aggression. If the Americans crossed the 38th parallel China would be forced to intervene in Korea. Otherwise he was most anxious for a peaceful settlement." Panikkar asked whether China intended to intervene if only the South Koreans crossed the parallel? Zhou responded, emphatically: "The South Koreans did not matter but American intrusion into North Korea would encounter Chinese resistance."[52]

338

Within hours, Zhou's statement was in the hands of American officials.[53] The next day, October 4, Ambassador Henderson sent in a full analysis from Delhi. "Panikkar said that Peiping officials had made clear that entry of South Korean armed forces into North Korea would not be considered as aggression and that therefore crossing 38th parallel by South Koreans would not necessitate Chinese intervention. Entry of forces other than South Korean into North Korea would be met, however, by Chinese intervention." Furthermore, he reported, China "would not recognize any decision re future Korea taken by UN unless it was member of the UN Commission on Korea."[54]

Henderson saw the making of a dilemma for the U.N. On the one hand, the pause by U.N. forces before crossing into North Korea has "almost placed" the U.N. in the position of being open to the Communist charge that "entry . . . into North Korea could . . . be widely acclaimed as a new war, not continuation of war brought about by North Korean aggression," which must be met by force. On the other hand, "if UN forces decide not to enter North Korea they might be compelled either to remain there indefinitely in order to defend South Korea . . . or withdraw sooner or later and permit North Korea . . . to complete the work of conquest which the UN had interrupted." This dilemma, however, was overcome by passage of the October 7 resolution authorizing immediate military operations throughout Korea.

By this time Mao had also reached the decision that China must fight, but not before he had squeezed the last drop out of the negotiations with Stalin. Between October 3 and 7, there had been yet another exchange between the two leaders.[55] In his reply to Mao's October 2 cable, Stalin adopted the tone of a disappointed parent addressing a child. "I considered it possible to turn to you with the question of five–six volunteer divisions because I was well aware of a number of statements made by the leading comrades regarding their readiness to move several armies in support of the Korean comrades if the enemy were to cross the 38th parallel." This was in reference to Zhou's comments to Panikkar and also Liu Shaoqi's remarks to Ambassador Roshchin.

Stalin assumed that China's readiness to send troops lay in her interest "in preventing the danger of the transformation of Korea into a USA springboard or a bridgehead for a future militaristic Japan against China." Then, he said, "while raising before You the question of dispatching troops to Korea, I considered 5–6 divisions a minimum, not a maximum." Stalin argued that "the USA, as the Korean events showed, is not ready at present for a big war." Nor was Japan "capable of rendering military assistance" to the U.S. From this Stalin drew several conclusions: that the U.S. "will be compelled to yield in the Korean question to China behind which stands its ally, the USSR." Thus, Korea will not become a springboard. Finally, he averred, the U.S. will "have to abandon Taiwan," and also abandon the idea of "a separate peace" with Japan. But, Stalin continued, China would not be able to

> extract these concessions if it were to adopt a passive wait-and-see policy. . . . [W]ithout serious struggle and an imposing display of force not only would China fail to obtain all these concessions but it would not be able to get back even Taiwan which at present the United States clings to as its springboard. . . .
>
> I took into account also that the U.S., despite its unreadiness for a big war could still be drawn into a big war, which, in turn, would drag China into the war, and along with this draw into the war the USSR, which is bound with China by the Mutual Assistance Pact. Should we fear this? In my opinion, we should not, because together we will be stronger than the USA and England, while the other European capitalist states . . . do not present serious military forces. If a war is inevitable, then let it be waged now, and not in a few years when Japanese militarism will be restored as an ally of the USA and when [they] . . . will have a ready-made bridgehead on the continent in a form of the entire Korea run by Syngman Rhee.[56]

Mao did not reply to Stalin's letter until October 7, following a stormy series of Politburo meetings in Beijing on October 4–5. The "majority" of Chinese leaders assembled for the meetings believed that "it would be too risky . . . to send troops to Korea." The reasons were familiar. China needed time for reconstruction. Liberation was not yet completed. The revolution had not yet been consolidated. Troops were poorly armed. The Americans were too powerful. The general view was that "unless there was no other choice . . . it was better not to send troops to Korea."[57]

But Mao turned the tide, asking: "When other people are in a crisis, how can we stand aside with our arms folded?" In accordance with the earlier decision to appoint Peng Dehuai to command the volunteers to Korea, Mao had brought him from his post in Xi'an to attend the meeting. Peng argued that for national security considerations, China must intervene. China's superior manpower would overcome superior American firepower. "If we can avoid committing serious mistakes in our strategy and tactics," he said, "we could be confident of beating the American aggressor's troops."[58]

Mao agreed, saying: "The Americans are now forcing us to enter the battle against them. It will be useless if we either retreat or are frightened by the American threat. . . . We have only one choice now, that is, to send troops to Korea *before Pyongyang falls* into the enemy's hands, regardless of whatever risks or difficulties might be involved."[59] Mao emphasized that "the situation in Korea is now extremely urgent, and we must act immediately, otherwise we could lose the opportunity." He declared that he would send a message to Kim on October 8 informing him of the Chinese decision, and still adhering to the original timetable of October 15 for the dispatch of troops into Korea.[60]

Before sending his cable to Kim, however, Mao replied to Stalin's letter, once again bargaining over terms without disclosing his own timetable, or revealing the fact that he had decided to intervene. In an October 7 cable, Mao expressed "solidarity with the fundamental positions" in Stalin's letter and said that he would "dispatch to Korea nine, not six, divisions." He would not send them now, however, "but after some time." Mao also reiterated his earlier proposal to send representatives for talks.[61] Here, Mao was holding out the carrot of greater involvement, but only after his representatives had arrived for talks. It was obvious that the outcome of these talks would determine Mao's decisions.

Stalin replied immediately, attempting to define the agenda in advance by agreeing to receive Mao's emissaries "to discuss with them a detailed plan of military assistance to Korea." If Mao's position was that his troop commitment would hinge on Stalin's decision, Stalin's position was how to arrange the aid package. Stalin also finally cabled a reply to Kim Il-sung's letter of September 29 requesting direct Soviet aid. Without responding to Kim's desperate plea for direct intervention, Stalin urged Kim to "stand firm and fight for every tiny piece of your land," and informed him of his discussions with Mao and his expectation that Chinese assistance would shortly be forthcoming.[62] However, while enjoining Kim to "stand firm and fight," Stalin was at that very moment ordering the complete evacuation of Soviet advisers from Korea, action entirely consistent with his aim of maneuvering China and the United States into conflict.

His order to Shtykov read, in part, "all the Soviet personnel of the air commandants offices and families of Soviet military advisers must be evacuated from the territory of Korea." In case of emergency, the cable continued, "all the Soviet citizens, including Soviet citizens of Korean nationality, [must] be evacuated to the territory of the USSR and China."[63] Once Mao committed troops, Stalin wanted no advisers present to compromise his position in any way. Stalin intended to leave the field to Mao and Truman—his own version of sitting on the mountain to watch two tigers fight.

Meanwhile on October 7, the U.N. General Assembly passed 47–5–7 the British-sponsored resolution authorizing immediate military operations in North Korea. Later that day, General Walker's First Cavalry began crossing the 38th parallel into North Korea near Kaesong. The passage of the October 7 U.N. resolution also set the stage for the climactic meetings between Zhou Enlai, Lin Biao, and Stalin.

STALIN CALLS MAO'S BLUFF

Before departing on October 8, Zhou Enlai met again with Indian Ambassador Panikkar to reemphasize that China would intervene if U.S. troops crossed into North Korea "to extend the war." "We favor a peaceful solution and the localization of the Korean incident. That is still our stand."[64] The devil, however, was in the details. Zhou's "peaceful solution" involved a cease-fire and the prompt withdrawal of U.N. forces. It should be left to "concerned countries," he said, of which China and Russia were most prominent, to negotiate the final outcome. This solution was worse than the one proposed by Stalin, having not even the fig leaf of elections to recommend it, and made clear that it was simply a ploy to buy additional time.

On the same day, the 8th, Zhou Enlai and Lin Biao set off for Moscow. Immediately after their departure and unbeknownst to them, Mao informed Kim that China would "send volunteers to Korea to help you fight against the aggressors."[65] But he did not say when. He also sent a circular directive to "leading comrades" changing the name of the Northeast Border Defense Army, in actuality the Thirteenth Army, to the "Chinese People's Volunteers." These forces, initially some 256,000 strong, were ordered to "get everything in readiness and await orders to set off."[66]

Upon receiving Mao's cable, Kim Il-sung reportedly shouted in delight.[67] He immediately sent a telegram to Stalin, in reply to his of the 7th, with a new request. As Stalin had effectively refused direct assistance, but Mao had agreed to send troops, Kim asked him to train pilots, tankers, radio operators, and engineers from among "Korean students" studying in, and from among those "Soviet Koreans" residing in, the Soviet Union. Kim's cable, reflecting his buoyed spirits, oddly said nothing about Mao's commitment, which seems highly unlikely under the circumstances. It arrived on October 9, just as Zhou and Lin were making their way to Stalin's dacha on the Black Sea.

Kim's cable to Stalin suggests that Stalin thus learned, or deduced, before his talks with Zhou and Lin had begun, that Mao had already made the decision to send troops to Korea. If so, Mao had undercut his own negotiators and strengthened the Soviet leader's hand.

Zhou, Lin, and their interpreter Shi Zhe arrived at Stalin's dacha late on the evening of October 10. After a brief rest, discussions began immediately, lasting until 5:00 the next morning. Although Stalin had brought his closest associates—Georgy Malenkov, Lazar Kaganovich, Lavrenty Beria, Anastas Mikoyan, Nicolai Bulganin, and Vyacheslav Molotov—for the discussion, the extant record indicates that only he, Zhou, and Lin spoke.[68] Zhou's opening remarks essentially reiterated Mao's earlier argument that China could not afford the economic burden of war, which would impinge upon national reconstruction. China's troops were poorly armed, and supply would be very difficult. Once committed to battle "we will not get away from it easily," he said. "Moreover, if this war expands, it might involve other fraternal countries," meaning the Soviet Union. Therefore, Zhou concluded, "we think it better not to send troops."[69]

Stalin replied with a variation on his own earlier argument to Mao, but one calculated to reassure the Chinese of Soviet support. He repeated his view that although the Soviet Union was too weak to enter into a world war against the United States, it was strong enough to deter the United States from attacking China. Therefore, he believed, China could send troops without fear of direct U.S. retaliation. "Any kind of U.S. attack against China," he said, "would trigger the mutual military assistance provision of the Soviet-Chinese Alliance Treaty and draw the U.S. into a global conflict with the USSR for which it was not ready." America, he concluded, was therefore "unlikely to risk a war with China on the latter's own territory."[70]

Of course, as noted above, "any kind of U.S. attack against China," was *not* covered by the treaty. There would have to be a prior, formal declaration of war to activate the treaty. Nor was it true that Mao had decided against sending troops to Korea. Both sides were quite obviously feeling each other out before getting down to the hard bargaining.

Observing the current situation, Stalin said that without immediate assistance Kim's regime would not last a week. If you do not intend to lend assistance, he told Zhou, it would be better for the North Koreans to withdraw from Korea entirely. China and the Soviet Union could provide "sanctuary" for Kim and his forces. He proposed that China accept the main NKA forces, along with their weapons, into Manchuria and that the Soviet Union provide accommodations for the "disabled and wounded," plus Koreans of Soviet origin, in the Soviet Far East.[71] "Both of us have to share this heavy burden. I suggest that we tell Kim Il-sung about our advice, which is to withdraw."[72]

Stunned at the prospect of thousands of North Korean troops, with their weapons, streaming into Manchuria, both Chinese leaders could well imagine the consequences. If their presence in Manchuria did not tempt American action against them, Stalin might incite them to resentment against the Chinese and stir up domestic strife. Lin Biao spoke up at this point to declare that it would not be "necessary to withdraw their main force; they can remain in Korea instead. As there are mountains and forests, they can stay there and carry on guerrilla warfare . . . and wait for the opportunity to fight back." Stalin, however, dismissed Lin's suggestion, saying, "I am afraid the enemy would not allow the guerrillas to exist. They will annihilate them soon."[73]

Stalin now made his pitch, promising far more than he would deliver. "If China can send a certain amount of troops, then we would provide weapons and equipment. During the fighting we can provide a certain number of aircraft for ground support. Of course, we have to avoid being struck by the enemy. Otherwise, it would cause very negative international repercussions." Stalin also sought to sweeten his offer further by dangling the prospect of re-equipping the Chinese army, air force, and navy, although he conceded that it would take a long time to develop the navy.[74]

Here was the nub of it. Zhou's mission was to gain Stalin's agreement to provide combat air support for Chinese troops in Korea and his threat was to refuse Chinese entry if air support were not forthcoming. Stalin initially appeared to say "yes," but as the discussion continued, it became clear that not only would he not provide combat air support for Chinese troops in Korea, he would not agree to commit the Soviet air force for the air defense of Manchuria for at least two-and-a-half months.[75] Zhou, perhaps confused by Stalin's disappearing commitment on air support, and with their discussion at an impasse, apparently insisted that Stalin put in writing precisely what the Soviet Union was willing to provide. This was the origin of what has come to be known as the Stalin-Zhou "joint telegram" to Mao.

Although some have questioned the existence of a joint telegram, the circumstances of the discussion at this critical moment in history, combined with Stalin's vague but extravagant promises, certainly called for establishing just what it was he was prepared to do, and when.[76] Furthermore, Zhou was not authorized to make the decision on sending troops, which would have to be considered by Mao and the Chinese leadership. In short, it would appear to me that some record of Soviet commitment would have been necessary to send to Mao. That Zhou would have appended his name to it also seems natural enough, since he was a principal to the discussion. It is in this sense only that they sent a "joint" telegram on October 11 (and probably explains why a text has not been found).

In any case, Stalin did commit to provide Chinese forces with artillery, tanks, trucks, airplanes, and other military equipment, but not combat air support in Korea.[77] Chinese sources claim that he promised to provide such support "later," two-and-a-half months after Chinese forces began fighting, then broke his commitment.[78] Stalin's intent was to prod Mao into the conflict and it was not out of the realm of possibility, or out of character, that he would promise something he had no intention of delivering to achieve his desired outcome. It is vital, however, not to lose sight of the true issue: by demanding the provision of combat air support in Korea, Mao sought to maneuver Stalin into war against the United States, a trap that Stalin eluded. Subsequent claims that Stalin "reneged" can only be classified as the sour residue of, and an attempt to obscure, this failed maneuver.

The arrival of the Stalin-Zhou telegram in Beijing raised a furor among the Chinese leadership, but Mao realized that his ploy had failed. While many leaders demanded that China not commit forces and Mao temporarily halted troop movements for a few days, to allow his commanders to voice their concerns, Mao had no choice but to send his forces into Korea while there was still time.[79] U.N. forces were already advancing on Pyongyang and Kim Il-sung and his entourage had already fled to a hideaway close to the Yalu River, to Kanggye near the border town of Manpolin. Indeed, in his last turn of the screw, and consistent with his proposal to Zhou, on October 12 Stalin ordered Kim to "evacuate North Korea and pull out his troops to the north," that is, into Manchuria. This decision made the seizure of the North Korean capital a certainty, and opened the way for a drive to the Yalu.[80]

For Mao the game was over for now. On October 13, Mao sent two telegrams, one to Zhou and one to Stalin, declaring his commitment to send troops to Korea. The telegram to Zhou was the shorter of the two, informing him that "we have reached a consensus that the entry of our army into Korea continues to be to our advantage." Chinese troops in this "first phase" would only fight the puppet army [ROK] and establish a base "north of the Wonsan-Pyongyang line." Mao justified his position on the grounds that it was "favorable to China, Korea, the East, and the world," and if we do not do so "the reactionaries at home and abroad would be swollen with arrogance when the enemy troops press on toward the Yalu River."[81]

The second telegram of October 13, known in the West as Mao's October 2 cable, was sent directly to Stalin. Ambassador Roshchin's cable to Stalin accompanying Mao's letter confirms that two telegrams were sent. In summarizing Mao's decision to commit troops, Roshchin notes that "Zhou Enlai is being sent new instructions."[82] Chinese authorities, as noted above (p. 335 and n. 49), placed the earlier date on this cable to expand the time frame and obscure the difficult bargaining session with Stalin, a negotiation in which Mao must be said to have been the loser. Mao's letter, read in context, makes plain that it was sent at this time and not earlier, even though some changes may have been made.

Mao opened with the statement that "we have decided to send a portion of our troops, under the name of Volunteers, to Korea, assisting the Korean comrades to fight the troops of the United States and its running dog Syngman Rhee." He explained that this was a necessary mission that would otherwise lead to an unfavorable situation in the entire Far East. Where, in the cable to Zhou, Mao confided that Chinese forces would only fight South Korean forces at first, he told Stalin "we have decided to send Chinese troops to fight the Americans."[83] (In fact, Chinese troops would engage ROK forces wherever and whenever possible.)

He assured Stalin that his forces were "ready to annihilate and drive out the invading armies of the United States," but we must be prepared for a "declaration of war by the United States and for the subsequent use of the U.S. air force to bomb many of China's main cities and industrial bases, as well as an attack by the U.S. navy on coastal areas." The main thing, he continued, was "whether or not the Chinese troops can annihilate the American troops in Korea and effectively resolve the Korean issue." Mao, still bargaining, now disclosed that while he would commit troops to battle, in the first stage his forces would only employ defensive tactics until Stalin actually delivered the promised weapons.

Accordingly, Mao said, we have decided, "starting on October 15, to move the 12 divisions transferred earlier to Southern Manchuria, into suitable areas in North Korea (not necessarily close to the 38th parallel); these troops will only fight the enemy that venture to attack areas north of the 38th parallel; our troops will employ defensive tactics, while engaging small groups of enemies and learning about the situation in every respect." Our troops will "wait for the delivery of Soviet weapons" before launching in cooperation with North Korean forces "a counter-offensive to destroy the invading American forces."

Mao then entered into a lengthy discourse describing the armament of an American army, the number and kind of artillery, tank guns, anti-tank guns, and anti-aircraft guns, noting the great disparity in armament and equipment of the Chinese army. Mao also acknowledged that "the enemy would control the air while our air force, which has just started its training, will not be able to enter the war with some 300 planes until February 1951." All this was his way of establishing Chinese requirements for the equipment that Stalin had promised to provide, including the continuation of the argument about air support.

Therefore, Mao concluded, "we are not assured that our troops will be able to annihilate an entire U.S. army once and for all. But since we have decided to go into the war against the Americans, we should be prepared that, when the U.S. high command musters up one complete army to fight us in a campaign, we should be able to concentrate our forces four times greater than those of the enemy . . . and to marshal firing power one and a half to two times stronger than that of the enemy . . . so that we can guarantee a complete and thorough destruction of one enemy army."

As soon as Stalin had received Mao's letter, he was overjoyed. On the verge of tears, he praised the Chinese. "The Chinese comrades are so good,"[84] he said, and immediately dashed off a handwritten note to Kim Il-sung via Ambassador Shtykov informing him that the Chinese had "decided after all to render military assistance to the Korean comrades, regardless of the insufficient armament of the Chinese troops." Therefore, "I ask You to postpone temporarily the implementation of the telegram sent to You yesterday about the evacuation of North Korea and the retreat of the Korean troops to the north."[85] Stalin's satisfaction, however, was a bit premature.

Mao was not yet finished with his attempt to draw Stalin into the conflict over the issue of air cover. In discussion with Ambassador Roshchin, pursuant to sending instructions to Zhou to reopen the discussions with Stalin, Mao wanted him to gain agreement to obtain the armaments "on credit," since they had no money to pay for them. But "the main thing that we need," said Mao, "is air power which shall provide us with air cover. We hope to see its arrival as soon as possible, but not later than in two months."[86] When Zhou presented these demands to Stalin, however, he declined to go over the same unfruitful ground of direct air support for Chinese troops in Korea and reportedly asked, instead, that Stalin send "volunteer pilots to support our military operations in Korea," in addition to dispatching regular Soviet air units to China's coastal cities for air defense.[87]

And in a last-ditch attempt to exert pressure on Stalin to provide air cover, Mao sent Zhou yet another, and in this case, final, telegram in this negotiation, on October 14. At last exhibiting the frustration he must have felt at failing to persuade Stalin to come into the conflict, he said that Chinese troops would establish "two or three defensive lines in the areas north of the Pyongyang-Wonsan railroad and south of the Tokch'on-Yongwon highway." This was the area spanning the northern portion of North Korea. "If the enemy attacks these lines," Mao said, "they will be cut off and destroyed." However, he said, "during the next six months, our troops will not initiate an attack on Pyongyang or Wonsan if the enemy remains in those place[s] and does not take the offensive."[88]

Continuing, Mao declared, "we will launch attacks on Pyongyang, Wonsan and other areas only *after* our troops are fully equipped and well trained, as well as having achieved an overwhelming air and land superiority to the enemy's troops. This is to say that we are not going to consider the question of launching an offensive for six months." He informed Stalin that Chinese troops would begin to enter Korea "on October 19" and complete their initial deployment of 260,000 troops by October 28. Then, as a final zinger, Mao said that if "the enemy remains in Pyongyang and Wonsan without venturing to make any attacks, we may withdraw about half of our troops back to China for training and supplies, and send them back when large-scale campaigns occur."

Of course, for Mao to say that his forces would only defend the immediate border area north of Tokch'on, and then withdraw half of his troops if the Americans didn't attack, was consistent with his scheme to preserve a North Korean buffer, but it threatened Stalin's entire strategy of pitting China against the United States. It was late in the game, however. Stalin undoubtedly recognized Mao's threat to take away what he had just given as improbable. We will never know, for if Mao's "game" depended on what the United States would do, then Stalin's worries were over. At that very moment, Truman was giving MacArthur the green light to strike for the Yalu and certain conflict with China.

CHAPTER THIRTEEN

Truman and the
New World Order

By THE BEGINNING of the second week of October, the United States and China were on a collision course. President Truman, implementing the U.N. resolution of October 7 to bring about the unification of Korea, authorized the forward movement of American forces. He knew that Chinese forces were massed at the border crossing points and, therefore, that China could intervene in an attempt to prevent unification. If he had knowledge of the Mao-Stalin negotiations, he also knew that Mao had declared his intention to intervene, but to decline major combat operations for several months, raising the prospect of establishing a small, buffer state between China and an enlarged Republic of Korea. Whether Truman realized that Mao's stance was part of his attempt to obtain a greater Soviet commitment is unknown.

For Truman, the moment of strategic opportunity had arrived. Chinese and American forces stood massed on either end of the North Korean battlefield, poised to enter the fray, and Truman was determined to take the step that would carry American strategy to fruition—the drive to the Yalu River. The movement of troops to the border, ostensibly to complete the unification of Korea, could not in fact "unify" Korea. The very mountainous border provinces would take months to clear and pacify, yet provided excellent terrain for forces determined to defend prepared positions. Thus, the drive north, particularly the manner in which American forces were deployed, would be both tempting and provocative, offering the most vulnerable of targets.

For Truman, therefore, the quest for Korean unity was the vehicle for conflict with China, a conflict that would polarize global politics into communist and noncommunist worlds in accordance with NSC-68. Therefore, disdaining a partial solution to avoid conflict, he sent U.N. forces northward to occupy North Korea, and did so in the face of undeniable and accumulating evidence that China had already deployed substantial forces into Korea. The resulting Sino-American conflict unequivocally defined the structure of global politics for a lengthy period thereafter.

Mao Zedong had decided to commit Chinese "volunteers" to battle in Korea to prevent its unification, and communicated that decision to Kim Il-sung on October 8. To Stalin, however, he had explained that his initial commitment would be completely defensive, seeking to ensure the survival of a small buffer zone beyond the Yalu River. He would engage American troops only if they advanced north of Pyongyang toward the Chinese border. Mao thereby appeared to leave open the possibility of a settlement of the Korean question without recourse to major warfare. Whether or not this seemingly defensive stance was an attempt to arrive at a settlement short of war, or yet another of his many attempts to prod Stalin into a full-fledged commitment to war against the U.N. in Korea, is unknown.

What is known is that Mao had failed repeatedly to obtain Stalin's partnership in a joint defense of North Korea, leaving Mao with little choice but to commit only his own forces to achieve his minimum, but still important, objective of ensuring the survival of a pro-Chinese North Korean buffer state. Mao would continue to press Stalin unsuccessfully for a full commitment for some time, but Stalin, despite his brave talk to Mao about the superiority of the Soviet Union in combination with China against the United States, prudently would not risk global war.

For the moment, but, historically speaking, only for the moment, Stalin had achieved his optimum outcome, of remaining on the sidelines and fueling the conflict between China and the United States, a conflict that would have been quite brief without his provision of armaments and supplies to Chinese forces. From Stalin's narrow, short-term viewpoint, keeping the conflict going prevented any possibility of a near-term improvement in relations between China and the United States. But it also provided the United States with the necessary political stimulus to move fully to the level of rearmament called for in NSC-68, a rearmament that Stalin and all Soviet leaders after him would never be able to match.

THE SIGINT CONUNDRUM

According to Christopher Andrew, President Truman was responsible for "the creation of the biggest peacetime intelligence community in the history of western civilization,"[1] including the Central Intelligence Agency and the National Security Agency (NSA). Both during his presidency and afterward, however, the president never mentioned the existence of the NSA, which he established by executive order, or any of its predecessors, and his biographers have shown "a similar disinclination to dwell on" sensitive intelligence issues. After half a century of writing on the Korean War, it is time for at least a tentative contemplation of the contribution of signals intercepts to the American military effort.

Simply speaking, among the various elements of intelligence collection, foreign broadcasts, embassy and attaché reports, aerial photographic reconnaissance, secret agents' reports, prisoner of war reports, and signals intercepts, the last is the most important, and most voluminous, yet least mentioned in the context of the Korean War. SIGINT, the contraction of the term signals intelligence, includes the radio interception and decoding of an adversary's telegram and telephone communications. As the previous chapter indicates, there was a significant volume of radio traffic between Moscow, Beijing, and Pyongyang, and among their various military units. There is no question that a great deal of it was collected. How much of what was collected was decoded?

The two fundamental questions regarding American intelligence and the Korean War—the North Korean attack and Chinese entry—are SIGINT-dominated issues. Radio intercepts, combined with force deployments, are the decisive indicators of a nation's intentions to undertake military action. In this regard, when the war began the Truman administration was faced with a conundrum. Truman could not say that SIGINT did not exist, yet to acknowledge its existence would imply advance knowledge that the war was coming and raise questions regarding the failure to take preventive action. His answer was to argue that America's intelligence capability had atrophied and Korea moreover had not been identified as a prime collection target. Scattered information was available, it was acknowledged, but it had not been properly evaluated or disseminated to higher officials. In short, the war came as a surprise because there had been an "intelligence failure."[2]

The administration could not also argue "intelligence failure" once the war began. As Andrew notes of the prewar situation, "had [Korea] been targeted, it is difficult to believe—given the success of SIGINT operations after the outbreak of the war—that there would not have been some warning of the massing of over ninety thousand North Korean troops and 150 T-34 tanks at 'jump off points' north of the 38th parallel before the invasion began."[3] Once the war began, the *New York Times* and other newspapers reported the gradual Chinese buildup of several hundred thousand troops along the Yalu River throughout the summer.

Also, once the war began, the American intelligence collection effort properly moved into high gear, focusing naturally on Moscow, Beijing, and Pyongyang. From collection points all around China's periphery, from Singapore to Japan and many points in between, a great volume of material was collected. As former Deputy Director of the CIA Ray Cline attested regarding China, "in particular ... Nationalist Chinese efforts, exploiting native language abilities and regional expertise ... greatly assisted the success of the U.S. signals processing machine and thus created a solid fund of knowledge on which analysts could draw in making their all-source studies of defense and foreign policy issues."[4]

Incredibly, however, the Truman administration did make the same argument with regard to Chinese intervention that it made with regard to the initial North Korean attack, even though a massive Chinese troop presence was undeniable in October. An attack was always possible, the CIA said, but "not probable in 1950." As Robert Donovan observes, "it was all a rerun of the story of the intelligence reports in June that the North Koreans would not attack. Washington did not wish to believe that the Chinese Communists would intervene. Washington did not believe it."[5] In fact, the administration's position was not credible.

One could not seriously argue (a) that the absence of intelligence capability accounted for the failure to anticipate the initial North Korean attack, and (b) that the presence of an intelligence capability also accounted for the failure to anticipate the Chinese attack. As this account testifies, the former was not true. As to the latter, the argument of this chapter will proceed on the assumption that the huge deployment of troops to border crossing points, the growing volume of communication between Beijing and its forces as well as the signals intercepts of those communications, clearly revealed Beijing's preparations to intervene. If, through intercepted communications, Truman had also learned of Mao's negotiations with Stalin, he knew of Mao's intention to intervene.

If Inchon marked the beginning of the end-game for Stalin, it signaled the beginning of the second stage of Truman's strategy. The first stage was to defeat the North Korean invasion, and the second to take the battle to China, sustaining a Sino-American conflict long enough to produce the desired structural effects, while avoiding escalation to global war. In the second stage, Truman would disdain a settlement of the war in favor of pressing forward with plans to unify Korea—in the face of clearly stated Chinese threats to counter any U.N. military operations in North Korea.

There were at least two and possibly three instances in October and November when Truman could have settled for substantially more than the status quo ante bellum, leaving South Korea the victor and North Korea perhaps terminally weakened and completely dependent on external support for survival, but he declined. In early October, with forces poised to attack Pyongyang, Truman could have settled for a restructured peninsula substantially favoring the Republic of Korea. A new dividing line from Pyongyang

351

to Wonsan, just north of the 39th parallel, would have marked a major improvement in the ROK position by incorporating a greater proportion of Korea's industrial capacity.

In truth, there would have been great difficulty for Truman to halt the momentum for complete victory generated by the success at Inchon. Indeed, it would have required more political courage to settle at this point, than to proceed. North Korean forces had been decimated and there was no sign at that point that China would intervene, except to provide logistical support for battered North Korean forces. The first week in October was, recall, when the Mao-Stalin negotiations were just entering high gear. Moreover, Washington's allies had been more or less mollified by Inchon, Syngman Rhee was demanding full unification, and the public expected victory.

In early November, however, the combat situation had changed, dramatically reviving prospects for a settlement. In late October, Chinese forces had entered the conflict in growing numbers, changing the political calculus for unification. Washington's allies began showing increased concern about an expanded war, although Rhee remained adamant in favor of unification. A settlement here, perhaps dividing the peninsula even further to the north across a line from Sinanju in the west to Hungnam on the Sea of Japan, just below the 40th parallel, would have left North Korea as no more than a rump regime supported completely by Russia and China as a buffer zone between them and a greatly enlarged ROK, with formidable if as yet unrealized economic capacity. In fact, Mao extended subtle feelers to explore such a solution, which were ignored.

Late November, prior to full-scale Chinese intervention, was the final opportunity for a settlement. Of the three instances noted, this was the most desirable moment for a settlement from the U.N. side, but the least likely possibility on the Chinese side because Beijing in the meantime had deployed over a quarter of a million troops into North Korea and had prepared for a defense in depth. In all three instances, it is important to realize, the nature of Chinese Communist involvement was as a response to advances by U.N. forces into prepared positions occupied by Chinese forces. Thus, even in late November, there would have been a chance for a standoff if U.N. forces had declined to advance and instead had prepared fortified defenses against attack along the Ch'ongch'on River.

In each instance, Truman disdained a settlement and decided to press forward toward the Yalu River and into prepared Chinese positions of strength. The two provinces bordering on the Yalu and Tumen Rivers are extremely mountainous areas. It is rough, trackless country, sparsely populated with few roads, but an excellent place to defend against an attacking force. It was close to Chinese supply lines, offered advantages to foot soldiers over motorized units, and was far distant from U.N. supply lines. It was not worth risking a major war over these two provinces, which would add little to a unified Korea beyond a hydroelectric capacity already integrated into Manchuria's power grid. Had an early end to the conflict been sought, this was an appropriate place to seek it.

The hard truth is that, despite increasing pleas from allies and growing concern from members of his own administration, Truman wanted no settlement and concealed his position behind a deference to the wishes of his field commander.[6] A settlement on any terms would have contradicted the strategy of containment, which required a sustained, public demonstration of the Communist monolith in action. Protracted Sino-American conflict would become the crucible of the structure of containment and American rearmament. Therefore, Truman decreed that U.N. forces should press forward to the Yalu River into certain conflict with China.

MACARTHUR WILL SHARE BLAME

In implementing NSC-68, President Truman had determined to reassert American supremacy in the face of a growing Soviet threat. A protracted conflict with China would provide the lengthy political stimulus for the rearmament that would thrust the United States into a position of hegemony. Among the problems associated with raising the United States to supremacy over the Soviet Union was the political price that would have to be paid— not least in the number of American dead. The president obviously could not escape a considerable share of the blame for enlarging the conflict in Korea, but he was determined not to take sole responsibility. He had decided, perhaps months earlier if previous efforts to misrepresent MacArthur's actions are any indicator, that some of that responsibility would be shared by General Douglas MacArthur.

In early October, just as Stalin and his cronies sped off to his Black Sea dacha to deal with the question of prodding Mao into war against the United States, President Truman was himself retreating with his close political advisers to his own hideaway, the presidential yacht *Williamsburg*, for a similarly difficult task regarding MacArthur and the next step ahead. While on board, the president was kept fully up to date by "a plane [that] would bring mail and newspapers every morning." (Truman referred to his daily intelligence summaries as his "newspapers.") In addition, as he notes, "powerful radio equipment . . . enabled me to talk to anybody . . . who could be reached by telephone," and vice versa.[7]

While on board the *Williamsburg*, the president decided on the set of measures he would employ to manage the next critical phase of the conflict. We have no records of his shipboard discussions, but several parts of his decision can be reconstructed. First, and foremost, it was necessary to determine whether Stalin would continue to limit the war to Korea. This required a determination as to whether or not the Soviet Union would after all enter the conflict to save Pyongyang. If so, NSC-76 would supersede NSC-73, which meant that the United States would curtail operations in Korea and prepare for World War III.

Had Truman been privy to the latest round of Mao-Stalin exchanges, he would have known that Mao had decided to send troops to Korea, but not immediately, and that Stalin was pulling out all of his advisers. Even setting aside any presumed SIGINT information on the Mao-Stalin negotiations, the passage of the October 7 U.N. resolution and the movement of U.N. troops across the 38th parallel would still have made it crucial to test Soviet readiness to contest Korean unification. Although Truman proceeded with planning on the assumption that Moscow would remain on the sidelines, to be on the safe side he decided to probe Soviet readiness to engage in conflict with the U.N. command.

The test came on October 8 when two American F-80 "shooting star" jets penetrated Soviet airspace to strafe an airbase located on the coast at Dry River, approximately midway between the North Korean–Soviet border and Vladivostok. The incident took place in the late afternoon, in sufficient daylight to dismiss the possibility of navigational error. Soviet markings on the planes and buildings of the airbase were clearly visible. Furthermore, the base lay well outside flight patterns of U.S. air operations in North Korea. The Russians, reportedly, neither returned fire, nor scrambled jets in an attempt to intercept the U.S. fighters. But Moscow immediately protested to the U.S. ambassador, who, in an unprecedented act, refused to accept the protest note on the grounds that it was a U.N. matter.[8]

For the same reason, the Defense Department made no investigation. At the same time, a spokesman for MacArthur's headquarters said that he "knew nothing of the Russian charges." It was clearly a U.S. runaround; but while Moscow was irked, it was not provoked. If the mild Soviet reaction was not enough of an answer to the question of whether the Soviet Union was preparing to join the conflict in Korea, a few days later, on October 13, the Soviet representative to the U.N., Andrey Vyshinsky, made it plain. In a speech before the council, he played the incident down, urging the United States to give up its "get tough" policy, and return to "wartime cooperation."[9]

A week later New York Times reporter Hanson Baldwin, on tour in Korea, provided added confirmation of the Russian decision. In a dispatch from Wonsan, he observed that "there are increasing evidences that the Russians have cut their losses in Korea and are pulling out altogether. The flow of traffic down the East Coast highway from Vladivostok apparently has been halted altogether and the Russian advisers and technicians, who were present in fairly large numbers here at Wonsan and elsewhere, apparently have fled over the border." However, Baldwin noted "an increased concentration of Chinese Communist forces near the Korean frontier . . . during the past week." This concentration was "apparently in reaction to the United States advances toward the north."[10]

While the test of Soviet intentions was in progress, Truman proceeded to plan for the next step ahead in Korea. In this regard, the main decision the president made on board the *Williamsburg* was to authorize MacArthur to occupy all of North Korea, but he crafted the decision in a way that suggested that he was responding to the recommendation of his field commander. This led to the decision to meet with MacArthur on Wake Island on October 15. The president's "spin" on the meeting was that "we had never had any personal contacts at all," and therefore ought to meet. More important, he said, "reports of threatened intervention in Korea by the Chinese Communists were another reason for my desire to confer with General MacArthur."

355

Truman's declared reason to discuss these "reports" was not to provide MacArthur with the latest intelligence the president possessed, but for the president "to get the benefit of *his* firsthand information and judgment."[11] Truman would have the reader believe that MacArthur was better informed about events in Beijing and Moscow, where a decision to intervene would be made, than he was, which, of course, was not remotely close to the truth. The president, in planting the notion that he would follow the recommendation of his field commander about a matter plainly outside his realm of professional competence, was setting the stage for tarring MacArthur with blame in case of failure. Indeed, when the Chinese Communists did intervene, Truman would claim that MacArthur had "misled" him.[12] The irony was that it was the other way round.

Truman's explanation for his trip was less than candid. The president disliked MacArthur intensely, as his diary entries before and after Wake attest.[13] Why not send a delegation of the JCS, which was the standard procedure whenever sensitive information had to be communicated? The president went himself, it can safely be surmised, because the decision to be communicated was too politically sensitive to be entrusted to the Joint Chiefs. Since China had already satisfied the criteria that would preclude military operations in North Korea, that is, Beijing had issued warnings and threatened to intervene, presidential authorization was necessary, and was the reason for the president's trip.

Moreover, what the president did on October 9 ensured that MacArthur would be eager to meet him and refuted any notion that Truman would be taking recommendations from his commander. On October 9, on the president's authorization, the Joint Chiefs of Staff sent MacArthur the following message: "In light of the possible intervention of Chinese Communist forces in North Korea," MacArthur was to be guided by the following policy.

Hereafter in the event of the open or covert employment anywhere in Korea of major Chinese Communist units, without prior announcement, you should continue the action as long as, in your judgment, action by forces now under your control offers a reasonable chance of success. In any case you will obtain authorization from Washington prior to taking any military action against objectives in Chinese territory.[14]

Parsing this brief but densely packed message, ostensibly a "full amplification" of the September 27 directive, reveals a reversal of three of its major policy propositions. First, it repaired the deficiency in NSC-81/1 and the September 27 guidance directive that dealt only with responses to Chinese Communist entry *south* of the 38th parallel. The October 9 directive stipulated that the current policy applied to Chinese Communist entry "anywhere" in Korea.

356   Second, whereas in NSC-81/1 and the September 27 directive MacArthur could conduct military operations in North Korea *only if* major Chinese Communist forces *had not* entered, announced an intention to enter, or threatened to counter U.N. operations militarily, the October 9 guidance reversed that condition and authorized that *even if* "major Chinese Communist units, without prior announcement" entered "you should continue the action as long as, in your judgment, action by forces now under your control offers a reasonable chance of success." If NSC-81/1 and the September 27 directive had placed limitations on military operations north of the 38th parallel, the October 9 directive removed them entirely. If they had sought to avoid a clash with "major" Chinese Communist forces, the October 9 directive ordered MacArthur to "continue the action."

Finally, the October 9 directive required MacArthur to "obtain authorization from Washington prior to taking any military action against objectives in Chinese territory." This stipulation, which no doubt focused MacArthur's attention, was a reversal from the command decision contained in NSC-73 regarding the way in which the United States would respond if China entered the war. This command language had been incorporated in NSC-81/1 but omitted from the September 27 guidance. Nevertheless, NSC-81/1 was the governing policy document. That decision was that *if* China entered *and* MacArthur engaged them, he would "be authorized to take appropriate air and naval action *outside* Korea against Communist China." That authority was now withdrawn. Instead, MacArthur was required to "obtain authorization from Washington," that is, from the president, for such action.

There can be little doubt that this directive, with its instructions to engage even major Chinese Communist forces, but withholding authorization to strike targets outside Korea, made MacArthur eager for a meeting with the president. It clearly limited the war to Korea and defined the way MacArthur could respond. If China intervened, MacArthur was prohibited from striking forward bases and supply points in Manchuria unless the president authorized it. Even more alarming was the suggestion that in the event of conflict with major Chinese Communist forces, MacArthur would receive no reinforcements, a suggestion indicated by the injunction that he "should continue the action as long as . . . action by forces now under your control offers a reasonable chance of success."

In other words, MacArthur was being placed in a position to engage major Chinese forces where he would not be permitted to use all of the weapons at his disposal. He would be forced to battle the Chinese hordes with one arm tied behind his back. He could neither strike at the logistical bases from which their attacks would be mounted nor destroy the bridges over which Chinese troops would cross into Korea. He would be required to wait until Chinese forces, whether ground or air, entered Korea before engaging them, and he would have to do it only with the forces currently under his command.

357

If the October 9 directive alarmed MacArthur, Truman's planned meeting with his general, decided upon by his political advisers with no apparent consultation with other agencies, generated immediate high-level concern in the State Department. Ambassador Jessup, who would accompany Truman to Wake Island, immediately recognized that Beijing would interpret the meeting "to foreshadow some major new American move in the Far East." And well they might. With passage of the U.N. resolution, lead elements of the First Cavalry Division crossed the 38th parallel. MacArthur had issued his second ultimatum to Kim Il-sung, who had replied defiantly, and the Chinese Foreign Ministry had also replied, declaring that "the American war of invasion in Korea has been a serious menace to the security of China from its very start."[15] Thus, Jessup thought it

> reasonable to assume that the Chinese Communists fear that we are mobilizing forces in North Korea to invade Manchuria or to engage the Chinese armies there while Chiang Kai-shek makes a landing on the mainland to the south. If the proposed conference closely followed or closely preceded another amphibious landing, the fears and suspicions would be heightened.[16]

Jessup felt that "the possible bad effects of such a dramatic meeting might be avoided through some very carefully prepared statement issued by the President in advance as well as by what he said in his California speech on his return." As it was precisely the president's purpose to prod China into conflict through a major show of force implied in a meeting with MacArthur, he accepted one part of Jessup's advice, but not the other. Before leaving, he issued a reassuring statement declaring that the United States had "no other aim in Korea than to carry out the great purpose of the United Nations." The United States wanted no bases, military installations, or "special position" in

Korea. After returning from Wake Island, however, he would send a quite different message.

Acheson also explored the possibility with Air Force Secretary Finletter of "a more explicit delimitation of air operations in the vicinity of the North Korean[–Chinese] border, in order to ensure against a repetition of border incidents." Acheson wanted to restrict air operations to a specified distance from the Manchurian and Soviet borders. This would certainly reduce if not eliminate border incidents, but it would also make it extremely difficult to conduct aerial reconnaissance along the border to assess any Chinese buildup. In any case, the Joint Chiefs refused, replying that "air interdiction operations in areas contiguous to the international boundaries of Korea is sufficient justification for not further delimiting air operations." Furthermore, anticipating MacArthur's later orders, the chiefs declared that

358

> in light of information currently available it appears that U.N. ground forces (including U.S.) operations will be required up to the international boundaries of Korea. Therefore, it is not considered desirable, from the military point of view, to deny these ground troops air and naval support in these areas. . . . Moreover, there will be a continuing requirement for aerial as well as ground reconnaissance in areas contiguous to the borders for an indefinite period.[17]

THE WAKE ISLAND MEETING

The president arrived at Wake Island at 6:30 A.M. on October 15 and departed at 11:35 A.M. Immediately upon arrival, he and MacArthur sped off a short distance in the only car on the island to a small Quonset hut for a private meeting lasting "more than one hour."[18] The president had flown over seven thousand miles for this private meeting. Although no minutes of their conversation were taken, there can be little doubt that the main topic of discussion during their tête-à-tête was China. Truman's Secret Service man, Henry Nicholson, accompanying them in the car to the Quonset hut, overheard Truman ask MacArthur "whether he thought the Chinese would enter the Korean War?" MacArthur reportedly replied that he thought not, but if they did, "the United Nations forces could defeat them." Truman replied: "I have been worried about that."[19]

There is thus no doubt about the topic of primary interest to the president. The president had with him the latest intelligence estimates of probable Chinese and Russian intervention, compiled by newly installed CIA Director Walter "Beetle" Smith just before he set off for Wake Island.[20] Whatever Truman did or did not know about Mao's decision to intervene in Korea, and I believe he did know, the president put before MacArthur a different interpretation—based on the latest CIA estimate—that Chinese intervention "was not probable in 1950." During the next two-and-a-half months, the CIA believed, "intervention will probably be confined to continued covert assistance to the North Koreans."[21] The implication was that overt intervention was more probable in 1951. Furthermore, the president would also have shown MacArthur the latest CIA estimate on the threat of Soviet entry, which was that Stalin would stay out of Korea because of the "grave risk of [world] war."[22] Finally, Truman would also have shown MacArthur State Department cables that reinforced this view.

Thus, if over the next couple of months Chinese intervention would be "confined to continued covert assistance," perhaps logistics support and a few "volunteers," MacArthur would have few worries, but still must move fast to destroy the NKA before it could be rebuilt and/or China intervened in 1951. Truman, as we shall see below, may even have reassured the general that in the event that China entered massively he would be authorized to strike targets in Manchuria. But the president's main thrust was clear: he authorized MacArthur to move promptly to wipe out all remaining resistance in North Korea, consolidate victory, and deploy an occupation force that would enable South Korean authorities to conduct nationwide elections.

Truman must also have warned MacArthur not to acknowledge the early presence of "major" Chinese forces in Korea should he encounter them, lest the allies demand a premature withdrawal. I draw this conclusion from the change in reporting of battlefield intelligence after the Wake meeting, which consistently minimized the Chinese presence in Korea after China had entered. For example, before Wake, MacArthur's intelligence chief, General Willoughby, had reported heavy concentrations of Chinese troops, between 90,000 and 180,000, "massed" at the border crossing points.[23] (There were a total of twelve bridges, but those at Antung and Manpolin were most important.)

On November 2, *after* Chinese troops in division strength had been positively identified in Korea (press accounts reported from 20,000 to 40,000), Willoughby estimated that only 16,500 Chinese troops were actually in Korea.[24] And in telecons of November 24 and 25, just before full-scale conflict began, when China had 300,000 troops in Korea, Willoughby estimated that there were "between 40,000 and 70,935" Chinese troops facing MacArthur, a gross underestimate.[25] Nearly three-quarters of a million troops were acknowledged to be in Manchuria, yet Willoughby's reporting would have one believe that most of the large number of troops he had identified earlier massing at the border crossing points had not crossed, but simply turned around.[26]

Clay Blair believed that "Willoughby falsified intelligence reports" on MacArthur's orders, but the CIA also minimized Chinese troop numbers, which indicates a wider phenomenon of under-reporting.[27] The point of ma-

359

nipulating the troop estimates was plainly to allay the concerns of Washington's allies, who were already expressing fears that Chinese intervention could lead to world war. When the true dimensions of the Chinese presence in Korea were realized, it was too late.

After their hour-long meeting, Truman and MacArthur joined the rest of their party in another building for a conference that lasted roughly one-and-a-half hours. As the conference began, Truman's press secretary, Charles Ross, noting that MacArthur's aide, Colonel Laurence Bunker, was taking notes, "turned to MacArthur and told him that no record was to be made of the talks."[28] Bunker stopped, yet all seven members of the president's entourage did take notes: Bradley, Harriman, Jessup, Rusk, Bradley's exec, Colonel Willis Matthews, Pace's aide, Colonel Archelous Hamblin, and Jessup's secretary, Vernice Anderson, all took notes. General Bradley later "compiled" the following record "from the combined notes" of the seven note-takers.[29]

During this conference, which by all accounts was devoid of serious content, Truman managed to elicit from MacArthur his views on the possibility of Chinese intervention, that is, the estimate that Truman had communicated to MacArthur during their private meeting.[30] However, Truman was only able to get what he wanted from MacArthur by subsequently manipulating the record. Remarkably, all seven note-takers apparently missed what MacArthur actually said in response to Truman's question about the "chances" for Chinese intervention. According to Bradley's "compilation," he said:

> Very little. Had they interfered in the first or second months it would have been decisive. We are no longer fearful of their intervention. We no longer stand hat in hand. The Chinese have 300,000 men in Manchuria. . . . Only 50–60,000 could be gotten across the Yalu River. They have no Air Force. Now that we have bases for our Air Force in Korea, if the Chinese tried to get down to Pyongyang there would be the greatest slaughter.[31]

What MacArthur says he said is markedly different.

> My views were asked as to the chance of Red Chinese intervention. I replied that the answer could only be speculative; that neither the State Department through its diplomatic listening posts abroad, nor the Central Intelligence Agency to whom a field commander must look for guidance as to a foreign nation's intention to move from peace to war, reported any evidence of intent by the Peiping government to intervene with major forces; that my own intelligence, which I regarded as unsurpassed anywhere, reported heavy concentrations near the Yalu border in Manchuria, whose movements were indeterminate; that my own military estimate was that with our largely unsurpassed air forces, with their potential capable of destroying, at will, bases of attack and

lines of supply north as well as south of the Yalu, no Chinese military commander would hazard the commitment of large forces upon the devastated Korean peninsula. The risk of their utter destruction through lack of supply would be too great. There was no disagreement from anyone.[32]

The differences are striking. Bradley's compilation paints MacArthur as the headstrong general eager to press onward, while MacArthur's recollection stresses his caution and executive branch culpability. That MacArthur was a headstrong leader is true, but irrelevant. Parsing MacArthur's statement leads back to his meeting with the president, particularly his references to State Department cables and CIA estimates that reported no "evidence of intent by the Peiping government to intervene with major forces." These were what Truman had shown to him. He immediately contrasted that view, however, with his own "unsurpassed" intelligence, which "reported heavy concentrations [of Chinese troops] near the Yalu border." Thus, while the CIA saw no "intent" to intervene with "major" forces, MacArthur reported a capability to intervene, noting a "heavy concentration" of forces, that is, "major" forces.

Nevertheless, MacArthur's own "military estimate" was that he could deter and if necessary defeat any small-scale Chinese aggression, which was the only likely possibility based on what he had been told by the president. Furthermore, he implied that he had been given, or would be given, the authority to conduct air strikes against Chinese "bases of attack" in Manchuria. Thus, he believed that with the capability "of destroying, at will, bases of attack and lines of supply *north as well as south of the Yalu*," no Chinese commander would commit "large forces" and risk their "utter destruction through lack of supply."

Truman's instructions to MacArthur at Wake Island, it is fair to conclude, were based on the interpretation that while the Chinese were massing troops at border crossing points, they were not prepared for a full-scale intervention in 1950. That was the CIA's view. Therefore, MacArthur should move quickly and present the Chinese with a fait accompli. MacArthur was plainly dubious, as his juxtaposition of his own "unsurpassed" intelligence alongside the CIA's makes clear. Nevertheless, if his commander in chief urged him forward and, it follows, promised to support him, he would obey.

Time was of the essence. Thus, when the president proposed lunch following their conference, MacArthur said: "If it's all right, I am anxious to get back as soon as possible and would like to leave before luncheon if that is convenient."[33] Truman agreed. When reporters attempted to question MacArthur about his meeting with the president, the general referred all inquiries to the president's press secretary, who released a communiqué "initialed . . . by both men as if they were heads of different governments."[34] (MacArthur, however, had been "curtly" denied permission to bring any members of the Tokyo press corps with him to Wake Island.)[35] The entire five-hour event was stage-managed by the president's people.

ON TO THE YALU

MacArthur was "anxious to get back" to Tokyo because his plans had been changed as a result of his meeting with Truman. With no need to counter a Chinese assault with the Wonsan gambit, he would redirect X Corps, whose forces were about to embark, northward toward the Yalu to mop up remnants of North Korean forces east of the Taebaek mountains, which divided North Korea into separate sectors. At the same time, he would urge General Walker's Eighth Army to complete the attack on Pyongyang and drive on to the Yalu River in the sector west of the Taebaek range. Upon MacArthur's departure from Wake Island, the Eighth Army was poised for the assault on the North Korean capital, having captured Kumchon on October 14.[36]

As General Joe Lawton Collins observed, "before a single unit of the X Corps had landed at Wonsan, both Pyongyang and Wonsan had fallen to the Eighth and ROK armies." Nor by that time had the First Marine Division "yet sailed from Inchon."[37] Thousands of mines (between 2,000 and 4,000) had been discovered at Wonsan and sweeping had begun on October 10, the day the ROK Third Division took the port city.[38] Nevertheless, X Corps forces were still loaded aboard ships, ostensibly bound for Wonsan. The original plan had called for the landing of the First Marines and the Seventh Division at Wonsan on the 20th and their subsequent drive westward toward Pyongyang. Had Chinese forces intervened, they would have been perfectly positioned for a flank attack against them.

The Seventh Division would not land at Wonsan, but at Iwon, a small port 105 miles north of Wonsan, beginning on October 27 and head for Hyesanjin on the Yalu. The attached ROK Third and Capital Divisions would head up the coast toward the port of Ch'ongjin and the Soviet frontier. The First Marine Division would not land at Wonsan until the mines had been cleared on October 28. From there they would move to Hamhung and then northwestward toward the Chosin reservoir. By the time X Corps forces landed on the east coast, Eighth and ROK Army units had already encountered Chinese forces north of the Ch'ongch'on River, beginning on October 25, a story best told in terms of MacArthur's new orders upon returning from Wake Island.

Immediately upon his return to Tokyo, on October 17 MacArthur issued Operations Order No. 4, which, as Collins notes, "assigned a new objective for the United Nations Forces, running from Sonch'on on the west coast to Pyongwon, northwest of the Chosin Reservoir, and thence to Pungsan to Songjin on the Sea of Japan." This line was forty miles south of the Yalu on the west coast and nearly one hundred miles from the Russian frontier on the east coast. Collins and most others erroneously viewed this as "the first, but not the last, stretching of MacArthur's orders beyond JCS instructions."[39]

On the same day Ops Order No. 4 was issued, President Truman delivered a major speech in San Francisco on his return from Wake Island. Referring to his meeting with MacArthur, the president wanted to "make it perfectly clear . . . that there is complete unity in the aims and conduct of our foreign policy." Truman told of their "plans for establishing a 'unified, independent, and democratic' government" of Korea. Without mentioning China, Truman emphasized that "no country in the world which really wants peace has any reason to fear the United States of America."[40] Truman's speech, timed to coincide with the issuance of MacArthur's orders for the advance to new objectives in North Korea, conveyed the clear message that the United States would attempt to unify Korea, and not stop halfway.

363

Ops Order No. 4 also called for an air drop by the 187th Airborne Regiment north of Pyongyang, which MacArthur said would "close the trap on the enemy." He anticipated entrapping some thirty thousand retreating North Koreans and "very shortly" bringing the war to an end. Although the airborne operation was executed on the 20th, the day after the capture of Pyongyang, the vast majority of retreating NKA escaped north of the Ch'ongch'on River. Part of the rationale for the air drop was to rescue U.S. POWs being taken north. Only twenty-one survivors were found among eighty-nine men whom the North Koreans attempted to massacre. Only one regiment of the NKA, the 239th, comprising some 2,500 men attempting to delay the U.N. advance, was rounded up in follow-on operations.[41]

On the basis of the administration's estimate that the Chinese would not intervene in force in 1950 and that the war would soon be over, MacArthur also began to plan postwar moves. MacArthur's planning office, the Joint Strategic Plans and Operations Group (JSPOG), issued Operations Order No. 202 on October 20 outlining procedures to be followed once resistance had dwindled. The planning assumptions were clearly based, as James Schnabel notes, on MacArthur's meeting with the president on Wake Island. The assumptions were that, as resistance continued to dwindle, some forces could be withdrawn from Korea, and only mopping-up actions against guerrillas would remain to be done.[42]

By the evening of October 24, Eighth Army forces, comprising the U.S. First Corps (the U.S. Twenty-fourth Division, the British Twenty-seventh Brigade, and the ROK First Division), and the ROK Second Corps (the ROK Sixth, Seventh, and Eighth Divisions) had crossed the Ch'ongch'on River and were preparing to attack toward the villages of Unsan, Taechon, and Onjong. Their objective was to gain control of the high ground between the Ch'ongch'on and the Yalu Rivers in order "to dominate the Yalu crossings."[43]

These villages lay in the valleys leading to the ridges beyond the Ch'ong-ch'on. It would be here that Mao decided to fight.

Mao had begun sending the first Chinese "volunteer" units across the Yalu River bridges into North Korea on the night of October 19.[44] Over the following three weeks, by early November, some 300,000 troops had surreptitiously entered North Korea. Along with 65,000 reformed and rearmed North Korean troops, Mao had a formidable force in place and in prepared positions when the Eighth Army began its advance beyond the Ch'ongch'on River and X Corps headed for the Yalu. In what must be counted as one of the more remarkable feats of military history, if true, the Chinese deployment, carried out at night and in radio silence, went completely undetected by American intelligence.

One source claims it is not. According to Henry Rositzke, "the key figure in providing firsthand evidence of the military situation north of the Korean-Chinese border was a CIA agent." A former high-ranking Chinese Nationalist officer was sent to China after the outbreak of the conflict and made contact with former officer colleagues who had defected to the Communists. From conversations and direct observation,

> he was able to establish with some precision the number and distribution of Chinese Communist troops along the Manchurian–North Korean border. His detailed reports, as well as others from Chinese Nationalist sources in the fall of 1950, gave fair warning to the UN command of the imminent Communist crossing of the Yalu River in November 1950.[45]

These reports were never acknowledged, yet Willoughby did report Chinese troops massing at the border crossings at this time. On the other hand, on October 18, "American reconnaissance planes flying close to the Yalu found almost one hundred Russian-built fighters lined up on Antung Airfield across the river in Manchuria." General Stratemeyer minimized the military significance of the Chinese deployment, believing that it was done to lend "color and credence to . . . threats of Chinese Communist leaders." He did not believe that the Chinese meant to employ these fighters in Korea. "If deployment for possible action in Korea were under way, it would be highly unlikely that aircraft would have been positioned to attract attention from south of the border."[46] Viewed in the context of the troop investment, the deployment probably served as a diversion.

In any case, on October 24, MacArthur issued new orders to the Eighth Army to accelerate its advance to the Yalu. He "removed all restrictions on the use of U.N. ground forces south of the border, and instructed his commanders to press forward to the northern limits of Korea, utilizing all their forces."[47] MacArthur's headquarters issued a statement formally denying repeated reports that U.N. forces would halt some distance south of the Yalu and establish a buffer zone. A spokesman declared that he was "authorized to state" that the mission was "to clear Korea."[48]

The Joint Chiefs immediately demanded an explanation for what appeared to be an outright violation of his September 27 directive prohibiting the use of non-Korean forces along the Yalu. MacArthur, unperturbed, replied. He justified lifting the restriction as a matter of military necessity because the ROK Army was not strong enough to handle the situation alone. Furthermore, he viewed his decision as being in consonance with Secretary Marshall's missive of September 29 urging him to feel "unhampered tactically and strategically . . . north of the 38th parallel." Finally, and most important, MacArthur said, "this entire subject was covered in my conference at Wake Island."[49] As all authors note, the record of the Wake Island conference contains no discussion of MacArthur's proposed military operations in North Korea. The general's reference was to "his" conference with Truman.   **365**

There can be little doubt that General Bradley, who attended the Wake Island conference and compiled the record for it, understood MacArthur's reference, or that he checked with the president for confirmation, which he undoubtedly received. Yet General Bradley did not bother to inform his colleagues on the JCS, who continued to assume that "MacArthur had violated their basic 27 September directive," even though they did not countermand his orders.[50] Incidentally, President Truman, quoting this exchange of messages in his memoirs, makes no objection to MacArthur's order, providing belated confirmation that he had approved it. Moreover, had MacArthur been in violation of his orders, the president would certainly have called it to his attention. Yet between the Wake Island meeting and the end of the month, Truman and MacArthur engaged in a mutually complimentary correspondence.[51]

The brouhaha over the October 24 order has overshadowed MacArthur's reasons for issuing it. The Ch'ongch'on River parallels the Yalu sixty-five miles to the south. Although MacArthur had no evidence of a Chinese decision to intervene and all the estimates suggested that they would not do so, he calculated that *if* they were to intervene it would be now, before U.N. forces reached the Yalu. If his own forces could reach the Yalu first and fortify the border and river crossings, Chinese intervention would be immensely more difficult. Therefore, MacArthur sought to move his forces as quickly as possible to the Yalu to preempt any last-minute intervention.

Unfortunately, unbeknownst to MacArthur, the Chinese were already streaming across the Yalu in sufficient strength to meet both Eighth Army and X Corps advances even before they reached the ridges overlooking the Yalu. Between October 25 and November 6 Chinese "volunteers" trapped and mauled ROK and U.S. forces as they advanced north of the Ch'ongch'on River in the west and toward the Yalu in the east. In the west, General

Walker sent three groups of forces forward, not expecting much resistance and therefore not heavily armed. He sent the ROK Second Corps toward Onjong, the ROK First Corps toward Unsan, and the British Twenty-seventh Brigade and elements of the Twenty-fourth Divisions to Anju, near the mouth of the Ch'ongch'on.

Around Onjong, Chinese forces surrounded the Third Battalion of the ROK Sixth Division's Second Regiment and "cut [it] to pieces." They "mauled" the Second Battalion and then attacked the Sixth Division at Onjong itself. The ROKs "broke in panic."[52] Other forces sent to assist were themselves badly beaten. Finally, the defeat at Onjong trapped yet another unit further north, the Seventh Regiment, which had earlier reached Ch'osan on the Yalu, apparently stumbling "close to the staging area where the Chinese troops were massing."[53] Completely isolated, only 875 of the Seventh Regiment's complement of 3,552 men escaped. Within four days, by October 29, the ROK Second Corps, comprising the ROK Sixth, Seventh, and Eighth Divisions, had been driven back south of the Ch'ongch'on River in disarray.

At Unsan, the Chinese employed two divisions to trap and overwhelm the ROK First Division's Fifteenth Regiment. Walker sent the U.S. Eighth Cavalry Regiment, in reserve at Pyongyang, to support the Fifteenth, but in the ensuing battle the Chinese surrounded and cut off the Eighth Cavalry's Third Battalion. General Walker sent out another rescue force, but it, too, failed to break through to the encircled battalion. Ordered to withdraw south of the Ch'ongch'on River, over 600 American soldiers of the Third Battalion were left behind to be "slaughtered."[54]

At Anju, the Chinese also sent two divisions against the British Twenty-seventh Brigade and the U.S. Twenty-fourth Division, but the combined British-American force successfully beat them back, holding their position. On November 6, the Chinese abruptly broke off their attacks and withdrew into the hills. Interrogation of POWs and examination of battlefield dead confirmed the presence of large but "undetermined" numbers of Chinese soldiers.[55]

In the east, General Almond sent the ROK Third Division's Twenty-sixth Regiment (of the ROK First Corps) to the Chosin reservoir. The First Marines at Hamhung were to relieve the ROK at the reservoir when the U.S. Third Infantry Division arrived on November 1. Almond sent the Seventh Division to Hyesanjin on the Yalu, and the bulk of the ROK First Corps and Capital Division up the east coast road to the Russian border. The Twenty-sixth Regiment encountered Chinese troops halfway to the Chosin reservoir, capturing one prisoner on October 25 and several more on the 30th. The Marines, relieving the Twenty-sixth Regiment, also encountered and drove back what appeared to be a regimental-size Chinese force in early November.

General Almond himself interrogated the prisoners, confirming Chinese intervention in his sector. During this period, October 25–November 6, other units also encountered increasing resistance from North Korean forces as they advanced, but no Chinese. Nevertheless, it was abundantly apparent by early November, at the latest, that there was an entirely new factor in the Korean equation—the presence of Chinese troops in significant strength contesting the advance of U.N. forces in the west and east.

President Truman wanted an up-to-date estimate of the situation from MacArthur, who responded on November 4. MacArthur thought it impossible to reach an authoritative appraisal "based upon the battle intelligence coming in from the front," but he saw several possibilities. Least likely was an all-out declaration of war. More likely, he thought, was some combination of covert assistance with "volunteers." He thought that "such intervention, as exists, has been in the belief that no UN forces would be committed in the extreme northern reaches of Korea except those of South Korea." MacArthur warned against "hasty conclusions," and recommended waiting for "a more complete accumulation of military facts."[56]

Over the next day and a half MacArthur got more "military facts" from his intelligence chief Willoughby and from his field commander Walker. On November 5 Willoughby reported that Chinese troops, who had been crossing into North Korea via the Yalu bridges in great numbers, "now had the capacity to launch a major counteroffensive."[57] And Walker, in a message to MacArthur the next day, declared that his offensive plans were being formed "to meet the new factor of organized Chinese Communist forces." To meet this new threat his supply lines would have to be rectified, for, at the moment, "there now exists in the forward areas only one day of fire."[58] Walker explained that his advance north of Pyongyang had been "based on a calculated logistical risk involving supply almost entirely by airlift. Available supplies were sufficient only for bare maintenance of combat operations against light opposition."[59]

Properly alarmed at the precarious position of his forces, on November 5 MacArthur ordered General Stratemeyer "to throw the full power of the Far East Air Forces into a 2-week effort to knock the North Koreans and their new allies out of the war." He wanted the destruction of "the Korean ends of all international bridges on the Manchurian border." Between the border southward to U.N. lines, he wanted to "destroy every means of communication and every installation, factory, city, and village," with the exception of the port of Najin and the hydroelectric facilities that had already been placed off limits.[60]

When word of MacArthur's orders reached Washington, via a message from Stratemeyer to the Pentagon, it immediately caused great consternation because it came at the precise moment that the British government was meeting to reconsider its attitude toward the Chinese Communist government. Washington also had a commitment with London not to take any action that might affect Manchuria without prior consultation. Finally, the State Department had sent MacArthur's "special report" of Chinese interventionist acts in Korea to the U.N., which was then being circulated. In view of the delicacy of the moment, the president, on Acheson's advice, ordered the postponement of the attacks.[61]

MacArthur's response on November 6 was close to apoplectic. "Men and material in large force are pouring across all bridges over the Yalu from Manchuria," threatening the "ultimate destruction" of his forces. Once Chinese troops crossed the river, "the distance between the river and our lines is so short that the forces can be deployed against our troops without being seriously subjected to air interdiction." In MacArthur's view, "the only way to stop this reinforcement of the enemy is the destruction of these bridges" as well as the maximum destruction of all facilities in the north.

368

MacArthur would suspend his ordered attack "under the gravest protest," but insisted that "the matter be immediately brought to the attention of the President as I believe your instructions may well result in a calamity of major proportion for which I cannot accept the responsibility without his personal and direct understanding of the situation." Time was essential, he concluded, and requested "immediate reconsideration" of the decision.[62] There is the slightest hint of MacArthur's realization here that the Joint Chiefs were not fully cognizant of the authority he had received from the president.

Truman was in Independence, Missouri, to vote, but Acheson immediately contacted him and after consultations the president reconsidered and authorized MacArthur to proceed with his plan, but with a restriction that effectively negated it. Truman authorized him "to go ahead with your planned bombing in Korea near the frontier including targets at Sinuiju and Korean end of Yalu bridges." But MacArthur was enjoined to exercise "extreme care . . . to avoid violation of Manchurian territory and airspace."[63] In his reply, Truman was saying to MacArthur that the provision in NSC-73 that authorized attacks "outside" Korea would not be implemented.

Meanwhile, Secretary of Defense Marshall, in an attempt to assuage MacArthur's feelings, sent him a personal message telling him that he had just spoken with the president. He wanted the general to know that he understood his problem and that "everyone here . . . is intensely desirous of supporting you." It happens, he said, that "discussions and decisions here are heavily weighted with the extremely delicate situation we have before the Security Council of the UN . . . whose meeting tomorrow may have fateful consequences." At the end of this note, Marshall asked, for his "personal information," whether MacArthur believed that the hydroelectric and reservoir issues were Beijing's "dominant consideration" in intervening.[64]

MacArthur replied to this message immediately, in the first of three messages he sent to Washington on November 7. Acknowledging Marshall's support, MacArthur expressed "complete agreement with the basic concept of localizing, if possible, the Korean struggle." As to the Chinese intervention, he discounted heavily the idea that the dams and reservoirs were the reasons for entering, because the hydroelectric stations were barely operable, having suffered severely from "Soviet post-war looting." He thought that Chinese "support of the North Koreans" was the dominant motivation and saw their interests "at present parallel to those of the Soviet," but he drew attention to Beijing's "lust for the expansion of power which has animated every would-be conqueror since the beginning of time."[65]

MacArthur sent two other messages on November 7 in response to the Joint Chiefs' authorization to carry out his air attacks. In his message numbered C-68411, MacArthur reported that "hostile planes are operating from bases west of the Yalu River against our forces in North Korea." Because of the short distances involved, it was "almost impossible to deal effectively with the hit and run tactics now being employed." He declared that affording the enemy a "sanctuary" in Manchuria was undermining the "morale and combat efficiency of both air and ground troops" and he thought that "this factor can assume decisive proportions" unless prompt corrective measures were taken.[66] MacArthur made no recommendations and simply requested instructions, but it was clear that he was raising a fundamental question. He was indirectly questioning Truman's refusal to implement NSC-73 and its provision to attack bases "outside" Korea once the Chinese had intervened.

MacArthur's third message of November 7, C-68465, was devoted to the issue of Chinese intervention. He reported that "organized units of Chinese Communist forces have been and are being utilized against our forces; that while the exact strength is impossible to accurately determine, it is sufficient to have seized the initiative in the west sector and to have materially slowed the offensive in the east sector." He believed that the Chinese were continuing to increase their strength. "If this augmentation continues, it can well reach a point rendering our resumption of advance impossible and even forcing a movement in retrograde. An effort will be made in the west sector in due course of time, possibly within ten days, to again assume the initiative provided the flow of enemy reinforcement can be checked. Only through such an offensive effort can any accurate measure be taken of enemy strength."[67]

With these messages, MacArthur had placed before the president the fundamental question of what should be done. Truman promptly scheduled a meeting of the NSC, which he himself did not attend, to consider whether MacArthur's mission should be changed. In preparation for the meeting, he requested that the JCS, CIA, State, and MacArthur, too, provide written assessments to guide their deliberations. The NSC meeting of November 9, and the president's response to it, would be the penultimate opportunity to determine whether or not there would be war with China.[68]

THE NOVEMBER 9 MEETING: MAINTAINING COURSE

The striking feature of the NSC meeting called by Truman to consider changing MacArthur's mission to unify Korea was the absence of the one man who could actually decide on the course of action—the president. The president's absence from what was the most important meeting since the war began (and arguably the most important meeting of his presidency), a meeting that would decide on war or peace, is particularly notable. Contrary to his presence at earlier meetings where key decisions were taken, especially the June 25 and 27 meetings at the outset of the conflict, his absence from the critical meeting of November 9 (and also the one of the 21st) requires an explanation.

In my view, Truman absented himself because he did not wish to be placed in a position where he would have to make a decision on the spot, particularly one contrary to the recommendations of his advisers. The proposals put forth at the November 9 meeting strongly suggest this motive for his absence. None of those present advocated the course of action the president finally chose, and the course he chose was that advocated by the second most important principal, who was of necessity absent—General MacArthur.

The principals attending the meeting were Acheson, who chaired the meeting, Marshall, Bradley, and Smith; MacArthur was also present in the form of his cable, which had arrived that morning. The Joint Chiefs had advised him of the coming NSC meeting to consider revision of his mission, so he sent in his very strong views. Buoyed by the start of his bombing campaign the day before, he argued vigorously for no abridgment of his mission, based on the JCS "amplification" of October 9. On November 8, and continuing until December 5, General Stratemeyer sent hundreds of aircraft against the twelve Yalu bridges and practically anything that moved between the river and U.N. lines. This included 79 B-29s, 300 F-80s and F-51s, and several hundred carrier aircraft.[69] It was this application of air power, rather than the withdrawal of Chinese forces, as Collins suggests, that "heartened" MacArthur.[70]

MacArthur's cable thus reflected an optimism that "with my air power, now unrestricted so far as Korea is concerned except as to hydroelectric installations, I can deny reinforcements coming across the Yalu." He planned to launch an attack on or about November 15 "with the mission of driving to the border and securing all of North Korea." He deplored "any program short of this" as destroying troop morale and having "inestimable" psychological consequences, akin to British appeasement at Munich in 1938.

"To give up any portion of North Korea to the aggression of the Chinese Communists would be the greatest defeat of the free world in recent times." Not only would it "bankrupt our leadership and influence in Asia," it would "condemn us to an indefinite retention of our military forces along difficult defense lines in North Korea." Moreover, it "would represent wishful thinking at its very worst," to assume that the Chinese Communists "after having achieved the complete success of establishing themselves within North Korea would abide by any delimitations upon further expansion southward."[71]

General Bradley, representing the Joint Chiefs, offered their latest assessment, as well as his own view. As for the latter, he thought MacArthur's argument that he could keep the Chinese out with his air power was "somewhat optimistic."[72] CIA Director Smith interjected that in any case the Yalu would soon be frozen and passable almost anywhere.[73] Intelligence indicated that the "Chinese Communists are entering North Korea both as individuals and as well organized, well-led and well-equipped Chinese Communist units, probably as large as divisions."[74]

The chiefs perceived three possible Chinese objectives: to protect the Yalu River and its reservoir complex and "possibly to establish a cordon sanitaire in North Korea"; to continue in an "active undeclared war" against us; or to drive the U.N. from Korea entirely.[75] They discounted the last, believing that the Chinese could not drive the U.N. from Korea without the assistance of Soviet air and naval power. Soviet materiel support in and of itself did not signal direct participation, but should direct Soviet participation occur, in the form of air and naval attacks against our forces, it would signal the outset of World War III and we should proceed according to NSC-76. As to the first, we could offer a U.N. guarantee to preserve their interests along the Yalu, which, if refused, would clarify their intentions and, essentially, leave the second possibility as the likely Chinese objective—an undeclared war against the U.N.

If we were, indeed, facing an undeclared war, the chiefs saw three possible courses of action. We could "force the action" to a successful conclusion, which would require a considerable augmentation of troop levels; we could "continue the action on a defensive line short of the Korean border"; or, we could "withdraw." In their view troop augmentation was infeasible in the light of other needs, especially in Europe, and of the production rate of new units, and withdrawal unthinkable and unnecessary. They felt that "the second course is apparently feasible now and it might be a temporary expedient pending clarification of the military and political problems raised by Chinese intervention."

However, while identifying as the "feasible" course a "defensive line short of the Korean border," the chiefs declined to advocate it. Instead, they waffled, urging Acheson to seek a political settlement through the U.N. "Pending further clarification as to the military objectives of the Chinese Communists and the extent of their intended commitments," they concluded, "the mission assigned to the Commander in Chief, UN Command, should be kept under review, but should not be changed." That "assigned" mission was, of course, to clear and occupy North Korea.

The chiefs did not believe the Chinese Communists alone could drive the U.N. command from Korea, although the Manchurian sanctuary could present problems. As "their army units are able to move from the Manchurian sanctuary to the fighting lines overnight ... such a situation may well become intolerable." In this case, "there appears strong likelihood that the tactical situation in Korea will demand that the United Nations commander 'be authorized to take appropriate air and naval action outside Korea against Communist China,' as provided in NSC-73/4 and NSC-81/1." Although not pressing for a clear-cut decision, in a very convoluted way, based on the command decision of NSC-73, the chiefs presented the two most likely options: either a withdrawal to defensive lines short of the Yalu, or an expansion of the war to Manchuria.

CIA Director "Beetle" Smith, basing his remarks on his agency's most recent estimate of Chinese capabilities, NIE-2 of November 8, responded to the JCS position with the view that the Chinese were "believed capable either of (a) halting further UN advance northward by matching any foreseeable UN buildup with piecemeal commitments of forces presently along the Yalu River; or (b) forcing UN withdrawal to defensive positions further south through a powerful assault."[76]

This conclusion was based on the estimate of Chinese forces already in Korea and on how many more could be deployed within two months. In a serious misjudgment, the CIA believed that Chinese Communist troop strength currently in North Korea was only 30,000–40,000, despite the fact that twelve different divisions had already been identified from at least four different armies. They arrived at this low number on the unusual theory that the Chinese had taken battalion-sized units "from each division of three or more of the Chinese Communist armies along the Korean border in Manchuria" and combined them "to form units of approximately division size."

The estimate of China's capabilities in Manchuria was far more accurate. Thus, while the Chinese Communists had deployed a relatively small force in North Korea to date, there were over three-quarters of a million troops assembled in Manchuria. Of these, the CIA estimated that Beijing could, within one to two months, deploy as many as 350,000 troops "for sustained ground operations in Korea and could provide limited air support and some armor."

During discussion, General Smith thought that the unanswered question was the "extent to which the Chinese . . . were willing to act as the pawn . . . of the Soviets."[77] He produced a memorandum formally restating an argument implied in the estimate. The CIA did not believe that the Soviet Union would enter the Korean conflict overtly, although Chinese intervention meant that Moscow was willing to raise the "risk of general war." Moscow "considers that the U.S. will not launch a general war over Chinese Communist intervention in North Korea." And, as the "principal risk of general war is through the exercise of Soviet initiative which the Kremlin continues to hold . . . there is a good chance that they will not in the immediate future take such a decision."[78]

On the basis of this analysis, Smith offered the opinion that "action by U.N. forces to attack troop concentrations or air fields north of the Yalu River, or to pursue enemy aircraft into Chinese territory would not increase the already substantial risk that the situation may degenerate into a general war involving Russia. In other words, the Kremlin's basic decision for or against war would hardly be influenced by this local provocation in this area. However, such provocation would probably materially increase the extent of Chinese Communist reaction in Korea proper."

As the discussion continued, Secretary Marshall, in his only recorded remark, observed that MacArthur's forces in the east sector were "vulnerable to an attack" because of their dispersed position. Bradley responded saying that "MacArthur had split his forces to carry out his directive to occupy the country and to hold elections." This prompted Acheson to ask whether there was "any line" that was better militarily than MacArthur's current position? Bradley's view was that "militarily the farther back the line, the better off we would be." But a withdrawal would cause political problems with the South Koreans.[79]

At this point, Acheson raised what he purported to be the British proposal of a buffer zone along the Yalu. His formulation of the concept—"a twenty-mile demilitarized area, ten miles on each side of the Yalu"—was quite different from the British idea and hardly likely to be acceptable to Beijing, as he well knew.[80] The British proposal called for a buffer zone only in North Korea from the Yalu River south to the Chongju-Hungnam line, the narrow neck of the peninsula.[81] Acheson had cleverly shifted the zone northward and extended it into Chinese territory.

A political settlement requiring Beijing to relinquish control of a ten-mile strip of its own territory along the Yalu River was an obvious non-starter, as Calum MacDonald notes, but Acheson's purpose was not to seek a solution so much as to divert the discussion away from its current thrust of proposing options that the president did not want.[82] These options were: either advance to the Yalu and attack Manchurian bases, according to NSC-73, or retreat to a more defensible position and seek a political settlement. Indeed, the discussion appeared to lean toward the retreat/settlement option.

The president's position, and the one Acheson decided upon at the meeting, was what can best be described as NSC-73 "minus," that is, an advance to the Yalu but no attacks outside Korea. Thus Acheson's introduction of the buffer zone concept. The result was an inconclusive end to the meeting, with Acheson offering to explore ways to contact the Beijing leadership, seek support in the U.N. for a resolution demanding the withdrawal of Chinese forces from Korea, and to raise the possibility of a buffer zone. In the meantime, he decided, MacArthur's mission would not be changed. He was "free to do what he militarily can do without bombing Manchuria."[83]

When Acheson briefed the president on the meeting the next day, Truman made no change. As Collins notes, "the most important outcome of this meeting was that it permitted General MacArthur to go ahead with his plans for an attack . . . a move that was destined to lead to one of the few military defeats in United States history."[84] It would be more precise to say, however, that it was the president who "permitted" MacArthur to go ahead with his plans.

PROPOSALS, COUNTERPROPOSALS, AND WAR

The two weeks before MacArthur's highly publicized advance to the Yalu River saw frenzied efforts by Washington and Moscow to place obstacles in the way of any possible settlement, proposals by London and Paris to craft a compromise, and (what appeared to be) trial balloons from Beijing for a settlement under certain (patently unacceptable) conditions. Lastly, the Truman leadership strove mightily to maintain discipline among its subordinates, as many within the administration saw, and voiced concern about, the looming specter of war.

Washington and Moscow sparred in the U.N. over Beijing. After assembling on November 8, the U.N. Security Council agreed, over Soviet protest, to discuss General MacArthur's November 5 "special report" on Chinese intervention in Korea.[85] The Security Council also agreed to invite Beijing to send a representative to join the discussion. Throwing a monkey wrench into this process, Acheson authorized the presentation of a resolution calling for the removal of all Chinese troops from Korea, but Malik threatened to veto any "resolution calling for the withdrawal of Chinese forces."[86]

At the same time the French proposed a resolution to take all necessary measures to prevent any damage to installations along the Yalu, on the assumption that the hydroelectric stations on the Yalu were the reason behind China's involvement. Although the Joint Chiefs initially balked at wording in the resolution terming the Chinese border "inviolate," they eventually acquiesced. When the resolution was presented on November 10, debate began over the objections of the Soviets, who insisted that the subject could be discussed only in the presence of a representative from Beijing. When Beijing notified the Security Council the next day that it would not participate in discussion of MacArthur's special report, the Security Council decided that no action was necessary.[87]

Zhou Enlai, China's foreign minister, issued a statement clarifying that Chinese representatives would "discuss the Korean problem on its own terms—that Formosa and Korea be regarded as part of the same picture of 'American aggression.' "[88] When he did that, the United States successfully lobbied the U.N. General Assembly to postpone debate on the Formosa issue "until it had disposed of all other items before it." The vote was 53–0. As John Foster Dulles explained, with China's "intervention in North Korea, the invasion of Tibet, the great aid to Ho Chi-minh in Indochina and the threats of invasion of Formosa—there is a risk that the whole area may be engulfed in aggressive war. If that is going to happen, then a discussion here of the long-range future of Formosa would be somewhat academic."[89]

Amid several requests from friendly governments, notably the British, French, Australian, Burmese, and Swedish, to exercise "military caution" in light of Beijing's involvement, came a variety of signals from China. Under the heading that war could, perhaps, be avoided, the November 10–11 edition of Hong Kong's *Ta Kung Pao* put forth a mixed bag of conditions: withdrawal of all foreign troops, that is, U.N. forces, and nationwide Korean elections were coupled with demands for an end to aid to Chiang Kai-shek and no rearmament of Japan.[90] On closer examination, it was clear that these demands were all non-negotiable.

On the other hand, reports from Hong Kong noted the "increasing scope and intensity of [China's] anti-American campaign." The Chinese press was no longer speaking of a long war of attrition, but of "turning [the] tide of war, annihilating and repulsing unconsolidated American invading troops."[91] A statement issued in the name of all China's non-Communist ruling parties, that is, political fronts, pledged full support to those Chinese who "voluntarily undertake the sacred task of resisting America, aiding Korea, protecting their homes and defending their country." The statement declared that "to save our neighbor is to save ourselves."[92] Reports out of Tokyo noted that "Chinese reinforcements continued to cross from Manchuria into North Korea, threatening a new drive against the United Nations forces as soon as the hostile buildup had been completed."[93]

On November 17, the Netherlands government passed on a report from its ambassador to China that Chinese intervention in Korea was motivated by fear of an attack on Manchuria and that there were already 160,000 Chinese troops in Korea. "If U.N. forces halted fifty miles south of the Yalu, the Netherlands believed, there would be no further intervention."[94] In light of this perceived opening, London redoubled efforts to gain consideration of its proposal for a buffer zone covering this area.[95] Foreign Secretary Bevin sought to discuss his proposal with the Beijing delegation to the U.N. when it arrived, but concerns regarding the impact on U.S. support for Europe dissuaded Bevin from immediately pressing the issue.[96]

Meanwhile, within the Pentagon and the State Department there was growing restiveness regarding the course of policy. On November 14, General James H. Burns, Assistant for Foreign Military Affairs and Military Assistance, spoke for a growing number of colleagues that the United States was headed for war with China. In a message to Marshall, he wrote: "Many people feel, and I am one of them, that if we continue to pursue our present military objectives in Korea we are running a serious risk of becoming involved in the world war we are trying to avoid."[97] Burns wanted to send a joint Defense-State delegation to Tokyo for an emergency conference with MacArthur. Marshall was dubious, but told him to explore the matter with the State Department, where Acheson turned it down.[98]

The State Department's Intelligence Bureau was also raising alarums. On November 17, in a memorandum to Ambassador Jessup, Fisher Howe offered an estimate as to the "immediate situation with regard to Chinese intervention in Korea." It was the view of the bureau that, while Chinese military action "so far is not sufficiently extensive to indicate a plan for major operations," he believed that "military preparations being carried out in Manchuria and China generally are on a scale that suggest (1) plans for a major operation of prolonged duration, (2) expectations of extensive US air attacks on Chinese, particularly Manchurian, cities."[99]

Considering all factors, the State Intelligence Bureau reached the conclusion that the Chinese would continue "holding operations in North Korea until Chinese over-all preparations have been completed and until prospects of securing US withdrawals from Korea through intimidations and diplomatic maneuvers have been exhausted." Should these tactics fail, they expected "increasing unofficial Chinese intervention in Korea to, if necessary, the point of large scale military operations." They also believed that the Soviet Union would provide "support of the Chinese in the form of equipment, planes, technical advisers, and, if necessary 'volunteers' to the extent required to prevent a Chinese defeat."[100]

This ferment prompted Acheson to attempt to maintain solidarity within government ranks as well as to reassure Beijing on Manchuria. On November 14, in remarks before some two hundred representatives of nongovernment organizations in the State Department, he declared that "the United States must employ all its wisdom . . . if it was to prevent the entry of Chinese Communists troops in Korea from causing a world-wide tragedy 'of the most colossal nature.'" Hinting that he would welcome discussions of China's "legitimate" interests, he declared that the United States has "no ulterior designs in Manchuria [and] everything possible must be done to disabuse them of such an illusion because it is not true."[101] President Truman did the same the next day, issuing a statement declaring that the United States had "never had" any intention of extending the war into Manchuria and would take every "honorable step" to avoid it.[102]

On November 19 came a cable from Everett Drumright, chargé d'affaires in Korea. He reported that although the lull in military action continued, more Chinese had been taken prisoner by elements of the U.S. Twenty-fourth Division. He spoke of "numerous reports being received [that] Chinese preparing defensive positions on line running from coast north of Chongju to Taechon, thence to Unsan and thence Northeast to point east of Huichon."[103] Secretary Marshall, too, reading the intelligence, learned that "the enemy had organized a strong-points defense of key terrain features in the area between the UNC front and the Yalu." The "lack of activity" reminded Marshall of "similar withdrawals . . . in the past . . . [that] preceded definite offensive action."[104] In other words, if permitted to commence his assault, MacArthur would be marching into the face of Chinese laying in wait behind prepared positions.

A few hours after Drumright's cable arrived, Ambassador Kirk in Moscow sent in a report on London's latest demarche, a renewed attempt to gain agreement on a demilitarized zone in North Korea. Kirk was "apprehensive at this proposed British initiative which seems to us to play into Soviet hands in the same fashion as British talks on this subject last July." Kirk was also "unhappy" that London was attempting to place this proposal before the Beijing authorities, fearing that the Chinese might assume they could act with "impunity" behind an inviolate frontier.[105] But of course, that was also the implication behind both Acheson's and Truman's statements of a few days earlier.

Such ferment, both within the administration and among the allies, precipitated another meeting of the high command—and the last before the crisis erupted—again without benefit of the president's presence. On November 21, Secretary Acheson, accompanied by Harriman, Rusk, Matthews, and Jessup, met with Secretary Marshall, the Joint Chiefs of Staff and the service secretaries. Acheson's concern, as he put it in his memoirs, was to deal with the two proposals developed so far for "easing the dangerous showdown that might be coming by such a method as Bevin favored—a cease-fire and a demilitarized zone along the border—or as others had urged by falling back to the neck of Korea, concentrating our forces, and doing our probing with Korean forces."[106]

Although in his memoir Acheson says, "I was sure that General MacAr-

377

thur would frustrate any such efforts until he had felt out Chinese strength," the record of the meeting does not bear out his view. Indeed, the record shows that the very opposite was his view. At the outset of the meeting, General Marshall "expressed satisfaction that Mr. Acheson had stated his belief that General MacArthur should push forward with the planned offensive." Thus, while it was true that MacArthur wished to probe the enemy's strength, so did Acheson.

On the question of Bevin's buffer zone idea, Acheson "expressed some doubt" about its feasibility, once again putting forth his own view that "if one were established south of the [Yalu] River another would have to be established to the north."[107] (After the meeting, Acheson would persuade Foreign Secretary Bevin to postpone his proposal "until after the Chinese arrive [at the U.N.] and talks have started with them.")[108] In other words, Acheson gained Bevin's agreement on an offensive first, then discussion of a buffer zone.

The main business of the Pentagon meeting of November 21 revolved around the question raised by Marshall's deputy, Robert Lovett, who asked whether "it would not be better . . . if General MacArthur withdrew to a defensible line *after* pressing his offensive forward successfully to the [Yalu] River?" On this all seemed to agree, the question then shifting to where to hold the line after driving to the Yalu. The chiefs concluded that "it would not be useful to hold the line at the River but rather the high ground back of the River."[109] (A message to this effect, drafted by General Collins, was sent to General MacArthur three days later just as the fateful offensive had begun.)[110]

There was a degree of surrealism surrounding this discussion. Everyone present had read the intelligence reports stating point blank that the Chinese were building positions of strength on the very high ground that MacArthur's forces would have to traverse to reach the Yalu River. However desirable it might have been to discuss a place to hold the line after reaching the Yalu, the intelligence estimates stating that the Chinese could halt any advance and force a withdrawal made the outcome of any decision to commit to an offensive certain—there would be large-scale *and unsuccessful* conflict with China.

Acheson got precisely what he came for, which was to quell the dissent in the Pentagon and gain the chiefs' agreement to proceed with the offensive. The agreed formula was: carry out the offensive, withdraw to the high ground afterward, and perhaps even negotiate a buffer zone between the high ground and the Yalu. Of course, as Acheson (if not the chiefs) certainly understood, once the offensive began and Chinese troops engaged in force, the rest would be academic. Nevertheless, having gotten what he came for, Acheson departed, leaving his aides to continue the discussion.[111]

Had an outcome short of all-out conflict with China been the objective, the November 21 meeting was the last opportunity to devise a formula for it. There were certainly a number of formulas circulating both inside and outside of the government offering a settlement short of war. Of course, as argued in this volume, that was never Truman's objective. A settlement would have contradicted the strategy of containment to which the president had committed the United States. That strategy required sustained conflict with China to be successful. Of course, the president sought a conflict short of all-out war, but he sought a conflict nevertheless. It is fair to conclude that he got more than he bargained for.

CONCLUSION

It was Stalin who triggered war in Korea to bring about a conflict that would avert his worst nightmare—the establishment of a Sino-American relationship. Stalin would achieve his objective of subordinating China to Soviet design and preventing the development of a Chinese-American relationship, but he got both more and less than he schemed for. The Sino-Soviet relationship would never be harmonious, although Soviet influence on China would continue down to the present—much to China's detriment. The vaunted Sino-Soviet alliance would in fact become a dead letter by the late 1950s, characterized more by conflict than by cooperation from then on.

Although Truman did not begin the war in Korea, he used the conflict to supreme national advantage. Chinese entry into the Korean conflict not only brought about, in MacArthur's words, "an entirely new war," but it also polarized global relations, which was in the long term its most important—and intended—effect. Chinese entry enabled the United States to rearm at a level sufficient to maintain military superiority over the Soviet Union. At the same time, Washington would undertake to organize a global set of alliances and strengthen its allies, including Japan, South Korea, and the Republic of China on Formosa, in constructing a forward American presence at key points around the Eurasian landmass to guard against the communist menace.[1] As conceived in NSC-68, containment would henceforth be the strategy that the United States would pursue.

Kim Il-sung had pressed Stalin to support a war of Korean unification, it is true, but it was Stalin who determined that it would be fought, when it would be fought, how it would be fought, and, most important, that it would be lost. For Stalin, too, the war would serve far larger ends than the conquest of South Korea. To avert a Sino-American relationship, Stalin employed war in Korea as the opening step in a two-step plan to maneuver China into conflict with the United States. Sino-American hostility removed for the foreseeable future any possibility of a Sino-American relationship, kept the United States off the East Asian landmass, and subordinated China to the Soviet Union.

Mao Zedong, holding the weakest hand, sought the most grandiose goal:

to occupy the middle position between the Soviet Union and the United States, leaning toward the former, but benefiting from both. He sought to ally with the Soviet Union, bring the civil war to an end with the conquest of Formosa, and eventually open up relations with the United States and other Western countries. Mao sought to terminate the unequal treaties imposed by the imperialist powers upon China in the past and establish relations with all countries based on equality.

Neither Stalin nor Truman would permit Mao to have his cake and eat it, too, both acting to thwart him. Stalin triggered war in Korea to forestall Mao's attempt to seize Formosa, while Truman responded promptly with the same object. Formosa would remain in the American sphere outside Mao's grasp, down to the present. As for war in Korea, Stalin pressed Mao to prepare for intervention as early as the second week, when victory seemed inevitable, while ultimately ensuring that the North Korean assault would fall short. **381**

Truman, on the other hand, having turned back the invasion at the Pusan perimeter and destroyed the North Korean Army by encirclement with the Inchon landing, authorized MacArthur to drive to the Yalu River with a full understanding that conflict with China would be the inevitable result. But Truman would not extend the conflict to Manchuria and risk general war with China. He sought stalemate, not victory, a decision that led to conflict with MacArthur, and MacArthur's dismissal.

Nevertheless, for all the Chinese claims of victory and American lamentations of defeat in Korea, almost the reverse was true. Although clearly both sides suffered militarily, Mao would squander nearly a million lives in Korea to secure his dubious goal of a divided regime, an outcome that remains to the present day. The additional cost to China in lost investment and development due to estrangement from the West, which perpetuated Chinese isolation and backwardness for decades, was a terrible price to pay. Both Truman and Stalin, acting independently but in parallel, subordinated China to their respective strategic designs. It is in this sense that Mao was Odd Man Out.

This study raises an important question, the answer to which must await further developments: Did the United States break Communist codes? The juxtaposition and timing of Chinese-Soviet and American decisions strongly suggests that Truman acted on the basis of special information. Three crucial points in the chronology raise this question.

First, Mao's December 19 cable from Moscow to Liu Shaoqi authorizing the opening of diplomatic relations with the United States was followed four days later by Acheson's formulation of a very attractive offer of relations with the United States. Second, Stalin's cable to Kim Il-sung of January 30 informing Kim that he would approve the Korean War was followed within forty-eight hours by Truman's command decisions to proceed with the hydrogen bomb and the formulation of a new strategy, NSC-68. And finally, after Mao's exchange of cables with Stalin through the first week of October, his cable of October 8 to Kim Il-sung informing him that China would send troops was followed the next day by Truman's authorization to MacArthur that he could engage Chinese forces "anywhere" he encountered them in Korea.

Defenders of the official wisdom will no doubt dispute these closely timed events as mere coincidence, and contend that the decision chains proceeded wholly independently of one another. They will no doubt adduce other reasons to explain the timing of Truman's decisions. All of these reasons may have validity, whether or not they are the truth. I do not expect revelations regarding American code-breaking to spill forth as a result of this book, although there would be much more to gain in admitting American intelligence prowess than to lose in acknowledging these secrets. So many changes in encryption systems have occurred in the meantime as to render innocuous any revelations about 1950.

NOTES

CHAPTER 1

1. "United States Policy Toward China," NSC-34/1, January 11, 1949. In "The Far East: China," United States Department of State, *Foreign Relations of the United States, 1949* (cited hereafter as *FRUS*), 9 (Washington, D.C.: GPO [Government Printing Office], 1974), 475.

2. "The British Embassy to the Department of State," January 5, 1949, and "The Secretary of State to the Consul General at Peiping (Clubb)," February 3, 1949, ibid., 2–5, 11.

3. "Testimony of Secretary of State Dean Acheson on March 18, 1949," Economic Assistance to China and Korea: 1949–1950, Hearings in Executive Session before the Senate Committee on Foreign Relations, *Historical Series of the Committee on Foreign Relations* (Washington, D.C.: GPO, 1974), 27–28.

4. Ibid., 43–44.

5. "The British Embassy to the Department of State," March 21, 1949, *FRUS*, 9: 11–12.

6. "The Secretary of State to the Ambassador in China (Stuart)," April 9, 1949, *FRUS*, 8: 230–31.

7. "The Ambassador in China (Stuart) to the Secretary of State," April 25, 1949, *FRUS*, 8: 723.

8. "The Ambassador in China (Stuart) to the Secretary of State," April 29, 1949, *FRUS*, 9: 12–14.

9. "The Ambassador in China (Stuart) to the Secretary of State," May 4 and May 5, 1949, *FRUS*, 9: 15–16.

10. *China and U.S. Far East Policy, 1945–1966* (Washington, D.C.: Congressional Quarterly, 1967), 47.

11. Robert M. Blum, *The United States and Communist China in 1949 and 1950: The Question of Rapprochement and Recognition*, staff study, U.S. Senate Committee on Foreign Relations (Washington, D.C.: GPO, 1973), 7–12.

12. "The Secretary of State to the Ambassador in China (Stuart)," May 13, 1949, *FRUS*, 9: 21–22.

13. "The Ambassador in China (Stuart) to the Secretary of State," May 14, 1949, *FRUS*, 8: 745–46. See also J. Leighton Stuart, *Fifty Years in China* (New York: Random House, 1949), 247.

14. Huang Hua, "My Contacts with John Leighton Stuart after Nanjing's Libera-

tion," *Chinese Historians* (Spring 1992), 51, confirms Stuart's "willingness to establish new relations with the New China."

15. Blum, *The United States and Communist China*, 8.

16. Huang Hua, "My Contacts With Stuart," 54, says that the initiative for Stuart's trip came from Undersecretary of State James Webb.

17. Blum, *The United States and Communist China*, 10–11.

18. "The Ambassador in China (Stuart) to the Secretary of State," July 14, 1949, *FRUS*, 8: 784.

19. Mao Zedong, "On the People's Democratic Dictatorship," (Peking: Foreign Languages Press, 1952), 10.

20. *Department of State Bulletin*, August 15, 1949, 236–37.

21. *United States Relations with China* (Washington, D.C.: Department of State, 1949), xvi–xvii.

22. *Department of State Bulletin*, August 15, 1949, 237.

23. Paul H. Nitze, *From Hiroshima to Glasnost: At the Center of Decision—A Memoir* (New York: Grove-Weidenfeld, 1989), 82.

24. Ibid., 87.

25. Blum, *The United States and Communist China*, 14.

26. "The Consul General at Peiping (Clubb) to the Secretary of State," October 1, 1949, *FRUS*, 8: 544–45.

27. Sergei N. Goncharov, John W. Lewis, and Xue Litai, *Uncertain Partners: Stalin, Mao, and the Korean War* (Stanford: Stanford University Press, 1993), 34.

28. *Hearings on the Institute of Pacific Relations*, U.S. Congress, Senate Committee on the Judiciary, Subcommittee to Investigate the Administration of the Internal Security Act (Washington, D.C.: GPO, 1951), 1554.

29. "Memorandum of Conversation by the Acting Deputy Director of the Office of Chinese Affairs (Freeman)," October 11, 1949, *FRUS*, 9: 120–21.

30. "Memorandum of the Secretary of State of a Conversation with President Truman," October 17, 1949, *FRUS*, 9: 132.

31. Ibid.; for Kirk's remarks, see 106–8; for Clubb's cable, see 121–22; and for the cable from London, see 124.

32. "Testimony of Secretary of State Dean Acheson on October 12, 1949," in *Reviews of the World Situation: 1949–1950*. Hearings held in Executive Session before the Senate Committee on Foreign Relations, in *Historical Series of the Committee on Foreign Relations*, 93rd Congress, 2nd session (Washington, D.C.: Government Printing Office, 1974), 96–97.

33. Ibid.

34. Ibid., 94.

35. "Testimony of Ambassador at large Philip Jessup on October 12, 1949," in *Reviews of the World Situation, 1949–1950*, 99–100.

36. "Memorandum of Conversation, by the Secretary of State (Acheson)," October 12, 1949, *FRUS*, 9: 124–25.

37. *New York Times*, October 13, 1949, 19.

38. For the full text of the charges, see "The Consul General at Peiping (Clubb) to the Secretary of State," June 19, 1949, *FRUS*, 8: 965–67. For the U.S. reaction, see

"The Consul General at Peiping (Clubb) to the Secretary of State," October 30, 1949, *FRUS*, 8: 993–95.

39. "Decisions Reached by Consensus at the Meetings with the Secretary and the Consultants on the Far East," November 2, 1949, *FRUS*, 9: 160–62.

40. "Memorandum of Conversation, by the Director of the Office of Chinese Affairs (Sprouse)," November 1, 1949, *FRUS*, 9: 149–51.

41. "Personal Message from Mr. Bevin to Mr. Acheson," December 16, 1949, *FRUS*, 9: 225–26, and "The British Embassy to the Department of State," December 27, 1949, ibid., 248.

42. "The Secretary of State to Certain Diplomatic and Consular Officers," December 16, 1949, *FRUS*, 9: 222–23.

43. "Mao Interview with a TASS Correspondent, January 2, 1950," in Goncharov et al., *Uncertain Partners*, 241–42.

CHAPTER 2

1. For an early adumbration of Mao's views of China's place in the world, see his interview with Anna Louise Strong in August 1946. Mao Zedong, *Selected Works* (Beijing: People's Press, 1977), 4: 1191–92.

2. *United States Relations with China* (Washington, D.C.: Department of State, 1949), 586.

3. "Stalin to Mao Zedong, 10 January 1949," *Cold War International History Project Bulletin*, 6–7: 27. (Hereafter referred to as *CWIHP*). See also Song Datu, trans., "Communications Between Mao and Stalin: Seven Telegrams, January 1949," *Chinese Historians* (Spring–Fall 1994), 163–72.

4. *United States Relations with China*, 290.

5. "Mao Zedong to Stalin, 13 January 1949," *CWIHP*, 6–7: 27–28.

6. "Stalin to Mao Zedong, 14 January 1949," *CWIHP*, 6–7: 28; and "Mao Zedong to Stalin, 14 January 1949," *CWIHP*, 6–7: 29.

7. Goncharov et al., *Uncertain Partners* (cited chap. 1, n. 27), 42 and 306n.25. For the recollection of Mao's interpreter, see Shi Zhe, "With Mao and Stalin: The Reminiscences of a Chinese Interpreter," trans. Chen Jian, *Chinese Historians* (Spring 1992), 35–46.

8. Goncharov et al., *Uncertain Partners*, 40 and 48n.

9. Ibid., 41.

10. Ibid., 48. Chen Jian, *China's Road to the Korean War* (New York: Columbia University Press, 1994), 40, places heavy anti-American emphasis on the admonition "not to be in a hurry" for recognition. But not hurrying does not mean "no recognition."

11. Goncharov et al., *Uncertain Partners*, 49.

12. "Stalin Cable to Mao re the Principles of Establishing Relations with the United States, April 1949," in ibid., 231.

13. Ibid., 53.

14. Ibid. See also "Mao Zedong to the CCP's General Front-line Committee, April 28, 1949," cited in Chen Jian, *China's Road*, 51 and 240.

15. Mao Zedong, "Statement by the Spokesman of the General Headquarters of the Chinese People's Liberation Army, April 30, 1949," cited in Chen Jian, *China's Road*, 51.

16. Kathryn Weathersby, "To Attack Or Not to Attack? Stalin, Kim Il-sung, and the Prelude to War," *CWIHP*, 5: 8.

17. Vojtech Mastny, *The Cold War and Soviet Insecurity* (New York: Oxford University Press, 1996), 90–91.

18. Chen Jian, *China's Road*, 56, agrees that the espionage charge was without evidence, but believes that it was used "to send the Americans a clear message."

19. Shi Zhe, "With Mao and Stalin: The Reminiscences of Mao's Interpreter, Part II: Liu Shaoqi in Moscow," *Chinese Historians* (Spring 1993), 71–72. See also Goncharov et al., *Uncertain Partners*, 65–67, and Chen Jian, *China's Road*, 71–73. Chen says that Liu took a prepared "memo" along with him, but Shi says that the memo was only prepared after he arrived in Moscow.

20. Goncharov et al., *Uncertain Partners*, 72.

21. Chen Jian, *China's Road*, 72.

22. Goncharov et al., *Uncertain Partners*, 67–68.

23. Ibid., 69.

24. Ibid., 70.

25. Chen Jian, *China's Road*, 74.

26. Goncharov et al., *Uncertain Partners*, 69.

27. Ibid., 71.

28. The Gao episode is based on Kovalev's unpublished memoirs, but is disputed by Shi Zhe. See Li Haiwen, "A Distortion of History: An Interview with Shi Zhe about Kovalev's Recollections," trans. Wang Xi, *Chinese Historians* (Fall 1992), 63.

29. Goncharov et al., *Uncertain Partners*, 75.

30. Ibid., 311n.128.

31. The resolution condemning Gao Gang can be found in *People's Daily*, April 10, 1955. Shi Zhe's account cited above, "With Mao and Stalin: . . . Liu Shaoqi in Moscow," 88–89, omits the episode with Gao, saying that he left before the others because "he had important administrative duties in the Northeast" and declaring that "every meeting during Liu's visit was filled with an atmosphere of respect, friendship, and sincerity."

32. He Di, "The Last Campaign to Unify China: The CCP's Unmaterialized Plan to Liberate Taiwan, 1949–1950," *Chinese Historians* (Spring 1992), 4, says simply that Stalin gave a "positive response." Goncharov et al., *Uncertain Partners*, 69–70 and 73–74, say Stalin refused, while Shi Zhe, "With Mao and Stalin: . . . Liu Shaoqi in Moscow," omits any mention of a request.

33. Goncharov et al., *Uncertain Partners*, 74, assert that Stalin deployed Soviet MIG-15s from Port Arthur to Shanghai in the summer of 1949 to provide defense against Nationalist bombing attacks, but this appears to be too early. Other sources say that the first appearance of Soviet MIGs over Shanghai came only in April 1950. See Steven J. Zaloga, "The Russians in MIG Alley," *Air Force Magazine* (February 1991), 75.

34. He Di, "The Last Campaign to Unify China," 2, and Goncharov et al., *Uncertain Partners*, 79.

35. Chen Jian, *China's Road*, 77–78.

36. Ibid., 98–99. Chen asserts that the Soviet Union had begun to send "air and naval aid . . . to strengthen the PLA's amphibious combat power . . . in September and October 1949." But the PLA's defeats on Quemoy and Dengbu were precisely the result of the absence of such air combat power. Therefore, one must question the assertion that Moscow began to send planes in September and October.

37. Ibid., 98.

38. Goncharov et al., *Uncertain Partners*, 80, 84, cite Kovalev's memoir. Shi Zhe, in Li Haiwen, "A Distortion of History: An Interview with Shi Zhe about Kovalev's Recollections," trans. Wang Xi, *Chinese Historians* (Fall 1992), 63, says that "Mao stayed in Shenyang for one day. He stayed in the Dahe Hotel, and did not go outside." The two positions are not necessarily in conflict. Mao's "tour" could have been the ride from the train station to the hotel and back.

39. For film footage of his arrival, see the informative documentary *Messengers from Moscow—The East* (London and Los Angeles: Pacem Productions, 1995).

40. "Mao Speech at the Railway Station on His Arrival in Moscow, December 16, 1949," Goncharov et al., *Uncertain Partners*, 237.

41. *Messengers From Moscow* (documentary), quoting Shi Zhe. In this documentary, Mikhail Kapitsa, one of the interpreters, states unequivocally that Stalin offered his apology to Mao with the words "beg your pardon." Goncharov et al., *Uncertain Partners*, 87, deny that Stalin apologized and quote a slightly different version of Mao's response from Shi Zhe's memoirs: "For a long time I was mistreated and pushed aside and had nowhere to complain"; Shi Zhe, *Zai Li Shi Ju Ren Shen Bian hui yi lu (Beside Great Historical Figures—The Memoirs of Shi Zhe)* (Beijing: Central Document Press, 1996), 434.

42. Chen Jian, *China's Road*, 80.

43. Shi Zhe claims that at this point KGB chief Lavrenty Beria "laughed at Mao's expression," but the official Soviet transcript of the Mao-Stalin conversation only lists Stalin, Malenkov, Molotov, Bulganin, and Vyshinsky as present, with Shi Zhe and Nikolai Fedorenko as the interpreters. See "Stalin's Conversations with Chinese Leaders: I: Conversation Between Stalin and Mao, Moscow, 16 December 1949," *CWIHP*, 6–7: 5–7.

44. Chen Jian, *China's Road*, 80, and Goncharov et al., *Uncertain Partners*, 86, both interpret Stalin's response as one of bewilderment and lack of understanding. The latter eventually comes closer, citing former Chinese ambassador Liu Xiao, who observed that Stalin "was not about to refer explicitly to the possibility of a new treaty until Mao did, which would put the Chinese in the position of supplicants."

45. "Conversation Between Stalin and Mao, Moscow, 16 December 1949," *CWIHP*, 6–7: 5. This official record begins with Mao's question about peace, omitting the introductory exchange noted above.

46. Ibid.

47. Ibid.

48. For the Yalta Agreement, see *United States Relations with China*, 113–14.

49. "The Consul General at Shanghai (McConaughy) to the Secretary of State," January 21, 1950, *FRUS*, 6: 91.

50. "Conversation Between Stalin and Mao, Moscow, 16 December 1949," *CWIHP*, 6—7: 6.

51. Ibid.

52. Richard A. Russell, *Project Hula: Secret Soviet-American Cooperation in the War Against Japan* (Washington, D.C.: Naval Historical Center, 1997), 39—40.

53. "Conversation Between Stalin and Mao, Moscow, 16 December 1949," *CWIHP*, 6—7: 6.

54. Ibid.

55. Mao's cable to Liu Shaoqi is found in Chen Jian, "Comparing Russian and Chinese Sources: A New Point of Departure for Cold War History," *CWIHP*, 6—7: 20.

56. "Mao's Conversation with Yudin, 31 March 1956," *CWIHP*, 6—7: 165. Pavel Yudin was the Soviet ambassador to China from 1956 to 1960.

57. "Mao Zedong to Liu Shaoqi and Zhou Enlai, 19 December 1949," in *CWIHP*, 8—9: 227. For a slightly different version, see "Mao Cable from Moscow re Establishing Diplomatic Relations with Burma, December 19, 1949," in Goncharov et al., *Uncertain Partners*, 238.

58. Headquarters, Far East Command, *History of the North Korean Army*, 92, as cited in Myung Lim Park, "North Korea's Inner Leadership and the Decision to Launch the Korean War," *Korea and World Affairs* (Summer 1995), 260.

59. Ibid., 247.

60. "Kovalev Report to Stalin re a Conversation with Mao, Dec. 20, 1949," Goncharov et al., *Uncertain Partners*, 238—39.

61. Ibid., 90.

62. "Mao Congratulatory Speech at the Ceremony in Honor of Stalin's Seventieth Birthday in Moscow, Dec. 21, 1949," ibid., 239—40.

63. "Mao Cable from Moscow re Preparations for a Trade Agreement with the Soviet Union, Dec. 22, 1949," ibid., 240.

64. "Mao Cable from Moscow re Sino-Soviet Cooperation, Dec. 29, 1949," ibid., 241.

65. "Mao's Conversation with Yudin, 31 March 1956," *CWIHP*, 6—7: 165.

66. Ibid.

67. Ibid. and Goncharov et al., *Uncertain Partners*, 92.

68. "Mao Cables from Moscow re Zhou Enlai's Departure for the Soviet Union to Participate in the Talks, Jan. 2, 1950, 2300; Jan. 3, 0400," Goncharov et al., *Uncertain Partners*, 242.

69. Ibid., 244.

70. Ibid.

CHAPTER 3

1. NSC-48/1, "The Position of the United States with Respect to Asia," *A Report to the National Security Council by the Executive Secretary*, December 23, 1949, 10. The National Security Archives, George Washington University.

2. Ibid., 2—3.

3. See Michael Schaller, *The American Occupation of Japan: The Origins of the*

Cold War in Asia (New York: Oxford University Press, 1985), chap. 11, for a discussion of the NSC-48 drafts. Bruce Cumings, *The Origins of the Korean War,* 2 vols. (Princeton: Princeton University Press, 1990), vol. 2, chap. 5, also discusses them.

4. "Testimony of Louis A. Johnson, Former Secretary of Defense," June 14, 1951, *Military Situation in the Far East,* Hearings before the Senate Committee on Foreign Relations and Senate Committee on Armed Services, 1st session, 82nd Congress (Washington, D.C.: GPO, 1951), 2578. (Hereafter cited as *MSFE.*)

5. Ibid.

6. For the meetings as scheduled in the secretary's appointment book, see Cumings, *The Origins of the Korean War,* 2: 420.

7. NSC-48/2, "The Position of the United States with Respect to Asia," *A Report to the President by the National Security Council,* December 30, 1949. The National Security Archives, George Washington University.

8. "Mao Interview with a TASS Correspondent, January 2, 1950," in Goncharov et al., *Uncertain Partners* (cited chap. 1, n. 27), 241–42.

9. "Memorandum of Conversation of V. M. Molotov and A. Y. Vyshinsky with the Chairman of the People's Central Government of the People's Republic of China, Mao Zedong, 17 January 1950," *CWIHP* (cited chap. 2, n. 3), 8–9: 233. See also below, chap. 4, p. 85.

10. "Memorandum of Conversation, by the Secretary of State (Acheson)," January 5, 1950, *FRUS,* 6: 258–64.

11. "United States Policy Toward Formosa," Statement by President Truman, *Department of State Bulletin,* January 16, 1950, 79.

12. "Extemporaneous Remarks by Secretary Acheson," ibid., 79–81.

13. Britain's representative to the U.N., Sir Alexander Cadogan, in conversation with Secretary General Trygve Lie, suspected that "the Soviet attitude was based on a calculated policy of discouraging rather than encouraging recognition.... China could thereby be kept more effectively in isolation from the West and under Soviet domination." Trygve Lie, *In the Cause of Peace* (New York: Macmillan, 1954), 258.

14. Thomas J. Hamilton, "Russian Quits U.N. Council on China Recognition Issue; Acheson Is Firm on Policy," *New York Times,* January 11, 1950, 1.

15. Thomas J. Hamilton, "Soviet to Attend the U.N. Assembly," *New York Times,* August 31, 1950, 1.

16. "Proclamation of Peking Municipal Military Control Commission of Chinese People's Liberation Army, PU Number 15," January 6, 1950, *Department of State Bulletin,* January 23, 1950, 121.

17. "Testimony of Secretary of State Dean Acheson on January 10, 1950," in *Reviews of the World Situation, 1949–1950* (cited chap. 1, n. 32), 125–27.

18. "Acheson Is Firm on Policy," *New York Times,* January 11, 1950, 1.

19. Secretary Acheson, "Crisis in Asia—An Examination of U.S. Policy," *Department of State Bulletin,* January 23, 1950, 111–18.

20. This is not the place to discuss Acheson's extraordinary assertion. Readers interested in the nature of the Kuomintang's defeat can consult any number of texts, including the author's *China: A Political History, 1917–1980,* (Boulder, Col.: Westview, 1982), chapter 8.

21. Walter Waggoner, "Sec Acheson Sees USSR 'Attaching' Manchuria, Inner and Outer Mongolia and Sinkiang Prov; Says Move Is Most Important Factor Shaping US Far East Policy," *New York Times*, January 13, 1950, 1.

22. Ferdinand Kuhn, "Russia Now Carving Up China, But Will Face Wrath of People Acheson Says in Policy Outline," *Washington Post*, January 13, 1950, 1.

23. "Text of the Wallace Report on China," *New York Times*, January 19, 1950, 3. See also the accompanying article discussing the report on page one.

24. "Memorandum of Conversation of V. M. Molotov and A. Y. Vyshinsky with the Chairman of the People's Central Government of the People's Republic of China, Mao Zedong, 17 January 1950," *CWIHP*, 8–9: 233.

25. "Communists Take U.S. Property in China," *Department of State Bulletin*, January 23, 1950, 119–21.

26. *New York Times*, January 15, 1950, 1.

27. Jay Wale, "Consular Holdings of French, Dutch Seized by Beiping," *New York Times*, January 16, 1950, 1.

28. "The Consul General at Shanghai (McConaughy) to the Secretary of State," January 21, 1950, *FRUS*, 6: 289–93.

29. "The Secretary of State to the Consulate General at Shanghai," January 25, 1950, ibid., 294.

30. "The Consul General at Shanghai (McConaughy) to the Secretary of State," January 26, 1950, ibid., 296–300.

31. Ibid.

32. "Memorandum by John P. Davies of the Policy Planning Staff," February 2, 1950, ibid., 305.

33. "I agree with your telegram dated 13 January about implementing the order to requisition foreign military barracks and preparing to force the United States to evacuate all the former U.S. consulates from China." Mao's remark suggests not only that the decision was made in Beijing, but also that he was not informed of it beforehand. See "Mao Zedong to Liu Shaoqi, 13 January 1950," *CWIHP*, 8–9: 232.

CHAPTER 4

1. Kim Philby, a British official and an agent for Moscow, had been assigned to Washington in 1949 and was in "as perfect a spot for the Soviets as they could possibly get a man." See David C. Martin, *Wilderness of Mirrors* (New York: Harper & Row, 1980), 44.

2. Goncharov et al., *Uncertain Partners* (cited chap. 1, n. 27), 102.

3. "Mao Cable from Moscow re an Official Statement Denying the Legitimacy of the Nationalist Government's Seat on the UN Security Council, January 7, 1950," ibid., 246. Vyshinsky's diary entry gives the same account with additional details. See "Memorandum of Conversation with the Chairman of the People's Central Government of the People's Republic of China, Mao Zedong, 6 January 1950," *CWIHP* (cited chap. 2, n. 3), 8–9: 230–31.

4. Thomas J. Hamilton, "Malik Again Quits Council as Chinese Ouster Is Beaten," *New York Times*, January 14, 1950, 1. Hamilton observed that the failure to

oust the Nationalists "would make the West the enemy of Mao's China and the USSR its only friend."

5. "Derevyanko, Aides Quit Tokyo Mission," *New York Times*, May 28, 1950, 21.

6. John Gittings, *The World and China, 1922–1972* (New York: Harper & Row, 1974), 160–62.

7. "Mao Cable from Moscow re Supporting the Cominform Bulletin's Criticism of the Japanese Communist Party Politburo Member Nosaka Sanzo," January 14, 1950, Goncharov et al., *Uncertain Partners*, 250.

8. Lindesay Parrott, "Japan's Reds Bow to Cominform But Hold Policy Is Best Possible," *New York Times*, January 13, 1950, 3.

9. "The Director of the Office of Northeast Asian Affairs (Allison) to the Acting United States Political Adviser for Japan (Sebald)," May 24, 1950, *FRUS*, 6: 1203.

10. Secretary of State Acheson, "Crisis in Asia," *Department of State Bulletin*, January 23, 1950, 115.

11. See for example, Goncharov et al., *Uncertain Partners*, appendix, 249–54. Mao's first mention of Acheson's speech is in his cable of January 19.

12. "Memorandum of Conversation of V. M. Molotov and A. Y. Vyshinsky with the Chairman of the People's Central Government of the People's Republic of China, Mao Zedong, 17 January 1950," *CWIHP*, 8–9: 232–33.

13. Ibid., 233.

14. For the response, see "Mao Cable from Moscow re the Release on U.S. Secretary of State Dean Acheson's Statement," January 19, 1950, in Goncharov et al., *Uncertain Partners*, 254–55.

15. "Memorandum of Conversation of V. M. Molotov and A. Y. Vyshinsky with the Chairman of the People's Central Government of the People's Republic of China, Mao Zedong, 17 January 1950," *CWIHP*, 8–9: 233.

16. Goncharov et al., *Uncertain Partners*, 99–100, 107–8.

17. "Mao Cable from Moscow Approving the Establishment of Diplomatic Relations with the Democratic Republic of Vietnam," Jan. 17, 1950, Goncharov et al., *Uncertain Partners*, 251.

18. "Order to Shtykov to elucidate North Korean position regarding return of Korean soldiers from China," January 8, 1950. The National Security Archives, George Washington University.

19. "Report to Moscow concerning Shtykov's conversation with Kim Il-sung about transfer of Korean troops from China to North Korea," January 11, 1950. The National Security Archives, George Washington University.

20. "Ciphered Telegram from Shtykov to Vyshinsky, 19 January 1950," *CWIHP*, 5: 8.

21. Chen Jian, *China's Road* (cited chap. 2, n. 10), 88.

22. Ibid., 110.

23. "Shtykov to Vyshinsky re Meeting with Kim Il-sung," May 12, 1950, *CWIHP*, 6–7: 38–39.

24. Chen Jian, *China's Road*, 87–88, based on an interview with Shi Zhe. Nikita Khrushchev, in *Khrushchev Remembers: The Glasnost Tapes*, Jerrold L. Schechter and Vyacheslav V. Luchkov, eds. (Boston: Little, Brown, 1990), 371–72, places a dif-

ferent spin on the conversation. Like Shi Zhe he portrays Stalin as the passive recipient of Kim's passionate plea for invasion, but claims that Mao was in positive agreement about the plan and believed that "the USA would not interfere since the war would be an internal matter." Hao Yufan and Zhai Zhihai, "China's Decision to Enter the Korean War: History Revisited," *China Quarterly*, no. 121 (March–April 1990), 100, say that Mao was "more cautious than both Kim and Stalin," and himself "raised the possibility of American military intervention."

25. Cf. Chen Jian, *China's Road*, 90.

26. Dieter Heinzig, "Stalin, Mao, Kim and Korean War Origins, 1950: A Russian Documentary Discrepancy," *CWIHP*, 8–9: 240. Heinzig points out that Russian censors omitted this fragment of Mao's talk with Yudin.

27. Goncharov et al., *Uncertain Partners*, 99–100.

28. See ibid., 98. Goncharov, Lewis, and Xue clearly pose the strategic implications of a Chinese conquest of Taiwan occurring before a war in Korea. "As Mao saw it, Washington's announced policy of staying clear of the Chiang regime was an invitation to accelerate the preparations for the 'liberation of Taiwan.' Stalin, however, saw the same realities through a quite different lens. Any 'Chinese' solution of the Taiwan problem without American interference, if linked to normalizing U.S.-PRC relations, constituted a serious danger to the agreements being transacted in Moscow. That solution could destroy the basis for China's willing acceptance of the Soviet security zone and could provide Mao with an excuse to seek a reconsideration of the most controversial sections of the proposed treaty of alliance" (ibid.). Korea first, in short, would thwart Mao's plans.

29. Present were Molotov, Malenkov, Mikoyan, Vyshinsky, Roshchin, and interpreter Fedorenko; Li Fuchun, Wang Jiaxiang, Chen Boda (Mao's political secretary), and interpreter Shi Zhe.

30. Chen Jian, *China's Road*, 84.

31. *Messengers from Moscow—The East* (documentary; cited chap. 2, n. 39).

32. "Record of Conversation Between Comrade I. V. Stalin and Chairman of the Central People's Government of the People's Republic of China Mao Zedong, 22 January 1950," *CWIHP*, 6–7: 7–9.

33. Ibid. This record includes only the "first group" of questions; the "second group" refers to the secret "additional agreement" on Manchuria and Sinkiang, which is not printed in *CWIHP*, but is discussed, along with several other secret protocols, in Goncharov et al., *Uncertain Partners*, 121–29.

34. Goncharov et al., *Uncertain Partners*, 122–23.

35. "Mao's Conversation with Yudin, 31 March 1956," *CWIHP*, 6–7: 166.

36. See Mark Kramer, "The USSR Foreign Ministry's Appraisal of Sino-Soviet Relations on the Eve of the Split," September 1959, *CWIHP*, 6–7: 183n.86.

37. "The Secretary of State to the Embassy in France," February 11, 1950, *FRUS*, 6: 309, and Mark Kramer, "The USSR Foreign Ministry's Appraisal of Sino-Soviet Relations on the Eve of the Split," September 1959, *CWIHP*, 6–7: 170.

38. "Mao Cable from Moscow re the Sino-Soviet Talks and the Drafting of the Treaty of Friendship," January 25, 1950, Goncharov et al., *Uncertain Partners*, 256–57.

39. Ibid., 125–26.

40. In "Mao's Conversation with Yudin, 31 March 1956," 166, he said that "in the course of the negotiations around this treaty, there was the most genuine trading going on. It was an unattractive way to pose the issue, in which Stalin's distrust and suspicion of the CPC was brightly expressed."

41. Goncharov et al., *Uncertain Partners*, 115–18, discusses the changes.

42. *United States Relations with China* (cited chap. 1, n. 21), 485–87. Goncharov et al., *Uncertain Partners*, 117, cite the White Paper, but substitute the term "military engagement," for "hostilities" used in the original. The Russian term is *voennie deistviia*, or "military actions."

43. "Treaty of Friendship, Alliance, and Mutual Assistance Between the People's Republic of China and the Union of Soviet Socialist Republics," February 14, 1950, in Goncharov et al., *Uncertain Partners*, 260–61 (emphasis supplied).

44. Ibid., 261–62 (emphasis supplied).

45. "Agreement Between the Republic of China and the U.S.S.R. Concerning the Chinese Changchun Railway," *United States Relations with China*, 593–96, and Goncharov et al., *Uncertain Partners*, 126–27.

46. "Mao Cable from Moscow re the Publishing of the Treaty," February 10, 1950, in Goncharov et al., *Uncertain Partners*, 257.

47. "Mao Cable from Moscow re Revisions in the Editorial 'A New Epoch in Sino-Soviet Friendship and Cooperation,'" February 14, 1950, at 0500, in Goncharov et al., *Uncertain Partners*, 258.

48. Goncharov et al., *Uncertain Partners*, 121.

CHAPTER 5

1. For the text of the telegram, see Dmitrii Volkogonov, "Should We Be Frightened by This?—Behind the Scenes of the Korean War," *Ogonek*, no. 25–26 (June 1993), 5. Volkogonov asserts without documentation that Stalin approved "Pyongyang's plans" on February 9. He also argues without documentation that Stalin sent at least two messages to Beijing to consult with Mao in late January and early February, evidently failing to recall that Mao was at that time still in Moscow.

2. "Shtykov to Stalin re Meeting with Kim, 31 January 1950," *CWIHP* (cited chap. 2, n. 3), 6–7: 36.

3. "Shtykov to Vyshinsky re Meeting with Kim, 7 February 1950," ibid., 36.

4. "Shtykov to Vyshinsky transmitting a note from Kim, 9 March 1950," ibid., 37.

5. "Shtykov to Vyshinsky transmitting 14 March message from Kim, 16 March 1950," ibid., 37.

6. "Stalin to Kim Il-sung (via Shtykov), 18 March 1950," ibid., 37.

7. "Shtykov to Vyshinsky re meeting with Kim, 21 March 1950," ibid., 38.

8. Goncharov et al., *Uncertain Partners* (cited chap. 1, n. 27), 144, claim that Yu Song-chol accompanied them, but in "Yu Song-chol's Testimony" December 27, 1990, *Foreign Broadcast Information Service—East Asian Survey* (*FBIS-EAS*) (Washington, D.C.: Central Intelligence Agency), 26, Yu says that he did not even learn of Kim's trip until told by Mun Il a year later.

9. Syn Song-kil and Sin Sam-soon, "Who Started the Korean War," *Korea and*

World Affairs (Summer 1990), 250. The authors were highly placed officials in North Korea at the time of the Korean War.

10. Ibid.

11. Lim Un, *The Founding of a Dynasty in North Korea: An Authentic Biography of Kim Il-sung* (Tokyo: Jiy v-sha, 1982), 168.

12. Syn and Sin, "Who Started the Korean War," 250.

13. Goncharov et al., *Uncertain Partners*, 145.

14. Interview with Yu Song-chol, as cited in ibid., 330, n.77.

15. "Soviet Representative Aleksei Ignatiev to Vyshinsky, 10 April 1950," *CWIHP*, 6–7: 38. Ignatiev was the Soviet representative while Shtykov was in Moscow with Kim and Pak.

16. Ibid.

17. "Shtykov to Maj. Gen. A. M. Vasilevsky, Head of the Soviet Military Advisory Group, 23 February 1950," ibid., 37.

18. Volkogonov, "Should We Be Frightened By This?," 6.

19. Goncharov et al., *Uncertain Partners*, 149.

20. Coded message N-2220, May 3, 1950, as cited in Evgueni Bajanov, "Assessing the Politics of the Korean War, 1949–1951," *CWIHP*, 6–7: 87. According to Mun Il, Kim's interpreter, it was only at this point, shortly after Kim had returned to Pyongyang, that "a dispatch authorizing an invasion of the south came down from the Soviet Union." See "Yu Song-chol's Testimony, Part 8," *FBIS-EAS*, December 27, 1990, 26.

21. "Shtykov to Vyshinsky re meeting with Kim Il-sung, 12 May 1950," *CWIHP*, 6–7: 38.

22. Syn and Sin, "Who Started the Korean War," 250.

23. "Shtykov to Vyshinsky re Meeting with Kim Il-sung, 12 May 1950," *CWIHP*, 6–7: 39.

24. Ibid.

25. "Roshchin to Filippov, 13 May 1950," *CWIHP*, 4: 61.

26. "Filippov to Mao Zedong, 14 May 1950," ibid.

27. Goncharov et al., *Uncertain Partners*, 146, citing interviews with an unidentified Chinese specialist and a senior Soviet diplomat.

28. Hao Yufan and Zhai Zhihai, "China's Decision to Enter the Korean War: History Revisited," *China Quarterly*, no. 121, (March–April 1990), 100.

29. Goncharov et al., *Uncertain Partners*, 146, citing an interview with a "well informed Chinese specialist." Goncharov's position is contradictory. On this page, he claims in one place that Mao gave Kim his "blessing," and in another that "the Soviets knew that the Chinese Politburo opposed the idea."

30. Goncharov et al., *Uncertain Partners*, 147, 153, quoting from an interview with General Chung Sang-chin.

31. Roy E. Appleman, *South to the Naktong, North to the Yalu* (Washington, D.C.: Office of the Chief of Military History, 1961), 12.

32. Central Intelligence Agency, "Current Capabilities of the Northern Korean Regime," Office of Regional Estimates 18, June 19, 1950, *FRUS*, 7: 120–22.

33. Ibid.

34. Ibid.

35. Goncharov et al., *Uncertain Partners*, 147.

36. See Appleman, *South to the Naktong*, 10–11.

37. Goncharov et al., *Uncertain Partners*, 149.

38. Ibid., 150, citing an interview with Yu Song chol, head of the KPA Operations Directorate.

39. "Yu Song-chol's Testimony, Part 8," 26.

40. Goncharov et al., *Uncertain Partners*, 150, citing an interview with Yu Song-chol.

41. See the highly informative article by Park, "North Korea's Inner Leadership" (cited chap. 2, n. 58), 240–68, from which this interpretation is drawn.

42. Headquarters, Far East Command, *History of the North Korean Army*, 92 (cited chap. 2, n. 58).

43. "Yu Song-chol's Testimony, Part 9," *FBIS-EAS*, December 27, 1990, 26–27.

44. See Lim Un, *Founding of a Dynasty*, chap. 6 passim.

45. Park, "North Korea's Inner Leadership," 261–62.

46. "Shtykov to Stalin, re Meeting with Kim Il-sung and Pak Hon-yong, 4 July 1950," *CWIHP*, 6–7: 42–43.

47. "Yu Song-chol's Testimony, Part 8," 26.

48. "Yu Song-chol's Testimony, Part 9," 26.

49. Goncharov et al., *Uncertain Partners*, 154.

50. "Shtykov to Comrade Zakharov, top secret report on military situation, 26 June 1950," *CWIHP*, 6–7: 39.

51. "Yu Song-chol's Testimony, Part 9," 26.

52. See Chen Jian, *China's Road* (cited chap. 2, n. 10), 102.

53. Goncharov et al., *Uncertain Partners*, 148, and "Mao Zedong to Liu Shaoqi, 10 February 1950," *CWIHP*, 8–9: 235.

54. "The Chargé in China (Strong) to the Secretary of State," June 7, 1950, *FRUS*, 6: 359. Strong estimated there were 410,000 troops on Taiwan and Jinmen. Robert Payne, *Chiang Kai-shek* (New York: Weybright and Talley, 1969), 290, says 800,000 troops and 600 planes, which was an exaggeration.

55. William Whitson, ed., *Military Campaigns in China: 1924–1950* (Taipei: Military History Office, 1970), 189.

56. "Remarks on the Situation in China by Consul General McConaughy at the Inter-Departmental Meeting on the Far East," June 1, 1950, *FRUS*, 6: 355.

57. See Steven J. Zaloga, "The Russians in MIG Alley," *Air Force Magazine* (February 1991), 75, and Chen Jian, "The Sino-Soviet Alliance and China's Entry into the Korean War," Working Paper No. 1, June 1992, *CWIHP*, 18n.58.

58. Goncharov et al., *Uncertain Partners*, 149.

59. "The Consul General at Shanghai (McConaughy) to the Secretary of State," March 16, 1950, *FRUS*, 6: 319.

60. Chen Jian, *China's Road*, 95.

61. Whitson, ed., *Military Campaigns in China*, 189.

62. "Memorandum by the Assistant Secretary of State for Far Eastern Affairs (Rusk) to the Secretary of State," April 26, 1950, *FRUS*, 6: 334.

63. "The Secretary of State to the Secretary of Defense (Johnson)," March 7, 1950, *FRUS*, 6: 316.

64. "The Secretary of State to the Secretary of Defense (Johnson)," April 14, 1950, *FRUS*, 6: 326.

65. "The Chargé in China (Strong) to the Secretary of State," May 17, 1950, *FRUS*, 6: 340.

66. "Memorandum by the Assistant Secretary of State for Far Eastern Affairs (Rusk) to the Secretary of State," April 17, 1950, *FRUS*, 6: 330.

67. "The Chargé in China (Strong) to the Secretary of State," May 17, 1950, *FRUS*, 6: 340.

68. Cumings, *The Origins of the Korean War* (cited chap. 3, n. 3), 2: 508.

69. *MSFE* (cited chap. 3, n. 4), Part 4, 2621. The secretary adjusted his estimate to "slightly more than 40,000" later in his testimony.

70. Chen Jian, *China's Road*, 97.

CHAPTER 6

1. Schaller, *American Occupation of Japan* (cited chap. 3, n. 3), 252–53.

2. On Truman's twofold decision, see Dmitrii Volkogonov, "Should We Be Frightened by This?—Behind the Scenes of the Korean War," *Ogonek,* nos. 25–26 (June 1993), 5. Ironically, U.S. and Soviet interception of Mao's December 19 cable not only prompted the formulation of the U.S. offer to Mao, but also Stalin's decision for war in Korea.

3. Robert J. Lamphere, *The FBI-KGB War: A Special Agent's Story* (Macon, Ga.: Mercer University Press, 1995), 79, 91, 311. See also Robert L. Benson and Michael Warner, eds., *Venona: Soviet Espionage and the American Response, 1939–1957* (Washington, D.C.: National Security Agency, 1996), and David Martin, "The Code War," *The Washington Post Magazine*, May 10, 1998, 14.

4. Lamphere, *FBI-KGB War,* 79.

5. *Emergence of the Intelligence Establishment, FRUS,* 1945–1950 (Washington, D.C.: GPO, 1996), 1117–18.

6. Ibid., "National Security Council Intelligence Directive No. 9," March 10, 1950, 1123–25.

7. "The Consul General at Shanghai (McConaughy) to the Secretary of State," January 5, 1950, *FRUS*, 6: 265.

8. Burton Crane, "Formosa Invasion by August Is Seen," *New York Times*, February 1, 1950, 8; see also his: "Chiang Gave Fund to Formosa Regime," February 2, 1950, 6; and "Seized Chinese Red Bares Peiping Plan," May 4, 1950, 14 (all in *New York Times*).

9. "The Chargé in China (Strong) to the Secretary of State," April 27, 1950, *FRUS*, 6: 335–38.

10. "The Chargé in China (Strong) to the Secretary of State," May 17, 1950, *FRUS*, 6: 340.

11. "The Acting Secretary of State to the Embassy in China," May 19, 1950, *FRUS*, 6: 343–44.

12. "Americans Urged to Go," *New York Times*, May 24, 1950, 20.

13. "Testimony of Louis A. Johnson, Former Secretary of Defense," June 14, 1951, *Military Situation in the Far East* (cited chap. 3, n. 4), Part 4, 2621.

14. "Soong Quits, Breaks with Chiang in Rift of the Chinese Nationalists," *New York Times*, June 10, 1950, 4.

15. "The Secretary of Defense (Johnson) to the Secretary of State," July 29, 1950, *FRUS*, 6: 401.

16. General Matthew B. Ridgway, *The Korean War* (New York: Doubleday, 1967), 13–14. For these and other intelligence reports, see James F. Schnabel, *Policy and Direction: The First Year* (Washington, D.C.: Office of the Chief of Military History, 1972), 63–64. It is Schnabel's view, however, that "no conclusions were drawn from these indications."

17. General John K. Singlaub, *Hazardous Duty: An American Soldier in the Twentieth Century* (New York: Summit Books, 1991), 164–65. As an army major Singlaub had been seconded to the CIA in 1948–1949 and assigned to duty in Manchuria, South Korea, and the CIA's "China desk." His account of Washington's foreknowledge is reinforced by an interview with Walter Pforzheimer, then legal counsel to CIA Director Roscoe Hillenkoetter, who helped prepare the director's testimony before Congress following the outbreak of the conflict.

18. "South Koreans Warned," *New York Times*, May 11, 1950, 14.

19. Joseph C. Goulden, *Korea: The Untold Story of the War* (New York: Times Books, 1982), 39.

20. Samuel F. Wells, "Sounding the Tocsin: NSC 68 and the Soviet Threat," Working Paper No. 7, The Wilson Center, International Security Studies Program, 13.

21. This is a reference to the espionage efforts of Kim Philby, Guy Burgess, and Donald Maclean, British agents for Moscow posted to Washington. After the escape of Burgess and Maclean on May 25, 1951, a senior intelligence officer of the Joint Chiefs of Staff observed that "it would appear that very nearly all U.S./U.K. high-level planning information prior to 25 May 1951 must be considered compromised." See David C. Martin, *Wilderness of Mirrors* (cited chap. 4, n. 1), 60.

22. Nitze, *From Hiroshima to Glasnost* (cited chap. 1, n. 23), 93–100.

23. "NSC-68, A Report to the National Security Council, April 14, 1950," *FRUS*, 1: 235–92.

24. Nitze, *From Hiroshima to Glasnost*, 96.

25. Despite the fact that the United States held a substantial advantage in economic capacity, the Soviets and the Chinese, in alliance, could each concentrate power on a single front, while the United States had to distribute its resources around the vast periphery of the alliance from Europe to Asia.

26. Melvyn P. Leffler, *A Preponderance of Power: National Security, the Truman Administration, and the Cold War* (Stanford: Stanford University Press, 1992), 355.

27. "Text of Acheson's Statement on Foreign Arms Aid Program," *New York Times*, June 4, 1950, 2.

28. John M. Hightower, "U.S. Expects Spring Offensive in Cold War," *Washington Post*, January 29, 1950, 3.

29. Dean Acheson, "United States Policy Toward Asia," *Department of State Bulletin*, March 27, 1950, 469.

30. Leffler, *Preponderance of Power*, 346.

31. Walter Waggoner, "West Asks Soviet to Disband 'Army' of East Germans," *New York Times*, May 24, 1950, 1. See page 11 for text of the note.

32. Leffler, *Preponderance of Power*, 347–48.

33. Benjamin Welles, "Bevin Warns West Against Civil Wars Inspired by Russia," *New York Times*, May 25, 1950, 1.

34. Hanson Baldwin, "Soviet Acts on 2 Salients," *New York Times*, June 1, 1950, 7.

35. NSC-48/1, "The Position of the United States with Respect to Asia," December 23, 1949 (cited chap. 3, n. 1).

36. Richard B. Finn, *Winners in Peace: MacArthur, Yoshida, and Postwar Japan* (Berkeley: University of California Press, 1992), 248.

37. Richard Deverall, *Red Star over Japan* (Calcutta: Temple Press, 1952), 247–48.

38. "Rusk File Memorandum," January 24, 1950, *FRUS*, 6: 1131.

39. "Memorandum by the Special Assistant to the Secretary (Howard) to the Assistant Secretary of State for Far Eastern Affairs (Butterworth)," March 9, 1950, *FRUS*, 6: 1138–49.

40. Lindesay Parrott, "Japan Hints West Can Build Bases," *New York Times*, January 24, 1950, 10.

41. Lindesay Parrott, "Japan Said to Back Giving Bases to U.S.," *New York Times*, February 7, 1950, 1.

42. Finn, *Winners in Peace*, 249.

43. "The Special Assistant to the Under Secretary of the Army (Reid) to the Assistant Secretary of State (Butterworth)," May 10, 1950, *FRUS*, 6: 1195–96.

44. Lindesay Parrott, "Yoshida Suports a 'Separate' Peace," *New York Times*, May 9, 1950, 14.

45. C. L. Sulzberger, "Security in Japan Held Vital to U.S.," *New York Times*, May 30, 1950, 1.

46. "Memorandum by the Supreme Commander for the Allied Powers (MacArthur)," June 23, 1950, *FRUS*, 6: 1227–28.

47. Schaller, *American Occupation of Japan*, 222–26, discusses the missions. For the documentary record, see *FRUS*, 6: passim.

48. See "Statement by the Secretary of State," February 1, 1950, "Memorandum from the Secretary of State to the President," February 2, 1950, and "Memorandum of Conversation by the Secretary of State," February 3, 1950, *FRUS*, 6: 711–19.

49. "Truman to Acheson," May 1, 1950, ibid., 791.

50. "Testimony of Secretary of State Acheson," May 1, 1950, in *Reviews of the World Situation* (cited chap. 1, n. 32), 287–90.

51. Cumings, *Origins of the Korean War*, 2: 529.

52. "Memorandum by Dulles for the Secretary of State," May 18, 1950, *FRUS*, 1: 314–16.

53. MacArthur is quoted in "The Acting Political Adviser in Japan (Sebald) to the Secretary of State," June 22, 1950, *FRUS*, 6: 366.

54. "Memorandum by the Special Assistant to the Secretary of Defense for Foreign Military Affairs and Assistance (Burns) to the Assistant Secretary of State for Far Eastern Affairs (Rusk)," May 29, 1950, *FRUS*, 6: 346–47.

55. "Extract from a Draft Memorandum by the Assistant Secretary of State for Far Eastern Affairs (Rusk) to the Secretary of State," May 30, 1950, *FRUS*, 6: 351. An

accompanying note declared that "this memorandum is identical with a memorandum prepared by Mr. Dulles for Secretary of State Acheson on May 18."

56. "Memorandum by the Deputy Special Assistant for Intelligence (Howe) to Mr. W. Park Armstrong, Special Assistant to the Secretary of State for Intelligence and Research," May 31, 1950, *FRUS*, 6: 348–49.

57. Cumings, *Origins of the Korean War*, 2: 539–40. The author also cites a late May intelligence report from Manila disclosing Chiang's discreet efforts to negotiate asylum in either the Philippines or South Korea. See ibid., p. 871n.78.

58. "The Secretary of State to the Secretary of Defense (Johnson)," June 1, 1950, *FRUS*, 6: 351–52.

59. Schaller, *American Occupation of Japan*, 265–66.

60. "3.2 Billions Aid Bill Signed, Truman Calls It 'Peace Step,'" *New York Times*, June 6, 1950, 1.

61. C. L. Sulzberger, "'Truman Doctrine' Held Set by U.S. for Southeast Asia," *New York Times*, May 14, 1950, 21.

62. "U.S. Agrees to Give Arms Aid to Iran," *New York Times*, May 24, 1950, 7.

63. "Text of Truman's Message on Arms Aid," *New York Times*, June 2, 1950, 2.

CHAPTER 7

1. "NSC 8/2," March 23, 1949, *FRUS*, 7: 977ff.

2. "Current Capabilities of the Northern Korean Regime," June 19, 1950, (cited chap. 5, n. 32), *FRUS*, 7: 120–21.

3. For text, see *FRUS*, 7: 969–78.

4. "Implications of a Possible Full-Scale Invasion from North Korea Subsequent to Withdrawal of U.S. Troops from Korea," June 10, 1949, Memorandum by the Chief of Staff, U.S. Army, *JCS 1776/2* (National Security Archive, George Washington University), 14.

5. "Memorandum by the Ambassador at Large, Philip C. Jessup," January 14, 1950, *FRUS*, 7: 5.

6. "The Ambassador in Korea (Muccio) to the Secretary of State," January 28, 1950, ibid., 19.

7. "Memorandum by the Ambassador at Large, Philip C. Jessup," 5.

8. Mary Spargo, "2 House Votes Beat Korea Aid: Slap at Truman," *Washington Post*, January 20, 1950, 1, and Clayton Knowles, "2 Votes Block Korea Aid Bill; House Test a Blow to Truman," *New York Times*, January 20, 1950, 1.

9. "Korea Aid Approval Urged by Truman," *Washington Post*, January 22, 1950, 4.

10. Clayton Knowles, "Korean Aid Change Accepted by G. O. P.," *New York Times*, February 1, 1950, 13.

11. Clayton Knowles, "Truman Keeps Ban on Aid to Formosa," *New York Times*, February 9, 1950, 2, and "Korea, Formosa Aid Is Passed by House in Reversing Stand," *New York Times*, February 10, 1950, 1.

12. "Bradley, Johnson Air Formosa View," *New York Times*, January 27, 1950, 9.

13. Knowles, "Truman Keeps Ban on Aid to Formosa."

14. See Cumings, *The Origins of the Korean War* (cited chap. 3, n. 3), 2: 508–12.

15. "The Ambassador in Korea (Muccio) to the Secretary of State," January 25, 1950, *FRUS*, 7: 15.

16. "The Chief of the United States Military Advisory Group to the Republic of Korea (Roberts) to the Ambassador in Korea (Muccio)," January 25, 1950, *FRUS*, 7: 16–19.

17. There is some confusion over the type of fighter aircraft the Russians supplied. The embassy source cited identifies the Yak-3, but other sources say the fighter was the Yak-9. See "Memorandum by the Central Intelligence Agency," June 19, 1950, ibid., 119, which identifies the Yak-9 and the IL-10, but not the Yak-3, fighter. Robert F. Futrell, *The United States Air Force in Korea: 1950–1953* (New York: Duell, Sloan and Pearce, 1961), 19, mentions no Yak-9, saying that "on the day the war began the North Koreans apparently possessed 62 IL-10 aircraft, [and] 70 Yak-3 and Yak-7B fighters."

18. "The Secretary of State to the Embassy in Korea," February 3, 1950, *FRUS*, 7: 25.

19. "The Chargé in Korea (Drumright) to the Secretary of State," February 10, 1950, ibid., 26.

20. "The Secretary of State to the Embassy in Korea," February 14, 1950, ibid., 28.

21. "Memorandum of Conversation, by the Officer in Charge of Korean Affairs (Bond), March 15, 1950, ibid., 30–33.

22. "The Ambassador in Korea (Muccio) to the Secretary of State," March 16, 1950, ibid., 34–35.

23. "The Secretary of State to the Embassy in Korea," March 23, 1950, ibid., 35–36.

24. "The Deputy Administrator of the Economic Cooperation Administration (Foster) to the Embassy in Korea," March 27, 1950, ibid., 36–37.

25. "The Ambassador in Korea (Muccio) to the Secretary of State," March 29, 1950, ibid., 37–38.

26. "The Secretary of State to the Embassy in Korea," March 31, 1950, ibid., 38–39.

27. "The Ambassador in Korea (Muccio) to the Secretary of State," April 1, 1950, ibid., 39–40.

28. "Memorandum of Conversation, by the Officer in Charge of Korean Affairs (Bond)," April 3, 1950, ibid., 40–41.

29. "The Secretary of State to the Embassy in Korea," April 13, 1950, ibid., 45–46.

30. "The Chargé in Korea (Drumright) to the Secretary of State," April 20, 1950, ibid., 46–47.

31. "Memorandum by Mr. W. G. Hackler of the Bureau of Far Eastern Affairs," April 27, 1950, ibid., 48–52.

32. Burton Crane, "Korea Transfers Farms, Industries," *New York Times*, June 2, 1950, 5.

33. "World Policy and Bipartisanship," *U.S. News & World Report*, May 5, 1950, 12.

34. For the Rusk memorandum, see "Memorandum by the Assistant Secretary of State for Far Eastern Affairs (Rusk) to the Under Secretary of State (Webb)," May 2,

1950, *FRUS*, 7: 64–65; for Secretary Acheson's actual remarks, see "The Chargé in Korea (Drumright) to the Secretary of State," May 5, 1950, ibid., 67, n1.

35. "The Chargé in Korea (Drumright) to the Secretary of State," May 5, 1950, *FRUS*, 7: 67, n1.

36. "Memorandum of Conversation, by the Chargé in Korea (Drumright)," May 9, 1950, *FRUS*, 7: 77.

37. Ibid., 78.

38. "Memorandum of Conversation, by the Officer in Charge of Korean Affairs (Bond)," May 10, 1950, ibid., 78–81.

39. "Memorandum by the Acting Director of the Mutual Defense Assistance Program (Ohly) to the Assistant Secretary of State for Far Eastern Affairs (Rusk)," May 10, 1950, ibid., 82–83.

40. Appleman, *South to the Naktong* (cited chap. 5, n. 31), 35.

41. Clay Blair, *The Forgotten War: America in Korea, 1950–1953* (New York: Times Books, 1987), 57.

42. Appleman, *South to the Naktong*, 35, 72.

43. Ibid., 17. Appleman claims that the U.S. provided 1,900 2.36″ rocket launchers, but that number is inflated. South Korean army rifle companies were assigned 6 bazookas each. In a 21 regiment infantry force, this amounts to no more than 600 bazookas. For a general discussion of arms supplied to South Korea, see Hanson Baldwin, "Ground Aid in Korea," *New York Times*, June 29, 1950, 4.

44. For the development history and the decision to begin production of the 3.5″ rocket launcher, see "Minutes of the Ordnance Committee Meeting No. 15," August 5, 1948, The National Archives, Record Group No. 156. Between July 1950 and July 1951 over 18,000 3.5″ rocket launchers had been withdrawn from National Guard stocks and delivered to forces in Korea. By the end of August 1950 alone, some 40,000 rockets for the launcher had been delivered. See James A. Huston, *U.S. Army Logistics in the Korean War* (Selinsgrove: Susquehanna University Press, 1989), 90, 133–34. Cf. Appleman, *South to the Naktong*, 157, who says that production of the 3.5″ had been delayed "because of the difficulty in perfecting its ammunition" and had been in production only fifteen days before the outbreak of the conflict. Therefore, "none had been issued to troops."

45. See Appleman, *South to the Naktong*, 179, for the T-34 tank total and Futrell, *United States Air Force in Korea*, 645, for the overall figure.

46. It would be learned later that North Korean tankers had received their training in the Soviet Union. See Department of State, *North Korea: A Case Study of a Soviet Satellite* (Washington, D.C.: GPO, May 20, 1951).

47. Major Robert R. Sawyer, *Military Advisors in Korea: KMAG in Peace and War* (Washington, D.C.: Office of the Chief of Military History, 1962), 105–6. Ridgway, *The Korean War* (cited chap. 6, n. 16), 9, carefully straddles the issue, but suggests that T-34s were delivered late. "In the first months of 1950, just prior to the irruption across the 38th parallel, Russia supplied the North Korean Peoples Army with large quantities of modern arms, including . . . T-34 tanks."

48. "The Chargé in Korea (Drumright) to the Secretary of State," May 11, 1950, *FRUS*, 7: 83–84.

49. "South Koreans Warned," *New York Times*, May 11, 1950, 14.

50. "The Chargé in Korea (Drumright) to the Secretary of State," May 11, 1950, *FRUS*, 7: 84–85.

51. "Memorandum by the Central Intelligence Agency," June 19, 1950, ibid., 118.

52. "The Chargé in Korea (Drumright) to the Secretary of State," May 11, 1950, ibid., 85n.2, and Cumings, *The Origins of the Korean War*, 2: 494.

53. "South Koreans Warned," *New York Times*, May 11, 1950, 14.

54. According to Goulden, *Korea* (cited chap. 6, n. 19), 39, from March 1 onward, there were no references to Korea in the CIA's daily summaries.

55. Ibid., 40. Appleman, *South to the Naktong*, 12n.19, says that United States intelligence did not "settle" on the identification of T-34s in North Korea "until the end of the third week of the war."

56. "The Acting Secretary of State to the Embassy in Korea," May 19, 1950, *FRUS*, 7: 85–86.

57. "The Ambassador in Korea (Muccio) to the Secretary of State," May 23, 1950, ibid., 86–88.

58. "The Ambassador in Korea (Muccio) to the Secretary of State," May 29, 1950, ibid., 93.

59. Charles R. Shrader, *Communist Logistics in the Korean War* (Westport: Greenwood Press, 1995), 11.

60. See Sherry Sontag and Christopher Drew, *Blind Man's Bluff: The Untold Story of American Submarine Espionage* (New York: Public Affairs, 1998), 25.

61. Austin Stevens, "War Games Uphold 'Shooting Airlift,'" *New York Times*, May 3, 1950, 9.

62. John Norris, "Combat Supply Goals Cut in Air Maneuvers," *The Washington Post*, May 2, 1950, 3. See also Norris, "Troop Carrier Forces Weak, Gavin Says," ibid., May 1, 1950, 1, and "Powerful Air Offensive Force Forged in Carolina Operation," ibid., May 3, 1950, 1.

63. Austin Stevens, "New Attack Style Seen in U.S. Airlift," *New York Times*, May 1, 1950, 7.

64. Austin Stevens, "Training to Stress Tactical Air Help," *New York Times*, June 15, 1950, 2.

65. Hanson Baldwin, "Pacific Northwest High in Army Plan," *New York Times*, May 22, 1950, 7.

66. "Readiness Urged on Troops in Japan," *New York Times*, June 10, 1950, 4.

67. Austin Stevens, "U.S. Orders Transport Service to Train Fliers for Global Airlift," *New York Times*, May 12, 1950, 10.

68. Malcolm W. Cagle and Frank A. Manson, *The Sea War in Korea* (Annapolis: U.S. Naval Institute, 1957), 36.

69. "7th U.S. Fleet Gathers at Guam," *New York Times*, May 26, 1950, 14.

70. Cagle and Manson, *Sea War in Korea*, 33.

71. John Norris, "Truman Sees 'Invasion' by Helicopter," *The Washington Post*, June 16, 1950, 1.

72. See Colonel Donald McB. Curtis, letter to the editor, *Army*, July 1985, 5–6 (emphasis in original). Curtis "was the staff officer in G4 Plans Division who wrote the strategic concept for SL-17." The finished plan can be found at the U.S. National

Archives, Adelphi, Md., in Records Group No. 319, Army G-4, Decimal 1949–1950, Box 39. See also Blair, *Forgotten War*, 87.

73. Futrell, *United States Air Force in Korea*, 7.

74. "Army Combat Units Alerted for Tests," *New York Times*, June 25, 1950, 26.

75. "Acheson Rules Out 'Preventive War,'" *New York Times*, June 14, 1950, 2.

CHAPTER 8

1. James Field, *History of United States Naval Operations—Korea* (Washington, D.C.: GPO, 1962), 51.

2. George F. Kennan, *Memoirs: 1925–1950* (Boston: Little, Brown & Co., 1967), 486, also expected to attend, but was told that "somehow or other . . . my name had been omitted from the list sent to the White House. . . . This dinner had the effect of defining—by social invitation, so to speak—the group that would be responsibly engaged in the handling of the department's end of the decisions in the ensuing days."   **403**

3. "Resolution Adopted by the United Nations Security Council," June 25, 1950, *FRUS*, 7: 155–56.

4. Glenn D. Paige, *The Korean Decision: June 24–30, 1950* (New York: The Free Press, 1968), 120.

5. Dean Acheson, *Present at the Creation: My Years in the State Department* (New York: Signet, 1969), 527.

6. "Memorandum of Conversations, by Mr. Charles P. Noyes, Adviser on Security Council Affairs, United States Mission at the United Nations," June 25, 1950, *FRUS*, 7: 147.

7. Harry S. Truman, *Memoirs*, vol. 2, *Years of Trial and Hope* (New York: Doubleday, 1956), 333.

8. Acheson, *Present at the Creation*, 528.

9. Schnabel, *Policy and Direction* (cited chapter 6, n. 16), 67. On the other hand, Truman, *Memoirs*, 335, asserts that it was during the first Blair House meeting that he "instructed the service chiefs to prepare the necessary orders for the eventual use of American units if the United Nations should call for action against North Korea."

10. Margaret Truman, *Souvenir* (New York: McGraw-Hill, 1956), 275.

11. Robert C. Albright, "Congress Eyes Chance of War; Keep Calm, Its Leaders Urge," *Washington Post*, June 27, 1950, 1.

12. See "The Acting Political Adviser in Japan (Sebald) to the Secretary of State," June 25, 1950, *FRUS*, 7: 140.

13. "Memorandum of Teletype Conference, Prepared in the Department of the Army," June 25, 1950, *FRUS*, 7: 136.

14. Hearings, *MSFE* (cited chap. 3, n. 4), 4: 2579–80.

15. Acheson, *Present at the Creation*, 528.

16. "Memorandum on Formosa, by General of the Army Douglas MacArthur, Commander in Chief, Far East, and Supreme Commander, Allied Powers, Japan," June 14, 1950, *FRUS*, 7: 161–65.

17. Paige, *Korean Decision*, 126.

18. "Korea Is 14 Hours Ahead of Daylight Time Here," *New York Times*, June 28, 1950, 5.

19. "Memorandum of Teletype Conference, Prepared in the Department of the Army," 0844 Washington time, June 25, 1950, *FRUS*, 7: 136. In response to a question about the North Korean objective, Far East Command said: "the north Koreans are engaged in an all-out offensive to subjugate South Korea."

20. Field, *History of United States Naval Operations: Korea*, 51.

21. "South Korea Chief Charges Russians Lead Northerners," *New York Times*, June 27, 1950, 3.

22. "The Ambassador in Korea (Muccio) to the Secretary of State," received 12:26 P.M., June 25, 1950, *FRUS*, 7: 141–43.

23. Appleman, *South to the Naktong* (cited chap. 5, n. 31), 31.

24. "Memorandum of Conversation, by the Ambassador at Large (Jessup)," June 25, 1950, *FRUS*, 7: 158 (hereafter referred to as "Jessup Memorandum, Blair I").

25. Paige, *Korean Decision*, 126.

26. Truman, *Memoirs*, 334. Johnson, *MSFE*, 4: 2580, says that Truman asked him for the views of Defense, but "since the Joint Chiefs had no recommendations to make, I should like to call on each of the members of the Joint Chiefs and the Chairman and each of the Secretaries." Truman, *Memoirs*, 333–36, omits Johnson entirely from his account of the meeting, except to note that he attended.

27. "Jessup Memorandum, Blair I," 160.

28. Ibid., 158. Truman, *Memoirs*, 335, omits Bradley's final comment questioning the advisability of putting in ground troops.

29. "Jessup Memorandum, Blair I," 158. Truman, *Memoirs*, 335, on the other hand, claims that "Collins said that if the Korean army was really broken, ground forces would be necessary."

30. "Jessup Memorandum, Blair I," 158–59. Truman, *Memoirs*, 335, says that "Vandenberg and Sherman thought that air and naval aid might be enough," but, as noted above, Sherman did not speak to the issue of ground troops at all, nor did Vandenberg. Both officers confined their remarks to their service responsibilities.

31. Acheson, *Present at the Creation*, 529.

32. "Jessup Memorandum, Blair I," 160. Johnson testified that at this point the president wished to adjourn the meeting, but he proposed "to start the fleet moving" and to "order the jets" to the three islands near Formosa. See Johnson's testimony, *MSFE*, 4: 2580–81.

33. Truman, *Memoirs*, 334–36.

34. Ibid., 336, and Acheson, *Present at the Creation*, 529–30. For the message, see "The Acting Political Adviser in Japan (Sebald) to the Secretary of State," June 25, 1950, *FRUS*, 7: 140.

35. Paige, *Korean Decision*, 147.

36. For an account of the episode based on informed sources, see Singlaub, *Hazardous Duty* (cited chap. 6, n. 17), 166–68. Acheson, *Present at the Creation*, 530, passes over this incident with a single sentence: "The appropriations hearing went off without too much trouble."

37. "War No Surprise, Intelligence Says," *New York Times*, June 27, 1950, 3.

38. Singlaub, *Hazardous Duty*, 166.

39. Ibid., 167.

40. "War No Surprise, Intelligence Says."

41. Singlaub, *Hazardous Duty*, 167.

42. "War No Surprise, Intelligence Says."

43. Singlaub, *Hazardous Duty*, 168. Later, before the same committee, Acheson denied that intelligence had provided a war warning and insisted that "the reported events in Korea were but a continuation of the wearing-away-by-border-raids strategy which the North Koreans had been pursuing for some time." See Senate Committee on Appropriations, 81st Congress, 2nd Session, *Supplemental Appropriations for 1951*, 290–91.

44. Paige, *Korean Decision*, 154.

45. See, for example, Ferdinand Kuhn, "Policy Now Bars Sending U.S. Troops," *Washington Post*, June 27, 1950, 1.

46. "The Ambassador in Korea (Muccio) to the Secretary of State," received 8:05 P.M., June 25, 1950, *FRUS*, 7: 165–66.

47. "The Ambassador in Korea (Muccio) to the Secretary of State," received 6:14 A.M., 6:24 A.M., and 9:31 A.M., June 26, 1950, *FRUS*, 7: 168, 170. In all a total of 2,001 people, 1,527 American nationals, were evacuated.

48. Ibid., 171.

49. "Memorandum of Conversation, by the Secretary of State (Acheson)," June 26, 1950, *FRUS*, 7: 172–73.

50. Ibid., 173.

51. Beverly Smith, "Why We Went to War in Korea," *Saturday Evening Post*, November 10, 1951, 80.

52. "The Ambassador in Korea (Muccio) to the Secretary of State," received 5:07 P.M., June 26, 1950, *FRUS*, 7: 173.

53. "The Ambassador in Korea (Muccio) to the Secretary of State," received 6:54 P.M., June 26, 1950, ibid., 176.

54. Smith, "Why We Went to War in Korea," 80. Undersecretary Freeman Matthews substituted for Webb, who was on duty at the department, and Secretary of the Navy Francis Matthews arrived just as the meeting ended.

55. Truman, *Memoirs*, 337.

56. For the data on each point, see Appleman, *South to the Naktong*, 28–30, 32, 43, 40, respectively. Ridgway, *Korean War* (cited chap. 6, n. 16), 19, says it was the 6th, not the 7th.

57. "Memorandum of Conversation, by the Ambassador at Large (Jessup)," June 26, 1950, *FRUS*, 7: 178–83. Unless otherwise noted, all quotations of the discussion are taken from this memorandum.

58. Acheson's masterful performance here and later this week stands in stark contrast to his timidity at the critical meeting of November 21 when he declared that he was "unwilling to urge on the President a military course that his military advisers would not propose." See Acheson, *Present at the Creation*, 605.

59. Paige, *Korean Decision*, 185.

60. Ibid.

61. See, for example, Ferdinand Kuhn, "Policy Now Bars Sending U.S. Troops," *Washington Post*, June 27, 1950, 1. Kuhn noted, however, that "this policy may change if the United Nations should call on its members to send armed forces."

62. Paige, *Korean Decision*, 185 (emphasis supplied).

63. Paik Sun-yup, *From Pusan to Panmunjon* (Washington, D.C.: Brassey's, 1992), 18.

64. "Statement Issued by the President," June 27, 1950, *FRUS*, 7: 202–3.

65. "Memorandum of Conversation, by the Ambassador at Large (Jessup)" June 27, 1950, ibid., 200–202.

66. "Testimony of Louis Johnson, Secretary of Defense," *MSFE*, 4: 2609.

67. Paige, *Korean Decision*, 191.

68. Acheson, *Present at the Creation*, 532, says it was Truman who averred that the U.S. was acting "in support of the United Nations."

69. "Memorandum of Conversation, by the Ambassador at Large (Jessup)," June 27, 1950, *FRUS*, 7: 200–202.

70. Kennan, *Memoirs*, 487.

71. Ibid.

72. Paige, *Korean Decision*, 191.

73. Kennan, *Memoirs*, 487.

74. Ferdinand Kuhn, "Policy Now Bars Sending U.S. Troops," *Washington Post*, June 27, 1950, 1.

75. Paige, *Korean Decision*, 203.

76. "Resolution Adopted by the United Nations Security Council," June 27, 1950, *FRUS*, 7: 211.

77. Smith, "Why We Went to War in Korea," 86.

78. Doris M. Condit, *The Test of War: 1950–1953*, 3 vols. (Washington, D.C.: OSD, 1988), 62.

79. Hanson Baldwin, "Blocking the Red Conquest Program," *New York Times*, June 28, 1950, 12.

80. Schnabel, *Policy and Direction*, 72. According to Futrell, *United States Air Force in Korea* (cited chap. 7, n. 17), 28, General Church felt that "if the ROKs could be made to hold anywhere, it would be behind the shelter of the broad and swiftly flowing Han River."

81. "The Secretary of State to the Secretary of Defense (Johnson)," June 28, 1950, *FRUS*, 7: 217.

82. See Paige, *Korean Decision*, 221, and Smith, "Why We Went to War in Korea," 86, who says that "on Wednesday, June twenty-eighth, no new decisions were made."

83. Baldwin, "Blocking the Red Conquest Program."

84. "Draft Policy Statement Prepared by the Secretary of State," June 28, 1950, *FRUS*, 7: 217.

85. "Memorandum of Conversation, (Ambassador Jessup)," NSC Meeting, June 28, 1950, as quoted in Robert J. Donovan, *Tumultuous Years: The Presidency of Harry S. Truman, 1949–1953* (New York: W. W. Norton, 1982), 210.

86. Acheson, *Present at the Creation*, 535.

87. Truman, *Memoirs*, 340, reports Acheson's admonition differently to include the possibility of "all out war" in the sentence that Acheson records as involving "casualties and taxes."

88. "Transcript of Press Conference," *New York Times*, June 29, 1950, 10.

89. The newsmen accompanying MacArthur were: Russell Brines, AP; Ernest Holberecht, UP; Howard Handleman, INS; and Roy MacCartney, Reuters.

90. Futrell, *United States Air Force in Korea*, 28–29, and Appleman, *South to the Naktong*, 44. Oddly, carrier air operations would have alleviated, if not solved, this problem, but no carrier air operations were conducted until after the commitment of combat troops. See Paige, *Korean Decision*, 231.

91. Schnabel, *Policy and Direction*, 77.

92. Appleman, *South to the Naktong*, 44.

93. Futrell, *United States Air Force in Korea*, 31.

94. Lindesay Parrott, "A Defense Line Set," *New York Times*, June 30, 1950, 1.

95. Marguerite Higgins, *War in Korea: The Report of a Woman Combat Correspondent* (New York: Doubleday, 1951), 34.

96. Appleman, *South to the Naktong*, 45, and Schnabel, *Policy and Direction*, 74. Oddly, in discussion of the trip, both authors cite the same source, MacArthur's pilot, Lieutenant Colonel Anthony Storey.

97. *FRUS*, 7: 248n.2.

98. Russell Brines, "B-29s Drive Reds Out of Seoul's Airport," *Washington Evening Star*, June 29, 1950, 1.

99. FRUS, 7: 228n.2, citing DA TT-3437, June 29, 1950.

100. Truman, *Memoirs*, 342.

101. General Edward Almond, "Orders from Washington Kept Us from Winning Korean War," *U.S. News & World Report*, December 10, 1954, 88.

102. Higgins, *War in Korea*, 34, and Courtney Whitney, *MacArthur: His Rendezvous with Destiny* (New York: Alfred A. Knopf, 1956), 332.

103. See *FRUS*, 7: 228n.2 for a summary of number 3437, and 250–53 for a transcript of number 3444.

104. Paige, *Korean Decision*, 239–40n.15, was the first and only author to question the accepted chronology, but ultimately decided "reluctantly and in the hope that some reader can explain satisfactorily what appears to be a 17-hour gap . . . to follow Appleman, Whitney, and all other accounts."

105. Truman, *Memoirs*, 342–43.

106. "The Commander in Chief, Far East (MacArthur) to the Secretary of State," June 30, 1950, *FRUS*, 7: 248–49.

107. "The Chargé in Korea (Drumright) to the Secretary of State," June 29, 1950, *FRUS*, 7: 227–28.

108. A brief, unsigned newspaper item, datelined June 30, described this sequence in general terms: "General Douglas MacArthur received broadened authority to prosecute his mission in Korea as a direct result of a message he sent here to his chiefs on the dangers of the situation as he had personally observed it a few hours before. The United States Far Eastern Commander's assessment of what was developing in Southern Korea was received here late yesterday and was transmitted promptly to the White House. The contents of the message were not disclosed." See "MacArthur Gets Wide Powers," *New York Times*, July 1, 1950, 2.

109. Alfred Friendly, "Not at War, Truman Says; Sees Success," *Washington Post*, June 30, 1950, 1.

110. See Paige, *Korean Decision*, 244–52, and Truman, *Memoirs*, 341–42.

111. "The Joint Chiefs of Staff to the Commander in Chief, Far East (MacArthur)," June 29, 1950, *FRUS*, 7: 240–41.

112. Truman, *Memoirs*, 341, omits any reference to the order to seize Pusan.

113. Ibid., 342.

114. Smith, "Why We Went to War in Korea," 88.

115. "Memorandum by the Deputy Assistant Secretary of State for Far Eastern Affairs (Merchant) to the Secretary of State," June 29, 1950, *FRUS*, 7: 239.

116. Truman, *Memoirs*, 342.

117. "The Commander in Chief, Far East (MacArthur) to the Secretary of State," June 30, 1950, *FRUS*, 7: 248–50.

118. Smith, "Why We Went to War in Korea," 88.

119. Paige, *Korean Decision*, 253.

120. "Memorandum of Teletype Conference, Prepared in the Department of the Army," June 30, 1950, *FRUS*, 7: 250–53.

121. Ibid.

122. Ibid.

123. Ibid.

124. Smith, "Why We Went to War in Korea," 88.

125. Ibid.

126. "Memorandum of Teletype Conference," June 30, 1950, 252.

127. Futrell, *United States Air Force in Korea*, 32.

128. Smith, "Why We Went to War in Korea," 88.

129. Ibid.

130. Truman, *Memoirs*, 343.

131. Ibid.

132. Ibid.

133. "The Joint Chiefs of Staff to the Commander in Chief, Far East (MacArthur)," June 30, 1950, *FRUS*, 7: 263.

CHAPTER 9

1. While maintaining that the war was at "the initiative of Comrade Kim Il Sung," Soviet leader Nikita Khrushchev said: "Our advisers, when they planned this operation, probably did not take everything into account and did not give everything needed. For this, of course, I think Stalin was to blame. Kim didn't need much more on top of what had already been given. We, of course, could have provided the tanks for another tank corps, which I think would have been enough." See Schechter and Luchkov, eds., *Khrushchev Remembers: The Glasnost Tapes* (cited chap. 4, n. 24), 146. In Strobe Talbott, ed., *Khrushchev Remembers* (London: André Deutsch, 1971), 370, he was even more emphatic on this point. "If we hadn't refused him aid in qualified personnel to assess the distribution of forces and to direct operations, there's no doubt that North Korea would have been victorious. I think if Kim had received just one [more] tank corps, or two at the most, he could have accelerated his advance south and occupied Pusan on the march. The war would have ended then and there."

2. "Yu Song-chol's Testimony, Part 8," *FBIS-EAS* (cited chap. 5, n. 8), December 27, 1990, 26.

3. Ibid.

4. "26 June 1950, top secret report on military situation by Shtykov to Comrade Zakharov," *CWIHP* (cited chap. 2, n. 3), 6–7: 39.

5. "Yu Song-chol's Testimony, Part 10," *FBIS-EAS*, December 27, 1990, 28.

6. Ibid., 29. Kim may have employed Pak as a scapegoat for failure, but it is true that there were no uprisings in South Korea accompanying the invasion. For more on their rivalry, see Park, "North Korea's Inner Leadership" (cited chap. 2, n. 58), 240–68.

7. Talbott, ed., *Khrushchev Remembers*, 370. Khrushchev had more to say in his later account. In Schechter and Luchkov, eds., *Khrushchev Remembers: The Glasnost Tapes*, 146, he said that the withdrawal of Soviet advisers "weakened the North Korean army, because they lacked qualified cadres knowledgeable in military tactics . . . [and] decreased North Korean combat capability and operational readiness," but omitted any comment on the impact of the advisers on the early stage of the war. The reader should read these accounts with a heavy dose of skepticism, for, as we now know from the few Soviet documents that have been released thus far, they are replete with errors.

8. "26 June 1950, top secret report on military situation by Shtykov to Comrade Zakharov," *CWIHP*, 6–7: 40.

9. "Yu Song-chol's Testimony, Part 10," 28–29.

10. Ibid., 29.

11. "1 July 1950, ciphered telegram, Fyn-Si (Stalin) to Soviet ambassador in Pyongyang (Shtykov)," *CWIHP*, 6–7: 40.

12. "2 July 1950, ciphered telegram, Shtykov to Fyn-Si (Stalin) re political mood in North Korea," *CWIHP*, 6–7: 42. (The annotation is misdated 1 July, but the telegram itself is 2 July.)

13. Harold B. Hinton, "U.S. Troops Land in South Korea, North Bombed on Truman Order; Suwon Lost as Defense Weakens," *New York Times*, July 1, 1950, 1.

14. "4 July 1950, ciphered telegram, Shtykov to Fyn-Si (Stalin) re meeting with Kim Il-sung and Pak Hon-yong," *CWIHP*, 6–7: 42–43.

15. Appleman, *South to the Naktong* (cited chap. 5, n. 31), 52–55.

16. "Yu Song-chol's Testimony, Part 9," *FBIS-EAS*, December 27, 1990, 27. Yu places the Second Division with the First Corps, but Appleman properly assigns it to the Second Corps. See Appleman, *South to the Naktong*, 26–27.

17. "Yu Song-chol's Testimony, Part 10," 29.

18. Appleman, *South to the Naktong*, 106.

19. Field, *History of United States Naval Operations: Korea* (cited chap. 8, n. 1), 65, 98. The *Juneau* and *Black Swan* appeared on the east coast for bombardment duty on July 4 and were joined by six other ships in subsequent days.

20. "4 July 1950, ciphered telegram, Shtykov to Fyn-Si (Stalin) re meeting with Kim Il-sung and Pak Hon-yong," 42.

21. "Yu Song-chol's Testimony, Part 10," 29. See also Lim Un, *Founding of a Dynasty* (cited chap. 5, n. 11), 175–76, who concurs.

409

22. "Yu Song-chol's Testimony, Part 9," 28.

23. "Yu Song-chol's Testimony, Part 10," 29.

24. "4 July 1950, ciphered telegram, Shtykov to Fyn-Si (Stalin) re meeting with Kim Il-sung and Pak Hon-yong," 42.

25. Park, "North Korea's Inner Leadership," 262.

26. "4 July 1950, ciphered telegram, Shtykov to Fyn-Si (Stalin) re meeting with Kim Il-sung and Pak Hon-yong," 42.

27. In his telegram, Shtykov referred to Mu Chang as Mu Den and Kim Ung as Kim Koo.

28. "Yu Song-chol's Testimony, Part 9," 27.

29. "4 July 1950, ciphered telegram, Shtykov to Fyn-Si (Stalin) re meeting with Kim Il-sung and Pak Hon-yong," 43.

30. "6 July 1950, ciphered telegram, Fyn-Si (Stalin) to Shtykov," *CWIHP*, 6–7: 43.

31. "Yu Song-chol's Testimony, Part 11," *FBIS-EAS*, December 28, 1990, 13.

32. "8 July 1950, ciphered telegram, Shtykov to Fyn-Si (Stalin), transmitting letter from Kim Il-sung to Stalin," *CWIHP*, 6–7: 43–44.

33. On at least one occasion, a Russian tank driver was identified among the battlefield dead. No doubt there were others. See Uzal W. Ent, *Fighting on the Brink: Defense of the Pusan Perimeter* (Paducah, Ky.: Turner Publishing, 1996), 38.

34. "U.S. Troops Moving to Battle Front; Reinforcements Leave Japan by Sea; Northern Korean Advance Is Stalled," *New York Times*, July 2, 1950, 1.

35. Ent, *Fighting on the Brink*, 31–55.

36. Higgins, *War in Korea* (cited chap. 8, n. 95), 71.

37. "The Chargé in Korea (Drumright) to the Secretary of State," July 9, 1950, *FRUS*, 7: 336–37.

38. Futrell, *United States Air Force in Korea* (cited chap. 7, n. 17), 85.

39. Appleman, *South to the Naktong*, 210–11.

40. Ibid., 247.

41. Ibid., 211.

42. Ent, *Fighting on the Brink*, 106, concurs. "The time it took the NK 6th Division to make the wide swing took it out of contact and battle long enough for the Americans to react."

43. Appleman, *South to the Naktong*, 222.

44. Ent, *Fighting on the Brink*, 106: "Sending the 4th and 6th Divisions . . . on a deep flanking movement was probably a North Korean mistake. A shallower, more concentrated envelopment would have had a good chance of crushing the Eighth Army's left flank, cutting it off from resupply via Pusan, and leading to its defeat."

45. Appleman, *South to the Naktong*, 264.

46. Ibid., 247.

47. "Telecon, TT 3573, Gens Bradley, Collins, Norstad, and Adm Sherman in Washington with General MacArthur in Tokyo, 24 July 1950," as cited in Schnabel, *Policy and Direction*, 113.

48. Appleman, *South to the Naktong*, 247.

49. "Logistic Study Covering Operations in Korea," National Archives, Records Group 319, Army G-4, Decimal 1949–1950, Box 39.

50. Appleman, *South to the Naktong*, 488–89, Schnabel, *Policy and Direction*, 139–40, and Robert D. Heinl, *Victory at High Tide: The Inchon-Seoul Campaign* (New York: Lippincott, 1968), 16–19.

51. See Blair, *Forgotten War* (cited chap. 7, n. 41), 87–88.

52. "CINCFE 58473 to DA (for JCS)," July 23, 1950, cited in Schnabel, *Policy and Direction*, 142.

53. Douglas MacArthur, *Reminiscences* (New York: McGraw-Hill, 1964), 346.

54. "Estimate of the Situation in Korea, decision on J. C. S. 1924/19," July 13, 1950, 318. National Security Archives, George Washington University.

55. Ibid., 318–19.

56. Ibid., 331–34.

57. Ent, *Fighting on the Brink*, 59, reprints a copy of General Walker's original perimeter trace line.

58. Toland, *In Mortal Combat: Korea, 1950–1953* (New York: William Morrow, 1991), 93.

59. "General MacArthur's Estimate of the Military Situation," July 19, 1950, *MSFE* (cited chap. 8, n. 14), 5: 3381–82.

60. Ent, *Fighting on the Brink*, 60.

61. See, for example, "Withdrawal Action," in Russel A. Gugeler, *Combat Actions in Korea* (Washington, D.C.: Office of the Chief of Military History, 1970), 3–19, for the experience of the First Battalion, Thirty-fourth Infantry, and Twenty-fourth Division.

62. Toland, *In Mortal Combat*, 131.

63. Ridgway, *Korean War* (cited chap. 6, n. 16), 17, attributes the NKA slowdown to the Lord. "Considering the relative strength and combat readiness of the forces that faced each other across the 38th Parallel in June 1950, it was a miracle that the North Korean armies were delayed at all in their drive to overrun all of South Korea."

64. Blair, *Forgotten War*, 115, believes that "these delays were not in any way decisive" and the cost disproportionately high, involving 3,000 American dead, wounded, missing, or captured.

65. Quoted in Schnabel, *Policy and Direction*, 114n.35.

66. *Public Papers of the Presidents of the United States: Harry S. Truman, 1950*, vol. 6 (Washington, D.C.: GPO, 1961–1966), 537.

67. "The President's Message to the Congress, July 19, 1950," in *MSFE*, 5: 3463–73.

CHAPTER 10

1. "8 July 1950, ciphered telegram, Filippov (Stalin) to Soviet Ambassador Roshchin in PRC transmitting message to Mao Zedong," *CWIHP* (cited chap. 2, n. 3), 6–7: 44.

2. Allen S. Whiting, *China Crosses the Yalu: The Decision to Enter the Korean War* (New York: Macmillan, 1960), 54.

3. "Mao Speech at the 8th Meeting of the Central People's Government Council, June 28, 1950," in Goncharov et al., *Uncertain Partners* (cited chap. 1, n. 27), 270–71.

4. Whiting, *China Crosses the Yalu*, 58.

5. "Roshchin cable to Moscow, 2 July 1950," as cited in Evgueni Bajanov, "Assessing the Politics of the Korean War, 1949–1951," *CWIHP*, 6–7: 89.

6. "War in Asia," *Time*, July 24, 1950, 20. See also the August 28 and September 4 editions for similar analyses.

7. "Roshchin cable to Moscow, 2 July 1950."

8. "5 July ciphered telegram, Filippov (Stalin) to Chinese Foreign Minister Zhou Enlai," *CWIHP*, 6–7: 43. I take the reference to the enemy crossing the 38th parallel to mean an amphibious landing in the NKA rear for the reason that the United States did not then and would not for months have any capability to stem the North Korean attack, counterattack, and drive them back across the parallel.

9. Whiting, *China Crosses the Yalu*, 54–55.

10. Field, *History of United States Naval Operations–Korea* (cited chap. 8, n. 1), 67.

11. Lei Yingfu, "Recollections of Several Important Decisions During the War to Resist America and Aid Korea," *Dang de wenxian* (Party Documents), (Beijing: People's Press, 1993), no. 6, 77–78. Lei was Zhou Enlai's military secretary and Director of the Operations Department of the PLA General Staff. For this translation, see Li Xiaobing, Donald Duffy, Zhang Zujian, and Glenn Tracy, "Chinese Generals Recall the Korean War," *Chinese Historians* (Spring–Fall 1994), 124–29.

12. Ibid.

13. He Di, "The Last Campaign to Unify China: The CCP's Unmaterialized Plan to Liberate Taiwan, 1949–1950," *Chinese Historians* (Spring 1992), 15. See also Chen Jian, *China's Road* (cited chap. 2, n. 10), 132.

14. "13 July 1950, ciphered telegram, Filippov (Stalin) to Zhou Enlai or Mao Zedong (via Roshchin)," *CWIHP*, 6–7: 44.

15. Hanson Baldwin, "Buying Time in Korea," *New York Times*, August 2, 1950, 5. MacArthur's intelligence section had produced an analysis estimating Communist casualties at 37,500 killed and wounded, tank losses of 304 destroyed or out of action, and an evaluation of NKA attacks as being "in less strength than a fortnight ago," although "equal in intensity." See "Korean Reds' Loss Set at 37,500 Men," *New York Times*, August 1, 1950, 5.

16. "Estimate of the Situation in Korea, decision on J. C. S. 1924/19," July 13, 1950, 318. National Security Archives, George Washington University.

17. See "C58993, CINCFE to JCS, 29 July 1950, cited in Schnabel, *Policy and Direction* (cited chap. 6, n. 16), 144–45.

18. Truman, *Years of Trial and Hope* (cited chap. 8, n. 7), 349.

19. JCS 87401 to CINCFE, July 28, 1950, as cited in Schnabel, *Policy and Direction*, 368.

20. Ibid., C58994 CINCFE to JCS, 29 July 1950.

21. "The Chargé in China (Strong) to the Secretary of State," July 14, 1950, *FRUS*, 6: 375.

22. "The Secretary of Defense (Johnson) to the Secretary of State," July 17, 1950, *FRUS*, 6: 379–80.

23. "The Chargé in China (Strong) to the Secretary of State," August 4, 1950, *FRUS*, 6: 417–18.

24. Higgins, *War in Korea* (cited chap. 8, n. 95), 171.

25. "The Secretary of Defense (Johnson) to the Secretary of State," July 29, 1950, *FRUS*, 6: 401.

26. "The Chargé in China (Strong) to the Secretary of State," August 3, 1950, FRUS, 6: 411–12.

27. Burton Crane, "MacArthur Rejects Chiang's Troop Bid," *New York Times*, August 1, 1950, 4. The communiqué was printed alongside.

28. "Statement of Generalissimo Chiang Kai-shek relative to visit of General MacArthur to Formosa, August 2, 1950," *MSFE* (cited chap. 8, n. 14), 5: 3383–84.

29. Ibid.

30. "The Chargé in China (Strong) to the Secretary of State," August 3, 1950, FRUS, 6: 411–12.

31. Ibid., 410.

32. "The Secretary of State to the Secretary of Defense (Johnson)," July 31, 1950, *FRUS*, 6: 402–3 (emphasis supplied). Acheson, *Present at the Creation* (cited chap. 8, n. 5), 548–50, presents a markedly different interpretation, blaming MacArthur.

33. Appleman, *South to the Naktong* (cited chap. 5, n. 31), 258–59.

34. "The Secretary of Defense (Johnson) to the Commander in Chief, Far East (MacArthur)," August 4, 1950, *FRUS*, 6: 423.

35. "The Commander in Chief, Far East (MacArthur), to the Secretary of Defense (Johnson)," August 5, 1950, *FRUS*, 6: 423–24.

36. Donovan, *Tumultuous Years* (cited chap. 8, n. 85), 261.

37. "Extracts of a Memorandum of Conversations, by Mr. W. Averell Harriman, Special Assistant to the President, With General MacArthur in Tokyo on August 6 and 8, 1950," *FRUS*, 6: 427–30.

38. Donovan, *Tumultuous Years*, 262.

39. James Reston, "MacArthur Visit to Formosa Viewed in U.N. as Mistimed," *New York Times*, August 11, 1950, 11.

40. Futrell, *United States Air Force in Korea* (cited chap. 7, n. 17), 67.

41. Roger Dingman, "Atomic Diplomacy During the Korean War," *International Security* 3 (1988–1989), 62–63.

42. Ibid., 63n.66. See also John Patton Davies memorandum, "Calculated Indiscretion by Ambassador Henderson," Box 19, Office of Chinese Affairs papers, RG 59, National Archives.

43. Austin Stevens, "More Medium Bombers Sent to Help in Korea—Air Marine Expands," *New York Times*, August 1, 1950, 1.

44. "Bomb-Laden B-29 Hits Trailer Camp; 17 Killed, 60 Hurt," *New York Times*, August 7, 1950, 1.

45. "Memorandum of Conversation, by Lieutenant General Matthew B. Ridgway, Deputy Chief of Staff for Administration, United States Army," August 8, 1950, *FRUS*, 7: 540–41.

46. Ibid., 542n.2.

47. Whiting, *China Crosses the Yalu*, 81–82.

48. Chen Jian, *China's Road*, 143.

49. Ibid. The phrase "further decided" should be understood as "decided later."

413

50. "Military Commission Telegram to Gao Gang re Completing the Northeast Frontier Force's Combat Preparations, August 5, 1950," in Goncharov et al., *Uncertain Partners*, 271. See also Li Xiaobing, Wang Xi, and Chen Jian (trans.), "Mao's Dispatch of Chinese Troops to Korea: Forty-Six Telegrams, July–October," *Chinese Historians* (Spring 1992), 64.

51. Du Ping, *My Experience at the Headquarters of the Chinese People's Volunteers* (Beijing: PLA Press, 1989), 17–22, as translated in "Chinese Generals Recall the Korean War," *Chinese Historians* (Spring–Fall 1994), 129–32.

52. "Mao Telegram to Gao Gang re Hastening the Frontier Force's Combat Readiness, August 18, 1950," in Goncharov et al., *Uncertain Partners*, 272. Du Ping, *My Experience at the Headquarters*, 22, says Nie Rongzhen sent the cable.

53. "Draft Memorandum Prepared by the Policy Planning Staff," July 22, 1950, *FRUS*, 7: 449–54.

54. "The Ambassador in the Soviet Union (Kirk) to the Secretary of State," July 2, 1950, *FRUS*, 7: 280–81. Callam A. MacDonald, *Korea: The War Before Vietnam* (New York: The Free Press, 1986), 43–45, deftly outlines early British policy toward the conflict.

55. "The Ambassador in the Soviet Union (Kirk) to the Secretary of State," July 10, 1950, *FRUS*, 7: 340–41.

56. K. M. Panikkar, *In Two Chinas: Memoirs of a Diplomat* (London: George Allen & Unwin Ltd., 1955), 104.

57. Kennan, *Memoirs* (cited chap. 8, n. 2), 491–93.

58. Kennan, *Memoirs*, 476.

59. "5 July 1950, ciphered telegram, Filippov (Stalin) to Chinese Foreign Minister Zhou Enlai (via Soviet ambassador to the People's Republic of China, N. V. Roshchin)," *CWIHP*, 6–7: 43.

60. "The Secretary of State to the Embassy in the United Kingdom," July 10, 1950, *FRUS*, 7: 347–48, and "The Secretary of State to the Embassy in India," July 22, 1950, ibid., 447–49.

61. For an account of these deliberations, see Leland M. Goodrich, *Korea: A Study of United States Policy in the United Nations* (New York: Council on Foreign Relations, 1956).

62. "The United States Deputy Representative at the United Nations (Gross) to the Secretary of State," August 11, 1950, *FRUS*, 7: 564–565.

63. For the contents of Zhou's telegram, see *Shi Jie Zhi Shi* (World Knowledge) (Beijing), August 26, 1950, 3. Cf. Whiting, *China Crosses the Yalu*, 79, 84–85, who translates the title of the magazine as *World Culture*.

64. Thomas J. Hamilton, "Hitler Lie Tactics Charged to Malik by U.S. and Britain," *New York Times*, August 23, 1950, 1. For the speeches, including Malik's, see pp. 18–20.

65. "The Ambassador in India (Henderson) to the Secretary of State," August 24, 1950, *FRUS*, 7: 446–47.

66. Ibid.

67. "Chinese Communist U. N. Note," *New York Times*, August 25, 1950, 4.

68. "Letter, Ambassador Austin to Secretary-General Lie, August 25, 1950," *MSFE*, 5: 3473–75.

CHAPTER 11

1. The administration had come to this conclusion over two weeks earlier, on July 10. See "Memorandum by the Joint Chiefs of Staff to the Secretary of Defense (Johnson)," July 10, 1950, *FRUS*, 7: 346. Department of State officials insisted that only the president could authorize implementation of the directive and only after aerial reconnaissance had verified Soviet involvement. See "Note by the Executive Secretary to the National Security Council on U.S. Courses of Action in the Event Soviet Forces Enter Korean Hostilities," ibid., July 25, 1950, 475–77.

2. See ibid., "Memorandum by Mr. Walter P. McConaughy, of the Staff of the Ambassador at Large (Jessup)," August 25, 1950, 649–52n.4.

3. Heinl, *Victory at High Tide* (cited chap. 9, n. 50), 24, 40. In attendance were: Admirals Arthur Radford and Turner Joy; Generals Edward Almond, Doyle Hickey, Clark Ruffner, Edwin Wright, and three unnamed officers from General Wright's Joint Strategic Plans and Operations Group (JSPOG). Since the Air Force would play no role at Inchon, General Idwall Edwards, USAF, represented JCS Chief Vandenberg. The Marines, who would play a critical role, were not invited. MacArthur, on the other hand, in *Reminiscences* (cited chap. 9, n. 53), 347, claims Marine General Lemuel C. Shepherd was there.

4. J. Lawton Collins, *War in Peacetime: The History and Lessons of Korea* (Boston: Houghton Mifflin, 1969), 119.

5. Ibid., 120.

6. Schnabel, *Policy and Direction* (cited chap. 6, n. 16), 144.

7. Heinl, *Victory at High Tide*, 41–42.

8. Collins, *War in Peacetime*, 126. Cf. MacArthur, *Reminiscences*, 349–50.

9. Cagle and Manson, *Sea War in Korea* (cited chap. 7, n. 68), 77.

10. Captain Walter Karig, Commander Malcolm W. Cagle, and Lieutenant Commander Frank A. Manson, *Battle Report VI, The War in Korea* (New York: Rinehart and Company, 1952), 167–68.

11. Schnabel, *Policy and Direction*, 150, 144.

12. Appleman, *South to the Naktong* (cited chap. 5, n. 31), 491–92.

13. Collins, *War in Peacetime*, 126, quoting Admiral Joy, suggests that Sherman was likewise not persuaded, but Heinl, *Victory at High Tide*, 39, shows otherwise.

14. Schnabel, *Policy and Direction*, 151.

15. Lei Ying-fu, "Recollections of Several Important Decisions During the War to Resist America and Assist Korea," *Dang de wenxian* (Party Documents), translated in *Chinese Historians* (Spring–Fall 1994), 133.

16. Ibid., 133–34.

17. Appleman, *South to the Naktong*, 501.

18. Lei Ying-fu, "Recollections," 136.

19. "Mao Telegram to Peng Dehuai re the Need for 12 Corps, August 27, 1950," in Goncharov et al., *Uncertain Partners* (cited chap. 1, n. 27), 272.

20. Chen Jian, *China's Road* (cited chap. 2, n. 10), 151–52.

21. Ibid., 155.

22. Ibid., 156.

23. See "July 25 1950, ciphered telegram, Vyshinsky to Roshchin transmitting

message from Filippov (Stalin) to Zhou Enlai," and "27 August 1950, ciphered tele-gram, Filippov (Stalin) to Zhou Enlai," *CWIHP* (cited chap. 2, n. 3), 6–7: 45.

24. "31 August 1950, ciphered telegram, Shtykov to Fyn-Si (Stalin) transmitting letter from Kim Il-sung to Stalin," ibid., 46 (emphasis supplied).

25. "Matthews Favors U.S. War for Peace," *New York Times*, August 26, 1950, 1.

26. Walter H. Waggoner, "U.S. Disowns Matthews Talk of Waging War to Get Peace," *New York Times*, August 27, 1950, 1, and Hanson Baldwin, "War of Preven-tion," ibid., September 1, 1950, 4.

27. "Message of General MacArthur to Veterans of Foreign Wars," *MSFE* (cited chap. 8, n. 14), 5: 3477–80. MacArthur, in *Reminiscences*, 341–43, says that he sent the message "through the Department of the Army ten days before the encamp-ment. The officials of that Department apparently found nothing objectionable in it." MacArthur concluded: "To this day I do not know who managed to construe my statement as meaning exactly the opposite of what it said, and how this person or persons could have so easily deceived the President. Were his political advisers play-ing strategist, and his military advisers playing politics?"

28. For an internal account of the president's decision-making procedure, see "Memorandum by Mr. Lucius D. Battle, Special Assistant to the Secretary of State, for the Record of Events of August 26, 1950," *FRUS*, 7: 453–60.

29. Donovan, *Tumultuous Years* (cited chap. 8, n. 85), 262–67.

30. "Memorandum by the Joint Chiefs of Staff to the Secretary of Defense," Sep-tember 8, 1950, FRUS, 6: 491.

31. "Memorandum by the Deputy Assistant Secretary of State for Far Eastern Affairs (Merchant) to the Deputy Under Secretary of State (Matthews)," August 28, 1950, FRUS, 6: 462, n.1.

32. "Memorandum by the Chief of Staff, United States Air Force (Vandenberg), to the Secretary of Defense (Johnson)," August 28, 1950, *FRUS*, 6: 463.

33. "Navy Bomber Is Attacked by U.S.-Built Red Planes," *New York Times*, Au-gust 13, 1950, 2.

34. Thomas J. Hamilton, "Foe Launches All-Out Push for Pusan; UN Considers Peiping Charge; Austin for a Study," *New York Times*, September 1, 1950, 1.

35. "Memorandum by the Chief of Staff, United States Air Force (Vandenberg), to the Secretary of Defense (Johnson)," August 28, 1950, *FRUS*, 6: 463.

36. Thomas J. Hamilton, "Nations Vote Formosa Study; Austin Held Outmaneu-vered," *New York Times*, August 30, 1950, 1.

37. Walter H. Waggoner, "Acheson Says U.S. Is Trying to Keep Peiping Out of War," *New York Times*, August 31, 1950, 1.

38. Anthony Leviero, "Fleet to Quit Formosa at End of Korea War, Says Truman," *New York Times*, September 1, 1950, 1.

39. "The Secretary of State to the Embassy in India," September 1, 1950, *FRUS*, 6: 478–80.

40. "Text of Truman's 'Report to Nation' on Korean War," *New York Times*, Sep-tember 1, 1950, 4.

41. Hanson Baldwin, "War of Prevention," *New York Times*, September 1, 1950, 4.

42. Acheson, *Present at the Creation* (cited chap. 8, n. 5), 577, saw it this way. "Two views were then locked in what seemed to me wholly unnecessary conflict. One was

that under no circumstances should General MacArthur's forces cross the 38th Parallel. The other denied this and advocated ... going wherever necessary to destroy the invader's forces and restore security in the area. The latter view seemed the right one if properly restricted. Troops could not be expected, as I put it, to march up to a surveyor's line and stop."

43. Paul Nitze was the current director. Key members included Dean Rusk, John D. Hickerson, Arthur Bonbright, and John Paton Davies.

44. See Acheson, *Present at the Creation*, 578, for his gentle appraisal of Kennan's memorandum as "good, even if purely negative."

45. "Memorandum by the Counselor (Kennan) to the Secretary of State," August 21, 1950, *FRUS*, 7: 623–28.

46. "Memorandum by the Director of the Office of Northeast Asian Affairs (Allison) to the Assistant Secretary of State for Far Eastern Affairs (Rusk)," July 15, 1950, *FRUS*, 7: 393.

47. "The President to the Secretary of State," July 17, 1950, *FRUS*, 7: 410.

48. "The President of the Republic of Korea (Rhee) to President Truman," July 19, 1950, *FRUS*, 7: 428–29.

49. "The Secretary of State to the Ambassador in Korea (Muccio)," August 10, 1950, *FRUS*, 7: 553–54.

50. "Memorandum by Mr. John Foster Dulles, Consultant to the Secretary of State, to the Director of the Policy Planning Staff (Nitze)," July 14, 1950, *FRUS*, 7: 386–87.

51. "Memorandum by the Director of the Office of Northeast Asian Affairs (Allison) to the Assistant Secretary of State for Far Eastern Affairs (Rusk)," July 15, 1950, *FRUS*, 7: 393–95.

52. "Draft Memorandum Prepared by the Policy Planning Staff," July 25, 1950, *FRUS*, 7: 469–73. The July 22 draft is located on pages 449–54.

53. "Memorandum by the Executive Secretary of the National Security Council (Lay)," July 25, 1950, *FRUS*, 7: 475–77.

54. "Draft Memorandum Prepared in the Department of Defense for National Security Council Staff Consideration Only," August 7, 1950, *FRUS*, 7: 528–35. The July 31 memorandum can be found on pages 502–10.

55. "Draft Memorandum by the Director of the Office of Northeast Asian Affairs (Allison)," August 12, 1950, *FRUS*, 7: 567–73.

56. "Memorandum by the Deputy Under Secretary of State (Matthews)," August 12, 1950, *FRUS*, 7: 566.

57. "Memorandum by the Counselor (Kennan) to the Secretary of State," August 14, 1950, *FRUS*, 7: 574–76.

58. "Memorandum by the Under Secretary of State (Webb)," August 18, 1950, *FRUS*, 7: 599–600.

59. "Memorandum by the Counselor (Kennan) to the Under Secretary of State (Webb)," August 21, 1950, *FRUS*, 7: 612–13, and "The Secretary of Defense (Johnson) to the Secretary of State," August 21, 1950, ibid., 613–14.

60. "Memorandum Prepared in the Central Intelligence Agency," August 18, 1950, *FRUS*, 7: 600–603.

61. "Draft Memorandum Prepared by the Policy Planning Staff," August 21,

1950, and "Memorandum by the Assistant Secretary of State for Far Eastern Affairs (Rusk) to the Planning Adviser, Bureau of Far Eastern Affairs (Emmerson)," September 8, 1950, *FRUS*, 7: 615–16 and 708, respectively.

62. "Draft Memorandum by Messrs. John M. Allison and John K. Emmerson of the Office of Northeast Asian Affairs," August 21, 1950, *FRUS*, 7: 617–23.

63. "Draft Memorandum Prepared in the Department of State for National Security Council Staff Consideration Only," August 23, 1950, *FRUS*, 7: 635–39.

64. "Memorandum of Conversation, by Mr. James W. Barco, Special Assistant to the Ambassador at Large (Jessup)," August 25, 1950, *FRUS*, 7: 646–48.

65. "Draft Memorandum Prepared in the Department of State for National Security Council Staff Consideration Only," August 30, 1950, *FRUS*, 7: 660–66.

66. "Draft Memorandum Prepared in the Department of State," August 31, 1950, *FRUS*, 7: 671–79.

67. "Memorandum by the Joint Chiefs of Staff to the Secretary of Defense," September 7, 1950, *FRUS*, 7: 707–8.

68. For NSC-81, see *FRUS*, 7: 685–93; for NSC-81/1, see pages 712–22.

69. Harold Faber, "Walker Declares Enemy Weakens," *New York Times*, September 14, 1950, 1.

70. Blair, *Forgotten War* (cited chap. 7, n. 41), 238–39 (emphasis supplied).

71. Ibid., 240.

72. Shrader, *Communist Logistics in the Korean War* (cited chap. 7, n. 59), 162–63.

73. Huston, *U.S. Army Logistics in the Korean War* (cited chap. 7, n. 44), 176–77.

74. "CINFE to JCS, 8 September 1950," as cited in Appleman, *South to the Naktong*, 495.

75. Cited in Cumings, *Origins of the Korean War*, 2: 447 and 853n.28.

76. See Alexandre Y. Mansourov, "Stalin, Mao, Kim, and China's Decision to Enter the Korean War, September 16–October 15, 1950: New Evidence from the Russian Archives," *CWIHP*, 6–7: 95, 106n.10.

CHAPTER 12

1. Walter Waggoner, "U.S. Will Propose Rearming by Japan," *New York Times*, September 16, 1950, 1.

2. See "Draft of Points to Be Included in the Formulation of the Terms of the United States–Japanese Bilateral Agreement on Security," October 27, 1950, *FRUS*, 6: 1336–42.

3. James Reston, "West Bars a German Army Under the Guise of Police," *New York Times*, September 15, 1950, 15.

4. Thomas J. Hamilton, "Bonn Arming Snags Atlantic Parleys; Talks Go On Today," *New York Times*, September 16, 1950, 1.

5. "Allies Announce Decisions on Bonn," *New York Times*, September 20, 1950, 13.

6. Walter Sullivan, "Russians and Chinese Reds Help Foe, MacArthur Says," *New York Times*, September 19, 1950, 1. For the full report, see *MSFE* (cited chap. 8, n. 14), 5: 3398–3406.

7. "Extracts of a Memorandum of Conversations, by Mr. W. Averell Harriman, Special Assistant to the President, with General MacArthur in Tokyo on August 6 and 8, 1950," *FRUS*, 6: 428.

8. "U.N. Assembly Bars Peiping, 33–16," *New York Times*, September 20, 1950, 1.

9. David Anderson, "China Shows New Voting Strength in Gaining a U.N. Vice Presidency," *New York Times*, September 21, 1950, 7.

10. Thomas J. Hamilton, "U.S. Bids Assembly Take Power of U.N. Council to Bar Aggression," *New York Times*, September 21, 1950, 1.

11. "The Secretary of State to the Acting Secretary of State," September 23, 1950, *FRUS*, 7: 763–64.

12. "Peiping Warns U.N.," *New York Times*, September 25, 1950, 6.

13. *Ren Min Ri Bao* (People's Daily), September 25, 1950, as cited in Whiting, *China Crosses the Yalu* (cited chap. 10, n. 2), 106.

14. Shi Zhe, *Memoirs of Shi Zhe* (cited chap. 2, n. 41), 492. On the cable, see also Goncharov et al., *Uncertain Partners* (cited chap. 1, n. 27), 174.

15. Alexandre Y. Mansourov, "Stalin, Mao, Kim, and China's Decision to Enter the Korean War, September 16–October 15, 1950: New Evidence from the Russian Archives," *CWIHP* (cited chap. 2, n. 3), 6–7: 96 and 106n.10. (Hereafter referred to as Mansourov, "China's Decision.")

16. Ibid., 96.

17. Ibid. (emphasis supplied).

18. Ibid.

19. Chen Jian, *China's Road* (cited chap. 2, n. 10), 163.

20. Mansourov, "China's Decision," 96.

21. Syn Song-kil and Sin Sam-soon, "Who Started the Korean War," *Korea and World Affairs* (Summer 1990), 251.

22. "Ciphered telegram from Matveyev (Zakharov) to Fyn Syi (Stalin), 26 September 1950," *CWIHP*, 6–7: 110.

23. "Telegram from Fyn Si (Stalin) to Matveyev (Army Gen. M. V. Zakharov) and Soviet Ambassador to the DPRK T. F. Shtykov, approved 27 September 1950 Soviet Communist Party Central Committee Politburo," *CWIHP*, 6–7: 109.

24. Mansourov, "China's Decision," 97.

25. "Ciphered Telegram, Shtykov to Deputy Foreign Minister Andre Gromyko and Instantsia (Stalin), 29 September 1950," *CWIHP*, 6–7: 111.

26. "Ciphered Telegram, DPRK leader Kim Il-sung and South Korean Communist leader Pak Hon-yong to Stalin (via Shtykov), 29 September 1950," *CWIHP*, 6–7: 111–12. The timing of the letter is important and the lengthy delay in transmission, some eleven hours, suspicious. It may be that the Soviets falsified the arrival time to place it after the September 30 Politburo meeting, which would put the Soviet decision to ask for a Chinese troop commitment before Kim asked Stalin for one.

27. Ibid. For the letter to Mao, with the same request for direct military assistance, see Goncharov et al., *Uncertain Partners*, 176.

28. "Draft Telegram, Chan Fu (Stalin) to Matveyev (Zakharov), 30 September 1950," *CWIHP*, 6–7: 113. Mansourov, "China's Decision," 98, without evidence, says that at the Politburo meeting "discussion focused on the need to avoid a direct mili-

tary confrontation between the USSR and the United States and the options still available to salvage the situation in Korea, including soliciting Chinese help and opening a last-ditch diplomatic maneuvering at the United Nations. The Politburo directed that the Foreign Ministry draft a new ceasefire resolution to be submitted to the UN."

29. See, for example, Donovan, *Tumultuous Years* (cited chap. 8, n. 85), 263–67.

30. Schnabel, *Policy and Direction* (cited chap. 6, n. 16), 177.

31. Both immediately before and after Inchon the issue of Chinese intervention was publicly discussed in the press. Thus, Hanson Baldwin, "Defense Gain Is Seen in Johnson Exit," *New York Times*, September 14, 1950, 8, noted that "factors that would determine success or failure would be" whether the NKA "had any sizable forces in their rear areas," and "the intervention or non-intervention of the Chinese Communists." Immediately afterward, Baldwin, in "The Landing at Inchon," ibid., September 18, 1950, 4, noted somewhat cryptically that "air observations ... indicated that enemy troops were moving toward Seoul from both north and south. How many are available and how quickly they can arrive will tell the tale of battle."

32. Most accounts credit the NKA with a force no larger than 100,000 concentrated around Pusan. It was later discovered to be closer to 70,000. Of that number, it was estimated that between 25,000 and 40,000 escaped to North Korea, or close to half. Acheson, *Present at the Creation* (cited chap. 8, n. 5), 578–79, claims that the southern force numbered 400,000, of which 30,000 escaped.

33. See Blair, *Forgotten War* (cited chap. 7, n. 41), 330–31, and Schnabel, *Policy and Direction*, 187–91, for a discussion of these plans. Schnabel, for example, says that MacArthur assumed there would be no outside interference.

34. Blair, *Forgotten War*, 280–81.

35. Blair, *Forgotten War*, 333. Ridgway, *Korean War* (cited chap. 6, n. 16), 48, noted that not only did MacArthur fail to close the trap on the NKA, the Eighth Army supply "suffered for weeks."

36. Goulden, *Korea* (cited chap. 6, n. 19), 253–54.

37. Collins, *War in Peacetime* (cited chap. 11, n. 4), 160–61, notes that the "JCS raised no question about the strategy to be employed," although he was skeptical about the "command arrangements." Ridgway, *Korean War*, 43, says that "even though some of the drawbacks to the plan were obvious and overriding," no one protested. He believed MacArthur's plans "did not outweigh the importance of closing the trap quickly on the fleeing North Koreans." Cagle and Manson, *Sea War in Korea* (cited chap. 7, n. 68), 119, cite Admiral Turner C. Joy: "None of us at COMNAVFE could see the necessity for such an operation ... since the 10th Corps could have marched overland to Wonsan in a much shorter time and with much less effort than it would take to get the Corps around to Wonsan by sea."

38. "The Acting Secretary of State to the United States Mission at the United Nations," September 26, 1950, *FRUS*, 7: 781–82; see also 792–93.

39. For the texts of both messages, see Schnabel, *Policy and Direction*, 183–84.

40. MacArthur implicitly acknowledged the essence of his plan years later, but without mentioning China. "The dispatch of Tenth Corps by sea was intended as a flanking movement against enemy remnants still trying to escape from the south to the north, and as an envelopment to bring pressure upon Pyongyang should the at-

tack upon that enemy capital result in a long drawn-out siege." See Cagle and Manson, *Sea War in Korea*, 114.

41. Panikkar, *In Two Chinas* (cited chap. 10, n. 56), 108.

42. "The Secretary of State to the Acting Secretary of State," September 28, 1950, *FRUS*, 7: 797–98.

43. "Excerpts from Zhou Enlai's Report to the Chinese People's Political Consultative Conference, September 30, 1950," in Goncharov et al., *Uncertain Partners*, 173–74.

44. "Memorandum by the Director of the Office of Chinese Affairs (Clubb) to the Assistant Secretary of State for Far Eastern Affairs (Rusk)," September 30, 1950, *FRUS*, 7: 829.

45. Whiting, *China Crosses the Yalu*, 110.

46. It should come as no surprise, therefore, to find that both sides to this crucial decision have been and are engaged in far-reaching efforts to manipulate the historical record to place themselves in the best light, place their negotiating partner in a **421** bad light, and cover up damaging issues, which reverberate down to the present. It appears to me that the historical record covering this two-week period has been manipulated to the point that the truth may never emerge completely. The best that can be hoped for is a rough approximation.

47. "Ciphered Telegram, Filippov (Stalin) to Mao Zedong and Zhou Enlai, 1 October 1950," *CWIHP*, 6–7: 114.

48. Zhang Xi, "Peng Tehuai and China's Entry into the Korean War," *Chinese Historians* (Spring 1993), 5–7.

49. Ibid., 8. At this point in the historical record, a major evidentiary conflict arises. There now exist two October 2 cables from Mao to Stalin, which are diametrically opposite. One, which appeared first, from a compilation of Mao's writings published in 1987, responds positively to Stalin's request for a troop commitment. The other is a newly released message from the Russian archives, in 1995, in which Mao hesitates to make an immediate commitment, wishing to consider the issue further. The paradox is that both documents are authentic. It is my view, arguing from the context, that the "Russian October 2 cable" contains Mao's initial response to Stalin, while the "Chinese October 2 cable" is a later cable sent on October 13 and mis-dated to appear to have been sent earlier. In any case, the obvious purpose of advancing the date of the cable to October 2 was to obscure the bargaining that ensued, which revealed the callous disregard shown by both sides for the North Korean "comrades" and the unsuccessful attempt by Mao to draw Stalin into the war. For a discussion of this controversy, including copies of both cables, see Mansourov, "China's Decision," 100.

50. "Ciphered telegram from Roshchin in Beijing to Filippov (Stalin), 3 October 1950, conveying 2 October 1950 message from Mao to Stalin," *CWIHP*, 6–7: 114–15.

51. "Ciphered Telegram, Chang Fu (Stalin) to Matveyev (Zakharov), 2 October 1950," *CWIHP*, 6–7: 114. Although dated October 2, the context argues strongly that this order does not precede, but follows, Stalin's reception of Mao's cable. A further suggestion that the dating of this cable was changed is provided by the absence of any enciphering or transmission data.

52. Panikkar, *In Two Chinas*, 109–10.

53. "The Ambassador in India (Henderson) to the Secretary of State," and "The

Ambassador in the Soviet Union (Kirk) to the Secretary of State," both October 3, 1950, *FRUS*, 7: 850–51.

54. "The Ambassador in India (Henderson) to the Secretary of State," October 4, 1950, *FRUS*, 7: 870–71.

55. The general contents of these exchanges are contained in Stalin's letter to Kim Il-sung. See "Letter, Fyn Si (Stalin) to Kim Il-sung (via Shtykov), 8 October 1950," *CWIHP*, 6–7: 116–17.

56. Ibid.

57. Zhang, "Peng and China's Entry," 11–13.

58. Ibid.

59. Ibid., 14 (emphasis supplied).

60. Ibid., 15.

61. "Letter, Fyn Si (Stalin) to Kim Il-Sung (via Shtykov), 8 October 1950," *CWIHP*, 6–7: 116.

62. Ibid.

63. "Gromyko and Vasilevsky to Stalin, 6 October 1950, attaching draft cable to Shtykov," *CWIHP*, 6–7: 117.

64. "Zhou Enlai Talk with Indian Ambassador K. M. Panikkar, October 8, 1950," in Goncharov et al., *Uncertain Partners*, 276–78. Oddly, Panikkar, *In Two Chinas*, 110–12, does not mention this vital meeting.

65. "Mao Zedong to Kim Il-sung, October 8, 1950," from "Mao's Dispatch of Chinese Troops to Korea: Forty-Six Telegrams," *Chinese Historians* (Spring 1992), 69.

66. "Mao Directive Creating the Chinese People's Volunteers, October 8, 1950," ibid., 68–69.

67. Goncharov et al., *Uncertain Partners*, 185.

68. Nikolai Fedorenko attended as interpreter for the Soviet side. Chen Jian, *China's Road*, 197, says the Chinese ambassador to the Soviet Union, Wang Jiaxiang, also attended.

69. Shi Zhe, *Memoirs of Shi Zhe*, 496.

70. Mansourov, "China's Decision," 102, based on the recollection of Soviet interpreter Nikolai Fedorenko, who was present.

71. Ibid. See also Mansourov, "China's Decision," 103.

72. Shi Zhe, *Memoirs of Shi Zhe*, 497.

73. Ibid.

74. Ibid. Shi Zhe's actual wording about providing aircraft for ground support is "zai, zuozhan shi, women keyi chu dong yiding shuliang de kongjun zuo yanhu."

75. See Chen Jian, *China's Road*, 196–200, for discussion.

76. See Mansourov, "China's Decision," 103.

77. Vladimir Petrov, "The Soviet Role in the Early Phase of the Korean War," *Journal of American–East Asian Relations* (Winter 1993), 438–58.

78. Chen Jian, *China's Road*, 196–200. See also Goncharov et al., *Uncertain Partners*, 190–93.

79. "Mao Zedong to Peng Dehuai and Others, 12 October 1950," and "The CCP Central Committee to Rao Shushi and Chen Yi, 12 October 1950," in "Mao's Dispatch of Chinese Troops to Korea," *Chinese Historians* (Spring 1992), 71.

80. Mansourov, "China's Decision," 104. See also "Ciphered Telegram, Shtykov to Fyn Si (Stalin), 14 October 1950," "Ciphered Telegram, Fyn Si (Stalin) to Kim Il-sung (via Shtykov), 13 October 1950," and "Ciphered Telegram, Fyn Si (Stalin) to Kim Il-sung, 14 October 1950," *CWIHP*, 6–7: 118–19.

81. This telegram, with minor variations, is available in several places. See "Mao Dispatch of Chinese Troops to Korea," 71–72, Goncharov et al., *Uncertain Partners*, 194, and Chen Jian, *China's Road*, 202. Shi Zhe, *Memoirs of Shi Zhe*, 498–99, describes Zhou's reaction to Mao's cable as one of disbelief.

82. "Ciphered Telegram, Roshchin to Filippov (Stalin), 14 October 1950, re Meeting with Mao Zedong," *CWIHP*, 6–7: 118.

83. "Mao Zedong to Stalin, 2 October 1950," in "Mao Dispatch of Chinese Troops to Korea," *Chinese Historians* (Spring 1992), 67–68. This letter can also be found in Goncharov et al., *Uncertain Partners*, 177–78, and in Chen Jian, *China's Road*, 175–77.

84. Goncharov et al., *Uncertain Partners*, 195.

85. "Ciphered Telegram, Fyn Si (Stalin) to Kim Il-sung (via Shtykov), 13 October 1950," *CWIHP*, 6–7, 119.

86. "Ciphered Telegram, Roshchin to Filippov (Stalin), 14 October 1950, re Meeting with Mao Zedong," *CWIHP*, 6–7: 118.

87. Chen Jian, *China's Road*, 203, and 287n.44. I say "reportedly," because this statement comes from an unverified and still classified Chinese report.

88. "Mao Zedong to Zhou Enlai, 14 October 1950," in "Mao's Dispatch of Chinese Troops to Korea," *Chinese Historians* (Spring 1992), 73–74.

CHAPTER 13

1. Christopher Andrew, *For the President's Eyes Only: Secret Intelligence and the American Presidency from Washington to Bush* (New York: Harper-Collins, 1995), 198.

2. For a discussion of the "intelligence failure" argument, see Schnabel, *Policy and Direction* (cited chap. 6, n. 16), 61–65.

3. Andrew, *For the President's Eyes Only*, 187. It is likewise difficult to believe his contradictory claim that it was only "after the Chinese offensive of November 25, 1950 [that SIGINT] came at last into its own."

4. Ray Cline, *Secrets, Spies and Scholars: Blueprint of the Essential CIA* (Washington: Acropolis Books, 1976) 126.

5. Donovan, *Tumultuous Years* (cited chap. 8, n. 85), 285.

6. Acheson, *Present at the Creation* (cited chap. 8, n. 5), put it most baldly. He had been "unwilling to urge on the President a military course that his military advisers would not propose. They would not propose it [a pullback] because it ran counter to American military tradition of the proper powers of the theater commander since 1864." Acheson confused the proper powers of the theater commander with the determination of national policy. In that regard, since 1864 and every war since, the executive had closely managed the theater commander's actions. MacArthur, in World War II, was perhaps the most closely managed of all American theater commanders,

as even a casual look at the record shows. See Louis Morton, *The War in the Pacific, Strategy and Command: The First Two Years* (Washington, D.C.: Office of the Chief of Military History, 1962).

7. Truman, *Memoirs* (cited chap. 8, n. 7), 361.

8. For the notes and discussion, see "The Ambassador in the Soviet Union (Kirk) to the Secretary of State," October 10, 1950, *FRUS*, 7: 917ff. See also "Moscow Protests U.S. Plane 'Attack,'" *New York Times*, October 10, 1950, 1.

9. For a deft treatment of the incident, see I. F. Stone, *The Hidden History of the Korean War* (Boston: Little, Brown & Co., 1952), 135–38. Nearly a week later, on October 19, the U.S. admitted and regretted the attack, attributing it to "navigation error and poor judgment," said that disciplinary action had been taken against those involved, and offered to pay damages.

10. Hanson Baldwin, "Reds Said to Mass Men in Manchuria," *New York Times*, October 22, 1950, 5.

424

11. Truman, *Memoirs,* 363 (emphasis supplied).

12. Clay James, *The Years of MacArthur* (Boston: Houghton Mifflin, 1985), 516.

13. Ibid., 514.

14. "The Joint Chiefs of Staff to the Commander in Chief, Far East (MacArthur)," October 9, 1950, *FRUS*, 7: 915.

15. See Whiting, *China Crosses the Yalu* (cited chap. 10, n. 2), 115.

16. "Memorandum by the Ambassador at Large (Jessup) to the Secretary of State," October 9, 1950, *FRUS*, 7: 915–16.

17. "The Deputy Secretary of Defense (Lovett) to the Secretary of State," November 4, 1950, *FRUS*, 7: 1037.

18. Truman, *Memoirs*, 365.

19. Donovan, *Tumultuous Years*, 285.

20. Andrew, *For the President's Eyes Only*, 188. Truman demanded that new CIA director Smith produce seven estimates twenty-four hours before his departure.

21. "Threat of Full Chinese Communist Intervention in Korea," October 12, 1950, *FRUS*, 7: 933–34.

22. "Threat of Soviet Intervention in Korea," October 12, 1950, ibid., 935–36.

23. In the Far East Command's Daily Intelligence Summaries (DIS) of October 8, 9, and 14, 1950, it was noted that "between nine and eighteen of the thirty-eight Chinese divisions believed to be in Manchuria were massing at the border crossings." See Schnabel, *Policy and Direction*, 200. There were ten thousand troops per division.

24. James, *Years of MacArthur*, 519. See Lindesay Parrott, "South Koreans at Frontier, Climax of 350-Mile March," *New York Times*, October 27, 1950, 1. And by the same reporter, "Korean Reds Turn and Fight 60 Miles from Manchuria," *New York Times*, October 28, 1950, 1.

25. Schnabel, *Policy and Direction*, 273.

26. Stone, *Hidden History of the Korean War*, 152, makes a similar point. "Every bit of evidence which might show, or be made to show, Chinese or Russian intervention was highlighted and exaggerated *except* during one short period. In that period, the three weeks after the Wake Island meeting, when Chinese military intervention

actually began, every effort was made by Tokyo Headquarters to discount and disparage reports of this intervention."

27. Blair, *Forgotten War* (cited chap. 7, n. 41), 377. For the CIA's estimate regarding possible Chinese intervention, see "Memorandum by the Central Intelligence Agency," November 8, 1950, *FRUS*, 7: 1101–1106.

28. Whitney, *MacArthur: His Rendezvous with History* (cited chap. 8, n. 102), 388. See also MacArthur, *Reminiscences* (cited chap. 9, n. 53), 361.

29. "Substance of Statements Made at Wake Island Conference on 15 October 1950," *FRUS*, 7: 948–60. When the MacArthur controversy erupted in 1951, Ms. Vernice Anderson would be tagged with the blame for surreptitiously recording what was said. At the same time, having no ulterior motive and being a mere secretary, her account gained veracity.

30. Truman, *Memoirs*, 366, leaves out his part of the story when he says, "then I gave MacArthur an opportunity to repeat to the larger group some of the things he had said to me in our private meeting."

31. "Substance of Statements Made at Wake Island Conference," 953.

32. MacArthur, *Reminiscences*, 362.

33. James, *Years of MacArthur*, 510.

34. Anthony Leviero, "Allies Tightening Arc on Pyongyang; President Impressed Upon M'arthur That Far East Policy Is Unchanged," *New York Times*, October 16, 1950, 1.

35. MacArthur, *Reminiscences*, 361.

36. Appleman, *South to the Naktong* (cited chap. 5, n. 31), 632, and Collins, *War in Peacetime* (cited chap. 11, n. 4), 165–68.

37. Ibid., 166.

38. Lindesay Parrott, "Allies in Wonsan, Fight in Streets; Foe's Resistance Rises on Wide Front," *New York Times*, October 10, 1950, 1.

39. Collins, *War in Peacetime*, 177. Schnabel, *Policy and Direction*, 216, also claims that "MacArthur removed the restrictions against using any but ROK forces north of the line Ch'ongju . . . Hamhung," but that restriction properly applied only to the two most northern provinces of North Korea, a restriction which MacArthur, at least for the moment, honored.

40. Truman, *Memoirs*, 369. For the text of the speech, see *New York Times*, October 18, 1950, 8.

41. "68 Americans Massacred by North Korean Captors," *New York Times*, October 22, 1950, 1. See also Appleman, *South to the Naktong*, 654–59.

42. Schnabel, *Policy and Direction*, 222.

43. Collins, *War in Peacetime*, 182–83, and Ridgway, *Korean War* (cited chap. 6, n. 16), 64. Walker's forces also included the U.S. Ninth Corps (the U.S. Second and Twenty-fifth Divisions, and the Turkish Brigade) and the First Cavalry Division in reserve.

44. Although POW reports date Chinese entry from October 13–14. See Appleman, *South to the Naktong*, 717.

45. Harry Rositzke, *CIA's Secret Operations: Espionage, Counterespionage and Covert Action* (New York: Readers' Digest Press, 1977), 53.

46. Schnabel, *Policy and Direction*, 230–31.

47. Appleman, *South to the Naktong*, 670.

48. Lindesay Parrott, "South Koreans at Frontier, Climax of 350-Mile March," *New York Times*, October 27, 1950, 1.

49. Truman, *Memoirs*, 372.

50. Appleman, *South to the Naktong*, 670, and Collins, *War in Peacetime*, 180, who maintained that MacArthur's "instructions were clearly counter to the policy of the administration."

51. James, *Years of MacArthur*, 513.

52. Collins, *War in Peacetime*, 183ff.

53. Ridgway, *Korean War*, 51.

54. "U.N. Troops Slaughtered at Unsan by Chinese Reds in Surprise Attack," *New York Times*, November 3, 1950, 4, and Lindesay Parrott, "Korean Reds Hit U.S. Unit; Now Use Jets," *New York Times*, November 2, 1950, 1, reported that the North Koreans were "reinforced by troops of the Chinese Red Army." Parrott also noted reports of "as much as two divisions" on the east coast.

55. Lindesay Parrott, "Korean Reds Press Attacks in Center with Fresh Help," *New York Times*, November 1, 1950, 1. It is of interest to note that Mao, having sent his troops into combat against U.N. forces, demanded from Stalin "high-speed torpedo boats, floating mines, armored ships, small patrol boats, minesweeping equipment, coastal fortress artillery and torpedo bomber planes" to support his assault on Taiwan. Mao was evidently still operating under the mistaken assumption that there was a quid pro quo involved between Korea and Taiwan, and that Stalin was committed to support his invasion. See "28 October 1950, ciphered telegram, Mao Zedong to Filippov (Stalin), via Roshchin," *CWIHP* (cited chap. 2, n. 3), 6–7: 47.

56. Truman, *Memoirs*, 373.

57. Schnabel, *Policy and Direction*, 241.

58. Collins, *War in Peacetime*, 197.

59. MacArthur, *Reminiscences*, 365. Collins, in the footnote above, omits Walker's important point regarding the "calculated logistical risk."

60. Schnabel, *Policy and Direction*, 241.

61. Acheson, *Present at the Creation*, 598–99. Acheson labeled MacArthur's actions "schizophrenic." For the general's U.N. report of November 5, see *MSFE* (cited chap. 8, n. 14), 5: 3492–93. For the discussion, see "Memorandum of Conversations, by the Secretary of State," November 6, 1950, *FRUS*, 7: 1055–57.

62. Truman, *Memoirs*, 374–75. Truman portrays MacArthur's plan as "a bombing mission to take out the bridge across the Yalu River from Sinuiju (Korea) to Antung (Manchuria)," but, as noted, MacArthur's plan was for a two-week-long bombing campaign.

63. Ibid., 376. Bombing the "Korean end" of the Yalu bridges would be nearly impossible without crossing into Chinese territory and, as a result, only four of the twelve were cut.

64. James F. Schnabel and Robert J. Watson, *The Joint Chiefs of Staff and National Policy, Vol. III, The Korean War* (Washington, D.C.: Office of Joint History, 1998), 128. (Hereafter referred to as Schnabel and Watson, *The JCS and the Korean War*.)

65. Ibid., 128–29. Marshall replied curtly to this message, telling MacArthur that he had "misunderstood" his query about the hydroelectric installations. He had not expected a philosophical treatise on Chinese behavior. He was referring, he explained, "only to the sudden developments of the past week."

66. "Memorandum by the Assistant Secretary of State for Far Eastern Affairs (Rusk) to the Secretary of State," November 7, 1950, *FRUS*, 7: 1077n.1. Allied governments, when queried about "hot pursuit," unanimously turned thumbs down on the request.

67. "The Commander in Chief, Far East (MacArthur) to the Joint Chiefs of Staff," November 7, 1950, *FRUS*, 7: 1076–77. For reasons that are obscure, Truman, Schnabel, and others place MacArthur's message C-68465 before his C-68411. See Truman, *Memoirs*, 376–77, and Schnabel, *Policy and Direction*, 244–46.

68. Acheson, *Present at the Creation*, omits the November 9 meeting. See his section, "the last clear chance," 602–5, in which he describes the key meeting as the November 21 meeting. Truman, *Memoirs*, 378–84, does discuss the November 9 meeting, but not the meeting of the 21st, spicing his account instead with a tirade against MacArthur.

69. James, *Years of MacArthur*, 524.

70. Collins, *War in Peacetime*, 205.

71. "The Commander in Chief, Far East (MacArthur) to the Joint Chiefs of Staff," November 9, 1950, *FRUS*, 7: 1107–1110.

72. "Memorandum for the President, November 10, 1950, meeting of NSC," cited in Goulden, *Korea* (cited chap. 6, n. 19), 315.

73. Collins, *War in Peacetime*, 207.

74. "Memorandum by the Joint Chiefs of Staff to the Secretary of Defense (Marshall)," November 9, 1950, *FRUS*, 7: 1117–21.

75. Ibid.

76. "Memorandum by the Central Intelligence Agency," November 8, 1950, *FRUS*, 7: 1101–1106.

77. "Memorandum for the President, November 10, 1950, meeting of NSC," cited in Goulden, *Korea*, 314.

78. "Memorandum by the Director of the Central Intelligence Agency (Smith) to the National Security Council," November 9, 1950, *FRUS*, 7: 1122.

79. Goulden, *Korea*, 315.

80. See Schnabel and Watson, *The JCS and the Korean War*, 137–38.

81. MacDonald, *Korea: The War Before Vietnam* (cited chap. 10, n. 54), 64.

82. Ibid., 67.

83. "Memorandum for the President, November 10, 1950, meeting of NSC," cited in Goulden, *Korea*, 316.

84. Collins, *War in Peacetime*, 208.

85. Lindesay Parrott, "M'Arthur Says 'Alien' Reds Have Reopened Korean War; Sees 'Gravest' Issue Raised," *New York Times*, November 6, 1950, 1.

86. Thomas J. Hamilton, "West Bids U.N. Ask Peiping to Withdraw Men in Korea," *New York Times*, November 11, 1950, 1, and, by the same reporter, "Malik Says Russia Will Bar Call to Chinese to Withdraw," ibid., November 17, 1950, 1.

87. Schnabel and Watson, *The JCS and the Korean War*, 136.

88. A. M. Rosenthal, "Peiping Rejects U.N.'s Bid to Answer Charge of Intervening in Korea War," *New York Times*, November 12, 1950, 1.

89. Thomas J. Hamilton, "U.N. Defers Formosa Debate in Light of Red China Threats," *New York Times*, November 16, 1950, 1.

90. William Stueck, *The Korean War: An International History* (Princeton: Princeton University Press, 1995), 116–17.

91. "The Consul General at Hong Kong (Wilkinson) to the Secretary of State," November 9, 1950, *FRUS*, 7: 1128.

92. Henry Lieberman, "Red Chinese Rally People Against U.S.," *New York Times*, November 6, 1950, 1.

93. Lindesay Parrott, "Chinese Continue March into Korea Despite Air Blows," *New York Times*, November 11, 1950, 1.

94. Schnabel, *Policy and Direction*, 266–67.

95. Thomas J. Hamilton, "Some in U.N. Favor Mission to Peiping on War in Korea," *New York Times*, November 21, 1950, 1.

96. MacDonald, *Korea: The War Before Vietnam*, 67.

97. Schnabel and Watson, *The JCS and the Korean War*, 135.

98. Doris M. Condit, *The Test of War: 1950–1953* (Washington, D.C.: OSD, 1988), 2: 81–82.

99. "Estimate of the Most Probable Course of Soviet-Chinese Action with Regard to Korea," November 17, 1950, *FRUS*, 7: 1188.

100. Ibid., 1190.

101. Walter Waggoner, "Acheson Hints at Readiness for Peiping Talks on Korea," *New York Times*, November 16, 1950, 1.

102. James Reston, "Truman Reassures Peiping That U.S. Plans No Invasion," *New York Times*, November 17, 1950, 1.

103. "The Chargé in Korea (Drumright) to the Secretary of State," November 19, 1950, *FRUS*, 7: 1190–91.

104. Condit, *Test of War*, 82.

105. "Ambassador in the Soviet Union (Kirk) to the Secretary of State," November 19, 1950, *FRUS*, 7: 1191–92.

106. Acheson, *Present at the Creation*, 604.

107. "Memorandum of Conversation, by the Ambassador at Large (Jessup)," November 21, 1950, *FRUS*, 7: 1204–1208. Attending for the Pentagon were Marshall, Lovett, Bradley, Collins, Vandenberg, Sherman, and Pace.

108. "The British Secretary of State for Foreign Affairs (Bevin) to the British Ambassador (Franks)," November 23, 1950, *FRUS*, 7: 1217–18.

109. "Memorandum of Conversation, by the Ambassador at Large (Jessup)," November 21, 1950, *FRUS*, 7: 1204–1208 (emphasis supplied).

110. "The Chief of Staff, United States Army (Collins), to the Commander in Chief, United Nations Command (MacArthur), November 24, 1950, *FRUS*, 7: 1222–24.

111. Condit, *Test of War*, 82.

CONCLUSION

1. Condit, *The Test of War* (cited chap. 13, n. 98), 255ff, offers a comprehensive budget analysis of the force and assistance buildup. For example, compared to the fiscal year 1950 budget of $12 billion, fiscal year 1951 and 1952 budgets for all national security programs totaled $140 billion. Between the outbreak of the war and mid-1952, the Army increased the number of infantry divisions from 10 to 20. The Navy increased the number of aircraft carriers from 18 to 29. The Marines increased the number of divisions from 2 to 3. The Air Force increased the number of combat air wings from 52 to 80. Total service personnel went from 1,729,472 to 3,621,487.

INDEX

432

ABOUT THE AUTHOR

DR. RICHARD C. THORNTON is professor of history and international affairs at George Washington University in Washington, D.C. His major works include *The Nixon-Kissinger Years: The Reshaping of American Foreign Policy; The Carter Years: Toward a New Global Order; The Falklands Sting: Reagan, Thatcher, and Argentina's Bomb* (Brassey's, 1998); and *China: A Political History, 1917–1980*. He lives in Arlington, Virginia.